To This Very Day
Fundamental Questions in Bible Study

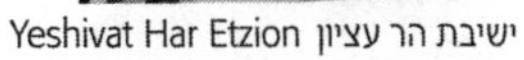

Amnon Bazak

עד היום הזה

To This Very Day

Fundamental Questions in Bible Study

TRANSLATED BY

Kaeren Fish with Elka Weber

Yeshivat Har Etzion
Maggid Books

To This Very Day
Fundamental Questions in Bible Study

First Edition, 2020

Maggid Books
An imprint of Koren Publishers Jerusalem Ltd.

POB 8531, New Milford, CT 06776-8531, USA
& POB 4044, Jerusalem 9104001, Israel
www.maggidbooks.com

Cover Photo: The Great Isaiah Scroll MS A (1QIsa), first century BCE; Koren Tanakh, twentieth century CE

ISBN 978-1-59264-515-2, *hardcover*

A CIP catalogue record for this title is available from the British Library

Printed and bound in the United States

"And purify our hearts to serve You in truth"

In memory of mori verabbi
Rosh Yeshivat Har Etzion and its founder

HaRav Yehuda Amital zt"l

Who taught us to seek out truth in avodat Hashem
With love, fear, and humility

הָאֱ־לֹהִים אֲשֶׁר הִתְהַלְּכוּ אֲבֹתַי לְפָנָיו...
Dedicated in loving memory of my father

Harold Singer z"l
חיים מנחם סינגער ז"ל

He and my mother Eva (חוה) *Singer*
Emerged from the Holocaust
As sole survivors of their families.
Through devotion to family and to the Jewish community
They ensured the passing down of their precious legacies
...עַד הַיּוֹם הַזֶּה (בראשית מח, טו)

Dr. Marc Singer

Contents

Introduction

For hundreds of years, Tanakh (Bible) study was relegated to near insignificance, even in the curricula of yeshivot and other educational institutions. In recent generations, however, an encouraging phenomenon has emerged: a renaissance of Tanakh study among Jewry in general, and in the study halls of the Religious-Zionist community in particular. Tanakh has become an integral component of every educational stream within the Israeli system. The return to the study of the biblical text includes a return to engagement with the *peshat* – the plain or literal meaning of the text – and has led to the exploration of profound and fascinating dimensions of the narrative. This, of course, goes hand in hand with the return of the Jewish people to its land, which has generated greater interest in the concrete and material aspects of the Bible. Students of Tanakh hike through the regions mentioned in the books before them and become familiar with the archaeological sites and artifacts relevant to the Tanakh.

The return to in-depth study of the plain text has naturally brought in its wake new challenges. In the past, the religious world dismissed questions of biblical criticism out of hand, either because of the non-Jewish origins of these questions, or because religious Jews were not heavily immersed in studying the *peshat* of Tanakh. For the last two hundred years or so, academic Bible scholarship has proposed views that are inconsistent with traditional Jewish belief. Biblical scholars who did not have a religious worldview took for granted that the Tanakh was a human document with no divine or prophetic source. This starting point was grounded in several different areas, including literary analysis of the text, archaeological discoveries, and the growing body of knowledge on the ancient Near East. In-depth study of the plain text has brought these questions to the fore and demanded clearer answers than those that might have sufficed in the past. Moreover, although these academic views were closely bound up with the secular – and sometimes even anti-Semitic – beliefs of the scholars themselves, the questions and problems that served as their raw material nevertheless deserve renewed attention, especially in light of the significant change of attitude toward text study of the last generation. The academic scene itself has also changed, with many scholars in Israel and around the world, among them religious Jews, taking a scientific approach to biblical literature. Biblical research has come into its own, both in the academic world and outside it, especially as technology grants wide audiences instant access to the sources.

How, then, should one respond to the complex questions raised by close textual reading, by new methodology, and by recent discoveries?

The recent changes demand a more in-depth examination of the basic assumptions of the academic world, and rabbis and Jewish thinkers have risen to the challenge. The few who first addressed biblical criticism in nineteenth-century Germany, such as Rabbi David Zvi Hoffmann and Rabbi Samson Raphael Hirsch, have had their work taken up by renowned scholars, such as Rabbis Mordechai Breuer and Yoel Bin-Nun, in the last generation in Israel. As part of this process, it became clear that some assumptions may actually be shared by the worlds of academia and of the yeshiva. Many of the fundamental differences between the two worlds arise not from the data itself, but from the different intellectual axioms, which create different points of departure and different interpretive methodologies, and therefore result in different interpretations of the data. Some of the fundamental questions at the center of biblical study had already been addressed by medieval rabbinic scholars, for example, who on many occasions provided answers that rarely were given the exposure they deserved, because so few in the traditional world focused on the issues of the biblical texts.

Indeed, academic study of the Bible has had a positive value in the traditional world for uncovering and illuminating new facets of the Torah. Rabbi Abraham Isaac HaKohen Kook articulates this approach of recognizing every contribution and enhancement in Torah:

> This is a great principle in the battle of ideas – that for every view that appears to contradict some matter in the Torah, we must first not necessarily deny it, but rather build the palace of Torah upon it. We are thereby elevated and as we are elevated, ideas are revealed. Then we are untroubled and we may wholeheartedly confront these difficult ideas.[1]

The aim of this work is to portray the unique approach that has arisen in the current generation among Bible scholars, who come to Tanakh study with deep, serious belief, on the one hand, and according to the prevailing methodology of Bible criticism, on the other. This new manner of study is grounded in a profound belief in the holiness and divine nature of the books of the Bible, and coupled with the understanding that new discoveries in the scholarly world need be neither rejected out of hand nor adopted in their entirety. Such scholarship demands of its students that they distinguish clearly between facts, tools, and speculation. They must refrain from rejecting truths that demand explanation, and from

1. Rabbi Abraham Isaac Kook, *Iggerot HaRe'aya*, vol. 1 (Jerusalem, 1962), letter 134, 164. Rabbi Kook (1865–1935) was a major figure in religious Zionist thought. He served as chief rabbi of the Ashkenazi community of British Palestine from 1921 until his death. His works on Jewish law and thought continue to be highly influential. The view noted above is also reflected in the following: "All the words and paths that lead to the ways of heresy themselves lead, fundamentally, if we seek out their source, to a greater depth of faith, one that is more illuminating and life-giving than the simple understanding that was illuminated prior to the revelation of that outburst" (*Orot HaKodesh*, vol. 2 [Jerusalem, 1964], 547). And more: "We cannot deny that there are many good things even in books that are deficient in many places… and truth is more beloved than all else, and it is specifically in that, that God is to be praised and the banner of the believer's faith is raised" (*Iggerot HaRe'aya*, vol. 2 [Jerusalem, 1985], letter 255, 20).

avoiding complex modern methods out of protective zeal for older methods. These exegetical and spiritual challenges have been accepted, both orally and in writing, at Yeshivat Har Etzion and at the affiliated Herzog College – institutions that, in recent years, have formed an unparalleled center for the study of Tanakh.

It is important to emphasize that my intention is not for this book to serve as a tool in a polemic against the world of academic scholarship. It is not to "know how to answer a heretic" (Avot 2:14), but to "know how to answer your own questions." Believers are pressed, first and foremost, to reconcile their beliefs with their internal truths, and if they encounter specific areas that interfere with their beliefs, they must seek ways to reconcile these challenges to their belief system. The challenge posed by critical theory is not a threat, but a means for deeper understanding of God's word as revealed in the Bible.

There is also, of course, a public and educational imperative in raising these issues. In recent years, I have witnessed more and more graduates of the religious educational system express profound distress when they are exposed to the world of academic Bible study at institutions of higher education. They sometimes encounter questions for which they feel they have no answers; at other times, they are dumbfounded by the dismissal of the thought processes upon which they were raised. On occasion, they even express anger at the religious educational system for failing to prepare them for this challenge. I cannot deny that this harsh criticism has some merit.

I believe that it is correct and appropriate to expose our students, at some point in their schooling, to the fundamental questions and problems of Bible study, together with the various solutions proposed by religiously committed scholars. If anything, these questions lead to a deeper and more genuine understanding of the Torah. Confronting these questions allows students to establish a firm religious foundation, with an awareness of the larger picture. They will then be able to chart their own path within their own system of belief.

This book contains three parts.

The first part, *Between Tradition and Criticism,* deals with questions of the authorship of books of the Bible and examines the relationship between the traditional approach and the critical one.

- In the first chapter, I present the relatively few references within Tanakh itself to the consolidation of the Torah, and then the various approaches of *Ḥazal* (the talmudic Sages) and the *Rishonim* (sages of the premodern era) to the issue.
- The second chapter addresses one of the first questions raised by the early biblical critics: the existence of verses that appear to be written subsequent to the rest of the Torah. I explore the approaches to this question among medieval Jewish scholars and discuss the ramifications of the phenomenon – according to those for whom it indeed exists – regarding when the Torah was actually written.
- The third chapter presents the phenomenon of contradictions and repetitions in biblical verses, and reviews the documentary hypothesis (Wellhausen hypothesis) with its underlying assumptions, its literary and historical aspects, and the problems and alternatives associated with it. As an alternative to the documentary hypothesis, I present an extensive review of the "aspects theory" (*shitat habeḥinot*), developed by Rabbi Mordechai Breuer, as well as its later expansions.
- The fourth chapter deals with the composition of the books of the Prophets and Writings (*Nevi'im* and *Ketuvim*), according to the midrash and the medieval commentators. I consider the possibility of implementing the "aspects theory" regarding these books too, and conclude with a detailed discussion of the composition of the book of Isaiah.
- The fifth chapter, which concludes this section of the book, deals with the traditional text of the Bible. Is it possible to identify the traditional text conclusively? This chapter considers the possibility of textual variations and whether introducing a textual variation as a way to solve an exegetical problem is legitimate.

The second section of the book, *Tanakh and Its World,* deals with archaeological discoveries and the physical realities of the biblical world.

- The sixth chapter weighs in on disputes raging between different schools of archaeologists regarding the period of the forefathers, the Egyptian servitude, the conquest and settlement of the Land of Israel, and the period of the monarchy of David and Solomon. This section reviews the questions arising from the existence or absence of archaeological finds, and discusses the general relationship between Tanakh and archaeology.

- The seventh chapter focuses on texts and artifacts from the ancient Near East, particularly those texts that predate the revelation of the Tanakh, featuring elements that parallel sections in the Torah, both in prose and in legal units. I also discuss the significance of such discoveries.

The last section of the book, *Between Peshat and Derash,* deals with the relationship between the *peshat* of Tanakh and the midrashim of the Sages.

- The eighth chapter investigates the relationship between the straightforward interpretation of the text and *midreshei aggada.*[2] It presents different approaches of medieval commentators, who respectively tackled the various levels on which verses can be understood.
- The ninth chapter discusses the relationship between the straightforward reading of the text and *midreshei halakha,*[3] which have legal standing. I present models for explaining the discrepancies that sometimes exist between these two realms, and examine fundamental questions pertaining to halakha and the ways in which its rulings are determined.
- The final chapter concerns a question arising from the study of *peshat* that has generated much public discussion in the national-religious community in recent years: how to understand misdeeds of characters in Tanakh, as seen according to the plain reading of the text. I examine the position of the talmudic Sages and the medieval commentators on this subject, and also discuss the theoretical and educational questions emerging from their positions.

Of course, the fundamental thinking and positions presented are not new. They draw on the opinions and understandings of the classical Jewish

2. The Sages' interpretations of the narrative sections of Tanakh.
3. The Sages' interpretations of the legal sections of Tanakh.

thinkers and sages and of recent scholars. If there is anything new in my presentation of them, it consists of the gathering of these views into a single collection. Granted, the questions that arise from this integrative way of approaching the biblical text are endless, and I shall not be able to address every detail and every aspect of every topic. Rather, I aim to cover only the central points, and to summarize the relevant problems and the various ways of dealing with them, so that we may engage with, rather than hide from, challenges to our faith.

I have entitled this book *To This Very Day* for a few reasons. This well-known biblical phrase reflects the reader's direct interaction with the text, at all times and in all places. *To This Very Day* expresses the everlasting relevance of Tanakh. No book in history has so aroused the passions of its students and readers for so many generations. No book has earned so much interpretation, or bequeathed so much wisdom, charm, and strength, to this very day. At the same time, the expression is an important source in discussing the time between when a biblical event occurred and when it was recorded. Sometimes, many years have elapsed, if one reads the expression literally (for more on this, see chapter 2). Finally, this book grapples with the questions that have challenged readers and students from the time the Tanakh was written to this very day.

Many partners brought this book to fruition. First, this book was written within the walls of Yeshivat Har Etzion and Herzog College, where I studied and where I have been privileged to teach for many years. The yeshiva and its affiliated college imbued in me a love of Torah and taught me to seek its truth, with humility and awe. This method was impressed upon me by the founders and heads of the yeshiva, Rabbi Yehuda Amital *zt"l*, in whose memory this book is dedicated, and Rabbi Aharon Lichtenstein, *zt"l*, who passed away after the publication of the Hebrew edition of this book. Their successors as *roshei yeshiva*, my revered teachers Rabbi Yaakov Medan, Rabbi Baruch Gigi, and Rabbi Mosheh Lichtenstein, *shlit"a*, aided me greatly with their wisdom and guidance. I cannot possibly thank them enough for their time and thoughtful comments.

My colleagues in the Tanakh department at Herzog College also helped a great deal. First and foremost, I want to acknowledge my debt to two dear childhood friends, who are with me to this day: Rabbi Dr. Joshua Reiss was the first to hear from me about this book, and, from the start, he encouraged, boosted, and accompanied the work with great dedication. Prof. Yonatan Jacobs read many of the chapters, and commented and improved upon them.

Thanks from the bottom of my heart to my dear friend Dr. Yoshi Farjun, who edited and improved the Hebrew edition of this book with dedication and professionalism. It is impossible to overestimate the value of his comments and their influence on the finished product.

My deepest thanks to Rabbi Dr. Yoel Bin-Nun and Professor Yoel Elitzur, who reviewed the book and offered important comments; to Professor Yosef Ofer for his comments on chapter 5, about the text of the Bible; and to Dr. Doron Sar-Avi, for help with chapter 6, on archaeology and the Bible. I am also grateful to the library staff at Yeshivat Har Etzion and Herzog College, who responded willingly and cheerfully to my requests.

This English edition would not have been possible without the contributions of many people. Thank you to Matthew Miller and my friend Rabbi Reuven Ziegler of Maggid Books, who spared no effort in ensuring the high quality of this edition; to Rabbi Ezra Bick of Yeshivat Har Etzion; to scholarly consultant Dr. Shawn Zelig Aster; to translators Kaeren Fish and Dr. Elka Weber; to editors Ita Olesker, Anne Gordon, Ilana Sobel, and Rabbi Joe Wolfson; and to my friends Dr. Marc Singer and Ezra Dyckman for their belief in this project and their support of it.

While I am grateful to all those who helped in many ways, all responsibility for what is written here rests with me alone.

Last but not least, thank you from the bottom of my heart to my dear and beloved family, who were a part of the writing of this book: my wife Anat, my devoted partner all along the journey, who gave the book its title; and our children, Rinat, Talia, Elnatan, and Hillel. Together, we climbed the ruins at Khirbet Qeiyafa to follow in the footsteps of the Davidic monarchy, and together at the Shabbat table we discussed essential questions relating to the composition of Tanakh and ways of studying it in our times. Whatever is mine is theirs.

I thank You, Lord, my God, and God of my fathers, for setting my lot with those who sit in the *beit midrash*, for giving us a Torah of truth, and for planting within us eternal life, to this very day.

Alon Shvut
Elul, 5779

Part I

Between Tradition and Criticism

Chapter 1

Composition of the Torah According to Tanakh and Jewish Tradition

INTRODUCTION

Tanakh is made up of two kinds of books: those composed by an author whose identity is explicitly stated, and those composed by an author whose identity is not stated. The first category includes, among others, some of the Later Prophets, written in the first person, in which the main character narrates the events and prophecies. The second category, books that describe events from the perspective of an anonymous narrator, includes, among others, the Five Books of the Torah, which are written from an external point of view rather than in the first person. Surprising though it may sound, the Tanakh itself does not engage directly with the question of who wrote the Five Books of the Torah, and it does not describe in detail the process by which they were written and transmitted to the Jewish people. Insight about the Five Books of the Torah may be gleaned, however, by reviewing verses in Tanakh and examining various approaches among the Sages and medieval commentators concerning the creation of the Torah and its transmission to the Jewish people.

TORAH AS A COLLECTION OF MITZVOT

The terms "Torah" and "*Sefer Torah*" appear many times in Tanakh, but in most cases, the plain meaning of the text does not refer to the Five Books of the Torah. In fact, the word "Torah" has multiple meanings in Tanakh, and only in some instances does it refer to a written text. The term appears in one of the first legal passages in the Torah in Exodus 12:49, and its meaning throughout Exodus as well as in Leviticus and Numbers is "a law, or collection of laws, on a specific subject." We see this, for example, in the following verses:

> זֹאת **הַתּוֹרָה** לָעֹלָה לַמִּנְחָה וְלַחַטָּאת וְלָאָשָׁם וְלַמִּלּוּאִים וּלְזֶבַח הַשְּׁלָמִים.
>
> This is the law (*torah*) of the burnt offering, of the meal offering, and of the sin offering, and of the guilt offering, and of the consecration offering, and of the sacrifice of the peace offering. (Lev. 7:37)

> זֹאת **הַתּוֹרָה** לְכָל נֶגַע הַצָּרַעַת וְלַנָּתֶק.
>
> This is the law (*torah*) for every *tzaraat*, and for the patch. (Lev. 14:54)

> זֹאת **תּוֹרַת** הַקְּנָאֹת אֲשֶׁר תִּשְׂטֶה אִשָּׁה תַּחַת אִישָׁהּ וְנִטְמָאָה.
>
> This is the law (*torah*) of jealousies: when a wife strays from her husband and is defiled. (Num. 5:29)[1]

---

1. There is one verse in these books that seems to be an exception: וַיֹּאמֶר ה' אֶל מֹשֶׁה, עֲלֵה אֵלַי הָהָרָה - וֶהְיֵה שָׁם וְאֶתְּנָה לְךָ אֶת לֻחֹת הָאֶבֶן, וְהַתּוֹרָה וְהַמִּצְוָה, אֲשֶׁר כָּתַבְתִּי, לְהוֹרֹתָם, "God said to Moses: Come up to Me, to the mountain, and be there, and I shall give you the tablets of stone, and the Torah, and the commandments which I have written, [for you] to teach them" (Ex. 24:12). Here it seems that the word "Torah" refers to a written collection in His possession, something broader than a specific collection of laws. However, the commentators note that the reference cannot be to such a written corpus, for "God did not write the Torah; rather, Moses wrote it, at God's word" (Ibn Ezra, ad loc.). Therefore, they (Ibn Ezra, Rashbam, Nahmanides, and others) conclude that the word "*katavti*" (I have written) refers only to the two tablets. Nahmanides interprets the word "Torah" as a general term, referring to different teachings within a larger collection (see Lev. 26:46, Deut. 5:27).

In other instances, the word "Torah" is a synonym for commandments, statutes, and judgments.[2]

In Deuteronomy, however, "Torah" refers explicitly to a text that is broader than just a single law or collection of laws relating to one subject, though the reference remains far more limited than the way the term is used today.

A review of the word's occurrences in Deuteronomy demonstrates that the corpus referred to as "Torah" is, in fact, Moses's main speech in Deuteronomy, commonly referred to as the "speech of the mitzvot," the speech of the commandments. This speech, which makes up chapters 5–26 of Deuteronomy, is one, continuous, uninterrupted monologue, containing an extensive list of mitzvot. At the beginning of this speech we read: וְזֹאת הַתּוֹרָה אֲשֶׁר שָׂם מֹשֶׁה לִפְנֵי בְּנֵי יִשְׂרָאֵל. אֵלֶּה הָעֵדֹת וְהַחֻקִּים וְהַמִּשְׁפָּטִים אֲשֶׁר דִּבֶּר מֹשֶׁה אֶל בְּנֵי יִשְׂרָאֵל בְּצֵאתָם מִמִּצְרָיִם, "This is *the Torah* that Moses placed before the Children of Israel. These are the testimonies and the statutes and the judgments that Moses spoke to the Children of Israel when they came out of Egypt" (Deut. 4:44–45). The plain meaning of the text here suggests that the "Torah" means the things Moses is going to say from this point onward.[3]

At the end of the "speech of the mitzvot," Moses commands the Children of Israel to set up great stones after passing over the Jordan: וְכָתַבְתָּ עֲלֵיהֶן אֶת כָּל דִּבְרֵי הַתּוֹרָה הַזֹּאת, "And you shall inscribe upon them all the words of this Torah" (Deut. 27:3). On the plain level of the text, this command, too, would seem to refer to the writing of the "speech of the mitzvot" – that is, the same "Torah" that was just concluded.[4]

It should be noted that, according to Ibn Ezra, the word "Torah" here refers to the first and fifth of the Ten Commandments. In any event, the verse itself indicates clearly that it cannot be referring to the Five Books of the Torah or to any other written corpus.

2. See Gen. 26:5; Ex. 16:28; Jer. 44:10, and elsewhere.
3. As Rashi comments there, "'This is the Torah': that which he is going to set forth after this unit."
4. There are many opinions among the Sages and the commentators as to what was written on the stones. The Mishna (Sota 7:1) states that the entire Torah was written on them – that is, the entire Five Books, and since the verse also adds "very clearly" (בַּאֵר הֵיטֵב, Deut. 27:8), one is left to conclude that it was also written in seventy languages. However, *Mekhilta* Deuteronomy (see S. Z. Schechter, "Mekhilta on Deuteronomy,

It is only in Deuteronomy that, for the first time, the "Torah" is mentioned as being committed to writing in a book. The book is mentioned for the first time in a very specific context, namely, concerning a future king: וְהָיָה כְשִׁבְתּוֹ עַל כִּסֵּא מַמְלַכְתּוֹ וְכָתַב לוֹ אֶת מִשְׁנֵה הַתּוֹרָה הַזֹּאת עַל סֵפֶר מִלִּפְנֵי הַכֹּהֲנִים הַלְוִיִּם, "And it shall be, when he sits upon the throne of his kingdom that he shall write for himself *a copy of this Torah,* in a written form, from that which is before the Levite priests" (Deut. 17:18). The conventional explanation of the Hebrew term *mishneh torah* is "copy of the Torah" (see *Targum Onkelos* and others), but the verse itself is unclear.

Toward the end of Deuteronomy, the "Torah" refers explicitly to something that is written:

> וַיִּכְתֹּב מֹשֶׁה אֶת **הַתּוֹרָה הַזֹּאת** וַיִּתְּנָהּ אֶל הַכֹּהֲנִים בְּנֵי לֵוִי הַנֹּשְׂאִים אֶת אֲרוֹן בְּרִית יְהוָה; וְאֶל כָּל זִקְנֵי יִשְׂרָאֵל.
>
> And Moses wrote *this Torah,* and he gave it to the *kohanim,* the sons of Levi, who bore the Ark of the Covenant of the Lord, and unto all the elders of Israel. (Deut. 31:9)

Parashat Re'eh," in *Tiferet Yisrael, Festschrift zu Israel Lewy's siebzigstem Geburtstag,* ed. M. Brann and J. Elbogen [Breslau, 1911, reprinted Jerusalem, 1972], 189–92), also cites the view of Rabbi Shimon bar Yoḥai, which accords better with the plain meaning of the text: "They wrote only the repetition [or copy – *mishneh*] of the Torah by Moses." This approach is based on the verse describing the fulfillment of the command, in the days of Joshua: וַיִּכְתָּב שָׁם עַל הָאֲבָנִים אֵת מִשְׁנֵה תּוֹרַת מֹשֶׁה אֲשֶׁר כָּתַב לִפְנֵי בְּנֵי יִשְׂרָאֵל, "And he wrote there upon the stones the repetition [or copy] of the Torah of Moses, which he wrote in the presence of the Children of Israel" (Josh. 8:32). From the limiting language of Rabbi Shimon bar Yoḥai's view, "they wrote only," one can deduce that he disagrees not only with the idea that the Torah was written in seventy languages, but also with the initial assertion that the Torah was written in its entirety. He maintains that only Deuteronomy was written on the stones.

The Mekhilta also cites a third opinion, which limits the inscription on the stones even further to include only those texts pertaining to the other nations, such as the unit, כִּי תָצוּר אֶל עִיר יָמִים רַבִּים לְהִלָּחֵם עָלֶיהָ, "When you besiege a city for a long time, to wage war against it" (Deut. 20:19).

The commentators raise other possibilities, with some limiting the written text still further. For extensive discussion of the entire subject, see M. Bar Ilan, "HaTorah HaKetuva al HaAvanim BeHar Eval," in Z. H. Ehrlich and Y. Eshel, eds., *Meḥkerei Yehuda VeShomron* 2 (Kedumim-Ariel, 1993), 29–42.

What is included in this "Torah"? Rashi and Nahmanides explain that it refers to the Five Books of the Torah, and the same point is stated explicitly at the beginning of *Sifrei* Deuteronomy (*piska* 1).[5] However, this interpretation raises some difficulties. First, as already noted, in previous units the word "Torah" refers specifically to the "speech of the mitzvot" and not to the entire Five Books. Second, the plain meaning of the text seems to suggest that this verse – and all those that follow – are not part of "this Torah" but rather serve as an introduction to the Torah itself. Moreover, just two verses later, the command concerning the "*hak'hel*" ceremony uses the term again.

> וַיְצַו מֹשֶׁה אוֹתָם לֵאמֹר מִקֵּץ שֶׁבַע שָׁנִים בְּמֹעֵד שְׁנַת הַשְּׁמִטָּה בְּחַג הַסֻּכּוֹת...תִּקְרָא אֶת הַתּוֹרָה הַזֹּאת נֶגֶד כָּל יִשְׂרָאֵל בְּאָזְנֵיהֶם.
>
> Moses commanded them, saying: "At the end of every seven years, at the time of the *Shemitta* year, on the festival of Sukkot...you shall read *this Torah* before all of Israel, in their hearing. (Deut. 31:10–11)

The Sages (Sota 7:8) agree that the command to read "this Torah" in the context of *hak'hel* does not refer to all Five Books of the Torah; rather, it indicates a few key selections from Deuteronomy. It therefore seems reasonable to suggest, as Abrabanel does in his commentary on this verse, that if the words "this Torah" in verse 11 do not refer to the Five Books of the Torah but only to parts of Deuteronomy, then the same words in verse 9, regarding Moses's writing of the text, should refer to that same text.[6]

The logical conclusion here is that the composition that the Torah records Moses as having written does not include all Five Books, but only the central portions of Deuteronomy.

---

5. Rashi (c. 1040–1105, northeastern France) is considered the preeminent biblical commentator in traditional Judaism, and was an important talmudist and halakhic decisor. Nahmanides (1194–1270, Spain) was a leading talmudist, philosopher, kabbalist, poet, physician, and commentator on the Torah.
6. Don Isaac Abrabanel (1437–1508, Spain and then Italy), philosopher and statesman, who authored a discursive non-allegorical Bible commentary.

Let us try to define more precisely what is included in the "Torah," which is described in Deuteronomy as having been written by Moses. Again, the Mishna tells us that the "Torah" that is read at the *hak'hel* ceremony includes only crucial parts of Deuteronomy:

> And he reads from the beginning of "These are the things" (Deut. 1:1) up to *Shema* (Deut. 6:4), and *Shema* (Deut. 6:4–9), and *Vehaya im shamoa* (Deut. 11:13–21), "You shall surely tithe" (Deut. 14:22–29), "When you finish tithing" (Deut. 26:12–15), and the unit on the king (Deut. 17:14–20), and the blessings and curses (Deut. 27:1ff.), until the end of that entire unit [apparently Deut. 28:69]. (Sota 7:8)

This mishnaic statement, which defines the word "Torah" in Deuteronomy 31:11, will serve as a means of identifying which passages the authors of this mishna considered to be "Torah." They include Moses's first speech (Deut. 1–4) in this rubric, an understanding clearly originating in the assumption that the first speech serves as a preface to the main speech – the "speech of the mitzvot."[7]

The Sages also maintained that the Book of the Torah included the passage that describes the blessings and curses that will befall the Children of Israel, depending on their future conduct, in chapter 28.

7. The main purpose of Moses's first speech is to convey that one must obey God and fulfill His commandments. In chapter 1, Moses reviews the failures of the first generation, who did not enter the land because they rebelled against God. In chapters 2 and 3, he describes the second generation, who did obey God. The conclusion to be drawn from this brief historical review is summed up nicely in the concluding chapter of the speech, which begins with a warning: וְעַתָּה יִשְׂרָאֵל שְׁמַע אֶל הַחֻקִּים וְאֶל הַמִּשְׁפָּטִים אֲשֶׁר אָנֹכִי מְלַמֵּד אֶתְכֶם לַעֲשׂוֹת לְמַעַן תִּחְיוּ וּבָאתֶם וִירִשְׁתֶּם אֶת הָאָרֶץ אֲשֶׁר ה׳ אֱלֹהֵי אֲבֹתֵיכֶם נֹתֵן לָכֶם, "And now, Israel, hearken to the statutes and the judgments which I teach you to perform in order that you may live and come in and possess the land which the Lord God of your forefathers gives you" (Deut. 4:1). Once this conclusion was established, it was possible to go on to teach the Jews the statutes and the judgments, as Moses indeed goes on to do in the "speech of the mitzvot." In light of this, it is possible that the "Book of the Torah" did indeed include the opening chapters, which serve as an introduction to the main speech.

This assertion is based on explicit references in the text, as the blessings and curses follow the "speech of the mitzvot," which concludes at the end of chapter 26.

A number of verses seem to indicate that the blessings and curses were written along with the "speech of the mitzvot" in the Book of the Torah. Moses warns concerning whoever worships idolatry: וְהִבְדִּילוֹ ה׳ לְרָעָה מִכֹּל שִׁבְטֵי יִשְׂרָאֵל כְּכֹל אָלוֹת הַבְּרִית הַכְּתוּבָה בְּסֵפֶר הַתּוֹרָה הַזֶּה, "God will set him aside for evil, out of all the tribes of Israel, according to all the curses of the covenant that are written in this Book of the Torah" (Deut. 29:20). Similarly, concerning Joshua: וְאַחֲרֵי כֵן קָרָא אֶת כָּל דִּבְרֵי הַתּוֹרָה הַבְּרָכָה וְהַקְּלָלָה כְּכָל הַכָּתוּב בְּסֵפֶר הַתּוֹרָה, "And thereafter he read all the words of the Torah – the blessing and the curse, according to all that is written in the Book of the Torah" (Josh. 8:34).[8] Hence, the blessings and curses were also included in the Book of the Torah, as they are part of the covenant to observe the "Torah."

Between chapter 26, with the end of the "speech of the mitzvot," and chapter 28, with its blessings and curses, is chapter 27, which includes the commands to build an altar on Mount Ebal and write the words of the Torah upon the stones there. It would seem that this chapter, too, is included in the Book of the Torah of Moses, as described in Joshua (8:30–31):

> אָז יִבְנֶה יְהוֹשֻׁעַ מִזְבֵּחַ לַה׳ אֱלֹהֵי יִשְׂרָאֵל בְּהַר עֵיבָל. כַּאֲשֶׁר צִוָּה מֹשֶׁה עֶבֶד ה׳ אֶת בְּנֵי יִשְׂרָאֵל כַּכָּתוּב בְּסֵפֶר תּוֹרַת מֹשֶׁה מִזְבַּח אֲבָנִים שְׁלֵמוֹת אֲשֶׁר לֹא הֵנִיף עֲלֵיהֶן בַּרְזֶל.

8. There are additional verses that mention the blessings and curses as included in the Book of the Torah: גַּם כָּל חֳלִי וְכָל מַכָּה אֲשֶׁר לֹא כָתוּב בְּסֵפֶר הַתּוֹרָה הַזֹּאת יַעְלֵם ה׳ עָלֶיךָ עַד הִשָּׁמְדָךְ, "Also every sickness, and every plague which is not written in this Book of the Torah, will God bring upon you, until you are destroyed" (Deut. 28:61); לֹא יֹאבֶה ה׳ סְלֹחַ לוֹ כִּי אָז יֶעְשַׁן אַף ה׳ וְקִנְאָתוֹ בָּאִישׁ הַהוּא וְרָבְצָה בּוֹ כָּל הָאָלָה הַכְּתוּבָה בַּסֵּפֶר הַזֶּה, "God will not spare him, but then the anger of God and His jealousy shall smoke against that man, and all the curses that are written in this Book will lie upon him" (Deut. 29:19); וַיִּחַר אַף ה׳ בָּאָרֶץ הַהִוא לְהָבִיא עָלֶיהָ אֶת כָּל הַקְּלָלָה הַכְּתוּבָה בַּסֵּפֶר הַזֶּה, "And God's anger burned against that land, to bring upon it all the curses that are written in this Book" (Deut. 29:26).

> Then Joshua built an altar to the Lord God of Israel, on Mount Ebal, as Moses, the servant of God, had commanded the Children of Israel, as it is written in the Book of the Torah of Moses – an altar of whole stones over which no iron had been lifted.

That verse represents an almost verbatim repetition of Deuteronomy 27:4–5:

> וְהָיָה בְּעָבְרְכֶם אֶת הַיַּרְדֵּן תָּקִימוּ אֶת הָאֲבָנִים הָאֵלֶּה אֲשֶׁר אָנֹכִי מְצַוֶּה אֶתְכֶם הַיּוֹם בְּהַר עֵיבָל...וּבָנִיתָ שָּׁם מִזְבֵּחַ לַה׳ אֱלֹהֶיךָ מִזְבַּח אֲבָנִים לֹא תָנִיף עֲלֵיהֶם בַּרְזֶל.

> And it shall be, when you have passed over the Jordan, you shall set up these stones which I command you this day, on Mount Ebal... and you shall build there an altar to the Lord your God, an altar of stones over which no iron has been lifted.

The repetition of the text of Deuteronomy in the book of Joshua, with its attribution to the "Book of the Torah of Moses," indicates that the "Torah of Moses" included at least chapters 5–28 of Deuteronomy, and perhaps also chapters 1–4.

It is interesting to note that, with regard to the famous command in Joshua (1:8), לֹא יָמוּשׁ סֵפֶר הַתּוֹרָה הַזֶּה מִפִּיךָ וְהָגִיתָ בּוֹ יוֹמָם וָלַיְלָה, "This Book of the Torah shall not depart from your mouth, and you shall meditate over it day and night," the midrash comments:

> R. Shimon ben Yoḥai said: "The book of the *mishneh torah*[9] was a banner for Joshua. When the Holy One, blessed be He, appeared to him, He found him sitting with the book of *mishneh torah* in his hand. He said to him, 'Be strong, Joshua; be of good courage, Joshua: this Book of the Torah shall not depart'" (Genesis Rabba 6:9, Theodor-Albeck edition, 49–50)

9. That is, Deuteronomy, which the Sages refer to in many places as "*mishneh torah*" (see, for example, Berakhot 21b).

According to R. Shimon ben Yoḥai, the expression "Book of the Torah" – at least in Joshua – refers to Deuteronomy, rather than to all five books of the Torah.[10]

The word "Torah" also occurs in the books of the Prophets. In most cases, the word is understood to be a general expression for observance of the commandments, which makes it difficult to determine whether the term refers to the Five Books of the Torah or only to the "speech of the mitzvot." However, when the term "Torah" is used to refer to the observance of specific commandments, it is clearly referring to the "speech of the mitzvot" (i.e., Deut. 12–27), and so it is likely that in other contexts as well, "Torah" refers to the "speech of the mitzvot."[11]

For example, we read of King Amatzia:

> וְאֶת בְּנֵי הַמַּכִּים לֹא הֵמִית כַּכָּתוּב בְּסֵפֶר תּוֹרַת מֹשֶׁה אֲשֶׁר צִוָּה ה׳ לֵאמֹר לֹא יוּמְתוּ אָבוֹת עַל בָּנִים וּבָנִים לֹא יוּמְתוּ עַל אָבוֹת כִּי אִם אִישׁ בְּחֶטְאוֹ ימות [יוּמָת קרי].
>
> He did not put to death the children of the murderers [of his father, King Yoash], according to that which is written in the Book of the Torah of Moses, whereby God commanded, saying: "Fathers shall not be put to death for children, nor shall children be put to death for fathers; rather, each shall be put to death for his own sin." (II Kings 14:6)

Here, too, the verse in II Kings repeats Moses's words in his "speech of the mitzvot" almost verbatim: א יוּמְתוּ אָבוֹת עַל בָּנִים וּבָנִים לֹא יוּמְתוּ עַל אָבוֹת אִישׁ בְּחֶטְאוֹ יוּמָתוּ, "Fathers shall not be put to death for children, nor shall children be put to death for fathers; each shall be put to death for his own sin" (Deut. 24:16).

---

10. R. Shimon ben Yoḥai's understanding that the "Book of the Torah" refers to Deuteronomy is consistent. With regard to writing of the Torah upon the stones, he explains that only the "*mishneh torah*" was written.
11. See, for example, Josh. 23:6, I Kings 2:3, and II Kings 23:25.

The book of Daniel (9:11) mentions "the curse and the oath that is written in the Torah of Moses" – referring to the section of blessings and curses in Deuteronomy, as noted above.

II Kings also recounts the discovery of a Book of the Torah in the days of King Josiah: וַיֹּאמֶר חִלְקִיָּהוּ הַכֹּהֵן הַגָּדוֹל עַל שָׁפָן הַסֹּפֵר סֵפֶר הַתּוֹרָה מָצָאתִי בְּבֵית ה׳, "And Hilkiya, the high priest, said to Shafan, the scribe: 'I have found a Book of the Torah in the house of God'" (II Kings 22:8). Again, the reference is most likely to Deuteronomy, as suggested in the commentary attributed to Rashi[12] on Chronicles (see II Chr. 34:14).[13]

TORAH AS THE FIVE BOOKS OF THE TORAH

Thus far we have seen, from the descriptions that appear in the Torah itself as well as from those in the books of the Prophets, that there is no way of knowing how, when, and by whom the Five Books of the Torah were committed to writing. In the later books, the picture changes somewhat, and the existence of a "Book of the Torah" that is more extensive than Deuteronomy itself is mentioned explicitly. For instance, the book of Nehemiah recounts:

> וַיֵּאָסְפוּ כָל הָעָם כְּאִישׁ אֶחָד אֶל הָרְחוֹב אֲשֶׁר לִפְנֵי שַׁעַר הַמָּיִם וַיֹּאמְרוּ לְעֶזְרָא הַסֹּפֵר לְהָבִיא אֶת סֵפֶר תּוֹרַת מֹשֶׁה אֲשֶׁר צִוָּה ה׳ אֶת יִשְׂרָאֵל. וַיָּבִיא עֶזְרָא הַכֹּהֵן אֶת הַתּוֹרָה לִפְנֵי הַקָּהָל מֵאִישׁ וְעַד אִשָּׁה וְכֹל מֵבִין לִשְׁמֹעַ בְּיוֹם אֶחָד לַחֹדֶשׁ הַשְּׁבִיעִי. וַיִּקְרָא בוֹ לִפְנֵי הָרְחוֹב... וַיִּקְרְאוּ בַסֵּפֶר בְּתוֹרַת הָאֱלֹהִים מְפֹרָשׁ וְשׂוֹם שֶׂכֶל וַיָּבִינוּ בַּמִּקְרָא... וּבַיּוֹם הַשֵּׁנִי נֶאֶסְפוּ רָאשֵׁי הָאָבוֹת לְכָל הָעָם הַכֹּהֲנִים וְהַלְוִיִּם אֶל עֶזְרָא הַסֹּפֵר וּלְהַשְׂכִּיל אֶל דִּבְרֵי הַתּוֹרָה. וַיִּמְצְאוּ כָּתוּב בַּתּוֹרָה אֲשֶׁר צִוָּה ה׳ בְּיַד מֹשֶׁה אֲשֶׁר יֵשְׁבוּ בְנֵי יִשְׂרָאֵל בַּסֻּכּוֹת בֶּחָג בַּחֹדֶשׁ הַשְּׁבִיעִי. וַאֲשֶׁר יַשְׁמִיעוּ וְיַעֲבִירוּ קוֹל בְּכָל עָרֵיהֶם וּבִירוּשָׁלַ͏ִם לֵאמֹר צְאוּ הָהָר וְהָבִיאוּ עֲלֵי זַיִת וַעֲלֵי עֵץ שֶׁמֶן וַעֲלֵי הֲדַס וַעֲלֵי תְמָרִים וַעֲלֵי עֵץ עָבֹת

12. As is well known, the commentary that appears as "Rashi" on the book of Chronicles was not written by him. For extensive discussion of this commentary, which was written in Germany in the twelfth century, see Eran Viezel, *HaPerush HaMeyuḥas LeRashi LeSefer Divrei HaYamim* (Jerusalem, 2010).

13. Chapter 3 addresses this matter at length, in the discussion of the writing of the book of Deuteronomy.

לַעֲשֹׂת סֻכֹּת כַּכָּתוּב... וַיִּקְרָא בְּסֵפֶר תּוֹרַת הָאֱלֹהִים יוֹם בְּיוֹם מִן הַיּוֹם הָרִאשׁוֹן עַד הַיּוֹם הָאַחֲרוֹן וַיַּעֲשׂוּ חָג שִׁבְעַת יָמִים וּבַיּוֹם הַשְּׁמִינִי עֲצֶרֶת כַּמִּשְׁפָּט.

All the people gathered themselves together as one man to the broad place that was before the water gate, and they spoke to Ezra the scribe to bring the Book of the Torah of Moses, which God had commanded to Israel. And Ezra the priest brought the Torah before the congregation, both men and women, and all who could hear with understanding, on the first day of the seventh month. And he read from it in front of the broad place.... And they read from the Book of God's Torah, distinctly; and they gave the sense, and caused them to understand the reading.... And on the second day, the heads of fathers' houses of all the people, the priests, and the Levites were gathered to Ezra the scribe, to study the words of the Torah. And they found it written in the Torah that God had commanded by the hand of Moses, that the Children of Israel should dwell in *sukkot* during the festival of the seventh month; and that they should publish and proclaim in all their cities, and in Jerusalem, saying: "Go forth to the mountain, and fetch olive branches, and branches of wild olive, and myrtle branches, and palm branches, and branches of thick trees, to make *sukkot,* as it is written."... And he read from the Book of God's Torah day by day, from the first day until the last day; and they observed the festival for seven days, with a convocation on the eighth day, as prescribed. (Neh. 8:1–18)

In this passage, Ezra reads from the "Book of the Torah of Moses," also called "the Book of God's Torah," verses about the festival of Sukkot. Yet in this case the "Book of the Torah" may not refer solely to Deuteronomy, since the description of Sukkot in the "speech of the mitzvot" (Deut. 16:13–17) makes no mention of such central details as the command to dwell in *sukkot,* the observance of the festival in the seventh month, the observance of the eighth day as a "convocation" (*atzeret*), or even the bringing of the four species. All of these details do, however, appear in

Leviticus (23:33–43).[14] It is clear, therefore, that the Book of the Torah that was read in the days of Ezra included at least Leviticus, and it was called "the Book of Moses."[15]

Chronicles presents a similar phenomenon, with the description of the observance of the second Passover (*Pesaḥ Sheni*) in the days of Hezekiah:

> וַיִּשְׁחֲטוּ הַפֶּסַח בְּאַרְבָּעָה עָשָׂר לַחֹדֶשׁ הַשֵּׁנִי... וַיַּעַמְדוּ עַל עָמְדָם כְּמִשְׁפָּטָם כְּתוֹרַת מֹשֶׁה אִישׁ הָאֱלֹהִים הַכֹּהֲנִים זֹרְקִים אֶת הַדָּם מִיַּד הַלְוִיִּם.
>
> Then they slaughtered the Passover [sacrifice] on the fourteenth day of the second month.... And they stood in their place as prescribed, according to the Torah of Moses, the man of God; the priests sprinkled the blood, which they received from the hands of the Levites. (II Chr. 30:15–16)

---

14. The present discussion will not address the differences between the species mentioned in Nehemiah and the description in Leviticus: וּלְקַחְתֶּם לָכֶם בַּיּוֹם הָרִאשׁוֹן פְּרִי עֵץ הָדָר כַּפֹּת תְּמָרִים וַעֲנַף עֵץ עָבֹת וְעַרְבֵי נָחַל, "You shall take for yourselves on the first day the fruit of the beautiful tree, branches of palm trees, the branches of thick trees, and willows of the brook" (Lev. 23:40). Despite the differences, the linguistic connection between the two sources is clear.
15. The same impression arises from the verses describing previous stages in the book of Ezra. At the beginning of Ezra, the text describes the building of the altar for offering the sacrifices of the festivals of the seventh month, in the days of Yehoshua ben Yehotzadak and Zerubavel ben Shealtiel:

    > וַיָּקָם יֵשׁוּעַ בֶּן יוֹצָדָק וְאֶחָיו הַכֹּהֲנִים וּזְרֻבָּבֶל בֶּן שְׁאַלְתִּיאֵל וְאֶחָיו וַיִּבְנוּ אֶת מִזְבַּח אֱלֹהֵי יִשְׂרָאֵל לְהַעֲלוֹת עָלָיו עֹלוֹת כַּכָּתוּב בְּתוֹרַת מֹשֶׁה אִישׁ הָאֱלֹהִים. וַיַּעֲשׂוּ אֶת חַג הַסֻּכּוֹת כַּכָּתוּב וְעֹלַת יוֹם בְּיוֹם בְּמִסְפָּר כְּמִשְׁפַּט דְּבַר יוֹם בְּיוֹמוֹ. וְאַחֲרֵי כֵן עֹלַת תָּמִיד וְלֶחֳדָשִׁים וּלְכָל מוֹעֲדֵי ה׳ הַמְקֻדָּשִׁים.
    >
    > And Yeshua, son of Yotzadak, and his brethren the *kohanim*, and Zerubavel, son of Shealtiel, and his brethren, arose, and they built the altar of the God of Israel, to offer burnt offerings upon it, as it is written in *the Torah of Moses, the man of God*.... And they observed the festival of Sukkot, as it is written, with the daily burnt offerings by number, as prescribed, fulfilling each day's requirement. And afterwards they offered the continual burnt offering, and of the New Moon, and of all the sanctified times appointed by God. (Ezra 3:2–5)

    Once again, the text reflects, in its plain meaning, commandments that appear in Leviticus and Numbers, but not in Deuteronomy.

It would therefore appear that extensive portions of the Five Books of the Torah were defined as part of the "Torah of Moses." Moreover, later in Nehemiah, the Jewish people commits to observe the Torah – clearly identified with "God's Torah," at the ceremony of the covenant: לָלֶכֶת בְּתוֹרַת הָאֱלֹהִים אֲשֶׁר נִתְּנָה בְּיַד מֹשֶׁה עֶבֶד הָאֱלֹהִים, "To follow God's Torah, which was given by the hand of Moses, God's servant" (Neh. 10:30).

There are no further explicit references in Tanakh that demonstrate how the Five Books of Torah were committed to writing and conveyed to the Jewish people. Analysis of the books of the Prophets and Writings does, however, strongly suggest that they relate to all Five Books of the Torah. This is readily apparent when books of Prophets and Writings refer to verses in the Torah, whether openly or through allusion. It is also evident in narratives that are built upon stories from the Torah – either in the narratives themselves, or in their literary structures. Both phenomena are widespread, as just a few examples will demonstrate.

The books of the Prophets contain many verses that are written in a way that indicates a clear connection to verses in the Torah.[16] An example is Rahab's words to Joshua's spies: יָדַעְתִּי כִּי נָתַן ה׳ לָכֶם אֶת הָאָרֶץ וְכִי נָפְלָה אֵימַתְכֶם עָלֵינוּ וְכִי נָמֹגוּ כָּל יֹשְׁבֵי הָאָרֶץ מִפְּנֵיכֶם, "I know that God has given you the land, and that the fear of you is fallen upon us, and that all the inhabitants of the land melt away from before you" (Josh. 2:9). This language clearly echoes the words of the Song at the Sea: נָמֹגוּ כֹּל יֹשְׁבֵי כְנָעַן, תִּפֹּל עֲלֵיהֶם אֵימָתָה וָפַחַד, "All the inhabitants of Canaan shall melt away; dread and fear shall fall upon them" (Ex. 15:15–16).

The second phenomenon, the literary parallels within Tanakh, have received a great deal of attention in the past generation.[17]

16. The *Daat Mikra* series includes, in the introduction to each book of the Prophets and Writings, an extensive list of parallels between that book and books of the Torah. Examples of such parallels include Joshua 2:9, which parallels Exodus 15:15–16; Judges 2:13, which reprises what God told Moses following the giving of the second set of Tablets in the book of Exodus 34:12–13; I Kings 8:10–11, which refers to Exodus 40:34–35; and even Jeremiah 4:23, which clearly alludes to Genesis 1:2. Further examples abound.

17. A significant contribution was made by Yair Zakovitch, who collated dozens of "mirror narratives," as he calls them, distilling their meaning in his *Mikraot BeEretz HaMarot* (Tel Aviv, 1985). For further reading, see my work, *Makbilot Nifgashot – Makbilot*

Scholars have studied various texts that display commonalities, whether in terms of language or content, where one may reasonably assume that the chronologically later passage alludes intentionally to the earlier one. The discussion of parallels between the books of the Prophets and Writings and the books of the Torah are particularly interesting and germane to this discussion. There are dozens of instances of clear connections between the books – in terms of both content and language. Here, too, a small sample shall suffice.

Several of the stories about Joshua are constructed along the same lines as those about Moses. For example, Joshua's and Moses's sending of spies (Josh. 2; Num. 13); the revelation in Jericho (Josh. 5:15) and the revelation at the burning bush (Ex. 3:5); and the crossing of the Jordan (Josh. 3:3–16) and the splitting of the Red Sea (Ex. 14:21–22).[18]

Similarly, many stories in the Prophets and Writings parallel narratives in the Five Books of Torah. For example, the incident of the concubine in Giv'a (Judges 19) pairs with the story of the angels visiting Lot in Sodom (Gen. 19); the story of Elkana, Hannah, and Penina (the first chapter of I Samuel) clearly echoes the story of Jacob, Rachel, and Leah (Gen. 30); Elijah at Horeb (I Kings 19) strongly aligns with Moses; and there are many other narratives as well that demonstrate a clear connection between the stories in the Prophets and Writings and those in the Torah. In the great majority of cases, the significance of the literary parallel is clear, and we are able to understand the literary benefit of writing the stories in this way so as to emphasize the messages that the Tanakh is seeking to convey.

In many cases, it is apparent that a story in the book of the Prophets consciously adopts the language of a story that appears in the Torah. Let us examine two examples.

Sifrutiot BeSefer Shmuel (Alon Shvut, 2006), 7–11, 194–200. (Although little has appeared in English on the subject of biblical parallels, one such work is that of Judy Klitsner, *Subversive Sequels in the Bible* [Maggid, 2019].)

18. A long list of parallels between Joshua and Moses appears in *Midrash Tanhuma, Tetzaveh*, 19.

1. The parallels between the story of David's marriage to Michal and the story of Jacob's marriage to Rachel are extensive.[19] In terms of content, the two narratives contain many common elements: a father-in-law who violates his commitment to the groom; a father-in-law who has two daughters; a groom who ultimately pays twice; a groom who flees from the father-in-law with the help of the father-in-law's daughters. In addition, the story of David's marriage to Michal uses an expression that is difficult to understand: "The matter pleased David well to be the king's son-in-law, and the days were not yet complete (*velo male'u hayamim*)" (I Sam. 18:26).[20] This opaque expression emphasizes the connection to the story of Jacob and Rachel, where Jacob uses the same phrase in speaking to Laban: "Give me my wife, for my days are complete (*ki male'u yamay*), that I may come to her" (Gen. 29:21). In the story of Jacob, however, the turn of phrase makes sense, since a specific period of time is indeed mentioned. The use of the phrase in Samuel is less logical and therefore calls attention to the narrative's connection to that of Genesis, highlighting the similarities between the two narratives.
2. The parallels between the story of Ruth and Boaz and that of Judah and Tamar are also extensive.[21] The deaths of Mahlon and Khilyon parallel the deaths of Er and Onan; the kinsman declines to marry Ruth, just as Onan avoided fathering a child that would be considered his brother's; both Ruth and Tamar take the initiative to reach out to the patriarch of the family, each of whom ultimately fathers the child, and so on. In Ruth, the story of Judah and Tamar is mentioned explicitly, in the blessing given to Boaz: וִיהִי בֵיתְךָ כְּבֵית פֶּרֶץ אֲשֶׁר יָלְדָה תָמָר לִיהוּדָה, "May your house be like the house of Peretz, whom Tamar bore to Judah" (Ruth 4:12). In both accounts, the root Y-B-M (levirate marriage) appears

19. I discuss this parallel at length elsewhere: see *Makbilot Nifgashot*, 109–21.
20. Rashi explains that he had not waited until the time allotted for his task of gathering a hundred foreskins was complete. Many commentators follow Rashi's lead in this explanation, despite the fact that earlier verses do not indicate that a time frame had been specified for completing the challenge.
21. For a discussion of the parallel between these stories and its significance, see Y. Zakovitch, *Mikra LeYisrael, Rut* (Tel Aviv, 1990), 26–28.

> prominently, which is particularly notable since it appears nowhere else in Tanakh outside of the actual commandment for levirate marriage (Deut., chapter 25). The author of the Book of Ruth demonstrates clear familiarity with the earlier sections of the Torah, and especially Genesis.

In the coming chapters, we shall discuss the critical approach, which suggests a late date for the writing of the Torah and Prophets – either in the late seventh or early sixth centuries BCE, immediately before the destruction of the First Temple, or even later, in the exilic or post-exilic period (dating roughly between 597 and 538 BCE).

I argue that some of the parallels between books of the Prophets and the Torah demonstrate that the passages in the Torah predate the Prophets. The critical approach, however, suggests that the parallels reflect the contemporaneous composition of the books, and the similarities between the texts simply attest to certain expressions being in use at the time of the writing of these passages. The claim of late authorship will be dealt with extensively, but at this stage, the two examples above may be understood to demonstrate that the authors of certain passages in the Prophets were familiar with, and assumed the readers' familiarity with, parts of the Torah.

That is to say, despite the absence of any explicit mention of an extensive written Book of the Torah – beyond sections of Deuteronomy – in the books of the Prophets and Writings (before Ezra and Nehemiah), there are nevertheless clear connections throughout the Prophets and Writings to the books of the Torah, and in some cases, the commonalities prove that parts of the Torah predate parts of the books of the Prophets.

"IT WAS GIVEN PART BY PART"

As noted, the tradition that Moses himself wrote the Five Books of the Torah goes back at least to the beginning of the Second Temple Era. By the time of the Sages, it was taken for granted;[22] in innumerable places, the Sages refer to Moses as having written the Torah, as dictated by God. To cite just one example: "This teaches us that Moses wrote what the

---

22. See the extensive discussion in Sid Z. Leiman, *The Canonization of Hebrew Scripture: The Talmudic and Midrashic Evidence* (Hamden, 1976).

Holy One, blessed be He, told him to. This is as it is written (Jer. 36:18), וַיֹּאמֶר לָהֶם בָּרוּךְ, מִפִּיו יִקְרָא אֵלַי, 'Then Baruch answered them: He dictated to me'" (*Sifrei* Deuteronomy, *piska* 357; and see Bava Batra 15a).[23]

That said, opinions are divided as to when, and in what manner, the Torah was committed to writing and given to the Jewish people. The Talmud (Gittin 60a) records a debate in this regard. According to R. Shimon ben Lakish, "The Torah was given in full and finished form." Rashi (ad loc.) explains: "It was not committed to writing until the end of the forty [years in the desert], after all of the sections had been given over [by God to Moses]. And those that had been given over to him in the first and second years were set forth orally, until he set them in writing."

In contrast, R. Yoḥanan teaches in the name of R. Bena'a: "The Torah was given *megilla megilla*" – that is, one part (literally, "scroll") at a time. The medieval commentators were divided in their understanding of the term "*megilla megilla*." Rashi explains: "When a unit was given over to Moses [by God], he would write it down. At the end of the forty years, when all the sections were complete, he sewed them together with sinews." Here, the repetition of the word *megilla* implies multiple scrolls.[24] According to this view, the Torah was given to Moses piecemeal over the forty years in the desert. It was made up of many different units, and in the fortieth year Moses joined them all together, creating the "Torah."

Nahmanides, in his introduction to Genesis, maintains that the term "*megilla megilla*" actually refers to only two parts, reflecting the literal meaning of the expression, "scroll, scroll," or two scrolls: "When he descended from the mountain, he wrote from the beginning of the Torah until the end of the matter of the Tabernacle, and the rest of the Torah he wrote at the end of the fortieth year."[25]

Although the Torah does not address this question directly, several verses offer support for the view that the Torah was given "one part

23. Meaning that Moses transcribed the Torah from God, just as Baruch transcribed the words of Jeremiah.

24. This is the generally understood meaning of repeated words, such as "*yom yom,*" "*shana shana,*" and "*ish ish.*"

25. For further discussion of this debate, see A. J. Heschel, *Heavenly Torah as Refracted through the Generations*, ed. and transl. G. Tucker with L. Levin (New York, 2005), 631–33.

at a time" and, in accordance with Rashi's understanding, that there were many parts given over the course of the years. There are several mentions of Moses writing down some subject that is part of the Torah.

For instance, after the war against Amalek, Moses is commanded: כְּתֹב זֹאת זִכָּרוֹן בַּסֵּפֶר וְשִׂים בְּאָזְנֵי יְהוֹשֻׁעַ כִּי מָחֹה אֶמְחֶה אֶת זֵכֶר עֲמָלֵק מִתַּחַת הַשָּׁמָיִם, "Write this for a memorial in a book, and repeat it for Joshua to hear – that I shall surely wipe out the remembrance of Amalek from under the heavens" (Ex. 17:14). It is therefore reasonable to conclude that at that time, Moses wrote down the episode of the war.

In the second description of the Revelation at Sinai, the Torah does not elaborate on what the people heard from Moses, but from the people's response we understand that the "Book of the Covenant" included several commandments, and not necessarily all the commandments in the Torah.[26]

> וַיִּכְתֹּב מֹשֶׁה אֵת כָּל דִּבְרֵי ה׳...וַיַּשְׁכֵּם בַּבֹּקֶר וַיִּקַּח סֵפֶר הַבְּרִית וַיִּקְרָא בְּאָזְנֵי הָעָם וַיֹּאמְרוּ כֹּל אֲשֶׁר דִּבֶּר ה׳ נַעֲשֶׂה וְנִשְׁמָע
>
> And Moses wrote all of God's words... and he arose early in the morning, and he took the Book of the Covenant, and read it for the people to hear, and they said: "All that God has spoken – we shall do and we shall hear." (Ex. 24:4–7)

---

26. In this regard there is a disagreement among the Sages of the Mishna (*Mekhilta DeRabbi Yishmael, Yitro, masekhta divehodesh, parasha* 3, Horowitz-Rabin ed., 211). According to Rabbi, the "book" indeed included only mitzvot: "The mitzvot that had been commanded to Adam, and the mitzvot that had been commanded to the sons of Noah, and the commandments that they [the Jewish people] had been given in Egypt and at Mara, and all the rest of the mitzvot." According to Rabbi Yossi, son of Rav Yehuda, the book recorded everything "from the beginning of Genesis up to that point." This opinion serves as the source upon which Nahmanides relies in his interpretation as noted above, concerning the expression "*megilla megilla*." Among biblical academics, the prevalent view is that the "Book of the Covenant" or "Covenant Code" consisted of the chapters preceding this one in *Parashat Mishpatim* – that is, chapters 21–23 of Exodus. See, for example, David P. Wright, "The Origin, Development, and Context of the Covenant Code (Ex. 20:23–23:19)," in *The Book of Exodus; Composition, Reception, and Interpretation*, eds. Thomas B. Dozeman, Craig A. Evans, Joel N. Lohr (Leiden and Boston: Brill, 2014), 220–44.

The journeys of the Jewish people in the wilderness were likewise recorded by Moses: וַיִּכְתֹּב מֹשֶׁה אֶת מוֹצָאֵיהֶם לְמַסְעֵיהֶם עַל פִּי ה׳, "And Moses wrote their departures by their journeys at God's command" (Num. 33:2). The verse presents the picture of Moses writing short units, allowing for the interpretation that the rest of the Torah's sections were recorded in this way, piecemeal, until the entire Torah was complete.[27]

The discussion regarding how Moses recorded the events that occurred during his lifetime – whether in many distinct scrolls or two long pieces of writing – applies, of course, only to the texts that describe those events contemporaneous with Moses. But what about Genesis? One might suggest that Genesis is another text written by Moses at God's command, a simple explanation for how Moses knew the details of events that had happened before his time. Yet another possibility lies in the presumption that the "Torah was given part by part" – perhaps Genesis already existed in written form prior to Moses's time, and Moses then copied the ancient text into the Torah that he wrote. According to a midrash in Exodus Rabba, Moses knew the stories of Genesis thanks to a book he had read prior to the giving of the Torah:

> וַיָּשָׁב מֹשֶׁה אֶל ה׳ וַיֹּאמַר אֲדֹנָי לָמָה הֲרֵעֹתָה לָעָם הַזֶּה, "And Moses went back to God and said: 'God, why have You dealt harshly with this people?'" (Ex. 5:22) .... This is what he said to the Holy One, blessed be He: "I took the Book of Genesis, and read it, and saw the actions of the generation of the Flood, [and] how they were judged – this was the Attribute of Justice; and the actions of the generation of the Dispersion, [and] of the people of Sodom, [and] how they were judged – this was the Attribute of Justice. But this nation – what have they done, that they have been enslaved and

27. It is interesting to note that according to *Ḥizkuni* (also known as *Ḥazzekuni*, a Torah commentary written by Rabbi Hezekiah b. Manoah, a thirteenth-century French rabbi), when Moses ultimately committed all the "parts" to writing, it was he himself who decided upon their order: "But the Torah was given as a scroll, for as Moses heard the commandments from the Holy One, blessed be He, he would write each one of them on a separate scroll. When his time came to leave this world, he organized the Book of the Torah and set the units in it, to this day, in accordance with the proper juxtapositions of them, as our Sages have taught" (*Ḥizkuni* on Ex. 34:32).

> punished more harshly than all the previous generations? And if it is because our forefather Abraham said, בַּמָּה אֵדַע כִּי אִירָשֶׁנָּה, 'By what shall I know that I shall inherit it [the land]?' (Gen. 15:8), and You answered him, יָדֹעַ תֵּדַע כִּי גֵר יִהְיֶה זַרְעֲךָ בְּאֶרֶץ לֹא לָהֶם, 'Know with certainty that your descendants will be strangers' (Gen. 15:13), then what about Esau and Ishmael? They too are his descendants, and they should have been enslaved too!" (Exodus Rabba 5:22)

This passage posits the existence of a "Book of Genesis," including the exact text of the stories of the forefathers, before Moses's time. The same source, Exodus Rabba, also indicates that the Jewish people were aware of these texts:

> תִּכְבַּד הָעֲבֹדָה עַל הָאֲנָשִׁים, "Increase the work load upon the men" (Ex. 5:9) – this teaches that they possessed texts that they would read every Sabbath, in which it was written that the Holy One, blessed be He, would redeem Israel. Because they rested on the Sabbath, Pharaoh decreed, תִּכְבַּד הָעֲבֹדָה עַל הָאֲנָשִׁים וְיַעֲשׂוּ בָהּ וְאַל יִשְׁעוּ בְּדִבְרֵי שָׁקֶר, "Increase the work load upon the men, that they may labor in it, and not pay heed to vain words." Let them not relax and let them not rest on the Sabbath.

The midrash offers no indication as to who wrote these texts, or how, but it clearly suggests that some parts of the Torah had originally been written at different periods of time, and by different people. According to this account, only afterwards did Moses integrate these texts at God's command into the Torah.[28]

Indeed, the existence of an ancient text is mentioned explicitly at least once in Genesis: זֶה סֵפֶר תּוֹלְדֹת אָדָם בְּיוֹם בְּרֹא אֱלֹהִים אָדָם בִּדְמוּת אֱלֹהִים עָשָׂה אתו, "This is the Book of the Generations of Man; on the day that God created man, in the likeness of God He made him" (Gen. 5:1). A genealogy of the ten generations from Adam to Noah apparently existed from antiquity as a separate work, and was later included – in whole or

28. See also Heschel, *Heavenly Torah as Refracted through the Generations*, 650–53.

in part[29] – as part of the Torah of Moses, perhaps having already been included in the ancient Book of Genesis, as per Exodus Rabba.

MOSES'S ROLE IN THE WRITING OF THE TORAH

A further question that must be addressed is whether Moses was involved in determining the wording of the Torah, or whether all its verses were dictated by God. The biblical text does not address this question; however, the Midrash offers two approaches. The first is already familiar:

> Moses wrote down whatever the Holy One, blessed be He, told him to write, as it is written (Jer. 36:18), וַיֹּאמֶר לָהֶם בָּרוּךְ, מִפִּיו יִקְרָא אֵלַי, "And Baruch said to them, 'He dictated all these words to me.'" (*Sifrei* Deuteronomy, *piska* 357)

According to this opinion, God dictated the Torah to Moses, word for word. Nahmanides adopts this view, writing in his introduction to Genesis:

> Thus, Moses was like a scribe copying an ancient text, and therefore he did the writing, but it is true and clear that the entire Torah, from the beginning of Genesis to "in the eyes of all Israel" [i.e., the end of Deuteronomy] was uttered by the Holy One, blessed be He, to Moses, in the same way that we find: מִפִּיו יִקְרָא אֵלַי אֵת כָּל הַדְּבָרִים הָאֵלֶּה וַאֲנִי כֹּתֵב עַל הַסֵּפֶר בַּדְּיו, "He dictated all these words to me, and I wrote them with ink in the book" (Jer. 36:18).[30]

---

29. The Sages refer to this book as "the Book of Adam" (Genesis Rabba, Vilna edition, 24:3–7), and explain that this prophetic book included the names of the people of all generations. Elsewhere we read that God showed this book to Moses: "What did the Holy One, blessed be He, do? He brought him the Book of Adam and showed him all the generations that were destined to arise, from the Beginning until the Resurrection" (Exodus Rabba, Vilna edition, 40). On this basis, it would seem that only the first part of the book was included as part of the Torah. It should be noted that there are commentators who interpret the word "book" not in the sense of an object – a written text – but rather as an "account": "These are the accountings of the generations of Man" (Rashi there; see also Radak).
30. On the question of whether the Torah was dictated to Moses orally or whether he copied it from an "ancient book," see Heschel, *Heavenly Torah as Refracted through the Generations*, 538–42.

In other midrashim, however, as well as in the writings of many medieval sages, Moses is identified as the "writer" of the Torah, though its content is presented as entirely received from God. A midrash in Exodus Rabba takes this approach:

> "Write for yourself" (Ex. 34:27): The ministering angels said to the Holy One, blessed be He: "You are giving license to Moses to write whatever he wishes; he might say to Israel, 'I gave you the Torah – I am the one who wrote it and gave it to you!'" The Holy One, blessed be He, told them: "Heaven forefend that Moses would do that, and even if he did, he is trusted, as it is written (Num. 12:7), לֹא כֵן עַבְדִּי מֹשֶׁה בְּכָל בֵּיתִי נֶאֱמָן הוּא, 'Not so My servant, Moses; in all of My house He is trusted.'" (Exodus Rabba, Vilna edition, *Ki Tisa* 47:9)

According to this midrash, God did not necessarily dictate the Torah to Moses, but trusted Moses to write in accordance with His will:

> Even if Moses were to write something in the Torah on his own initiative, it would not be, heaven forefend, with the intention of being able to say that he himself had written and initiated that element; rather, he is "trusted in all the house" of Torah, and to him I have handed over all the principles and ways of the Torah." (Commentary of Rabbi Ze'ev Wolf Einhorn)[31]

This midrash stipulates, therefore, that Moses wrote the Torah in accordance with his own understanding, with God's permission, for God trusted that Moses's writings would align with the divine will.

It should be noted, however, that a mishna in Sanhedrin (10:1) lists, among those who have no share in the World to Come, one who says, "The Torah is not divine in origin." Two of the Talmud's teachings regarding this statement pertain to the actual writing of the Torah:

---

31. One of the greatest of the commentators on the midrash; he lived in Vilna in the nineteenth century.

> Our Sages taught: "For he has despised God's word and has violated His commandments; that soul shall utterly be cut off" (Num. 15:31) – this refers to one who says, "The Torah is not divine."... Another opinion says: "For he has despised God's word" – this refers to one who says that the Torah is not divine, and even to one who says: "The entire Torah is divine, except for this verse, which was not said by God but rather Moses said it himself," this is, "for he has despised God's word." And even if he says, "The entire Torah is divine, except for this detail, this *kal vaḥomer*, this *gezera shava"* [i.e., Torah laws that are deduced by means of the hermeneutical rules], this is, "for he has despised God's word." (Sanhedrin 99a)

These two opinions reflect very different positions. According to the first view, following the plain meaning of the mishna, the punishment stated in the verse refers only to one who denies altogether that the Torah was conveyed by God to Israel. According to the second view, the required belief in the Torah's divinity is far more extensive in scope, and it requires one to believe that not even a single verse was uttered by Moses on his own. It also requires one to accept the divine origin of the lessons derived through the hermeneutical laws, within the framework of the Oral Law.

This second approach, established as one of Maimonides's Thirteen Principles of Faith,[32] appears at first glance to contradict the description in Exodus Rabba cited above. However, this is not necessarily the case. Faith in "the divine origin of the Torah" (*Torah min haShamayim*) to the extent that Moses did not act of his own accord, does not rule out the possibility that

32. See Maimonides's *Commentary on the Mishna,* Introduction to chapter "*Helek*" in Tractate Sanhedrin and *Mishneh Torah, Hilkhot Teshuva* 3:8. The eighth of Maimonides's Thirteen Principles of Faith is the belief that Torah is from Heaven, "that is, that we believe the entire Torah which we have in our hands today is the Torah that was given to Moses, that it is all divinely spoken: that is to say that all of it reached him through a mechanism that we refer to as speech.... The idea that Torah is not from Heaven means that one who says, 'All of Torah is from the mouth of the Holy One, blessed be He, except for one verse that the Holy One, blessed be He, did not say but rather Moses said it himself,' of him, we say, 'He has reviled God's word.'" Thus Maimonides ruled in the *Mishneh Torah* (*Hilkhot Teshuva* 3:8): "Anyone who says that the Torah, even one verse or one word of it, is not from God, or who says: 'Moses made these statements independently,' denies the Torah completely."

God gave Moses license to write the Torah in his own words, and that Moses did not deviate from the framework of the license given to him.

Indeed, several medieval sages of northern France, well acquainted with the talmudic concern, maintain that Moses had God's permission to formulate the text.

Rashbam (c. 1085–1146), the grandson of Rashi and a leading biblical commentator and halakhist in his own right, offers a unique view. He advances the "introductory approach," arguing that many units or verses in the Torah were written not for their own sake, but rather as a preface or background to units that appear later in the Torah. Rashbam suggests that these preambles were written by Moses in order to clarify certain points later on in the Torah. Consider, for instance, his explanation of why the Book of Genesis needed to start with the story of Creation:

> This entire unit on the work of the six days is brought by Moses as a preface to explain what God says later, at the time of the giving of the Torah: זָכוֹר אֶת יוֹם הַשַּׁבָּת לְקַדְּשׁוֹ...כִּי שֵׁשֶׁת יָמִים עָשָׂה ה׳ אֶת הַשָּׁמַיִם וְאֶת הָאָרֶץ, אֶת הַיָּם וְאֶת כָּל אֲשֶׁר בָּם, וַיָּנַח בַּיּוֹם הַשְּׁבִיעִי, "Remember the Sabbath day, to sanctify it...for [over] six days God made the heavens and the earth, the sea, and all that is in them, and He rested on the seventh day" (Ex. 20:8–11). And this is the meaning of the verse, וַיְהִי עֶרֶב וַיְהִי בֹקֶר יוֹם הַשִּׁשִּׁי, "And it was evening and it was morning, the sixth day" (Gen. 1:31) – that sixth day, which was the conclusion of the six days of which God spoke at the giving of the Torah. Therefore Moses told this to Israel, so they would know that God's word is truth: "Do you then maintain that the world has always been built up as you see it now, full of all kinds of goodness? It was not so; rather, בְּרֵאשִׁית בָּרָא אֱלֹהִים, 'In the beginning, God created.'" (Rashbam, Gen. 1:1)

According to Rashbam, Moses wrote the account of Creation to teach the Jewish people the significance of God's declaration at Sinai that He had created the world in six days.

Elsewhere, Rashbam explains why the Torah records the stories of Joseph and his brothers: "All of this was necessary for Moses to write, for by means of this, he rebuked them (Deut. 10:22): בְּשִׁבְעִים נֶפֶשׁ יָרְדוּ

אֲבֹתֶיךָ מִצְרָיְמָה, 'As seventy souls, your forefathers went down'" (Rashbam, Gen. 37:2).[33]

A similar approach is adopted by Rabbi Yosef Bekhor Shor, in his commentary on the Torah, discussing Jacob's instructions to the messengers who carry his gift to Esau:[34]

> וַאֲמַרְתֶּם גַּם הִנֵּה עַבְדְּךָ יַעֲקֹב אַחֲרֵינוּ כִּי אָמַר אֲכַפְּרָה פָנָיו בַּמִּנְחָה הַהֹלֶכֶת לְפָנָי וְאַחֲרֵי כֵן אֶרְאֶה פָנָיו אוּלַי יִשָּׂא פָנָי.
>
> And you shall say, "Moreover, behold, your servant, Jacob, is behind us" – for he said, "I shall appease him with the gift that goes before me, and afterwards I shall see his face; perhaps he will accept me." (Gen. 32:21)

The end of Jacob's message to Esau is absent from these instructions to the messengers. What were the messengers supposed to convey to Esau? Some of the commentators contend that the final words – "and afterwards I shall see his face; perhaps he will accept me" – are not part of the message at all. Rather, they express Jacob's inner monologue at the time. Ibn Ezra, for example, writes: "'For he said' – [this refers to] Jacob, in his heart; and these are the words of Moses."[35] Rabbi Yosef Bekhor

33. For more on this subject, see E. Touitou, *HaPeshatot HaMit'ḥadshim BeKhol Yom – Iyunim BePerusho Shel Rashbam LaTorah* (Jerusalem, 2003), 120–22. Touitou expands on Rashbam's approach and posits that the entire narrative aspect of the Torah, along with Deuteronomy, were written by Moses, of his own accord, while only the halakhic aspects, including the commandments, were written by Moses at God's command. The justification for this expansion is not sufficiently proven. See M. Sabbato, "Perush Rashbam LaTorah," *Maḥanayim* 3 (5753/1993): 116–17, and A. Kislev, "VaAni Lefaresh Peshutan Shel Mikra'ot Bati," *Shenaton LeḤeker HaMikra VeHaMizraḥ HaKadum* 15 (5765/2005): 321.

34. Rabbi Yosef Bekhor Shor, who lived in the twelfth century, was a disciple of Rabbenu Tam and one of the Tosafists. He wrote a commentary on the Torah (a critical edition edited by Y. Nevo was published by Mossad HaRav Kook (Jerusalem, 1994) and on Psalms, as well as *piyutim* (liturgical poems) and commentaries on the Talmud. See E. E. Urbach, *Baalei HaTosafot*, vol. 1 (Jerusalem, 1954), 132–40, and Y. Jacobs, *Bekhor Shoro Hadar Lo* (Jerusalem, 2017).

35. Ibn Ezra often employs the phrase "the words of Moses" to mean the narrator's interpolation (generally to explain something that is not direct speech). See, for example, his commentary on Genesis 20:16, 28:11, and 32:11.

Shor adopts the same view, but expresses it in a more radical way: "The author of the book (*baal hasefer*) is explaining that this is why Jacob did all of this – in order to dissipate Esau's anger, were his intentions to have been evil; but the shepherds did not say this [to Esau]."

Rabbi Yosef Bekhor Shor explains other background comments in the Torah narrative using the same manner of interpreting phrases as narrative comment. For instance, with regard to the verse וַיַּצֵּב יַעֲקֹב מַצֵּבָה עַל קְבֻרָתָהּ הִוא מַצֶּבֶת קְבֻרַת רָחֵל עַד הַיּוֹם, "Jacob set up a pillar upon her grave; that is the pillar of Rachel's grave to this very day" (Gen. 35:20), he writes: "So says the author of the book (*baal hasefer*) – that that is the pillar of Rachel's grave, which still existed until his day."[36]

Another commentator who takes this approach is Rabbi Yehuda HeHasid.[37] He maintains, for example, that the final chapter of the Torah, describing how Moses saw the entire land, actually preceded – chronologically – the writing of the section that sets forth the boundaries of the land, at the end of Numbers (chapter 34). Were this not the case, he argues, Moses would not have been able to describe the land in such detail:

---

36. For more on Rabbi Yosef Bekhor Shor's approach, see R. Harris, "Muda'ut LeArikhat HaMikra Etzel Parshanei Tzefon Tzarfat," *Shenaton LeḤeker HaMikra VeHaMizraḥ HaKadum* 12, 302–5.

37. Rabbi Yehuda son of Shmuel HeHasid, of Speyer, was born around the year 1140 and died in 1217. He was one of the leaders of the group known as *Ḥasidei Ashkenaz* (the pietists of Ashkenaz) – a movement that developed during the twelfth and thirteenth centuries and involved various practices related to Kabbalah, with its members adopting a life of asceticism and self-mortification. The students of Rabbi Yehuda HeHasid included some of the most important sages of Ashkenaz, such as Rabbi Yitzhak, author of the *Ohr Zaru'a*, and Rabbi Moshe of Coucy, author of the *Sefer HaMitzvot HaGadol* (*Semag*). Rabbi Yehuda's best known work is *Sefer Ḥasidim*, which includes moral teachings, matters of halakha and customs, explanations of prayers, and various commentaries. He is also known for his ethical will, *Tzvaat Rabbi Yehuda HeHasid*, which includes ten "legacies" and practices, some of which are highly unusual.

Some fifty years ago, a book entitled *Perushei HaTorah LeRabbi Yehuda HeḤasid* was published in Jerusalem by Yitzhak Shimshon Lange, based on two manuscripts, as well as various commentaries that appeared in other books and were attributed to Rabbi Yehuda HeHasid. The commentary was written by Rabbi Yehuda's son, Rabbi Moshe Zaltman, who found some of the material among his father's writings, heard other parts directly from his father, and gathered additional material from others who conveyed teachings in his father's name. The book gave rise to extensive debate, which will be discussed in the next section.

> וַיַּרְאֵהוּ ה' אֶת כָּל הָאָרֶץ, "And God showed him the entire land" (Deut. 34:1), and this was...prior to the end of *Parashat Masei,* where it says, "And the border shall go down to Zifron,"[38] and likewise concerning all [the borders], for how could Moses have written all this if he had not seen it all from Har HaAvarim, Mount Nebo? For the Torah does not follow chronological order. (Commentary of Rabbi Yehuda HeHasid, Deut. 3:25)

The basic assumption here is that Moses could not have written a description of the borders of the land without having seen it with his own eyes; hence, the conclusion is that God did not dictate this to him. Elsewhere in his commentary, Rabbi Yehuda HeHasid is quoted as saying that a chronological distinction should be drawn between the writing of the two verses in the Torah that pertain to the command to build *sukkot.* In his view, the verse, בַּסֻּכֹּת תֵּשְׁבוּ שִׁבְעַת יָמִים, כָּל הָאֶזְרָח בְּיִשְׂרָאֵל יֵשְׁבוּ בַּסֻּכֹּת, "You shall dwell in *sukkot* for seven days, every citizen in Israel shall dwell in *sukkot*" (Lev. 23:42), was written in the first year after the Exodus. The explanation for this command, which appears in the following verse, is לְמַעַן יֵדְעוּ דֹרֹתֵיכֶם כִּי בַסֻּכּוֹת הוֹשַׁבְתִּי אֶת בְּנֵי יִשְׂרָאֵל בְּהוֹצִיאִי אוֹתָם מֵאֶרֶץ מִצְרָיִם, "in order that your generations will know that I caused the Children of Israel to dwell in *sukkot* when I brought them out of the land of Egypt." Rabbi Yehuda HeHasid suggests that this explanation was added by Moses in the fortieth year, and refers to the *sukkot* in which the Children of Israel dwelled on the plains of Moab, during the conquest of the land:

> This verse was uttered in the fortieth year, when they were encamped on the plains of Moab, and dwelled in *sukkot,* and were conquering territories.[39] God had commanded it in the

---

38. Num. 34:9; the Masoretic, traditional, text reads, וְיָצָא הַגְּבֻל זִפְרֹנָה, "And the border shall emerge (*veyatza hagevul*) to Zifron."

39. Apparently, Rabbi Yehuda HeHasid's argument that dwelling in *sukkot* is related to war arises from the fact that, in various places, "*sukkot*" appear in the description of preparations for war. For example, in the words of Uriah the Hittite: הָאָרוֹן וְיִשְׂרָאֵל וִיהוּדָה יֹשְׁבִים בַּסֻּכּוֹת וַאדֹנִי יוֹאָב וְעַבְדֵי אֲדֹנִי עַל פְּנֵי הַשָּׂדֶה חֹנִים, "The Ark, and Israel, and Judah, dwell in *sukkot,* and my lord Yoav, and my master's servants, are encamped

> wilderness of Sinai, and Moses wrote this in the fortieth year in order to provide an explanation for what He had commanded concerning *sukkot* – because it was God's intention to cause you to dwell in *sukkot* and to conquer territory for you" (*Perushei HaTorah LeRabbi Yehuda HeḤasid*, Lev. 23:43).[40]

This approach is also employed by the compilers of the medieval midrashim – *Lekaḥ Tov* and *Sekhel Tov*. Rabbi Tuvia ben Eliezer, compiler of the *Midrash Lekaḥ Tov* (also known as *Pesikta Zutreta*), in addressing the story of the Creation, explains why on the sixth day the Torah says, "*the* sixth day" (Gen. 1:31), using the definite article, in contrast to the other days ("*a* fifth day," "*a* fourth day," etc.):[41]

> Another explanation: "The sixth day" – when the Holy One, blessed be He, gave the Torah to Moses at Mount Sinai, He recounted to him the entire act of Creation, from beginning to end. When the Holy One, blessed be He, said, זָכוֹר אֶת יוֹם הַשַּׁבָּת לְקַדְּשׁוֹ...כִּי שֵׁשֶׁת יָמִים עָשָׂה ה׳ אֶת הַשָּׁמַיִם וְאֶת הָאָרֶץ...וַיָּנַח בַּיּוֹם הַשְּׁבִיעִי, "Remember the Sabbath day, to sanctify it … for in six days God made the heavens and the earth … and He rested on the seventh day" (Ex. 20:8–11), and Moses arranged the entire work of Creation in a book, and wrote, "*the* sixth day," the day upon which there was an end to the labor of the world. Likewise he says, וְהָיָה בַּיּוֹם הַשִּׁשִּׁי וְהֵכִינוּ אֵת אֲשֶׁר יָבִיאוּ, "And it shall be on *the* sixth day that they shall prepare that which they

in the field" (II Sam. 11:11). Or in the war that Ahab wages against Aram, where we read of Ben Hadad: וְהוּא שֹׁתֶה הוּא וְהַמְּלָכִים בַּסֻּכּוֹת וַיֹּאמֶר אֶל עֲבָדָיו שִׂימוּ וַיָּשִׂימוּ עַל הָעִי, "And he was drinking – he and the nobles – in *sukkot*, and he said to his servants, 'Set yourselves in array,' and they set themselves in array against the city" (I Kings 20:12).

40. For additional places where Rabbi Yehuda HeHasid follows this approach, see G. Brin, "Kavim LePerush HaTorah Shel Rabbi Yehuda HeḤasid," in *Te'udah – Meḥkarim BeSifrut HaTalmud, BeLashon Ḥazal, U'VeParshanut HaMikra* (Tel Aviv, 1983), vol. 3, 221–23.

41. This midrash was compiled in the eleventh century, apparently in Greece. Concerning the midrash (and the source of the name *Pesikta Zutreta*, which seems to have been based on an error), see H. L. Strack and G. Stemberger, *Introduction to the Talmud and Midrash*, transl. M. Bockmuehl (Minneapolis, 1992), 356–57.

will bring in" (Ex. 16:5). Therefore, he said, "*the* sixth day" here too – in other words, the sixth day of activity. (*Lekaḥ Tov*, Gen. 1:31, Buber edition, 16)

According to the *Midrash Lekaḥ Tov*, God "recounted" to Moses all of Creation, and Moses "arranged" it all in a book; and it was Moses who decided on the expression, "the sixth day." This view conforms with the introduction of this midrash to the Torah:

> Moses wrote, with divine inspiration, the creation of the world, in accordance with all that is written in the book of the Torah of Moses, the man of God, from God's mouth, so as to make His might known to His nation, Israel. (*Lekaḥ Tov*, Buber edition, 70a–b)

Moses heard the story from God, but he was the one who wrote it down, with his divine inspiration and in his own words.[42]

In light of this interpretation, we can also understand the midrashic comment on the verse: וּמָה הָאָרֶץ הַשְּׁמֵנָה הִוא אִם רָזָה הֲיֵשׁ בָּהּ עֵץ אִם אַיִן, וְהִתְחַזַּקְתֶּם וּלְקַחְתֶּם מִפְּרִי הָאָרֶץ וְהַיָּמִים יְמֵי בִּכּוּרֵי עֲנָבִים, "And what is the land – is it fat or lean? Is there a tree in it or none? And you shall gird yourself and take of the fruit of the land – and the season was the season of the first of the grapes" (Num. 13:20). Here, too, one can ask which of Moses's words are addressed to the spies, and which are not. The final words of the verse appear to be independent of his message to them, which aligns with Rashbam's understanding of the verse.

---

42. It seems that this is how we should understand the midrashic teaching concerning God's words to Moses: בֹּא אֶל פַּרְעֹה: כִּי אֲנִי הִכְבַּדְתִּי אֶת לִבּוֹ, וְאֶת לֵב עֲבָדָיו, לְמַעַן שִׁתִי אֹתֹתַי אֵלֶּה, בְּקִרְבּוֹ. וּלְמַעַן תְּסַפֵּר בְּאָזְנֵי בִנְךָ וּבֶן בִּנְךָ, אֵת אֲשֶׁר הִתְעַלַּלְתִּי בְּמִצְרַיִם, "Come to Pharaoh, for I have hardened his heart, and the heart of his servants, in order that I may set these signs of Mine in his midst. And in order that you will tell it in the hearing of your children and your children's children, that which I performed in Egypt" (Ex. 10:1–2). According to the midrash, God's command to Moses related to the writing of the story of the Exodus in the Torah: "This verse was said to Moses, in order that he would tell it in the Torah, to make it known to future generations." Here, too, the text gives the impression that God dictates the content to Moses, but leaves the wording to the prophet's own judgment.

The *Midrash Lekaḥ Tov* presents this approach slightly differently: "This is a note by the editor (*hasadran*), to speak the praises of the Land of Israel" (*Lekaḥ Tov*, Num. 13, Buber edition, 210). This term, *hasadran*, is used in the midrash to refer to the writer, or compiler, of the Torah in other places too.[43]

This writer or compiler also turns up in the work of Rabbi Menahem ben Shlomo, compiler of the *Yalkut Sekhel Tov*.[44] In five different places in his commentary, the collection of midrashim mentions the "*sadran*" – in contexts that are similar to the instances treated in *Midrash Lekaḥ Tov*.[45] For instance, concerning the verse, וַיָּשֶׂם אֹתָהּ יוֹסֵף לְחֹק עַד הַיּוֹם הַזֶּה עַל אַדְמַת מִצְרַיִם לְפַרְעֹה לַחֹמֶשׁ, "And Joseph made it a law over the land of Egypt, to this very day, that a fifth part goes to Pharaoh" (Gen. 47:26), *Midrash Sekhel Tov* writes: "'To this very day' – this is a comment by the *sadran*" (Buber edition, 298).[46]

Thus, we have seen that there are two main approaches to understanding the way in which Moses wrote the Torah. According to one approach, exemplified by certain midrashim and Nahmanides, God dictated the Torah to Moses, word for word, and Moses served merely as

---

43. The midrash notes that when Jacob's sons report Joseph's words to them, they claim that he told them, וְהָבִיאוּ אֶת אֲחִיכֶם הַקָּטֹן אֵלַי וְאֵדְעָה כִּי לֹא מְרַגְּלִים אַתֶּם כִּי כֵנִים אַתֶּם, אֶת אֲחִיכֶם אֶתֵּן לָכֶם וְאֶת הָאָרֶץ תִּסְחָרוּ, "And bring your youngest brother to me, that I may know that you are not spies, but that you are honest men; I shall deliver your brother to you, and you shall conduct commerce in the land" (Gen. 42:34). In the Torah's account of the actual exchange, there was no mention of commerce at the end (Gen. 42:16). *Midrash Lekaḥ Tov* explains this as follows: "The *sadran* was sparing with words, for the Torah did not previously report [that Joseph said], 'and you shall conduct commerce in the land'; yet they reported to their father [that Joseph had said], 'and you shall conduct commerce in the land'" (Buber edition, 105b–106a). For more on the matter of the "*sadran*" in this midrash, see G. Brin, "HaSadran VeHaMesader," *Leshonenu* 66 (5765/2005): 341–46.

44. This midrash was compiled in 1139, apparently in Italy.

45. Aside from the examples treated below, see Genesis 26:32, Buber edition, 107; Genesis 36:31, 210; Genesis 41:4, 250; Genesis 43:34, 265 (in this instance, the commentary parallels that which appears on the same verse in the *Midrash Lekaḥ Tov*).

46. For more on the attitude of this midrash toward the "*sadran*," see Y. Elbaum, "Yalkut 'Sekhel Tov': Derash, Peshat, VeSugyat HaSadran," in *Davar Davur Al Ofnav: Meḥkarim VeParshanut HaMikra VeHaKoran BiYemei HaBenayim, Mugashim LeHaggai Ben Shammai*, ed. M. M. Bar Asher, et al. (Jerusalem, 2007), 82–93.

a scribe, having no influence on a single word in the Torah. The other approach appears in the works of medieval Ashkenazic commentators, such as Rashbam, R. Yosef Bekhor Shor and R. Yehuda HeHasid, as well as in collections of midrashim, such as *Lekaḥ Tov* and *Sekhel Tov*. It can be summarized as follows: God conveyed the contents of the Torah to Moses, and authorized him to formulate at least some of the text in his own style, or to arrange the materials as he saw fit.

SUMMARY

The Tanakh does not state clearly or explicitly how, and by whom, the Five Books of the Torah were written. The Tanakh generally uses the term "Torah" in its narrowest sense, to mean collections of laws, or in a slightly broader sense that includes central portions of Deuteronomy, which Moses was explicitly commanded to write. The tradition of the Sages maintains unequivocally that it was Moses who wrote all five books, and this tradition is based on explicit verses in Nehemiah. The books of the Prophets, too, make extensive use of the language of the Torah and its content, testifying to the Torah's antiquity.

Among the Sages, however, there are different opinions as to how exactly the Torah came to be written. Among other approaches, the plain text suggests strongly that "the Torah was given one part ('scroll') at a time" – that is, that the Torah is composed of various parts that were written at different times, some perhaps even before Moses's lifetime (such as Genesis), and it was only at the end that Moses joined them all into a single book. Likewise, we noted two approaches among the Sages and medieval commentators for understanding the way in which Moses wrote the Torah: One approach is that the entire Torah was dictated by God to Moses, word for word, from beginning to end. The other view suggests that Moses was given the role of editing and collating, or perhaps even formulating in his own words, the content he had received from God.

Chapter 2

Verses Added to the Torah at a Later Date: The Phenomenon and Its Ramifications

FROM EIGHT VERSES TO THE SECRET OF THE TWELVE

The previous chapter addressed Moses's role in the writing of the Torah, as well as questions of how and when the Torah was written and transmitted to the Children of Israel. Now, the verses in the Torah that appear to have been written after Moses died merit attention.

The earliest discussion of this question arises with regard to the final eight verses of the Torah, which describe Moses's death:

> וַיָּמָת שָׁם מֹשֶׁה עֶבֶד ה׳... וְלֹא יָדַע אִישׁ אֶת קְבֻרָתוֹ עַד הַיּוֹם הַזֶּה... וְלֹא קָם נָבִיא עוֹד בְּיִשְׂרָאֵל כְּמֹשֶׁה אֲשֶׁר יְדָעוֹ ה׳ פָּנִים אֶל פָּנִים.

> And Moses, servant of God, died there.... No man knows the place of his burial to this very day.... No other prophet like Moses has arisen in Israel, who knew God face to face. (Deut. 34:5–10)

Assuming that Moses wrote these verses raises two problems. First, how could Moses describe, in the past tense, events that occurred after his death? Second, one gets the impression from the verses that they are written from a distant perspective.

The Sages offer two different approaches to the issue:

> This follows the opinion that maintains that the eight [final] verses in the Torah were written by Joshua, as the *baraita* [an oral tradition not included in the Mishna] teaches: "And Moses, servant of God, died there" – is it then possible that Moses died and then wrote, "And Moses died there"?[1] [Obviously not;] rather, up to this point Moses wrote, and from this point onwards, it was Joshua who wrote. This represents the view of R. Yehuda, and some say it was R. Neḥemia.
>
> But R. Shimon said to him: Can a *Sefer Torah* be lacking even a single letter? And yet, the verse states, "Take this Book of the Torah (*Sefer Torah*)"! Therefore [we must conclude that Moses wrote and transmitted the entire Torah, including these verses]; up to this point God dictated and Moses repeated and wrote it down, and from this point onwards God dictated and Moses wrote and wept, as we read later (Jer. 36:18), וַיֹּאמֶר לָהֶם בָּרוּךְ מִפִּיו יִקְרָא אֵלַי אֵת כָּל הַדְּבָרִים הָאֵלֶּה, וַאֲנִי כֹּתֵב עַל הַסֵּפֶר בַּדְּיוֹ, "Baruch said to them: All of these things he dictated to me, and I wrote them in a book with ink." (Bava Batra 15a)

According to Rabbi Shimon, Moses himself wrote the final eight verses of the Torah. This seems to suggest that since the Torah is not primarily about the life of Moses, but rather about a wider history of which

1. "Is it possible that Moses died?" is found in *Sifrei,* Deuteronomy 3, 457, Finkelstein edition. This passage in the *Sifrei* is the product of combining two versions, which appear in different sources. The rejected version, which appears in parentheses in that edition, raises the objection that it is impossible for a dead man to write a book. The printed, accepted version, "Is it possible that Moses was alive?" appears in *Midrash Tanna'im* Deuteronomy 44:5, Hoffman edition, 255, and it assumes that a living man cannot write about his death in the past tense, as that would obviously be false.

Moses is a part, the prophet might well receive dictation from God concerning his own death.

By contrast, the first talmudic view posits that it is not possible for one who is alive to write (in the past tense!) about his own death and its aftermath, making it impossible for the concluding verses of the Torah to have been written by Moses himself. Instead, they were written by Joshua bin Nun.

Why Joshua? The Sages discuss an ambiguous verse at the end of the book of Joshua that suggests Joshua added something to the Torah. Following Joshua's speech prior to his own death, the text records:

> וַיִּכְרֹת יְהוֹשֻׁעַ בְּרִית לָעָם בַּיּוֹם הַהוּא וַיָּשֶׂם לוֹ חֹק וּמִשְׁפָּט בִּשְׁכֶם. וַיִּכְתֹּב יְהוֹשֻׁעַ אֶת הַדְּבָרִים הָאֵלֶּה בְּסֵפֶר תּוֹרַת אֱלֹהִים.

> "And Joshua forged a covenant for the nation on that day, and set them a law and a judgment in Shekhem. And Joshua wrote these things in the Book of God's Torah." (Josh. 24:25–26)

Although the chapter that gives this verse its context describes events that do not appear in the Torah, neither in the limited sense (referring to the "speech of mitzvot"), nor in its broader sense (the Five Books of the Torah, as they are known), this verse presents a difficulty in that it seems to suggest that Joshua added to the Torah.

The Talmud suggests two possible meanings: "This was debated by Rabbi Yehuda and Rabbi Neḥemia. One said, '[This refers to] the eight [final] verses,' while the other said, '[This refers to the commandment concerning] the cities of refuge'" (Makkot 11a). According to the first view, Joshua's addition to the Torah is its final eight verses – namely, he wrote them, and Moses did not.[2] This view is an important step in

2. From the language of the *baraita*, one may conclude that both rabbis agree that Joshua added this section to the Torah. They differ only in what constitutes this section – the last eight verses of the Torah, or the section on cities of refuge (Num. 35:9–44 or Deut. 19:1–13). Another possibility is that the unit on cities of refuge is not the commandment to set apart the cities, but rather a description of Moses's designating them (Deut. 4:41–43). See A. J. Heschel, *Heavenly Torah as Refracted through the Generations*, 620–22. The Talmud does not go on to adopt

dealing with the question of authorship for the end of the Torah, as it is based first and foremost on a logical consideration – how could Moses have written, during his lifetime, that he had already died? It relates to the compilation of the Torah from a rational perspective, while the interpretation that presents Moses as having taken dictation from God deals with the issue from an idealistic point of view. This essential difference in outlook underpins many differences on the subject. We shall analyze some of those differences below.

The question of whether there are verses in the Torah that were not written by Moses extends beyond the issue of the final eight verses. Some of the medieval commentators who took the rationalist approach raised the question of his authorship elsewhere in the Torah, and in so doing, broadened the question to include a discussion of the last verses in the Torah. We must emphasize that this was not the prevailing opinion; nevertheless, this understanding was not considered beyond the pale.

In fact, the medieval Spanish commentator Rabbi Abraham ibn Ezra (c. 1093–1167, poet and biblical commentator) notes that the question arises not only concerning the final eight verses, but also concerning all twelve verses of Deuteronomy 34, starting with the words וַיַּעַל מֹשֶׁה מֵעַרְבֹת מוֹאָב אֶל הַר נְבוֹ, "And Moses went up from the plains of Moab to Mount Nebo." Since Moses never descended after this ascent, then, according to the view of R. Neḥemia that Moses did not write about events that had not yet happened, he also could not have written the four verses describing his ascent to Mount Nebo. Commenting on the first verse of this chapter, Ibn Ezra writes: "To my view, from this verse onwards it was Joshua who wrote, since after his ascent Moses did not write anymore. It was written through prophecy."[3]

---

this conclusion, but rather assumes that the unit on the cities of refuge referred to is the one in Joshua 20. (Indeed, the special introduction that appears at the beginning of chapter 20 suggests as much: "And God spoke to Joshua, saying." This formula is found almost nowhere else except in the verses of the Torah that record instances of God speaking to Moses.) However, if we accept this interpretation, it is difficult to understand why there is any need to state specifically that Joshua wrote this unit, since it appears in his book and not in the Torah.

3. See Ibn Ezra's commentary on Deuteronomy 34:6: "'To this very day' – these are the words of Joshua. It is possible that he wrote this at the end of his [Joshua's] life."

In using the expression "through prophecy," Ibn Ezra seems to be trying to reconcile the apparent contradiction between R. Neḥemia's approach, which the exegete adopts and expands upon, and the view that delegitimizes anyone who claims that even a single verse "was not uttered by God, but rather by Moses on his own initiative," as discussed in the previous chapter. This reconciliation understands all of the Torah to have been said as a prophecy from God, but not necessarily to Moses.[4]

Ibn Ezra also addresses other verses whose ascription to Moses is no less problematic than the conclusion of the Torah is, in that their formulation suggests they were written after Moses's time. In his commentary at the beginning of Deuteronomy, Ibn Ezra writes:

> Likewise, the interpretation of the expressions: כְּכֹל אֲשֶׁר צִוָּה ה' אֹתוֹ, "according to all that God commanded him" (Deut. 1:3), בְּעֵבֶר הַיַּרְדֵּן בַּמִּדְבָּר בָּעֲרָבָה, "on the other side of the Jordan, in the wilderness, in the Arava" (Deut. 1:1). If you understand the secret of the twelve, then also in וַיִּכְתֹּב מֹשֶׁה אֶת הַשִּׁירָה הַזֹּאת בַּיּוֹם הַהוּא,

4. Most commentators disagree with R. Yehuda's approach, and unequivocally prefer the approach of R. Shimon, maintaining that Moses himself wrote even the last eight verses of the Torah. For example, Rabbenu Bahya ben Asher writes in his commentary on the Torah: "However, it is proper to believe, as per the true tradition that we have, that Moses wrote the entire Torah, from 'In the beginning' to 'in the eyes of all of Israel'; all from God's mouth… and it seems to me that there is nothing remarkable about Moses having written, 'And Moses, the servant of God, died there, and He buried him in the valley,' while he was still alive, for he wrote what was going to happen…. For all the prophets do the same in their words, speaking in the past tense instead of [but with reference to] the future."

Rabbi Hayim ben Attar, in the eighteenth century, was aware of the ramifications of Ibn Ezra's interpretation, as will be addressed further on. In his commentary on the Torah, *Ohr HaḤayim,* he wrote as follows: "It is not proper to write such things concerning the plain meaning of the text – that Moses did not complete the *Sefer Torah* when he transmitted it to the Levites. With my own ears I have heard some of our people becoming confused in this regard, and ending up with conclusions that deny the Torah. This is the argument of the other nations – that the text was written by some among Israel, and that it describes things that did not happen, or that did not happen in the way that they are described, and such ideas and their like have become entrenched, and one should pay them no regard. The main principle is that the entire Book of the Torah was written by Moses, as our Sages teach: 'Moses completed it, weeping.'"

> "And Moses wrote this song the same day" (Deut. 31:22); וְהַכְּנַעֲנִי אָז בָּאָרֶץ, "And the Canaanites were then in the land" (Gen. 12:6); בְּהַר ה׳ יֵרָאֶה, "he shall be seen in God's mountain" (Gen. 22:14); and עַרְשׂוֹ עֶרֶשׂ בַּרְזֶל הִנֵּה, "Behold, his bed is a bed of iron" (Deut. 3:11) – you will perceive the truth.

Ibn Ezra's meaning here is obscure. His intention becomes clear in the context of one of the verses that he quotes, Genesis 12:6: וַיַּעֲבֹר אַבְרָם בָּאָרֶץ עַד מְקוֹם שְׁכֶם עַד אֵלוֹן מוֹרֶה וְהַכְּנַעֲנִי אָז בָּאָרֶץ, "And Abram passed through the land, to the place of Shekhem, to Elon Morei, and the Canaanites were then (*az*) in the land." Ibn Ezra comments: "It may be that [the meaning here is that] the land of Canaan had [already] been conquered from some other nation by the Canaanites. And if this is not so, then there is a secret here. And one who understands remains silent."

Now the problem that Ibn Ezra is addressing becomes comprehensible. The expression "the Canaanites were then in the land" implies that at the time the verse was written, the Canaanites were no longer in the land. Ibn Ezra offers two possible explanations: First, that the word be understood in the sense of "by then," or "already." That is, by Abraham's time, the Canaanites were already living in the land, having conquered it from its previous inhabitants. The second explanation mentions a secret, and, given the infrequency of such a comment, it is reasonable to infer that it is the same secret identified in his commentary on Deuteronomy as "the secret of the twelve."

The "secret of the twelve" has long been understood to be the secret of the final twelve verses of the Torah, which, according to Ibn Ezra, were not written by Moses. The issue is explained by Rabbi Yosef ben Eliezer HaSefaradi, one of the sages of Spain in the fourteenth century, in his supercommentary on Ibn Ezra, *Tzofnat Paaneaḥ*:[5]

> Ibn Ezra hints at this secret at the beginning of Deuteronomy. His explanation is as follows: How could the text say here the word "then," meaning "the Canaanites were in the land at that

5. Commonly – and mistakenly, it seems – identified as Rabbi Yosef Tov Elem (Bonfils). See M. Wilansky, *Meḥkarim BeLashon U'VeSifrut* (Jerusalem, 1978), 344–48.

> time [of Abraham], but now are no longer in it" – for did Moses not write the Torah, and in his time the land was [still] in the hands of the Canaanites?!... Accordingly, it would seem that Moses did not write that word ["*az*"] here, but rather it was written by Joshua or one of the other prophets.... And since we must believe in the tradition and in the words of the prophecies, what does it matter whether [this word] was written by Moses or by some other prophet, since the words of all of them were truth, and all were spoken through prophecy.[6]

According to this interpretation, Ibn Ezra maintained that there are verses throughout the Torah that, like the final verses of Deuteronomy, were written after Moses's death, either by Joshua or by one of the other prophets.[7] Rabbi Yosef ben Eliezer explains that this in no way contradicts our faith, since the entire text was written through prophecy, regardless of which prophet brought it from God to the people.[8]

---

6. The same direction is adopted by other commentaries in explanation of Ibn Ezra. Among others, Rabbi Moshe Almosnino (Greece, c. 1518–1581) wrote: "Thus, it cannot be that this was said by Moses, for in his time, [the land] was still in the hands of the Canaanites; rather, it was uttered by Joshua, or perhaps Ezra wrote it. And this is the 'secret' – meaning, that it was not written by Moses" (cited also in N. ben Menachem, "*Tosefet Biur Al Divrei HaIbn Ezra LeRabbi Moshe Almosnino*," *Sinai* 59, 153). For more on Rabbi Almosnino see N. ben Menachem, *Rabbi Moshe Almosnino* (Jerusalem, 1946).
7. One might argue that Ibn Ezra does not choose between his two approaches, but the commentary on Deuteronomy 1:3 makes clear that "*az*" means "then, and not now."
8. Further on, Rabbi Yosef ben Eliezer addresses the statement of the Sages, cited above, condemning one who claims that even a single verse of the Torah "was not uttered by God, but rather that Moses said it on his own initiative." I proposed above that Ibn Ezra himself solved this problem by drawing a distinction between the assertion that Moses made up some words in the Torah on his own, and the assertion that some words in the Torah may have been added by someone else, through prophecy. Rabbi Yosef ben Eliezer takes a different approach: "The answer is that [the condemnation by the Sages applies to one who makes this statement] in matters of the mitzvot, as we have explained above, but not concerning the narratives." In light of this distinction, Rabbi Yosef explains why Ibn Ezra only hinted at his understanding of the origin of the verses, rather than spelling it out explicitly: "It is not proper to make this secret known to people, in order that they will not hold the Torah in scorn, for one who

This principle also helps clarify other points of Ibn Ezra's commentary, such as the verse at the end of the story of the binding of Isaac: וַיִּקְרָא אַבְרָהָם שֵׁם הַמָּקוֹם הַהוּא ה׳ יִרְאֶה אֲשֶׁר יֵאָמֵר הַיּוֹם בְּהַר ה׳ יֵרָאֶה, "And Abraham called the name of that place *Hashem Yireh,* concerning which it is said today, 'in the mountain, God will be seen'" (Gen. 22:14). The use of the word "today" indicates that the end of the verse refers to a time subsequent to the events of the chapter, when the place had already been chosen for the Temple and was then known as "God's mountain."[9] Ibn Ezra appears to view this verse, too, as a later addition, introduced at a time when the Temple already existed.[10]

Ibn Ezra also mentions the verse:

> כִּי רַק עוֹג מֶלֶךְ הַבָּשָׁן נִשְׁאַר מִיֶּתֶר הָרְפָאִים, הִנֵּה עַרְשׂוֹ עֶרֶשׂ בַּרְזֶל הֲלֹה הִוא בְּרַבַּת בְּנֵי עַמּוֹן, תֵּשַׁע אַמּוֹת אָרְכָּהּ וְאַרְבַּע אַמּוֹת רָחְבָּהּ בְּאַמַּת אִישׁ.
>
> For only Og, king of the Bashan, remained from the rest of the Refa'im; behold, his bed is a bed of iron; is it not in Rabba, of the children of Amon? Nine cubits is its length, and four cubits is its width, according to the cubit of a man. (Deut. 3:11)

This, too, seems to have been written long after the death of Og, when all that remained as testimony to his tremendous size was his bed.

---

is not knowledgeable will not distinguish between verses that convey mitzvot and verses that convey a narrative. Also, [the concealment] is meant for the benefit of the other nations, who tell us, 'Your Torah was originally true, but you replaced and changed some words'; therefore Ibn Ezra writes, 'One who understands remains silent' – for one who understands knows that this [knowledge] does no harm; only the ignorant use this for attack."

9. Contrast this with the language in Deuteronomy, which refers to the Temple in the future: הַמָּקוֹם אֲשֶׁר יִבְחַר ה׳, "the place which God will choose" (Deut. 12:5, and others).
10. In his comment on the verse itself in Genesis, Ibn Ezra merely hints at this. Other commentators tried to solve the difficulty in other ways. Rashi adopts the view that the verse is speaking of the future: "That in the times of later generations they would say of it, 'On this mountain God is revealed to His people.'" Radak writes, "An altar will be built on this mountain, and then the Temple – and then it shall be said, and they shall tell about this day, when I came to offer up my son Isaac as a sacrifice."

Finally, Ibn Ezra introduces his far-reaching idea at the beginning of Deuteronomy, in relation to the verse, אֵלֶּה הַדְּבָרִים אֲשֶׁר דִּבֶּר מֹשֶׁה אֶל כָּל יִשְׂרָאֵל בְּעֵבֶר הַיַּרְדֵּן בַּמִּדְבָּר בָּעֲרָבָה מוֹל סוּף, "These are the words that Moses spoke to all of Israel on the other side of the Jordan, in the wilderness, in the Arava, facing Suf" (Deut. 1:1). The expression, "on the other side of the Jordan" (*be'ever haYarden*), which refers here, and throughout Deuteronomy, to the *eastern* side of the Jordan River, appears to be the phrase that troubles Ibn Ezra. Since the Children of Israel were still located east of the Jordan at the opening of Deuteronomy, surely there was no reason to describe it as "the other side." Ibn Ezra's solution is to see the phrase as a later addition by a prophet who was located in Israel, on the *western* side of the Jordan.[11]

It would seem, therefore, that as far as Ibn Ezra was concerned, the Torah was not given as a fixed text with no possibility of future additions. Even after the Torah was completed by Moses, it was still open to a very limited degree, and in select instances where it was important to add certain clarifications or elucidations to the text, the prophets did so.

Ibn Ezra was not the only medieval commentator to raise the possibility that the Torah includes some verses that were added after the death of Moses.[12] Ibn Ezra's "secret of the twelve" is perhaps the

---

11. Admittedly, this question poses less of a problem, since the appellation here may reflect the more objective, fundamental situation, in which the tribes of Israel are destined to live their lives on the western side of the Jordan, and, for this reason, the area where they are encamped prior to their entry into the land is already at this stage referred to as "the other side of the Jordan."

12. According to Abrabanel, there is one instance in which Nahmanides also follows Ibn Ezra's approach. In Numbers (21:1–3), the Torah recounts the war waged against the Canaanites:

    וַיִּשְׁמַע הַכְּנַעֲנִי מֶלֶךְ עֲרָד יֹשֵׁב הַנֶּגֶב כִּי בָּא יִשְׂרָאֵל דֶּרֶךְ הָאֲתָרִים וַיִּלָּחֶם בְּיִשְׂרָאֵל וַיִּשְׁבְּ מִמֶּנּוּ שֶׁבִי. וַיִּדַּר יִשְׂרָאֵל נֶדֶר לַה׳ וַיֹּאמַר אִם נָתֹן תִּתֵּן אֶת הָעָם הַזֶּה בְּיָדִי וְהַחֲרַמְתִּי אֶת עָרֵיהֶם. וַיִּשְׁמַע ה׳ בְּקוֹל יִשְׂרָאֵל וַיִּתֵּן אֶת הַכְּנַעֲנִי וַיַּחֲרֵם אֶתְהֶם וְאֶת עָרֵיהֶם וַיִּקְרָא שֵׁם הַמָּקוֹם חָרְמָה.

    And the Canaanite king of Arad, who dwelled in the Negev, heard that Israel were coming by the way of Atarim; he fought against Israel and took some of them captive. And Israel made a vow to God and said, "If You will give this people into my hand, then I will utterly destroy their cities." And God heard the voice of Israel, and He delivered up the Canaanites, and they destroyed them utterly, along with their cities, and they called the name of the place Horma.

best known treatment of the subject, but a far more explicit discussion may be found in the writings of – surprisingly enough – Rabbi Yehuda HeHasid.[13] In his commentary on the Torah, Rabbi Yehuda HeHasid notes several times that certain verses were added to the Torah at a later stage; however, in contrast to Ibn Ezra, who attributes later verses to Joshua, Rabbi Yehuda HeHasid raises the possibility that these verses were introduced much later, by the Men of the Great Assembly![14]

When did Israel utterly destroy the cities of the Canaanites? Ibn Ezra notes, at the beginning of this episode, "Many have said that this incident was written by Joshua, and as proof they cite the verse, מֶלֶךְ עֲרָד אֶחָד, "the king of Arad – one" (Josh. 12:14). However, he himself rejects this position by arguing that the passages in Numbers and Joshua refer to different locations with the same name, and that therefore the passage in Numbers is really referring to an event that took place during Moses's lifetime on the eastern side of the Jordan.

Nahmanides (commentary to Num. 21:1) proposes two possibilities. Perhaps the Torah is indeed telling us here about an event that took place later, after Moses's death: "And the text completes its account here, for Israel destroyed their cities completely, after they reached the land of Canaan, after the death of Joshua, to fulfill the vow which they had made [in the wilderness], and they called the name of these cities Horma [meaning destruction]."

Alternatively, the event described took place during Moses's time: "It is also correct to say that Israel destroyed this king and his people by the sword right now, during Moses's time, and they called the site of the battle 'Horma.'" The simplest reading of the first explanation is that the Torah is recording a prophecy of Moses, rather than the record of something which had already happened. However, Abrabanel, in his commentary on this chapter, maintains that Nahmanides understood this verse as a later addition – in accordance with the view recorded by Ibn Ezra.

Abrabanel himself vehemently attacks this possibility: "But our teacher shames himself in proposing that Joshua wrote this verse... and Ibn Ezra took this view in its entirety from the Karaites, who, in their commentaries on the Torah, maintain that this was not written by Moses. Nahmanides tends toward the view of Ibn Ezra, and it is astonishing that from the mouth of one with such wholeness of Torah and purity could come the suggestion that the Torah contains something that was not written by Moses. And this being so, they are included in the category of 'he has despised God's word.'"

13. Concerning Rabbi Yehuda HeHasid and his commentary on the Torah, see chapter 1, note 40.
14. By "Men of the Great Assembly" *Ḥazal* refer (Avot 1:4 and elsewhere) to sages in the period starting with the time of Ezra and Nehemiah, and continuing on into the Second Temple Period, until the time of Shimon HaTzaddik – namely, the fifth through the third centuries BCE.

Rabbi Yehuda HeHasid attributes verses of the Torah from three different passages to the Men of the Great Assembly.[15] First, in his commentary to the second chapter of Deuteronomy, he asks how the Children of Israel could have encamped at Etzion Gever (Num. 33:35). After all, Etzion Gever is known to have been situated in the land of Edom (as II Chronicles recounts about Solomon, 8:17), and the Children of Israel were not permitted to enter the land of Edom (Deut. 2:8). His solution is that Etzion Gever fell into the hands of Edom only at a later stage, with the marriage of Meheitavel, daughter of Matred, to the king of Edom: וַיִּמְלֹךְ תַּחְתָּיו הֲדַר וְשֵׁם עִירוֹ פָּעוּ וְשֵׁם אִשְׁתּוֹ מְהֵיטַבְאֵל בַּת מַטְרֵד בַּת מֵי זָהָב, "And he was succeeded by Hadar, and the name of his city was Pa'u, and the name of his wife was Meheitavel, daughter of Matred, daughter of Mei Zahav" (Gen. 36:39). Rabbi Yehuda HeHasid explains:

> This was not yet done in the time of Moses, but rather in the period before the kingship, that is, before Saul. But in the days of Solomon, this had already happened; therefore it (i.e., the verse in Genesis) was written into the Five Books of the Torah in the days of the Great Assembly, so that you will not wonder how Etzion Gever came to belong to Edom, as is written in Chronicles."[16]

Another verse attributed by Rabbi Yehuda HeHasid to the Men of the Great Assembly describes Jacob's blessing to Ephraim and Menashe: וַיְבָרְכֵם בַּיּוֹם הַהוּא לֵאמוֹר בְּךָ יְבָרֵךְ יִשְׂרָאֵל לֵאמֹר יְשִׂמְךָ אֱלֹהִים כְּאֶפְרַיִם וְכִמְנַשֶּׁה וַיָּשֶׂם אֶת אֶפְרַיִם לִפְנֵי מְנַשֶּׁה, "And he blessed them on that day, saying: 'With you, Israel will bless, saying: May God make you like Ephraim and Menashe' – and he set Ephraim before Menashe" (Gen. 48:20). Rabbi Moshe, son of Rabbi Yehuda HeHasid, wrote:

---

15. For more on this subject, see G. Brin.
16. It is possible that Rashbam, too, maintained this position. See the article by Y. Jacobs, "Nusaḥ Perush Rashbam LaTorah Al Pi Ketav-Yad Breslau VeAl Pi Mekorot Nosafim," in *Zer Rimmonim: Meḥkarim BaMikra U'VeFarshanuto Mukdashim Lifrofesor Rimmon Kasher*, ed. Elie Assis, Michael Avioz, Yael Shemesh (Atlanta, 2013), 468–88.

> My father's explanation [of "and he set Ephraim before Menashe"] was that this is said not of Jacob, but rather of Moses: Moses placed Ephraim as the leader of one camp, because Jacob had said, "His younger brother will be greater than he." And Joshua wrote this, or the Men of the Great Assembly.

This is a startling interpretation even on the literal level of the text, and it certainly comes as a surprise that Rabbi Yehuda HeHasid sees fit to suggest that this verse, which contains no inherent chronological difficulties, was a later addition.[17]

There is an even more startling assertion elsewhere in Rabbi Yehuda HeHasid's commentary, according to which not only were later sections added to the Torah, but sections were also removed. Thus, for example, he writes explicitly, with regard to the Song of the Well (Num. 21):

> "Then Israel sang this song" – my father and teacher explained this as a reference to the Great *Hallel* (Ps. 136), which followed their deliverance from Sihon and Og, and the crossing of Wadi Arnon. Then this song was created, and it was [originally] written in the Five Books of the Torah, until David came and removed Moses's psalm, and included it in the Book of Psalms.

This assertion – that Moses's words were removed from the Torah – amid the other comparable comments, aroused such controversy that some argued that Rabbi Yehuda HeHasid could not have written such things and the text must be a forgery.[18]

It turns out, however, that the same controversial views are cited in another work from the Middle Ages, written by Rabbi Menahem

---

17. For more on this commentary, see Y. Schwartz, "Perush Rabbi Yehuda HeHasid LeBereshit 48:20–22," *Tarbiz* 80:1 (5772/2012), 29–39.
18. The issue was put to a number of authorities, among them Rabbi Moshe Feinstein *zt"l*. In a letter dated 28 Adar I 5736/1976 (*Iggerot Moshe, Yoreh De'ah*, part III, *siman* 114), he expressed vehement opposition to the publication of the book: "One who suggests that Moses wrote even a single letter on his own initiative, denies the Torah, and is included in the category of 'he has despised God's word.' And all the more so

Tzioni ben Meir, with attribution to Rabbi Yehuda HeHasid.[19] Owing to the surrounding controversy, this work too was subject to polemic and debate.[20] Indeed, as a result of this controversy, the first edition of

---

one who says that there is some matter which was written not even by Moses, but rather by others, or that others came and removed some matter from the Torah – they deny the Torah and are included in the category of 'he has despised God's word.'" However, here too one might argue that a careful look at what is actually written in this commentary reveals no hint of the idea that Joshua, David, or even the Men of the Great Assembly wrote these things on their own initiative; rather, they were written through prophecy and divine inspiration. Rabbi Feinstein also argues that what was written makes no sense even in relation to the text itself, and therefore concludes: "These wicked heretics forged this within a book that is attributed to Rabbi Yehuda HeHasid, in order to mislead everyone into the heretical view that Rabbi Yehuda HeHasid said this, too. Therefore, it is clear that it is forbidden to print this book; it is even worse than the books of the heretics, which are [at least] attributed to the heretics [themselves], and many among even the least learned Jews will not believe them. But where the name of Rabbi Yehuda HeHasid appears, one has to take into consideration the possibility that it will also lead others astray, to deny the Torah."

19. Rabbi Menahem Tzioni, *Sefer Tzioni*, Lemberg 1882, *Parashat Ḥukkat*, 64b. This explanation of Rabbi Yehuda HeHasid is mentioned also in the Hamburg manuscript, 45, attributed to the thirteenth-century Tosafist R. Avigdor Katz. See also H. J. Zimmels, "Ketav Yad Hamburg Cod. hebr. 45 VeYihuso LeRav Avigdor Katz," *Maamarim LeZikhron R. Zevi Perez Chajes*, ed. A. Aptowitzer and Z. Schwartz (Vienna, 1993), 261, n. 70.

    Rabbi Menehem Tzioni ben Meir lived in Germany, c. 1340–1410. He wrote a kabbalistic commentary on the Torah, called *Sefer Tzioni*, as well as several liturgical poems. For more about this interesting figure, see Y. Peles, "Rabbenu Menahem Tzion ('HaTzioni')," in *Moriah* 11, 5–6 (125–26) (5742/1982): 9–15; Y. Yuval, *Ḥakhamim BeDoram* (Jerusalem, 1989), 282–310.

20. Rabbi Moshe Feinstein, at the end of his responsum cited above in note 18, writes: "We do not have conclusive knowledge of who Rabbi Menahem Tzioni was, and it seems that he copied what he found in some book with Rabbi Yehuda HeHasid's name on it, without paying attention. I would say that it is forbidden to sell or buy *Sefer Tzioni*, too, since it contains this heretical statement, and it would also be proper to write this to the leading authorities in the Land of Israel."

    However in the response *Mishneh Halakhot* (part XII, siman 214), Rabbi Menashe Klein (the "Ungvarer Rav") expresses surprise at this questioning of the credentials of Rabbi Menachem Tzioni, and uses the same tactic against Rabbi Feinstein's response: "But the truth is I do not believe that this was said by Rabbi Feinstein; rather, it seems to me that some misguided student wrote it, and included it among his letters after his death. And the hands of strangers reigned over him

Rabbi Yehuda HeHasid's commentary, from which the above quotations were taken, was set aside, and a new edition appeared with most of the controversial excerpts removed.[21] A laconic note was appended to the new edition. "I consider it correct to inform you that, after consultation with giants of Torah, and in accordance with their opinions, I have eliminated a few passages that cannot possibly have come from the holy mouth of our teacher Yehuda HeHasid, of blessed memory. We must assume that they were interpolated by others."[22] However, the prevailing view among academic scholars is that the original commentary was genuine and not a forgery, based, among other things, on sources that we shall examine later on.

---

and chose themselves a reputed scholar. For I do not believe that Rabbi Moshe Feinstein had never seen *Sefer HaTzioni*, which is well known; he must surely have been familiar with it."

Further on in the same responsum, he writes: "In truth, in light of this, the manuscript of Rabbi Yehuda HeHasid should likewise not be hidden away… and thank God I have reviewed what they wrote and I have seen that they should be interpreted in accordance with his approach, in accordance with the halakha, but this is not their place."

21. Not all were removed. Concerning the verse, וְלֹא תַשְׁבִּית מֶלַח בְּרִית אֱלֹהֶיךָ מֵעַל מִנְחָתֶךָ עַל כָּל קָרְבָּנְךָ תַּקְרִיב מֶלַח, "You shall not cause the salt of the covenant of your God to be lacking from your meal offering; with all your sacrifices you shall offer salt" (Lev. 2:13), even the new edition included the proposition that this was written after Moses's time. Rabbi Yehuda HeHasid actually suggests this in view of the Gemara in Menahot (21a), stating that the salt referred to here is *melaḥ sedomit* (salt of Sodom). This interpretation, according to Rabbi Yehuda HeHasid, is based on Moses's rebuke to the nation. לְעָבְרְךָ בִּבְרִית ה׳ אֱלֹהֶיךָ וּבְאָלָתוֹ... גָּפְרִית וָמֶלַח שְׂרֵפָה כָל אַרְצָהּ לֹא תִזָּרַע וְלֹא תַצְמִחַ וְלֹא יַעֲלֶה בָהּ כָּל עֵשֶׂב כְּמַהְפֵּכַת סְדֹם וַעֲמֹרָה אַדְמָה וצביים [וּצְבוֹיִם קרי] אֲשֶׁר הָפַךְ ה׳ בְּאַפּוֹ וּבַחֲמָתוֹ, "To cause you to pass into the covenant of the Lord your God and His oath.… Brimstone and salt, burning throughout the land, which is not sown, nor does it produce, nor does any grass grow upon it, like the overthrow of Sodom and Gomorrah, Admah and Zeboim, which God overthrew in His anger and His wrath" (Deut. 29:11–22). How could an idea first mentioned in the last days of Moses already appear in Leviticus? One of his proposed solutions to the problem is that "perhaps originally the text simply read, 'You shall not cause salt to be lacking from your meal offering,' and after Moses wrote this in [*Parashat*] *Nitzavim*, they then elaborated on this 'salt' – the 'salt of the covenant of your God'" (commentary of Rabbi Yehuda HeHasid on Lev. 2:13).
22. Yitzhak Shimshon Lange, ed., *Perushei Rabbi Yehuda HeHasid* (Jerusalem, 1975), 5 (table of errors and changes).

Indeed, an approach similar to that of Rabbi Yehuda HeHasid may be found in the writing of his student, Rabbi Shlomo ben Shmuel HeHasid.[23] In his study on the commentary of Ibn Ezra, Rabbi Shlomo addresses Ibn Ezra's understanding of the word "*Azazel*," namely: "If you could understand the secret that lies behind the word *Azazel*, you would understand its secret and the secret of its name, for it has parallels in the Torah."

Rabbi Shlomo understands Ibn Ezra to mean that this word hints to the "secret of the twelve." Ibn Ezra, he explains, knew that the word "*Azazel*" means "wilderness" in Aramaic, while Moses obviously wrote the Torah in Hebrew.[24] Therefore, Rabbi Shlomo continues:

> Do not be surprised at the fact that he [Moses] wrote this Aramaic word in the Torah, for it was not he who wrote this verse. And this is the secret that is referred to here – that it was not Moses who wrote this verse, but rather someone else. And do not be surprised at what I say – that "someone else wrote it," for there are other such instances in the Torah. In other words, there are many verses that were not said by Moses."[25]

---

23. Rabbi Shlomo ben R. Shmuel lived in France, c. 1160–1240. His work, *Te'amim Shel Ḥumash*, includes commentary and allegories on the Torah, and is still extant in some manuscripts. Concerning this sage and his approach to later verses in the Torah, see Y. M. Ta-Shma, *Kenesset Meḥkarim: Iyyunim BeSifrut HaMeḥkarit BiYemei HaBenayim* 1 (Jerusalem, 2004), 274–77.
24. *Ta-Shma, Kenesset Meḥkarim*, 276–77. It should be noted that in this specific instance, Rabbi Shlomo did not understand Ibn Ezra correctly and was mistaken in saying that the word *Azazel* means "wilderness" in Aramaic. The "secret" that Ibn Ezra refers to here is not related to later additions to the Torah. Rather, it relates to the phenomenon of he-goats (*se'irim*) in the wilderness. Ibn Ezra himself alludes to this, further on: "And I shall reveal to you part of this secret with the hint that when you are 33, you will know." Nahmanides comments here that Ibn Ezra is hinting to a verse that appears 33 verses hence.
25. Further on, Rabbi Shlomo notes the relevant verses cited by Ibn Ezra, as discussed earlier. Concerning the verse about Og's bed in the Ammonite city of Rabba, Rabbi Shlomo raises the possibility that Moses could indeed have written this verse as a prophecy, but then goes on to reject it: "And if you might say, even though Moses had never been in Rabba of the Ammonites, he could have prophesied through his divine spirit and said, 'Is it not in Rabba?' so why say that Moses did not write

The most startling aspect of the commentaries of these German pietists (Rabbi Yehuda HeHasid and Rabbi Shlomo HeHasid) is that they openly and explicitly articulated the same ideas that Ibn Ezra had expressed with great caution and cloaked language, and even in places where suggesting such an interpretation was not the only way of making sense of a textual problem.[26] Clearly, some medieval commentators supported the assertion that, based on the simple, literal text, some verses in the Torah have later origins than the main text. They did not regard this view as contradicting or denying the divine origin of the Torah.

There are several other verses that seem to feature language that testifies to the verses' later origins – and in which this conclusion is far more compelling than it seems to be in those passages discussed by the sages of Germany. Consider, for example, Moses's words to the nation in the first speech in Deuteronomy, which appear to be interrupted suddenly by a parenthetical statement:

> וַיֹּאמֶר ה׳ אֵלַי אַל תָּצַר אֶת מוֹאָב וְאַל תִּתְגָּר בָּם מִלְחָמָה כִּי לֹא אֶתֵּן לְךָ מֵאַרְצוֹ יְרֻשָּׁה כִּי לִבְנֵי לוֹט נָתַתִּי אֶת עָר יְרֻשָּׁה. הָאֵמִים לְפָנִים יָשְׁבוּ בָהּ עַם גָּדוֹל וְרַב וָרָם כָּעֲנָקִים. רְפָאִים יֵחָשְׁבוּ אַף הֵם כָּעֲנָקִים וְהַמֹּאָבִים יִקְרְאוּ לָהֶם אֵמִים. וּבְשֵׂעִיר יָשְׁבוּ הַחֹרִים לְפָנִים וּבְנֵי עֵשָׂו יִירָשׁוּם וַיַּשְׁמִידוּם מִפְּנֵיהֶם וַיֵּשְׁבוּ תַּחְתָּם כַּאֲשֶׁר עָשָׂה יִשְׂרָאֵל לְאֶרֶץ יְרֻשָּׁתוֹ אֲשֶׁר נָתַן ה׳ לָהֶם
>
> And God said to me: Do not harass Moab, nor goad them into battle, for I shall not give you their land for a possession, since I have given Ar to the children of Lot as a possession. (The Emim had previously lived there – a great and populous and tall people,

---

it? To this one must answer that he could have prophesied and said something through the divine spirit, if there was some need for it, but concerning something that need not necessarily be said [since it makes no practical difference], such as this verse, 'Is it not in Rabba?' he would not have received the divine spirit. And since the divine spirit did not visit him, and he had never been in Rabba of the Ammonites, where would he know this from? Hence, it certainly could not have been written by Moses."

26. Many studies have addressed the scope of this phenomenon. For a summary of these, see Jacobs's article "Nusaḥ Perush Rashbam" (see note 16 above).

> like the Anakim; they too were considered Refa'im, as were the Anakim, but the Moabim called them "Emim." The Horim had also previously dwelled in Se'ir, but the children of Esau succeeded them, and annihilated them from before them, and dwelled there in their stead – as the Children of Israel did to the land of their possession, which God gave to them.) (Deut. 2:9–12)

According to Nahmanides, verses 10–12 do indeed interrupt God's message to Moses, and their role is to explain why the Children of Israel are not receiving the inheritance of the children of Lot and the children of Edom. Namely, as descendants of Abraham, the children of Lot and the children of Edom retained the areas that had belonged to the Refa'im and the Anakim, which had been conquered by Abraham. Similarly, the children of Esau merit to conquer the Horim in Se'ir – yet, for the purposes of this discussion, they have not yet done so at the time of the verse in Deuteronomy. That is, the children of Esau conquered the Horim, כַּאֲשֶׁר עָשָׂה יִשְׂרָאֵל לְאֶרֶץ יְרֻשָּׁתוֹ אֲשֶׁר נָתַן ה' לָהֶם, "as the Children of Israel did [past tense] to the land of their possession, which God gave to them" (Deut. 2:12). In fact, at the time of Moses's speech, Israel had not yet entered – much less conquered – the land.

The commentators offer different explanations for this difficulty. According to Nahmanides, this verse was a forecast of future events. Even Ibn Ezra offers a standard interpretation in this case, suggesting that the text refers to the already-completed conquest of the areas to the east of the Jordan. However, adopting the same logic that Ibn Ezra employs elsewhere, it is not unreasonable to posit that here too these verses might represent a later addition.[27]

---

27. Two more examples of verses presenting a similar difficulty:
    (1) Exodus 16:35 – וּבְנֵי יִשְׂרָאֵל אָכְלוּ אֶת הַמָּן אַרְבָּעִים שָׁנָה עַד בֹּאָם אֶל אֶרֶץ נוֹשָׁבֶת אֶת הַמָּן אָכְלוּ עַד בֹּאָם אֶל קְצֵה אֶרֶץ כְּנָעַן, "And the Children of Israel ate the manna for forty years, until they reached inhabited land; they ate the manna until they reached the border of the land of Canaan." From the formulation of the verse, it would seem that it speaks of the arrival of Israel in the land as an event that had already taken place in the past, as a parallel to what we find in Joshua 5:11–12.
    (2) Deuteronomy 3:14 – יָאִיר בֶּן מְנַשֶּׁה לָקַח אֶת כָּל חֶבֶל אַרְגֹּב עַד גְּבוּל הַגְּשׁוּרִי וְהַמַּעֲכָתִי וַיִּקְרָא אֹתָם עַל שְׁמוֹ אֶת הַבָּשָׁן חַוֹּת יָאִיר עַד הַיּוֹם הַזֶּה, "Yair ben Menashe took all

Once one accepts the possibility raised by R. Yehuda (Bava Batra 15a) – that the final eight verses of the Torah were a later prophetic addition written by Joshua – there is room to investigate whether they should be attributed specifically to Joshua. Two of the eight verses seem to have been written from a far broader and more distant perspective than that of Joshua, who replaced Moses as leader immediately after his death.

That is, the expression וְלֹא יָדַע אִישׁ אֶת קְבֻרָתוֹ עַד הַיּוֹם הַזֶּה, "but no man knows his grave to this very day" (Deut. 34:6), suggests the sense of great distance in time. Moreover, the text asserts, וְלֹא קָם נָבִיא עוֹד בְּיִשְׂרָאֵל כְּמֹשֶׁה אֲשֶׁר יְדָעוֹ ה׳ פָּנִים אֶל פָּנִים", "There arose no prophet since then in Israel like Moses, whom God knew face to face" (Deut. 34:10) – an assessment that could only have been made years after the event, given its use of the past tense. This seems to reflect a perspective from at least a few generations after Joshua. Yet Ibn Ezra, as we have seen, attributes these verses to Joshua specifically, and does not even raise the possibility that they might have been written by someone else.

Thus, we have seen that among the medieval commentators there are two different approaches to verses that appear to have been added at a later time. The more widely accepted approach attributes them to Moses, who wrote them in a spirit of prophetic foresight. The other approach, advocated by Ibn Ezra and some of the sages of Germany, maintained that the Torah contains verses that were added by prophets of later generations.

THE LATER VERSES IN THE THOUGHT OF EARLY BIBLICAL CRITICS

Ibn Ezra's approach was both innovative and complex, and he was careful not to articulate it openly, so as not to lead those who might not understand him properly into error.[28] Despite his efforts to keep a low profile, however, he was called inspirational five hundred years after he wrote his commentary. Benedict Spinoza (1632–1677), who may be regarded

---

of the region of Argov, up until the border of the Geshuri and the Maakhati, and he named them, that is, the Bashan, after himself – *Havot Yair* – to this very day." Here again, the language appears to reflect a description from the perspective of a later period.

28. See Rabbi Yosef ben Eliezer below, note 34.

as the first of the biblical critics,[29] arrived at the following sweeping conclusion: "In these few words, he [Ibn Ezra] discloses and, at the same time, demonstrates that it was not actually Moses who wrote the Pentateuch, but some other person who lived much later, and that the book Moses wrote was a different work."[30]

It must be pointed out immediately, however, that attributing this claim to Ibn Ezra is unquestionably misleading and a misrepresentation, as noted by Rabbi Shmuel David Luzzatto, in his commentary at the beginning of Deuteronomy:[31]

> Now that Spinoza's books have already been disseminated in the world... I am forced to state that Spinoza wrote a complete lie... when he said that Ibn Ezra hinted that it was not Moses who wrote the Book of the Torah. It is true that Ibn Ezra alluded, via the hidden wisdom, that there exist in the Torah a few additional verses from after Moses's time, but nowhere in all his words and all his allusions is there any room to regard him as not believing that Moses wrote his book.... Spinoza, aside from having made some errors in his studies, also unquestionably spoke duplicitously, and in several places misled his readers, with cunning and guile.[32]

29. Along with Thomas Hobbes, who arrived at similar conclusions to those of Spinoza; see T. Hobbes, *Leviathan*, ed. C. B. Macpherson (Baltimore, 1968), e.g., 418.
30. Benedict de Spinoza, *Theological-Political Treatise*, ed. Jonathan Israel, transl. M. Silverthorne and J. Israel, Cambridge Texts in the History of Philosophy (Cambridge, 2007), 119.
31. The biblical commentator Rabbi Shmuel David Luzzatto (Shadal) (1800–1865) was also a philosopher, educator, and historian. He headed the rabbinical academy in Padua and engaged in every branch of Jewish study, integrating his faith in God and in the Torah with critical research. Much has been written about Luzzatto's approach, particularly by Shmuel Vargon. See especially, "The Controversy between I. S. Reggio and S. D. Luzzatto on the Date of the Writing of the Pentateuch," *Hebrew Union College Annual*, vol. 72 (2001), 139–53; "Luzzatto's Attitude towards Higher Criticism of the Torah," in S. Japhet, ed., *Shnaton* 13 (2002), 271–304; "The Dispute between Samuel David Luzzatto and His Colleagues on the Relationship of R. Abraham ibn Ezra and Part of the Haskalah Movement," in *Samuel David Luzzatto: The Bicentennial of His Birth*, eds. R. Bonfil, I. Gottleib, and H. Kasher (Jerusalem, 2004), 25–54.
32. Concerning Spinoza's distortion of Ibn Ezra, see also M. Haran, *Mikra VeOlamo* (Jerusalem, 2009), 546–49.

Indeed, even Ibn Ezra himself speaks against broadening the idea of later additions to the Torah. In Genesis, we find a list of the kings of Edom:

> וְאֵלֶּה הַמְּלָכִים אֲשֶׁר מָלְכוּ בְּאֶרֶץ אֱדוֹם לִפְנֵי מְלָךְ מֶלֶךְ לִבְנֵי יִשְׂרָאֵל. וַיִּמְלֹךְ בֶּאֱדוֹם בֶּלַע בֶּן בְּעוֹר...וַיָּמָת בַּעַל חָנָן בֶּן עַכְבּוֹר וַיִּמְלֹךְ תַּחְתָּיו הֲדַר וְשֵׁם עִירוֹ פָּעוּ וְשֵׁם אִשְׁתּוֹ מְהֵיטַבְאֵל בַּת מַטְרֵד בַּת מֵי זָהָב.
>
> These are the kings who reigned in the land of Edom before any king reigned over the Children of Israel. And Bela, son of Be'or, reigned in Edom… and Baal Hanan, son of Akhbor, died, and Hadar reigned in his stead, and the name of his city was Pa'u, and his wife's name was Meheitavel, daughter of Matred, daughter of Mei Zahav. (Gen. 36:31–39)

This unit could seem to be a later addition, since it implies that there is already a king ruling over Israel. Ibn Ezra cites a presumably Karaite commentator by the name of "Yitzhaki,"[33] who suggests that "this unit was written in the days of Jehoshaphat," but Ibn Ezra rejects his view with great vehemence: "It is with good reason that he is called 'Yitzhaki,' for all who hear will laugh at him… and Heaven forefend, Heaven forefend that the matter is as he says, in the days of Jehoshaphat; and his book should be burned."

Instead, the Spanish exegete proposes a different interpretation: "And in truth, the meaning of 'before any king reigned over the Children of Israel' refers to [the leadership of] Moses, as it is written, וַיְהִי בִישֻׁרוּן מֶלֶךְ, 'And there was [or "he became"] a king in Yeshurun' (Deut. 33:5)."

Given that Ibn Ezra accepts in principle that some verses were added to the Torah at a later stage, why does he attack Yitzhaki so fiercely, especially considering that his alternative to Yitzhaki's approach is a fairly weak interpretation. Ibn Ezra does not explain himself, but perhaps

33. Opinions are divided as to his identity, but the prevailing view identifies him as Yitzhak ben Yashush of Toledo (982–1057). For more on this subject, see U. Simon, "Yizchaki: A Spanish Biblical Commentator Whose 'Book Should be Burned' According to Abraham ibn Ezra," in M. Brettler and M. Fishbane, eds., *Minḥa LeNaḥum* (Sheffield, 1993), 217–32.

he was willing to accept the idea of later additions only with regard to fragments or single verses, and not with regard to entire textual units – making exception, of course, for the Torah's conclusion, which does not read like an appendix.[34] In any event, his objection speaks for itself when it comes to Spinoza's claim that Ibn Ezra himself believed that Moses did not write the Torah.

Spinoza's sweeping claim invited the first critical polemic concerning the period of the composition of the Torah, and the debate continues to this day. Obviously, the central point of contention surrounding verses that appear to be later additions is whether they are the exceptions that prove the rule, as Ibn Ezra and the sages of Germany understood them to be, or whether they are only a small sample of a phenomenon that in fact characterizes the biblical text as a whole, as argued by Spinoza and many of the scholars who followed him.

Of course, these differences in approach are due not to literary analysis but to the worldview of the respective thinkers. The medieval sages based themselves on the ancient tradition that the Torah was written by Moses at God's command, even when they were willing, in principle, to recognize the occasional later addition. Essentially, they do not depart from the approach of those commentators in the periods of the *Geonim* or *Rishonim* who identified later interpolations in the Mishna and the Talmuds but did not reject the notion that these works were authored by the Sages.

By the same token, the critics who contend that the phenomenon of later additions to the biblical text is not a matter of a few isolated examples, but indicative of a later composition date for the work as a whole, are not objective either, but subject to their own preexisting attitudes. Baruch Schwartz explains:

---

34. As Rabbi Yosef ben Eliezer (*Tuv Elem*) writes: "For if it had been written in the days of Jehoshaphat, then an entire unit would have been added to the Torah, while the Torah itself stipulates, לֹא תֹסֵף עָלָיו, 'You shall not add to it' (Deut. 13:1). And if someone should raise the question, 'Did R. Avraham (ibn Ezra) himself not hint, at the beginning of Deuteronomy, that the later prophets added words and verses to the Torah,' the answer is that to add a word or verse in explanation of what Moses had written, to clarify it, is not the same as adding an entire unit; for a word or a verse is commentary, whereas an entire unit is a textual addition."

> These excerpts are not addenda; they are integral to the narrative and necessary in their context, and do not bear the signs of later addenda at all. They do not interrupt the flow of the narrative; they cannot easily be removed in such a way as to leave a logical text, and their language and style in no way differs from that which precedes or follows them.[35]

Schwartz concludes therefore that all of the Torah was composed after the time of Moses.

This position is difficult to accept – specifically because such fragments as "And the Canaanites were then in the land," and "Concerning which it is said today" – the possible indicators of (occasional) later addenda – are easy to delete from the text without marring the narrative itself; they are not integral to it. One might have expected Schwartz to have come to the opposite conclusion!

Indeed, the supposed additions to the Mishna and the Talmuds take this same form: the addenda may be eliminated without changing the text. They therefore cannot prove anything about the date or authorship of the text as a whole, a point that can in turn be applied to the Torah as well. That is, there is no reason to stray from the accepted position of the medieval sages who saw these verses as exceptions that do not demonstrate anything about the broader text.

Further Critical Arguments for Late Dating of the Text

Spinoza and his followers based their argument not only on verses whose language seems to suggest that they were written after Moses's death, but on other points as well.

One of the main arguments is as follows: If the Torah were written by Moses, how is it that Moses refers to himself in the third person, writing, among other things, וְהָאִישׁ מֹשֶׁה ענו [עָנָיו קרי] מְאֹד מִכֹּל הָאָדָם אֲשֶׁר עַל פְּנֵי הָאֲדָמָה, "And the man Moses was extremely humble, more than any other person upon the face of the earth" (Num. 12:3)?[36] But

35. B. Y. Schwartz, "HaTorah: Ḥameshet Ḥumasheha VeArba Te'udoteha," in Z. Talshir (ed.), *Sifrut HaMikra – Mevo'ot U'Meḥkarim* (Jerusalem, 2011), 177.

36. Spinoza made a mistake when he argued that only in part of the Torah does Moses speak in the third person, while in Deuteronomy he speaks about himself in the

this argument may be rejected out of hand: the Torah was never presented as Moses's personal book, and it is written in the third person for the simple reason explained by Nahmanides:

> Moses wrote the lineage of all the early generations, as well as his own lineage and his actions and the events of his life, in the third person. Therefore the Torah says, "And God spoke to Moses and said to him" – as a narrator talking about two other characters. This being so, there is no mention of Moses in the Torah until he is born, and then he is mentioned as though someone else were talking about him.... And the reason for the Torah's being written in this way is because it preceded the creation of the world, and obviously also the birth of Moses, as the Kabbala teaches – it was written in black fire upon white fire. And thus Moses is like a scribe who copies from an ancient book and writes, and therefore he writes impersonally. (Nahmanides, Introduction to Genesis)

The Torah cannot be Moses's own book, since parts of it describe events that precede his birth, and other parts describe events of which Moses could not have had any direct knowledge. More fundamentally, the Torah's importance is derived specifically from the assumption that it expresses God's word – and not because it narrates the events of Moses's life and his actions. There is therefore no contradiction between the fact that the Torah speaks about Moses in the third person and the assumption that Moses wrote the Torah – as the traditional view has it – like a scribe copying from an ancient book.[37]

---

first person. Spinoza did not pay attention to the fact that nowhere does Moses speak about himself in the first person as the "narrator"; every instance of his use of the first person, throughout Deuteronomy, is a quotation from one of the lengthy speeches that he delivers before his death. As Nahmanides notes in his introduction to Genesis: "Do not be troubled by the matter of Moses speaking about himself in Deuteronomy – 'And I pleaded and prayed to God, and I said' – since the beginning of that book states, 'These are the things which Moses spoke to all of Israel' – and thus the text records his speech in the first person."

37. M. Z. Segal (*Mavo HaMikra* [Jerusalem, 1977], 124) argues that the argument of the Bible critics is "founded on the norms of secular literature, in which the author highlights himself. But this is not the approach taken by narrators of the Tanakh,

Let us now examine a far weightier argument that was first raised by Spinoza, though it has since been echoed by others. The issue is that many of the places mentioned in the Torah are identified by names that were given to those places only after Moses's time. The best-known example of this conundrum concerns Abraham's battle against the five kings:

> וַיִּשְׁמַע אַבְרָם כִּי נִשְׁבָּה אָחִיו וַיָּרֶק אֶת חֲנִיכָיו יְלִידֵי בֵיתוֹ שְׁמֹנָה עָשָׂר וּשְׁלֹשׁ מֵאוֹת וַיִּרְדֹּף עַד דָּן. וַיֵּחָלֵק עֲלֵיהֶם לַיְלָה הוּא וַעֲבָדָיו וַיַּכֵּם וַיִּרְדְּפֵם עַד חוֹבָה אֲשֶׁר מִשְּׂמֹאל לְדַמָּשֶׂק.
>
> And when Abram heard that his brother had been taken captive, he led forth his trained servants, born in his house – three hundred and eighteen – and he pursued them until Dan. And he divided [his camp] against them by night, he and his servants, and he smote them and pursued them until Hobah, which is north of Damascus. (Gen. 14:14)

Abram pursues the kings northward, up until Dan, which is in the region of Damascus. The name "Dan" raises an immediate question, for the original inheritance of the tribe of Dan was supposed to be in the center of the coastal region and the interior lowlands, as set forth in the book of Joshua (19:40–48). The tribe of Dan only found itself in the north because its members had not conquered their intended inheritance (see Judges 1:34), and were forced to find an alternative portion of land, as described toward the end of the book of Judges. The children of Dan moved to the north, conquered the city of Layish, and only then changed the city's name: וַיִּקְרְאוּ שֵׁם הָעִיר דָּן בְּשֵׁם דָּן אֲבִיהֶם אֲשֶׁר יוּלַּד לְיִשְׂרָאֵל וְאוּלָם לַיִשׁ שֵׁם הָעִיר לָרִאשֹׁנָה, "And they called the name of

---

who generally minimize their own presence." This argument is also made by Robert Alter (*The World of Biblical Literature* [New York 1992], chapter 8). The third person is used in cases of official, formal literature, such as Josephus in his *Wars of the Jews*. Surprisingly, this same claim – that the Torah cannot have been authored by someone who appears in the text in the third person – is still being propounded in our generation, despite the simple fact that nowhere is there any suggestion that the Torah is presented as Moses's own book. See, for example, R. E. Friedman, *Who Wrote The Bible?* (San Francisco, 1997), 24; B. Y. Schwartz, 176.

the city Dan, after the name of Dan, their father, who was born to Israel. But the original name of the city was Layish" (Judges 18:29). How, then, does Genesis speak of the city of Dan, when, as far as anyone knew in the time of Moses, the tribe of Dan was not even supposed to live there? It would seem that Genesis should refer to the city by its original name – Layish (or Leshem).[38]

Biblical commentators throughout the generations have wrestled with this question, and have proposed various explanations. Radak offers two solutions. The first is that the name "Dan" was written in Genesis with prophetic insight for the future:

> [Thus named] because of its ultimate destiny, because when Moses wrote this it was not yet called by this name; it was called "Leshem." And when it was conquered by the children of Dan, they called it "Dan" after Dan, their father.[39]

---

38. In the brief parallel description in Joshua 19:47, the original name of the city is recorded as "Leshem." The same difficulty arises concerning the verses at the end of the Torah, where we read: וַיַּעַל מֹשֶׁה מֵעַרְבֹת מוֹאָב אֶל הַר נְבוֹ רֹאשׁ הַפִּסְגָּה אֲשֶׁר עַל פְּנֵי יְרֵחוֹ וַיַּרְאֵהוּ ה' אֶת כָּל הָאָרֶץ אֶת הַגִּלְעָד עַד דָּן וְאֵת כָּל נַפְתָּלִי וְאֶת אֶרֶץ אֶפְרַיִם וּמְנַשֶּׁה וְאֵת כָּל אֶרֶץ יְהוּדָה עַד הַיָּם הָאַחֲרוֹן, "Moses ascended from the plains of Moab to Mount Nebo, to the top of Pisga, facing Jericho. And God showed him the entire land of Gilead, up to Dan; and all of Naftali, and the land of Ephraim and Menashe, and all the land of Judah, up until the utmost sea" (Deut. 34:1–2). The impression arising from a simple reading of the text is that the reference here is to "Dan" in the north. However, in this context – at least according to Ibn Ezra's approach – this does not present a problem, since according to his view the final eight verses of the Torah were not written in Moses's time.
39. This interpretation follows Ibn Ezra's "secret of the twelve," maintaining that some verses in the Torah were written through prophetic vision with reference to the future, even though they are formulated in the past tense. Yet this approach is somewhat problematic, for there is no hint in the text that it refers to a future reality. It is therefore difficult to understand why the generation that received the Torah was presented with a place name unfamiliar to them. The difficulty is noted by Rabbi Baruch Epstein (1860–1942) in his *Torah Temima*: "Even though we find instances where the Torah names something on the basis of the future [as explained above, in *Parashat Bereshit* (10:11), on the verse, 'From that land emerged Ashur'], this applies only where it had no previous name. Therefore, the Torah now names it according to the way it will be called in the future. But this is not the case here: until the name of the place was changed to 'Dan' it had a name that was known – Layish, or Leshem – and so why does the text refer to it by its later name?"

Radak's second solution is that "perhaps there was another place that, in those days, was called Dan."[40]

Ibn Ezra addresses this question with regard to other verses as well. The story of the spies reads:

> וַיָּבֹאוּ עַד נַחַל אֶשְׁכֹּל וַיִּכְרְתוּ מִשָּׁם זְמוֹרָה וְאֶשְׁכּוֹל עֲנָבִים אֶחָד... לַמָּקוֹם הַהוּא קָרָא נַחַל אֶשְׁכּוֹל עַל אֹדוֹת הָאֶשְׁכּוֹל אֲשֶׁר כָּרְתוּ מִשָּׁם בְּנֵי יִשְׂרָאֵל.
>
> And they came as far as Nahal Eshkol, and they cut down from there a branch with a cluster of grapes.... That place was called Nahal Eshkol on account of the cluster (*eshkol*) of grapes which the Children of Israel cut from there. (Num. 13:23–24)

This seems paradoxical: at first, the spies arrive at a place called "Nahal Eshkol," and then the text seems to claim that the name only took hold in the wake of their visit. Ibn Ezra suggests two possible ways of understanding these verses. The first is as he writes: "[These are] the words of Moses" – meaning that the verse was written from the later perspective of Moses, while at the time when the spies arrived there, it did not yet have that name. Of course, this approach does not explain the case of Dan, as even in the time of Moses Layish had not yet been conquered by the tribe of Dan.

To explain Dan, we need Ibn Ezra's second suggestion: "Perhaps the same possibility exists here as in the verse, 'And he pursued them until Dan' – as though another name." The plain meaning of Ibn Ezra's alternative seems to be that the place had been called by that name in the

40. Y. M. Grintz, *Yiḥudo VeKadmuto Shel Sefer Bereshit* (Jerusalem, 1983), 69–70, finds support for this possibility in the fact that had the text been speaking about the same place, it should have read, "Dan, which is Layish/Leshem," in the same way that we find reference, in the same chapter, to other places known by more than one name: מֶלֶךְ בֶּלַע הִיא צֹעַר, "the king of Bela, which is Tzoar" (Gen. 14:2); עֵמֶק הַשִּׂדִּים הוּא יָם הַמֶּלַח, "the valley of Sidim, which is the Salt Sea" (Gen. 14:3); וַיָּשֻׁבוּ וַיָּבֹאוּ אֶל עֵין מִשְׁפָּט הִוא קָדֵשׁ, "And they returned and they came to Ein Mishpat, which is Kadesh" (Gen. 14:7); אֶל עֵמֶק שָׁוֵה הוּא עֵמֶק הַמֶּלֶךְ, "to the valley of Shaveh, which is the king's valley" (Gen. 14:17).

past, for a different reason, and the events recounted in the text simply provided further reason to call the place by that name.[41]

We should add that some commentators understood Ibn Ezra to mean that he included this verse in the "secret of the twelve," and concluded that it too represents a later addition to the Torah. In one of the early commentaries written on Ibn Ezra, known as *Ot Nefesh,* the author incorrectly understands Ibn Ezra as suggesting that the verse "he pursued

41. It is a widespread phenomenon that reasons for names and places in the Bible are not necessarily the original source of the name, but a sort of explanation for a name, giving new meaning to a name that already existed. One well-known example will suffice. Following the covenant and oath between Abraham and Avimelekh: עַל כֵּן קָרָא לַמָּקוֹם הַהוּא בְּאֵר שָׁבַע כִּי שָׁם נִשְׁבְּעוּ שְׁנֵיהֶם, "Therefore he called that place Be'er Sheva, for there the two of them swore (*nishbe'u*)" (Gen. 21:31). However, in Isaac's time a completely different explanation is given for the name: וַיְהִי בַּיּוֹם הַהוּא וַיָּבֹאוּ עַבְדֵי יִצְחָק וַיַּגִּדוּ לוֹ עַל אֹדוֹת הַבְּאֵר אֲשֶׁר חָפָרוּ וַיֹּאמְרוּ לוֹ מָצָאנוּ מָיִם. וַיִּקְרָא אֹתָהּ שִׁבְעָה עַל כֵּן שֵׁם הָעִיר בְּאֵר שֶׁבַע עַד הַיּוֹם הַזֶּה, "And it was on that day that the servants of Isaac came and told him about the well which they had dug, and they told him, 'We have found water.' And he called it Shiva; therefore, the name of the city is Be'er Sheva, to this very day" (Gen. 26:32–33). In other words, the place had been known by the same name previously, and the "renaming" was simply a matter of imbuing the existing name with new significance. As Ibn Ezra comments there, "It was named for two events, or it was a different city."

Ibn Ezra's innovation here is that the city's name went through three iterations. First it was called Dan, then it was known as Layish or Leshem, and then the tribe of Dan revived the previous name, in honor of their ancestor. This interpretation is adopted by A. Weiser, in his commentary *Tanakh Meforash* on Genesis (Jerusalem, 1981). He adds that it was perhaps the fact that the city had originally borne that name that drew the descendants of Dan to conquer it.

Ibn Ezra mentions this again when a similar problem arises. Moses describes to the Jews the location of the mountains Ebal and Gerizim: מוּל הַגִּלְגָּל אֵצֶל אֵלוֹנֵי מֹרֶה, "Opposite [or, on the way to] Gilgal, near the plains of Moreh (Deut. 11:30). How could Moses have called the place "Gilgal" when it was only given that name later, by Joshua? וַיֹּאמֶר ה׳ אֶל יְהוֹשֻׁעַ הַיּוֹם גַּלּוֹתִי אֶת חֶרְפַּת מִצְרַיִם מֵעֲלֵיכֶם וַיִּקְרָא שֵׁם הַמָּקוֹם הַהוּא גִּלְגָּל עַד הַיּוֹם הַזֶּה, "And God said to Joshua, today I have removed the shame of Egypt from upon you, and he called the name of the place Gilgal to this very day" (Josh. 5:9). Ibn Ezra explains, just as for "and he pursued up to Dan" – either by way of prophecy, or they are two different places. In other words, the place was already called Gilgal, but the name was given added meaning because of the events that transpired there.

them until Dan" (as well as the verse concerning Nahal Eshkol) is a later addition, "from the time of the Judges."[42]

Additional suggestions have been put forth,[43] but it seems that the most satisfying solution to this question is an analysis proposed by Yehuda Elitzur.[44]

He begins with two central points. First, the text itself makes clear that the general division of the land among the tribes was known from ancient times – from the time of Jacob – and would therefore have been known to Moses as well when he wrote the Torah. When Jacob blesses his sons prior to his death, he mentions geographical areas in relation to some of the tribes. To Zebulun, he says, זְבוּלֻן לְחוֹף יַמִּים יִשְׁכֹּן וְהוּא לְחוֹף אֳנִיּוֹת וְיַרְכָתוֹ עַל צִידֹן, "Zebulun shall dwell at the shore of the sea, and he shall be a haven for ships, and his border shall be at Sidon" (Gen. 49:13). His blessing to Judah mentions an inheritance that provides an abundance of wine (Gen. 49:11). Similarly, Moses's blessings to the tribes before his death are also partly related to geographical areas recognized for their landmarks, agriculture, and the like. The blessings to Benjamin (Deut. 33:12) and to Joseph (Deut. 33:13–15) allude to such geographic areas. Moreover, the description of Gilead son of Machir son of Manasseh (Num. 26:28–29) clearly refers to the tribal inheritance in the region named Gilead.

---

42. We do not know who wrote the *Ot Nefesh*. N. ben Menahem, *MeGinze Yisrael BaVatikan* (Jerusalem, 1954), 30, points to various fifteenth- and sixteenth-century manuscripts which identify the author as Rabbi Asher, son of Abraham Cresques, but the introduction to the book also raises the possibility that it was written by Yedaya HaPnini (c. 1270–1334), a French sage, who was a proponent of Maimonidean philosophy.
43. Y. Kiel, in *Daat Mikra* on Genesis (Jerusalem, 1997), raises the possibility that the text is referring not to a city called "Dan" but rather to a region – "the land of Dan" – so called because of its proximity to the sources of the Jordan, and as we find in Psalms 42:7, כֵּן אֶזְכָּרְךָ מֵאֶרֶץ יַרְדֵּן וְחֶרְמוֹנִים, "For I remember You from the land of the Jordan and from the Hermonim." See Y. Bin-Nun, *Eretz HaMoriah* (Alon Shvut, 2006), 17.
44. In a lecture he delivered in 1981, published in *Al Atar* 4–5 (Nissan 5749/1989): 243–49. The essence of the explanation below is based on his words, with slight changes and some additions.

In this vein, the fact that when Judah "goes down from his brothers," he wanders in the Timna region (Gen. 38:12) and that the same area ultimately becomes part of his inheritance (Josh. 14:57) is too neat to be a coincidence. Similarly, it is difficult to ignore the connection between Jacob's words to Joseph – וַאֲנִי נָתַתִּי לְךָ שְׁכֶם אַחַד עַל אַחֶיךָ אֲשֶׁר לָקַחְתִּי מִיַּד הָאֱמֹרִי בְּחַרְבִּי וּבְקַשְׁתִּי, "I have given you one portion (*shekhem eḥad*) more than your brothers, which I took from the hand of the Emori, with my sword and with my bow" (Gen. 48:22) – and the fact that the city of Shekhem ends up within the inheritance of Joseph, between the portions of Menashe and Ephraim, as stated above.[45] It seems clear that Jacob's sons were quite aware of the division of the land that their descendants were later to apportion to each respective tribe.[46]

45. Similarly, Issachar calls one of his sons "Shimron" (Gen. 46:13), and there is a city by this name that is located in the portion of Zebulun (Josh. 19:15), which is adjacent to the portion of Issachar.

46. In keeping with this approach, Elitzur argues that the casting of lots for the inheritance of the land, at God's command (Num. 26:52–56; 33:54), and its implementation over the course of the book of Joshua (14:2; 15:1; 16:1, and elsewhere), is not meant to establish a division *ex nihilo*; instead, it merely confirms the general division that is already known, defining the boundaries more accurately. Support for Elitzur's argument may be found in the fact that the command in the Torah is already formulated to indicate a combination between human agency and the intentions of God. On the one hand, Israel is commanded to divide the land in a just and fair manner: לָרַב תַּרְבֶּה נַחֲלָתוֹ וְלַמְעַט תַּמְעִיט נַחֲלָתוֹ אִישׁ לְפִי פְקֻדָיו יֻתַּן נַחֲלָתוֹ, "For a bigger [tribe] you shall give a bigger inheritance, while to a smaller [tribe] you shall give a smaller inheritance; each in accordance with his census shall be given his inheritance" (Num. 26:54). However, immediately thereafter we find: אַךְ בְּגוֹרָל יֵחָלֵק אֶת הָאָרֶץ לִשְׁמוֹת מַטּוֹת אֲבֹתָם יִנְחָלוּ. עַל פִּי הַגּוֹרָל תֵּחָלֵק נַחֲלָתוֹ בֵּין רַב לִמְעָט, "But by lot shall the land be divided, according to the names of the tribes of their fathers shall they inherit" (Num. 26:55–56). These verses appear to be in tension with each other – the second part of the command seems to indicate that the lot is decided by God, and has nothing to do with the relative size of each tribe. If the division of the land is ultimately carried out on the basis of a lot that depends on fate, then why the command to divide the land fairly? It would seem that the basic division indeed rests in human hands, and must be carried out in a just way. The casting of lots thus represents God's confirmation of the division. There are other instances in Tanakh of this sort of phenomenon, where the result is known before a selection is made. An example is the story of the appointment of Saul as king (I Sam. 10:17–27).

But this assumption, in and of itself, is not sufficient to answer the question concerning "Dan." It seems to suggest that the original inheritance of the tribe of Dan was supposed to be in the north, yet we know that they were explicitly allotted their portion in the south (Judges 1:34). Elitzur argues, however, that the reality was exactly the opposite: the original inheritance of Dan *was* indeed supposed to be in the north.

The location of Dan's inheritance is based on two main sources. The first is a hint in Moses's blessing to the tribe of Dan: דָּן גּוּר אַרְיֵה יְזַנֵּק מִן הַבָּשָׁן, "Dan is a lion's cub that leaps from Bashan" (Deut. 33:22), where Moses speaks to the tribe as though its inheritance lies in the Bashan area (in the north).[47] Second, according to the layout of the Israelite camp, as described in the second chapter of Numbers, the tribes of Judah, Issachar, and Zebulun encamp in the east; Reuben, Simeon, and Gad in the south; Ephraim, Menashe, and Benjamin in the west, and finally – Dan, Asher, and Naphtali in the north. As we can see,[48] the layout of the "banners" of the tribes essentially mirrors the structure of their settlement of the land.[49] The tribes of Dan, Asher, and Naphtali settle in the north, just as their banner in the wilderness was on the northern side of the camp – another indication that the tribe of Dan was identified with the north prior to the inheritance of the land.

Why, then, did Dan not inherit their portion in the north at the outset? It seems that when the tribes of Reuben and Gad relinquish their portion on the western side of the Jordan, requesting instead the land on the eastern side, the original plan for the division of the land underwent some changes. The most prominent amendment to the original plan concerns the portion of Zebulun, which was originally meant to be "at the shore of the sea ... and his border at Sidon," but is ultimately

Another is the discovery of Jonathan as the person who has violated the oath of Saul, his father; from the way the lot is carried out, it is clear that Saul is well aware that it was Jonathan who had violated the oath (I Sam. 14:40–42).

47. There is certainly room to contemplate the allusion in the expression "a lion's cub" (*gur aryeh*), with regard to the city called "Layish," a word that means "lion" (see M. Garsiel, *Midreshei Shemot BaMikra* [Ramat Gan, 1988], 48–49).

48. See *Daat Mikra* commentary on Numbers (Jerusalem, 1988), 16, n. 2.

49. Except for an obvious deviation concerning the tribes of Reuben and Gad. The visual parallel suggests that their portion was originally meant to be in the southern region. Ultimately, the portion that Reuben receives *is* in the south – but on the other side of the Jordan.

limited to the lower Galilee (see Joshua 19:10–16, 34). In the wake of these alterations, the tribe of Dan received its inheritance in the central region – which may originally have been meant for the tribe of Reuben or Gad. However, after the tribe of Dan failed to conquer this region, they moved northward and conquered the inheritance that had always been intended for them, since the time of Jacob and his sons.

Yehuda Elitzur's understanding of the tribal inheritances, supported by the plain meaning of the text, therefore rejects the claim that verses such as "he pursued them until Dan" indicate a later authorship of the Torah. Rather, the Torah hints again and again to the fact that the division of the land – including the northern inheritance of the tribe of Dan – existed and was known in general form from ancient times.

Another possible understanding is implied by the book of Chronicles, which strongly suggests that the connection between the sons of Jacob and the Land of Israel was not broken by the descent into Egypt and slavery there (most notably in I Chronicles 7:20–24). The traditions associating the families descended from Jacob's sons with particular regions in the land of Canaan would therefore have existed long before larger groups of Israelites entered the Land of Israel in the era of the "Conquest and Settlement."

SUMMARY

The Sages raise the possibility that, logically, some verses must have been added to the Torah after the death of Moses. Their discussion concerns the final eight verses of the Torah, but some of the medieval sages – especially Ibn Ezra – extend that line of reasoning and point to other verses whose plain meaning raises the possibility that they, too, were added to the Torah after Moses's time, by one of the prophets.

The thesis of the Bible critics, from Spinoza's time onwards, which seeks to extrapolate from a few exceptional verses that the entire Torah was written later, does not stand up to scrutiny. Using an exception to prove the rule is both subjective and incorrect.

Additionally, the claim that early mention of places in the Torah whose names were given only after Moses's time establishes later authorship is insufficient. Rather, careful reading is critical, before insisting that such place names necessarily require a late date of composition.

Chapter 3

Duplication and Contradiction

BACKGROUND

There is nothing new in the awareness that the Torah contains many instances of duplication, as well as contradictions between different sources. The Sages address these phenomena in many places, and note them using expressions such as, "Two biblical verses contradict one another";[1] or "one verse says...while another verse says..." (Mishna Arakhin 8:7). The medieval commentators broaden the discussion and propose different explanations for the phenomena of repetition and contradiction in Tanakh, both between different textual units, and within one single unit.[2]

Some of the better-known duplications and contradictions serve to illustrate the phenomena. Consider the description of Creation, famously presented as two different accounts, as set forth in the first and second chapters of Genesis. In chapter 1, plants were created (verses

1. *Torat Kohanim Baraita Divrei Yishmael,* chapter 1, Finkelstein edition, 4.
2. For the meantime we will concern ourselves with these phenomena as they are found in the Torah. The phenomena and the applicability of the solutions proposed in relation to the rest of Tanakh will be discussed in a later chapter.

11–12), followed by animals (verses 20–25), and finally man – male and female together (verse 27). In chapter 2, by contrast, man is created first (verse 7), followed by vegetation (verses 8–9), with the text emphasizing that there was no point in creating plants prior to the appearance of man,[3] and animals are created only in order to serve as a "helpmate" to man (verses 18–20). Woman, too, is created at a later stage, from one of man's ribs (verses 21–23).

Duplications and contradictions of this sort pepper the narrative of the book of Genesis. The story of the Flood, for example, employs an intentional duality: twice, God sees the evil of man and decides to destroy mankind from upon the earth (Gen. 6:5–8; 6:9–13); twice God commands Noah to bring the animals into the Ark, and twice the Torah recounts that Noah does everything as God commands him (Gen. 6:14–22; 7:1–5). Furthermore, different verses blatantly contradict each other regarding the number of animals that Noah is required to bring on the Ark. He is first told, וּמִכָּל הָחַי מִכָּל בָּשָׂר שְׁנַיִם מִכֹּל תָּבִיא אֶל הַתֵּבָה, "And of all the living things, of all flesh, *two of everything* shall you bring to the Ark" (Gen. 6:19–20). And then just four verses later he is told, מִכֹּל הַבְּהֵמָה הַטְּהוֹרָה תִּקַּח לְךָ שִׁבְעָה שִׁבְעָה אִישׁ וְאִשְׁתּוֹ, "Of all the pure animals shall you take for yourself by *sevens*, male and female" (Gen. 7:2).

At the end of *Parashat Noaḥ,* Terah leads Abram, Sarai, and Lot from Ur Kasdim, in the direction of Canaan, but they stop in Haran (Gen. 11:31–32). Later, they continue from Haran to Canaan (Gen. 12:5). But at the beginning of *Parashat Lekh Lekha,* God commands Abram, לֶךְ לְךָ מֵאַרְצְךָ וּמִמּוֹלַדְתְּךָ וּמִבֵּית אָבִיךָ אֶל הָאָרֶץ אֲשֶׁר אַרְאֶךָּ, "Go forth from your land and from your birthplace and from your father's house, to the land which I will show you" (Gen. 12:1), which implies that Abram was still in his birthplace and his father's house

---

3. As it says there, וְכֹל שִׂיחַ הַשָּׂדֶה טֶרֶם יִהְיֶה בָאָרֶץ וְכָל עֵשֶׂב הַשָּׂדֶה טֶרֶם יִצְמָח כִּי לֹא הִמְטִיר ה' אֱלֹהִים עַל הָאָרֶץ וְאָדָם אַיִן לַעֲבֹד אֶת הָאֲדָמָה, "No shrub of the field was yet in the earth, and no herb of the field had yet sprung up; for the Lord God had not caused it to rain upon the earth, and there was not a man to till the ground." Rashi there adds a midrashic understanding. In his words: "And why does it say that it did not rain? Because there was no man to work the land, and so there would be no one to be grateful for rain. When Adam arrived and saw that rain was needed, he prayed for rain and it fell, and trees and grass grew."

when God commanded him to go to Canaan. This circumstance is also suggested by God's words later on, in the Covenant between the Parts: אֲנִי ה' אֲשֶׁר הוֹצֵאתִיךָ מֵאוּר כַּשְׂדִּים, "I am the Lord who brought you forth from Ur Kasdim" (Gen. 15:7).

The boundaries of the Land of Israel, as stated at this Covenant between the Parts, are "from the River of Egypt to the great river, the Euphrates," מִנְּהַר מִצְרַיִם עַד הַנָּהָר הַגָּדֹל נְהַר פְּרָת (Gen. 15:18), but then two chapters later, the boundaries are limited to "the land of Canaan" (Gen. 17:8), located between the great sea (Mediterranean) and the Jordan River (see also Num. 34:1–13).

God appears to Abraham and tells him that his son, Isaac, will be born in a year's time (Gen. 17:15–19), and Abraham responds with laughter. In the next chapter, angels reveal themselves to Abraham and inform him that in a year's time a son will be born to him (Gen. 18:10). This time it is Sarah who laughs.

When Jacob returns from Haran to Canaan, he sends messengers to Esau, in Se'ir (Gen. 32:4). At the end of their encounter, Esau returns home: וַיָּשָׁב בַּיּוֹם הַהוּא עֵשָׂו לְדַרְכּוֹ שֵׂעִירָה, "Esau returned that day on his way unto Se'ir" (Gen. 33:16).

But chapter 36 (vv. 6–8) indicates that Esau only returns to Se'ir later:

> וַיִּקַּח עֵשָׂו אֶת נָשָׁיו...וְאֵת כָּל קִנְיָנוֹ אֲשֶׁר רָכַשׁ בְּאֶרֶץ כְּנָעַן וַיֵּלֶךְ אֶל אֶרֶץ מִפְּנֵי יַעֲקֹב אָחִיו. כִּי הָיָה רְכוּשָׁם רָב מִשֶּׁבֶת יַחְדָּו וְלֹא יָכְלָה אֶרֶץ מְגוּרֵיהֶם לָשֵׂאת אֹתָם מִפְּנֵי מִקְנֵיהֶם.
>
> And Esau took his wives ... and all his possessions, which he had gathered in the land of Canaan; and went into a land away from his brother Jacob. For their substance was too great for them to dwell together; and the land of their sojournings could not bear them because of their cattle.

Regarding the sale of Joseph, וְהַמְּדָנִים מָכְרוּ אֹתוֹ אֶל מִצְרָיִם לְפוֹטִיפַר סְרִיס פַּרְעֹה שַׂר הַטַּבָּחִים, "the *Midianites* sold him to Egypt, to Potiphar, Pharaoh's chamberlain, the captain of the guard" (Gen. 37:36). And then further on we read, וַיִּקְנֵהוּ פּוֹטִיפַר...מִיַּד הַיִּשְׁמְעֵאלִים אֲשֶׁר הוֹרִדֻהוּ שָׁמָּה,

"And Potiphar bought him … from the *Ishmaelites* who had brought him down there" (Gen. 39:1).

The same phenomenon continues into Exodus. For instance, in the plague of blood, Moses says, הִנֵּה אָנֹכִי מַכֶּה בַּמַּטֶּה אֲשֶׁר בְּיָדִי עַל הַמַּיִם אֲשֶׁר בַּיְאֹר וְנֶהֶפְכוּ לְדָם, "Behold, I will smite with the staff that is in my hand upon the water that is in the river, and it shall turn into blood" (Ex. 7:17). That is, Moses himself will strike the Nile with his staff. But two verses later God tells Moses, אֱמֹר אֶל אַהֲרֹן קַח מַטְּךָ וּנְטֵה יָדְךָ עַל מֵימֵי מִצְרַיִם עַל נַהֲרֹתָם עַל יְאֹרֵיהֶם וְעַל אַגְמֵיהֶם וְעַל כָּל מִקְוֵה מֵימֵיהֶם וְיִהְיוּ דָם, "Say to Aaron: Take your staff and stretch your arm over the water of Egypt, over their streams, over their rivers, over their lakes, and over all their pools of water, and they shall be blood." In other words, it is Aaron who strikes the water with his staff, turning not only the Nile, but all bodies of water throughout Egypt, into blood.

At the time of the Exodus, Moses tells the Jews, וְאַתֶּם לֹא תֵצְאוּ אִישׁ מִפֶּתַח בֵּיתוֹ **עַד בֹּקֶר**, "No man shall emerge from the door of his house until the morning" (Ex. 12:22), suggesting that the Exodus was to take place the next day. But a few verses later,

> וַיִּקְרָא לְמֹשֶׁה וּלְאַהֲרֹן **לַיְלָה** וַיֹּאמֶר קוּמוּ צְּאוּ מִתּוֹךְ עַמִּי... וַתֶּחֱזַק מִצְרַיִם עַל הָעָם לְמַהֵר לְשַׁלְּחָם מִן הָאָרֶץ... כִּי גֹרְשׁוּ מִמִּצְרַיִם וְלֹא יָכְלוּ לְהִתְמַהְמֵהַּ וְגַם צֵדָה לֹא עָשׂוּ לָהֶם.
>
> [Pharaoh] called for Moses and Aaron by night, and he said: "Arise and get out from among my people," … and the Egyptians urged the people to hurry, that they might send them out of the land … for they were driven out of Egypt, and could not delay, nor had they prepared themselves any provisions. (Ex. 12:31–39)

This tells us that they left by night – as supported by the verse in Deuteronomy (16:1), כִּי בְּחֹדֶשׁ הָאָבִיב הוֹצִיאֲךָ ה׳ אֱלֹהֶיךָ מִמִּצְרַיִם **לָיְלָה**, "For in the month of spring the Lord your God brought you out of Egypt by night."

Contradictions abound in legal units, too. In the laws concerning a Hebrew servant, in *Parashat Mishpatim* (Ex. 21:2–7) and *Parashat Re'eh* (Deut. 15:12–18), a servant who does not wish to go free in the seventh year has his ear pierced with an awl by his master, and then "he shall serve him forever (לְעֹלָם)" (Ex. 21:6 and similarly Deut. 15:17). On the verse in Exodus, Rashbam explains, "The literal meaning is 'all the days of his life,' as it says in the book of Samuel: וְיָשַׁב שָׁם עַד עוֹלָם, 'And he shall remain there forever' (I Sam. 1:22)." By contrast, in *Parashat Behar*, the Torah rules out the possibility of a Hebrew servant's serving beyond the Jubilee year: עַד שְׁנַת הַיֹּבֵל יַעֲבֹד עִמָּךְ... כִּי עֲבָדַי הֵם אֲשֶׁר הוֹצֵאתִי אֹתָם מֵאֶרֶץ מִצְרָיִם לֹא יִמָּכְרוּ מִמְכֶּרֶת עָבֶד, "Until the Jubilee year, he shall work with you ... for they are My servants, those whom I brought out of the land of Egypt; they shall not be sold as bondsmen" (Lev. 25:40–42).

In the commandment of *Shemitta*, the Sabbatical year, the book of Exodus establishes that the produce of the land is meant for consumption by the poor: וְהַשְּׁבִיעִת תִּשְׁמְטֶנָּה וּנְטַשְׁתָּהּ וְאָכְלוּ אֶבְיֹנֵי עַמֶּךָ וְיִתְרָם תֹּאכַל חַיַּת הַשָּׂדֶה, "But in the seventh year you shall let it rest and lie fallow, that the poor of your people may eat, and what they leave, the beasts of the field shall eat" (Ex. 23:11). In Leviticus, however, the essence of the *Shemitta* year is to allow everyone to eat of the produce freely and equally. The poor are not singled out:

> וְהָיְתָה שַׁבַּת הָאָרֶץ לָכֶם לְאָכְלָה לְךָ וּלְעַבְדְּךָ וְלַאֲמָתֶךָ וְלִשְׂכִירְךָ וּלְתוֹשָׁבְךָ הַגָּרִים עִמָּךְ. וְלִבְהֶמְתְּךָ וְלַחַיָּה אֲשֶׁר בְּאַרְצֶךָ תִּהְיֶה כָל תְּבוּאָתָהּ לֶאֱכֹל
>
> And the Sabbath produce of the land shall be for you for food, and for your servants, and for your maidservants, and for your hired workers, and for the stranger who sojourns with you. And for your cattle, and for the beasts in your land shall all its produce be, for food. (Lev. 25:6–7)

Especially prominent are the seeming contradictions between Deuteronomy and the preceding books – both in the narrative and legal sections. Chapter 1 of Deuteronomy begins with a description of the appointment of judges (Deut. 1:9–18), and it differs in several significant respects from the narrative in the eighteenth chapter of Exodus. In Exodus, Jethro is given credit for the suggestion to appoint judges, whereas in Deuteronomy, the appointment of the judges is depicted as Moses's initiative. Furthermore, in Exodus it is Moses who selects the judges, while in Deuteronomy he appeals to the people to choose them.

When, in the first chapter of Deuteronomy, Moses recounts the episode of the spies, the account is quite different from the one recorded in *Parashat Shelaḥ* in Numbers. The most glaring and well-known difference is that in *Parashat Shelaḥ*, the initiative of appointing spies comes from God; in Deuteronomy, it is the people who request this scouting mission. There are also many other differences – the purpose of the mission, the question of whether the conclusion drawn from the mission is stated by the spies or by the people, Joshua's role, and more.

In Deuteronomy 2:2–8, the Children of Israel approach Edom, and we read of the warnings they are given in advance: they will not be able to enter the land of Edom, and they will be permitted only to purchase food and water there (Deut. 2:5–6) – and indeed they did pay for the food and water provided by the Edomites (Deut. 2:28–29). In Numbers, chapter 20, however, the Children of Israel express interest in journeying through the land of Edom, and Edom refuses, not even permitting them to purchase food and water along the way.

Likewise, the accounts of the circumstances of the Golden Calf differ. Exodus, chapter 32, describes how God tells Moses of His intention to wipe out the nation, and Moses immediately begs and pleads and succeeds in annulling this decree. In Deuteronomy, chapter 9, however, Moses descends the mountain with the feeling that the fate of the nation has been sealed; only afterwards does he ascend to God and ask that He annul the decree.

In the legal realm, recall the well-known differences between the Sabbath, as presented in the Ten Commandments in Exodus (20:8–11) as compared to Deuteronomy (5:12–15). The discrepancy goes beyond the opening command ("Remember" vs. "Observe"), extending to the reason behind the mitzva. Exodus situates the meaning of the Sabbath in the context of human beings' relationship to God (Ex. 20:11), while Deuteronomy emphasizes the social context of allowing slaves to rest (Deut. 5:15).

In the passages describing the Passover sacrifice, there are again discrepancies between Deuteronomy and the previous books. For example, in Exodus, chapter 12, sacrificial animals should be taken מִן הַכְּבָשִׂים וּמִן הָעִזִּים, "from the sheep or from the goats" (verse 5), and the meat must be roasted. Further, אַל תֹּאכְלוּ מִמֶּנּוּ נָא וּבָשֵׁל מְבֻשָּׁל בַּמָּיִם,

"you shall not eat of it raw, nor boiled at all in water" (verse 9). In Deuteronomy, chapter 16: וְזָבַחְתָּ פֶּסַח לַה׳ אֱלֹהֶיךָ צֹאן **וּבָקָר** "You shall offer a Passover to the Lord your God, of the flock and of the herd [cattle]" (verse 2), and as to its form: שָׁם תִּזְבַּח אֶת הַפֶּסַח...**וּבִשַּׁלְתָּ** וְאָכַלְתָּ בַּמָּקוֹם אֲשֶׁר יִבְחַר ה׳ אֱלֹהֶיךָ בּוֹ, "There you shall offer the Passover…and you shall cook it [boil it] and eat it in the place which the Lord your God will choose" (verses 6–7).

One final example: in Exodus, a Hebrew maidservant לֹא תֵצֵא כְּצֵאת הָעֲבָדִים, "shall not go out as the slaves go out" (21:7). The plain meaning is that she is not automatically freed when a Hebrew servant would be – "after six years" (Rashbam, ad loc.), as mentioned in the previous verse. In Deuteronomy, however: כִּי יִמָּכֵר לְךָ אָחִיךָ הָעִבְרִי **אוֹ הָעִבְרִיָּה** וַעֲבָדְךָ שֵׁשׁ שָׁנִים וּבַשָּׁנָה הַשְּׁבִיעִת תְּשַׁלְּחֶנּוּ חָפְשִׁי מֵעִמָּךְ, "If your brother, a Hebrew man *or Hebrew woman*, is sold to you, he shall serve you for six years, and in the seventh year you shall let him go free from you" (Deut. 15:12).

The examples above are just that – examples of a larger phenomenon – and not an exhaustive list. Their meanings and implications have been debated over the generations, and various explanations have been proposed. Many of the solutions are less than satisfactory, for they too often interpret the text in a manner that does not sit well with its plain meaning.

For instance, the textual description of Abraham journeying with Terah, his father, until they reach Haran, followed by Abraham's journey to Canaan, is in contrast to the revelation in which God calls upon him to leave מֵאַרְצְךָ וּמִמּוֹלַדְתְּךָ וּמִבֵּית אָבִיךָ, "your land and your birthplace and your father's house," implying that this command came while he was still in Ur Kasdim, as indeed he was, according to the account of his journey as recalled in Genesis 15:7. The commentators offer various ways of resolving this contradiction, but the difficulty is fundamentally unresolved. Rashi comments (Gen. 12:2): "But did he not leave there already, with his father, and come as far as Haran? Rather, this is what God told him: Distance yourself even further from there, and leave your father's house."

On the plain level of the text, it is difficult to interpret the command "*Lekh lekha*" – literally, "go for yourself" – to mean "distance yourself even further," especially in light of the fact that a similar command appears in the context of the *Akeda* (the story of the Binding of Isaac) in Genesis 22:2, where the plain meaning is to leave the place where he was right then, and not to "distance himself even further." Ibn Ezra and Radak therefore explain that this command was indeed given to Abraham in Ur Kasdim before Terah took his family to Haran, and the verse in fact is meant in the sense of the past perfect tense – that God "had commanded" Abraham. Yet the verse gives no hint of this chronological ordering.[4] Other commentaries give rise to comparable questions.[5]

In legal portions of the Torah, some of the resolutions to contradictions do not work well with the plain meaning of the text. Concerning the Hebrew servant, for example, we noted the contradiction between "and he shall serve him forever (*le'olam*)" in *Parashat Mishpatim*, and the mandatory release in the Jubilee year, as mentioned in *Parashat Behar*.

---

4. Hebrew grammar does not offer a fixed form for complex tenses such as the past perfect. Generally, when the biblical text seeks to convey the past perfect, the usual order of the verse is changed around so that the subject appears before the object. An example is the verse וְהָאָדָם יָדַע אֶת חַוָּה אִשְׁתּוֹ, "And Adam had known Eve, his wife" (*veha'adam yada* – that is, Adam engaged in marital relations with her) (Gen. 4:1), where Rashi comments, "This was prior to the matter just discussed; it was before he sinned and was expelled from the Garden of Eden, and likewise the pregnancy and birth [preceded the sin and expulsion]. If the verse had read, '*vayeda ha'adam*,' it would mean that his children were born only after he was expelled." Similarly, we may point to the verse, וַה׳ גָּלָה אֶת אֹזֶן שְׁמוּאֵל יוֹם אֶחָד לִפְנֵי בוֹא שָׁאוּל "And God had revealed (*vaHashem gala*) to Samuel a day before Saul's arrival" (I Sam. 9:15).

   In the case of God's command to Abraham, too, according to the explanation of Ibn Ezra and Radak, the text should logically have read, "And God had said (*vaHashem amar*) to Abram, 'Go forth from your land.'" Nahmanides points out another difficulty with understanding the verse in this way: If Abraham had indeed started out on his journey in response to God's command, then he should be depicted as the dominant figure on the journey. But it is Terah who, at the end of chapter 11, seems to be the main character: וַיִּקַּח תֶּרַח אֶת אַבְרָם בְּנוֹ...לָלֶכֶת אַרְצָה כְּנַעַן, "And Terah took Abram, his son ... to go to the land of Canaan" (Gen. 11:31).
5. Nahmanides, for example, rejecting the interpretations of Rashi and Ibn Ezra, argues that Abraham had not been born in Ur Kasdim at all, but rather in Haran. This forces him to explain Genesis 15:7 with reference to Abraham's miraculous deliverance from the fiery furnace. This direction of interpretation, quite uncharacteristic of Nahmanides, is based on a homiletic interpretation and is difficult to reconcile with the plain meaning of the text.

The Sages' well-known solution to the contradiction? "'Forever' means 'for as long as there is until the Jubilee'" (Kiddushin 21b).

However, the term "*le'olam*" appears dozens of times in Tanakh, and it always means "forever," rendering the Sages' solution difficult to reconcile with the plain sense of the text, as noted by Rashbam. For instance, לֹא תִדְרֹשׁ שְׁלֹמָם וְטֹבָתָם כָּל יָמֶיךָ לְעוֹלָם, "You shall not seek their peace and their welfare all the days of your life, forever (*le'olam*)" (Deut. 23:7); וָאֹמַר לֹא אָפֵר בְּרִיתִי אִתְּכֶם לְעוֹלָם, "And I said, I shall never (*le'olam*) break My covenant with you" (Judges 2:1). Why would the Torah use an expression whose meaning is clearly understood in other contexts as meaning "forever," rather than simply stating "until the Jubilee year"?

Beyond the unsatisfactory nature of the solutions to the various contradictions, the sheer number of contradictions poses a more fundamental difficulty. One cannot help but ask why the Tanakh is written in this way. Would it not be more appropriate for the text to be written in an organized, smooth style, devoid of repetition and contradiction? Indeed, as the study of the biblical text and criticism spread, it became necessary to address this phenomenon from a broader and more all-encompassing perspective, rather than on a case-by-case basis.

THE DOCUMENTARY HYPOTHESIS[6]

In 1753, a French doctor named Jean Astruc published a book in which he proposed a revolutionary explanation for the authorship of the book of Genesis. He pointed out that the book is full of contradictions and repetitions, but that generally they arise when two different names of

6. Much has been written on this subject. Some of the major reviews in Hebrew may be found in the following sources: M. Weinfeld, ed., "Torah, Meḥkar HaTorah BaEt HaḤadasha," *Encyclopedia Mikra'it* 8 (Jerusalem, 1982), columns 495–507; Z. Weisman, *Mavo LaMikra*, Open University series (Tel Aviv, 1989), vol. 3, unit 6, 32–97; A. Rofe, *Mavo LeSifrut HaMikra* (Jerusalem, 2006), 26–82; B. Y. Schwartz, "HaTorah: Ḥameshet Ḥumasheiha VeArba Te'udoteiha," in Z. Talshir, ed., *Sifrut HaMikra – Mevo'ot U'Meḥkarim* (Jerusalem, 2011), 177–225. Similarly, much has been written in English on the documentary hypothesis; an excellent summary of the history and nature of it can be found in Joshua Berman's introduction to Umberto Cassuto's *The Documentary Hypothesis* (Jerusalem, 2010). See also Jon D. Levenson, *The Hebrew Bible, the Old Testament, and Historical Criticism: Jews and Christians in Biblical Studies* (Louisville, 1993), 1–32.

God are used: HVYH[7] and Elohim. He concluded that Moses wrote Genesis by combining two distinct sources ("documents") that described creation, each referring to God by a different name. These two documents, he explained, were consolidated by Moses, but imperfectly, and that accounts for the many contradictions and duplications found in the text. Thus, the contradictions between the first and second chapter of Genesis can be resolved by understanding that chapter 1 is the version that speaks of "Elohim," while chapter 2 speaks of "HVYH Elohim."

A similar distinction explains the discrepancies in the two foretellings of the birth of Isaac. The first, in Genesis 17, belongs to the Elohim source (see verses 15, 18, and 19), while the second (Gen. 18) was taken from the HVYH source (see verses 1, 13 and 17).

Astruc's theory is useful in explaining not just contradictions and duplications between different narratives, but even problems within a single narrative. For example, the story of the Flood may be unraveled into two separate narrative strands, one that employs only verses using HVYH and another that uses Elohim. This untangling yields two complete stories, each internally consistent. And so it becomes possible to suggest that the flood narrative as it appears in the Bible is in fact a hybrid of two different flood narratives.

Astruc's theory did not attract much attention among critics of his time, perhaps because he was an amateur. Many years later, Johann Gottfried Eichhorn, considered the father of modern biblical criticism, expanded upon Astruc's theory in a three-volume book that appeared in the years 1780 to 1783 (*Historisch-Kritische Einleitung ins Alte Testament*, "Historical and Critical Introduction to the Old Testament"). He distinguished the literary and thematic indications of separate sources, even where different names of God did not appear in the text. He called the first source E for Elohim, and the second J, for the transliteration of the first letter of Y-H-V-H.

At first, Eichhorn suggested that Moses combined these two sources, but by the time the book had reached its fourth edition, he changed his mind. He proposed a later date for the combining of the sources, based primarily on claims already addressed in previous chapters,

7. This is a traditional substitute for writing the Tetragrammaton, Y-H-V-H.

concerning verses that appear to have been written at a later time than the events they describe.

Over the years, the basic theory was further developed and broadened. Scholars argued for the existence of additional sources, and tried to define and characterize the nature and style of the different sources from which, in their view, the Torah had been constructed. The central challenge was to isolate each source, and then attempt to demonstrate how all the parts of the Torah belonging to that source connect to form a continuous text with a unique literary and theological approach. At the same time, the scholars argued that the various documents reflect views that had developed and changed over the course of many generations, rendering some of the contradictions in the biblical text the product of inter-generational differences of view. Some pointed to contradictions among the various textual units that use the name "Elohim," and posited the existence of an additional source, which included the commandments pertaining to the priests. In 1805, the German scholar Wilhelm de Wette published his theory that the book of Deuteronomy represented a separate source, composed during the period of King Josiah (649–609 BCE).

In 1878, Julius Wellhausen reformulated this documentary hypothesis, proposing four separate sources, each reflecting a different stage in the evolution of Jewish faith. He considered the earliest phase to be that of natural religion, followed by the ethical moralism of the prophets, which eventually became the priestly theocracy of Judaism, which was the basis for Pharisee and Rabbinic Judaism of the Second Temple Period – a form of Judaism that Wellhausen considered a spiritual step backwards. On the basis of de Wette's theory that Deuteronomy was composed during the period of King Josiah, Wellhausen hypothesized as to the period when each of the four sources appeared:

1. The "J" source is the most ancient, dating to the beginning of the period of the monarchy.
2. The "E" source (referring to the name "Elohim") is slightly later (eighth century BCE), with visual descriptions of God and extensive attention to nature.
3. The "D" (Deuteronomist) source, consisting mainly of Deuteronomy, as well as a major portion of the books of the Early Prophets, is

dated to the period of Josiah (seventh century BCE), and serves as the basis for the dating of the other documents.[8]

4. The "P" (Priestly) source, including the chapters concerning the Mishkan (the Tabernacle) in Exodus and major portions of Leviticus. This source is totally disconnected from nature and deals with detailed rituals and the superior status of the priests. Wellhausen thought this source was composed as late as the Second Temple Period (sixth century BCE), when the faith of Israel had become more focused on details, and the priests formed the major religious leadership.

These four sources, according to the documentary hypothesis, were combined by a number of editors, until the final form of the Torah was achieved in the fifth century BCE.

The documentary hypothesis rests on two central pillars: a literary focus, addressing the contradictions and repetitions in the text, which can be explained by dividing the Torah into four separate documents;[9] and a historical focus, explaining the contradictions as a result of cultural and religious developments within Judaism.

We shall first address the historical aspect of the documentary hypothesis.

HISTORICAL FOCUS OF THE DOCUMENTARY HYPOTHESIS

Let us begin our discussion of the historical aspect of the documentary hypothesis with the main arguments for the dating of the Deuteronomist source, as this serves as the basis for the dating of the other documents.[10]

---

8. The word "Deuteronomy" is derived from the Greek and means "second law." *Ḥazal* often use the Hebrew equivalent "*mishneh torah*" in referring to Deuteronomy.
9. It should be noted that the documentary hypothesis does not necessarily imply that the Torah was composed from four complete parallel texts. Rather, some of the original documents overlapped incompletely. Only in cases where two (or, rarely, three) different versions of a law or narrative existed would they leave behind traces in the form of duplications or contradictions.
10. Historical questions arose once again in the wake of archaeological discoveries in the Middle East. The implications of these discoveries, most of which were made after the formulation of the documentary hypothesis, will be discussed in future chapters.

The prevalent view in academic circles, going back to the time of de Wette, is that a major part of the book of Deuteronomy was written in the seventh century BCE as part of the battle waged by Hezekiah and Josiah for centralized ritual worship, and that there is a connection between this source and the discovery of the Book of the Torah by Hilkiyah the *kohen* in the Temple, in the days of Josiah (II Kings 22).[11] This assertion is based mainly on the argument that Deuteronomy is the only book of the Torah that speaks of the selection of a single location for Divine service, and rejects worship outside of this location, as emphasized over and over in chapter 12:

> הִשָּׁמֶר לְךָ פֶּן תַּעֲלֶה עֹלֹתֶיךָ בְּכָל מָקוֹם אֲשֶׁר תִּרְאֶה. כִּי אִם בַּמָּקוֹם אֲשֶׁר יִבְחַר ה׳ בְּאַחַד שְׁבָטֶיךָ שָׁם תַּעֲלֶה עֹלֹתֶיךָ.
>
> Guard yourself lest you offer up your burnt offerings in every place which you see; but only in the place which God will choose, among one of your tribes – there shall you offer up your burnt offerings. (Deut. 12:13–14)

According to this understanding, the polemic against multiple places of divine worship in the land appears for the first time in the days of Hezekiah (II Kings 18:4, 22), and especially in the words of his great-grandson, Josiah (II Kings 23), immediately after the discovery of the Book of the Torah. This chronology in turn led to the hypothesis that

11. De Wette had offered the hypothesis that the rediscovered Book of the Torah was actually a forgery, and that it was authored by the priests in the time of Josiah, with the aim of having it viewed as holy in order to gain acceptance by the people. For this reason, they placed it in a concealed place in the Temple. Chapter 1 discussed the possibility that the "Book of the Torah" discovered by Hilkiah may well have included only the main parts of Deuteronomy, noting that the commentary on Chronicles attributed to Rashi maintains this view. However, it is not easy to believe that the work was a forgery accepted unquestioningly by the public. Indeed, many scholars today do not accept this theory, arguing instead that the book had been written during the time of Hezekiah, was hidden during the period of Menashe, and was rediscovered during the reign of Josiah (see M. Weinfeld, *Deuteronomy 1–11*, Anchor Bible Commentary 5 [New York, 1991], especially 50–57 and 65–77, presenting a more complex view).

the book in question was composed during this period, as a means of reinforcing a single location for divine worship, and as part of the war on idolatry around Jerusalem. That also explains why it is only in the book of Kings, which was necessarily composed after the period of Josiah, that mention is made of the fact that the people offer sacrifices on "*bamot*" (altars outside of the Temple). The implication is that this accusation was added to the narrative by a later editor.

Because the proposed period of authorship of the Deuteronomist source rests upon a specific historical event, the dating of this source served as the cornerstone for the dating of the other documents. The documents' initial dating was based more on an analysis of the ideas and literary form of their respective texts, and correlating them to different historical periods, with no clear historical anchor. The following passage, attributed to the "Elohist" ("E") source, seems to indicate that sacrifice is possible anywhere and is not limited to a single location:

> מִזְבַּח אֲדָמָה תַּעֲשֶׂה לִּי וְזָבַחְתָּ עָלָיו אֶת עֹלֹתֶיךָ וְאֶת שְׁלָמֶיךָ אֶת צֹאנְךָ
> וְאֶת בְּקָרֶךָ בְּכָל הַמָּקוֹם אֲשֶׁר אַזְכִּיר אֶת שְׁמִי אָבוֹא אֵלֶיךָ וּבֵרַכְתִּיךָ.
>
> You shall make for Me an altar of earth, and you shall offer upon it your burnt offerings and your peace offerings and your sheep and your oxen; in every place where I cause My Name to be uttered, I shall come to you and I shall bless you. (Ex. 20:20)

The argument runs that this source must have preceded the Deuteronomist source, and that it was only at a later stage of history that the idea of centralized worship in a single location arose.

However, this claim – central to the documentary hypothesis – raises several difficulties. Consider the following:[12]

---

12. For reviews of the difficulties surrounding the hypotheses of de Wette and Wellhausen, concerning the essence and dating of Deuteronomy, see M. Z. Segal, *Mavo HaMikra* (Jerusalem, 1977), 140–42; U. Cassuto, "Devarim," *Encyclopedia Mikra'it* 2 (Jerusalem, 1954), column 611; Y. M. Grintz, "Devarim," *HaEncyclopedia HaIvrit* 11 (Jerusalem, 1957), columns 887–90. In English, see U. Cassuto, *The Documentary Hypothesis* (Jerusalem, 2011).

1. Deuteronomy makes no mention of the name of Jerusalem; rather, it speaks (more than twenty times!) of הַמָּקוֹם אֲשֶׁר יִבְחַר ה׳, "the place which God will choose." Had Deuteronomy indeed been written only toward the end of the First Temple Period with a view to strengthening Jerusalem's centrality, why not mention Jerusalem explicitly?

2. De Wette's hypothesis grants disproportional weight to the opposition to divine worship outside of God's chosen place. Restricting ritual to Jerusalem occupies only a minor place in Josiah's revolution, and the same in Deuteronomy. The crux of Josiah's battle was against idolatry, which features throughout the Torah.[13] The Tanakh devotes twenty-one verses to its description of Josiah's actions, in the wake of the discovery of the Book of the Torah, and the great majority of them describe explicitly the extermination of the various types of idolatry: the *baal* and the *ashera* (verses 4–7); worship of Molekh (verse 10); sun worship (verse 11); the altars built for idolatrous purposes by the kings of Judah, from the time of Solomon until the days of Ahaz and Menashe (verses 12–14); worship of the calves by Jeroboam ben Nebat (verses 15–18), and so on. Only a single verse discusses divine worship outside of the Temple (verse 8). The argument that Deuteronomy was composed for the purpose of reinforcing such a relatively minor issue as the centralization of divine worship in the book of Kings seems difficult to sustain. At the same time, even in Deuteronomy itself, this prohibition is mentioned in chapter 12, but cannot be regarded as a central motif of the book as a whole, when one considers the many mitzvot and other subjects.

13. In the Ten Commandments: לֹא יִהְיֶה לְךָ אֱלֹהִים אֲחֵרִים עַל פָּנָי, "You shall have no other gods beside Me" (Ex. 20:2), and further on, וְשֵׁם אֱלֹהִים אֲחֵרִים לֹא תַזְכִּירוּ לֹא יִשָּׁמַע עַל פִּיךָ, "You shall make no mention of the name of other gods; it shall not be heard from your mouth" (Ex. 23:13). See Ex. 34:11–16; Lev. 19:4; and elsewhere. From the finds at Kuntillet Ajrud, it is clear that worship of HVYH outside Jerusalem became linked to considering HVYH as limited to a specific place and connected to an *ashera*, and therefore the battle against idolatry may be connected to the need to centralize the worship of HVYH at a single cult-site (Zeev Meshel et al., *Kuntillet Ajrud (Horvat Teman): An Iron Age II Religious Site on the Judah-Sinai Border* [Jerusalem, 2012]). Nevertheless, the verses concerning Josiah's revolution focus on the battle against idolatry.

3. The book of Kings mentions repeatedly that "the people were still sacrificing and offering incense on the *bamot*" (I Kings 22:44; II Kings 12:4, and elsewhere), and the word "*bamot*" appears dozens of times. If Deuteronomy were composed for the sake of the book of Kings' struggle against divine worship outside of the Temple, one would expect Deuteronomy to make explicit mention of the *bamot*. However, the word does not appear in Deuteronomy at all.

4. Opposition to the centralization of divine worship in Kings appears following the construction of the altar in Beit El, by Jeroboam (I Kings 12:32–33). Concerning this, the "man of God" who comes from Judea chastises Jeroboam, and foretells a gruesome end for the altar:

    מִזְבֵּחַ מִזְבֵּחַ כֹּה אָמַר ה׳ הִנֵּה בֵן נוֹלָד לְבֵית דָּוִד יֹאשִׁיָּהוּ שְׁמוֹ וְזָבַח עָלֶיךָ אֶת כֹּהֲנֵי הַבָּמוֹת הַמַּקְטִרִים עָלֶיךָ וְעַצְמוֹת אָדָם יִשְׂרְפוּ עָלֶיךָ.

    Altar, altar, so says God: Behold, a child will be born to the house of David, by the name of Josiah, and he shall offer upon you the *kohanim* of the *bamot* who burn incense upon you, and they shall burn human bones upon you. (I Kings 13:2)

    According to the documentary hypothesis, one would have to conclude that this narrative was composed only after Josiah's religious revolution, and was deliberately "planted" in the text in order to support his campaign.[14] The problem is that an approach that accepts the reliability of the biblical narrative only when that narrative fits the hypothesis, and rejects the reliability of the text when it does not

14. See, for example, M. Haran, *HaAssufa HaMikra'it: Tahalikhei HaGibbush Ad Sof Yemei Bayit Sheni VeShinuyei HaTzura Ad Motza'ei Yemei HaBenayim* (Jerusalem, 2004), 28–32. Haran attempts to prove that the story is chronologically later on the basis of the mention of Josiah as the one to destroy the altar. However, this hypothesis relies on two prior assumptions. First, Haran rejects outright the existence of the phenomenon of prophecy; if this were true, then even if the words "by the name of Josiah" did not appear here, there would be no room for a prophet to say anything about the future. Therefore, to his view, any story about a prophecy concerning the future is actually based on later authorship, after that "future" had already come to pass; only then could historical events be presented as having been prophesied in advance. Obviously, for a person who believes that prophecy did exist, there is no

meet the critic's assumptions, is untenable. To illustrate that limitation, consider Jeremiah's prophecy (Jer. 34:13–14):

> כֹּה אָמַר ה׳ אֱלֹהֵי יִשְׂרָאֵל אָנֹכִי כָּרַתִּי בְרִית אֶת אֲבוֹתֵיכֶם בְּיוֹם הוֹצִאִי אוֹתָם מֵאֶרֶץ מִצְרַיִם מִבֵּית עֲבָדִים לֵאמֹר: מִקֵּץ שֶׁבַע שָׁנִים תְּשַׁלְּחוּ אִישׁ אֶת אָחִיו הָעִבְרִי אֲשֶׁר יִמָּכֵר לְךָ וַעֲבָדְךָ שֵׁשׁ שָׁנִים וְשִׁלַּחְתּוֹ חָפְשִׁי מֵעִמָּךְ.
>
> So says the Lord God of Israel: I forged a covenant with your forefathers on the day I brought them out of the land of Egypt, from the house of slavery, saying: "At the end of seven years, every man shall release his Hebrew brother who has been sold to you; when he has served you for six years, you shall let him go free from you."

Jeremiah refers here to a covenant that had been forged already at the time of the Exodus – and then goes on to cite almost verbatim Deuteronomy 15:12: כִּי יִמָּכֵר לְךָ אָחִיךָ הָעִבְרִי אוֹ הָעִבְרִיָּה וַעֲבָדְךָ שֵׁשׁ שָׁנִים וּבַשָּׁנָה הַשְּׁבִיעִת תְּשַׁלְּחֶנּוּ חָפְשִׁי מֵעִמָּךְ, "If your brother, a Hebrew man or a Hebrew woman, is sold to you, when he has served you for six years, then in the seventh year you shall let him go free from you." Thus, Jeremiah clearly testifies that Deuteronomy was written during the period of the Exodus, and he makes extensive use of Deuteronomy throughout his prophecies[15] to reinforce the messages that he seeks to convey.[16]

---

difficulty in accepting the possibility that a prophet would foretell the future. This assumption does not rule out the concept of prophecy concerning the future (as noted, for example, by Y. Elitzur, *Yisrael VeHaMikra* [Jerusalem, 2000], 19–20).

15. For a discussion of the ways in which Jeremiah makes use of verses from Deuteronomy, see D. Rom-Shiloni, "HaTorah BeSefer Yermiya: HaTekhnikot HaParshaniot VeHaMegamot HaIdeologiot," *Shenaton LeḤeker HaMikra VeHaMizraḥ HaKadum* 17 (5767/2007): 43–87, and, by the same author, "Actualization of Pentateuchal Legal Traditions in Jeremiah: More on the Riddle of Authorship," in *Zeitschrift für Altorientalische und Biblische Rechtsgeschichte* 15 (2009): 254–81.
16. Many additional arguments in this regard are raised in the sources cited in the previous note. above. Among others, the following difficulties are treated: Had Deuteronomy been written in the time of Josiah, there would be no reason for it to have mentioned the obligation of acting in a positive way toward Edom

5. Let us proceed to the central argument of the documentary hypothesis, namely the contradiction between centralized worship, espoused by Josiah and the book of Deuteronomy, and that which is recorded in Exodus – בְּכָל הַמָּקוֹם אֲשֶׁר אַזְכִּיר אֶת שְׁמִי אָבוֹא אֵלֶיךָ וּבֵרַכְתִּיךָ, "In every place where I cause My Name to be mentioned, I shall come to you and I shall bless you." This argument is problematic, since the passage cited could be understood not as permitting the building of an altar anywhere, but permitting it only in specific places where God causes His Name to be mentioned. In the words of Ibn Ezra: "In every place where I place awareness of My Name, since My glory dwells there – such as Shiloh and Nov, where the Ark stood [at different periods]."

The contradiction between the verse in Exodus and the command in Deuteronomy about "the place which God will choose" is artificial, for both books agree that sacrifices may be offered only in a place that God chooses and mentions His name. This can be either the Tabernacle, which was the center of ritual for hundreds of years, or, in due time, Jerusalem.[17]

In fact, in Deuteronomy itself, we find the commandment to build an altar on Mount Ebal (Deut. 27:4–7) and to offer sacrifices upon it. Hence, we must conclude that building altars and offering sacrifices in

(see Deut. 23:4–9), since Edom was an enemy kingdom during this period (see II Kings 8:22). Furthermore, the text affirms that Amaziah, who reigned before Hezekiah and Josiah, also fulfilled the commandment set forth in Deuteronomy not to put children to death for the transgressions of their fathers (see II Kings 14:6; cf. Deut. 23:18). In addition, the depiction of the prophet-leader set forth in Deuteronomy 18:16 sits well in relation to such figures as Joshua and Samuel, but not with regard to the prophets at the end of the First Temple Period.

17. Yechiel Bin Nun (in *Eretz HaMoriah – Pirkei Mikra VeLashon* [Alon Shvut, 2001], 29) notes that the verse in Exodus does not speak of "every place" but "all of *the* place," meaning anywhere in that particular place where God mentions His name. Each generation will have a place of its own, until a time when a permanent abode is determined. His son, Rabbi Dr. Yoel Bin-Nun, expands on the idea in a comment there, pp. 30–32.

different places, at least prior to God's selection of one specific location for that purpose, was not at all problematic.[18]

The adherents of de Wette's view, who believe that the prohibition of worship outside the Temple was renewed only in the days of Hezekiah, rely upon the fact that altars existed in the (earlier) time of Elijah, after the establishment of the Temple. Elijah himself says, עָזְבוּ בְרִיתְךָ בְּנֵי יִשְׂרָאֵל אֶת מִזְבְּחֹתֶיךָ הָרָסוּ וְאֶת נְבִיאֶיךָ הָרְגוּ בֶחָרֶב, "For the Children of Israel have abandoned Your covenant; they have destroyed Your altars and have slain Your prophets by the sword" (I Kings 19:10).

But if the altars were forbidden, why was Elijah bothered by their destruction? Moreover, the early prophets, who follow the era of Elijah and his successor, Elisha, such as Amos, Hosea, Micah, and Isaiah, do not mention a need to refrain from sacrifices outside of Jerusalem.[19]

One answer suffices for both objections. After the split of the monarchy in 930 BCE, most of the people in the Kingdom of Israel were essentially disconnected from the Temple. It is reasonable to surmise that many of them reverted to the earlier practice of building altars outside Jerusalem as a familiar means of worshipping God. Elijah bemoaned the destruction of the then-forbidden altars, since even this form of worship was infinitely preferable to the alternative of idolatry. The altars were

---

18. As Cassuto notes, the proponents of the documentary hypothesis indeed argue that the unit in Deuteronomy concerning the altar on Mount Ebal does not belong to the Deuteronomist source, but represents a later addition. However, this is a superficial and *ad hoc* manner of solving textual difficulties.

19. Scholars who adopt de Wette's view also base their opinion on the absence of any negative view regarding the multiplicity of altars from the period of the Judges or from the time of King David, and the fact that these sources indicate evidence of many altars during the period of the settlement of the land and the period of the Judges (see, for example, A. Rofe, 59). However, these arguments are puzzling: Deuteronomy itself emphasizes that the prohibition applies specifically in the context of "the place which God shall choose," and God's choice of Jerusalem became apparent only during the time of Solomon (see I Kings 8:12–21). The plain meaning of the text gives no indication of a prohibition on sacrificing at other locations prior to the selection of the site of the Temple. The Sages discuss the question of the permissibility of *bamot* and the different periods in which this license was used (for a summary of the discussion, see "*bama,*" *Encyclopedia Talmudit* 3, 339–41), but they address mainly the verses in Leviticus 17, which are not relevant to our discussion at this stage.

destroyed in order to prevent the people from worshipping God, and thus even Elijah bemoaned their destruction.

Of course, this hierarchy of worship also helps explain why the prophets of Israel do not prophesy about the altars: their campaign against idolatry left no room to criticize worshipping of God in inappropriate places. Instead, those in the Kingdom of Israel who constructed altars to God were evidently regarded by the prophets in a positive light, since they had not fallen into the far greater evil of outright idolatry.

In any event, it should be emphasized that the book of Kings, which according to these scholars was edited under the influence of Josiah's revolution, and was aimed at advancing the idea of concentrating the ritual in Jerusalem, is the very same source that presents the story of Elijah – and it does not necessarily mean a contradiction of the principle. Unless we posit that the editor of Kings did not understand the contradiction between his goals and his narratives, we must conclude that this book maintains that although one single location had been chosen in Jerusalem, there is no contradiction between that and the gravity of the shattering of altars to God outside of Jerusalem.

The central argument for the claim of late authorship of Deuteronomy may therefore be understood to have multiple serious flaws. And since the dating of this document is the basis for dating the other documents, the timeline proposed for the other documents is highly questionable.

The dating of the Priestly source to the Second Temple Period is another argument that is central to Wellhausen's approach, though it was contested by many in the previous generation. Wellhausen claimed that, at the time of Ezra and Nehemiah (end of the sixth and beginning of the fifth century BCE), the Jewish religion was shaped and influenced by the priestly regime, a fundamental transition from religion based around natural life, to one focused on historical events and to ceremonial and symbolic frameworks.

Wellhausen argued further that it was during this period that the idea of sacrifices that could atone for sin (the sin-offering and guilt-offering) emerged, and the idea of sacrifice in general took hold. In addition, the entire subject of priestly gifts, he contended, appeared during this period of the priestly regime, along with the festivals that were not agricultural in nature – Rosh HaShana and Yom Kippur – which drew on the sense of iniquity of the Jewish community in its Babylonian exile. The agricultural celebrations were thus imbued with additional historical significance.

These speculative claims as to the nature of the Priestly source and its relationship to the preceding books were countered, from different directions, by Rabbi David Zvi Hoffmann and Prof. Yeḥezkel Kaufmann.[20] Three of the major arguments found in their works against this approach are as follows:[21]

1. Given that the Priestly source includes major sections of Exodus and Numbers and almost all of Leviticus, it is difficult to understand why it includes so many laws that have no connection with the Second Temple Period – such as the instructions to build the Temple and its vessels, and the division of the land among the tribes. Conversely, some laws that were extremely relevant during that period – particularly the issue of mixed marriages, which was a central issue treated by Ezra and Nehemiah – do not appear in this source at all.

2. Archaeological finds from the ancient Near East[22] have established that a significant number of rituals and sacrifices existed as many as hundreds of years prior to Israel's entry into the land. "The argument that during the period of exile new sacrifices, new festivals and new

---

20. Rabbi David Zvi Hoffmann (1843–1921) was one of the leaders of German Jewry, a halakhic authority, and a commentator on Tanakh, who headed the Hildesheimer Rabbinical Seminary in Berlin. In his book *Decisive Refutations of Wellhausen*, originally written in German, Rabbi Hoffmann presented a moderate and objective refutation of Wellhausen's claims of a Priestly source dating to the Second Temple Period.

    Yehezkel Kaufmann (1889–1963), a professor at the Hebrew University of Jerusalem, accepted the documentary hypothesis in principle, but was vehemently opposed to Wellhausen's claim that the Priestly source can be dated to the Second Temple Period. See his work, *Toledot HaEmuna HaYisraelit*, vol. 1 (Jerusalem, 1976), 113–20 (translated and abridged by Prof. Moshe Greenberg as *The Religion of Israel* [Chicago, 1960]).
21. See M. Weinfeld, *MiYehoshua VeAd Yoshiyahu* (Jerusalem, 1992), 499–502.
22. The relationship between these finds and the biblical text will be discussed in a later chapter.

religious institutions were invented, seems absurd to anyone who is familiar with the cultures of the ancient Near East.... Wellhausen viewed institutionalized and complex ritual as the fruit of later development. He had no idea of the existence of orderly and fixed ritual in the major cultural centers of the ancient Near East."[23]

3. Scholars have noted profound linguistic differences between biblical Hebrew and the language developed in the Second Temple Period.[24] For instance, the word "*edah*" (congregation), which appears dozens of times in different parts of the Torah that are attributed to the Priestly source, was cited extensively by Wellhausen's school as evidence of its late origin.[25] However, the frequency of this word declines over time. In the books of the Early Prophets, it appears twenty times; in the Later Prophets – only three times; and in the books from the time of the return from the

---

23. Weinfeld, *MiYehoshua*, 500.
24. See, for example, the following by A. Hurvitz: *A Linguistic Study of the Relationship between the Priestly Source and the Book of Ezekiel* (Paris, 1982); "The Historical Quest for Ancient Israel and the Linguistic Evidence of the Hebrew Bible: Some Methodological Observations," *Vetus Testamentum* 47 (1997): 301–15; "Al Kama Munaḥim MiTeḥum HaKedusha VeHaTahara HaMeshamshim BeSefer Yeḥezkel BeMishkal 'Mekutal,'" in Y. Zakovich and A. Rofe, eds., *Sefer Yitzhak Aryeh Zeligman* (Jerusalem, 1983), 247–56; "HaVikuaḥ HaArkheologi-Histori Shel Kadmut HaSifrut HaMikrait Le'or HaMeḥkar HaBalshani Shel HaIvrit," in Y. L. Levin and A. Mazar, eds., *HaPulmus Al HaEmet HaHistorit BaMikra* (Jerusalem, 2001), 34–46. This approach has been attacked in recent years by Young, Rezetko, and Ehrensvärd. See I. Young, R. Rezetko, and M. Ehrensvärd, *Linguistic Dating of Biblical Texts: An Introduction to Approaches and Problems*. 2 vols. (London, 2008), and more recently R. Rezetko and I. Young, *Historical Linguistics and Biblical Hebrew: Steps toward an Integrated Approach*, ANEM 9 (Atlanta, 2014), with references there to further literature. Responses to their radical suggestions can be found in Avi Hurvitz, "The Recent Debate on Late Biblical Hebrew: Solid Data, Experts' Opinions, and Inconclusive Arguments," *Hebrew Studies* 47 (2006): 191-210; in the essays in C. Miller-Naude and Z. Zevit, eds., *Diachrony in Biblical Hebrew*, LSAWS 8 (Winona Lake, 2012); and in Nili Samet's study "The Validity of the Masoretic Text as a Basis for Diachronic Linguistic Analysis of Biblical Texts: Evidence from Masoretic Vocalisation," *Journal for Semitics*, vol. 25 (2016): 1064–79.
25. See Rabbi Hoffmann, 62, n. 1; A. Hurvitz, "LeShimusho Shel HaMunaḥ HaKohani 'Edah' BeSifrut HaMikrait," *Tarbiz* 40, 3 (5731/1971): 261–67.

Babylonian exile (Ezra and Nehemiah),[26] it makes no appearance at all – although seemingly, it should be quite popular. Instead, these books make extensive use of the word "*kahal*." The decrease in the number of appearances of the word "*edah*" indicates the gradual abandonment of this term, which points to the conclusion that it belongs to the linguistic context of a period long before that of the Second Temple.

In addition, there are striking differences between the language of Ezekiel and that of Leviticus, despite the relatively extensive treatment of Temple matters in Ezekiel. For example, the verb used in the Priestly source to describe the washing of the parts of the sacrifices is "*raḥatz*,"[27] while in Ezekiel, the verb "*davaḥ*" is used instead (for example, 40:38 – יָדִיחוּ אֶת הָעֹלָה, "they would wash the burnt offering," and likewise in Chronicles, e.g., II Chr. 4:6).

In view of these discrepancies, some scholars agree that biblical Hebrew is indeed different from the Hebrew of the Second Temple Period, but argue that the latter is the invention of scholars who lived during that era, and it existed as a literary language rather than a living one. This position not only seems tenuous on its own terms, but also seems to ignore archaeological findings that appear to corroborate the development of the Hebrew language as it is presented in the different books of the Tanakh.[28] Thus we find that ancient biblical Hebrew matches inscriptions from the period of the monarchy,[29] and later biblical Hebrew matches external testimonies that we have from the Second Temple Period, such as the Book of Ben Sira and the Dead Sea Scrolls.

---

26. In Chronicles, it appears just once (II Chr. 5:6), but there, too, the verse has a parallel in I Kings 8:5, such that the appearance of the word here does not represent any new content.
27. See, for example, Ex. 29:17; Lev. 1:9, 13; 8:21; 9:14.
28. See Hurvitz 1997, 308–13.
29. Relevant findings from the period of the monarchy will be discussed in chapter 6.

These arguments have led many scholars, even those who generally subscribe to the idea of the documentary hypothesis, to reject Wellhausen's hypothesis concerning the later authorship of the Priestly source.[30]

Linguistic Layers

Beyond the historical challenges to the claims of the documentary hypothesis with regard to the dating of the Deuteronomist source and the Priestly source, the linguistic difficulties call it into question even further. That is, the study of the development of biblical Hebrew strongly indicates that the Five Books of Moses predate not only the later books of Tanakh, as discussed above, but also the books of the Prophets.[31] Contrast the language of the Five Books of Moses with the Books of the Prophets, and the number of motifs that appear exclusively in each one and not the other is striking – despite the general similarity between them.

For example, some common expressions in the prophetic literature are completely absent from the Torah. Three prominent examples:

1. The expression "*Hashem Tzeva'ot*" ("Lord of Hosts") appears 260 times in the later books of Tanakh – beginning in the book of Samuel.[32] This description of God is not used in the Torah, or in the Books of Joshua and Judges.
2. The expression, "So may God do, and so may He add," appears eight times as an oath in the books of Samuel and Kings, but is not used in conjunction with any of the oaths in the Torah.
3. "*Naveh*" refers to the place where shepherds sit as they pasture their flocks. The word is used in this sense some twenty times in Tanakh – all from the book of Samuel onwards.[33] Given that the biblical

30. See, among others, Weinfeld, *MiYehoshua*, 502; Schwartz, 209.
31. The examples cited here were presented in a lecture by Y. Elitzur, "*Revadim BeIvrit HaMikrait HaKeduma*," at the Study Days in Tanakh held in Alon Shvut during the summer of 2006. Prof. Elitzur plans a fuller monograph on the subject.
32. The Sages note: "Rabbi Elazar said: From the time that the Holy One, blessed be He, created His world, no one called Him '*Tzeva-ot*' until Hannah [mother of Samuel], who called Him by this name" (Berakhot 31b).
33. It appears in the Torah only once, and in a metaphoric sense: נֵהַלְתָּ בְעָזְּךָ אֶל נְוֵה קָדְשֶׁךָ, "To Your holy habitation (*el neveh kodshekha*)" (Ex. 15:13).

forefathers lived a nomadic, shepherding life, one would expect this word to appear in the Torah as well.[34] Its absence suggests that the word was not widely used in that earlier time, only taking on the now-accepted meaning during the period of the monarchy, much later on.

The absence of these common expressions from the Torah suggests that the Torah's Hebrew is more ancient than the language that is found in the Books of the Prophets. Were some parts of the Torah to have been written from the period of the monarchy onwards, those turns of phrases would be expected to appear in the text. There is no reason for the absence of such common expressions.

Additionally, there are many instances of spelling differences between the Torah and the Books of the Prophets. To cite just two examples:

1. The word "*hi*" (היא, meaning "she") is spelled just eleven times in the Torah with the letter *yod*. Far more often (199 times!), the word appears with the same spelling as the word "*hu*" (הוא, meaning "he") – i.e., with a *vav*, and only the vowel (*ḥirik*) indicating the feminine form הִוא. The rest of Tanakh, in contrast, contains the word spelled with a *yod* 474 times, and not a single time with the letter *vav*. It is reasonable to infer that this difference in spelling reflects a difference in the way the word was pronounced, but, in any event, it points to a difference between the period of the Torah and that of the prophets.
2. The word "*naarah*" (נערה, meaning "girl") appears twenty-two times in the Torah, mostly in Deuteronomy. Once, it is spelled with the letter *heh* at the end (Deut. 22:19); in every other instance, it ends with the letter *resh*, accompanied by the "*kamatz*" vowel to signify the feminine form. In contrast, the rest of Tanakh includes the word twenty-three times – all spelled with a "*heh*" at the end. Again, it

34. Other examples: (1) the root K-L-M ("shame"), as a verb and as a noun, appears some seventy times in Tanakh, but never in the Torah. (2) The word "*dim'a*" ("tear" – as in weeping) appears in its various forms twenty-five times in Tanakh, but never in Torah (except for Ex. 22:28, where the root is used in a completely different sense: "You shall not delay to offer the first of your ripe fruits [*mele'atekha*] and of your liquors [*vedim'akha*]").

would seem that in the most ancient form of Hebrew, the same word was used for the masculine and feminine forms of the word, and that the traditional pronunciation of the word נער as "*naara*" represents a later development.[35]

These discrepancies of spelling are easy to understand if we assume that the period of the Torah was characterized by a more ancient stage of the Hebrew language, as these examples imply.[36] Indeed, by comparing the various Books of the Tanakh with one another, as well as with external findings, the development of the Hebrew language and the building of its various layers into the Tanakh as it progresses are readily apparent.

THE LITERARY ASPECT OF THE DOCUMENTARY HYPOTHESIS

Like the historical aspect of the documentary hypothesis, the literary aspect presents significant difficulties, to the extent that scholars of recent generations have gradually rejected parts of the approach as well.[37] The attempt to create continuity within each of the various documents was

35. Further examples: (1) The phenomenon of defective spelling (where on occasion a word is spelled with a letter missing) is far more prevalent in the Torah than it is in the Books of the Prophets. For instance, the word "*eleihem*" (to them) appears in defective form (without the *yod*) in the vast majority of cases in the Torah (86 out of 103 instances); in the Books of the Prophets, in contrast, it appears in defective form only rarely (19 out of 150 instances). This example is cited from J. Barr, *The Variable Spellings of the Hebrew Bible* (New York 1989), 135. (2) The word "*ha'el*," in the sense of "*ha'eleh*" ("these"), appears 8 times in the Torah, but nowhere in the Books of the Prophets. (In I Chr. 20:8 we find one instance of "*el noldu*," אֵל נוּלְּדוּ – "these were born.")
36. Linguistic scholar Gotthelf Bergsträsser addressed these phenomena. In his book *Dikduk HaLashon HaIvrit* (*Hebräische Grammatik: mit Benutzung der von E. Katzsch bearbeiteten 28. Auflage von Wilhelm Gesenius' hebräischer Grammatik*) transl. M. Ben Asher (Jerusalem, 1972), he writes that they "should be attributed solely to later editing." However, the claim that a later editor would alter the language in such a peculiar way seems highly unlikely.
37. Reviews of approaches opposing the documentary hypothesis may be found in sources cited previously: A. Rofe, 83–112; B. Y. Schwartz, 218–25. See also M. Z. Segal, 127–47; R. Alberts, "Tahalikh Tzemiḥatah shel HaTorah – Gishot BaMeḥkar HaModerni," *Beit Mikra* 55, 2 (5771/2011): 5–38.

unsuccessful, and led to various attempts to instead divide the documents into sub-sources. But official subdivision of the four central sources gave rise to a great deal of controversy among scholars, with especially contentious debate over the division between the "E" source and the "J" source.

It should be noted that it is especially difficult to determine such phenomena as the stages of development within these sources. Divergences of opinion spread to other aspects of the hypothesis as well, including: the dating of the various documents, the relationship between their various sub-units, the degree to which the redactor was involved in the writing, the question of how and when the sources were joined into a single Torah, and more. To a certain degree, these disagreements undermined the reliability of the approach as a whole.

But beyond any and all of these debates, the crucial difficulty in the documentary hypothesis is the very notion that several sources were brought together to form a single work – not an anthology, with several sources combined together in succession, but a single, continuous text that intertwines the various sources, and preserves continuity of themes, despite the disparate origins of the sources. Precedent for such an enormous editorial enterprise is limited;[38] few known documents from the ancient world were compiled in such a manner.[39] Moreover, what would prompt

38. As noted by M. Z. Segal, 144: "No work has ever been composed through this approach of joining fragments – neither in biblical literature, nor in world literature.... This entire idea, set forth by the proponents of the documentary hypothesis, runs contrary to common sense and to scientific truth."

39. This problem troubled many scholars, prompting them to seek sources for this sort of compilation. The question was broached by Jeffrey H. Tigay in his study of an important Mesopotamian text, *The Evolution of the Gilgamesh Epic* (Philadelphia, 1982), and then addressed in the essays in the volume he edited, *Empirical Models for Biblical Criticism* (Philadelphia, 1985). The question of parallels between the editing of the Samaritan Torah and that of the Pentateuch were also addressed in his essay "HaḤumash HaShomroni KeDegem Empiri LeBikkoret HaSifrutit Shel HaTorah," *Beit Mikra* 22, 3 (70) (5737/1977): 348–61. Tigay noted (360) that since in the Samaritan Torah, the fragments that were integrated into Exodus remained unchanged in their place in Deuteronomy, "the proto-Samaritan redactor is revealed as having added into one fundamental text an addendum from another text, instead of presenting them equally or creating a completely new version through his own free workings of them. A greater measure of freedom than this is attributed to the redactor of the Torah" (Tigay, 360.). Beyond this, however, there is a significant

the anonymous redactor to weave disparate sources into a single work? Worse (for the hypothesis), not one of the sources for this interwoven text is mentioned anywhere outside of its presence in the Torah. There is no attestation of independent existence for any of these individual documents prior to their combined presence in the Torah, and no archaeological discovery has ever unearthed any of them in pristine, independent form.

As a result of the diminishing persuasiveness of the documentary hypothesis, many contemporary scholars turned away from analyzing the distinctions between the various sources (even as they continue to recognize their existence in principle, in the process of the consolidation of the Torah).

Many modern German scholars, in particular, have almost completely abandoned the documentary hypothesis, and have proposed alternative models to explain the process of the writing of the Torah.[40] At the beginning of the twentieth century, German scholar Hermann Gunkel (1862–1932) initiated a further critical approach known as form criticism. He suggested that the text is the consolidation of various oral traditions, not necessarily written ones; thus, one need not necessarily posit a collection of contradictory written sources.[41] While this approach was not meant to replace the documentary hypothesis, it did lead to

---

difference between these sources and what appears in the Torah: in these sources some changes have been introduced in order to create a single narrative continuum. Therefore, even in the Samaritan Torah and other similar sources, there are no contradictory narratives that are presented in juxtaposition.

40. See Alberts, 6–7.

41. Gunkel did, however, accept Wellhausen's theory regarding written narratives, though he tried to uncover the earliest elements of the stories, which he considered to have grown out of ancient folk tales. The basic assumption of the documentary hypothesis was that each document was internally consistent, and so exceptions testify to the consolidation process. However eclectic the form of the narratives that preceded the consolidation, there's no reason to assume that minor changes in vocabulary, lack of consistency, or even overt contradictions necessarily demonstrate the shift from one document to another, as Gunkel noted. Gunkel also noted that the different types of tales are an important feature in classification. So, for example, the Abraham narratives are structured as a series of short stories, while the Joseph narrative is built on a novelistic structure. This categorization creates further problems in dividing the original material (which served as the basis for composing the biblical text) into separate documents. Thus, instead of a collection of four sources in order, one would find sources combined haphazardly.

the development of other scholarly views that tended not to accept the documentary hypothesis in its entirety. Some scholars, having concluded that little is to be gained from trying to discover the origins of the biblical text, instead engage in literary analysis of the text in its present form.

Yet despite all the difficulties that weaken the claims of the documentary hypothesis and similar models, the textual problems that prompted these theories still remain. The contradictions and duplications present in the Tanakh, and the impossibility of reading the Torah as a single continuum, have not been solved. The fact remains that one is often able to discern a pattern to the contradictions between different passages, in terms of the different terminology they use, including different names of God. Any student of the Torah must therefore confront the challenge of how the contradictions and duplications within the Torah should be addressed.

THE "ASPECTS" APPROACH

The documentary hypothesis stands, of course, in direct contradiction to the traditional Jewish worldview, which regards the Torah as a unified creation emanating from a divine source. Much of the religious Jewish public has never been exposed to the documentary hypothesis, and even those who have partial familiarity with it have waved off its concerns, for the most part. This disinterest has many reasons. For starters, fear of the possible influences of the Enlightenment and its attendant views, which had penetrated the Jewish world as well, led to a general distaste for this academic realm – and to some extent, to a diminished Tanakh study among Jews. Moreover, the major proponents of the documentary hypothesis were also outspoken anti-Semites who used their theory as a means of launching attacks on Jews and on Judaism.[42]

The modern Jewish scholars who did address the documentary hypothesis essentially rejected it out of hand.[43] That approach was taken by Malbim (1809–1879), Rabbi Samson Raphael Hirsch (1808–1888),

42. For a general discussion of the topic see Y. Shavit and M. Eran, *Milḥemet HaLuḥot – HaHagana al HaMikra BeMea HaTesha Esreh U'Pulmus Bavel VeHaTanakh* (Tel Aviv, 2004), esp. 68–80.
43. A review of Jewish Orthodox grappling with the documentary hypothesis is presented by Shavit and Eran, 72–75.

Rabbi Yitzchak Isaac HaLevy Rabinowitz (1847–1914),[44] and – especially – Rabbi David Zvi Hoffmann (1843–1921).[45] Indeed, it was the prevailing approach. However, none of these scholars, not even Rabbi Hoffmann, who was the only one to tackle the documentary hypothesis head-on, supplied a satisfactory answer to the original main question: What is the meaning of the obvious contradictions and duplications in the Torah, and how do they fit in with the traditional faith in the unity of the Torah? What is the meaning of the systematic nature of these contradictions?

Toward the end of the twentieth century, however, Rabbi Mordekhai Breuer (1921–2007), a Torah sage as well as a scholar of world renown in the field of biblical study, developed the "aspects approach," or in Hebrew, *shitat habeḥinot*, and brought about a revolution in the attitude toward research by biblical scholars among those Jews who believe in the unity of the Torah.[46] The principal innovation of the approach was to acknowledge and use the claims of the documentary hypothesis, which saw the Torah as a compilation of multiple and frequently contradictory texts, while maintaining that these differences and contradictions were nevertheless divinely authored and intended, and not a combination by a later editor of multiple human authors and traditions. Rabbi Breuer believed that there was no reason to ignore the literary element of the criticism.

> These conclusions of biblical scholarship are based on firm evidence which can in no way be refuted, and anyone who seeks the truth and acknowledges the truth cannot deny the truth that arises from the words of these scholars. And since our tradition teaches that one cannot deny that which the eye sees and the ear

---

44. In his book *Dorot Rishonim*, vol. 6 (Jerusalem, 1939).
45. In his book *Decisive Refutations of Wellhausen*, Rabbi Hoffmann deals extensively with the critical approach in his commentaries on Leviticus and Deuteronomy.
46. This new approach was first published in the journal *Deot* 11 (1960): 18–25, and after that he wrote several more articles on the subject. His own articles, and other articles written about his approach, appear together in the book *Shitat HaBeḥinot shel HaRav Mordekhai Breuer* (Alon Shvut, 2005); the references from this point onwards are to this book. The best discussion in English of Rabbi Breuer's work appears in *Modern Scholarship in the Study of Torah*, ed. S. Carmy (The Orthodox Forum, Lanham, MD, 1996), which features a number of articles by Rabbi Breuer and others about his approach.

> hears, we too – as faithful Jews – shall not deny that which the human intellect indicates with certainty. We cannot deceive our souls in turning a lie into truth, and truth into a lie."[47]

He maintained that the contradictions do not change our belief that the Torah is divine. Rather, these inconsistencies are part of God's intent – a method of writing the Torah in such a way as to present different subjects in their full complexity. As he explains, the Torah presents different aspects of reality – on both the narrative and the halakhic level – through the technique of multiple descriptions of a given topic or event. Each description can be presented individually and discretely, expressing one aspect of reality in its pristine form, or more than one description can be presented in combination with others that may conflict, presenting different aspects of the issue. When one steps back from the text and considers the multiple aspects of a topic that have been presented, the differences cease to appear as contradictions, but are rather expressions of the multifaceted nature of a given topic, which, taken together, give us the whole picture. Rabbi Breuer continues:

> The man of science sees in the Torah a collection of documents, written by J, E, D, P, and redacted later on by R.... The man of great faith, in contrast, sees in the Torah the work of God. This man believes that God Himself wrote J, E, D, and P, and He Himself also took on R's redaction work.[48]

Rabbi Breuer develops his approach in his written works.[49] A few examples will help clarify his approach.

Consider first the opening chapters of Genesis, a well-known example of two seemingly different versions of the same event appearing alongside one another; both describe the creation of the world.[50] Rabbi Breuer argued that these two chapters represent two different

---

47. Breuer, *Shitat HaBeḥinot*, 112.
48. Breuer, 132–33.
49. *Pirkei Moadot* (Jerusalem, 1986); *Pirkei Bereshit* (Alon Shvut, 1998); *Pirkei Mikraot* (Alon Shvut, 2008).
50. For a more extensive discussion, see *Pirkei Bereshit*, 82–122.

aspects of God's relationship with, and guidance of, the world. Chapter 1 represents the world of nature, where the order of Creation follows a natural progression from plant life, via animals, to the creation of man, or humankind. Humans are created, male and female together, to ensure the continuation of the species. In this natural world, man's role is to rule over nature – but he has no creative role that separates him fundamentally from the animal kingdom. In this chapter, God is called "Elohim."

Chapter 2, in contrast (starting from verse 4), expresses the connection between God and humanity. Man stands at the center of this world, and until he is created, there is no point in creating plants and animals (which are created after he was). Man's role in chapter 2 is "to cultivate it [the world] and to guard it": he has a creative role, relating to his obligation to develop the world. He is a creature with intelligence, able to give names to the animals, and he is given special prohibitions by God – he may not eat from the Tree of Knowledge. In this world, the creation of woman, who is created in this version after man, is not intended solely for the purpose of continuing the human race; her role is also, perhaps fundamentally, to alleviate man's loneliness by providing him with a partner, a "helpmate," whom he can love and in whom he can rejoice. This chapter sees the name "HVYH" added to God's name.

It appears that the Torah's account of creation is not supposed to be simply a record of how the world was created. Rather, it presents each aspect as though it stands alone: how the world would have been created had it been a world of nature alone, and how it would have been created had it been a world only of revelation and direct contact between God and man. In reality, "both these and those are the words of the living God," where the divine truth is a combination of these two ideas together, going far beyond the basic facts of the event.[51] Man is at one and the same time

---

51. If the biblical text presents "aspects" of the full truth, how can we know what actually happened? Counterintuitively, Rabbi Breuer suggests that we look in the midrash: "Someone who believes that only the plain, literal level of the text is the 'correct' or 'true' interpretation of the Torah, will have trouble believing that the plain level of the text does not describe what 'actually' happened, 'in reality.' But their view is the view of the Sadducees and the Karaites. Faithful Jews believe that both the *peshat* (literal level) and the *derash* (homiletical level) provide correct and true interpretations of

a part of the natural world and the most sophisticated creature in it, with the natural role of reproducing and continuing the human race, but also fundamentally separate from nature and a part of God Himself – a creature endowed with intelligence, who may be commanded, and whose connection with his partner is not like that which exists among the animals, but has a strong social-spiritual component as well.[52]

Another example of "two aspects" in the text is the description of the plague of blood in Egypt, mentioned earlier. In this case, the two aspects are intertwined in the text, rather than being neatly contained in different chapters. Nevertheless, it would seem that the Torah is

---

the Torah. The *derash* describes what actually happened in reality, while the *peshat* describes what should have happened. This principle is well known and universally accepted in the halakhic realms of the Torah; my 'aspects approach' merely applies this method to the narrative, as well. This being the case, where is the problem, and where is the innovation?" (*Shitat HaBeḥinot*, 299–300).

52. Obviously, there are also other ways of understanding the nature of the contradictions, and especially the significance of the two different names for God in the two accounts of creation. Rabbi Breuer makes extensive use of the expressions "*middat hadin*" (the divine attribute of strict justice, reflected in the name "Elohim"), and "*middat haraḥamim*" (the divine attribute of mercy, reflected in the name "HVYH"), based on the Sages' teachings in this regard. U. Cassuto, *The Documentary Hypothesis* (Jerusalem, 1959), explains the relationship between the two names in a slightly different way. He posits that the name "Elohim" is a "general name" and therefore appears in various possessive forms, implying the definite article: "Eloheinu" (our God), "Elohekha" (your God), etc. The name HVYH, on the other hand, is a "private name" which is not made explicit and does not appear in any possessive form; this is the Lord God of Israel. Hence, the name "Elohim" expresses a general, objective description of a universal God and transcendental Being, while the name "HVYH" expresses the unmediated relationship between God and His creations in general, and Israel in particular. For this reason, chapter 1 presents a general, overall description of Creation, while in chapter 2 the description is personal and subjective. Likewise, the dual description of the Flood: the first description, which employs "HVYH," as God's personal name, describes God in personal terms, as having "regretted … and was sorrowed in His heart," since the text is speaking here of the direct relationship between God and man. The description using God's "general name," on the other hand, makes no mention and gives no hint of this relationship. The Torah begins with both descriptions in order to express the two aspects of God's relationship with man and to convey both the required "fear of God" – arising from a sense of distance, and "love of God" – arising from a sense of closeness.

describing two distinct aspects of the plague.[53] First, the biblical text presents God's specific command to Moses to address Pharaoh and to strike the water of the Nile. This blow seems to represent the beginning of Pharaoh's punishment, "measure for measure," for his command that all boys born to Jews be cast into the Nile:

> לֵךְ אֶל פַּרְעֹה בַּבֹּקֶר הִנֵּה יֹצֵא הַמַּיְמָה וְנִצַּבְתָּ לִקְרָאתוֹ עַל שְׂפַת הַיְאֹר וְהַמַּטֶּה אֲשֶׁר נֶהְפַּךְ לְנָחָשׁ תִּקַּח בְּיָדֶךָ. וְאָמַרְתָּ אֵלָיו ה׳ אֱלֹהֵי הָעִבְרִים שְׁלָחַנִי אֵלֶיךָ לֵאמֹר שַׁלַּח אֶת עַמִּי וְיַעַבְדֻנִי בַּמִּדְבָּר וְהִנֵּה לֹא שָׁמַעְתָּ עַד כֹּה. כֹּה אָמַר ה׳ בְּזֹאת תֵּדַע כִּי אֲנִי ה׳ הִנֵּה אָנֹכִי מַכֶּה בַּמַּטֶּה אֲשֶׁר בְּיָדִי עַל הַמַּיִם אֲשֶׁר בַּיְאֹר וְנֶהֶפְכוּ לְדָם. וְהַדָּגָה אֲשֶׁר בַּיְאֹר תָּמוּת וּבָאַשׁ הַיְאֹר וְנִלְאוּ מִצְרַיִם לִשְׁתּוֹת מַיִם מִן הַיְאֹר.
>
> Go to Pharaoh in the morning – behold, he goes out to the water – and you shall stand at the bank of the Nile to meet him, and you shall take in your hand the staff which turned into a snake. And you shall say to him, "The Lord God of the Hebrews has sent me to you, to say: Let My people go, that they may serve Me in the wilderness, for behold, you have not obeyed until now. So says the Lord: By this shall you know that I am the Lord: behold, I shall smite with the staff that is in my hand upon the water that is in the Nile, and it shall turn to blood. And the fish that are in the Nile will die, and the Nile will stink, and the Egyptians will no longer be able to drink water from the Nile." (Ex. 7:15–17)

The same Nile in which Moses had been hidden as an infant, and where he was saved from the bloodbath that was the fate of the other Jewish babies, becomes – at Moses's command – a river of blood.[54]

---

53. The explanation proposed here is slightly different from that given by Rabbi Breuer himself: see *Pirkei Moadot*, 208–18.
54. The connection between the striking of the Nile and the casting of the newborn boys into the Nile is apparent not only in the repetition of the word "*yeor*" (Nile) multiple times in both narratives, but also in another linguistic link: Moses is sent to Pharaoh prior to the plague, and God commands him, וְנִצַּבְתָּ לִקְרָאתוֹ עַל שְׂפַת הַיְאֹר, "You shall stand (*venitzavta*) at the bank of the Nile (*al sefat hayeor*) to meet him" (Ex. 7:15). The language here is highly reminiscent of the description of Moses's

The Torah then goes on to describe the other aspect of the plague of blood, this time as part of a more general theme within the plagues as a whole that are intended as a response to Pharaoh's demand תְּנוּ לָכֶם מוֹפֵת, "Show a sign for yourselves" (Ex. 7:9). From this perspective, the plague on the Nile represents an "escalation" in the power of the sign, after the sign involving the serpent does not have the desired effect, and וַיֶּחֱזַק לֵב פַּרְעֹה וְלֹא שָׁמַע אֲלֵהֶם, "Pharaoh's heart was hardened, and he did not listen to them" (7:13). The plague is therefore understood to have affected not only the Nile, but also every source of water in Egypt. For this purpose the staff of Aaron is used, just as it had been for the sign of the serpent:

> וַיֹּאמֶר ה׳ אֶל מֹשֶׁה אֱמֹר אֶל אַהֲרֹן קַח מַטְּךָ וּנְטֵה יָדְךָ עַל מֵימֵי מִצְרַיִם עַל נַהֲרֹתָם עַל יְאֹרֵיהֶם וְעַל אַגְמֵיהֶם וְעַל כָּל מִקְוֵה מֵימֵיהֶם וְיִהְיוּ דָם וְהָיָה דָם בְּכָל אֶרֶץ מִצְרַיִם וּבָעֵצִים וּבָאֲבָנִים.
>
> And God said to Moses: Say to Aaron, "Take your staff and stretch out your arm over the water of Egypt – over their rivers, over their canals, over their ponds, and over every pool of water, that they shall become blood, and there shall be blood throughout the land of Egypt, both in [vessels of] wood and in [vessels of] stone." (Ex. 7:19)

The Torah thereafter records the execution of both aspects together: וַיַּעֲשׂוּ כֵן מֹשֶׁה וְאַהֲרֹן כַּאֲשֶׁר צִוָּה ה׳, "And Moses and Aaron did so, as God had commanded" (7:20), detailing first the one aspect of the plague and then the other:[55]

---

concealment as an infant: וַתָּשֶׂם בַּסּוּף **עַל שְׂפַת הַיְאֹר**. וַתֵּתַצַּב אֲחֹתוֹ מֵרָחֹק לְדֵעָה מַה יֵּעָשֶׂה לוֹ, "And she placed him in the reeds at the bank of the Nile (*al sefat hayeor*). And his sister stood (*vatetatzav*) at a distance, to know what would be done with him" (Ex. 2:3–4). Notably, the expression "*al sefat hayeor*" ("at the bank of the Nile") is not mentioned in the other plagues.

55. The same is said after the plague of lice, where Moses also tells Aaron to stretch out his hand. There too it says, וַיֹּאמֶר ה׳ אֶל **מֹשֶׁה** אֱמֹר אֶל אַהֲרֹן נְטֵה אֶת מַטְּךָ וְהַךְ אֶת עֲפַר

> וַיָּרֶם בַּמַּטֶּה וַיַּךְ אֶת הַמַּיִם אֲשֶׁר בַּיְאֹר לְעֵינֵי פַרְעֹה וּלְעֵינֵי עֲבָדָיו וַיֵּהָפְכוּ כָּל הַמַּיִם אֲשֶׁר בַּיְאֹר לְדָם. וְהַדָּגָה אֲשֶׁר בַּיְאֹר מֵתָה וַיִּבְאַשׁ הַיְאֹר וְלֹא יָכְלוּ מִצְרַיִם לִשְׁתּוֹת מַיִם מִן הַיְאֹר.
>
> And he lifted the staff[56] and he struck the water that was in the Nile, before the eyes of Pharaoh and before the eyes of his servants, and all the water that was in the Nile turned into blood. And the fish that were in the Nile died, and the Nile stank, and the Egyptians were unable to drink water from the Nile. (Ex. 7:20–21)

This description corresponds exactly to the warning that had been issued concerning the striking of the Nile by Moses. The Torah then immediately goes on to describe the second aspect of the plague: וַיְהִי הַדָּם בְּכָל אֶרֶץ מִצְרָיִם, "And there was blood throughout the land of Egypt" (Ex. 7:21).

Just as the two aspects of the plague of blood are intertwined in both the introduction and the enactment of the plague of blood, the end of the plague is likewise described from both perspectives. According to the aspect that describes Aaron's striking of the water, the main purpose of the plague is to serve as proof of God's existence. It becomes apparent, however, that, just as after the sign of the snake, the plague has not achieved its aim.

> וַיַּעֲשׂוּ כֵן חַרְטֻמֵּי מִצְרַיִם בְּלָטֵיהֶם וַיֶּחֱזַק לֵב פַּרְעֹה וְלֹא שָׁמַע אֲלֵהֶם כַּאֲשֶׁר דִּבֶּר ה׳. וַיִּפֶן פַּרְעֹה וַיָּבֹא אֶל בֵּיתוֹ וְלֹא שָׁת לִבּוֹ גַּם לָזֹאת.

הָאָרֶץ... וַיַּעֲשׂוּ כֵן וַיֵּט אַהֲרֹן אֶת יָדוֹ בְמַטֵּהוּ, "God said Moses: Say to Aaron, 'Stretch out your staff and strike the dust of the land.' So they did: Aaron stretched out his hand with his staff" (Ex. 8:12–13).

56. The reference here is to Moses, as we see later on: וַיֹּאמֶר ה׳ אֶל מֹשֶׁה עֲבֹר לִפְנֵי הָעָם וְקַח אִתְּךָ מִזִּקְנֵי יִשְׂרָאֵל וּמַטְּךָ אֲשֶׁר הִכִּיתָ בּוֹ אֶת הַיְאֹר קַח בְּיָדְךָ וְהָלָכְתָּ, "And God said to Moses, 'Pass before the people and take with you some of the elders of Israel, and the staff with which you struck the Nile take in your hand as you go" (Ex. 17:5).

> And the magicians of Egypt did the same with their secret arts, and Pharaoh's heart was hardened, nor did he listen to them, as God had said. And Pharaoh turned and went to his house, and did not take even this[57] to heart. (Ex. 7:22–23)

It would seem, then, that according to this aspect, the plague of blood was already over before the magicians performed their trick – for if all the water in Egypt were blood, the Egyptian magicians would not have had any fresh water to use. Thus, Aaron's sign ended after a while, and so Pharaoh once again did not take Aaron's sign seriously.

However, from the perspective of the "Moses angle," which is directed against the waters of the Nile, the plague had not yet ended. The Torah immediately goes on to note:

> וַיַּחְפְּרוּ כָל מִצְרַיִם סְבִיבֹת הַיְאֹר מַיִם לִשְׁתּוֹת כִּי לֹא יָכְלוּ לִשְׁתֹּת מִמֵּימֵי הַיְאֹר. וַיִּמָּלֵא שִׁבְעַת יָמִים אַחֲרֵי הַכּוֹת ה׳ אֶת הַיְאֹר.

> And all the Egyptians dug around the Nile for water to drink, for they could not drink of the water of the Nile. And seven days were completed, after God had struck the Nile. (Ex. 7:24)

In this description, the plague lasted a week, and the Egyptians were unable to drink water from the Nile – the same Nile which had previously been full of the corpses of Jewish babies. It was only at the end of the week that the plague was seen to have ended, and it was time for another plague.[58]

The plague of blood may therefore be understood to have had a dual purpose. The Torah presents both aspects through the intertwining of their various elements, giving us a multifaceted and nuanced presentation of this plague.

A third example of Rabbi Breuer's *shitat habeḥinot* is a legal one. How is an Israelite slave to be freed? The answer depends on the point

57. The expression "even this" alludes to the sign of the snake and the plague of blood (Rashi).
58. Two distinct aspects are apparent in the plague of frogs, too, as Rabbi Breuer notes.

of view. *Parashat Behar*, where this mitzva is detailed, expresses the idea that God owns the world, the Land of Israel, and humanity itself; it emphasizes that this ownership is expressed partly in freeing slaves every fiftieth year.

> וְכִי יָמוּךְ אָחִיךָ עִמָּךְ וְנִמְכַּר לָךְ לֹא תַעֲבֹד בּוֹ עֲבֹדַת עָבֶד. כְּשָׂכִיר כְּתוֹשָׁב יִהְיֶה עִמָּךְ עַד שְׁנַת הַיֹּבֵל יַעֲבֹד עִמָּךְ. וְיָצָא מֵעִמָּךְ הוּא וּבָנָיו עִמּוֹ וְשָׁב אֶל מִשְׁפַּחְתּוֹ וְאֶל אֲחֻזַּת אֲבֹתָיו יָשׁוּב. כִּי עֲבָדַי הֵם אֲשֶׁר הוֹצֵאתִי אֹתָם מֵאֶרֶץ מִצְרָיִם לֹא יִמָּכְרוּ מִמְכֶּרֶת עָבֶד.
>
> If your brother who is with you grows poor and is sold to you, you shall not cause him to serve as a slave. He shall be a hired worker and sojourner with you; he will serve with you until the Jubilee year. Then he shall depart from you – he and his sons with him – and return to his family, and he shall return to the inheritance of his fathers. For they are My servants, whom I brought out of the land of Egypt; they shall not be sold as slaves. (Lev. 25:39–42)

These verses emphasize the identity of every individual in the nation as a servant of God, for none can be sold into perpetual servitude, in the manner that a servant who is not an Israelite may be sold. The release of Israelite slaves in the Jubilee year is a function of the concept of God's ownership over Israel, which is why the slaves' release is automatic – not only is a master not required to conduct any formal act to release the slave, but the slave is released without any human action, and there is no mechanism whatsoever to prevent the release.

Yet in *Parashat Re'eh*, in contrast, the Torah illuminates a different perspective of the relations between the master and servant:

> כִּי יִמָּכֵר לְךָ אָחִיךָ הָעִבְרִי אוֹ הָעִבְרִיָּה וַעֲבָדְךָ שֵׁשׁ שָׁנִים וּבַשָּׁנָה הַשְּׁבִיעִת תְּשַׁלְּחֶנּוּ חָפְשִׁי מֵעִמָּךְ. וְכִי תְשַׁלְּחֶנּוּ חָפְשִׁי מֵעִמָּךְ לֹא תְשַׁלְּחֶנּוּ רֵיקָם. הַעֲנֵיק תַּעֲנִיק לוֹ מִצֹּאנְךָ וּמִגָּרְנְךָ וּמִיִּקְבֶךָ אֲשֶׁר בֵּרַכְךָ ה׳ אֱלֹהֶיךָ תִּתֶּן לוֹ. וְזָכַרְתָּ כִּי עֶבֶד הָיִיתָ בְּאֶרֶץ מִצְרַיִם וַיִּפְדְּךָ ה׳ אֱלֹהֶיךָ עַל כֵּן אָנֹכִי מְצַוְּךָ אֶת הַדָּבָר הַזֶּה הַיּוֹם. וְהָיָה כִּי יֹאמַר אֵלֶיךָ לֹא אֵצֵא מֵעִמָּךְ כִּי אֲהֵבְךָ וְאֶת בֵּיתֶךָ כִּי טוֹב לוֹ עִמָּךְ. וְלָקַחְתָּ אֶת הַמַּרְצֵעַ וְנָתַתָּה בְאָזְנוֹ וּבַדֶּלֶת וְהָיָה לְךָ עֶבֶד עוֹלָם וְאַף לַאֲמָתְךָ תַּעֲשֶׂה כֵּן.

> If your brother, a Hebrew man, or a Hebrew woman, is sold to you, he shall serve you for six years, and in the seventh year you shall let him go free from you. And when you send him free from you, you shall not send him empty-handed: you shall surely give him from your flock and from your threshing floor and from your vineyard; of that with which the Lord your God has blessed you shall you give to him. And you shall remember that you were a servant in the land of Egypt, and the Lord your God redeemed you; therefore I command you this thing today. And it shall be, if he says to you, "I will not go out from you, for I love you and your house," for he is happy with you, then you shall take an awl and thrust it through his ear to the door, and he shall be your servant forever; and also to your maidservant shall you do thus. (Deut. 15:12–17)

According to this perspective, what obligates the master to free the servant is not the religious aspect of *Parashat Behar* – that Israel are God's servants and not man's servants – but rather the moral aspect: since the Israelites were once slaves in Egypt, they must treat their own servants in a moral fashion. For this reason, they have a practical obligation to let all servants go in the seventh year. This release is not automatic, like the release in the Jubilee year; rather, it is a release that is incumbent upon and initiated by the master, who is enjoined not to send the servant away empty-handed – just as Israel did not leave Egypt empty-handed (see Ex. 3:21). But unlike the automatic release of the Jubilee year, in this instance, if the servant wishes to stay, then the master has no further obligation to effect the release. To the contrary: because the master has met his moral obligation, the servant remains "a servant forever."

In practice, "both these and those are the words of the living God" – and therefore the laws arising from both sections are combined when it comes to the actual halakha: the master bears a moral obligation to release the servant in the seventh year, and if the servant foregoes freedom and prefers to stay, the master is exempt forthwith from initiating his release, forever. However, in the Jubilee year, the servant goes free automatically – since an Israelite cannot be sold into perpetual servitude. By distinguishing between the two aspects of servitude – theocentric (Israel are God's servants) and anthropocentric (the people must learn from their experience in Egypt) – the topic as a whole is presented with greater complexity and nuance than would have been possible had the laws appeared combined in a single section of the Torah.[59]

These three examples are only a few of the many instances in which the aspects approach makes use of, and thereby recognizes in principle, the scholarly analysis of Wellhausen et al., which exposed the contradictions and the independent ideas expressed in the various units. But Rabbi Breuer's approach explains the nature of the phenomenon in a radically different way, for it maintains that these contradictions are not the unparalleled and unprecedented work of an anonymous editor, who joined together contradictory sources from different periods, managing to weave them into a reasonably coherent continuum – not to mention succeeding in passing off his work to the Israelites as God's Torah; rather, his sober and logical explanation views the contradictions as God's way of conveying the complexity that characterizes different realms in the Torah. This composition is indeed unparalleled and unprecedented – precisely because only God could have created it.

Of course, this approach depends on the belief that God gave the Torah. This faith lies beyond the specific textual questions that are addressed here, but ultimately it is the fundamental basis for the entire debate between the documentary hypothesis and the aspects approach. In Rabbi Breuer's words:

> All that separates us is faith in the Divine origin of the Torah. They believe that the sources of the Torah were written by man, and that a mortal redactor edited them into a single book. We, on the other hand, believe that the sources of the Torah were written by God, and that it is He who also edited them into a single book. This debate between us and the Bible critics cannot be decided by the intellect, for the intellect has nothing to say on the matter.[60]

59. See *Shitat HaBeḥinot*, 69–70. Further on, I shall address the question of the relationship between the plain meaning of the text and the *midreshei halakha* (the rabbinic analysis of the legal sections of the Torah), in instances where there are different aspects that contradict one another on the practical level. We will see how the *midrash halakha* in fact integrates the different approaches into a practical solution.
60. *Shitat HaBeḥinot*, 343–44.

It should be noted that Rabbi Breuer's extensive and minute analysis of the textual units, attributing even half-verses to different aspects, is not always convincing. He accepts almost unquestioningly the literary analysis of the classical Bible critics, while recent scholars have questioned the possibility of arriving at a clear, systematic division of sources. They acknowledge that the text is sometimes so intertwined and convoluted that the proposed division is difficult to accept. For this reason, those seeking to implement the aspects approach do not view themselves as being obligated by the precise claims of the early critics' division of the text, any more than contemporary academic scholars do. Instead, they may propose a different division of the aspects, based on more clearly defined ideas.[61]

One might argue that the aspects approach allows us to conclude that no clear division between the various documents actually exists. However, this is an oversimplification. Rabbi Breuer's fundamental insight should be seen as highlighting the Torah's tendency to express the complexity of various concepts and narratives through repetition, ambiguity, and contradiction. This insight does not depend on the ability to divide and separate the text into a number of clearly defined documents. Instead, it acknowledges the phenomenon of different and contradictory aspects in the Torah, but without insisting on drilling down to the details, and certainly not in a dogmatic fashion.[62]

---

61. As we have noted in the past, even the division between the "divine attribute of strict justice" and the "divine attribute of mercy," as Rabbi Breuer proposes it (paralleling, in literary terms, the division between the "E" source and the "J" source), neither requires nor admits of systematic adherence to these concepts. See the wide-ranging and perceptive treatment of Rabbi Yehuda Rock, "Shitat HaBeḥinot: Bikkoret Metodologit VeYissum Meḥudash," *Megadim* 53 (Tevet 5772/2012): 9–73.
62. Some proponents of Rabbi Breuer's approach deviated from his strict line, arguing that it is still possible to accept the fundamental historical argument of the documentary hypothesis and to say that the Torah was indeed written by prophets throughout the First Temple Period, and not by Moses alone. Proponents of this approach claim that this does not contradict faith in the divine origin of the Torah, since everything was written and redacted with a prophetic spirit, even if not by Moses personally. Rabbi Breuer rejected such approaches vehemently (*Shitat HaBeḥinot*, 156–68), arguing that they were to be regarded as "a new faith which these people invented on their own" (ibid., 162), since the Torah is not a prophetic book written in the language of the prophet, but rather God's direct word as conveyed to Moses. Yisrael Knohl (cited by Rabbi Breuer, ibid., 301–5) attempted to defend these

The Aspects Approach and Deuteronomy

Biblical scholars from de Wette onwards have been entirely correct in identifying many contradictions between the contents of Deuteronomy and that of the other books of the Torah. Some of these have already been addressed above, as in the discussion of the release of the Hebrew servant.

With regard to Deuteronomy, therefore, we need not use the aspects approach in order to resolve the abundant contradictions – because of the special character of the text in Deuteronomy. The great majority of the book is made up of Moses's own lengthy speeches, after all – especially the opening speech (Deut. 1:6–4:40) and the "speech of the mitzvot" (Deut. 5:1–26:19).[63] It would therefore seem that the apparent contradictions between other parts of the Torah and Deuteronomy arise from differences between the more divinely formulated parts of the Torah in earlier books, and the more personal words of Moses as recorded in Deuteronomy.

In some places the Sages note the special nature of Moses's speeches, pointing out that his delivery of these speeches even has halakhic significance.

> "And there is no interruption of the section on the curses." Abaye said: "This applies only to the verses in Leviticus, but in the curses in Deuteronomy, it is permitted to interrupt. What is the reason for this? These are stated in the plural, and Moses uttered them at God's instruction. Those are stated in the singular, and Moses stated them on his own." (Megilla 31b)

---

approaches, positing that some of the medieval commentators recognized that certain verses in the Torah were not written by Moses (as was discussed at length), and that it is therefore possible to grant legitimacy to the argument that different aspects in the Torah were written by prophets. However, Rabbi Breuer argued (ibid., 306–13) that a few individual verses do not serve as the basis for drawing conclusions as to the writing of the Torah as a whole. For more on this polemic, see Uriel Simon, "Shenayim Oḥazim BeSod HaSheneim Asar shel R. Avraham Ibn Ezra," *Megadim* 51 (Iyar 5770/2010): 77–85. Rabbi Breuer also made this point in an article published in English, "The Study of Bible and the Primacy of the Fear of Heaven: Compatibility or Contradiction?" in *Modern Scholarship in the Study of Torah*, ed. S. Carmy (Jersey City, 1995), 159–81.

63. See Nahmanides at the beginning of his commentary on Deuteronomy 1:1.

In other words, when the Torah is read publicly, the curses enumerated in *Parashat Beḥukotai* in Leviticus must be completed in a single reading, without interruption, whereas the curses in *Parashat Ki Tavo* in Deuteronomy may be interrupted in the middle, since these are not a quote of God's words, but rather Moses's own words in the speech where he bids farewell to the nation.[64] These words of Moses are therefore regarded as equivalent to any other reported speech in the Torah, and not the same as his words in Leviticus, which "Moses uttered at God's instruction."[65]

Elsewhere, the Sages note another difference with regard to Deuteronomy: in analyzing Moses's speeches in Deuteronomy, one can speculate as to the reason for the juxtaposition of two particular subjects, even if one were to maintain that in general there is no special significance to the ordering of topics in the Torah:

> And Rav Yosef said: Even one who does not usually delve into the reason behind the juxtaposition of different units in the Torah – with relation to Deuteronomy, he does so, as evidenced by R. Yehuda, who usually did not seek to explain, but in Deuteronomy he did. (Yevamot 4a)[66]

---

64. Of course, this teaching of the Sages in no way implies any distinction between the status of Deuteronomy and the status of the other books of the Torah. The Sages simply mean to note that the great majority of Deuteronomy consists of Moses's speeches, and therefore these quotes may indeed reflect Moses's own individual style, where he speaks "on his own," not having been commanded to say these words by God – just like the words of anyone else as recorded in the Torah.
65. This principle is extended by Rabbi Haim ben Attar, in the introduction to his commentary *Ohr HaḤayim*: "Our Sages taught that the curses in Deuteronomy were uttered by Moses himself. Even though he was repeating and explaining God's prior words, he was not commanded to do so; rather, he repeated it on his own initiative.... Therefore, Deuteronomy starts with the words, 'These are the words which Moses spoke' – meaning, these alone are the things which Moses said of his own initiative, whereas in everything that preceded this, in the other four books [of the Torah], he did not utter so much as a single letter on his own; rather, it was conveyed directly as God commanded."
66. As noted by Rabbi Eliezer ben Natan of Mainz, one of the great sages of Ashkenaz in the twelfth century, in his Responsa, no. 34: "The entire Torah was uttered by God, and there is no chronological order; but Moses ordered Deuteronomy, section after section, in such a way as to impart certain lessons."

In light of this different character of Deuteronomy that the Sages attribute to the book, based on these two passages, the discrepancies between Deuteronomy's laws and those of earlier books may be resolved without resorting to the aspects approach. Rather, one can consider them as emerging from two "standpoints," with Deuteronomy presenting a more "subjective" view, and the earlier books, more "objective."

A discrepancy between the Torah's objective description and the subjective account of an individual describing events from a personal point of view is not unusual in the Torah – and the differences between these standpoints were seen as meaningful by the talmudic Sages and the medieval commentators who interpreted these passages. For instance, the report that Abraham's servant conveys to Rebecca's family concerning his quest to find a wife for Isaac and the objective narrative that precedes it in the Torah diverge widely. One of the most prominent differences concerns the initial dialogue between Abraham and his servant. The objective account records the servant asking Abraham: אוּלַי לֹא תֹאבֶה הָאִשָּׁה לָלֶכֶת אַחֲרַי אֶל הָאָרֶץ הַזֹּאת, הֶהָשֵׁב אָשִׁיב אֶת בִּנְךָ אֶל הָאָרֶץ אֲשֶׁר יָצָאתָ מִשָּׁם?, "Perhaps the woman will not agree to follow me to this land; shall I then take your son back to the land from whence you departed?" (Gen. 24:5). Abraham responds: הִשָּׁמֶר לְךָ פֶּן תָּשִׁיב אֶת בְּנִי שָׁמָּה... וְאִם לֹא תֹאבֶה הָאִשָּׁה לָלֶכֶת אַחֲרֶיךָ וְנִקִּיתָ מִשְּׁבֻעָתִי זֹאת רַק אֶת בְּנִי לֹא תָשֵׁב שָׁמָּה, "Guard yourself lest you take my son back to there.... If the woman will not agree to follow you, you shall be free of this oath to me; only do not take my son back there" (Gen. 24:6–8).

Yet when the servant recounts these events, the entire discussion and its topic of whether Isaac would relocate is omitted. All the servant relates from his conversation with Abraham pertains to Rebecca:

> וָאֹמַר אֶל אֲדֹנִי אֻלַי לֹא תֵלֵךְ הָאִשָּׁה אַחֲרָי. וַיֹּאמֶר אֵלָי ה׳ אֲשֶׁר הִתְהַלַּכְתִּי לְפָנָיו יִשְׁלַח מַלְאָכוֹ אִתָּךְ וְהִצְלִיחַ דַּרְכֶּךָ וְלָקַחְתָּ אִשָּׁה לִבְנִי מִמִּשְׁפַּחְתִּי וּמִבֵּית אָבִי. אָז תִּנָּקֶה מֵאָלָתִי כִּי תָבוֹא אֶל מִשְׁפַּחְתִּי וְאִם לֹא יִתְּנוּ לָךְ וְהָיִיתָ נָקִי מֵאָלָתִי.
>
> I said to my master, "Perhaps the woman will not follow me." And he said to me, "The Lord before Whom I walk will send His angel with you, and cause your path to prosper, and you shall take a wife

> for my son from my family and from my father's household. Then you shall be free of my oath, when you come to my family; and if they do not grant it to you, you shall be free of my oath." (Gen. 24:39–41)[67]

This approach may also be applied to the apparent contradictions between Deuteronomy and earlier biblical books. Like the speech of the servant in Genesis 24, Deuteronomy's speeches are the unique perspective of a particular person. From an interpretive point of view, both the short speeches of Abraham's servant and the long monologue that is Moses's second speech in Deuteronomy may be seen through the lens of their subjectivity.

Of course, this explanation still begs the question: Why does the Torah incorporate both subjective and objective reporting? And more: Since the words of Moses were included in the Torah, and since he was God's servant and the greatest of the prophets, his words are part of God's word. But the Torah's choice to record them in a manner that reflects their subjective nature is an important key to resolving the contradictions; this is true both of narrative and of halakhic sections.

Let us examine three of the main characteristics of Moses's speeches, which can help us understand Moses's intentions and thereby the nature of the contradictions between his own words and what we find elsewhere in the Torah.

---

67. Another example of discrepancies between objective and subjective accounts is the meeting between Joseph, as governor of Egypt, and his brothers (Gen. 42). The Torah records that after Joseph accuses his brothers of being spies, they deny the charge and willingly offer the information that they have another brother: וַיֹּאמְרוּ שְׁנֵים עָשָׂר עֲבָדֶיךָ אַחִים אֲנַחְנוּ בְּנֵי אִישׁ אֶחָד בְּאֶרֶץ כְּנָעַן וְהִנֵּה הַקָּטֹן אֶת אָבִינוּ הַיּוֹם וְהָאֶחָד אֵינֶנּוּ, "And they said, 'Your servants are twelve; we are brothers, the son of one man in the land of Canaan, and behold – the youngest is with our father today, and one is gone'" (Gen. 42:13). But when Judah approaches Joseph later on, and recalls all that has transpired in the encounters between them, he offers a different account: אֲדֹנִי שָׁאַל אֶת עֲבָדָיו לֵאמֹר הֲיֵשׁ לָכֶם אָב אוֹ אָח. וַנֹּאמֶר אֶל אֲדֹנִי יֶשׁ לָנוּ אָב זָקֵן וְיֶלֶד זְקֻנִים קָטָן וְאָחִיו מֵת וַיִּוָּתֵר הוּא לְבַדּוֹ לְאִמּוֹ וְאָבִיו אֲהֵבוֹ, "My lord asked his servants, saying: 'Do you have a father or a brother?' And we said to my lord, 'We have a father, who is old, and a young child of his old age; and his brother died, and he alone remains of his mother, and his father loves him'" (Gen. 44:19–20). Further in Judah's dramatic speech, there are other significant differences between his subjective account and the objective description that precedes it in the previous chapters.

1. Morality as the Basis for Commandments in Deuteronomy

When Moses discusses the Hebrew servant, he emphasizes the ethical obligations of the master toward the servant: וְזָכַרְתָּ כִּי עֶבֶד הָיִיתָ בְּאֶרֶץ מִצְרַיִם – the master must "remember that you were a slave in the land of Egypt" (Deut. 5:14).

This expression appears five times in Deuteronomy. Its recurrence reflects the emphasis in Moses's speeches on the moral dimension of relations among humans as a motivating factor in the commandments. This approach differs substantially from the emphasis on God's supremacy as the motivating factor in mitzva observance, as is found in other passages outside Deuteronomy. The best-known example in this regard is the rationale for the Sabbath as set forth in the two different formulations of the Ten Commandments. In *Parashat Yitro* in Exodus, the mitzva is presented as pertaining to the man-God relationship, with its purpose being to remember the creation of the world:

> זָכוֹר אֶת יוֹם הַשַּׁבָּת לְקַדְּשׁוֹ... כִּי שֵׁשֶׁת יָמִים עָשָׂה ה׳ אֶת הַשָּׁמַיִם וְאֶת הָאָרֶץ אֶת הַיָּם וְאֶת כָּל אֲשֶׁר בָּם וַיָּנַח בַּיּוֹם הַשְּׁבִיעִי עַל כֵּן בֵּרַךְ ה׳ אֶת יוֹם הַשַּׁבָּת וַיְקַדְּשֵׁהוּ.
>
> Remember the Sabbath day to sanctify it.... For [in] six days God made the heavens and the earth, the sea, and all that is in them, and He rested on the seventh day; therefore God blessed the Sabbath day and sanctified it. (Ex. 20:7–10)

In *Parashat Va'etḥanan* in Deuteronomy, however, Moses repeats the Ten Commandments and presents the Sabbath day in a very different light: the Sabbath is a moral-social commandment whose goal is to provide rest for the servant.

> שָׁמוֹר אֶת יוֹם הַשַּׁבָּת לְקַדְּשׁוֹ...לְמַעַן יָנוּחַ עַבְדְּךָ וַאֲמָתְךָ כָּמוֹךָ. וְזָכַרְתָּ כִּי עֶבֶד הָיִיתָ בְּאֶרֶץ מִצְרַיִם וַיֹּצִאֲךָ ה׳ אֱלֹהֶיךָ מִשָּׁם בְּיָד חֲזָקָה וּבִזְרֹעַ נְטוּיָה עַל כֵּן צִוְּךָ ה׳ אֱלֹהֶיךָ לַעֲשׂוֹת אֶת יוֹם הַשַּׁבָּת.

> Observe the Sabbath day to sanctify it … in order that your manservant and your maidservant shall rest like you. And you shall remember that you were a servant in the land of Egypt, and the Lord your God brought you out of there with a strong hand and an outstretched arm; therefore the Lord your God commands you to observe the Sabbath day (Deut. 5:11–14).

Here too, the rationale for the command rests upon recalling Israel's experience of servitude in Egypt.

Another commandment whose description takes on a distinctly moral character when it appears in Deuteronomy is that of rejoicing on the festivals. When the commandment appears in Leviticus, it is mentioned in the context of the four species:

> וּלְקַחְתֶּם לָכֶם בַּיּוֹם הָרִאשׁוֹן פְּרִי עֵץ הָדָר כַּפֹּת תְּמָרִים וַעֲנַף עֵץ עָבֹת וְעַרְבֵי נָחַל וּשְׂמַחְתֶּם לִפְנֵי ה׳ אֱלֹהֵיכֶם שִׁבְעַת יָמִים.

> And you shall take for yourselves on the first day the fruit of a beautiful tree, branches of the date palm, and twigs from the tree with thick bark, and willows of the river, and you shall rejoice before the Lord your God seven days. (Lev. 23:40)

The rejoicing appears here as an expression of thanks to God, performed through the bringing of the four species.[68]

In Deuteronomy, with fair knowledge of what was to come, the joy of the festival is far more socially oriented, involving the vulnerable sectors of society – again based on the moral imperative that arises from the memory of slavery in Egypt:

> וְזָכַרְתָּ כִּי עֶבֶד הָיִיתָ בְּמִצְרָיִם...וְשָׂמַחְתָּ בְּחַגֶּךָ אַתָּה וּבִנְךָ וּבִתֶּךָ וְעַבְדְּךָ וַאֲמָתֶךָ וְהַלֵּוִי וְהַגֵּר וְהַיָּתוֹם וְהָאַלְמָנָה אֲשֶׁר בִּשְׁעָרֶיךָ.

68. The Jerusalem Talmud (Sukka 3:11; 54a) records a dispute as to whether the rejoicing here is over the four species or over the festive sacrifices, but the plain reading of the text contains no mention of the sacrifices in these verses, and it therefore seems more reasonable to accept the view that the rejoicing is over bringing the four species.

> And you shall remember that you were a servant in Egypt … and you shall rejoice in your festival – you and your son and your daughter, and your manservant and your maidservant, and the Levite and the stranger and the orphan and the widow who are in your gates. (Deut. 16:12–14)

This principle finds expression in several more commandments.[69] Of course, in the context and setting of Deuteronomy, this undercurrent of meaning makes sense. Moses is delivering his speeches as the nation is about to cross the Jordan and enter the land, undergoing a great transformation from a nomadic people to a nation living in its own land. Moses therefore regards it as essential to emphasize the social aspect of the commandments as a fundamental condition to sustain Israel's presence in the land for the coming generations. The memory of the exodus from Egypt will accompany them as the basis of their commitment to behave morally and ethically toward the weak and the vulnerable among them.

2. God's Love of Israel in Deuteronomy

Moses's speeches are the only sources in the Torah that treat the relationship between God and Israel from a perspective of love. Deuteronomy is where the Torah speaks of God's love for Israel. For example:

69. A brief note on an interesting example: the story of Amalek is presented in Exodus (17:8–16) as the first war waged against Israel, and as the first blow to God's "deterrent effect," which is described at length in the Song of the Sea (Ex. 15:14–16). For this reason, God Himself fights against Amalek, and promises to do so also in the future: כִּי מָחֹה אֶמְחֶה אֶת זֵכֶר עֲמָלֵק מִתַּחַת הַשָּׁמָיִם, "For I shall surely erase the memory of Amalek from under the heavens" (Ex. 17:14). In the description in Deuteronomy (25:17–19), in contrast, the emphasis is on the negative moral aspect of Amalek's act toward Israel: אֲשֶׁר קָרְךָ בַּדֶּרֶךְ וַיְזַנֵּב בְּךָ כָּל הַנֶּחֱשָׁלִים אַחֲרֶיךָ וְאַתָּה עָיֵף וְיָגֵעַ, "For meeting you on the way, and attacking the stragglers who trailed after you, while you were tired and weary" (Deut. 25:18). Hence, the obligation concerning Amalek is placed specifically upon Israel: תִּמְחֶה אֶת זֵכֶר עֲמָלֵק מִתַּחַת הַשָּׁמָיִם לֹא תִּשְׁכָּח, "You shall erase the memory of Amalek from under the heavens; you shall not forget" (Deut. 25:19).

לֹא מֵרֻבְּכֶם מִכָּל הָעַמִּים חָשַׁק ה׳ בָּכֶם וַיִּבְחַר בָּכֶם כִּי אַתֶּם הַמְעַט מִכָּל הָעַמִּים. כִּי מֵאַהֲבַת ה׳ אֶתְכֶם וּמִשָּׁמְרוֹ אֶת הַשְּׁבֻעָה אֲשֶׁר נִשְׁבַּע לַאֲבֹתֵיכֶם...

> It is not because you are more numerous than any other nation that God set His love upon you and chose you, for you were the fewest among all the nations; [rather,] it was out of God's love for you, and for Him to keep the oath which He swore to your forefathers. (Deut. 7:7–8)

וְלֹא אָבָה ה׳ אֱלֹהֶיךָ לִשְׁמֹעַ אֶל בִּלְעָם וַיַּהֲפֹךְ ה׳ אֱלֹהֶיךָ לְּךָ אֶת הַקְּלָלָה לִבְרָכָה כִּי אֲהֵבְךָ ה׳ אֱלֹהֶיךָ.

> The Lord your God would not listen to Balaam, and the Lord your God transformed the curse into a blessing, for the Lord your God loves you. (Deut. 23:6)

By the same token, only in Deuteronomy is there a reciprocal command for Israel to love God: וְאָהַבְתָּ אֵת ה׳ אֱלֹהֶיךָ בְּכָל לְבָבְךָ וּבְכָל נַפְשְׁךָ וּבְכָל מְאֹדֶךָ, "You shall love the Lord your God with all your heart, and with all your soul, and with all your might" (Deut. 6:5). And, וְאָהַבְתָּ אֵת ה׳ אֱלֹהֶיךָ וְשָׁמַרְתָּ מִשְׁמַרְתּוֹ וְחֻקֹּתָיו וּמִשְׁפָּטָיו וּמִצְוֹתָיו כָּל הַיָּמִים, "You shall love the Lord your God and observe His charge and His statutes and His judgments and His commandments for all time" (Deut. 11:1).

This message of love appears to be connected to the timing of most of Deuteronomy, as the Children of Israel stand on the cusp of entry into the land, and it is acknowledged in Moses's parting speech at the end of the book, where he describes the process of repentance that Israel will undergo after being exiled from the land as punishment for their sins:

וְשַׁבְתָּ עַד ה׳ אֱלֹהֶיךָ וְשָׁמַעְתָּ בְקֹלוֹ...וְשָׁב ה׳ אֱלֹהֶיךָ אֶת שְׁבוּתְךָ וְרִחֲמֶךָ וְשָׁב וְקִבֶּצְךָ מִכָּל הָעַמִּים...וֶהֱבִיאֲךָ ה׳ אֱלֹהֶיךָ אֶל הָאָרֶץ אֲשֶׁר יָרְשׁוּ אֲבֹתֶיךָ וִירִשְׁתָּהּ וְהֵיטִבְךָ וְהִרְבְּךָ מֵאֲבֹתֶיךָ.

> And you shall return to the Lord your God, and obey Him ... and the Lord your God will bring back your captivity, and have mercy

> upon you, and gather you back from all of the nations… and the Lord your God will bring you to the land which your forefathers inherited, and you shall take possession of it, and He shall be good to you, and multiply you more than your fathers. (Deut. 30:2–5)

Only afterwards does Moses say, וּמָל ה׳ אֱלֹהֶיךָ אֶת לְבָבְךָ וְאֶת לְבַב זַרְעֶךָ לְאַהֲבָה אֶת ה׳ אֱלֹהֶיךָ בְּכָל לְבָבְךָ וּבְכָל נַפְשְׁךָ לְמַעַן חַיֶּיךָ, "And the Lord your God will circumcise your heart and the heart of your descendants, to love the Lord your God with all your heart, and with all your soul, that you may live" (Deut. 30:6).

Apparently, love of God is possible only in the Land of Israel – the land upon which God's eyes rest "from the beginning of the year until the end of the year" (see Deut. 11:12). Only in the land can the relationship between God and Israel reach a level that may properly be called "love." Moses therefore refrains from mentioning this concept as a description of the bond between God and the nation – until just prior to entry into the land.

3. The Sanctity of the People in Deuteronomy

The special level of sanctity attributed to the people as a whole is also prominent in Moses's "speech of the mitzvot" (chapters 5–26 of Deuteronomy), especially in contrast to the other books of the Torah that focus on a special level of sanctity prescribed for a select group within the people. *Parashat Emor* in Leviticus sets forth various laws pertaining to the sanctity of the *kohanim* (priests), including the following prohibition:

> לֹא יקרחה [יִקְרְחוּ קרי] קָרְחָה בְּרֹאשָׁם וּפְאַת זְקָנָם לֹא יְגַלֵּחוּ וּבִבְשָׂרָם לֹא יִשְׂרְטוּ שָׂרָטֶת. קְדֹשִׁים יִהְיוּ לֵאלֹהֵיהֶם וְלֹא יְחַלְּלוּ שֵׁם אֱלֹהֵיהֶם כִּי אֶת אִשֵּׁי ה׳ לֶחֶם אֱלֹהֵיהֶם הֵם מַקְרִיבִם וְהָיוּ קֹדֶשׁ.

> They shall not make a bald patch on their head, nor shall they shave the corners of their beard, nor make any cut in their flesh. They shall be holy to their God, and shall not profane the name of their God, for it is the offerings of the Lord made by fire, the

> bread of their God, that they offer up; therefore they shall be holy. (Lev. 21:5–6)

The *kohanim* minister in the Mishkan and administer the sacrificial services, granting them a special holiness. That is, because of their role, they needed to conduct themselves in certain ways that distinguished them from the rest of the people. For example, *kohanim* are forbidden to make a bald spot or cut themselves (in mourning). They are also prohibited from eating forbidden foods: נְבֵלָה וּטְרֵפָה לֹא יֹאכַל לְטָמְאָה בָהּ, "That which dies of itself, or is torn by beasts, he [the *kohen*] shall not eat of it, to defile himself with it" (Lev. 22:8).

Moses, however, treats the entire people as holy in Deuteronomy. Indeed, the entire nation bears the same restrictions as those given only to the *kohanim* in Leviticus:

> בָּנִים אַתֶּם לַה׳ אֱלֹהֵיכֶם לֹא תִתְגֹּדְדוּ וְלֹא תָשִׂימוּ קָרְחָה בֵּין עֵינֵיכֶם לָמֵת. כִּי עַם קָדוֹשׁ אַתָּה לַה׳ אֱלֹהֶיךָ וּבְךָ בָּחַר ה׳ לִהְיוֹת לוֹ לְעַם סְגֻלָּה מִכֹּל הָעַמִּים אֲשֶׁר עַל פְּנֵי הָאֲדָמָה.

> You are children to the Lord your God; you shall not gash yourselves, nor make a baldness between your eyes for the dead. For you are a holy nation unto the Lord your God, and the Lord your God has chosen you to be a special possession for Himself out of all the nations that are upon the face of the earth. (Deut. 14:1–2)

> לֹא תֹאכְלוּ כָל נְבֵלָה לַגֵּר אֲשֶׁר בִּשְׁעָרֶיךָ תִּתְּנֶנָּה וַאֲכָלָהּ אוֹ מָכֹר לְנָכְרִי כִּי עַם קָדוֹשׁ אַתָּה לַה׳ אֱלֹהֶיךָ.

> You shall not eat any animal that dies of itself; you shall give it to the stranger who is in your gates that he may eat it, or you may sell it to a foreigner, for *you* are a holy nation unto the Lord your God. (Deut. 14:21)

The discrepancy between Leviticus and Deuteronomy in this context is not necessarily contradictory. We may posit that there are two levels of holiness, and that where Leviticus speaks of the holiness of the *kohanim*,

Moses in the "speech of the mitzvot" in Deuteronomy proceeds to apply those laws to the entire nation.[70] Indeed, Moses finds the expression of the halakhic dimension of the holiness of Israel not only in these prohibitions, but also in the rights and entitlements normally reserved for the *kohanim* or *leviim*. For example, after the rebellion of Korah, the Torah addresses the *kohanim* and speaks of their obligations and their rights – including the giving of the firstborn to the *kohen*:

> אַךְ בְּכוֹר שׁוֹר אוֹ בְכוֹר כֶּשֶׂב אוֹ בְכוֹר עֵז לֹא תִפְדֶּה קֹדֶשׁ הֵם אֶת דָּמָם תִּזְרֹק עַל הַמִּזְבֵּחַ...וּבְשָׂרָם יִהְיֶה לָּךְ כַּחֲזֵה הַתְּנוּפָה וּכְשׁוֹק הַיָּמִין לְךָ יִהְיֶה.
>
> But the firstborn of an ox, or the firstborn of a sheep, or the firstborn of a goat, you shall not redeem, they are holy; you shall sprinkle their blood upon the altar...and their meat shall be yours, just as the breast of elevation offering and the right thigh are yours. (Num. 18:17–18)

Further on, the Torah talks about the tithes given to the *leviim*: וְלִבְנֵי לֵוִי הִנֵּה נָתַתִּי כָּל מַעֲשֵׂר בְּיִשְׂרָאֵל לְנַחֲלָה חֵלֶף עֲבֹדָתָם אֲשֶׁר הֵם עֹבְדִים אֶת עֲבֹדַת אֹהֶל מוֹעֵד, "And to the children of Levi, behold, I have given all the tithes in Israel as their share, in return for the service which they perform – the service of the Tent of Meeting" (Num. 18:21).

Moses's speech in Deuteronomy, however, indicates that all Israelites are entitled to partake of the firstborn animals:

> כָּל הַבְּכוֹר אֲשֶׁר יִוָּלֵד בִּבְקָרְךָ וּבְצֹאנְךָ הַזָּכָר תַּקְדִּישׁ לַה׳ אֱלֹהֶיךָ...לִפְנֵי ה׳ אֱלֹהֶיךָ תֹאכְלֶנּוּ שָׁנָה בְשָׁנָה בַּמָּקוֹם אֲשֶׁר יִבְחַר ה׳ אַתָּה וּבֵיתֶךָ.
>
> Every firstborn male that is born of your cattle and your flocks you shall dedicate to the Lord your God...you shall eat it before

70. As Nahmanides comments (Deut. 14:1): "Now it is made clear that Moses commanded them thus not only owing to the stature of the *kohanim*; rather, all of the congregation is holy: 'You are all sons of the Lord your God' – like the *kohanim*; hence you too should observe this commandment, just as they do."

> the Lord your God, year by year, in the place which the Lord shall choose – you and your household. (Deut. 15:19–20)

And in the only place in Deuteronomy where mention is made of tithes, it is again applied to the entire people:

> כָּל הַבְּכוֹר אֲשֶׁר יִוָּלֵד בִּבְקָרְךָ וּבְצֹאנְךָ הַזָּכָר תַּקְדִּישׁ לַה׳ אֱלֹהֶיךָ...לִפְנֵי ה׳ אֱלֹהֶיךָ תֹאכֲלֶנּוּ שָׁנָה בְשָׁנָה בַּמָּקוֹם אֲשֶׁר יִבְחַר ה׳ אַתָּה וּבֵיתֶךָ.

> You shall surely tithe all of the increase of your seed that the field brings forth, year by year. And you shall eat it before the Lord your God, in the place where He will choose to cause His name to rest – the tithe of your corn, of your wine, of your oil, and the firstborn of your herds, and of your flocks. (Deut. 14:22–23)[71]

This phenomenon of the sanctity of Israel, which appears so prominently in Deuteronomy, bears explanation.

It would seem that on the eve of the entry into the land Moses presents a utopian reality. Namely, that the whole nation of Israel was ideally supposed to be imbued with the same sanctity as that of the *kohanim*, but only if they were truly deserving of their status as a holy nation. This question – whether Israel merits God's benevolence and designation as a holy nation – is one of the central themes of Moses's speeches throughout Deuteronomy.

On the one hand, he asserts that the people are holy: כִּי עַם קָדוֹשׁ אַתָּה לַה׳ אֱלֹהֶיךָ בְּךָ בָּחַר ה׳ אֱלֹהֶיךָ לִהְיוֹת לוֹ לְעַם סְגֻלָּה מִכֹּל הָעַמִּים אֲשֶׁר עַל פְּנֵי הָאֲדָמָה, "For you are a holy nation unto the Lord your God; the Lord your God has chosen you to be a special possession for Himself out of all the nations that are upon the face of the earth" (Deut. 7:6). This continues the vision that was presented prior to the revelation at Sinai: כִּי עַם קָדוֹשׁ אַתָּה לַה׳ אֱלֹהֶיךָ בְּךָ בָּחַר ה׳ אֱלֹהֶיךָ

71. Rashi explains, in accordance with the halakha set down by the Sages: "'You shall eat it before the Lord your God' – this is addressed to the *kohen*, for we already know that this is one of the gifts given to the *kohanim*." However, this interpretation is difficult to reconcile with the plain meaning of the text.

לִהְיוֹת לוֹ לְעַם סְגֻלָּה מִכֹּל הָעַמִּים אֲשֶׁר עַל פְּנֵי הָאֲדָמָה, "You will be My special possession out of all the nations, for all the earth is Mine. And you shall be for Me a kingdom of *kohanim* and a holy nation" (Ex. 19:5–6).

On the other hand, this vision hints strongly to the fact that this holiness is not automatic, but contingent upon observance of the commandments. This idea, too, recurs in Moses's speeches on the eve of the entry into the land: יְקִימְךָ ה׳ לוֹ לְעַם קָדוֹשׁ כַּאֲשֶׁר נִשְׁבַּע לָךְ כִּי תִשְׁמֹר אֶת מִצְוֹת ה׳ אֱלֹהֶיךָ וְהָלַכְתָּ בִּדְרָכָיו, "The Lord shall establish you for Himself as a holy nation, as He promised you, if you keep the commandments of the Lord your God and follow in His ways" (Deut. 28:9). The holiness of Israel would be expressed only in the event that the nation observes the commandments and follows the way of God.

The dependence of the people's well-being on their observance of the commandments is introduced by Moses with regard to an idyllic economic situation as well. Fundamentally, Moses's speech presents the utopian vision and gritty reality side by side: כִּי לֹא יֶחְדַּל אֶבְיוֹן מִקֶּרֶב הָאָרֶץ עַל כֵּן אָנֹכִי מְצַוְּךָ לֵאמֹר פָּתֹחַ תִּפְתַּח אֶת יָדְךָ לְאָחִיךָ לַעֲנִיֶּךָ וּלְאֶבְיֹנְךָ בְּאַרְצֶךָ, "For the poor shall never cease from the midst of the land; therefore I command you, saying, you shall surely open your hand to your brother, to your poor and to your needy who are in your land" (Deut. 15:11).

Yet Moses had just declared in that same speech that there would seemingly be no need for the legislation regarding cancellation of debts, since there would be no loans and no poor people:

> אֶפֶס כִּי לֹא יִהְיֶה בְּךָ אֶבְיוֹן כִּי בָרֵךְ יְבָרֶכְךָ ה׳ בָּאָרֶץ אֲשֶׁר ה׳ אֱלֹהֶיךָ נֹתֵן לְךָ נַחֲלָה לְרִשְׁתָּהּ. רַק אִם שָׁמוֹעַ תִּשְׁמַע בְּקוֹל ה׳ אֱלֹהֶיךָ לִשְׁמֹר לַעֲשׂוֹת אֶת כָּל הַמִּצְוָה הַזֹּאת אֲשֶׁר אָנֹכִי מְצַוְּךָ הַיּוֹם.
>
> But there shall be no poor person among you, for the Lord shall surely bless you in the land which the Lord your God gives to you as an inheritance, to possess it – only if you diligently obey the Lord your God, to observe and to perform all of these commandments which I command you this day. (Deut. 15:4–5)

Even this formulation, however, suggests that ultimately the idyllic economic situation is dependent upon observance of the commandments.

The same idea applies to Israel and its holy status. Moses describes the nation in an ideal state, where the people are worthy of eating of the firstborn of the animals and of the tithes of the produce, just as the priests who serve in the Temple do. In practice, however, these laws may well never be implemented – for Israel must first reach the level of holiness that creates this reality. Nevertheless, as the people are about to enter the land, Moses presents them with the aspiration to be a holy nation, something for which they should strive in their life in the land.

The points that we have examined here illustrate the special nature of Deuteronomy with its idiosyncratic style and unique ideas. We have seen why, in his speeches, Moses purports to treat identical topics with different emphases. Identification of the themes in Deuteronomy allows us to explain the variations between Moses's words in Deuteronomy and the text elsewhere. Obviously, the scope of this chapter does not allow for an exhaustive discussion of the entire book, but the examples addressed here offer an overall approach to Deuteronomy as a whole.

The Roots of the Aspects Approach

While Rabbi Breuer pioneered the systematic application of the "aspects approach," the approach has much earlier – perhaps even ancient – roots. The most obvious foundation for such an approach is the well-known teaching of the Sages that contradictory verses were said "as a single utterance" (*bedibbur eḥad*), appearing in a number of variations:

> "*Shav*" and "*shaker*"[72] emerged as a single utterance, which is impossible for the human mouth to say, or for the ear to perceive; "*zakhor*" [remember] and "*shamor*" [observe][73] emerged

72. This refers to the discrepancy in the ninth of the Ten Commandments, לֹא תַעֲנֶה בְרֵעֲךָ עֵד שָׁקֶר, "You shall not bear false witness against your neighbor": in Exodus (20:12), the expression for "false witness" is "*ed shaker*"; in Deuteronomy (5:16), the verse reads "*ed shav*."

73. The different terms express different ways of relating to the day, as we saw above.

> as a single utterance, which is impossible for the human mouth to say, or for the ear to perceive; מְחַלְלֶיהָ מוֹת יוּמָת, "Those who desecrate it shall be put to death" (Ex. 31:14) and שְׁנֵי כְבָשִׂים בְּנֵי שָׁנָה תְּמִימִם, "Two lambs of the first year, without blemish" (Num. 28:9), emerged as a single utterance, which is impossible for the human mouth to say or for the ear to perceive;[74] עֶרְוַת אֵשֶׁת אָחִיךָ לֹא תְגַלֵּה, "You shall not uncover the nakedness of your brother's wife" (Lev. 18:16) and יְבָמָהּ יָבֹא עָלֶיהָ, "Her husband's brother shall go to her" (Deut. 25:5) emerged as a single utterance....[75] And so it is written, אַחַת דִּבֶּר אֱלֹקִים, "One thing was said by God" – in speech – שְׁתַּיִם זוּ שָׁמָעְתִּי, "yet two things have I heard" (Ps. 62:12); and it is written (Jer. 23:29), הֲלוֹא כֹה דְבָרִי כָּאֵשׁ נְאֻם ה׳ וּכְפַטִּישׁ יְפֹצֵץ סָלַע, "Is My word not like a fire, says the Lord; like a hammer that shatters rock." (Y. Nedarim chapter 3, col. 37d)[76]

This passage draws a clear distinction between God and man – God is able to utter multiple ideas in a single utterance, but humans do not have the capacity to absorb these ideas all at once. The text of the Torah is primarily concerned with describing events and understanding their significance, and, in order to express a multiplicity of ideas, the text emphasizes different angles which may create irreconcilable factual contradiction. This approach is comparable to the working assumption of the "aspects theory": when one encounters contradictory accounts of an event, one cannot know from the text which version actually happened or how to reconcile the contradictory accounts.[77]

---

74. The contradiction relates to the prohibition of slaughtering animals on Shabbat while at the same time mandating sacrificial offerings on Shabbat.
75. Here, again, this is not a clear contradiction, since the Torah does not state explicitly that one may not marry the wife of a brother who has died. The other examples which *Ḥazal* go on to cite, omitted here, are of a similar nature.
76. A similar discussion may be found in *Mekhilta deRabbi Yishmael, Yitro, "BaḤodesh"* 7, Horowitz-Rabin edition.
77. As above, Rabbi Breuer maintained that in aggadic midrashim, the Sages attempt to reconcile narratives, and in halakhic midrashim, they reconcile the various legal aspects to arrive at the law.

A proof that the disparities between the verses are to be appreciated in and of themselves without reference to any potential resolution can be found in a well-known talmudic text regarding the disputes between the School of Hillel and the School of Shammai. The Gemara concludes that "both these and those are the words of the living God" (Eruvin 13b). One of the most prominent Tosafists of the thirteenth century, Rabbenu Peretz bar Eliyahu of Corbeil, questions this statement in a way that is pertinent to our own discussion, for how can "these and those" be the "words of the living God" in questions of material fact?[78] For example, there are differing opinions, based on biblical sources, concerning the size of the altar in the Temple (see Zevaḥim 62a). One opinion states it was sixty cubits in size, while the other maintains it was twenty cubits. Surely the actual size of the altar accorded with only one of the opinions?

Rabbenu Peretz answered his own question, explaining that even with regard to the details of material fact, the text offers no decisive ruling. The verses may be interpreted in different ways, and as long as the method of exegesis is rooted in the text itself, then "both these and those are the words of the living God" – even though only one opinion could have been historically accurate. He understands that the text does not necessarily describe physical reality, but instead offers the possibility of multiple interpretations, which, for the purposes of the Tanakh's message, are able to coexist.

If this is so where the seeming contradiction is of a technical nature, such as the size of the altar, then it surely also applies to a matter of different perspectives on reality, or to different elements of a worldview. The text may express truths that appear contradictory to human beings, but are nevertheless considered "the words of the living God."

Rabbi Breuer himself found a basis for his approach in the works of Rabbi Aryeh Leib Gunzburg, author of *Shaagat Aryeh,* one of the greatest Lithuanian scholars of the eighteenth century.[79] The Gemara states that the expression "to this very day," which appears many times

78. For further discussion, see my article in *Shitat HaBeḥinot,* 295–98, and Rabbi Breuer's response, 299–300.

79. See *Shitat HaBeḥinot,* 92ff.

in Tanakh, means up until the time of the writing (and not until the reader's time) (Yoma 54a). A verse in Chronicles makes the point: מִן בְּנֵי שִׁמְעוֹן הָלְכוּ לְהַר שֵׂעִיר... וַיַּכּוּ אֶת שְׁאֵרִית הַפְּלֵטָה לַעֲמָלֵק וַיֵּשְׁבוּ שָׁם עַד הַיּוֹם הַזֶּה, "Some of them, of the children of Simeon, went to Mount Seir... and they smote the remnant of Amalek, who had escaped, and they dwelled there to this very day" (I Chr. 4:42–43). Clearly, this passage does not describe the current day, for "Sennacherib, king of Assyria, mixed the different ethnicities together" (Mishna Yadayim 4:4), so the nations no longer dwell in the locations that they did.

Relegating the "contemporary" nature of this verse to the era of its author does not explain the meaning of this phrase, however, given that Ezra composed Chronicles long after the time of Sennacherib, at least according to the Sages (Bava Batra 15a). How, then, could Ezra have written about Simeon dwelling in Mount Seir "to this very day" long after that fact? Rabbi Aryeh Leib Gunzburg suggests an answer:

> We must conclude that Ezra copied the Chronicles from some books which he found, as I have written. Because in any case the lineage of the generations is not properly ordered; it includes several internal contradictions, and also some between Chronicles and the book of Ezra, for in one book he found such and such, and in another book something else, and he copied what he found. It seems most likely to suggest that he found written, in an ancient book that had been written before Sennacherib's upheaval, "And some of the children of Simeon went," up until "And they dwelled there to this very day," and he copied it word for word, not wishing to introduce any changes [although this was no longer the reality]. (*Gevurat Ari* on Yoma)

The assertion that Ezra used external source material in composing Chronicles and the book of Ezra, and that he copied it verbatim into his books, despite the resulting contradictions, is indeed an original and audacious idea. While it seems that Rabbi Gunzburg never contemplated the possibility of applying this approach to the Five Books of the Torah, despite his application of it to the latter books of Tanakh, the foundation for such an approach appears in the writings of two of the greatest Jewish philosophers of the twentieth century: Rabbi Abraham Isaac HaKohen Kook, and Rabbi Joseph B. Soloveitchik. The aspects approach aligns well with Rabbi Kook's fundamental approach of seeking out the positive, even in opinions and beliefs that contradict the Torah and Jewish faith. For him, grappling with such approaches is what creates the possibility of deepening our understanding of the Torah. Indeed, he believes in building the "palace of Torah" upon new ideas, as mentioned at the beginning of this book:

> And in general, this is an important rule in the struggle of ideas: we should not immediately refute any idea which comes to contradict anything in the Torah, but rather we should build the palace of Torah upon it; in doing so we are exalted by the Torah, and through this exaltation the ideas are revealed, and thereafter, when we are not pressured by anything, we can confidently also struggle against it.[80]

80. *Iggerot HaRe'aya* 1 (Jerusalem, 1962), *iggeret* 134 (translation from Tzvi Feldman in *Selected Letters* [Maaleh Adumim, 1986], 14). Rabbi Breuer himself cites this passage as the heading of his second article on the subject of his exegetical approach; see *Shitat HaBeḥinot*, 28. Rabbi Kook writes a similar idea in other places, such as in *Orot HaKodesh* 2 (Jerusalem, 1964), 547: "The very same declarations and paths that lead to the ways of heresy, also lead in their essence – if we seek their source – to the depths of a faith that is more exalted, more illuminating and life-giving, out of the same simple understanding that shone prior to the appearance of this rift." Concerning the relationship between the story of the Creation and the theory of evolution, Rabbi Kook wrote: "A comparison between the story of the Creation and recent studies is a noble endeavor. There is no problem with interpreting the biblical account, 'These are the generations of the heavens and the earth,' as containing within itself worlds of millions of years, until man arrived at some awareness that he was differentiated from all animals, and that through some sort of vision it appeared to him that he had to establish a family that would be stable and of noble spirit, by choosing a wife, who would be more connected to him than his father and his mother – his natural family members. The deep sleep could be interpreted as visions, and this could also last for some time, until the consolidation of the idea of 'bone of my bones and flesh of my flesh'" (*Shemona Kevatzim* [Jerusalem, 2004], *kovetz* 1, *siman* 594, 163).

More specifically, the conceptual basis of the aspects approach conforms to Rabbi Kook's harmonious approach, which views contrasts and contradictions as part of an overarching, all-encompassing unity. This idea appears in many different places in Rabbi Kook's writings. For example, in *Orot HaKodesh,* he compares different worldviews to saplings that must be planted at some distance from one another in order for each to be able to grow and develop fully, expressing all of its unique, individual characteristics.[81] Were the distances between them eliminated, the identity and features of each would be less distinct; they would blur into one another. Only the distance and sharp contrast between them allow for appreciation of the connections between the separate parts, so that true unity can eventually develop.

Rabbi Kook thereby laid the foundation for an approach that views contradictions in the biblical text, too, not as problems that require solutions, but as part of an overall harmony and a more complete truth. As he comments, at the end of a discussion on the nature of prophecy and its relationship to science, "Reality is not afraid of contradictions as science is, for it is inestimably greater than science."[82]

Rabbi Soloveitchik took this idea a step further, explaining some of the contradictions between chapter 1 and chapter 2 of Genesis in a manner similar to the aspects approach:[83]

> We all know that the Bible offers two accounts of the creation of man. We are also aware of the theory suggested by Bible critics attributing these two accounts to two different traditions and sources. Of course, since we do unreservedly accept the unity

81. *Orot HaKodesh* 1 (Jerusalem, 1963), 15. This, too, is cited by Rabbi Breuer, at the end of a different article; see *Shitat HaBeḥinot,* 70. The idea that Rabbi Kook sets forth here is part of a more comprehensive discussion that he develops over the course of *Orot HaKodesh,* especially in part 1, chapters 8–13.
82. *Iggerot HaRe'aya,* 2 (Jerusalem, 1962); *iggeret* 478, 120. At the same time, Rabbi Kook was vehemently opposed to the study of biblical criticism: see, for example, *Iggerot HaRe'aya* 1, *iggeret* 279, 317; *Iggerot HaRe'aya* 2, *iggeret* 363, 27.
83. On more than one occasion, I heard Rabbi Breuer express his regret that Rabbi Joseph B. Soloveitchik did not expand his approach beyond the specific aspect noted here. See *Shitat HaBeḥinot,* 188–89.

> and integrity of the Scriptures and their divine character, we reject this hypothesis which is based, like much Biblical criticism, on literary categories invented by modern man, ignoring completely the eidetic-noetic content of the Biblical story. It is, of course, true that the two accounts of the creation of man differ considerably. This incongruity was not discovered by the Bible critics. Our sages of old were aware of it. However, the answer lies not in an alleged dual tradition but in dual man, not in an imaginary contradiction between two versions but in a real contradiction in the nature of man. The two accounts deal with two Adams, two men, two fathers of mankind, two types, two representatives of humanity, and it is no wonder that they are not identical.[84]

Thus, although Rabbi Breuer was the first to apply his method in a consistent and specific manner, the roots of his approach are firmly rooted in generations of Jewish philosophy.

BIAS IN THE WRITING OF TANAKH?

The documentary hypothesis and the aspects approach make nearly identical use of the same literary tools. We have seen, however, that the fundamental difference between the approaches concerns the question of whether the Torah is of divine or human origin.

The natural next question for the Bible critics, which does not arise for those who believe in Divine authorship of the Torah, is: Who authored the various documents and collated them into a single textual anthology? The prevailing historical approach used general terms such as "priestly groups," "groups close to the kingdom of Judea or Israel," and the like. In recent generations, however, there have been attempts to identify the authors with greater precision – both in relation to the documentary hypothesis and independently of it – by identifying the various different political interests or ideological

84. *The Lonely Man of Faith* (Maggid, 2012), 8. Rabbi Soloveitchik goes on to develop these two aspects of man, Adam I and Adam II (corresponding to the Torah's description of his creation, in chapter 1 and chapter 2 of Genesis).

biases evident in the text, implying authors who sought to convey their own messages by means of these documents. These attempts have largely been rather forced, and run counter to the impression that arises from the biblical text as a whole.

One brief example suffices to illustrate the shortcomings of these efforts.

The story of Judah and Tamar (Gen. 38) is one of the most dramatic episodes in the Torah. A review of the story demonstrates that its central theme is Judah's process of repentance. In the previous chapter, Judah is the main protagonist in the sale of his brother Joseph. His sin lies primarily in his attempt to gain the best of both worlds, as it were: he wants to rid the family of Joseph, but he does not want to kill him, thereby evading the difficult moral problem of murder (Gen. 37:26–27). Selling a person into slavery is also a very grave act, however, for which the Torah mandates the death sentence, just as it does for murder (Deut. 24:7). And from Jacob's perspective, the blow is exactly as painful as it would have been had the brothers really killed Joseph.[85] The brothers all adopt Judah's deceptive approach, as they show Jacob the coat belonging to Joseph that they had dipped in blood, and ask with seeming innocence, technically without lying: הַכֶּר נָא הַכְּתֹנֶת בִּנְךָ הִוא אִם לֹא – See now, is it your son's coat or not?" (Gen. 37:32).

At the beginning of chapter 38, the shameful path of combining sin with evasion of responsibility reappears in the behavior of Onan, Judah's son. Outwardly, he fulfills his moral responsibility in marrying Tamar, the wife of his deceased brother, Er. However, in truth, he does not want to bear a son, and therefore, וְהָיָה אִם בָּא אֶל אֵשֶׁת אָחִיו וְשִׁחֵת אַרְצָה לְבִלְתִּי נְתָן זֶרַע לְאָחִיו, "when he came to his brother's wife, he spilled [his seed] on the ground so as not to give seed to his brother" (Gen. 38:9),

85. The Sages note this and emphasize that the sale of Joseph was not a positive act on Judah's part, but the opposite: "Rabbi Meir said: The term *botze'a* is mentioned only in connection with Judah, as it is written: 'Judah said to his brothers: What profit (*betza*) is it if we kill our brother.' And anyone who praises Judah is in fact a blasphemer. Concerning this it is said, וּבֹצֵעַ בֵּרֵךְ נִאֵץ ה׳, 'The compromiser (*botze'a*) blasphemes and renounces God' (Ps. 10:3)" (Sanhedrin 6b).

and he himself dies.[86] With two of Judah's sons dead,[87] one might have expected Judah to deduce that there was some problem with his path and the way he was educating his children.

But Judah does not take heed at this stage; instead, he continues to sin. His daughter-in-law, Tamar, is obligated to undergo a second levirate marriage, given that Er died without children, and the first levirate marriage, to Onan, did not result in children to carry on his dead brother's name. But Judah prevents her from marrying his third son, Shela, because he blames her for the deaths of his sons. He makes it impossible for her to rebuild her life. He does not explain to her what he is doing, or why, instead stalling her with an excuse that the Torah itself indicates does not reveal his true concern: וַיֹּאמֶר יְהוּדָה לְתָמָר כַּלָּתוֹ

86. The son born of a levirate marriage is considered the child of the deceased brother: וְהָיָה הַבְּכוֹר אֲשֶׁר תֵּלֵד יָקוּם עַל שֵׁם אָחִיו הַמֵּת וְלֹא יִמָּחֶה שְׁמוֹ מִיִּשְׂרָאֵל, "And the firstborn that she bears shall succeed in the name of his deceased brother, so that his name will not be wiped out from Israel" (Deut. 25:6). The Torah demonstrates awareness of the natural aversion to this situation and therefore permits *ḥalitza* – a ceremony of exemption – although this is clearly regarded as the less preferable option; hence, the degrading procedure to be followed by a person who chooses it.

87. It would seem that their fate is not the result of their actions alone. Despite the severity of Onan's behavior, the Torah does not mandate the death penalty for his sin. It appears that their deaths are related to Judah's own sin – especially since the sin of the father and the sin of the sons share a common background. This idea is also echoed in Reuben's words to Jacob, following the encounter with Joseph – the viceroy of Egypt – who demands that the brothers bring Benjamin down to Egypt. When Jacob initially refuses, Reuben pledges, אֶת שְׁנֵי בָנַי תָּמִית אִם לֹא אֲבִיאֶנּוּ אֵלֶיךָ, "Slay my two sons if I do not bring him to you" (Gen. 42:37). How does Reuben arrive at such a peculiar idea? It seems that he sought to hint that someone who does not bear responsibility toward his brother is deserving of losing two sons – as indeed happened to Judah. (It must be remembered that at this stage Reuben already had four sons [Gen. 46:9], such that the emphasis on *two* sons, specifically, is not coincidental.)

A connection between the sale of Joseph and the death of Judah's two sons is drawn already in the midrash: "Rabbi Yehuda son of Rabbi Simon [son of] Rabbi Ḥanin taught in the name of Rabbi Yoḥanan: A person who does part of a mitzva, but does not complete it, will bury his wife and his sons. From whom do we learn this? From Judah: 'And Judah said to his brothers: "What profit"' – [i.e., he sufficed with saving him from active murder, but left him to die of hunger and thirst while] he should have taken him back to his father. What happened to him [Judah]? He buried his wife and his sons" (Genesis Rabba 85:3, Theodor-Albeck edition, 1034).

שְׁבִי אַלְמָנָה בֵית אָבִיךְ עַד יִגְדַּל שֵׁלָה בְנִי כִּי אָמַר פֶּן יָמוּת גַּם הוּא כְּאֶחָיו, "Judah said to Tamar, his daughter-in-law: 'Remain as a widow in your father's house until Shela, my son, is grown,' for he said [to himself]: Lest he, too, die as his brothers did" (Gen. 38:11).[88]

Later in the same chapter, Judah sinks to the lowest moral point of his life when he visits Tamar, whom he mistakes for a prostitute (Gen. 38:15–18), and when he hears that Tamar is pregnant, he is quick to sentence her to death by burning.

Tamar does not accuse him outright in the public forum; rather, she hints at the facts of the matter to him in a way that would allow him, once again, to evade responsibility: הִוא מוּצֵאת וְהִיא שָׁלְחָה אֶל חָמִיהָ לֵאמֹר לָאִישׁ אֲשֶׁר אֵלֶּה לּוֹ אָנֹכִי הָרָה; וַתֹּאמֶר הַכֶּר נָא לְמִי הַחֹתֶמֶת וְהַפְּתִילִים וְהַמַּטֶּה הָאֵלֶּה, "As she was being brought out and she [had] sent word to her father-in-law, saying: 'The man to whom these belong – I am pregnant by him.' And she said, 'See now to whom this seal and this cloak and this staff belong'" (Gen. 38:25).

At this dramatic moment, Judah reaches a turning point. Though he does not respond to her first statement,[89] the second shakes him out of his complacency. Perhaps it is Tamar's use of the expression "*hakker na*" – "see now" – the same phrase used by Judah and his brothers when they presented their father with Joseph's coat: הַכֶּר נָא הַכְּתֹנֶת בִּנְךָ הִוא אִם לֹא, "See now, is this your son's coat or not?"

88. This may be what the Torah alludes to at the beginning of the chapter: וַתֹּסֶף עוֹד וַתֵּלֶד בֵּן וַתִּקְרָא אֶת שְׁמוֹ שֵׁלָה וְהָיָה בִכְזִיב בְּלִדְתָּהּ אֹתוֹ, "She conceived yet again and she bore a son and she named him Shela, and he was at Keziv when she bore him" (Gen. 38:5). The seemingly redundant mention of the name of the place may hint at the deceit (*kazav*) and illusion that Judah practices in relation to this son. The connection between *keziv* and *shela* is highlighted once again in the story of the Shunnemite woman: At first, when Elisha promises that she will bear a child, she answers: אִישׁ הָאֱלֹהִים אַל תְּכַזֵּב בְּשִׁפְחָתֶךָ, "Do not lie (*tekhazev*) to your handmaid" (II Kings 4:16). Later, when her son dies, she tells him, הֲלֹא אָמַרְתִּי לֹא תַשְׁלֶה אֹתִי, "Did I not say: Do not deceive (*tashleh*) me?" (II Kings 4:28).

89. The first part of the verse is formulated in the past perfect tense – *vehi shalḥa*: וְהִיא שָׁלְחָה אֶל חָמִיהָ לֵאמֹר, "And she had sent word," rather than *vatishlaḥ*, the usual consecutive past. This suggests that she had already sent messengers to Judah with the seal and the cloaks, but he had not yet responded (see commentary of Rabbenu Bahya there).

(Gen. 37:32).[90] Apparently this echo, this allusion, stops Judah in his tracks. And suddenly, the many similarities between what Tamar does to Judah and what the brothers had done to their father draw the attention of discerning readers.

1. Just as Joseph's brothers used a garment (Joseph's special coat) to deceive their father, so does Tamar deceive Judah using a garment – her veil.
2. Just as it occurs with the brothers: וַיִּקְחוּ אֶת כְּתֹנֶת יוֹסֵף וַיִּשְׁחֲטוּ שְׂעִיר עִזִּים וַיִּטְבְּלוּ אֶת הַכֻּתֹּנֶת בַּדָּם. וַיְשַׁלְּחוּ אֶת כְּתֹנֶת הַפַּסִּים, "And they took Joseph's coat and they slaughtered a goat kid (*se'ir izim*) and dipped the coat into its blood. And they sent (*vayeshalleḥu*) the coat" (Gen. 37:31–32) – so Yehuda proposes to Tamar, אָנֹכִי אֲשַׁלַּח גְּדִי עִזִּים, "I will send (*ashallaḥ*) a goat kid from the flock (*gedi izim*)" (Gen. 38:17).[91]
3. Just as Judah preferred that the brothers adopt a course of action that would not necessitate the "covering" of blood – מַה בֶּצַע כִּי נַהֲרֹג אֶת אָחִינוּ וְכִסִּינוּ אֶת דָּמוֹ, "What profit is there if we kill our brother and cover (*vekhisinu*) his blood?" (Gen. 37:26) – he is misled by Tamar in a comparable way: וַתְּכַס בַּצָּעִיף...וַיַּחְשְׁבֶהָ לְזוֹנָה כִּי כִסְּתָה פָּנֶיהָ, "She covered herself (*vatekhas*) with a veil...and he thought her a prostitute, for she covered (*khista*) her face" (Gen. 38:15).

Thus, the Torah clearly connects the two narratives, which implicitly alludes to their thematic connection. Judah is forced to wrestle with himself and ultimately acknowledge his misdeeds, despite the shame that

---

90. It should be noted that these are the only two instances in Tanakh where this expression occurs. The Sages comment on the connection between the two narratives and its effect on Judah: "He sought to deny it, but she said to him, 'See now' your Creator: They belong to you and your Creator. 'See now' to whom the signet belongs. Rabbi Yoḥanan taught: God said to Judah, You said to your father, 'See now'; by your life, Tamar now tells you, 'See now'" (Genesis Rabba, Vilna edition, 85:25).
91. This too is noted by the Sages: "God said to Judah: You deceived your father with garments of the goat; by your life, Tamar will deceive you with garments of a goat" (Genesis Rabba 85:9, Theodor-Albeck edition, 1043).

doing so may entail,[92] thanks to the full weight of responsibility that Tamar places upon him even as she refuses to accuse him openly. Indeed, Judah assumes responsibility for his actions for the first time since the beginning of the story: he not only acknowledges that Tamar did not prostitute herself, but also takes responsibility for his neglect of her over the course of so many years: וַיַּכֵּר יְהוּדָה וַיֹּאמֶר צָדְקָה מִמֶּנִּי כִּי עַל כֵּן לֹא נְתַתִּיהָ לְשֵׁלָה בְנִי, "And Judah recognized, and he said, 'She has been more righteous than I, for I did not give her to Shela, my son'" (Gen. 38:26). Just as Jacob had "recognized" his son's bloodstained cloak, so too did Judah "recognize" his own fault.[93] The story ends with the birth of Peretz and Zerah; Peretz is ultimately the progenitor of the royal dynasty of the House of David.

Moreover, Judah goes on to assume responsibility for all that happens to his brothers in Egypt. His entire personality has changed – from the moment he acknowledged his poor conduct regarding Tamar. Prior to that point he evaded all responsibility for his own actions, but from the moment of that wake-up call by Tamar, he assumes moral responsibility even for that which he personally did not do:

> וַיֹּאמֶר יְהוּדָה מַה נֹּאמַר לַאדֹנִי מַה נְּדַבֵּר וּמַה נִּצְטַדָּק הָאֱלֹהִים מָצָא אֶת עֲוֹן עֲבָדֶיךָ הִנֶּנּוּ עֲבָדִים לַאדֹנִי גַּם אֲנַחְנוּ גַּם אֲשֶׁר נִמְצָא הַגָּבִיעַ בְּיָדוֹ.
>
> Judah said, "What shall we say to my lord; what shall we speak and how shall we justify ourselves? God has found the transgression of your servants; behold, we are servants to my lord – both we and him with whom the goblet was found." (Gen. 44:16)

The climax of his transformation comes, of course, when he does what he can to protect his father from additional pain, especially given that he

92. As Judah himself had previously said: תִּקַּח לָהּ פֶּן נִהְיֶה לָבוּז הִנֵּה שָׁלַחְתִּי הַגְּדִי הַזֶּה וְאַתָּה לֹא מְצָאתָהּ, "Let her take it herself, lest we be shamed; behold, I sent this kid, but you have not found her" (Gen. 38:23).

93. Although, at first glance, the intention of the verse would seem to be that Judah recognized the belongings as his own, the absence of a direct object from the phrase "Judah recognized" indicates that the recognition taking place was on a deeper, more profound level (in contrast to Gen. 37:33, where the verse merely says of Jacob, "He recognized it").

himself was responsible for the first terrible blow to Jacob.[94] He expresses his readiness to take the place of Benjamin, the only other son of Rachel, and remain a slave in Egypt in his stead. Ultimately, this narrative teaches the importance of taking responsibility, of the possibility of repair, the power of repentance, and the danger of evading responsibility by misleading others. That profound understanding of what it means to take responsibility, grounded in the act of taking responsibility, explains why Judah and his descendants are blessed by Jacob to rule among the people of Israel: לֹא יָסוּר שֵׁבֶט מִיהוּדָה וּמְחֹקֵק מִבֵּין רַגְלָיו, "The staff shall not depart from Judah, nor the lawmaker from among his offspring" (Gen. 49:10). R. Akiva sums up the plain sense of this verse as follows: "Why was Judah granted royalty? Because he acknowledged [his guilt] concerning Tamar."[95]

This literary analysis emerges easily from a review of the verses and the way various midrashim approach this episode. Yet some biblical critics turn a blind eye to the important lessons this narrative contains, so entrenched are they in the assumption that biblical narrative is agenda-driven, created by people promoting their own views by disseminating them. They ignore the possibility that this profound and complex story was written in order to convey those messages about responsibility and kingship.

Moreover, the biblical critics can be queried on their own terms, with regard to their interpretation of this narrative. As background, note scholars generally regard the "J" source as originating in documents composed in the kingdom of Judah, while the "E" source originates from those composed in the kingdom of Israel.[96] Thus, the documents tend to reveal the interests of the polities to which they are loyal. Friedman theorizes that the authors of the E documents may be Levitical priests from Shiloh, who emphasize the role of Moses, their presumed ancestor. The authors of the J documents, by contrast, express support for the Judahite origins

94. There is a linguistic connection between chapter 38 and Judah's declaration in which he takes responsibility for Benjamin: the root A-R-V (guarantor, or pledge) appears only five times in the entire Torah – in chapter 38, the word "pledge" (*eravon*) appears three times (in verses 17, 18, and 20), and twice the Torah mentions that Judah is a guarantor (*arev*) for Benjamin (Gen. 43:9; 44:32).

95. Tosefta Berakhot 4:18, Lieberman edition, 23.

96. See Richard Elliot Friedman, *Who Wrote the Bible* (New York, 1987), 62–67, 85–88.

of the house of David.[97] The narrative of Judah and Tamar, however, uses the name HVYH and is therefore assigned to the J documents[98] – a direct contradiction to the critics' assumptions that the Judah and Tamar narrative disqualifies Judah from a leading role in history.[99]

Some scholars have argued that, since the end of the episode depicts Judah in a positive light, this narrative should be viewed as supportive of Judah[100] – but that suggestion smacks of "too little, too late," a most unsatisfactory resolution of the problem. Judah is portrayed as neglecting his family, withholding levirate marriage from his daughter-in-law via false excuses, and abandoning her to a bitter fate. One is hard pressed to find the superiority of the tribe of Judah in this text, no matter how much one might want to write support for the royal house of David. Would someone seeking to glorify Judah really describe him as mistaking his daughter-in-law for a harlot, and engaging in relations with her himself?

Indeed, those scholars who are not blindly committed to the pro-Judah view might suggest a completely different interpretation. Thus, for example, Y. Zakovitch writes:

---

97. Ibid., 70–80.

98. Verses 7–10 mention *shem Hashem* (the name of God attributed to the J source) three times.

99. Friedman pays no attention to this episode in his book, although (or perhaps because) it is highly problematic in light of his theory.

100. See Y. Amit, "Hidden Polemics in the Story of Judah and Tamar," in *A Critical Engagement: Essays on the Hebrew Bible in Honour of J. Cheryl Exum,* D. Clines and E. van Wolde, eds. (Sheffield, 2011), 1–20. Amit's view raises many questions. Proceeding from the assumption that the narrative does indeed mean to convey support for the house of Judah – and thus, naturally, for the royal house of David – she is left only with the question of why David himself is not mentioned in the text(!). Amit argues that the Torah is not devoid of anachronism – as evidenced in the unit of Layish and Dan, as discussed in a previous chapter. This argument is, of course, baseless, since even according to those who maintain that the phenomenon of anachronism does exist in Tanakh, it is certainly not deliberate; at most, it testifies to a lack of attention on the part of the writer. The idea that the Torah, which is clearly oriented toward the nation of Israel on the verge of entering the land, could make explicit mention of someone who would live hundreds of years later is simply untenable, regardless of one's religious or ideological position.

> The story of Judah and Tamar is an anti-Judah narrative; it is a narrative that puts Judah – patriarch of the tribe, patriarch of the house of David – to shame. Whoever placed chapter 38 at the heart of the story of Joseph, after chapter 37, sought to diminish Judah's stature.[101]

Granted, Zakovitch's understanding begs the opposite question: why would someone who seeks to embarrass Judah include the narrative's conclusion, in which the biblical figure ultimately acknowledges his misdeeds, despite the personal hardship that doing so entails and when he could easily have avoided admitting his guilt? More, how is one to explain Judah's "reward," the birth of sons, let alone his eventual standing as the progenitor of the Davidic dynasty that comes about as a result of this story?

To be sure, other scholars read the story as pointing toward a completely different lesson. Y. Amit argues that the central theme of the story is the controversy surrounding foreign women – a prominent issue during the Persian (early Second Temple) period.[102] According to her theory, Tamar was a Canaanite who accepted upon herself the customs of Judah's family, and thereby the text justifies marriage with foreign – even Canaanite – women. This theory is problematic from the very outset, however, first and foremost because the text does not mention Tamar's Canaanite origins; rather, it ignores the issue of her lineage altogether. From a literary point of view, Amit's interpretation warrants some explicit mention of the message regarding foreign women among all the complicated details of Judah's exploits. The fact that none is present in the text calls her understanding into question.

This example illustrates the pitfall of those seeking the bias in biblical narratives: their searches themselves may reflect the scholars' own biases and demonstrate the risk of misunderstanding and misrepresenting the meaning of a given story and its messages. The

---

101. Y. Zakovitch, *Mikraot BeEretz HaMarot* (Tel Aviv, 1995), 55. See also, at greater length, Y. Zakovitch and A. Shinan, *Maaseh Yehuda VeTamar* (Jerusalem, 1992), 219–20.

102. See note 100 above.

episode of Judah and Tamar conveys important, objective messages – and an objective search for bias in this story leads nowhere, as the extreme differences between the respective conclusions of those undertaking the search demonstrate. Indeed, the insistence on the presence of bias in Tanakh is a mistake not only with regard to the interpretation of a given passage, but also because doing so may lead to ignoring the narrative's messages, to the degree that Bible study loses all independent value.

While our argument has been based on only one narrative and its interpretations, the same idea arises from the most cursory familiarity with Tanakh as a whole. Anyone who reads the Tanakh cannot fail to notice that it shows no favoritism. For example, in contrast to the attention paid to the outstanding successes of rulers in ancient cultures, biblical characters – including the leaders – are always complex and never free from criticism. Consider the forefathers (the "she is my sister" episodes; Jacob's theft of the birthright from Esau); the stories of the fathers of the tribes (the slaughter of Shekhem, the sale of Joseph); Moses (hitting the rock at the waters of Meribah); and, of course, the complex picture and description of the royal house of David – these events all criticize the biblical figures rather than engage in idealization of them. Surely, these episodes are recounted in a way that nullifies any concern of vested interest on the part of the writer. For that matter, would any nation in the world invent a past that involved slavery and hard labor, as the story of the Exodus does? Would anyone writing about a contemporaneous monarchy criticize the king's behavior as sharply as the book of Samuel rebukes King David?[103]

> Why did this author invent the story of David and Bathsheba? Why did he seek to present David, at the beginning of his career, as a robber living off "protection money"? Why, as part of his

103. Even Friedman (*Who Wrote the Bible*) notes that the writing describing the kingdom of David, in the book of Samuel, is "remarkable because it openly criticizes its heroes, a practice that is all but unknown among ancient Near Eastern kings" (p. 39). However, he makes no attempt to explain this most unusual phenomenon, nor does he draw any conclusions from it.

> imaginary tale, does he attribute the building of the Temple not to the founder of the dynasty, David, but rather to Solomon? All of this stands in complete contrast to what we would expect, considering the norms of the Ancient East.... Why did he invent a story about Saul, the king chosen by God before David, despite the theological difficulties that this story raises? The invention of these stories makes no sense.[104]

By the same token, no entity or group ever had a real vested interest in the dissemination of the Torah. For all that the *kohanim* and *leviim*, for example, receive "priestly gifts" and serve in important positions, their involvement is not particularly influential, given that they have no inheritance in the land.[105] More sharply, the very notion of a monarchy for Israel is set forth in the Torah only with strict limitations, which no king would have any interest in publicizing (Deut. 17).

It would seem, then, that assertions of bias in Tanakh are themselves suspect, and likely themselves emerge from biased motives.

---

104. Y. Hoffman, "Historia, Mitos U'Politika," in Y. L. Levine and A. Mazar, eds., *HaPulmus Al HaEmet HaHistorit BaMikra* (Jerusalem, 2001), 31–32.

105. It is interesting to note the literary manner in which the Torah emphasizes the difference between *kohanim* in Israel and the priests of other nations, in this regard. In describing Yosef's regime in Egypt during the years of famine, the Torah states: רַק אַדְמַת הַכֹּהֲנִים לֹא קָנָה כִּי חֹק לַכֹּהֲנִים מֵאֵת פַּרְעֹה וְאָכְלוּ אֶת חֻקָּם לָהֶם פַּרְעֹה **עַל כֵּן** לֹא מָכְרוּ אֶת אַדְמָתָם אֲשֶׁר נָתַן, "Only the land of the priests he did not buy, *for* the priests had a portion assigned to them by Pharaoh, and they ate their portion which Pharaoh gave to them; *therefore* they did not sell their lands" (Gen. 47:22). In other words, the fact that they received their food directly from the king was an expression of their status – and for this reason they were not required to sell their inheritance, in contrast to the rest of Egypt. The Torah uses similar language in describing the status of the tribe of Levi – but with precisely the opposite meaning: **כִּי** אֶת מַעְשַׂר בְּנֵי יִשְׂרָאֵל אֲשֶׁר יָרִימוּ לַה׳ תְּרוּמָה נָתַתִּי לַלְוִיִּם לְנַחֲלָה **עַל כֵּן** אָמַרְתִּי לָהֶם בְּתוֹךְ בְּנֵי יִשְׂרָאֵל לֹא יִנְחֲלוּ נַחֲלָה, "For the tithes of the Children of Israel, which they offer as a gift to God, I have given to the Levites to inherit; *therefore* I have said to them, among the Children of Israel they shall receive no inheritance" (Num. 18:24). It is specifically because the Levites receive their food from God that they receive no inheritance in the land, for God's servants must engage in their labor for the sake of heaven, with no personal interest.

SUMMARY

The Torah contains many instances of duplication and contradiction. The general approach throughout the generations was to address these instances individually and locally, without attending to the more general question of why these phenomena exist and why the Torah was written in this way. Then, biblical scholars discovered that many of the contradictions are systematic, and arrived at the "documentary hypothesis," wherein the duplications and contradictions arise from the premise that the "single work" of the Torah is made up of four main documents, each composed in a different period and possessing its own characteristics. Yet the documentary hypothesis poses some difficulties as well, on both the historical and the literary levels, and biblical scholars of the last generation have expressed growing reservations toward this hypothesis in its classic form.

At the same time, the documentary hypothesis advanced the study and understanding of the Torah, in recognizing that the Torah itself was written in such a way as to suggest multiple perspectives. This observation gave rise to the "aspects approach," developed by Rabbi Mordekhai Breuer, which maintains that complex and nuanced messages arise specifically from the juxtapositions and contradictions, to the extent that there is no need to resolve every contradiction on its own terms upon a first reading.

Finally, we noted the problematic interpretations ensuing from the efforts of biblical scholars trying to detect political bias in the various narratives and units of the Torah, an approach that developed in the wake of the documentary hypothesis. Our review of one narrative unit showed this view to be untenable and led to the conclusion that the Tanakh is a unique and unprecedented work insofar as it shows no favoritism toward anyone.

Chapter 4

Authorship of the Books of the Prophets and Writings

"AND WHO WROTE THEM?"

In contrast to the complexity surrounding the question of the Torah's authorship, as discussed in previous chapters, the authorship issues are somewhat clearer when it comes to the Prophets (*Nevi'im*) and Writings (*Ketuvim*). Indeed, some books, especially among the Later Prophets, are written in the first person by the prophet himself, apart from some introductory verses that indicate a measure of editorial activity. In those cases, the matter is rather straightforward. Some other books, such as the Early Prophets, share the complications of the Five Books of the Torah – for they too are written in the third person, with no direct indication of the author's identity in the text.

The Sages address the question of the authorship of these books, and are in agreement concerning most of them:

> And who wrote them?
> Moses wrote his book and the episode of Baalam,[1] and Job.

1. The commentators question the need to specify the story of Balaam, since it is part of "Moses's book." Rashi notes that this comes to teach that Moses included this

> Joshua wrote his book and eight verses [at the end] of the Torah. Samuel wrote his book, and [the books of] Judges and Ruth. David wrote Psalms, including the contribution of ten elders.... Jeremiah wrote his book and the book of Kings and Lamentations. Hezekiah and his companions wrote Isaiah, Proverbs,[2] Song of Songs, and Ecclesiastes.
>
> The Men of the Great Assembly wrote [the book of] Ezekiel and the Twelve [Minor Prophets], Daniel, and the Scroll of Esther. Ezra wrote his book and the genealogy of Chronicles up to himself (or "up to *lo*").[3] (Bava Batra 14b–15a)

---

episode "even though it did not serve any purpose of Moses, or his teaching, or the record of his actions." The Ritva raises a different possibility: "Some say that this does not refer to the story of Balaam that is recorded in the Torah, for that was written by God, just like all the rest of the Torah. Rather, it is a document in its own right, which Moses wrote in greater details, and it was in their [the Sages'] possession." Rabbi Menahem Azariah (Immanuel) da Fano (1548–1620) in his *Asarah Maamarot* (*Maamar Ḥakor Din*, sec. 8, ch. 8) was of the opinion that this refers to a unit that appears in Joshua 13:15–33, dealing with Moses's apportioning of land to tribes on the eastern bank of the Jordan River, and reminding them of their victory over Midian and Balaam. See A. J. Heschel, *Heavenly Torah as Refracted through the Generations*, 654–56.

2. The basis for the attribution of Proverbs to Hezekiah is, of course, the verse, גַּם אֵלֶּה מִשְׁלֵי שְׁלֹמֹה אֲשֶׁר הֶעְתִּיקוּ אַנְשֵׁי חִזְקִיָּה מֶלֶךְ יְהוּדָה, "These, too, are the proverbs of Solomon which were copied by the men of Hezekiah, king of Judah" (Prov. 25:1).
3. The commentators are divided as to the meaning of these closing words. Rashi explains, "up until his own lineage," but the later commentators point out that Ezra is not mentioned anywhere in Chronicles. The Maharsha proposes that the reference is to Ezra's father, Seraya ben Azarya (Ezra 7:1), who is mentioned in I Chronicles 5:40. Rabbenu Hananel writes that what the Sages mean is that he wrote up until the word "*lo*" (לוֹ) in the verse, וְלוֹ אַחִים בְּנֵי יְהוֹשָׁפָט עֲזַרְיָה וִיחִיאֵל וּזְכַרְיָהוּ וַעֲזַרְיָהוּ וּמִיכָאֵל וּשְׁפַטְיָהוּ כָּל אֵלֶּה בְּנֵי יְהוֹשָׁפָט מֶלֶךְ יִשְׂרָאֵל, "And he had (*velo*) brothers, the sons of Jehoshaphat – Azarya and Yehiel and Zekharyahu and Azaryahu and Mikhael and Shefatyahu; all of these were the sons of Jehoshaphat, king of Israel" (II Chr. 21:2). This would suggest that Ezra concluded his writing with the end of the life of King Jehoshaphat. However, this interpretation is difficult to accept, since it is not clear why Ezra would end his account specifically at this point. (Interestingly, the Ritva seems to have understood that the individual referred to in the verse as Azaryahu was actually Ezra himself!) In addition, as *Tosafot* point out (ad loc.), why would the Sages have written "until *lo*" if the word as it appears in the verse is actually "*velo*"? Maharshal takes a completely different view of the Gemara here.

This passage suggests that there are two categories of authorship: a single author, where a prophet is credited with writing the book, such as Jeremiah and Ezra; and multiple authors of works that were compiled, edited, and put into their final form at a later date than the events or prophets they describe. Thus, Jeremiah is identified as the redactor of Kings, Hezekiah and his companions as the redactors of Isaiah, and the wisdom literature is attributed to Solomon, while the Men of the Great Assembly (roughly 530–500 BCE) are considered to be the redactors of the later books of the Tanakh.

Jeremiah is the only one of the later prophets to whom the Sages attribute the authorship of the book named after him, presumably because of the extensive detail in the documentation of his prophecies, as set forth in chapter 36 of his book. This chapter records the divine command: קַח לְךָ מְגִלַּת סֵפֶר וְכָתַבְתָּ אֵלֶיהָ אֵת כָּל הַדְּבָרִים אֲשֶׁר דִּבַּרְתִּי אֵלֶיךָ עַל יִשְׂרָאֵל וְעַל יְהוּדָה וְעַל כָּל הַגּוֹיִם מִיּוֹם דִּבַּרְתִּי אֵלֶיךָ מִימֵי יֹאשִׁיָּהוּ וְעַד הַיּוֹם הַזֶּה, "Take a scroll and write in it all the words which I have spoken to you concerning Israel, and concerning Judah, and concerning all the nations, from the day I spoke to you in the days of Josiah, until this day" (Jer. 36:2). It also describes its fulfillment, in Jeremiah's words to Baruch ben Nerya (Jer. 36:4), and the detailed description by Baruch himself: וְאֶת בָּרוּךְ שָׁאֲלוּ לֵאמֹר הַגֶּד נָא לָנוּ אֵיךְ כָּתַבְתָּ אֶת כָּל הַדְּבָרִים הָאֵלֶּה מִפִּיו. וַיֹּאמֶר לָהֶם בָּרוּךְ מִפִּיו יִקְרָא אֵלַי אֵת כָּל הַדְּבָרִים הָאֵלֶּה וַאֲנִי כֹּתֵב עַל הַסֵּפֶר בַּדְּיוֹ, "They asked Baruch, saying, 'Tell us now: How did you write all of these words from his mouth?' And Baruch said to them, 'He dictated all these words to me, and I wrote them with ink, in the book'" (Jer. 36:17–18).

The chapter ends with testimony to that effect:

> וְיִרְמְיָהוּ לָקַח מְגִלָּה אַחֶרֶת וַיִּתְּנָהּ אֶל בָּרוּךְ בֶּן נֵרִיָּהוּ הַסֹּפֵר וַיִּכְתֹּב עָלֶיהָ מִפִּי יִרְמְיָהוּ אֵת כָּל דִּבְרֵי הַסֵּפֶר אֲשֶׁר שָׂרַף יְהוֹיָקִים מֶלֶךְ יְהוּדָה בָּאֵשׁ וְעוֹד נוֹסַף עֲלֵיהֶם דְּבָרִים רַבִּים כָּהֵמָּה.

He maintains that the words should not be read as "*ad* (until) *lo*," but rather "*ed* (a witness) to him" – i.e., "evidence for his own lineage in the book of Ezra." He goes on to propose that the words of the Gemara that we will quote below, testifying that the end of the book was written by Nehemiah, actually refer to the book of Ezra, and not Chronicles.

> Then Jeremiah took another scroll, and gave it to Baruch, the scribe, the son of Neriyahu; and he wrote in it from the mouth of Jeremiah all the words of the book that Jehoiakim, king of Judah, had burned in the fire, as well as many other words in the same spirit. (Jer. 36:32)

The very fact of this description implies that the other prophets did not record their prophecies, leaving the Sages to conclude that their works were redacted in a subsequent era.

The *baraita* in Bava Batra continues with the clarification of several points:

> "Ezra wrote his book and the genealogy of Chronicles until *lo*" – and who completed it? Nehemiah, son of Hakhalia.
>
> "Joshua wrote his book" – but the text says, "Joshua bin Nun, God's servant, died" (Josh. 24:29)! This was completed by Pinhas.
>
> "Samuel wrote his book" – but the text says, "Samuel died" (I Sam. 28:3)! This was completed by Gad, the visionary, and Nathan the prophet.[4]

In other words, the books of Joshua, Samuel, and Chronicles were written by more than one prophet – a different prophet stepped in to complete what the primary prophet had written, especially for the sake of recounting the death of that primary prophet for whom the book is named. Granted, the Talmud does not explain why it assumes that the books of Joshua and Samuel were completed by others, rather than that they wrote their own books in their entirety through prophecy, for example, as with Moses.

Elsewhere, the Sages make additional observations concerning the authorship of these books. Some opinions maintain that, like the

4. This final statement would seem to be based on the penultimate verse of I Chronicles (29:29): וְדִבְרֵי דָּוִיד הַמֶּלֶךְ הָרִאשֹׁנִים וְהָאַחֲרֹנִים הִנָּם כְּתוּבִים עַל דִּבְרֵי שְׁמוּאֵל הָרֹאֶה וְעַל דִּבְרֵי נָתָן הַנָּבִיא וְעַל דִּבְרֵי גָּד הַחֹזֶה, "The acts of King David, from beginning to end, are written in the book of Samuel the seer, and in the book of Nathan the prophet, and in the book of Gad the visionary."

books of Joshua and Samuel, the book of Jeremiah was not written entirely by the eponymous prophet. Even the plain sense of the text seems to suggest that Jeremiah wrote the book of Jeremiah only up to a certain point:

> Up to what point is Jeremiah's prophecy recorded? R. Yaakov and R. Abba disagree with R. Elazar and R. Yoḥanan. One opinion says, "Until, 'He that scattered Israel will gather them up'" (Jer. 31:9), while the other says, "Until, 'There is hope for your future,' says God, 'and your children will return to their border'" (Jer. 31:16).[5]

Another book with disputed authorship going as far back as the Talmud is the book of Job. The *baraita* in Bava Batra attributes the work to Moses, but the talmudic discussion includes other opinions as to when the book was written; the various views place the composition of this work during the period of the Judges, the time of Ahasuerus, or upon the return from the Babylonian exile in 539 BCE.

Clearly, the nature of the authorship of the books of the Prophets is a less sensitive topic than that of the Torah. With regard to the Torah, very few medieval commentators mention later addition of Torah verses – and when they do, their references sometimes appear only by way of allusion. Those same commentators have no objection to stating openly that a given verse of the Prophets or the Writings was added by a redactor. Indeed, the Talmud itself establishes that most of these books had redactors who well could have added clarifications as needed – just as any faithful editor would do.

Moreover, the commentators also felt free to offer additional possibilities as to the identities of the various authors. Of particular note is the view of Abrabanel. In his introduction to the Early Prophets, he argues against Bava Batra's identification of the authors of these books, among others, because the phrase "to this very day" appears therein, implying that they were written at a later time. Regarding the book of Joshua, Abrabanel writes:

---

5. Lamentations Rabba, *Petiḥta* 34, Buber edition, 20. (The midrash is also cited in *Yalkut Shimoni*, Jer. 281.)

> Upon examining the verses, I perceived that the view maintaining that Joshua wrote his book is extremely unlikely – not only because the end of the text notes that "Joshua died" (and this issue in fact gives rise to the discussion in the Gemara), but also because of other places in the text which indicate that they were not written by Joshua. About setting up the stones in the Jordan River, the text says, וַיִּהְיוּ שָׁם עַד הַיּוֹם הַזֶּה, "And they remained there to this very day" (Josh. 4:9)....[6] If Joshua wrote all of this, how could he say, "to this very day"? For he wrote close to the time of the events, while the expression "to this very day" necessarily implies that it was written a long time after this happened. Likewise we find, concerning the inheritance of the tribe of Dan, that the text specifies, וַיֵּצֵא גְבוּל בְּנֵי דָן מֵהֶם וַיַּעֲלוּ בְנֵי דָן וַיִּלָּחֲמוּ עִם לֶשֶׁם, "And the border of Dan was too small for them, so the children of Dan went up to fight against Leshem" (Josh. 19:47) – but we know that this [fight] took place at the time of the statue of Micah, at the end of the period of the Judges. This is decisive evidence that the text could only have been written many years after Joshua's death, and hence Joshua could not have written it.... And on the basis of all of this, I conclude that Joshua did not write his book; rather, Samuel the prophet wrote his book [Joshua], as well as the book of Judges.... And do not be surprised that I differ in this matter from the view of the Sages, for even in the Gemara, the Sages are not unanimous in this regard, and there are dissenting opinions as to whether it was Moses who wrote the book of Job, and whether Joshua wrote the final eight verses of the Torah. And since the Sages themselves question the authorship in some cases, it is not so far-fetched for me, too, to propose a more logical explanation in keeping with the verses and their sense.

Abrabanel proves, from the various disagreements that are apparent already in *Ḥazal*'s discussion, that the *baraita* is not based on a longstanding tradition, but rather on logical deduction from a review of the verses of the text. He concludes, therefore, that identifying the authors of the

6. Here Abrabanel adds other instances in Joshua where the same expression appears.

books of Tanakh must be decided on the basis of the content of texts themselves. Because the book of Joshua, for example, includes verses that, demonstrably, could not have been written by Joshua himself,[7] Abrabanel proposes that it was written by Samuel, presumably because the Sages had named him as the author of the book of Judges. The exegete also offers a more moderate alternative interpretation, in the idea that the book underwent later redaction by some other later figure, perhaps Samuel or Jeremiah: "If you wish to say that Joshua wrote his book, as the Sages maintain, then we must posit that Jeremiah, or Samuel, gathered these narratives and put them together into a book, making additions, as they saw fit with their divine inspiration."

Abrabanel is not the first to take this approach; Rashi understands the verses that describe the conquest of Kiryat Arba and Kiryat Sefer (Josh. 15:13–19) to have been written later than the time of Joshua – at the start of the book of Judges (1:10–15): "after the death of Joshua, for during Joshua's time, Hebron had not yet been conquered, as the book of Judges recounts, and the matter is noted here only because of the division of the land." Rashi and Radak likewise maintain that the verse Abrabanel cites, mentioning the battle of the children of Dan at Leshem, refers to an event that occurred during the period of the Judges, and is thus recorded there.

A similar phenomenon occurs in the book of Samuel. Here too the expression "to this very day" appears in several places,[8] and here too it testifies to a distance from the time of the events. This distance of time is especially apparent in the verse: לְפָנִים בְּיִשְׂרָאֵל כֹּה אָמַר הָאִישׁ בְּלֶכְתּוֹ לִדְרוֹשׁ אֱלֹהִים לְכוּ וְנֵלְכָה עַד הָרֹאֶה כִּי לַנָּבִיא הַיּוֹם יִקָּרֵא לְפָנִים הָרֹאֶה, "In early times (*lefanim*) in Israel, a person who went to inquire of God would say, 'Come and let us go to the seer' – for the prophet of our days was previously called a 'seer' (*ro'eh*)" (I Sam. 9:9). The writer of this verse

7. In addition to the verses cited by Abrabanel, one might add: וַיָּשָׁב יְהוֹשֻׁעַ בָּעֵת הַהִיא וַיִּלְכֹּד אֶת חָצוֹר וְאֶת מַלְכָּהּ הִכָּה בֶחָרֶב כִּי חָצוֹר לְפָנִים הִיא רֹאשׁ כָּל הַמַּמְלָכוֹת הָאֵלֶּה, "And Joshua turned back at that time and he captured Hazor, and he killed its king by the sword, for Hazor had previously been the chief of all of these kingdoms" (Josh. 11:10). This suggests that the redactor treats the preeminence of Hazor as a fact that was once well known in the past, but would not be obvious to contemporary readers.

8. See I Sam. 5:5; 6:18; 27:6; 30:25; II Sam. 4:3; 6:8; 18:18.

found it necessary to explain Saul's use of the word "seer" in reference to the prophet, since the word was already obsolete at the time of the writing. Rabbi Yosef Kara notes this point in his commentary on this verse:[9]

> A person who would be referred to in that generation as a "*navi*" (prophet), would in previous generations have been called a "*ro'eh*" (seer). In other words, when this book was written, the seer was once again referred to as a "*navi*," because this book was not written in the time of Samuel.... And our Sages, of blessed memory, stated that Samuel wrote the book. He Who illuminates the world turns darkness into light, and turns a twisted path into a straight road.

The same approach is adopted by Abrabanel, and he offers a similar explanation:

> What appears correct to me in this matter is that Samuel, Nathan, and Gad all wrote their works individually – each writing what happened during his own lifetime – and all of these testimonies were gathered together by Jeremiah the prophet, and he joined them together into a single book. For if this was not so, who gathered these texts, which were composed by different people? For the text does not record that the prophets wrote their testimonies consecutively; rather, each wrote a book in his own right. It seems, then, that when Jeremiah sought to write the book of Kings, he knew that the book of Samuel was proximate to it, and he gathered the testimonies of the prophets mentioned in the book – and there is no doubt that he also added comments of clarification, as he saw fit. This explains the expression "to this very day," and this explains the verse, "In early times in Israel."

Opinions are similarly divided concerning the authorship of Psalms. In the *baraita* in Bava Batra quoted above, the Sages maintain that King David wrote the book "through [or, incorporating] ten elders," and the

9. Chapter 8 examines Rabbi Kara and his exegetical approach in detail.

list includes ten individuals, some of whom lived earlier than David, while others were his contemporaries: "Adam, and Melchizedek, and Abraham, and Moses, and Heiman, and Yedutun, and Asaf, and the three sons of Korah." Rashi understands David to have been not only the author of many of the psalms, but also the redactor of the book as a whole, collating psalms that had been uttered by others – some in previous generations, some in his own. He comments: "He [David] wrote the things which these elders had said, for they lived before him, and some lived in his own period."

The midrash on Song of Songs cites other opinions:

> Ten people uttered the book of Psalms: Adam, Abraham, Moses, David, Solomon – concerning these five there is no argument. Concerning the other five there is disagreement between Rav and R. Yoḥanan. Rav counts Asaf, Heiman, [and] Yedutun individually, and the three sons of Korah as one, and Ezra. R. Yohanan counts Asaf and Heiman and Yedutun as one, and the three sons of Korah individually, and Ezra.[10]

This midrash stipulates not that David wrote what ten people had said, but rather that "ten people uttered the book of Psalms," and David is listed as one of them, among five whose authorship is agreed upon unanimously. The midrash also counts Ezra among the authors of psalms – which means that some psalms that were included in the book of Psalms were composed after the time of David. The text itself appears to bear out this dating, since a number of psalms describe exile and destruction, the most famous of them being chapter 137, "By the Rivers of Babylon."[11]

Another opinion concerning the authorship of Psalms appears in the commentary of Rabbi Saadia Gaon (882–942), which attributes

10. Song of Songs Rabba, *parasha* 4, 1, 4.
11. Rashbam adopts this approach in his commentary on Psalms, which was only recently discovered, and parts of which were published by A. Mondshein in his article, "Al Gilui HaPerush 'HaAvud' Shel Rashbam LeSefer Tehillim," *Tarbiz* 79, 1 (5770–5771/2010–2011): 91–141. Rashbam argues that some of the "songs of ascent" (*shirei hamaalot*), such as chapters 120 and 123, were composed in Babylonian exile, or at the beginning of the Second Temple period (see there, 130, 133).

the entire work to David, composed through prophecy, and awarding no authorship status to the ten elders mentioned in Bava Batra:

> The entire book is a prophecy that was prophesied by David, just as the entire Jewish people unanimously refers to it as the "songs of David"; likewise, in many sources it is attributed to him.... And even though one might think that it also contains prophecies or psalms of others, in addition to David – such as Asaf, and Heiman, and Yedutun, and Eitan, and Moses the man of God, and others – one must know that it is not so. Rather there is nothing in it that was not of David.... And since this is clear, Yedutun is mentioned along with David in some places only to tell us that that psalm was a prophecy of David, yet named after Yedutun; Yedutun is a partner together with Asaf, and the sons of Korah, and Heiman – all the participants in the name of that psalm declare it and sing it together. But the [seventieth] psalm, "A prayer unto Moses the man of God," is a song that was conveyed to the sons of Moses who lived at the time of David, in order that they could sing it.[12]

While this opinion is certainly representative of and integral to a broader philosophical context,[13] it is clear that Rabbi Saadia Gaon did not regard the view presented in Bava Batra as binding.

These commentators leave us with the impression that the description in Bava Batra was not accepted unanimously, and that authorities – both in the times of the talmudic Sages and in the medieval period – differed in their understanding of the authorship of these books. In any event, our subsequent discussion will be conducted on the basis of the text itself, and will attempt to address in depth the questions surrounding the redaction of the various books.

12. R. Saadia Gaon's introduction to his *Commentary on the Book of Psalms*, Kapah edition, 28–29.
13. As part of his dispute with the Karaites. See U. Simon, *Four Approaches to the Book of Psalms, from R. Saadia Gaon to Abraham Ibn Ezra*, transl. L. Schram (Albany, 1991), 5–11.

THE BOOK OF ISAIAH

The book of Isaiah is a focal issue in the discussion of the authorship of the books of Tanakh. The Sages attribute the authorship of Isaiah to Hezekiah and his colleagues – suggesting early on that Isaiah was not the sole author of the work that bears his name.

In recent years, the question of the authorship of Isaiah has been the subject of wide-ranging debate. Many claim that the second half of the book, from chapter 40 onwards, was not written by Isaiah but rather by another prophet who lived long after the destruction of the Temple, and who describes a reality very different from the one depicted in the first part (the first half describes events from the eighth century BCE, well before the destruction of the Temple in 586 BCE). Let us review the main arguments.

First, the book of Isaiah mentions events in the past tense that had not yet happened. In the first part of the book (chapters 1 to 39), Isaiah addresses a nation that is ruled by the kings of Israel, while in the second part (chapter 40 onwards), he seems to be addressing the nation in exile, with the land and its cities lying in ruin and desolation. On several occasions in the second half, the destruction of the Temple is described as a known, familiar fact, leading the prophet to cry out in supplication and ask God to have mercy on His people in exile:

> אַל תִּקְצֹף ה׳ עַד מְאֹד וְאַל לָעַד תִּזְכֹּר עָוֹן הֵן הַבֶּט נָא עַמְּךָ כֻלָּנוּ. עָרֵי קָדְשְׁךָ הָיוּ מִדְבָּר צִיּוֹן מִדְבָּר הָיָתָה יְרוּשָׁלַם שְׁמָמָה. בֵּית קָדְשֵׁנוּ וְתִפְאַרְתֵּנוּ אֲשֶׁר הִלְלוּךָ אֲבֹתֵינוּ הָיָה לִשְׂרֵפַת אֵשׁ וְכָל מַחֲמַדֵּינוּ הָיָה לְחָרְבָּה. הַעַל אֵלֶּה תִתְאַפַּק ה׳ תֶּחֱשֶׁה וּתְעַנֵּנוּ עַד מְאֹד.
>
> Do not be exceedingly angry, O Lord, and do not remember iniquity forever; behold, see, we pray You – we are all Your people. Your holy cities have become a wilderness; Zion is a wilderness, Jerusalem is a desolation. Our holy and beautiful Temple, where our fathers praised You, has been burned with fire, and all our pleasant things have been laid waste. Will You restrain Yourself at these things, O Lord? Will You hold Your peace and afflict us so severely? (Is. 64:8–11)

> הַבֵּט מִשָּׁמַיִם וּרְאֵה מִזְּבֻל קָדְשְׁךָ וְתִפְאַרְתֶּךָ אַיֵּה קִנְאָתְךָ וּגְבוּרֹתֶךָ הֲמוֹן מֵעֶיךָ וְרַחֲמֶיךָ אֵלַי הִתְאַפָּקוּ... לָמָּה תַתְעֵנוּ ה׳ מִדְּרָכֶיךָ תַּקְשִׁיחַ לִבֵּנוּ מִיִּרְאָתֶךָ שׁוּב לְמַעַן עֲבָדֶיךָ שִׁבְטֵי נַחֲלָתֶךָ. לַמִּצְעָר יָרְשׁוּ עַם קָדְשֶׁךָ צָרֵינוּ בּוֹסְסוּ מִקְדָּשֶׁךָ.
>
> Look down from heaven and see, from the habitation of Your holiness and Your glory – where is Your zeal and Your might? Your acts of compassion and Your mercies are withheld from me.... Why, O Lord, have You caused us to stray from Your ways, and hardened our hearts, for fear of You? For the sake of Your servants, bring back the tribes of Your inheritance. The people of Your holiness possessed it for only a short while; our enemies have trodden down Your Sanctuary (Is. 63:15–18).

Many of the prophets mention the destruction of the Temple, but they speak of it using the future tense, while the book of Isaiah describes it in the past tense. It is clear from the prophet's language that he is crying out over a known reality.

The exile of Israel is also depicted as an established reality, even though there is no prophecy in Isaiah that foretells exile: כֹּה אָמַר ה׳ גֹּאַלְכֶם קְדוֹשׁ יִשְׂרָאֵל לְמַעַנְכֶם שִׁלַּחְתִּי בָבֶלָה וְהוֹרַדְתִּי בָרִיחִים כֻּלָּם, "So says the Lord, your Redeemer, the Holy One of Israel: For your sake I have sent to Babylon, and I will bring them all down as fugitives... (Is. 43:14); and צְאוּ מִבָּבֶל בִּרְחוּ מִכַּשְׂדִּים בְּקוֹל רִנָּה הַגִּידוּ הַשְׁמִיעוּ זֹאת הוֹצִיאוּהָ עַד קְצֵה הָאָרֶץ אִמְרוּ גָּאַל ה׳ עַבְדּוֹ יַעֲקֹב, "Go forth out of Babylon, flee from the Kasdim; declare in a voice of song; tell this, spread it to the ends of the earth, say: The Lord has redeemed His servant Jacob" (Is. 48:20).

Moreover, during the reign of Hezekiah, the last king in whose lifetime Isaiah is said to have prophesied (Isaiah 1:1), Jerusalem's destruction had not yet been decreed. That happened only in the reign of Hezekiah's son Manasseh (see II Kings 21:10–17).

The second argument for a late composition of the second half of Isaiah is its mention of Cyrus, the king of Persia who conquered the Babylonian empire in 539 BCE and decreed that the exiles could return to their homeland (see the first chapter of Ezra). His name is mentioned twice in the second half of the book, despite the fact that he lived approximately two hundred years after Isaiah: הָאֹמֵר לְכוֹרֶשׁ רֹעִי וְכָל חֶפְצִי יַשְׁלִם וְלֵאמֹר לִירוּשָׁלִַם תִּבָּנֶה וְהֵיכָל תִּוָּסֵד, "[He] Who says of Cyrus, 'He is My shepherd, and shall perform all that I desire,' and saying to Jerusalem, 'You shall be rebuilt,' and to the Temple, 'Your foundation shall be laid'" (Is. 44:28); and כֹּה אָמַר ה׳ לִמְשִׁיחוֹ לְכוֹרֶשׁ אֲשֶׁר הֶחֱזַקְתִּי בִימִינוֹ לְרַד לְפָנָיו גּוֹיִם וּמָתְנֵי מְלָכִים אֲפַתֵּחַ לִפְתֹּחַ לְפָנָיו דְּלָתַיִם וּשְׁעָרִים לֹא יִסָּגֵרוּ, "So says the Lord to His anointed one, to Cyrus, whose right hand I have held, that I might subdue nations before him, and loosen the loins of kings, that I might open before him doors and gates which shall not be shut" (Is. 45:1).

These verses give the impression that Cyrus was a historical figure, known to the original audience. It is difficult to ascribe this prophecy to Isaiah, for the prophets did not speak of matters that would take place so far in the future, and they did not use such detail as to specify names of people not yet born.[14] If Isaiah himself did prophesy these verses, then it is difficult to understand why he would mention by name a king who would live two hundred years in the future.[15]

---

14. My rabbi and teacher, Rabbi Yaakov Medan, in his article "Mavo LeMaamaro Shel H. Hefetz Al Malkhut Paras U'Madai," *Megadim* 14 (5751/1991): 64, likewise rules out the possibility of the prophecy about Cyrus presenting specific details about a person not yet born. He proposes a different solution to the problem, arguing that Isaiah was not speaking of Cyrus, king of Persia, whom we know as the king who declared the Jews of Babylon free to return to the Land of Israel, but rather of his grandfather, who lived in the period of Isaiah. However, the suggestion that there were two different kings named Cyrus is itself revolutionary, and beyond this, in the prophet's appellation of Cyrus as "God's anointed" it seems most unlikely that he would be referring to some king about whom we know nothing, rather than to the king whose promise to facilitate the rebuilding of the Temple concludes the Tanakh. The proposal that the Cyrus of Isaiah 44:28 and 45:1 was not Cyrus the Great had been made earlier. Aware of the problematic nature of this proposal, Y. Zlotnick, in his *Aḥdut Yeshayahu* (Tel Aviv, 1920), 56, noted, "it would be better to have two Cyruses than two Isaiahs."

15. Admittedly, there is one such instance in Tanakh – in the prophecy of the man of God who tells Jeroboam son of Nevat that a king is destined to arise from the house of David, who will profane the altar that Jeroboam has established in Beit El: וַיֹּאמֶר מִזְבֵּחַ מִזְבֵּחַ כֹּה אָמַר ה׳ הִנֵּה בֵן נוֹלָד לְבֵית דָּוִד **יֹאשִׁיָּהוּ שְׁמוֹ** וְזָבַח עָלֶיךָ אֶת כֹּהֲנֵי הַבָּמוֹת הַמַּקְטִרִים עָלֶיךָ וְעַצְמוֹת אָדָם יִשְׂרְפוּ עָלֶיךָ "And he said: Altar, altar, so says the Lord: 'Behold, a child will be born to the house of David, Josiah by name, and he shall slay the priests of the high places that burn incense upon you, and they shall burn bones of men upon you'" (I Kings 13:2). Here too, the prophet seems to be

A third argument for the late date of chapter 40 and onwards of Isaiah is the linguistic differences between the two sections of the book. A number of expressions that appear numerous times in the second part of the book are entirely absent from the first part. For example, "all flesh" (כָל בָּשָׂר, *khol basar*), which appears in the following verses: 40:5, 6; 49:26; 66:16, 23, 24. Similarly, "to heart" (עַל לֵב, *al lev*), in 42:25; 46:8; 47:7; 57:1, 11.[16]

In terms of content, too, there are conspicuous differences between the two parts of the book. One of the best known examples is the subject of "God's servant," which appears repeatedly as a central motif in the second part of the book (see the following verses: 41:8, 9; 42:1, 19; 43:10; 44:1, 2, 21; 45:4; 49:3; 52:13; 53:11), but is altogether absent from the first part.[17]

Additionally, the structure of the book of Isaiah reflects the division into two parts quite clearly. The first section of Isaiah's prophecies concludes with the prophecy of consolation in chapter 35, ending with the words, וּפְדוּיֵי ה׳ יְשֻׁבוּן וּבָאוּ צִיּוֹן בְּרִנָּה וְשִׂמְחַת עוֹלָם עַל רֹאשָׁם שָׂשׂוֹן

---

speaking of Josiah by name about three hundred years before the king would be born and the prophecy fulfilled – as described in II Kings 23:15–16. However, this does not represent any proof in the above case, for it is reasonable to suppose that the words "Josiah by name" were not uttered in the original prophecy, but were added later on by the redactor of the book (Jeremiah, according to the *baraita* cited above), who was writing later, and had witnessed the fulfillment of the prophecy. If the words "Josiah by name" are understood to be part of the original prophecy, then Josiah's repentance in the wake of the discovery of the *Sefer Torah* was actually planned and foretold by God in advance. Why, then, would the text testify, וְכָמֹהוּ לֹא הָיָה לְפָנָיו מֶלֶךְ אֲשֶׁר שָׁב אֶל ה׳ בְּכָל לְבָבוֹ וּבְכָל נַפְשׁוֹ וּבְכָל מְאֹדוֹ כְּכֹל תּוֹרַת מֹשֶׁה וְאַחֲרָיו לֹא קָם כָּמֹהוּ "And there had never before been a king like him who returned to God with all his heart and with all his soul and with all his might, according to all of the Torah of Moses; nor did any like him arise afterwards" (II Kings 23:25)? Conceivably, the prophecy was meant to have been fulfilled much earlier, but the inability of the kings of Judah to completely eradicate the practice of idolatry postponed its fulfillment to the days of Josiah.

16. For a partial list of such expressions, see M. Z. Segal, *Mevo HaMikra* (Jerusalem, 1977), 323.
17. The expression "My servant" (*avdi*) does appear twice in the first part, but in these instances it refers to a specific person – first Isaiah himself (Is. 20:3), and then Eliyakim ben Hilkiyah (Is. 22:20) – rather than as a general thematic motif of "God's servant."

וְשִׂמְחָה יַשִּׂיגוּ וְנָסוּ יָגוֹן וַאֲנָחָה, "And the ransomed of God shall return, and come to Tzion with song and everlasting joy upon their heads; they shall obtain joy and gladness, while sorrow and sighing shall flee" (Is. 35:10).

Following this are four chapters (Is. 36–39) that focus on King Hezekiah: his war against Assyria, his illness, his relations with the prophet Isaiah, and his failure in dealings with the king of Babylon. To a great extent, these chapters repeat chapters 18–20 of II Kings. A parallel phenomenon exists in Jeremiah, in that the actual prophecies end in chapter 51, while the final chapter (Jer. 52) repeats chapter 25 in II Kings. If the repetition of the chapter from Kings represents the conclusion of the book of Jeremiah, it seems reasonable to suggest that the repetition of the chapters from Kings in the book of Isaiah fill the same function.

Finally, Isaiah's name is mentioned fifteen times in the first part of the book – of which six appearances occur in the section of the actual prophecies (chapters 1–35) and nine times in the appendix that parallels the chapters from II Kings (chapters 36–39). By contrast, his name is not mentioned in the second part of the book at all.

The first person to suggest that the second part of the book of Isaiah was not actually written by Isaiah, was Rabbi Avraham ibn Ezra. In his commentary to the beginning of chapter 40, he writes:

> This unit was joined [to the preceding prophecies] because it is mentioned previously that all of the king's treasures, as well as his children, would be exiled to Babylon, and therefore this is followed by the consolations. And these first consolations from the second half of the book, according to the opinion of Rabbi Moshe HaKohen, concern the [building of the] Second Temple, while to my view it is all meant concerning our own exile, but within the book there are matters of the Babylonian exile, as a memorial, for Cyrus allowed the exiles back. However, the matters in the latter part of the book concern the future, as I shall explain. And know that while the Sages said that the book of Samuel was written by Samuel – this is only true until, "And Samuel died" (I Sam. 25:1)... and proof of this is the verse מְלָכִים יִרְאוּ וָקָמוּ שָׂרִים וְיִשְׁתַּחֲווּ, "Kings shall see and arise, and princes shall prostrate themselves" (Is. 49:7)... and he who is wise will understand.

Ibn Ezra writes cryptically, as is his custom when it comes to sensitive subjects,[18] but his meaning seems clear.[19] He maintains that this unit was "joined" to the preceding chapters, and he distinguishes between the content of the two sections of the book. He then immediately goes on to note that, despite Bava Batra's statement that "Samuel wrote his book," it does not refer to the entire book – only up to the point where the text explicitly notes his death. Presumably, Ibn Ezra mentions the authorship of Samuel in this context because he believes that Isaiah, like the book of Samuel, was not written in its entirety by the prophet after whom the book is named, but was completed by someone else.

Indeed, the Sages themselves note explicitly that there are verses in the book of Isaiah that were not written by Isaiah himself, but by a different prophet:

> R. Simon said: There were two verses that were prophesied by Be'era,[20] but they were not sufficient to comprise a book in their own right, so they were included in Isaiah. And these are they: וְכִי יֹאמְרוּ אֲלֵיכֶם דִּרְשׁוּ אֶל הָאֹבוֹת, "And when they say to you: 'Consult the mediums'" (Is. 8:19), and the following verse (Is. 8:20).[21]

Given that the Sages attribute the redaction of Isaiah to Hezekiah and his colleagues, the idea that the book is composed of the prophecies of more than one prophet in no way contradicts their view. As with other books, the attribution of authorship may apply to most of the book but not its entirety. Indeed, the idea that Isaiah is composed of

18. As seen previously, concerning the "secret of the twelve."
19. Concerning the meaning of his words see, *inter alia*, R. N. Krochmal, *Moreh Nevukhei HaZeman* (Lemberg, 1851), 114; M. Friedlander, *Perush Rabbi Avraham ben Ezra Al Yeshayahu* (London, 1873), 170–71.
20. The midrash refers here to Be'eri, father of Hosea, who was also a prophet – as the midrash goes on to explain. In some versions the midrash does indeed read "Be'eri," but this version points to an identification of Hosea's father as Be'era, prince of the tribe of Reuben (I Chr. 5:6). See Margaliot in his edition of Leviticus Rabba, n. 6.
21. Leviticus Rabba 6, 6, Margaliot edition, 142–43.

the prophecies of more than one prophet arises from a simple reading of the second half of the book.

The authorship of the book of Isaiah is not the only question, however. For even if later authorship of the second half of the book is accepted as fact, the question of how it came to be joined to the first half of the book remains. It also must be noted that the unity of the book of Isaiah goes back to antiquity: a clear allusion to the book as a single work (including both parts) is found as early as the Book of Ben Sira,[22] which offers the following comment on Isaiah: "He foretold the end with a mighty spirit, and comforted the mourners of Zion. He told eternal hidden matters before they transpired" (Ben Sira 48:33–34, Segal edition, 334). These verses of Ben Sira clearly refer to the prophecies in the second part of the book (see, for instance Is. 42:9; 61:2–3). Isaiah also appears as a single unit in its Septuagint translation, dating to the second century BCE. Moreover, the "Complete Scroll of Isaiah" that was discovered at Qumran, dating to the mid-second century BCE, likewise shows no division between the two parts.

Interestingly, alongside the differences in language and style noted above, the opposite phenomenon also exists: expressions – including some that are unique to Isaiah – that appear in both parts of the book. Some examples: יאמר ה', "*yomar Hashem*" (the future form of "says the Lord" – Is. 1:11, 18; 33:10; and also Is. 41:21; 66:9), an expression that appears nowhere else in the books of the Prophets);[23] רם ונשא, "*ram venissa*" ("high and elevated" – appearing only twice in all of Tanakh, namely, Is. 6:1 and Is. 57:15); ארח משפט, "*oraḥ mishpat*" ("the path of judgment" – Is. 26:8 and Is. 40:14); and others.[24] Clearly, the prophet who

22. The Book of Ben Sira was written at the end of the third or beginning of the second century BCE. See M. Z. Segal, *Sefer Ben Sira HaShalem* (Jerusalem, 1953), 3–6.

23. It appears not as a rhetorical expression, but as a regular future-tense verb in Jeremiah 42:20. We might add that Isaiah features other similar expressions which are likewise unique to this book: "*yomar Elo-heikhem*" (Is. 40:1); "*yomar kadosh*" (Is. 40:25); and "*yomar melekh Yaakov*" (Is. 41:21).

24. For more expressions appearing in both parts of the book, see M. Z. Segal, Y. T. Radday, and D. Wickman, *The Unity of Isaiah in Light of Statistical Linguistics* (Hildesheim, 1973). These expressions and their development have given rise to the proposal that the book as a whole bears many traces of the editorial activity of the author or authors of chapters 40–66, as is argued by H. G. M. Williamson, *The Book Called*

wrote the prophecies of the second part of Isaiah was well acquainted with the first part of the book, and was influenced by it in terms of both content and style, even as he also developed his own style and introduced new ideas. Presumably due to Isaiah's influence on the later prophet, the two collections were brought together to form a single unit.

All of the above accords with traditional Jewish biblical commentary and certainly with contemporary religious scholars of Tanakh, especially given the widespread popular re-engagement with Tanakh study in general, and the book of Isaiah in particular. However, the history of Bible studies has derailed the conversation.

That is, hundreds of years after Ibn Ezra wrote his veiled words, early Bible critics[25] arrived at the same conclusion – that the second part of Isaiah was not written by the prophet of that name, but rather by someone they refer to as "Second Isaiah" or "Deutero-Isaiah." Their main argument in support of this conclusion is the description of the Temple and the Babylonian exile in the second part of Isaiah – a reality that did not exist in Isaiah's time and therefore must have been written by someone who lived later. Implicit in this argument is a denial of the concept of prophecy; it suggests that a prophet could not describe events that would happen in the future. This, of course, is a very different approach from the one above that assumes that a prophet of God can know the future, but analysis of the style and content of this text suggests its later composition in any case. Certainly, prophecies concerning the future often depict future events in general terms – albeit, not in detail, as noted above. The Bible critics shifted the discussion from the question of whether the character of the prophecy and various stylistic elements necessarily indicate that a different prophet wrote the second part of Isaiah, to the question of whether any prophet is capable of knowing the future. Their approach caused great agitation among the Torah scholars, who were quick to reject their hypothesis.

Isaiah: Deutero-Isaiah's Role in Composition and Redaction (Oxford, 1994). For the argument for the near absence of later editing in much of chapters 1–39, see S. Z. Aster, *Reflections of Empire in Isaiah 1–39: Responses to Assyrian Ideology* (Atlanta, 2017).

25. This hypothesis was first suggested in 1775, by Johann Döderlein in his Latin commentary on Isaiah. It was later publicized by Johann Gottfried Eichhorn, in 1883, and has since become universally accepted by all academic biblical scholars.

One of the great Torah scholars who confronted the claim of a "Second Isaiah" head-on was Shadal, Rabbi Shmuel David Luzzatto (1800–1865). Despite his extensive academic scholarship, Rabbi Luzzatto rejects this view with great vehemence in his letters[26] and in his commentary on Isaiah. Another who does so is the modern biblical commentator Rachel Margaliot, who devotes an entire book to this subject – *Eḥad Haya Yeshayahu*.[27] In these works, as well as in works by other prominent Jewish scholars,[28] the controversy over the essence of prophecy features prominently:

> The idea of the division of the book arises from a realist, historical approach that places the prophet within the background of his prophecies. This approach does not view prophecy as a vision of the future, but rather as an overview of reality as it is unfolding. According to this approach, the prophet stands at the very point where the events that he is prophesying about are unfolding. The prophet is a sort of conscientious, insightful politician who

26. Published in *Kerem Hemed* 7 (Prague, 1843), 225–42. Concerning Shadal's position on this subject see S. Vargon, "S. D. Luzzatto's Approach Regarding the Unity of the Book of Isaiah," *Review of Rabbinic Judaism* 4, 2 (2001): 272–96. Vargon acknowledges that Shadal polemicizes against those who deny that prophets can foretell the future. He also notes that Shadal did not view in the same light all arguments against unified authorship of Isaiah; he recognized that the Sages, who had arrived at the same conclusion on the basis of different premises, expressed a legitimate view.
27. R. Margaliot, *Eḥad Haya Yeshayahu* (Jerusalem, 1954). Most of the book is devoted to a review of the linguistic style that is common to both parts of Isaiah, as set forth above. However, as we have seen, there are also stylistic differences, and the similarities in style could be evidence of the influence of Isaiah's prophecies on those of the prophet who composed the second part, rather than evidence of Isaiah having written all of it – as intimated by M. Z. Segal, *Mevo HaMikra* (Jerusalem, 1977), 323–24: "In general, there is a great discrepancy between the two parts in the stylistic qualities of the language. In the second part the language is lyrical, magnanimous and flowing, full of softness, gentleness, pathos and enthusiasm, while the prophecies of Isaiah, in the first part of the Book, are conveyed in elevated, intensive and dense language. Hence, the argument from language does not support the traditional view that the second part, too, was written by Isaiah son of Amotz, since the linguistic differences contradict this view."
28. For other works rejecting the division of the book of Isaiah, see R. Margaliot, *Eḥad Haya Yeshayahu*, 17; Y. Yaakobson, *Chazon HaMikra* II (Tel Aviv, 1957), 47.

> observes the reality around him, knows what is going on politically, and senses what awaits just beyond the horizon. He might be described as a talented publicist who dares to guess what is going to happen next, based on accumulated information as to what is happening now. This view led the scholars to reject any prophecy that was not within the scope of the prophet's natural vision.[29]

Indeed, there is no way around this fundamental difference of opinion between the secular, critical view of Tanakh and the religious view. Those who believe that the Tanakh possesses sanctity, and that the prophet receives his messages from God through prophecy and divine inspiration, will obviously regard the view that a prophet is simply an eloquent and insightful member of the general population with no real ability to discern the future as illegitimate. The latter approach represents a denial of the whole concept of prophecy, regardless of one's position on the question of the authorship of the book of Isaiah. These divergent starting points spawned a great controversy concerning "Second Isaiah."

Regardless of a prophet's status and abilities, however, the arguments against the book of Isaiah as a single work are substantial, valid, and compelling. They are based on the content of the prophecy itself,[30] and on simple, clear proofs from the style and structure of the text, as well as the conspicuous absence of any mention of Isaiah himself from chapter 40 onwards. There is no doubt that these considerations were borne in mind by Ibn Ezra, too, when he wrote his commentary to chapter 40 of Isaiah. The discussion of Isaiah's authorship, therefore, need

---

29. R. Margaliot, 20.
30. Concerning the nature of the prophecy, even Margaliot acknowledges: "Certainly, referring to someone by name two hundred years before he is to be born, is not an ordinary vision encountered in the Books of the Prophets.... We cannot pretend to know the power and depths of prophecy; whether a prophet can prophesy only concerning the near future, or also concerning more distant events; whether only in obscure metaphors, or also explicitly." Once again, though, our discussion does not concern the question of whether or not the prophet could know Cyrus's name, but rather whether there is any point in the prophet knowing, and stating, the name of a person to be born in the future, when this name in no way adds to or detracts from what he is saying.

not trespass into the territory of fundamental Jewish beliefs.[31] Positing the existence of two separate prophets is certainly compatible with a religious worldview that is willing to address the text itself.[32]

REDUNDANCIES AND CONTRADICTIONS IN THE BOOKS OF THE PROPHETS

The phenomenon of seeming redundancies and contradictions between chapters, as well as within literary units themselves, that is so challenging in the Torah exists in the books of the Prophets as well. Is the discussion of this phenomenon, as well as the two different approaches of explaining it – the documentary hypothesis, and the aspects approach of Rabbi Mordekhai Breuer – relevant to the prophetic literature as well?

Examples abound in the chapters describing the establishment of the monarchy in the book of Samuel (I Sam., chapters 8–17), for example. I will propose here only a brief solution to the problems raised above.

According to the aspects approach, the text seeks to illuminate different dimensions and perspectives on the narratives, and does so

---

31. As Rabbi Y. Cherlow points out in his *Yireh LaLevav* (Tel Aviv, 2007), 246, n. 52.
32. Indeed, in our times, the question is discussed without the passionate emotion that surrounded it in previous generations. The following are some of the Hebrew sources that address the issue: Z. Okashi, "Emunat HaMada – Yeshayahu HaSheni KeMashal," *Derekh Efrata* 7 (5758/1998): 99–105, argues that from a scientific point of view there is no absolute truth concerning the authorship of the second part of Isaiah, but he too believes that both positions are legitimate in terms of a religious worldview. A. Hacohen, "HaOmnam Eḥad Haya Yeshayahu?" *Derekh Efrata* 10 (5760/2000): 79–88, voices a strong protest against the silence of the Religious-Zionist world concerning the legitimacy of the view that the book of Isaiah comprises the writings of two prophets. Y. Rosenson, "Yiḥudo, Aḥduto U'Murkavuto Shel Sefer Yeshayahu – MeHashkafot Ḥazal Al Yeshayahu," *Derekh Aggada* 3 (5760/2000): 179–202, treats the question at length, *inter alia*, from the perspective of *midreshei Ḥazal*. A review of further sources may be found in N. Ararat's article, "Divrei HaNavi Menaḥem – Hatzaa LeLimmud HaYeḥidot HaNevuiyot BiYeshayahu 40–66," *Shaanan* 11 (5766/2006): 9, n. 1, and 53–55. For understandable reasons, the topic has generated little attention in English. Many years ago, the British Chief Rabbi, Joseph Hertz, reached a similar conclusion: "This question can be considered dispassionately. It touches no dogma, or any religious principle in Judaism; and, moreover, does not materially affect the understanding of the prophecies, or of the human conditions of the Jewish people that they have in view" (*Hertz Chumash* [London, 1938], 942).

by combining overlapping, and sometimes contradictory, accounts.[33] Bible critics maintain that contradictions arise from the fact that the texts are actually compilations of different sources,[34] yet the degree to which the attempted explanations by the Bible critics solve the difficulties has been questioned.

Without embarking on a lengthy discussion of all the details,[35] we may note that these chapters display a dual character, with two different perspectives on the monarchy. In chapter 8, Samuel is adamantly opposed to the nation's demand for a king. God, too, takes a dim view of the demand and tells Samuel:

> כִּי לֹא אֹתְךָ מָאָסוּ כִּי אֹתִי מָאֲסוּ מִמְּלֹךְ עֲלֵיהֶם. כְּכָל הַמַּעֲשִׂים אֲשֶׁר עָשׂוּ מִיּוֹם הַעֲלֹתִי אֹתָם מִמִּצְרַיִם וְעַד הַיּוֹם הַזֶּה וַיַּעַזְבֻנִי וַיַּעַבְדוּ אֱלֹהִים אֲחֵרִים כֵּן הֵמָּה עֹשִׂים גַּם לָךְ.
>
> For it is not you that they have rejected; rather, they have rejected Me from ruling over them. According to all the deeds that they have done, from the day I brought them up out of Egypt, and until this day, in that they have forsaken Me and served other gods – so they are doing also to you. (I Sam. 8:7–8)

Nevertheless, God does not reject the demand outright, and ultimately acquiesces. In chapter 9, Saul's appointment is presented as a decision originating with God Himself:

---

33. It should be noted that Rabbi Breuer himself preferred not to apply his approach to the books of the Prophets. He maintained that this approach was unique to the Torah, specifically because the Torah represents God's direct word, and that only God could encompass and contain all the contrasting perspectives in a single text. See S. Carmy, "Introducing Rabbi Breuer," in S. Carmy, ed., *Modern Scholarship in the Study of Torah* (New Jersey, 1996), 147.
34. See, for example, M. Z. Segal, *Sifrei Shmuel* (Jerusalem, 1971), 6–16; S. Bar-Efrat, *Perush Shmuel Alef* in the *Mikra LeYisrael* series (Jerusalem-Tel Aviv, 1996), 15–16.
35. I heard the essence of this approach from my teacher Dr. Mordekhai Sabbato, and I set it forth in detail in my book *Shmuel Alef: Melekh BeYisrael* (Maggid, 2013). An English version of the extended thesis on the application of "aspects theory" to these chapters in the book of Samuel can be found at https://www.etzion.org.il/en/16-chapter-9-part-iii-contradictions-book-shmuel.

וַה' גָּלָה אֶת אֹזֶן שְׁמוּאֵל יוֹם אֶחָד לִפְנֵי בוֹא שָׁאוּל לֵאמֹר. כָּעֵת מָחָר אֶשְׁלַח אֵלֶיךָ אִישׁ מֵאֶרֶץ בִּנְיָמִן וּמְשַׁחְתּוֹ לְנָגִיד עַל עַמִּי יִשְׂרָאֵל וְהוֹשִׁיעַ אֶת עַמִּי מִיַּד פְּלִשְׁתִּים כִּי רָאִיתִי אֶת עַמִּי כִּי בָּאָה צַעֲקָתוֹ אֵלָי.

And God had revealed to Samuel a day before Saul arrived, saying, "Tomorrow at about this time I will send you a man from the land of Benjamin, and you shall anoint him as prince over My people, Israel, and he shall save My people from the hand of the Philistines, for I have looked upon My people, for their cry has come to Me" (I Sam. 9:15–16).

This contradictory treatment of the notion of a king expresses the ambivalence toward monarchy that exists all through Tanakh. On the one hand, the monarchy is viewed in a positive light in many cases. For instance, going back as far as the forefathers, God promises Abraham, וּמְלָכִים מִמְּךָ יֵצֵאוּ, "And kings shall emerge from you" (Gen. 17:6); similarly, Jacob is told, וּמְלָכִים מֵחֲלָצֶיךָ יֵצֵאוּ, "And kings shall emerge from your loins" (Gen. 35:11).

Perhaps most significant is the positive attitude toward the concept of a monarchy that is found in the concluding chapters of Judges. These chapters describe a deplorable moral condition that expresses itself in terrible sins: idolatry (Judges 17, Micah's idol); sexual immorality (Judges 19, the concubine in Giv'a); and murder (Judges 20–21, the war against Benjamin). This reality is explained in a verse that is repeated like a refrain throughout the book: בַּיָּמִים הָהֵם אֵין מֶלֶךְ בְּיִשְׂרָאֵל אִישׁ הַיָּשָׁר בְּעֵינָיו יַעֲשֶׂה, "In those days there was no king in Israel; every man did what was right in his own eyes" (Judges 17:6; 21:25; see also 18:1; 19:1). The book of Judges perceives a monarchy as the solution to the anarchy reigning in the political, religious, and moral spheres of the day, and therefore concludes with an appeal for a king. A positive attitude to the monarchy also appears in I Chronicles 29:23, regarding a later era: וַיֵּשֶׁב שְׁלֹמֹה עַל כִּסֵּא ה' לְמֶלֶךְ תַּחַת דָּוִיד אָבִיו, "And Solomon sat on the seat of the Lord to rule in place of his father David."

A king can be a religious force for good. Consider worthy kings like David, Jehoshaphat, and Josiah.

On the other hand, the biblical text warns of the dangers inherent in monarchy. In the book of Judges, Gideon cautions the people, when they offer him a sort of dynasty whereby he and his sons would rule over Israel: לֹא אֶמְשֹׁל אֲנִי בָּכֶם וְלֹא יִמְשֹׁל בְּנִי בָּכֶם, ה׳ יִמְשֹׁל בָּכֶם, "I shall not rule over you, nor shall my sons rule over you; God shall rule over you" (Judges 8:23). Notably, in the Torah itself, the highest office in Israel is that of "*nasi*," prince (Ex. 22:27; Leviticus 4:22), until the request for a king in Deuteronomy. The danger of appointing a king – that is, the concentration of tremendous power in the hands of a single person – is clear: if the king is driven by improper motives, he may cause a complete collapse of the entire nation's divine service, as happened under such kings as Jeroboam ben Nevat and Ahab.

This complex attitude toward kingship appears to characterize the unit in the Torah that details the appointment of a king, as well:

> כִּי תָבֹא אֶל הָאָרֶץ אֲשֶׁר ה׳ אֱלֹהֶיךָ נֹתֵן לָךְ וִירִשְׁתָּהּ וְיָשַׁבְתָּה בָּהּ וְאָמַרְתָּ אָשִׂימָה עָלַי מֶלֶךְ כְּכָל הַגּוֹיִם אֲשֶׁר סְבִיבֹתָי. שׂוֹם תָּשִׂים עָלֶיךָ מֶלֶךְ אֲשֶׁר יִבְחַר ה׳ אֱלֹהֶיךָ בּוֹ מִקֶּרֶב אַחֶיךָ תָּשִׂים עָלֶיךָ מֶלֶךְ לֹא תוּכַל לָתֵת עָלֶיךָ אִישׁ נָכְרִי אֲשֶׁר לֹא אָחִיךָ הוּא.
>
> When you come to the land which the Lord your God gives to you, and you take possession of it and settle in it, and you will say, "Let us appoint a king over us, like all the nations around us" – you shall surely appoint over you a king whom the Lord your God will choose; from among your brethren shall you appoint a king over you; you cannot appoint over you a foreign man who is not of your brethren. (Deut. 17:14–15)

It is not clear whether this is meant as a command to appoint a king, or as license to do so. The Sages are divided on the issue.

> R. Yehuda said: "There are three commandments which the Jewish people were commanded upon their entry into the land: to appoint a king, to cut off the descendants of Amalek, and to build the Temple." R. Nehorai said: "This unit [concerning the king]

> was said only to pacify their discontent, as it is written, 'And you shall say: Let us appoint a king over ourselves.'"[36]

These differing opinions clearly reflect the two perspectives presented throughout Tanakh. A monarchy offers both risks and opportunities, advantages and disadvantages. The Tanakh expresses this tension by presenting both sides of the issue in the chapters in Samuel that pertain to the establishment of the monarchy.

The topic of kingship is introduced in I Samuel, chapter 8, as an essentially negative phenomenon, permitted only as a concession to human weakness. Chapter 9, however, treats the monarchy as a positive institution that was intended by God from the outset. The subsequent chapters align with each of these two approaches, viewing a failure on Saul's part and an encounter between him and David from both perspectives. The scope of the present discussion does not allow for a detailed presentation;[37] suffice it to note that this example of ambivalence regarding the monarchy suggests that repetition in Tanakh may be deliberate,

---

36. A similar difference of opinion exists among the commentators. Nahmanides understands the unit in Deuteronomy as representing a mitzva, and Maimonides (Laws of Kings 1:1) concurs. Abrabanel sees the unit as merely giving license to appoint a king, as an example of "the Torah speaks here only in response to the evil inclination," following the view of Rabbi Nehorai ("to pacify their discontent"). The plain meaning of the text seems to lend itself more to Abrabanel's view, which reflects more accurately the language of the command. If this is indeed an obligation, why would the Torah present it as a description of a situation – "You will say, 'Let us appoint a king over ourselves like all the nations around about us'"? Nahmanides addresses this question, suggesting that the Torah is hinting here at what will happen in the future: the nation will ask for a king "like all the nations." Were this not the meaning, he claims, it would indeed be difficult to understand why the Torah presents their request in this way: "For what reason would the Torah say, in relation to a commandment, 'like all the nations around about us'? For the Jews should not learn from them, nor envy those who act unjustly." However, this explanation seems slightly forced. The Netziv (*Haamek Davar*), in his commentary on Deuteronomy, explains that the Torah does not issue an absolute command in matters pertaining to national policy, since such matters are influenced by the circumstances at any given time, and no particular form of government is appropriate for every generation.
37. Interested readers are encouraged to examine the analysis in detail in my aforementioned book, *Shmuel Alef: Melekh BeYisrael.*

for the sake of presenting a more complete picture by means of diverse perspectives on the same reality – and not because diverse sources were collated together by an editor.

Internal contradictions and redundancies within the same textual unit demand a fresh eye as well. Consider the several contradictions in the description of the crossing of the Jordan in Joshua, chapters 3–4.

In chapter 3, Joshua addresses the people and tells them of the miracle that is going to happen when they cross the Jordan (Josh. 9–13). As part of his speech, he commands them, seemingly of his own initiative, וְעַתָּה קְחוּ לָכֶם שְׁנֵי עָשָׂר אִישׁ מִשִּׁבְטֵי יִשְׂרָאֵל אִישׁ אֶחָד אִישׁ אֶחָד לַשָּׁבֶט, "And now, take yourselves twelve men of the tribes of Israel, one man for each tribe" (Josh. 3:12).

Later, after the people have crossed the Jordan, God appears to Joshua with a command employing almost identical language, though it also describes the responsibilities of the people:

> קְחוּ לָכֶם מִן הָעָם שְׁנֵים עָשָׂר אֲנָשִׁים אִישׁ אֶחָד אִישׁ אֶחָד מִשָּׁבֶט. וְצַוּוּ אוֹתָם לֵאמֹר שְׂאוּ לָכֶם מִזֶּה מִתּוֹךְ הַיַּרְדֵּן מִמַּצַּב רַגְלֵי הַכֹּהֲנִים הָכִין שְׁתֵּים עֶשְׂרֵה אֲבָנִים וְהַעֲבַרְתֶּם אוֹתָם עִמָּכֶם וְהִנַּחְתֶּם אוֹתָם בַּמָּלוֹן אֲשֶׁר תָּלִינוּ בוֹ הַלָּיְלָה.
>
> Take yourselves from the people twelve men, one man for each tribe. And command them, saying: "Take yourselves from this place, from the midst of the Jordan, from where the feet of the *kohanim* stood firm, twelve stones, and you shall carry them over with you, and leave them in your lodging place where you will lodge tonight." (Josh. 4:2–3)

If Joshua had already commanded the people to choose men from among the nation before crossing the Jordan, why must God command Joshua regarding this same point?

The chronology as presented in the text suggests that after Joshua spoke to the people, they then crossed the Jordan, and then God commanded Joshua to choose twelve men: וְכָל יִשְׂרָאֵל עֹבְרִים בֶּחָרָבָה עַד אֲשֶׁר תַּמּוּ כָּל הַגּוֹי לַעֲבֹר אֶת הַיַּרְדֵּן. וַיְהִי כַּאֲשֶׁר תַּמּוּ כָל הַגּוֹי לַעֲבוֹר אֶת הַיַּרְדֵּן וַיֹּאמֶר ה׳ אֶל יְהוֹשֻׁעַ לֵאמֹר, "All of Israel passed over on dry land, until all of the nation had finished crossing over the Jordan. And it was, when the entire nation had passed over the Jordan that God spoke to Joshua, saying" (Josh. 3:17–4:1). Then the people fulfill the commandment and set up the pile of stones at the lodge:

> וַיַּעֲשׂוּ כֵן בְּנֵי יִשְׂרָאֵל כַּאֲשֶׁר צִוָּה יְהוֹשֻׁעַ וַיִּשְׂאוּ שְׁתֵּי עֶשְׂרֵה אֲבָנִים מִתּוֹךְ הַיַּרְדֵּן כַּאֲשֶׁר דִּבֶּר ה׳ אֶל יְהוֹשֻׁעַ לְמִסְפַּר שִׁבְטֵי בְנֵי יִשְׂרָאֵל וַיַּעֲבִרוּם עִמָּם אֶל הַמָּלוֹן וַיַּנִּחוּם שָׁם.
>
> And the Children of Israel did so, as Joshua had commanded, and they carried twelve stones from the midst of the Jordan, as God had spoken to Joshua, for the number of the tribes of the Children of Israel, and they carried them over with them to the lodge, and laid them down there. (Josh. 4:8)

But afterwards, the text reverts to the previous situation:

> וְהַכֹּהֲנִים נֹשְׂאֵי הָאָרוֹן עֹמְדִים בְּתוֹךְ הַיַּרְדֵּן עַד תֹּם כָּל הַדָּבָר אֲשֶׁר צִוָּה ה׳ אֶת יְהוֹשֻׁעַ לְדַבֵּר אֶל הָעָם כְּכֹל אֲשֶׁר צִוָּה מֹשֶׁה אֶת יְהוֹשֻׁעַ וַיְמַהֲרוּ הָעָם וַיַּעֲבֹרוּ.
>
> And the *kohanim,* who bore the Ark, stood in the midst of the Jordan, until the entire episode was finished, which God had commanded Joshua to speak to the people, in accordance with all that Moses had commanded Joshua, and the people hastened and crossed over. (Josh. 4:10)

There is also repetition in relation to the *kohanim.* First, the *kohanim,* bearing the Ark, emerge from the Jordan:

> וְהַכֹּהֲנִים נֹשְׂאֵי הָאָרוֹן עֹמְדִים בְּתוֹךְ הַיַּרְדֵּן... וַיְמַהֲרוּ הָעָם וַיַּעֲבֹרוּ. וַיְהִי כַּאֲשֶׁר תַּם כָּל הָעָם לַעֲבוֹר וַיַּעֲבֹר אֲרוֹן ה׳ וְהַכֹּהֲנִים לִפְנֵי הָעָם.
>
> And the *kohanim,* who bore the Ark, stood in the midst of the Jordan...and the people hastened and crossed over. And it was, when all the nation had finished crossing over, that the

> Ark of God passed over, and the *kohanim*, before the people. (Josh. 4:10–11)

Then the narrative closes: בַּיּוֹם הַהוּא גִּדַּל ה׳ אֶת יְהוֹשֻׁעַ בְּעֵינֵי כָּל יִשְׂרָאֵל וַיִּרְאוּ אֹתוֹ כַּאֲשֶׁר יָרְאוּ אֶת מֹשֶׁה כָּל יְמֵי חַיָּיו, "On that day God magnified Joshua in the eyes of all of Israel, and they feared him as they had feared Moses, all the days of his life" (Josh. 4:14). Except that once the entire episode is over, the text returns to describing the *kohanim*'s exit from the Jordan:

> וַיֹּאמֶר ה׳ אֶל יְהוֹשֻׁעַ לֵאמֹר. צַוֵּה אֶת הַכֹּהֲנִים נֹשְׂאֵי אֲרוֹן הָעֵדוּת וְיַעֲלוּ מִן הַיַּרְדֵּן. וַיְצַו יְהוֹשֻׁעַ אֶת הַכֹּהֲנִים לֵאמֹר עֲלוּ מִן הַיַּרְדֵּן. וַיְהִי בעלות [כַּעֲלוֹת קרי] הַכֹּהֲנִים נֹשְׂאֵי אֲרוֹן בְּרִית ה׳ מִתּוֹךְ הַיַּרְדֵּן נִתְּקוּ כַּפּוֹת רַגְלֵי הַכֹּהֲנִים אֶל הֶחָרָבָה וַיָּשֻׁבוּ מֵי הַיַּרְדֵּן לִמְקוֹמָם וַיֵּלְכוּ כִתְמוֹל שִׁלְשׁוֹם עַל כָּל גְּדוֹתָיו.
>
> And God said to Joshua, saying: "Command the *kohanim*, who bear the Ark of Testimony, and let them come up from the Jordan." And Joshua commanded the *kohanim*, saying, "Come up from the Jordan." And it was, when the *kohanim*, bearing the Ark of God's Covenant, arose from the midst of the Jordan, and the soles of the *kohanim*'s feet were lifted onto the dry ground, that the waters of the Jordan returned to their place, and flowed over all their banks, as they did before. (Josh. 4:15–18)

The repetition goes on to explain the need for the twelve stones taken by the representatives of the tribes. First:

> לְמַעַן תִּהְיֶה זֹאת אוֹת בְּקִרְבְּכֶם כִּי יִשְׁאָלוּן בְּנֵיכֶם מָחָר לֵאמֹר מָה הָאֲבָנִים הָאֵלֶּה לָכֶם. וַאֲמַרְתֶּם לָהֶם אֲשֶׁר נִכְרְתוּ מֵימֵי הַיַּרְדֵּן מִפְּנֵי אֲרוֹן בְּרִית ה׳ בְּעָבְרוֹ בַּיַּרְדֵּן נִכְרְתוּ מֵי הַיַּרְדֵּן וְהָיוּ הָאֲבָנִים הָאֵלֶּה לְזִכָּרוֹן לִבְנֵי יִשְׂרָאֵל עַד עוֹלָם.
>
> In order that this might be a sign in your midst, that when your children ask in the future, saying, "What are these stones to you?" Then you shall say to them, "That the waters of the Jordan were cut off before the Ark of God's Covenant; when it crossed

> over the Jordan, the waters of the Jordan were cut off; and these stones shall be a memorial for the Children of Israel forever." (Josh. 4:6–7)

The description is repeated after the second description of the *kohanim* emerging from the Jordan:

> וַיֹּאמֶר אֶל בְּנֵי יִשְׂרָאֵל לֵאמֹר אֲשֶׁר יִשְׁאָלוּן בְּנֵיכֶם מָחָר אֶת אֲבוֹתָם לֵאמֹר מָה הָאֲבָנִים הָאֵלֶּה. וְהוֹדַעְתֶּם אֶת בְּנֵיכֶם לֵאמֹר בַּיַּבָּשָׁה עָבַר יִשְׂרָאֵל אֶת הַיַּרְדֵּן הַזֶּה. אֲשֶׁר הוֹבִישׁ ה׳ אֱלֹהֵיכֶם אֶת מֵי הַיַּרְדֵּן מִפְּנֵיכֶם עַד עָבְרְכֶם כַּאֲשֶׁר עָשָׂה ה׳ אֱלֹהֵיכֶם לְיַם סוּף אֲשֶׁר הוֹבִישׁ מִפָּנֵינוּ עַד עָבְרֵנוּ.
>
> And he said to the Children of Israel, saying: "When your children ask their fathers in the future, saying, 'What are these stones?' Then you shall make known to your children, saying: 'Israel crossed over this Jordan on dry land. For the Lord your God dried up the waters of the Jordan before you, until you had passed over, as the Lord God did at the Red Sea, which He dried up before us until we had passed over.'" (Josh. 4:21–23)

The establishment of the monument of stones likewise appears twice. First we read:

> וַיַּעֲשׂוּ כֵן בְּנֵי יִשְׂרָאֵל כַּאֲשֶׁר צִוָּה יְהוֹשֻׁעַ וַיִּשְׂאוּ שְׁתֵּי עֶשְׂרֵה אֲבָנִים מִתּוֹךְ הַיַּרְדֵּן כַּאֲשֶׁר דִּבֶּר ה׳ אֶל יְהוֹשֻׁעַ לְמִסְפַּר שִׁבְטֵי בְנֵי יִשְׂרָאֵל וַיַּעֲבִרוּם עִמָּם אֶל הַמָּלוֹן וַיַּנִּחוּם שָׁם.
>
> And the Children of Israel did so, as Joshua had commanded, and they carried twelve stones from the midst of the Jordan, as God had spoken to Joshua, for the number of the tribes of the Children of Israel, and they carried them over with them to the lodge, and laid them down there. (Josh. 4:8)

And then we are told: וְאֵת שְׁתֵּים עֶשְׂרֵה הָאֲבָנִים הָאֵלֶּה אֲשֶׁר לָקְחוּ מִן הַיַּרְדֵּן הֵקִים יְהוֹשֻׁעַ בַּגִּלְגָּל, "And those twelve stones, which they took out of the Jordan, did Joshua set up in Gilgal" (Josh. 4:20).

The multiplicity of repetitions and contradictions has been explained by Bible critics as proof that different sources were compiled to create one narrative, though they have not identified the different source materials.[38] Here, too, it seems that the aspects approach may be applied to show how the text endeavors, by means of overlapping descriptions, to convey the different aspects of the miracle.[39]

Note that the story itself offers three distinct approaches. First, the consciousness among the Jews of Divine Providence: לְמַעַן תִּהְיֶה זֹאת אוֹת בְּקִרְבְּכֶם...וְהָיוּ הָאֲבָנִים הָאֵלֶּה לְזִכָּרוֹן לִבְנֵי יִשְׂרָאֵל, "In order that this may be a sign in your midst... and these stones shall be a memorial to the Children of Israel forever" (Josh. 4:6–7). And later on, לְמַעַן יְרָאתֶם אֶת ה׳ אֱלֹהֵיכֶם כָּל הַיָּמִים, "In order that you will fear the Lord your God all the days" (Josh. 4:24).

Second, Joshua's personal status among the people. Early in the story, the text states, הַיּוֹם הַזֶּה אָחֵל גַּדֶּלְךָ בְּעֵינֵי כָּל יִשְׂרָאֵל אֲשֶׁר יֵדְעוּן כִּי כַּאֲשֶׁר הָיִיתִי עִם מֹשֶׁה אֶהְיֶה עִמָּךְ, "This day I have started to magnify you in the eyes of all of Israel, that they may know that as I was with Moses – so I will be with you" (Josh. 3:7). By the end of the dramatic crossing of the Jordan, this aim has indeed been attained: בַּיּוֹם הַהוּא גִּדַּל ה׳ אֶת יְהוֹשֻׁעַ בְּעֵינֵי כָּל יִשְׂרָאֵל וַיִּרְאוּ אֹתוֹ כַּאֲשֶׁר יָרְאוּ אֶת מֹשֶׁה כָּל יְמֵי חַיָּיו, "On that day God magnified Joshua in the eyes of all of Israel, and they feared him as they had feared Moses, all the days of his life" (Josh. 4:14).

Third, there is a message to other nations: לְמַעַן דַּעַת כָּל עַמֵּי הָאָרֶץ אֶת יַד ה׳ כִּי חֲזָקָה הִיא, "In order that all the people of the earth may know the hand of God, that it is mighty" (Josh. 4:24).

These three approaches are interwoven in the chapter in ways too elaborate for the scope of this discussion. The key point, however, is that "their integration naturally brings about repetitions which illuminate, in each instance, the different aims of this miracle."[40] Thus, for example, the monument of stones is described twice, the first a description for the Jewish people and the second directed toward the nations of the world. In the repeated descriptions of the command to appoint the

38. A concise and clear review of the various approaches is presented by E. Assis, *MiMoshe LiYehoshua U'MiNes LeTeva* (Jerusalem, 2005), 85–89.

39. My presentation here is based on Assis's discussion, 92–108.

40. Assis, 107.

twelve men, or for the *kohanim* to exit the Jordan, the action is presented in one case as God's command (Josh. 4:2, 15–16), and in the other case, without any divine command (Josh. 3:11; 4:11). The actions therefore symbolize God's guidance of the Jewish people, and, at the same time, an elevation of Joshua's status in the eyes of the people.

These examples demonstrate that the aspects approach can provide an effective and practical way of understanding textual difficulties in the books of the Prophets, just as it does for similar difficulties that arise in the Torah itself.

Chapter 5

Accuracy of the Masoretic Text

INTRODUCTION

In previous chapters we addressed what is known as "higher criticism" – the processes by which the body of biblical literature came into being, along with the conclusions drawn by academic research in this area. In this chapter we will discuss what is known as "lower criticism," namely, the accuracy and history of the biblical text itself.[1] This type of scholarship seeks to explore the emergence of the precise biblical text that we possess today and the changes that this text has undergone over the course of generations, by comparing manuscripts, examining textual witnesses, and employing various philological tools. The aim of lower criticism is largely to evaluate the relative accuracy of textual variants. This realm of study is therefore not committed to any particular version

1. The following are some sources offering extensive reviews of the subject: H.D. Hummel, "Bible: Bible Research and Criticism," *Encyclopedia Judaica* 4 (Jerusalem, 1971), columns 914–15; Z. Talshir, "Synchronic and Diachronic Approaches in the Study of the Hebrew Bible: Text Criticism within the Frame of Biblical Philology," *Textus* 23 (2007): 1–32; Z. Talshir, in Z. Talshir (ed.), *Sifrut HaMikra: Mevo'ot U'Meḥkarim* 1 (Jerusalem, 2011), 37–85; Emanuel Tov, *Textual Criticism of the Hebrew Bible*, 2nd ed. (Minneapolis and Assen, 2001).

of the biblical text, and that openness to other versions creates another fundamental gap between the traditional Jewish approach maintained over the generations, and the academic approach. In general, the traditional approach would not dream of addressing the possibility of textual variants:

> There is a concept in Judaism, deeply rooted in the consciousness of the nation, concerning the sanctity of the biblical text, even its very letters. This is usually explained in historical terms: namely, the text, down to the last letter, has reached us in the same original form in which it was first composed. Over the course of many generations, this concept has come to assume something of the validity of a fundamental principle of Judaism, by virtue of many statements surrounding this subject, in both halakha and aggada, as well as in Jewish thought. Thus, any method that casts doubt on the absolute reliability of the transmission causes a believing Jew to recoil.[2]

This chapter therefore addresses two main questions: First, is the text that is considered sacrosanct by the traditional world today indeed the original text of the Tanakh? Second, if it is not identical in every detail to the original text, what are the implications of those discrepancies for the possibility of proposing emendations to the text? The discussion will address the history of the text through the generations, as well as the various textual witnesses, including, among others, the Dead Sea Scrolls, the Samaritan Torah, the Septuagint, and other translations.

THE TANAKH TEXT DURING THE PERIOD OF THE SAGES[3]

From time immemorial, the precise transmission of the biblical text has been undertaken with great care. Josephus, writing in the first century CE,

2. M. Cohen, "HaIde'a BiDevar Kedushat HaNusaḥ LeOtiotav UBikkoret HaText," in U. Simon (ed.), *HaMikra VaAnaḥnu* (Tel Aviv, 1979), 42–43.
3. For the purposes of this discussion, "the period of the Sages" is defined as extending from the Destruction of the Second Temple to the completion of the Talmud (roughly from the years 70 to 500), without noting the subdivisions within this period, which are not pertinent to the matter at hand.

testifies: "The scribes have taken care to maintain extreme accuracy, and – if I may be so bold – they will continue to do so (for all generations)."[4] The care taken in preserving the precise text is obvious throughout many rabbinic sources. For instance, R. Meir teaches:

> When I came to R. Yishmael, he said to me: "My son, what is your occupation?" I told him, "I am a scribe." He said to me, "Be meticulous in your work, for your occupation is a sacred one. If you were to omit or add a single letter, you would thereby destroy the entire world." (Eruvin 13a)

In addition to the Sages' great familiarity with the biblical text – clear from the corpus of midrashim that deal with verses from throughout the Tanakh[5] – the Sages were concerned with precise textual details. For example,[6] concerning the verse אֶחֱזוּ לָנוּ שׁוּעָלִים שֻׁעָלִים קְטַנִּים מְחַבְּלִים כְּרָמִים, "Take for us the foxes (*shualim*), the small foxes that spoil the vineyards" (Song of Songs 2:15), a midrash clarifies that the two appearances of the word "*shualim*" in the verse are spelled differently – the first time with a *vav* and the second time without it. "R. Berakhia said: The first [appearance of the word] '*shualim*' is written in plene, or full, form; the second – in defective form."[7] Similarly, attention is paid to the tiny *yod* in the word "*teshi*," in the verse צוּר יְלָדְךָ תֶּשִׁי, "Of the

4. Josephus, *Against Apion*, 1, 6.
5. As noted by S. Lieberman, *Hellenism in Jewish Palestine* (New York, 1950), 52–53. Admittedly, there were exceptions, as noted already by the *Rishonim* – "Sometimes they were not proficient in the verses" (*Tosafot*, Bava Batra 113a); see the anecdote recounted in Bava Kamma 54b concerning R. Ḥiyya bar Abba. However, as Lieberman notes, these were exceptions to the rule.
6. See E. Tov, "The Rabbinic Tradition Concerning the 'Alterations' Inserted into the Greek Pentateuch and Their Relation to the Original Text of the LXX," *Journal for the Study of Judaism in the Persian, Hellenistic and Roman Period* 15 (1984): 65–89.
7. R. Berakhia's teaching is reflected in the Koren edition of the Tanakh, but most manuscripts and printed versions do not follow this rule. For instance, in the Aleppo Codex, the word is missing the *vav* in both instances (see also *Minḥat Shai*), while MS Leningrad includes the *vav* in both instances.

Rock that begot you, you are unmindful (*teshi*)" (Deut. 32:18),[8] noting the unusual phenomenon of the letter being written even smaller than its usual size: "The *yod* is small."[9]

These examples imply that the Sages interpreted one single version of the text that they worked to understand precisely. That said, a number of sources suggest that there was disagreement with regard to some details of the accepted version, which gave rise to the need to choose among the different versions, as well as establishing ways of determining authenticity. The *Sifrei* Deuteronomy provides valuable examples:

> Three books [of Tanakh] were found in the *azara* (Temple courtyard): one of the "*me'onim*," another of "*hi-hi*," and one called *Sefer Zaatutim*. [The explanation for these appellations for the books follows:] In one book (the verse in Deut. 33:27) was written, מעון אלהי קדם, "The Eternal God is a dwelling place ("*ma'on*"), while in the other two it was written "*me'ona*." The Sages [therefore] rejected [the version appearing only in] the one copy, and accepted [the version that appeared in] the other two. In one version the word "*hi*" (היא, "it" or "she") appeared nine times, while in the others the word "*hi*" appeared eleven times. The Sages [therefore] rejected the one copy and accepted the other two. In one version the text read, וישלח את זעטוטי בני ישראל, "and he sent the young men (*zaatutei*) of the Children of Israel" (Ex. 24:5), and ואל זעטוטי בני ישראל, "upon the young men (*zaatutei*) of the Children of Israel" (24:11), while the other two read, וישלח את נערי בני ישראל, "he sent the young men (*naarei*) of the Children of Israel" and ואל אצילי בני ישראל, "upon the nobles (*atzilei*) of the Children

8. Here, too, the "authentic" spelling is a matter of debate. While the letter *yod* in this verse is mentioned in all Masoretic lists of letters that are written in diminutive form, it does not actually appear in this form in some important witnesses, including the Aleppo Codex and MS Leningrad.

9. Leviticus Rabba 23:14, Margaliot edition, 548.

of Israel" (Ex. 24:11). The Sages [therefore] rejected the one copy and accepted the other two.[10]

The three books found in the courtyard of the Temple surely represented the most sacred and important textual proofs available to the Sages during the Second Temple Period. Indeed, they were used to establish a standard text for all Torah scrolls. Nonetheless, no two were identical in every detail. The decision of the Sages to establish the "majority version" in each case of discrepancy created an interesting and surprising reality: after these three "models" were used to determine that standard text, each of the three of them became unfit for use, owing to the specific "defect" that it contained (when it did not align with the other two).

Despite this standardization, a *Sefer Torah* containing at least seven divergences from the accepted text,[11] belonging to Rabbi Meir, is

10. *Sifrei* Deuteronomy, *piska* 356, Finkelstein edition, 423. For various sources offering this description and the differences between them, see S. Talmon, "The Three Scrolls of the Law That Were Found in the Temple Court," *Textus* 2 (1962): 14–27.

11. Some of these variants appear to be midrashic in nature, since it is difficult to make sense of them on the plain level in the context of the verse. Especially well known are two examples. One concerns the verse, וַיַּרְא אֱלֹהִים אֶת כָּל אֲשֶׁר עָשָׂה וְהִנֵּה טוֹב מְאֹד, "And God saw all that He had done, and behold, it was very good (*tov me'od*)" (Gen. 1:31). In Genesis Rabba (*parasha* 9, 5, Theodor-Albeck edition, 70), we find, "The Torah of R. Meir was found to read, instead of והנה טוב מאד, 'And behold it was very good (*tov me'od*)' – **והנה טוב מות**, 'and behold it was good to die (*tov mot*).'" The second concerns the verse, וַיַּעַשׂ ה׳ אֱלֹהִים לְאָדָם וּלְאִשְׁתּוֹ כָּתְנוֹת עוֹר וַיַּלְבִּשֵׁם, "And the Lord God made for the man and for his wife coats of skins [*'ohr,'* written with the letter *ayin*], and He clothed them" (Gen. 3:21). Genesis Rabba (*parasha* 20, 12, Theodor-Albeck edition, 196) teaches, "The Torah of R. Meir was found to read **כותנות אור**, 'coats of light,' (*'ohr,'* written with the letter *alef*)." In both of these cases, the discrepancy in the text has a simple phonetic explanation, but given the content R. Meir's version seems to be aimed at conveying a certain homiletic message, rather than reflecting an actual textual version.

Another variant with conceptual or homiletic significance concerns the national struggle against Rome: the verse in Isaiah that starts with the words מַשָּׂא דּוּמָה, "The burden of Duma" (21:11) is replaced in R. Meir's version with "the burden of Rome." In this case, too, the substitution is easily explained in terms of the graphic similarity between the letters *dalet* and *resh*, but here again, the orientation seems to be midrashic – i.e., conveying a homiletic message, rather than simply featuring a textual variant.

mentioned in several places in rabbinic literature. An example is where the Masoretic text reads, וּבְנֵי דָן חֻשִׁים, "And the sons (*benei*) of Dan, Hushim" (Gen. 46:23), displaying a lack of correlation between the plural form (*benei* – "sons of") and the fact that only one son is named;[12] the verse in R. Meir's Torah is cited in the midrash as the simpler, more grammatically accurate "and the son (*ben*) of Dan, Hushim."[13]

Another discrepancy concerns the verse in which, in the Masoretic text, Joseph declares, וַיְשִׂימֵנִי לְאָב לְפַרְעֹה, "[God] has made me (*vayesimeni*) a father for Pharaoh" (Gen. 45:8). In R. Meir's Torah, the midrash reports, the equivalent verse reads: וישני לאב, "[God] has made me a creditor (*vayasheni*) as a father [to Pharaoh]," going on to cite a proof text, שנאמר אשר ישה ברעהו, "which he lends (*yasheh*) to his neighbor" (Deut. 15:2).[14] The midrash explains that this is "one of the words written in the Torah that left Jerusalem with the captives and was taken to Rome, where it was hidden in the synagogue of Severus."[15] It goes on to list all thirty instances where the text of this *Sefer Torah* differed from the accepted version,[16] most of them minor variations.[17]

---

12. The commentators note the difficulty in the verse, and Ibn Ezra offers two possible explanations: either Dan had two sons, one of whom died, and therefore the verse mentions only Hushim; or the verse adopts in relation to Dan the same standard formula that appears for each of the other sons of Jacob ("And the *sons of*"), even though in this case there was only one son.
13. Genesis Rabba 94, 9, Theodor-Albeck edition, 1182.
14. Genesis Rabba 45, 8, Theodor-Albeck edition, 209.
15. Two Roman emperors (Septimius and Alexander), who reigned during the second and third centuries CE, were called by the name Severus. The reference here is most likely to Severus Alexander (222–235), who was known for his positive relations with the Jews.
16. The list in the Albeck edition is somewhat corrupted, but with the aid of other manuscripts it is possible to arrive at the full list. Concerning manuscripts, see Talshir (above, n. 1), 40, n. 14.
17. Some of the differences include the versions unique to the Torah of R. Meir; others involve remnants of an ancient script in which no distinction is made between final letters and regular letters (for instance, יומ מותי, Gen. 27:2). A small number represent reasonable possible alternatives to the textual version with which we are familiar, such as the verse containing God's statement about Sodom: אֵרְדָה נָּא וְאֶרְאֶה הַכְּצַעֲקָתָהּ, "I shall go down now and see whether they have done altogether according to the cry of it (*haketzaakata*)" (Gen. 18:21); the text in this *Sefer Torah* reads הכצעקתם, "whether they have done altogether according to their cry (*haketzaakatam*)."

It is noteworthy that, with the exception of these thirty instances, the text of the Torah taken to Rome was identical to that of the accepted text, established by the Sages.

With an understanding that the words of the Torah were finalized, the dots that are written above certain words in the Torah came into question.[18] The dots and their placement are very ancient traditions, and they are among the very few markings of any sort that are found in a Torah scroll, which otherwise contains no punctuation or cantillation marks. One instance of these dots is the verse (Deut. 29:28), הַנִּסְתָּרֹת לַה׳ אֱלֹהֵינוּ וְהַנִּגְלֹת לָנוּ וּלְבָנֵינוּ עַד עוֹלָם לַעֲשׂוֹת אֶת כָּל דִּבְרֵי הַתּוֹרָה הַזֹּאת, "The hidden things are for the Lord our God, while the revealed things are for us and for our children forever (*lanu ulevanenu ad olam*), to perform all the words of this Torah." Dots are found above the words, "*lanu ulevanenu*" and above the letter *ayin* in the word "*ad*." A passage in *Avot deRabbi Natan* depicts the following scene:

> Ezra said: "If Elijah were to appear to me and ask, 'Why did you write it this way?' I would say to him, 'I have already placed dots above the letters.' If he says to me, 'You have done well in writing [the Torah text in this way],' then I will remove the dots from above the letters."[19]

The midrash implies that Ezra the Scribe had some doubt as to the proper rendering of this verse and therefore wrote it in a way that would give expression to both versions of the text.[20] Indeed, marking words with

18. This phenomenon occurs in ten different places in the Torah, four places in *Nevi'im* (Prophets), and once in *Ketuvim* (Writings). The phenomenon is noted in several sources in *Ḥazal*, including *Sifrei* Numbers, *Behaalotekha* 69, Horowitz edition 164.
19. *Avot deRabbi Natan*, version A, chapter 34. Schechter edition 51a.
20. Regarding the same verse in Deuteronomy, the Gemara quotes R. Yehuda asking: "Why are there dots over the words *lanu ulevanenu*, and upon the letter *ayin* in the [next] word, *ad* (forever)? This teaches that God did not punish for hidden things until the Jews had passed over the Jordan River" (Sanhedrin 43b). From this, we understand that there are indeed two possible ways of reading the verse, each pertaining to a different historical period: one reading of the text expresses the idea that is relevant only after the nation's entry into the land – i.e., that the Jewish people are punished even for hidden sins of the individuals among them,

dots over them to indicate that they have been "erased" was a well-known practice, found in manuscripts ranging from the Dead Sea Scrolls to those from the Middle Ages.

Given this clarification, and in light of Ezra's uncertainty, it is not difficult to read a verse where the phenomenon of dotting occurs in multiple ways. For instance, the verse dealing with the census of the Levites includes dots above the name Aaron: כָּל פְּקוּדֵי הַלְוִיִּם אֲשֶׁר פָּקַד מֹשֶׁה וְאַהֲרֹן עַל פִּי ה׳ לְמִשְׁפְּחֹתָם כָּל זָכָר מִבֶּן חֹדֶשׁ וָמַעְלָה שְׁנַיִם וְעֶשְׂרִים אָלֶף, "All who were counted of the Levites, whom Moses counted, and Aaron, at God's command, by their families – every male from a month old and upward, were 22,000" (Num. 3:39). The dots presumably appear here because the command at the beginning of the census is given solely to Moses (Num. 14–15), which calls into question the implication in the verse that Aaron was also directly commanded with regard to the census. Indeed, Rabbi Hayim Paltiel addresses this very concern in his commentary on verse 39:[21]

---

since the idea of mutual responsibility entails punishment even for sins that are not committed in public. However, the other reading indicates that prior to the entry into Israel, the nation was not punished for hidden sins. How does this idea arise from the placing of dots, indicating words that should be "erased," as it were? Rashi writes (ad loc.): "The dots should have been placed over the words 'for the Lord our God' – teaching that these (hidden) things do not remain within the realm of the Lord our God forever. However, it is not the way of the world to place dots over the name of God, and therefore they are placed over the words 'for us and for our children,' indicating that this is not their proper place." In other words, the dots should really have been placed over the words "the Lord our God," such that the alternative reading, without these words, would render the Jews responsible even for hidden matters: "The hidden and revealed things are for us and for our children forever." The only reason that the dots appear over different letters is because it is not proper to place dots over God's name. The *Tosafot* (ad loc.) note that according to Rashi's understanding, the letter *ayin* in the following word "*ad*" is likewise dotted, to indicate that there are a total of eleven letters that should be dotted (the Tetragrammaton [God's name] + the name "Elokeinu"), and therefore an alternative set of eleven letters is so marked ("*lanu ulevanenu*" + the letter *ayin*).

21. Rabbi Hayim Paltiel lived in France and in Germany during the thirteenth century, and was a disciple and friend of Rabbi Meir (ben Barukh) of Rothenburg (Maharam). The commentary that is named after him is a collection of commentaries on the Torah by the Tosafists, which was edited by the son of R. Hayim.

> Why are there dots on the word "Aaron"? Because he did not perform the counting; it was undertaken by Moses alone, since he alone had been commanded. For this reason the text says "whom [Moses] counted" [in the singular], and not "whom [Moses and Aaron] counted" [in the plural].

The version of this verse that is familiar from the Masoretic text implies that Aaron participated and aided Moses in the census, although he was not commanded to do so.

Another ambiguous phrasing is found in the verses describing the encounter between Jacob and Esau: וַיָּרָץ עֵשָׂו לִקְרָאתוֹ וַיְחַבְּקֵהוּ וַיִּפֹּל עַל צַוָּארָו וַיִּשָּׁקֵהוּ וַיִּבְכּוּ, "And Esau ran to meet him, and he embraced him, and he fell upon his neck, and he kissed him, and they wept" (Gen. 33:4). Dots appear above the word "and he kissed him" (*vayishakehu*). Those dots suggest two interpretations of the verse, each representing a different understanding of the warmth of Esau's response to Jacob. It seems that this is the meaning of the teaching that actually creates a balance between the two viewpoints: "He did not kiss him wholeheartedly."[22]

In another example of the presence of dots over a word in the Torah scroll, it is clear that the verse would retain its meaning, were it to be read without the dotted word. Specifically, when the angels visit Abraham, וַיֹּאמְרוּ אֵלָיו אַיֵּה שָׂרָה אִשְׁתֶּךָ וַיֹּאמֶר הִנֵּה בָאֹהֶל, "They said to him, 'Where is Sarah, your wife?' And he said, 'Behold, in the tent'" (Gen. 18:9) – here, the term "to him" (*elav*) is dotted. Ralbag, commenting on this verse, writes:[23]

> To my mind, the dots that are above [the word] "*elav*," and similar examples, appear to me to indicate an intermediate situation between the presence of the dotted word and its absence. For the dots are placed over a word [in order] to

22. Commentary of the *Sifrei* there.
23. Rabbi Levi ben Gershom, 1288–1344, lived in France and the Netherlands. His extensive commentaries on the *Ḥumash* and much of *Nevi'im* and *Ketuvim* address both exegetical and philosophical questions.

> erase that which appears under the dots. But since the word remains written in the text with the dots above it, it indicates that it is not erased altogether, nor is it written in its [usual] entire manner.[24]

The *Amora'im* stated explicitly that they were not experts in the exact text of the Tanakh. In the Gemara (Kiddushin 30a) we find:

> Therefore the early Sages were called "*Sofrim*" (literally, "counters") (II Chr. 55), for they would count all the letters in the Torah. They established that the *vav* of the word "*gaḥon*" (Lev. 11:42) is the halfway mark of all the letters in a *Sefer Torah*; the words "*darosh darash*" (Lev. 10:16) are the middle words [of a *Sefer Torah*]; and the verse that begins "*vehitgalaḥ*" (Lev. 13:33) is the middle verse [of a *Sefer Torah*].

In other words, the early *Sofrim* (a reference to the sages at the time of Ezra) possessed an extremely accurate version of the text, and they had a tradition as to the middle letter, word, and verse of the Torah.[25] In the continuation of the Gemara, R. Yosef raises a question: Assuming that the number of words in the Torah is an even number, such that there is no exact "middle letter," does the letter *vav* represent the last letter of the first half of the Torah, or the first letter of the second half? The Gemara proposes counting the letters in a *Sefer Torah* in order to arrive at the answer to this question, but then rejects the idea, stating: "They were

---

24. See Ralbag's commentary on the Torah, Brenner and Freiman edition (Maaleh Adumim, 1993), 248, n. 10.

25. These locations are quite far removed from the "middles" as we know them today: The middle letter in our *Sefer Torah* is the letter "*alef*" in the word "*hu*" (Lev. 8:28) – almost five thousand letters away from the letter mentioned here. The midpoint in our *Sefer Torah* in terms of words is to be found in between the words "*el yesod*" (Lev. 8:15) – about a thousand words away from the location cited. The middle verse of the Torah as we know it is Leviticus 8:8 – about 60 verses away from the one given. The *Minḥat Shai* (Lev. 8:8) notes this considerable discrepancy, noting first the possibility that "we might say that we are not experts in the verses," but goes on to acknowledge, "But my mind is not reconciled with this, since the discrepancy is very great.... [Elijah] the Tishbi will bring the solution."

experts in the traditional plene and defective spellings, but we are not." Further on, the Gemara explains that modern students of the text are likewise unable to locate the "middle verse" of the Torah:

> When R. Aha bar Adda came he said, "In the west [i.e., in the Land of Israel], the following verse is read as three [separate] verses: וַיֹּאמֶר ה׳ אֶל מֹשֶׁה הִנֵּה אָנֹכִי בָּא אֵלֶיךָ בְּעַב הֶעָנָן, "And God said to Moses, 'Behold, I come to you in a thick cloud.'" (Ex. 19:9)[26]

These discussions make it clear that, as long ago as the period of the *Amora'im,* the Sages addressed questions concerning textual variants – involving plene and defective spellings, and even the division of verses.[27] Obviously, this matter has significant halakhic ramifications, which are discussed by the commentators and authorities throughout the generations.[28]

---

26. The full verse reads: וַיֹּאמֶר ה׳ אֶל מֹשֶׁה הִנֵּה אָנֹכִי בָּא אֵלֶיךָ בְּעַב הֶעָנָן בַּעֲבוּר יִשְׁמַע הָעָם בְּדַבְּרִי עִמָּךְ וְגַם בְּךָ יַאֲמִינוּ לְעוֹלָם, וַיַּגֵּד מֹשֶׁה אֶת דִּבְרֵי הָעָם אֶל ה׳, "And the Lord said to Moses, 'Behold, I come to you in a thick cloud, in order that the people may hear when I speak with you, and believe you forever'; and Moses told the words of the people to the Lord." This may be broken down into three parts (see commentary of Maharsha [Samuel Eliezer b. Judah HaLevi Edels, 1555–1631, Poland] to the Gemara in Kiddushin, ad loc.).
27. The *Amora'im* in the Gemara cited here ask about the letters and the verses, but do not ask a similar question regarding the "middle word" of the Torah. On this basis, the *Tosefot HaRid* (Isaiah di Trani, thirteenth century, Italy) stated that "concerning the words there is no room for doubt as there is concerning the [middle] letters and verses." However, a counting of the words in the Torah shows that according to the version of the text as we know it, the middle words are found a whole two chapters earlier: אֶל יְסוֹד הַמִּזְבֵּחַ וַיְקַדְּשֵׁהוּ, "at the bottom of the altar and sanctified it" (Lev. 8:15). This calculation is cited in the word of Rabbi Yaakov Shor on the Tosefta (*Mishnat Rabbi Yaakov,* Pieterkov, 1930). For this reason it would appear that concerning words, too, the *Sofrim* had a different tradition (although Rabbi Yaakov Shor rightly asks how it is possible for there to be such a great discrepancy between the tradition of the *Sofrim* and the text as we have it), and the reason that the Gemara does not ask the same question about the words is, as the Ramah (Rabbi Meir HaLevi Abulafia, 1170?–1244, Spain) suggests in his commentary, ad loc., that the tradition was that the words "*darosh darash*" are exactly the middle: the first word concludes the first half, and the second word starts the second half.
28. Rabbi Menahem b. Solomon Meiri (1249–1316, Provence), in his commentary on

We may therefore conclude that during the time of the Sages, the version of the Tanakh was for the most part fixed and uniform, but in some instances there arose questions of textual variants; where such details as plene or defective spelling were concerned, there was a lack of clarity, which became more pronounced during the period of the *Amora'im*.

THE VERSION OF THE SAGES AND THE MESORA VERSION

Despite what we have seen above, there exists no complete, clear copy of the Tanakh from the period of the Sages. The text was handed down from generation to generation in the form of manuscripts, and, while the

---

the Gemara in Kiddushin, concludes as follows: "The guidelines that we have been given by the *Sofrim* that we rely on for the purposes of writing a *Sefer Torah* are based on the most precise texts in our possession, but it is not to say that we have absolute clarity on the matter. And on account of this I feel it is wise to be lenient and not invalidate a *Sefer Torah* on account of this [a missing or additional letter], for this could only apply to experts."

The Rema (Rabbi Moses b. Israel Isserles, halakhic codifier whose record of Ashkenazic rulings was incorporated into the *Shulḥan Arukh*) rules similarly that the law concerning a *Sefer Torah* in which a mistake has been found – i.e., that it is returned to the Holy Ark and a different Torah scroll is taken out to be read – applies "specifically when a definite mistake has been found, but one does not take out another scroll merely on account of plene or defective spelling of words, since our Torah scrolls are not so accurate that we can be sure that the second scroll will be any better [than the first]" (*Shulḥan Arukh, Oraḥ Ḥayim* 143:4). The *Shaagat Aryeh* (Rabbi Aryeh Leib Gunzburg, 1695–1785, Lithuania and France) (36) writes that on the basis of the Gemara's discussion, we may indeed conclude that in our times there is no possibility of writing a "kosher" *Sefer Torah*, and therefore the commandment of writing a *Sefer Torah* does not apply in our times: "Because even in the times of the *Amora'im*, they were not expert in plene and defective spellings... and, after all, a *Sefer Torah* that lacks even a single letter, or has one extra letter, is invalid. Therefore, we are unable to observe this commandment." The Hatam Sofer (*Orah Haim* 52) used this reasoning to explain why we do not recite a blessing over the writing of a *Sefer Torah*. (Admittedly, there were other authorities who disagreed on this point, maintaining that the version that has been handed down to us by the Masoretes, as is clear below, is the version that one is halakhically required to follow. Therefore writing such a scroll does fulfill the commandment to write a *Sefer Torah* in every respect, and a scroll lacking a single letter must not be read from in public. See *Shu"t Ginat Veradim, Orah Ḥaim* 2:6 and elsewhere.)

scribes who undertook this work undoubtedly attached great importance to the accurate transmission of the texts and regarded them as holy, they were after all human beings – in the copying of such lengthy manuscripts, human error inevitably creeps in.[29] Thus, over the years, a large number of manuscripts were produced, with very slight differences among them – until the time of the Masoretes.

The Masoretes lived between the eighth and tenth centuries, and sought to establish a uniform version of the text that would be accepted, from that point onwards, in all Jewish communities. To that end, they instituted Masoretic notes (to be discussed below), which served to set down, among other things, the number of times that certain words appeared in plene or defective form (*maleh veḥaser*) throughout the entire Tanakh. They wrote books discussing the exact wording and spelling of the biblical text, and they developed the system of vowels and cantillation marks to preserve the proper form of reading. The prevailing Tanakh text of the modern era is based, for the most part, on the Masoretic version of the text.[30]

The Talmud mentions two main textual traditions: that of Babylonia (the "eastern") and that of the Land of Israel (the "western"). These differ from one another in their letters, vowelization, cantillation, and "*keri ukhetiv*" variants (where a word is vocalized differently from the way it is written). Thus, there developed the "Babylonian tradition"[31] and the "Tiberian tradition," which reflected these differences.[32] The

29. Today, this fact is borne out by checking Torah scrolls using scanners. It turns out that even well-known scribes make mistakes. According to data published by websites dedicated to this field, the vast majority of Torah scrolls checked by computer are found to contain errors.

30. For a general overview of the subject, see A. Dotan, "Masorah," *Encyclopedia Judaica* 16 (Jerusalem, 1972), columns 1401–82, and Geoffrey Khan, *A Short Introduction to the Tiberian Masoretic Bible and Its Reading Tradition* (Piscataway, 2012). A much more detailed discussion appears in Israel Yeivin, *Introduction to the Tiberian Masorah*, translated and edited by E. J. Revell (Atlanta, 1980).

31. For a comprehensive review of the Babylonian tradition, see Y. Ofer, *HaMasoret HaBavlit LaTorah – Ekronoteha U'Derakheiha* (Jerusalem, 2001). For a briefer overview, see his "Masora, Babylonian," *Encyclopedia of Hebrew Language and Linguistics* 2, 585–88.

32. In the southern part of Israel, there developed a third *mesora*, known as the "*mesora*

Tiberian tradition, or *Mesora*, regarded as more accurate, was ultimately accepted as the authoritative text.

The Masoretes of Tiberias were active from the eighth through the tenth centuries, and were themselves split between two traditions – that of Aharon Ben-Asher, and that of Moshe Ben-Naphtali. There were hundreds of differences between them, mostly small discrepancies in matters of vowelization and cantillation.[33] The version of Ben-Asher came to be considered authoritative, and books of Tanakh published today are almost identical to it, with the exception of a few minor details. The *Mesora* text was preserved with great accuracy and meticulousness by various means, especially the mechanism of the "*Mesora Gedola*" and the "*Mesora Ketana*," which together provide tens of thousands of notations above, below, and at the sides of the columns of the text, which ensured the precise way that words were to be written throughout the Tanakh.

In particular, "Keter Aram Tzova" (the Aleppo Codex), a tenth-century manuscript of the Tanakh that was kept in Aleppo, Syria from the fourteenth century until 1947, came to be regarded as the definitive text, since its notations had been written by Aharon Ben-Asher himself. It is generally agreed that Maimonides's mention of a certain *Sefer Torah* in Egypt (where the Codex was kept prior to its move to Aleppo) refers to this manuscript:

> The manuscript that we have relied upon in these matters [the list of "open" and "closed" units] is the well-known scroll in Egypt, containing [all] twenty-four books [of Tanakh], which was kept in Jerusalem for some years for other manuscripts to be checked against, and everyone relied upon it because its notations were written by Ben-Asher, who worked on it painstakingly for many years, and checked it many times as he copied it. This is what I

of Eretz Yisrael," but it is marginal in relation to the two main traditions.

33. Lists of these variants were noted in manuscripts, the best-known of these being *Sefer HaḤilufin* (the Book of Variants), a scientific edition of which was published by A. Lipschitz (Jerusalem, 1965).

relied upon [also] for the *Sefer Torah* that I wrote in accordance with its laws."[34]

The particular merit of this manuscript lies in the almost perfect correlation between its text and its Masoretic notes, demonstrating the impressive degree of accuracy with which it was written. The Aleppo Codex serves as the basis for the Breuer edition of the Tanakh,[35] and later also Prof. Menahem Cohen's edition, *Mikraot Gedolot – HaKeter*[36] and the *Mifal HaMikra* edition published by the Hebrew University.[37]

In general, the Sages used the *Mesora* version of the text, which means that the questions and uncertainties discussed earlier remain. It should be noted, however, that in dozens of instances, the *Mesora* version differs from the text used by the Sages, and sometimes those differences carry broader ramifications – for example, the discussion in Kiddushin (30a) that reflects the discrepancies between the text as cited by the Sages and the text as it is known today, concerning the middle word and the middle letter of the Torah.

Another key discrepancy appears later in that same discussion: "Our Sages taught: 'The verses of a *Sefer Torah* number 5,888; the verses of the book of Psalms number eight fewer than that, and the number of verses of Chronicles number eight more.'" In the Tanakh in use today, which follows the specifications of the Masoretes, the number of verses in the Torah is 5,845 – forty-three fewer than the number cited in the Gemara, while the number of verses in Psalms (2,527) and in Chronicles

34. *Mishneh Torah, Hilkhot Sefer Torah* 8:4.

35. Rabbi Mordekhai Breuer published a number of editions of the Tanakh based on the Aleppo Codex. For his discussion of the Codex and its influences on the Tanakh accepted today, see M. Breuer, *Keter Aram Tzova VeHaNusaḥ HaMekubal Shel HaMikra* (Jerusalem, 1977); H. Tawil and S. Schneider, *The Crown of Aleppo: The Mystery of the Oldest Hebrew Bible Codex* (Philadelphia, 2010); Y. Ofer, "The Preparation of the 'Jerusalem Crown' Edition of the Bible Text," *Hebrew Studies* 44 (2003): 87–117.

36. At the time of writing, not all the volumes of this edition have been printed yet, but the entire Tanakh is available in this edition on DVD. The books of the Torah, the Prophets, Psalms, and the Five Megillot are available from Bar Ilan University Press, at http://www.mgketer.org.

37. This edition, too, is not yet complete; only a few volumes have been published.

(1,556) are even further removed from the Gemara's count. The *Geonim* and *Rishonim* offer various explanations of this discrepancy regarding the Books of Psalms and Chronicles,[38] but in any event these details indicate that the accepted division of the verses during the time of the Sages was different from that of the Masoretes.

Other differences pertain to matters of content and meaning. Many of the Sages' teachings cite verses that differ from the *Mesora* text. The medieval commentators note that "in several places there was controversy between the redactors of the Talmud and the sages of the *Mesora*" (Responsa of Ridbaz, III, 594).[39] Sometimes these discrepancies involve plene or defective spelling, and the shifts in meaning they present. For example, the Gemara (Shabbat 55b) cites Rav's opinion that, of the two sons of Eli, only Hofni sinned, and not Pinhas. He maintains that, although the text states that Eli told his sons that bad rumors were circulating, suggesting that they were "causing [in the plural] God's people to sin (*maavirim am Hashem*)" (I Sam. 2:24), he was in fact referring only to one of them. Rav proves this by noting, "It is written '*maaviram*' [in the singular]." In the *Mesora* version, the letter *yod* appears before the final *mem*, such that the verb is unquestionably in the plural, as noted by the *Tosafot*, who comment on the term: "The Gemara disagrees with the version as written in our Tanakh."[40] Elsewhere, this

38. The *Tosefot Yeshanim*, ad loc., question the count of the verses in Psalms, and the matter remains unresolved. Rabbi Hai Gaon (939–1038, head of the Babylonian yeshiva of Pumbedita), in a responsum, writes that the figures noted in the Gemara refer to "that *Sefer Torah* which they found in Jerusalem, which was unusual in its script and in its number of verses, and likewise the Psalms and also the Chronicles, but now there is only one [accepted] version of the Torah, and only one [accepted] version of Psalms, and one [accepted] version of Chronicles" (*Teshuvot HaGeonim*, Harkaby, *siman* 3). He refers here to the *Sefer Torah* found in the Synagogue of Severus, mentioned above. This explanation raises its own difficulties, since a *Sefer Torah* contains no division into verses, and in any case it is difficult to see how Psalms could possibly contain anywhere near as many verses as a *Sefer Torah*. For additional proposals see Segal, 886.

39. An extensive discussion of the responsum of Rabbi David Ibn Zimra regarding the *Mesora* and inaccuracies in the Torah text appears in B. Levy, *Fixing God's Torah: The Accuracy of the Hebrew Bible Text in Jewish Law* (Oxford, 2001).

40. Rashi, in contrast, maintains that the *Mesora* version is correct: "This [opinion of Rav] is greatly mistaken, and we do not accept that the word should be written that

divergence happens the other way around: "We find that the accepted [textual] tradition differs from what the Gemara says" (*Tosafot*, Nidda 33a).[41] Rabbi Akiva Eiger (1761–1837), in his *Gilayon HaShas* to Tractate Shabbat, notes many similar examples.[42]

Sometimes the discrepancies are more substantial. *Tosafot* on Shabbat 55b quote the Jerusalem Talmud (Y. Sota 1:8, 17b):

> In one place we read [regarding Samson], "He judged Israel for forty years," while in a different place, we read, "He judged Israel for twenty years." Rabbi Aḥa said: "This teaches that the Philistines were as fearful of him [and therefore refrained from attacking] for twenty years after his death as they had feared him for twenty years in his lifetime."

However, as *Tosafot* note, in our *Mesora* version, the first verse that is cited reads, וַיִּשְׁפֹּט אֶת יִשְׂרָאֵל עֶשְׂרִים שָׁנָה, "He judged Israel in the days of the Philistines for twenty years" (Judges 15:20).

Another example: the Gemara twice presents the following:

---

way, for our manuscripts read *'maavirim.'*"

41. The approach of the *Tosafot* and other *Rishonim* contrasts with that of the Sages of Babylonia, who consistently maintain that it is impossible for there to be any contradiction or discrepancy between the version noted in the Gemara and the version of the *Mesora*. If there are "verses that we find in the Talmud that do not appear [in that form] in the Tanakh," they are not the result of the talmudic Sages using a text with errors. Rather, "our Sages would not make a mistake with a verse, for in their teachings, they invest great effort so that the teaching of one Sage would not become muddled with the teaching of a different Sage, each taking care to cite [the law] as he heard it from his teacher; how much more so, then, [would they exercise caution] with the words of the Torah and Tanakh" (*Teshuvat Rav Hai Gaon, Teshuvot Geonim Kadmonim, siman* 78). Therefore, in this view, the phenomenon must be explained in one of three ways: "Either it is a scribal error, or the teachings were disseminated by disciples who were not proficient [in the text], or the words were never uttered in the first place as the quotation of a verse."
42. Rabbi Isaiah Pick-Berlin, in his comments scattered throughout the Gemara (Vilna edition), notes this phenomenon and compiles a list of instances in his work entitled *Haflaah SheBeArakhin* (on the *Arukh*), under the entry "*me'ah*."

> Rav Naḥman said: "Manoah was an ignoramus, as it is written, 'Manoah went after his wife' (Judges 13:11)." Rabbi Naḥman bar Yitzhak disagreed: "But what about Elkana, concerning whom it says, 'Elkana went after his wife,' and what about Elisha, concerning whom it is written, 'And he arose and went after her' (II Kings 4:30)? Are we then to understand that [in these latter instances, too, where the men were clearly knowledgeable and pious,] the man literally walked behind the woman? [Surely not;] it means he followed her words and her advice. Therefore here too, [with regard to Manoah,] he followed her words and her advice." (Berakhot 61a; Eruvin 18a)

The verse about Elkana does not appear in the Tanakh that is considered authoritative today. The verse closest in meaning to the one cited is וַיֵּלֶךְ אֶלְקָנָה הָרָמָתָה עַל בֵּיתוֹ, "Elkana went to Rama, to his house" (I Sam. 2:11). The Tosafists comment on the Berakhot passage: "This is a corruption [of the text], for there is no such verse in all of the Tanakh and we do not follow this tradition" – a position that was upheld by many other *Rishonim*.[43] Still, other medieval commentators – first and foremost Rashi and Rabbenu Hananel on Eruvin – do not reject the textual version upon which this discussion is based, accepting it at face value. Indeed, in most of the manuscripts of both tractates, the passage appears as cited above, with no alteration to the verse – even though it does not conform to the Masoretic version.[44] It would therefore seem

43. Including *Tosefot HaRosh* (Rabbi Asher b. Yeḥiel, c. 1250–1327, Germany and France) on Berakhot, ad loc.; and Rashba (Rabbi Solomon b. Abraham ibn Aderet, 1235–1310, Spain); and Ritba (Rabbi Yom Tov b. Abraham Ashbili, c. 1250–1330, Spain), on the parallel unit in Eruvin.

44. Maharshal (Rabbi Solomon Luria, 1510–1573, Poland), in his commentary *Ḥokhmat Shlomo* on Berakhot, ad loc., writes: "The comments of *Tosafot*, who completely erase the [Gemara's] version of the text, are difficult in my opinion. Of course, textual variants can be expected from time to time in the Talmud, but to utterly dismiss a version of the text and to maintain that it was mistakenly written is hard to accept."

Maharshal maintains that the quote in the Gemara is referring to the verse that appears in different form in the *Mesora* text, and that "it is the way of the Gemara to alter verses." As we find in the *Hagahot HaShas* there, Maharshal's explanation contradicts Rashi's approach.

that these *Rishonim* believed that this was the version that the Sages had before them, and for this reason they did not remove the verse.[45]

The discrepancies between the version of the Tanakh that the Sages used and the Masoretic text give rise to the obvious question: How is one to determine the proper and accurate version of the text? This question occupied *Rishonim* and *Aḥaronim* alike.[46] One approach, espoused by Rashba[47] and adopted by many *Rishonim,* is to distinguish between those instances where the discrepancy between the versions would have bearing on the law derived from the verse – in which cases, "we rely on the Sages of the Talmud" – and instances where the textual variants have no practical bearing, and then, "we rely on the sages of the *Mesora*."[48] In practice, however, the *Mesora* version is considered authoritative in every instance, a rule formulated by the *Minḥat Shai*:[49] "In every place where the Gemara or midrash differs from the *Mesora* in matters of additions or omissions, the decision is to follow the *Mesora* … even when the law is derived from them."[50]

A similar opinion is expressed by Rabbi Shlomo Ganzfried, redactor of the *Kitzur Shulḥan Arukh,* in his work *Keset HaSofer.*[51] These discussions reflect a clear awareness by authorities and commentators through the ages of the many discrepancies between the Masoretic version of Tanakh and the version used and cited by the talmudic Sages.

45. See Rosenthal, 400–401 and notes.
46. See Y. Maori, "Midrash Ḥazal KeEdut LeḤilufei Nusaḥ BaMikra," in M. Bar-Asher, et al. (eds.), *Iyyunei Mikra U'Parshanut* 3 (Ramat Gan, 1993), 273 n. 32, and in the appendix, 283–86.
47. In the Responsa of the Rashba attributed to Nahmanides, *siman* 232.
48. The citations are from the Responsa of the Ridbaz noted above (part III, *siman* 592). A similar view is expressed by the Meiri in his *Kiryat Sefer* (*maamar sheni,* part II, Herschler edition, 58).
49. *Minḥat Shai* is the name of an important work by Rabbi Shlomo Yedidia Norzi, published in 1626, that is a guide in matters relating to textual variants of the Tanakh. For more about the work and the author, see Z. Betzer, *Minḥat Shai Al Ḥamisha Ḥumshei Torah* (Jerusalem, 2005), 3–50, and Abraham Liebermann, "Jedidiah Solomon Norzi and the Stabilization of the Textus Receptus," *Masoretic Studies* 8 (1996): 37–47.
50. On Leviticus 4:34, Betzer edition, 237.
51. Introduction to Part II, *siman* 28, Shlomo Gantzfried, *Keset HaSofer.*

Keri UKhetiv

The phenomenon of "*keri ukhetiv*" variants (where a word is vocalized differently from the way it is written) is evident, to a limited extent, in the Sages' teachings[52] and among the Masoretes, who began to note the vocal form in the margins of Bible manuscripts, a practice that became very common. The origins of this custom have received some attention. One explanation of it was suggested by Radak:

> During the first exile, the books were lost or carried away, and the sages who knew the Bible passed away, and the Men of the Great Assembly, who restored the Torah to its previous honor, found discrepancies in the books and [therefore] followed the majority [of them] to the best of their understanding. Where their conclusions were not decisive, they wrote one option without vowels [thereby leaving room for more than one possibility for vocalization], or wrote on the outside, but not on the inside, or wrote the word one way in the text itself, but in a different way on the outside."[53]

According to Radak, this phenomenon represents a method of preserving different versions of a word in those instances where the Men of the

---

52. The most common example, of course, is the Ineffable Name of God, which is voiced differently from the way it is written. The Gemara teaches, "The textual reading as established by the *Sofrim*, and the embellishments of the *Sofrim*, and the letters that are pronounced but not written, and those that are written but not pronounced – all these were handed down as a law given to Moses at Sinai" (Nedarim 37b). The Gemara then enumerates instances of words that are voiced even though they are not written, and vice versa. (Incidentally, this indicates that the formula "a law given to Moses at Sinai" is used by the Sages, not necessarily in the literal sense, but rather in the sense of an ancient tradition, since the examples cited in the Gemara are from the book of the Prophets and Writings, rather than from the Five Books of Torah [as noted by Rabbi Yisrael Lipschitz in his commentary on Yoma, *Tiferet Yisrael*, 2:12].) Rabbinic literature includes several teachings about "*keri ukhetiv*" in the more familiar sense, i.e., that the text is written in one form, but read in a different form. See, for example, Sota 42b, pertaining to the *keri ukhetiv* in I Sam. 17:6, 23.
53. See Y. Ofer, "Ketiv U'Keri: Pesher HaTofaa, Darkei HaSimmun Shela VeDeot HaKadmonim Aleiha," *Leshonenu* 70 (5768/2008): 55–73; *Leshonenu* 71 (5769/2009): 255–79.

Great Assembly were unable to reach a final decision. In recognition of these deliberations, Radak labors to explain the text according to both *keri* and *ketiv* throughout his commentary, with the assumption that the latter represents a textual version that existed in the manuscripts used by the Men of the Great Assembly. Abrabanel, in his introduction to the book of Jeremiah, attacks Radak's position in the strongest terms, and on multiple grounds. First, he asserts the "argument from faith" against raising the possibility of any doubt as to the correct textual version:

> How can I believe or suggest that Ezra the Scribe found a book of God's Torah and books of the Prophets and other works written with divine inspiration, to contain any doubt or confusion? For, a book of Torah that lacks even a single letter is unfit for use; how much more so [is one that contains errors] in *keri ukhetiv*, which come with the Torah.

It must be noted, however, that the Sages themselves acknowledged their lack of expertise as to the exact text.

Abrabanel also invokes an "argument from probability." Namely, if indeed the *keri ukhetiv* phenomenon came about because of some doubt that arose in Ezra's mind concerning the proper version,

> Why, then, in explaining the text, do we always follow the version that is read, rather than the version that is written? If Ezra had any doubt in the matter, why would the vocalization always agree with the *keri* and not with the *ketiv*? This itself indicates that, in his view, the *keri* (vocalized version) is the correct one, and therefore he vocalized it thus, and not as it is written. And if indeed this was his opinion, then he should have placed the *keri* version in the text, for this would be the proper variant, in accordance with the vocalization, and the *ketiv* should have been placed outside!

But Ezra did not vocalize (add vowels to) the text. That was done about a thousand years later, by the Masoretes themselves. Moreover, the vocalization does not, in and of itself, express any preference for the read version over the written version, since there would be no point in adding vowels to a word that, by its very definition, is not vocalized. Finally, the *keri* version is in the margins and not in the body of text because it is not an integral part of the text, but an instruction as to how the text is to be read. It therefore seems reasonable to assume that the *ketiv* version does reflect the majority of the manuscripts, even if that is counterintuitive.[54]

Abrabanel reflects on that counterintuitive detail, recognizes the *ketiv* as more difficult to understand, and concludes that the *keri* represents the interpretation of Ezra the Scribe:

> For one of two reasons: Either because the person who wrote these strange words had in mind some secret of the Torah in keeping with his level of prophecy and the profundity of his wisdom.... Or because he who uttered them was not sufficiently precise, either because of insufficient knowledge of the Hebrew language or because of insufficient knowledge of proper writing, such that this emerged from the prophet or the individual speaking with divine inspiration כִּשְׁגָגָה שֶׁיֹּצָא מִלִּפְנֵי הַשַּׁלִּיט, "like an error in a royal edict" (Eccl. 10:5).

In other words, Abrabanel suggests that the problematic *ketiv* form may have arisen from a linguistic error on the part of the prophet, rather than entertaining the possibility of multiple versions of the text. He draws on this explanation when considering that the phenomenon of *keri ukhetiv* is particularly prevalent in the book of Jeremiah. He proposes that Jeremiah was "young in years when he began prophesying, and was

54. Abrabanel raises further arguments: (1) Sometimes the *keri* and *ketiv* distinctions are consistent, such as the word "צביים" which is read as "צְבוֹיִם" (Gen. 14:2, 8; Deut. 29:2. In the first instance the letter *yod* appears twice even in the *keri* version, after the letter *vav*). How is it logical to suggest that the same scribal error occurred in every instance of this word? (2) How are we to explain the statement in the Gemara (Megilla 25b) that "all descriptions that are written in the Tanakh in explicit terms, are read in a euphemistic way? For example, "but another man shall lie with her (ישגלנה/ישכבנה) (Deut. 28:30); בעפולים/בטחורים (Deut. 28: 27); חריונים/ דביונים (II Kings 6:25)? Obviously, Radak would respond that this is a different sort of "*keri ukhetiv*" that has nothing to do with textual variants, but rather reflects the guidelines for how verses containing sensitive or potentially offensive words are to be read in public.

therefore not yet proficient in the ways and rules of language, and the beauty of metaphor; indeed, he said of himself, הִנֵּה לֹא יָדַעְתִּי דַּבֵּר כִּי נַעַר אָנֹכִי, 'I cannot speak, for I am but a child' (Jer. 1:6)."

Contemporary scholars have offered other possible explanations for *keri ukhetiv*,[55] and a review of different instances of the phenomenon suggests that there are different types of *keri ukhetiv*, with no single explanation covering them all.

For example, many instances of variants arise from the graphic similarity between letters such as *vav/yod* (ו/י);[56] *bet/kaf* (ב/כ);[57] or *dalet/resh* (ד/ר).[58] Some other exchanges are less common, such as *dalet* (ד) and final *khaf* (ך),[59] or even exchanges involving adjacent letters.[60] Other instances involve an inversion of the order of letters in the word

---

55. See I. Yeivin, *Introduction to the Tiberian Masorah*, 61–62. Rabbi M. Breuer, "Emuna U'Mada BeNusaḥ HaMikra," *Deot* 47 (5738/1978): 102–14, reprinted in Y. Ofer (ed.), *Shitat HaBeḥinot Shel HaRav Mordechai Breuer* (Alon Shvut, 2005), 71–91, proposes that the "*ketiv*" represents the tradition of the *Sofrim* (Scribes) who engaged in the copying of manuscripts in accordance with the customs of earlier generations of scribes, while the "*keri*" represents the tradition of the scholars who learned these texts from their teachers. As a result, there were discrepancies between the versions.
56. See Y. Ofer, "Ḥilufei Vav-Yod BaMikra VeHishtakfutam BeHe'arot HaMesora," *Meḥkerei Morashtenu* 2–3 (5764/2004): 69–84, noting that there are some 315 instances of *vav/yod keri ukhetiv* variants in Tanakh – almost a third of the total number of such variant pairs.
57. See, for example, I Sam. 11:6, 9; II Sam. 5:24; II Sam. 12:31.
58. See, for example, II Sam. 13:37; II Kings 16:6; Jer. 31:39; Prov. 19:19.
59. A good example is to be found in the verse, וַיָּבוֹא וְהִנֵּה עֵלִי יֹשֵׁב עַל הַכִּסֵּא יך [יַד קרי] דֶּרֶךְ מְצַפֶּה, "And he came, and behold, Eli was sitting upon his seat by (יך [יַד קרי]) the wayside, watching" (I Sam. 4:13). The logic of the *keri* version is clear, as Rashi articulates it: "He was waiting by (*al yad*) the way." The *ketiv* is less clear. Radak – who, as noted above, consistently explains both the *keri* and the *ketiv* – proposes a somewhat forced explanation here: "Meaning, his heart was pounding (*makkeh*) within him, fearing for the Ark of God which had gone out [to battle], and this is the reason that the text uses the word יך."
60. A good example involving adjacent letters is to be found in the verse: וַיְהִי כִשְׁמֹעַ כָּל מַלְכֵי הָאֱמֹרִי...אֵת אֲשֶׁר הוֹבִישׁ ה׳ אֶת מֵי הַיַּרְדֵּן מִפְּנֵי בְנֵי יִשְׂרָאֵל עַד עברנו (עָבְרָם קרי) וַיִּמַּס לְבָבָם וְלֹא הָיָה בָם עוֹד רוּחַ מִפְּנֵי בְּנֵי יִשְׂרָאֵל, "And it was, when all the kings of the Emori heard ... that God had dried up the waters of the Jordan before the Children of Israel until they had passed over (עברנו [עָבְרָם קרי]), their hearts melted and they no longer had any spirit in them before the Children of Israel" (Josh. 5:1). Here, too, the *keri*

and other such linguistic phenomena.[61] Thus, in many dozens of cases, the differences between the written version and that which is read relate to the normal linguistic phenomena that commonly lead to textual variations. These variants seem to support Radak's view that there were different versions in the manuscripts, and, in most cases, the *keri* variant, with its vowels, represents the more probable alternative.

There are other instances, however, where the written text (*ketiv*) displays ancient grammatical forms, and the reading form (*keri*) replaces them with later forms. In those cases, the discrepancies presumably do not reflect multiple manuscript versions, but suggest instead deliberate changes, in keeping with Abrabanel's approach.[62] For instance, in ancient Hebrew, the letter *yod* is a suffix for the feminine second-person-singular,[63] and in various places the *keri* version replaces this with the grammatical form more prevalent in Tanakh. Examples include the verses:

> Judges 17:2 – ואתי [וְאַתְּ קרי] אָלִית וְגַם אָמַרְתְּ בְּאָזְנַי, "Concerning which you (ואתי [וְאַתְּ קרי]) swore, uttering it also in my hearing."
>
> II Kings 4:2–3 – מַה יֶּשׁ לכי [לָךְ קרי] בַּבָּיִת...שַׁאֲלִי לָךְ כֵּלִים מִן הַחוּץ מֵאֵת כָּל שכנכי [שְׁכֵנָיִךְ קרי], "What have you (לכי [לָךְ קרי]) in the house...borrow vessels from outside from all your neighbors (שכנכי [שְׁכֵנָיִךְ קרי])."

---

makes more sense, since the verse is part of the narrator's account, which maintains the third person (see Radak). The *ketiv* reflects the graphic similarity between the pair of letters *nun-vav* and a final *mem*.

61. See, for example, I Sam. 19:18, 19, 23, 24; II Sam. 20:14; II Kings 2:16.

62. This does not necessarily mean that at some stage someone amended the text as it appeared in the manuscripts. It may be that the reading tradition was consolidated in a different way from the writing tradition, as is usually the case in a language, and eventually someone added a comment reflecting this (following the introduction of vowelization).

63. This ancient form has been preserved in lyrical units in various places in Tanakh, such as: "He Who forgives all your sins (עֲוֹנֵכִי), Who heals all your diseases (תַּחֲלֻאָיְכִי), Who redeems your life (חַיָּיְכִי) from the pit, Who encircles you (הַמְעַטְּרֵכִי) with love and compassion" (Ps. 103:3–4); and "Return to your rest (לִמְנוּחָיְכִי), my soul, for the Lord has dealt with you (עָלָיְכִי) bountifully" (Ps. 116:7).

> II Kings 4:7 – וְאַתְּ בניכי [וּבָנַיִךְ קרי] תִּחְיִי בַּנּוֹתָר, "And you and your children (בניכי [וּבָנַיִךְ קרי]) shall live off the remainder."

Similarly, in ancient Hebrew, the feminine third-person-plural suffix in the past tense was a *heh* rather than a *vav*, and again, the ancient form became the basis for a *keri ukhetiv* distinction. Examples include:

> Deut. 21:7 – יָדֵינוּ לֹא שפכה [שָׁפְכוּ קרי] אֶת הַדָּם הַזֶּה, "Our hands have not spilled (שפכה [שָׁפְכוּ קרי]) this blood."
>
> I Kings 22:49 – כִּי נשברה [נִשְׁבְּרוּ קרי] אֳנִיּוֹת בְּעֶצְיוֹן גָּבֶר, "for the ships were wrecked (נשברה [נִשְׁבְּרוּ קרי]) at Etzion-Gaver."[64]

And, finally, it appears that some instances of *keri ukhetiv* indicate the existence of different textual versions, reflecting discrepancies between different manuscripts.

DEVELOPMENT OF THE MASORETIC TEXT

Even after Ben-Asher's *Mesora* text became the accepted authoritative version of Tanakh, various manuscripts continued to diverge in small ways from each other. The phenomenon is evident from Rashi's commentary, where he cites the biblical text from Ashkenazic manuscripts, and his citations differ in dozens of minute ways from the text of Ben-Asher.[65] One interesting example of this kind of discrepancy appears in Rashi's commentary on Isaiah. In the Masoretic text, one of Isaiah's prophecies reads:

---

64. See further M. Cohen, *HaKetiv VeHaKeri SheBaMikra* (Jerusalem, 2007).

65. See J. S. Penkower, "Nusaḥ HaMikra SheAmad Lifnei Rashi," in A. Grossman and S. Japhet (eds.), *Rashi – Demuto ViYetzirato* (Jerusalem, 2009), 99–122. Penkower examined manuscripts of Rashi's commentary and enumerates no fewer than sixty-three instances – in the Books of Genesis and Exodus alone – in which the Torah text that Rashi used was different from the one familiar to us. To rule out the possibility that these discrepancies arose from errors in copying the commentary itself, Penkower took the trouble to investigate proof texts of the Bible from the Middle Ages, in which the verses that Rashi cites appear in the identical form to his quotes. Most of the variants involve the inclusion or omission of the letter *vav* at the beginning of a word, but Penkower also notes four instances in the book of Exodus in which Rashi's commentary contains a different word:

בַּיּוֹם הַהוּא יִפְקֹד ה׳ בְּחַרְבּוֹ הַקָּשָׁה וְהַגְּדוֹלָה וְהַחֲזָקָה עַל לִוְיָתָן נָחָשׁ
בָּרִחַ וְעַל לִוְיָתָן נָחָשׁ עֲקַלָּתוֹן וְהָרַג אֶת הַתַּנִּין אֲשֶׁר בַּיָּם... אֲנִי ה׳ נֹצְרָהּ
לִרְגָעִים אַשְׁקֶנָּה פֶּן יִפְקֹד עָלֶיהָ לַיְלָה וָיוֹם אֶצֳּרֶנָּה״

On that day, the Lord with his fierce and great and mighty sword will punish Leviatan, the flying serpent, and Leviatan, the crooked serpent, and will slay the crocodile that is in the sea.... I, the Lord, guard it; I will water it every moment lest any punish it (*pen yifkod*), I will keep it night and day." (Isaiah 27:1–3)

Rashi comments: "'I will water it every moment' – little by little, I will water it with the cup of punishment that will come upon it, lest I punish it (*pen efkod*) in a moment and consume it."

Rashi's comment indicates clearly that the wording of the version he used is "*pen efkod*" ("lest I punish it"), and not, as above, "*pen yifkod*" ("lest any punish it"). Rashi's disciple and colleague, Rabbi Yosef Kara, notes these two variants in his commentary (on verse 3):[66]

"*Pen yifkod aleiha*" – thus it is written in all the texts in Spain. Accordingly, the meaning of the verse is: "I am the Lord Who guards it (Israel) from the crocodile, lest the crocodile punish them and make them like thorns and weeds." In our texts,

---

Exodus 20:5 – The Masoretic version reads וְעֹשֶׂה חֶסֶד לַאֲלָפִים, "and performing (*ve'oseh*) kindness to the thousandth [generation]," while Rashi's version reads ונוצר חסד לאלפים, "and preserving (*venotzer*) kindness to the thousandth";

Exodus 23:18 – The Masoretic version reads לֹא תִזְבַּח עַל חָמֵץ דַּם זִבְחִי, "You shall not offer the blood of My sacrifice with leavened bread," while Rashi's version reads לא תשחט על חמץ, "You shall not slaughter [it] with leavened bread";

Exodus 24:17 – The Masoretic version reads וּמַרְאֵה כְּבוֹד ה׳ כְּאֵשׁ אֹכֶלֶת בְּרֹאשׁ הָהָר לְעֵינֵי בְּנֵי יִשְׂרָאֵל "And the appearance of God's glory was like a consuming fire atop the mountain, in the sight of the Children of Israel," while Rashi's version (as he quotes it in his commentary on Exodus 24:30) reads לעיני כל ישראל, "in the sight of all of (*kol*) Israel";

Exodus 26:24 – the Masoretic version reads וְיַחְדָּו יִהְיוּ תַמִּים עַל רֹאשׁוֹ, "And they shall be coupled together above the head of it (*al rosho*)," whereas Rashi's version reads אל ראשו, "*el rosho*."

66. For more on Rabbi Yosef Kara, see chapter 8.

> where the verse reads *"pen efkod aleiha,"* the commentators have explained the verse as meaning, "Lest I punish it in a moment – for if I were to punish their transgression every time they sin, I would consume them in a moment." And only God knows which is the proper version.

Other commentators present the same phenomenon in their works.[67] That is, the medieval manuscripts that they cite contain thousands of tiny discrepancies, because the scribes who wrote them did not take pains to mirror the *Mesora* version precisely.[68]

A clear example of a divergent version that has been preserved, even though it contradicts the Masoretic version, is found in the inclusion or omission of two verses in the book of Joshua. Chapter 21 of Joshua deals with the cities of the Levites, and the beginning of the chapter recounts that the children of Merari received twelve cities from three tribes: לִבְנֵי מְרָרִי לְמִשְׁפְּחֹתָם מִמַּטֵּה רְאוּבֵן וּמִמַּטֵּה גָד וּמִמַּטֵּה זְבוּלֻן עָרִים שְׁתֵּים עֶשְׂרֵה, "The children of Merari by their families [received] from the tribe of Reuben and from the tribe of Gad and from the tribe of Zebulun – twelve cities" (Josh. 21:7). Afterwards, however, the Masoretic text lists eight cities given to the children of Merari: four from the tribe of Zebulun (verses 34–35) and four from the tribe of Gad (verses 36–37), followed by a concluding verse: כָּל הֶעָרִים לִבְנֵי מְרָרִי לְמִשְׁפְּחֹתָם הַנּוֹתָרִים מִמִּשְׁפְּחוֹת הַלְוִיִּם וַיְהִי גּוֹרָלָם עָרִים שְׁתֵּים עֶשְׂרֵה, "All the cities for the children of Merari by their families, which remained of the families of the Levites, were by their lot twelve cities" (Josh. 21:38). Clearly, the account of the four cities given by the tribe of Reuben is missing from the Masoretic text – though they do appear in the parallel chapter in the book of Chronicles:

67. For instance, see S. Japhet, *Dor Dor U'Parshanav* (Jerusalem, 2008), 189–206 and appendix.
68. See M. Cohen, "Mavo LeMahadurat HaKeter," in *Mikraot Gedolot – HaKeter: Yehoshua-Shofetim* (Jerusalem, 1992), 4.

> וּמֵעֵבֶר לְיַרְדֵּן יְרֵחוֹ לְמִזְרַח הַיַּרְדֵּן מִמַּטֵּה רְאוּבֵן אֶת בֶּצֶר בַּמִּדְבָּר וְאֶת מִגְרָשֶׁיהָ וְאֶת יַהְצָה וְאֶת מִגְרָשֶׁיהָ. וְאֶת קְדֵמוֹת וְאֶת מִגְרָשֶׁיהָ וְאֶת מֵיפַעַת וְאֶת מִגְרָשֶׁיהָ.
>
> And on the other side of the Jordan, by Jericho, in the east side of the Jordan, [they were given] from the tribes of Reuben – Betzer in the wilderness with its pasture lands, and Yahatz and its pasture lands. And Kedemot with its pasture lands and Mefaat with its pasture lands." (I Chr. 6:63–64)[69]

Radak addresses these different versions in his commentary on Joshua 21:7:

> And there are versions [of the book of Joshua] that have been redacted to include, "And from the tribe of Reuben, [the city of] Betzer and her pasture lands, Yahatz and her pasture lands, Kedemot and her pasture kinds, and Mefaat and her pasture lands – four cities." Yet I have not seen these two verses included in any ancient and authentic manuscript; rather, they have been added to a small number of texts. And I saw that Rabbenu Hai Gaon *z"l* had been asked regarding this, and he responded that even though here [in Joshua], they [the cities of Reuven] are not enumerated, nevertheless, in Chronicles they are enumerated. Thus, it would appear from his response that the verses are not written in the authentic versions of Joshua.

Radak rejects the manuscripts in which these verses appear as unreliable, though the presence of this text solves the difficulty posed by the Masoretic version.

Still another version of the first verse is cited by the author of *Minḥat Shai,* in the name of "ancient manuscripts from Spain": "And

69. In the Septuagint, which will be discussed further on, the verses in Chronicles appear also in Joshua. However, it must be remembered that the Septuagint displays a tendency toward harmonization of the Tanakh, and one therefore cannot rule out the possibility that these verses were simply copied from Chronicles, rather than being an integral part of the textual version upon which the translation was based. See below in our discussion of the attitude toward translations of Tanakh.

from the tribe of Reuben – the city of refuge for murderers, Betzer in the wilderness and its pasture lands and Yahatz and its pasture lands."[70]

It seems that the Masoretic version, for all that it was considered authoritative, was not relied upon for all commentary, and that the variants in other manuscripts reflected a more logical understanding of this particular verse in Joshua.[71]

Today, the various contemporary printed editions may include these verses, present them in the margins, or omit them. That said, with the advent of the printing press, discrepancies among manuscripts arising from scribal errors no longer exist, and most editions rely on the *Mikraot Gedolot* edition of the Tanakh, which was published in 1524–1525, based on the textual version established by the editor Yaakov ben Haim ibn Adonijah. This edition, although much closer to the Masoretic version than the manuscripts that were used in Germany, is still far from perfect, and sages such as Rabbi Menahem de Lonzano, Rabbi Eliyahu Bahur,[72] and Rabbi Yedidia Norzi criticized its defects.[73]

Today there are different editions of the Tanakh available, based on manuscripts that have many slight variations.[74] There are nine known

70. In his commentary on Joshua 13:26, *Minḥat Shai* points out – correctly – that based on the number of verses that make up the book of Joshua and the midpoint of the book, according to the *mesora*, "the two verses that are to be found in some of the manuscripts in chapter 21 should be removed, since in any case the calculation is inaccurate."

71. Concerning these manuscripts, too, it is of course possible that the additional verses – וַיַּעֲשׂוּ כֵן בְּנֵי יִשְׂרָאֵל כַּאֲשֶׁר צִוָּה יְהוֹשֻׁעַ וַיִּשְׂאוּ שְׁתֵּי עֶשְׂרֵה אֲבָנִים מִתּוֹךְ הַיַּרְדֵּן כַּאֲשֶׁר דִּבֶּר ה׳ אֶל יְהוֹשֻׁעַ לְמִסְפַּר שִׁבְטֵי בְנֵי יִשְׂרָאֵל וַיַּעֲבִרוּם עִמָּם אֶל הַמָּלוֹן וַיַּנִּחוּם שָׁם – were an addendum introduced on the basis of the version in Chronicles, rather than an ancient variant that had been preserved.

72. Rabbi Eliyahu Bahur, one of the most important grammarians and Masoretic scholars in the early sixteenth century, expressed praise for the *Mikraot Gedolot* edition, in the second introduction to his book *Masoret HaMasoret* (Sulzbach 1771), declaring it the most orderly, accurate, and beautiful set of Tanakh volumes that he had ever seen; but he also expresses reservations concerning errors (as well as concerning the editor, Yaakov ben Haim, who converted to Christianity at the end of his life).

73. See Cohen, 10–11, and Levy, *Fixing God's Torah*, 137–55.

74. The five best-known Hebrew editions are as follows: (1) The *Koren Tanakh* was first published in 1962, and its text was based on the editorial comments of E. D. Goldschmidt, A. M. Haberman, and M. Medan, "on the basis of the opinions

discrepancies between the text of Yemenite Torah scrolls (which follow the version of the Aleppo Codex) and that of Ashkenazi scrolls, including one difference that is expressed in the manner of reading: while the version in the Ashkenazi manuscripts starts the verse detailing the age of Noah when he died (Gen. 9:29), וַיְהִי כָּל יְמֵי נֹחַ תְּשַׁע מֵאוֹת שָׁנָה וַחֲמִשִּׁים שָׁנָה וַיָּמֹת, with the word "*vayehi,*" the Yemenite manuscripts read וַיִּהְיוּ, "*vayihyu.*"[75]

These very slight discrepancies demonstrate the careful transmission of the Masoretic text, but at the same time they also show that even with regard to the text of the Five Books of the Torah, there are some slight differences even today. Among the different printed editions that exist today there are a total of about one hundred variants.[76] Obviously, the number of discrepancies in the Tanakh as a whole is greater than the number found in the Torah.

---

of the Masoretes and of the grammarians and the commentators, and in accordance with the majority of the manuscripts and printed editions generally regarded as authoritative" – i.e., without relying on any specific manuscript as the textual basis. (2) The *Dotan Tanakh* was first published in 1973 and is based on the Leningrad Codex. This important manuscript was written in Cairo in the year 1008 and served as the basis for many Tanakh editions. In the colophon the scribe notes that it was copied "from the checked manuscripts produced by the teacher Aharon ben Moshe Ben-Asher," but its text contains hundreds of discrepancies with regard to the Aleppo Codex. (3) The *Breuer Tanakh* is based on the Aleppo Codex and other very similar manuscripts, although Rabbi Breuer occasionally deviates from the Aleppo Codex version with regard to vowels. (4) *Mikraot Gedolot HaKeter*, published beginning in 1992, edited by M. Cohen. This edition, too, is based on the Aleppo Codex and remains more closely dependent on it without the changes introduced by Rabbi Breuer ("except for a handful of instances which are unquestionably corruptions"; M. Cohen, 44). (5) The *Simanim Tanakh* (Jerusalem, 2010), based for the most part on the Aleppo Codex, and where this version is lacking, on the Leningrad Codex. The Artscroll Tanakh, commonly used in the United States, is based on rabbinic Bibles printed in Eastern Europe and not on any single manuscript. The NJPS Tanakh uses the Leningrad Codex, but modifies it in several places.

75. Concerning this difference and the different textual versions, see *Minḥat Shai*, ad loc. Aside from these differences there are also a few discrepancies in the division of the *parshiot*, the paragraphs, as well as in the Song of the Sea and the Song of *Haazinu*, and in the division of letters, as for example the name "Poti Fera" (Gen. 41:45, 50).
76. In most cases, the differences arise from discrepancies between the Leningrad Codex and other manuscripts.

We may therefore summarize by saying that the Masoretic version is indeed accepted as authoritative, but since the Tanakh is such a remarkably complex work, including tens of thousands of details (letters, vowels, cantillation marks, etc.), in many instances the general acceptance of an authoritative version was not sufficient for it to be implemented with perfect accuracy throughout the Jewish Diaspora.

Textual Supports

The Masoretic text is the "most complete and most accurate extant testimony" for the Tanakh.[77] Nevertheless, there are many other ancient textual supports, or witnesses, that contain numerous instances of different versions of words or verses. Let us first conduct a general review of these proof texts, and then address the question of how they should be regarded.

The textual supports may be divided into two main types – Hebrew texts and translations.

The Hebrew texts consist of the ancient Hebrew textual supports, first and foremost among them the Dead Sea Scrolls.[78] Hundreds of manuscripts were discovered in the caves on the western side of the Dead Sea, especially around the Khirbet Qumran area, mostly during the years 1947–1956. These manuscripts were written between the third century BCE and the first century CE – that is, more than a thousand years before the earliest Hebrew manuscripts known to that date. The majority of the scrolls appear to belong to a cult that split away from mainstream Judaism, and much of the material is devoted to their cultic ideology, including the "War of the Children of Light against the Children of Darkness" and the "Temple Scroll." However, this collection also included some two hundred biblical scrolls, with remnants of all of the books of Tanakh except the Scroll of Esther. Most of these are written in

77. Talshir, 52.

78. For more on the scrolls see Talshir, 56–67. See also E. Tov, "The Myth of the Stabilization of the Text of Hebrew Scripture," in *The Text of the Hebrew Bible from the Rabbis to the Masoretes*, eds. E. Martin-Contrers and L. Miralles-Macia (Gottingen, 2014), 37–46.

the square script used today, while a few copies of the books of the Torah and the book of Job are written in the ancient Hebrew script (*ketav Ivri*).

The biblical scrolls that were discovered at Qumran may be divided into those that reflect the normative Masoretic tradition and those that do not. The former group adheres to the letter-text very strictly. For example, within this category we find the Second Scroll of Isaiah (including parts of chapters 53–60). Although a thousand years separate this scroll from the earliest versions of the Masoretic text, the differences between them are minor. The latter group has letter-texts that differ from the Masoretic Tanakh and, in general, displays a fully "plene" spelling and elongated language forms (such as הואה instead of הוא; היאה instead of היא; and אתמה instead of אתם). They are also characterized by a freer version of the letter-text, sometimes to the point of carelessness.

Until the discovery of the Qumran scrolls, many biblical scholars had dismissed the significance of the Masoretic text owing to its relatively late appearance. The scrolls brought about a change in attitude, since they demonstrated that the *Masora* preserved a tradition that was a good millennium older than thought, and that had been passed down meticulously. It is therefore legitimate to conclude that the text upon which the Masoretic version is based was one of the textual versions that existed in the centuries prior to the Common Era. In addition, even those scrolls that cannot be easily categorized with the textual tradition of the Masoretic version do not display far-reaching deviations from it; the differences can be attributed to the normal processes of copying. Moreover, the instances of significant deviations from the Masoretic version do not necessarily reflect a version that is earlier than the *Mesora*. There is a strong correlation between some of the scrolls and the version that appears in the Septuagint, a translation discussed below, as well as links between some of the scrolls and the Samaritan version of the Torah.

The Samaritan Torah is a Hebrew textual witness for the Five Books of the Torah.[79] The Samaritans – or, as the Sages refer to them, "Kuttim" (Cuthites) – accepted only those five books and rejected the

79. For a discussion of the relationship between the Samaritan Torah and the Masoretic text, see Tov, 62–80; Talshir, 67–76; A. Tal and M. Florentin, *Ḥamisha Ḥumshei Torah:*

rest of the Tanakh.[80] The fact that the Kuttim possessed a *Sefer Torah* was mentioned by the Sages, who noted differences in spelling between this version and the Jewish Torah:

> Mar Zutra (or some say Mar Ukva) said: "In the beginning, the Torah was given to Israel in Hebrew script and in the holy tongue. In the times of Ezra, it was given to them over again in Assyrian script and in the Aramaic tongue. Ultimately, they settled on the Assyrian script and Hebrew tongue, leaving the (ancient) Hebrew script and the Aramaic tongue for the *hedyotot*." Who is referred to by the term "*hedyotot*"? Rav Ḥisda said: "The Kuttim." (Sanhedrin 21b)

Indeed, the Samaritan Torah is written in ancient Hebrew script, and also in the Hebrew language. There are no extant ancient manuscripts of the Samaritan Torah; the oldest scroll that the Samaritan community has in its possession dates back to approximately the twelfth century. It is generally agreed today that the Masoretic text predates the Samaritan one, especially owing to the addenda and corrections found in the latter.

There are some six thousand differences between the Samaritan text and the Masoretic text, and in about a third of the instances, the Samaritan version is identical to the Septuagint. A great many of the differences concern linguistic phenomena (such as plene spelling), exegetical addenda, and the like; these seem to derive from a text of a late date. There are also differences that reflect the Samaritan ideology, especially in matters relating to the unique status that the Samaritans attributed

---

Nusaḥ Shomron VeNusaḥ HaMesora (Tel Aviv, 2011), 11–57; J. Zsengellér, "Origin or Originality of the Torah? The Historical and Text-Critical Value of the Samaritan Pentateuch," *From Qumran to Aleppo* (Göttingen, 2009), 189–202.

80. Regarding the Sages' attitude toward the Kuttim in general, see "*kuttim*," *Encyclopedia Talmudit* 27 (Jerusalem, 1992), columns 649–730; A. Lehnardt, "The Samaritans (Kutim) in the Talmud Yerushalmi: Constructs of "Rabbinic Mind" or Reflections of Social Reality?" in *The Talmud Yerushalmi and Graeco-Roman Culture*, vol. 3, ed. by P. Schäfer (Tübingen, 2002), 139–60; and M. Lavie-Levkovitch, "The Samaritan May Be Included: Another Look at the Samaritan in Talmudic Literature," *Samaritans – Past and Present; Current Studies*, eds. M. Mor and F. V. Reiterer (Berlin, 2010), 147–73.

to Mount Gerizim.[81] Many other differences, however, may reflect the existence of a version more ancient than that of the *Mesora*, in light of the connection between the Samaritan text and some of the Qumran scrolls.[82]

The ancient translations of the Tanakh also provide textual supports for the Masoretic text.[83] The most significant translation, for the purposes of our discussion, is the Septuagint. The Letter of Aristeas speaks of a delegation, composed of seventy-two elders, that arrived

81. For instance, in the Samaritan Torah, the tenth commandment concerns the building of an altar on Mount Gerizim. Similarly, the expression that appears repeatedly in Deuteronomy, הַמָּקוֹם אֲשֶׁר יִבְחַר ה׳, "the place which God will choose (*yivḥar*)" (Deut. 12:5, 11, 21, and others), is replaced with the expression המקום אשר בחר ה׳, "the place which God has chosen (*baḥar*)" – in other words, the place is already designated (this, of course, being understood as a reference to Mount Gerizim). The Sages note these ideological differences: In Deuteronomy 11:30, there is a description of the exact location of Mount Gerizim and Mount Ebal: הֲלֹא הֵמָּה בְּעֵבֶר הַיַּרְדֵּן אַחֲרֵי דֶּרֶךְ מְבוֹא הַשֶּׁמֶשׁ בְּאֶרֶץ הַכְּנַעֲנִי הַיֹּשֵׁב בָּעֲרָבָה מוּל הַגִּלְגָּל אֵצֶל אֵלוֹנֵי מֹרֶה, "Are these not on the other side of the Jordan, by the way where the sun goes down, in the land of the Canaanites who dwell in the Arava opposite Gilgal, beside Elonei Moreh." The Samaritan version appends two words to the end of the verse: "*mul Shekhem*" (opposite Shekhem) (Tal and Florentin edition, 559). The Sages heap scorn on this addendum: "R. Elazar son of R. Yossi said: In this matter I proved the Samaritan scrolls to be false. I said to them, 'You have falsified your Torah but have gained nothing by doing so. For you say that 'Elonei Moreh' refers to Shekhem; we, too, agree that 'Elonei Moreh' is Shekhem. We infer this using the principle of *gezera shava*; but [since you do not accept the sanctity and authority of the hermeneutical laws,] on what basis do *you* infer it?!" (*Sifrei* Deuteronomy, 56; see also Y. Sota 7:3).
82. Unlike the *Mesora*, the Samaritan Torah has no uniform text, and the various manuscripts reflect different versions. The textual discrepancies between various Samaritan texts do not trouble the Samaritans, since their tradition places greater emphasis on an oral, rather than a written, tradition.
83. On Tanakh translations, see, *inter alia:* Y. Komlos, *HaMikra BeOr HaTargum* (Tel Aviv, 1984); C. Rabin, *Targumei HaMikra* (Jerusalem, 1984); P. Flesher (ed.), "Targum Studies, II: Targum and Peshitta" (Tübingen, 1998); M. McNamara, *Targum and New Testament: Collected Essays* (Tübingen, 2011). On the Septuagint, see E. Tov, *The Text-Critical Use of the Septuagint in Biblical Research* (Winona Lake, 2015).

in Alexandria, at the order of King Ptolemy, to translate the Torah.[84] A similar account of the story appears in the Gemara:[85]

> It is related concerning King Ptolemy that he brought together seventy-two elders[86] and placed them in seventy-two [separate] rooms, without telling them why he had brought them together. He went in to each one of them and said to him, "Write for me the Torah of Moses your teacher." (Megilla 9a)[87]

Without getting into the details of the account and the many questions that surround it, note that while the story concerns only the Five Books of the Torah, it has served as the source for applying the name "Septuagint" to the Greek translation of Tanakh as a whole – a project that

84. An extra-canonical work from the second century BCE and the earliest source relating to the translation of the Torah into Greek. The letter was written in Greek, and several translations exist. Hebrew translations include that of A. Kahana, *HaSefarim HaḤitzoniim*, vol. 2 (Tel Aviv, 1937), 1–71; and A. S. Hartoum, *HaSefarim HaḤitzoniim: Sippurim VeDivrei Ḥokhma* (Tel Aviv, 1968). For more on the period of the letter and its author, as well as on the nature of the Septuagint, see the introductions to the above editions, as well as Z. Doribel, "Al HaMekorot Shel Targum HaShivim LaTorah," *Beit Mikra* 50, 1 (180) (5765/2005): 3–19. An English translation of the letter can be read here: http://www.ccel.org/c/charles/otpseudepig/aristeas.htm.
85. The Gemara makes no explicit mention of a translation into Greek, but it can be deduced both from the content of the narrative and from a comparison to the account in the Letter of Aristeas.
86. *Avot deRabbi Natan*, version B, chapter 37, Schechter edition, 94, and *Masekhet Sofrim* 1:7, Higger edition, 101, mention "five elders."
87. Rabbinic sources recount how the king placed the elders in separate buildings and how each of them miraculously emended the biblical text in their translations in precisely the same way as the others, owing to different problems – mostly theological questions – that might have arisen from a literal translation. For instance, the verse "Let us [in the plural form] make man in our image and in our likeness" (Gen. 1:26) might create the impression of a multiplicity of divinities, or of God's corporeality. For this reason, each of the sages translated the verse "I shall make man in the image and in the likeness." The various sources offer differing counts of the instances where the translators introduced amendments: *Avot deRabbi Natan* asserts that "they changed ten things in the Torah." Tractate Sofrim puts the count at thirteen, and Megilla 9a enumerates fifteen emendations. The version of the Septuagint that we have today features only four of the changes mentioned (see Kahana, 16, n. 6).

was undertaken by different translators using different styles. There are various extant manuscripts of the Septuagint, the oldest of them dating to the fourth century CE.

The Septuagint deviates in many instances from the Masoretic text. In some places the differences may be attributed to the nature of the translation, exegetical problems, or different emphases. However, some discrepancies may shed light on the Hebrew manuscript from which the translators worked, and the differences between that text and the Masoretic version. As noted, the Dead Sea Scrolls also include some manuscripts that reflect a Hebrew text similar to the one used by the creators of the Septuagint.

In addition to the Septuagint and other translations that were based upon or influenced by it, the Aramaic translations from the first through eighth centuries of the Common Era, including the translations of Onkelos and Yonatan ben Uzziel, and the Syriac translation – the *Peshitta* – function as textual support for the Masoretic text. They generally adhere closely to it, and the occasional differences are instructive.

Proposed Textual Emendations

As we have seen, the issue of the accuracy of the Tanakh text involves many questions. First, we must consider instances where there is a discrepancy between the version found in the Dead Sea Scrolls and the currently accepted text. Then there are the instances where the Sages based their teachings on a version that is different from the Masoretic text. In addition there are the disagreements between the various Masoretes: "Easterners" vs. "Westerners," and among the "Westerners" themselves, between Ben-Asher and Ben-Naphtali. Add to that the range of textual versions in use during the Middle Ages, and, finally, the discrepancies between different contemporary printed editions of the Tanakh. One is thus hard-pressed to assert that the textual version that appears in any Tanakh today is in every detail a perfect copy of the "original" text. As Rabbi Mordechai Breuer writes:

> Anyone today who seeks to prove that the biblical manuscripts of the Second Temple Period – or of the period following the destruction – differed from one another in some lettering or some words, will find that this assertion is in no way revolutionary. I

> might apply to him the words of Job (12:9), מִי לֹא יָדַע בְּכָל אֵלֶּה, "Who knows not among all these"! Admittedly, the Jewish Sages of earlier generations could not have been aware of the full scope of the problem. Perhaps they did not imagine the number of textual variants, or the extent of the discrepancies between different versions. However, this is of no fundamental importance, since the principle itself is what matters – this being that the early Sages were aware of the fact that the scribes were divided concerning the textual version, and the Sages decided among the alternative versions on the basis of the majority.[88]

All that said, the version that is universally accepted today, with its very slight variations, is the version that was decided upon by the Masoretes, and it is, of course, the version that is halakhically binding.

The question that emerges from this history of textual variation, of course, is whether it opens the door to proposing emendations to the text, when the existing text is difficult. The inclination to do so is especially pertinent when a given verse in the Masoretic text is more problematic than its parallels in other textual witnesses. Furthermore, how should one approach the notion of a textual change where the emendation has no basis in earlier textual witnesses?

Once, academic biblical scholars would propose textual emendations on the slightest pretext, because they had little confidence in the accuracy of the Masoretic text. The work of some of these scholars gives the impression that there is no verse in Tanakh that is free of corruption. But while textual emendations may be an easy and convenient solution for textual difficulties, they may turn out – and have often turned out – to be a superficial and unsatisfying solution.

A comprehensive response to the premise of textual emendation is found in Rabbi David Zvi Hoffmann's introduction to his commentary on Leviticus:

88. R. M. Breuer, "*Emuna U'Mada BeNusaḥ HaMikra*," reprinted in Y. Ofer (ed.), *Shitat HaBeḥinot shel HaRav Mordekhai Breuer* (Alon Shvut, 2005), 71–72.

> Even if we acknowledge that certain places in the text are not free of error, we lack the necessary means to restore the version [originally] written with divine inspiration. There is no textual emendation – even if it rests on arguments drawn from exegesis and from history – that can force us to believe that the prophet, or the author of the holy books, wrote the text in the exact form proposed by the emender.

This approach demands that one strive to understand the version as it stands. Despite the possibility that errors have crept into the text, they are not provable in any conclusive way. The theoretical possibility of textual errors should not, therefore, inhibit any and all efforts to make sense of the Masoretic text.

Another reason to invest in understanding the seemingly less coherent or illogical text is that, often enough, it is actually accurate. Ironically, because scribes aspired to produce clear and intelligible manuscripts, they tended to "improve" the text to the best of their abilities, when the ancient version was puzzling. The problem is that their emendations frequently were made because the given scribe did not have the scholarship to understand the original text correctly, or as a result of attempted independent, unfounded exegesis. In recognition of these skewed readings, scholars understand that the general rule is "*lectio difficilior potior*" – "the more difficult reading is the stronger one."

This need to struggle with the Masoretic text is especially pronounced when the material has been translated. A transition into a different language is highly dependent on subjective interpretation, and capturing every meaning in one language and expressing it in another is a challenge all its own. As noted in Tractate Sofrim (1:7, Higger edition 101), concerning the Septuagint: "That day was as vexing for Israel as the day when the Golden Calf was fashioned, for the full meaning of the Torah could not be translated."

In recent generations, the trend of exaggerated reliance on textual emendations by academic scholars has been kept in check somewhat, and scholars are more cautious when proposing such solutions.[89]

89. As noted by Cohen, 69: "The need to avoid imaginary speculation and to exercise

Their suggested changes too often missed significant literary messages that the text manages to convey, specifically by means of the seemingly more complicated wording. In-depth familiarity with the linguistic and literary character of the Tanakh shows that the text consistently and systematically uses various means to emphasize the messages conveyed by the content. The scholar therefore needs to be sensitive to these techniques, in order to better understand the text. Nowadays, those who study the text have a broader and deeper knowledge of the idiosyncrasies of ancient Hebrew, so the forms of expression that previous generations might have dismissed as scribal errors are now understood to preserve a certain tradition of writing or pronunciation.

We will now examine different types of proposed textual emendations to textual difficulties that may be unnecessary in light of a deliberate literary expression.

One of the most common scribal errors is known as the *homeoteleuton*. It refers to the omission of text that occurs because a word, or a series of words, appears twice in close proximity, so that the scribe's eye jumps from the first instance of the word(s) to the second, while copying the text, and the text in between is inadvertently left out.[90]

This phenomenon has been cited, on occasion, as justification for proposing amending various verses in the Bible. For example, during the inauguration of the Temple, Solomon cites God's words:

> מִן הַיּוֹם אֲשֶׁר הוֹצֵאתִי אֶת עַמִּי אֶת יִשְׂרָאֵל מִמִּצְרַיִם לֹא בָחַרְתִּי בְעִיר
> מִכֹּל שִׁבְטֵי יִשְׂרָאֵל לִבְנוֹת בַּיִת לִהְיוֹת שְׁמִי שָׁם וָאֶבְחַר בְּדָוִד לִהְיוֹת
> עַל עַמִּי יִשְׂרָאֵל.

caution in the examination and assessment of facts is heard increasingly today among scholars themselves as one of the fundamental conditions for sound exegetical conclusions."

90. This phenomenon exists not only in the scribal copying of texts but also in the reading of them. For instance, a well-known halakha pertains to a person who is reciting the *Shema* by heart and skips from the words, "And you shall inscribe them upon the doorposts of your house and at your gates," in the first section of the *Shema* (Deut. 6:9), to the same words in the second section (Deut. 11:20). See Berakhot 16a and *Shulḥan Arukh, Oraḥ Ḥayim* 64:4.

> From the day when I brought My nation, Israel, out of Egypt, I have not chosen any city out of all the tribes of Israel for the building of a House, that My Name should be there, but I have chosen David to be over My nation, Israel. (I Kings 8:16)

This verse is seemingly problematic. At first, God states that, in the past, He had not chosen any *city* in which His House was to be built; the logical continuation should be that He has now chosen Jerusalem. Instead, the verse goes on to speak of choosing *David*. In the parallel chapter in Chronicles, the verse appears in a more elaborate form, and the problem is solved:

> מִן הַיּוֹם אֲשֶׁר הוֹצֵאתִי אֶת עַמִּי מֵאֶרֶץ מִצְרַיִם לֹא בָחַרְתִּי בְעִיר מִכֹּל שִׁבְטֵי יִשְׂרָאֵל לִבְנוֹת בַּיִת לִהְיוֹת שְׁמִי שָׁם וְלֹא בָחַרְתִּי בְאִישׁ לִהְיוֹת נָגִיד עַל עַמִּי יִשְׂרָאֵל. וָאֶבְחַר בִּירוּשָׁלַםִ לִהְיוֹת שְׁמִי שָׁם וָאֶבְחַר בְּדָוִיד לִהְיוֹת עַל עַמִּי יִשְׂרָאֵל.

> Since the day that I brought My people out of the land of Egypt, I have not chosen a city out of all the tribes of Israel for the building of a House, that My Name should be there, nor have I chosen any man to be ruler (*nagid*) over My people, Israel. But I have chosen Jerusalem, that My Name should be there, and I have chosen David, to be over My people, Israel. (II Chr. 6:5–6)

In this passage, God states that, in the past, He had chosen neither a city nor a king, and that now He has chosen both a city and a king. In light of this parallel, many scholars have proposed that the form of the verse in the book of Kings is a *homeoteleuton*, owing to the scribe having mistakenly skipped from the first appearance of the words "that My Name should be there" to the second "that My Name should be there." Indeed, in the Septuagint, the wording of the verse in Kings is identical to the wording in Chronicles.

Closer inspection reveals, however, the extent to which this proposed amendment is mistaken. The books of Samuel and Kings emphasize David's choice of Jerusalem, without any divine intervention, as well as the fact that the resting of the Divine Presence in Jerusalem was a function of his choice. It is David who chooses Jerusalem as his royal capital (II Sam. 5:6–9), and he decides, on his own initiative, to bring the Ark of the Covenant up to Jerusalem (II Sam. ch. 6). It is he who raises the idea of building a House for God in Jerusalem (II Sam. 7:1–2), and God accepts this suggestion – with a slight change: it is not David himself who will build it, but rather his son, Solomon (II Sam. 7:12–13). In contrast, Chronicles states explicitly that the choice of Jerusalem as the site of the Temple is divinely guided. This guidance is manifest when a plague that breaks out in the wake of the census ordered by David is halted. In Chronicles, the narrative ends with David's understanding that God is hinting that Ornan's threshing-floor is the site destined for the Temple:

> וּמַלְאַךְ ה׳ אָמַר אֶל גָּד לֵאמֹר לְדָוִיד כִּי יַעֲלֶה דָוִיד לְהָקִים מִזְבֵּחַ לַה׳ בְּגֹרֶן אָרְנָן הַיְבֻסִי. וַיַּעַל דָּוִיד בִּדְבַר גָּד אֲשֶׁר דִּבֶּר בְּשֵׁם ה׳...וַיִּבֶן שָׁם דָּוִיד מִזְבֵּחַ לַה׳ וַיַּעַל עֹלוֹת וּשְׁלָמִים וַיִּקְרָא אֶל ה׳ וַיַּעֲנֵהוּ בָאֵשׁ מִן הַשָּׁמַיִם עַל מִזְבַּח הָעֹלָה...בָּעֵת הַהִיא בִּרְאוֹת דָּוִיד כִּי עָנָהוּ ה׳ בְּגֹרֶן אָרְנָן הַיְבוּסִי וַיִּזְבַּח שָׁם...וַיֹּאמֶר דָּוִיד זֶה הוּא בֵּית ה׳ הָאֱלֹהִים וְזֶה מִזְבֵּחַ לְעֹלָה לְיִשְׂרָאֵל.
>
> Then the angel of God told Gad to tell David that David should go up and set up an altar to God on the threshing floor of Ornan the Jebusite. So David went up at Gad's word which he had spoken in God's name.... And David built there an altar to God, and he offered up burnt-offerings and peace-offerings, and he called upon God, and He answered him with fire from the heaven upon the altar of burnt offering.... At that time, when David saw that God had answered him at the threshing floor of Ornan the Jebusite, he sacrificed there.... And David said, "This is the House of the Lord God, and this is the altar of the burnt offering for Israel." (I Chr. 21:18 – 22:1)

The two versions of Solomon's prayer – in Kings and in Chronicles – reflect two fundamentally different aspects of the choice of Jerusalem as the resting place for the Divine Presence: human choice and divine choice. To amend the wording in Kings to bring it in line with that of

Chronicles would miss the significant message that is embodied specifically in the difference between them.

Changing the text in Kings to accord with the text in Chronicles appears to be an error for another reason, too. According to Chronicles, God declares that, up until the time of David, He had not chosen "any man to be ruler over My people, Israel" (לֹא בָחַרְתִּי בְאִישׁ לִהְיוֹת נָגִיד עַל עַמִּי יִשְׂרָאֵל). This formulation sits well with the focus of Chronicles, which almost completely ignores the reign of Saul, recording only the story of Saul's death (I Chr. 10). However, it is difficult to imagine how such an expression could appear in the book of Kings, which is a continuation of the book of Samuel. In Samuel, God explicitly defines Saul as a "*nagid*" (ruler) in his promise to Samuel: כָּעֵת מָחָר אֶשְׁלַח אֵלֶיךָ אִישׁ מֵאֶרֶץ בִּנְיָמִן וּמְשַׁחְתּוֹ לְנָגִיד עַל עַמִּי יִשְׂרָאֵל, "Tomorrow about this time I shall send to you a man from the land of Binyamin, and you shall anoint him as ruler (*nagid*) over My people, Israel" (I Sam. 9:16). Likewise, as Samuel anoints Saul, he tells him, הֲלוֹא כִּי מְשָׁחֲךָ ה׳ עַל נַחֲלָתוֹ לְנָגִיד, "Has God not anointed you as ruler (*nagid*) over His inheritance?" (I Sam. 10:1).

This, therefore, is an example of a seemingly simple and logical textual amendment which, upon closer examination, appears to be mistaken.

Note also that the biblical text on occasion deliberately omits a word or series of words from a verse as a literary device to convey a certain message. One example is the openly disdainful attitude of the text toward the son of Saul, Ish Boshet. Despite his royal status, Ish Boshet is depicted as a weak and almost insignificant character. With a view to expressing Ish Boshet's weakness, the text omits his name over and over again, even when doing so results in verses with peculiar syntax:

> וּלְשָׁאוּל פִּלֶגֶשׁ וּשְׁמָהּ רִצְפָּה בַת אַיָּה וַיֹּאמֶר אֶל אַבְנֵר מַדּוּעַ בָּאתָה אֶל פִּילֶגֶשׁ אָבִי – And Saul had a concubine whose name was Ritzpa, daughter of Aya, and he said[91] to Abner, "Why have you come to my father's concubine?" (II Sam. 3:7)

91. Who is the subject of the verb "said"? At first glance it would seem to be Saul, but,

וְלֹא יָכֹל עוֹד לְהָשִׁיב אֶת אַבְנֵר דָּבָר מִיִּרְאָתוֹ אֹתוֹ – But he could not answer Abner a word again, for his fear of him. (II Sam. 3:11)

וַיִּשְׁמַע בֶּן שָׁאוּל כִּי מֵת אַבְנֵר בְּחֶבְרוֹן וַיִּרְפּוּ יָדָיו וְכָל יִשְׂרָאֵל נִבְהָלוּ. וּשְׁנֵי אֲנָשִׁים שָׂרֵי גְדוּדִים הָיוּ בֶן שָׁאוּל – And when Saul's son heard that Abner had died in Hebron, his hands became feeble and all of Israel were afraid. And Saul's son[92] had two men who were captains of bands. (II Sam. 4:1–2)

These verses emphasize Ish Boshet's weakness, especially in contrast with Abner, captain of the army and the "strong man" in the kingdom, the mover behind Ish Boshet's coronation.

The same idea may explain other instances where the biblical text seems to be "deficient." For instance, one of the most difficult verses to explain is בֶּן שָׁנָה שָׁאוּל בְּמָלְכוֹ, "Saul was a year when he reigned" (*ben shana Shaul bemolkho*) (I Sam. 13:1). Since the suggestion that Saul was only one year old when he ascended to the throne is nonsensical, commentators have offered more "reasonable" interpretations of the verse. Rashi cites the Sages' well-known teaching (Yoma 22b) that the descriptive phrase "a year (old)" is to be understood metaphorically – "like a one-year-old, who had never sinned." He also offers an alternative explanation (suggested also by Radak) that the events recounted in the chapter took place during the first year of Saul's reign, representing the "*peshat*" (the literal level of the text). That interpretation is not as simple is it should be, however, because the verse follows the classic structure of a pattern of verses that introduce the reign of any number of kings, including both Ish Boshet and David in the book of Samuel (II Sam. 2:10; 5:4) and most of the kings listed in the book of Kings: "Y was X years old when he began to reign, and he reigned for Z years over Israel/Yehuda." It is therefore difficult to propose that the

---

as we know, Saul is already dead, and from the context it is clear that the reference is to Ish Boshet. Ish Boshet was last mentioned by name in the text dozens of verses previously, and thus our expectation is that his name should appear again in this verse. The text deliberately avoids this, so as to emphasize his weakness.

92. When the biblical text refers to someone by his father's name alone, it usually signifies disdain (see, for example, I Sam. 10:11; 20:31). The expression "Saul's son" implies a certain scorn toward Ish Boshet.

expression "Saul was a year when he reigned" refers to either the amount of time that he has reigned up to this point or to his moral character.

How, then, are we to understand the verse? One interpretation is that of R. Tanḥum the Jerusalemite,[93] who proposes that the verse was written in deficient form intentionally, as a sort of placeholder, where the number that was to specify Saul's age when he came to the throne had not yet been filled in: *ben X shana Shaul bemolkho* (Saul was X years old when he reigned).[94] What drives the unusual interpretation? Many modern biblical scholars maintain that Saul's age was not written clearly in the original manuscript from which the scribe copied this problematic text, and that he presumably intended to check a different source text and fill in the correct age later – but never ended up doing so. And then, for generations, the verse was passed down without Saul's age ever being filled in.[95]

Yet this approach misses the essence of the literary message underlying the unusual formulation. It would seem that the text seeks from the very outset, through the deficient introductory verse to Saul's reign, to hint that the king failed in his role and that he should not be regarded as a true king. He is not "deserving" of the standard introductory verse that appears in relation to the other kings of Israel.[96]

In Samuel's parting speech to the nation (I Sam. 12) there are several verses that are written in obscure form, representing prominent and puzzling departures from the clear language that characterizes the rest of the book.

Examples include the following:

93. A thirteenth-century commentator and grammarian. Little is known about his life. His original interpretation of the verse is cited by Y. Kiel in the *Daat Mikra* commentary on the Book of Samuel (Jerusalem, 1981), 113.

94. Indeed, some manuscripts of the Septuagint add the word "*sheloshim*" (thirty), but it is clear that this is a later addition, since this would present a highly unlikely chronology: Would it really be possible that at the age of thirty, Saul could already have a son who defeated the Philistines in battle?

95. See, for example, M. Garsiel, *Olam HaTanakh: Shmuel Alef* (Tel Aviv, 1993), 117.

96. For another example of the deliberate literary omission of a word in order to convey a certain lesson, see my article "Zeman Matan Torah," *Megadim* 13 (5751/1991): 107–12.

ה׳ אֲשֶׁר עָשָׂה אֶת מֹשֶׁה וְאֶת אַהֲרֹן וַאֲשֶׁר הֶעֱלָה אֶת אֲבֹתֵיכֶם מֵאֶרֶץ מִצְרָיִם – [It is] God who made Moses and Aaron (*asher asah et Moshe ve'et Aharon*),[97] and who brought our forefathers up from the land of Egypt. (I Sam. 12:6)

An unfamiliar name that appears in the list of judges:

אֶת יְרֻבַּעַל וְאֶת בְּדָן וְאֶת יִפְתָּח וְאֶת שְׁמוּאֵל – Yerubaal and Bedan[98] and Yiftah and Samuel. (I Sam. 12:11)

A condition that is left incomplete:

אִם תִּירְאוּ אֶת ה׳ וַעֲבַדְתֶּם אֹתוֹ וּשְׁמַעְתֶּם בְּקֹלוֹ וְלֹא תַמְרוּ אֶת פִּי ה׳ וִהְיִתֶם גַּם אַתֶּם וְגַם הַמֶּלֶךְ אֲשֶׁר מָלַךְ עֲלֵיכֶם אַחַר ה׳ אֱלֹהֵיכֶם – If you will fear the Lord and serve Him, and obey Him, and not rebel against God's command, and (if) both you and also the king who rules over you will follow the Lord your God.[99] (I Sam. 12:14)

---

97. The difficulty is that the verse states that God "made" Moses and Aaron, rather than stating, as other verses do, that he sent Moses and Aaron. Commentators address this difficulty and propose different interpretations: see Rashi, Radak, and *Metzudat David*. The language here seems to anticipate the next verse: וְאִשָּׁפְטָה אִתְּכֶם לִפְנֵי ה׳ אֵת כָּל צִדְקוֹת ה׳ **אֲשֶׁר עָשָׂה** אִתְּכֶם וְאֶת אֲבוֹתֵיכֶם, "Let me plead with you before God concerning all the victories which God has done for you (*asher asa itekhem*) and for your forefathers."

98. The Sages (Rosh HaShana 25a) maintain that this refers to Samson, who was a "son of Dan" (*ben Dan*), and most of the classical commentators follow this view. However, Radak points out the chronological difficulty that this entails, since Bedan is mentioned in between Yerubaal and Yiftah, while in Judges, Samson appears after Yiftah. He concludes that although Yiftah preceded Samson chronologically, Samson was more important and therefore Samuel mentions him first.

99. This difficulty leads some of the commentators to explain that the second part of the verse is meant as the outcome: "*then* both you and also the king who rules over you will follow the Lord your God"; that is, "both you and the king will survive for a long time" (Rashi). However, this interpretation is also problematic, since the word וִהְיִתֶם, "*vihyitem*," does not suggest long-term survival, and the verse seems to suggest that this is a continuation of the condition: "and (if) both you and also the king will follow God."

A puzzling word at the end of a verse:

> וְאִם לֹא תִשְׁמְעוּ בְּקוֹל ה׳ וּמְרִיתֶם אֶת פִּי ה׳ וְהָיְתָה יַד ה׳ בָּכֶם וּבַאֲבֹתֵיכֶם – But if you do not obey God, but rebel against God's command, then the hand of God shall be against you and against your forefathers (*uva'avotekhem*).[100] (I Sam. 12:15)

The word "*ki*" which appears redundant in its (first) appearance in the verse:

> וְלֹא תָּסוּרוּ כִּי אַחֲרֵי הַתֹּהוּ אֲשֶׁר לֹא יוֹעִילוּ וְלֹא יַצִּילוּ כִּי תֹהוּ הֵמָּה – Turn not astray except (*ki*) after vain things which cannot profit nor save, for they are vain.[101] (I Sam. 12:21)

Most of these difficulties can be resolved fairly easily by proposing textual changes. And in fact the Septuagint does introduce the following changes: The word "*ed*" (witness) is introduced before the phrase "God Who made Moses and Aaron"; "Barak" appears instead of "Bedan"; "against you and against your king" replaces "and against your forefathers"; and the seemingly superfluous word "*ki*" is omitted.

---

100. Seemingly, the word expected here is וּבְמַלְכְּכֶם, "*uvemalkekhem*" – "and against your king" – which would make sense in light of the previous verse. Likewise, later on we read, וְאִם הָרֵעַ תָּרֵעוּ גַּם אַתֶּם גַּם מַלְכְּכֶם תִּסָּפוּ, "But if you continue to act wickedly, *both you and your king* will be swept away" (I Sam. 12:25). It seems that the expression "and against your forefathers" appears here as a result of its appearance in verses 7 and 8, but its significance in our verse is unclear. Radak attempts to solve the problem by explaining the word "*uva'avotekhem*" as follows: "[The meaning of this word is] like 'and against your king,' for the sovereign over a nation is like a father toward a son."
101. Radak offers two possibilities: "Turn not astray from God, for (*ki*) if you turn away from Him, you will be turning to vanity – that is, the gods that cannot profit or save you, for they are vanity"; or "Turn not astray to vanity, for (*ki*) they cannot profit or save." *Targum Yonatan* ignores the word "*ki*" and omits it from his translation of the verse.

The conventional view thus maintains that the text is corrupted and that it should be corrected, either in accordance with the Septuagint or in a different manner.[102]

However, in-depth familiarity with the literary style of the Bible would point us in a different direction entirely. Most of the difficulties above arise from the fact that Samuel's words are out of order, as far as the flow of ideas is concerned, several times in this chapter. Given that this kind of irregularity is indeed quite common when a person, in a state of great excitement or emotion, speaks without thinking his words through, the text seems to depict Samuel's inner state as he addressed the nation. By preserving the exact formulation of his speech, with its unusual, recurring language, the text escalates the drama of the moment. That is, the text indicates that Samuel's speech was not a pre-planned and well-structured address, uttered in a clinical and precise manner. Rather, he spoke from the depths of his heart, with the heat and passion of a concerned leader who fears that his entire life's work is about to be lost. Thus the text records here – as it does elsewhere[103] – the speaker's emotions, by means of the words that are spoken, in a direct and unmediated manner.

Support for this idea comes from a speech that appears in two versions in the biblical text – in one case, a clearly articulated formula, and in the other, the same idea articulated in the heat of the moment. When the prophet Nathan sends Bathsheba to David to prevent the coronation of Adoniyahu, she addresses David with the following words: אֲדֹנִי אַתָּה נִשְׁבַּעְתָּ בַּה׳ אֱלֹהֶיךָ לַאֲמָתֶךָ כִּי שְׁלֹמֹה בְנֵךְ יִמְלֹךְ אַחֲרָי וְהוּא יֵשֵׁב עַל כִּסְאִי, "My lord, you swore by the Lord your God to your handmaid, that Solomon, your son, will reign after me, and he will sit upon my throne" (I Kings 1:17). And she immediately adds וְעַתָּה הִנֵּה אֲדֹנִיָּה מָלָךְ וְעַתָּה אֲדֹנִי הַמֶּלֶךְ לֹא יָדָעְתָּ, "And now, behold, Adoniyahu reigns, and now, my lord, the king, [you] do not know it" (I Kings 1:18).

102. See, for example, S. Bar Efrat, *Mikra LeYisrael – Shmuel Alef* (Jerusalem, 1996), 163; M. Z. Segal, *Sifrei Shmuel* (Jerusalem, 1964), 90.

103. Other examples of this phenomenon include David's emotional words of thanksgiving after Nathan's prophecy concerning the future building of the Temple and the establishment of the royal dynasty (II Sam. 7:18–29), and the emotional words that the woman of Tekoa addresses to David (II Sam. 14:13–17).

Seemingly, the second appearance of the word "*ve'ata*" ("and now") should have been spelled with an *alef* instead of an *ayin,* in which case, the verse would have read, "and you, my lord, the king, do not know it." But then, later on, Bathsheba says, וְאַתָּה אֲדֹנִי הַמֶּלֶךְ עֵינֵי כָל יִשְׂרָאֵל עָלֶיךָ לְהַגִּיד לָהֶם מִי יֵשֵׁב עַל כִּסֵּא אֲדֹנִי הַמֶּלֶךְ אַחֲרָיו, "And you, my lord, the king – the eyes of all of Israel are upon you, to tell them who shall sit upon the throne of my lord the king after him" (I Kings 1:20). This time, it would seem that "*ve'ata*" (with an *ayin* – "and now") should have replaced "*ve'ata*" (with an *alef* – "and you").

Radak was aware that the exchange of "*ve'ata*" ("and you") and "*ve'ata*" ("and now") would have been more logical than the extant text, and was also aware of versions of the text that included these amendments. Nevertheless, he remained committed to the manuscripts he had studied, refusing to accept the amendments. Concerning verse 18, he writes: "Many scribes have been mistaken concerning this word, and have written it with an *alef* since that seemed to make more sense, but it is clear to us that the proper spelling is with an *ayin,* both according to the accurate manuscripts and according to tradition." Commenting on verse 20, he writes: "This should be '*ve'ata,*' with an *alef,* and some have mistakenly written it with an *ayin,* since that seems to make more sense."

An alternative version does seem to have been in use at the time: *Targum Yonatan,* which appears in the standard printed editions, translates verse 18: "And now, behold, Adoniyahu reigns, and you, my lord, the king, do not know it." The Septuagint adopts the same editing. Indeed, the *Minḥat Shai* notes: "In a certain old book, I found it written '*ve'ata*' ('and you'), and likewise the *Targum Yonatan,*" and he refers to the Masoretic note cautioning against this version, written with an *alef*: "In three places [this being one of them] the word '*ata*' is mistakenly read as though written with an *alef* instead of an *ayin* [since this version appears to make more sense]."

But the Masoretic version again appears to possess a deeper literary significance, though, in this case, the ancient manuscripts do attest to the existence of the simpler variant as well. Consider, for example, the way these verses demonstrate that Bathsheba deviated from the message that Nathan had given her to convey to David: הֲלֹא אַתָּה אֲדֹנִי הַמֶּלֶךְ נִשְׁבַּעְתָּ לַאֲמָתְךָ לֵאמֹר כִּי שְׁלֹמֹה בְנֵךְ יִמְלֹךְ אַחֲרַי וְהוּא יֵשֵׁב עַל כִּסְאִי וּמַדּוּעַ מָלַךְ אֲדֹנִיָּהוּ, "Did not you, my lord, the king, swear to your maidservant, saying that 'Solomon, your son, will reign after me, and he shall sit upon my throne' – why, then does Adoniyahu reign?" (I Kings 1:13).

Nathan's message is much sharper than the one that Bathsheba actually conveys to David. She dares not accuse David of not carrying out his promise; instead, she presents the coronation of Adoniyahu as an event that has taken place without David's knowledge. Instead of addressing David in what might be construed as an accusatory tone – "and you, my lord, the king, do not know it" – she changes her statement, perhaps at the last minute, to "and now," thereby softening even further any hint of accusation. Thus, it is entirely possible that there is no scribal error in this biblical text, and that Bathsheba herself changed the words she was expected to utter, in light of the fear she felt standing before King David, presenting a request that might seal her own fate and that of her son.

Amending the biblical text may miss key literary messages in the text, and this indicates that the greatest degree of caution must be exercised by those who would make such changes. Rabbi Breuer makes this point particularly well:

> There are many places in the Bible that are similar to the two examples cited above. In each instance it appears to the scientific scholar that our text has become "corrupted." In each instance, one might question whether the scientific proof is absolutely certain, beyond any doubt. However, one is always entitled to postulate that perhaps the scientific hypothesis is in fact correct. But this will not suffice for a man of science; he will seek the reason for this "corruption." And as a believing Jew whose desire is only to study Torah, he will seek the religious significance behind this "corruption" – transforming it into Torah.[104]

Linguistic Phenomena in the Biblical Text

Of course, the classical commentators often suggest exegetical interpretations that seem to resemble the proposals for emending the text coming out of the modern academic world of scholarship. One key difference in their approaches – which may influence the degree to which

104. R. M. Breuer, "Emuna U'Mada BeNusaḥ HaMikra," 91.

the respective suggestions are accepted – is that the scholars regard their emendation as correcting a corruption in the text, and the commentators are delving into the richness of possibility that is biblical exegesis. Furthermore, the textual versions reflected in the translations may well have been written without any knowledge of other versions of the text or suggested emendations of it. And the linguistic phenomena of the Bible may simply have given rise to the need for commentary on the existing version. The principle of the exchangeability of similar letters and that of economical writing are two examples of such phenomena.

A. Exchangeability of similar letters

Commentators frequently note the phenomenon of "exchangeable letters," and interpret verses on the basis of this principle. Rashi, for example, establishes the rule that letters belonging to the same phonetic group are interchangeable:

> I therefore say that the term "*rakhil*" (gossiper) is related to the idea of going about gathering information (*meragel*), for the letter *kaf* replaces the letter *gimmel*. The letters that share the same place of articulation are interchangeable: *bet, peh,* and *vav*; *gimmel, kaf* and *kuf*; *nun* and *lammed*; *resh, zayin* and *tzaddi*. (Rashi on Lev. 19:16)

Another example is Nahmanides's explanation of the exchange of *bet* and *peh,* in his commentary on the verse נָשַׁפְתָּ בְרוּחֲךָ כִּסָּמוֹ יָם, "You exhaled (*nashafta*) with Your wind; the sea covered them" (Ex. 15:10):

> I also maintain that the meaning of this word is as though it were spelled with a *bet* – i.e., *nashavta,* in the same sense as "when God's spirit blew (*nashva*) upon it" (Is. 40:7).... For these two letters can be used interchangeably.... Likewise in the case of names: Shovakh (II Sam. 10:16) and Shofakh (I Chr. 19:16).

The medieval commentators also point out exchanges of the letters *alef, heh, vav,* and *yod*. Consider the nation's request that Samuel anoint a king over them: וַיְמָאֲנוּ הָעָם לִשְׁמֹעַ בְּקוֹל שְׁמוּאֵל וַיֹּאמְרוּ לֹּא כִּי אִם מֶלֶךְ יִהְיֶה

עָלֵינוּ, "But the people refused to listen to Samuel, and they said, '**No**' ('*lo*' – *lamed alef*), but let there be a king over us" (I Sam. 8:19). When Saul is crowned, Samuel repeats the nation's words, but this time, the text reads: וְאַתֶּם הַיּוֹם מְאַסְתֶּם אֶת אֱלֹהֵיכֶם אֲשֶׁר הוּא מוֹשִׁיעַ לָכֶם מִכָּל רָעוֹתֵיכֶם וְצָרֹתֵיכֶם וַתֹּאמְרוּ **לוֹ** כִּי מֶלֶךְ תָּשִׂים עָלֵינוּ, "And you, today, have despised your God Who Himself saves you from all your evils and troubles, and you have said **to Him** ('*lo*' – *lamed vav*), 'For You shall place a king over us'" (I Sam. 10:19).

Radak raises the possibility that, in the latter verse, the word "*lo*" is actually meant to reflect the negative connotation of the people's original statement, "for the letters *alef, heh, vav,* and *yod* are interchangeable." He similarly explains the exchange of names Peniel and Penuel in Genesis 32:31–32.

Rabbenu Bahya ben Asher, too, invokes the principle of the exchangeability of letters. For example, he explains the cry of "*avrekh*" (Gen. 41:43), proclaimed before Joseph's chariot, in the sense of "*havrekh*" ("bend the knee"), since "the letters *alef, heh, vav,* and *yod* are interchangeable."

Sometimes, the similarity between the letters is not phonetic, but visual. The *dalet-resh* exchange was already discussed in the context of *keri ukhetiv,* and similar discrepancies are found elsewhere in the different manuscripts of the Masoretic text. For example, in the story of the Giv'onim in Joshua (9:4), we read: וַיַּעֲשׂוּ גַּם הֵמָּה בְּעָרְמָה וַיֵּלְכוּ וַיִּצְטַיָּרוּ וַיִּקְחוּ שַׂקִּים בָּלִים לַחֲמוֹרֵיהֶם, "And they, too, acted with cunning, and they went and took provisions (*vayitztayaru*), and took old sacks upon their donkeys."

The word "*vayitztayaru*" is difficult to understand. Rashi comments: "They pretended to be journeying on a mission; the word recalls the phrase 'an emissary (*vetzir*) has been sent among the nations' (Ob. 1:1)," and most commentators follow his lead. However, *Targum Yonatan* translates this word in the sense of "taking provisions," as though it were written "*vayitztayadu,*" with a *dalet* replacing the *resh*. Although Radak questions the interpretation of the word in the sense of "provisions," it does make sense in view of the continuation of the chapter, where the word "*tzeida*" (provisions) appears several times, including in the words of the Giv'onim themselves: זֶה לַחְמֵנוּ חָם הִצְטַיַּדְנוּ אֹתוֹ מִבָּתֵּינוּ

בְּיוֹם צֵאתֵנוּ, "This, our bread, we took for ourselves [still] hot as provisions (*hitztayadnu*) from our houses on the day we set out" (Josh. 9:12).

For this reason, Rabbi Yosef Kara writes: "There are some books in which the word appears in the form *vayitztayadu*.... Both approaches cite support for their view.... But I tend to side with those books that say *vayitztayadu*, based on the mention further on." It should be noted that the version preferred by Rabbi Yosef Kara is also reflected in the Septuagint, but the real significance of this example in this context is the attestation to the fact that the exchange of *dalet* and *resh* in the various manuscripts appears in many other places, too.[105]

Sometimes, the commentators suggest that a verse should be understood on the basis of such exchangeability of letters, without even explicitly citing different versions.[106] Thus, for example, on the verse יְבַעֲתֻהוּ צַר וּמְצוּקָה תִּתְקְפֵהוּ כְּמֶלֶךְ עָתִיד לַכִּידוֹר, "Trouble and anguish make him afraid; they prevail against him as a king ready to the battle (*lakidor*)" (Job 15:24), Rashi proposes:

105. For instance, the author of *Minḥat Shai* notes several instances of interchanged *dalet* and *resh* in various manuscripts: Joshua 15:52 – וְדוּמָה, "and Duma" (and accordingly in the Koren edition), while some manuscripts feature וְרוּמָה, "and Rumah" (as in R. Breuer's edition; for more, see Y. Elitzur, "Ir BeSefer Yehoshua U'Teḥumei Mamlakhto Shel Yoshiyahu Teluyim BeKotzo Shel Dalet," in M. Bar-Asher [ed.], *Sefer HaYovel LaRav Mordekhai Breuer* [Jerusalem, 1992], 615–20); in II Sam. 8:3 and elsewhere, we find "Hadad'ezer," while in some manuscripts the name appears as "Hadar'ezer"; I Chr. 12:8 reads "the sons of Yeruham from Gedor" (מן הגדור), while some manuscripts read "from Gedud" (מן הגדוד); and many other similar examples. See the commentary of R. Shmuel bar Hofni Gaon (Greenbaum edition, Jerusalem, 1979) on Gen. 41:18 (and editor's note 79).

Sometimes the differences are reflected in the commentaries. For instance, concerning the verse כִּי תִכְתֹּב עָלַי מְרֹרוֹת וְתוֹרִישֵׁנִי עֲוֹנוֹת נְעוּרָי, "For You write bitter things (*merorot*) against me, and make me inherit the transgressions of my youth" (Job 13:26), Rashbam comments, "*merudot* – causing me to rebel (*lehamrideni*)" (S. Japhet, *Perush Rabbi Shmuel ben Meir [Rashbam] LeSefer Iyov* [Jerusalem, 2000], 374). Here, too, the different versions concern an interchange of *dalet* and *resh* as manifest from two manuscripts of Tanakh from the Middle Ages (see Japhet, 196).

106. Several examples in which Rabbi Shmuel David Luzzatto (Shadal) invokes this principle throughout his commentary on Tanakh are cited by S. Vargon, "Shadal KeḤalutz Ḥokre HaMikra HaYehudim: Al Gishato BeVaayot LeNosaḥ HaMikra" (Shadal as an Early Jewish Bible Researcher: His View Regarding Textual Problems in the Bible), *Iyyune Mikra UFarshanut* 6 (2003): 71–148, here 98–110.

> I have found no similar word; it should be understood as an interchange of the letters *resh* and *dalet*. Similar examples include "Ashkenaz and Rifat" in the Torah (Gen. 10:3) [as compared to] "Ashkenaz and Difat" (I Chr. 1:6). Likewise, we find "Kittim and Rudanim" (I Chr. 1:7).[107] Here, too, "*lakidor*" should be understood as the same as "*lakidod*," the same king who will eventually burn (*liykod*) in the fire of Gehennom – and that is Sennacherib.

Another example of this kind of letter exchange is וַיֵּרָא עַל כַּנְפֵי רוּחַ, "He was seen (*vayera*) upon the wings of wind" (II Sam. 22:11), as opposed to וַיֵּדֶא עַל כַּנְפֵי רוּחַ, "He soared (*vayede*) upon the wings of wind," as found in the parallel verse in Psalms (18:11). So too the description of the lean cows in Pharaoh's dream: the text describes cows that are רָעוֹת מַרְאֶה וְדַקּוֹת בָּשָׂר, "ill-favored and lean of flesh (*dakot basar*)" (Gen. 41:3); but when Pharaoh himself retells the dream to Joseph, he uses the expression וְרַקּוֹת בָּשָׂר, "*rakot basar*" (Gen. 41:19).

This approach works when solving problems of word comprehension, and sometimes helps explain variant texts. Consider two examples.

The story of the binding of Isaac culminates as follows: וַיִּשָּׂא אַבְרָהָם אֶת עֵינָיו וַיַּרְא וְהִנֵּה אַיִל אַחַר נֶאֱחַז בַּסְּבַךְ בְּקַרְנָיו, "Abraham lifted his eyes and he saw, and behold, behind (*aḥar*) [him] a ram caught in the thicket by its horns" (Gen. 22:13). The meaning of the word "*aḥar*" pres-

---

107. As opposed to "Kittim and Dodanim" (Gen. 10:4). Radak, commenting on the verse in Chronicles, likewise adopts the approach that the *dalet* and *resh* are interchangeable, but he limits this phenomenon specifically to names, based on the assumption that owing to the visual similarity between the letters, both forms of the name developed:

> Since the form of the *dalet* and the *resh* are similar, among those reviewing books of lineage written in ancient times some would have read [the name] with a *dalet*, while others would have read it with a *resh*, and these names became familiar to people in both forms. Thus it happens that it appears in Genesis in one form and in this book [Chronicles] in the other – showing that both are actually the same name, whether it is read with a *dalet* or with a *resh*. And a similar example is "Rivleta" (meaning, "to Rivla") (II Kings 25:6), with a *resh*, versus "Divleta" (meaning, "to Divla") (Ezek. 6:14), with a *dalet*. Likewise "Re'uel" (Num. 2:14) with a *resh* and "De'uel" (Num. 1:14) with a *dalet*.

ents a problem, and the commentators offer different solutions. Rashi explains, "After (*aḥarei*) the angel told him, 'Do not lay your hand…' (Gen. 22:12), he saw it, caught." Rashi understands the word "*aḥar*" as meaning "afterwards" – but this creates a rather peculiar syntax in the sentence. Ibn Ezra rejects this interpretation ("If this were so, the text would say '*aḥarei*,' '*aḥar ken*,' or '*aḥarei zot*,' as it does everywhere else"), and proposes instead, "after (*le'aḥar*) it was caught in the thicket." The problem with this explanation is that it renders the word "*aḥar*" superfluous. *Targum Yerushalmi*[108] resolves this difficulty by reading the word as "*aḥad*," meaning "one," instead of "*aḥar*" – with the *resh* switched for a *dalet*. It is possible that *Targum Yerushalmi* had a manuscript that reflected this exchange – as the same version, or interpretation, is reflected in the Septuagint.[109]

Moreover, this interpretation sits well with biblical language in other contexts – first and foremost among them, for these purposes, the verse in Daniel 8:3: וָאֶשָּׂא עֵינַי וָאֶרְאֶה וְהִנֵּה אַיִל אֶחָד עֹמֵד לִפְנֵי הָאֻבָל, "Then I lifted my eyes and I saw, and behold, there stood before the river one ram (*ayil eḥad*)." The verse appears to allude to the story of the binding of Isaac.[110] Indeed, both Radak and *Minḥat Shai* recognize that the principle of interchangeable letters has any number of applications.[111]

---

108. On the *Targum Yerushalmi* and its erroneous attribution to Yonatan ben Uzziel, see Y. Komlos, *HaMikra BeOhr HaTargum*, columns 748–49.

109. As well as in the Samaritan version (Tal and Florentin edition, 111), in the Syriac translation (*Peshitta*), and in other sources. See M. Tzippor, *Targum HaShivim LeSefer Bereshit* (Ramat Gan, 2006), 272.

110. The expression "And behold…one…" also appears in I Kings 20:13; Ezekiel 1:15; 8:7, 8; Daniel 10:5.

111. Let us consider two further examples.
(1) In the war of Israel and Judah against Aram, we find a difficult phrase in the words addressed to Jehosafat by Ahab: וַיֹּאמֶר מֶלֶךְ יִשְׂרָאֵל אֶל יְהוֹשָׁפָט הִתְחַפֵּשׂ וָבֹא בַמִּלְחָמָה וְאַתָּה לְבַשׁ בְּגָדֶיךָ וַיִּתְחַפֵּשׂ מֶלֶךְ יִשְׂרָאֵל וַיָּבוֹא בַּמִּלְחָמָה, "The king of Israel said to Jehoshaphat, 'Disguise yourself (*hitḥapes*) and enter the battle, and you – put on your robes.' So the king of Israel disguised himself and went into battle" (I Kings 22:30). What is the meaning of the seeming repetition in the words of Ahab, and why are we afterwards told that it is the king of Israel himself (i.e., Ahab and not Jehoshaphat) who disguises himself? *Targum Yonatan* translates the verse as, "I

B. A letter or word that should be read as though repeated

The phenomenon of "economical writing" finds expression in the omission of one of two identical (or similar) consecutive letters or words. It is particularly likely to happen when two identical letters follow each other, one ending a word and the other starting the next word. More striking examples involve entire words.

Rashbam comments on this phenomenon, noting three instances.[112] The first difficulty arises out of a contradiction between a genealogical verse in the Torah and a verse on the same genealogy in Chronicles. Compare: וַיִּהְיוּ בְּנֵי אֱלִיפָז תֵּימָן אוֹמָר צְפוֹ וְגַעְתָּם וּקְנַז. וְתִמְנַע הָיְתָה פִילֶגֶשׁ לֶאֱלִיפַז בֶּן עֵשָׂו וַתֵּלֶד לֶאֱלִיפַז אֶת עֲמָלֵק, "And the sons of Elifaz were Teiman, Omar, Tzefo, and Ga'tam and Kenaz. And Timna was a concubine to Elifaz, son of Esau, and she bore Elifaz [a son:] Amalek" (Gen. 36:11–12), and: בְּנֵי אֱלִיפָז תֵּימָן וְאוֹמָר צְפִי וְגַעְתָּם קְנַז וְתִמְנָע וַעֲמָלֵק, "The sons of Elifaz were Teiman and Omar, Tzefi and Ga'tam, Kenaz and Timna and Amalek" (I Chr. 1:36).

Why is Timna, the son of Elifaz, mentioned in Chronicles, but not listed in Genesis? Rashbam explains:

> I saw in *Shoḥar Tov*:[113] "And Timna" is connected to the previous verse... and here, too, "And the sons of Elifaz were Teiman,

shall disguise myself and enter the battle," indicating that the manuscript he had in front of him differed from our own. The same interpretation is reflected in the Septuagint and in the *Peshitta*, and Radak himself offers a similar interpretation. (2) Before he is executed, Agag says, אָכֵן סָר מַר הַמָּוֶת, "Surely the bitterness of death is come (*sar mar hamavet*)" (I Sam. 15:32). Most of the commentators interpret the word "*sar*" (spelled *samekh-resh*) in the sense of "coming" or "passing." However, *Targum Yonatan* understands the phrase as an exclamation: "[Please,] sir, the bitterness of death!" In other words, Agag is actually trying to arouse Samuel's compassion, so that he will spare him the death sentence. The *Targum* is treating the word "*sar*" as though written with the letter *sin* (cf. *Targum Yonatan* on I Sam. 22:14; Jer. 6:28).

For additional examples see Y. Komlos, under "Tanakh, Targumim" in *Encyclopedia Mikra'it* 8 (Jerusalem, 1982), column 745.

112. Other commentators follow his example, e.g., *Ḥizkuni* on Genesis 36:12; Rabbi Yosef Bekhor Shor on Genesis 36:12.

113. This explanation does not appear in the *Midrash Shoḥar Tov* as we know it. See

> Omar, Tzefo, and Ga'tam, and Kenaz, and Timna. And Timna was a concubine." The first Timna is a male, one of the sons of Elifaz; the second is female – "And the sister of Lotan – Timna."

In his view, the word "and Timna" should indeed have appeared in the verse in Genesis twice – once at the end of the first verse, which lists the sons of Elifaz, as the name of a man who was one of Esau's descendants, and again at the beginning of the second verse, as the name of a woman – Elifaz's concubine. Though the word appears only once, the meaning of the verses suggest that it should be read twice.

Rashbam observes this phenomenon again in the description of God's command to Joshua to divide the land among the tribes: וְעַתָּה חַלֵּק אֶת הָאָרֶץ הַזֹּאת בְּנַחֲלָה לְתִשְׁעַת הַשְּׁבָטִים וַחֲצִי הַשֵּׁבֶט הַמְנַשֶּׁה. עִמּוֹ הָראוּבֵנִי וְהַגָּדִי לָקְחוּ נַחֲלָתָם אֲשֶׁר נָתַן לָהֶם מֹשֶׁה בְּעֵבֶר הַיַּרְדֵּן מִזְרָחָה, "And now, divide this land for an inheritance to the nine tribes and the half tribe of Menashe. With him (*imo*), the Reuveni and the Gadi have received their inheritance, which Moses gave them, beyond the Jordan, eastward" (Josh. 13:7–8).

Verse 7 refers to the tribes that are destined to inherit land on the western side of the Jordan, including the half tribe of Menashe; verse 8 deals with the two tribes that have inherited on the eastern side. "With him," the expression with which verse 8 opens, is supposed to refer to the half tribe of Menashe that is to remain on the eastern side of the Jordan, inheriting alongside the tribes of Reuben and Gad. Rashbam again proposes reading "the half tribe of Menashe" twice: "We have no choice but to say that the second verse is deficient, for it should have said, 'And the other half of the tribe of Menashe has received its inheritance.'"[114]

While Rashbam notes only three such omissions, other verses do appear to reflect a similar phenomenon. For instance, the well-known verse, דַּבֵּר אֶל כָּל עֲדַת בְּנֵי יִשְׂרָאֵל וְאָמַרְתָּ אֲלֵהֶם קְדֹשִׁים תִּהְיוּ כִּי קָדוֹשׁ אֲנִי

Y. Jacobs, "LeBerur Hekef Ḥekeruto Shel Rashbam Im Midrash Lekaḥ Tov," in A. Reiner, et al. (eds.), *Ta Shema – Meḥkarim BeMada'ei HaYahadut LeZikhro Shel Yisrael M. Ta Shema* (Alon Shvut, 2012), 480–83.

114. Rashbam's third example pertains to the contradiction between two texts in I Chronicles: 8:35–36 and 9:41–42.

ה׳ אֱלֹהֵיכֶם, "Speak to all the congregation of the Children of Israel and say to them: 'You shall be holy, for I, the Lord your God, am holy (*ki kadosh ani Hashem Elokeihem*)'" (Lev. 19:2). To which part of the verse does the word "I" (אני, "*ani*") belong? On the one hand, it continues the first phrase – "You shall be holy, for I am holy" – a formulation found in many other verses, such as: וְהִתְקַדִּשְׁתֶּם וִהְיִיתֶם קְדֹשִׁים כִּי קָדוֹשׁ אָנִי וְלֹא תְטַמְּאוּ אֶת נַפְשֹׁתֵיכֶם...וִהְיִיתֶם קְדֹשִׁים כִּי קָדוֹשׁ אָנִי, "You shall sanctify yourself and be holy, for I am holy, and you shall not defile your souls ... you shall be holy for I am holy" (Lev. 11:44–45).

Yet many of the verses in chapter 19 of Leviticus (e.g., 3, 4, 10) conclude with the words, "I am the Lord your God." Here, too, we might raise the possibility – following the example of Rashbam – that the word "*ani*" should be read twice: "For *I* am holy; *I* am the Lord your God."

Far more common than the omission of complete words, however, is the omission of one letter of two consecutive identical letters; here too, commentators of different generations have noted the phenomenon. In describing the attitude of Ben-Hadad's servants toward Ahab, for example, the Masoretic text reads: וְהָאֲנָשִׁים יְנַחֲשׁוּ וַיְמַהֲרוּ וַיַּחְלְטוּ הֲמִמֶּנּוּ וַיֹּאמְרוּ אָחִיךָ בֶן הֲדַד, "The men took it for a [good] sign, and they hastily caught at his words (*vayaḥletu hamimenu*), and they said, 'Your brother, Ben-Hadad'" (I Kings 20:33). In some of the early Hebrew manuscripts, the letters are grouped differently – ויחלטוה ממנו, "*vayaḥletuha mimenu*." The *Targum Yonatan*'s wording shows that it follows this alternative division of the words, as does the Septuagint. Rashi (according to the *Keter* edition) maintains that the letter *heh* at the end of the word "*vayaḥletuha*" belongs not just to that word, but also to the beginning of the next word – "*vayaḥletu**ha** **ha**mimenu*" – meaning, "they wondered whether his words had been uttered intentionally."

Similarly, a linguistic difficulty appears in the law that obligates a man who rapes a woman to marry her if she desires: לֹא יוּכַל שַׁלְּחָהּ כָּל יָמָיו, "he may not send her away (*lo yukhal shalḥah*) all his days" (Deut. 22:29). After the words "*lo yukhal*," the verb should appear in the infinitive, as it does a few verses previously, with regard to a man who marries and then slanders his wife, claiming that she was not a virgin: וְלוֹ תִהְיֶה לְאִשָּׁה לֹא יוּכַל לְשַׁלְּחָהּ כָּל יָמָיו, "She shall be his wife; he may not send her away (*lo yukhal **le**shalḥah*) all his days" (Deut. 22:19). It appears, then, that in verse 29 too the letter *lamed* should be read as belonging to both words, concluding the word "*yukhal*" and starting the word "*leshalḥah*."

Rabbi Baruch Epstein, author of *Torah Temima*, cites many instances of places where, in his view, this phenomenon exists (in his commentary on Genesis 14, note 10):

> It is the way of the language that in some places, a letter that is at the end of a word also serves as the beginning of the following word, where this letter is required there. Hence the letter is omitted from the second word, or from the end of the first word. Examples include:
>
> 1. "*Balayla hu*" – "on that night" (בלילה הוא) (Gen. 19:33; 30:16; 32:23; I Sam. 19:10), instead of "*balayla **ha**hu*" (בלילה ההוא).[115]
> 2. "*Ozi vezimrat Y-h*" – "God is my strength and [my] song" (עזי וזמרת יה) (Ex. 15:2; Is. 12:2; Ps. 118:14), instead of "*ozi vezimrati Y-h*" (עזי וזמרתי יה).
> 3. "*Hishameru lakhem alot bahar*" – "guard yourselves [not] to ascend the mountain" (השמרו לכם עלות בהר) (Ex. 19:12), instead of "***me**'alot bahar*" (מעלות בהר).
> 4. "*Lo tikaḥ haem al habanim*" – "you shall not take the mother with the young" (לא תקח האם על הבנים) (Deut. 22:6), instead of "***me**'al habanim*," i.e., "from atop the young" (מעל הבנים).
> 5. "*Lo yukhal shalḥa*" – "he shall not be able to send her away" (לא יוכל שלחה) (Deut. 22:29), instead of "***le**shalḥa*" (לשלחה).
> 6. "*Vayikatev sefer zikaron*" – "a book of remembrance was written" (ויכתב ספר זכרון) (Malachi 3:16), instead of "*vayikatev **be**sefer zikaron*" (i.e., "it was written in the book of remembrance" (ויכתב בספר).

115. Indeed, in all three instances that the *Torah Temima* cites from the Torah, the Samaritan text reads "*balayla hahu*."

7. *"Yadati ki kol tukhal"* – "I know that You can do everything" (ידעתי כי כל תוכל) (Job 42:2), instead of *"ki yakhol tukhal"* (כי יכול תוכל).[116]

We have seen, therefore, that it is possible, in the context of exegesis – delving into the potential understandings of any given verse – to raise suggestions that explain a word as if it were written differently, without resorting to the argument that the text is corrupt. Indeed, in many cases, an apparent textual difficulty simply reflects a linguistic phenomenon that characterizes the biblical text, rather than serving as evidence of its corruption.

"IF THERE WERE TO BE FOUND, IN AN ACCURATE MANUSCRIPT"

We have discussed the problematic nature of proposals for textual emendations that may obscure or even erase the important literary messages conveyed by a seemingly erroneous word or phrase. We have also seen that some textual difficulties are easily solved if one is familiar with common biblical linguistic phenomena – indeed, such familiarity often renders superfluous the attempt at textual emendation. Even after all such instances have been resolved in a satisfactory manner, however, we are still left with some places where the Masoretic text presents a difficulty, and other textual witnesses may help solve the problem.

Still, even with all due caution, both from a religious perspective and in terms of textual analysis, we are left with Rabbi David Zvi Hoffmann's assertion that the extant biblical text is not perfect. While we uphold the exegetical effort to maintain the Masoretic version, we do not rule out categorically the possibility of textual emendations. It is important to emphasize that even where the commentators find no

116. A more extensive list of this type of linguistic phenomena is found in R. Reuven Margaliot's work *HaMikra veHaMesora* (Jerusalem, 1989), 66–70. To the examples cited by Rabbi Baruch Epstein and Rabbi Margaliot, we may add: I Kings 21:21; Jer. 19:15; Jer. 39:16 (see also Num. 32:42). For further examples, taken from the commentary of Shadal, see S. Vargon, "Shadal KeḤalutz Ḥokre HaMikra HaYehudim," 111–13.

way of explaining the Masoretic text, the proposals of textual emendations nevertheless remain nothing more than suggestions or hypotheses.

An interesting example of this approach is to be found in the commentary of Rabbi Yosef Kara on the verse, והבאיתי [וְהֵבֵאתִי קרי] עַל הָאָרֶץ הַהִיא אֶת כָּל דְּבָרַי אֲשֶׁר דִּבַּרְתִּי עָלֶיהָ אֵת כָּל הַכָּתוּב בַּסֵּפֶר הַזֶּה אֲשֶׁר נִבָּא יִרְמְיָהוּ עַל כָּל הַגּוֹיִם, "And I shall bring upon that land all My words (*et kol devarai*) that I have uttered concerning it, all that is written (*et kol hakatuv*) in this book, which Jeremiah prophesied concerning all the nations" (Jer. 25:13). He comments:

> "And I shall bring … concerning it" – as uttered by Isaiah. If an accurate manuscript were to show the word "*ve'et*" in this verse [that is, introducing the next phrase – "*and* all that is written"], then this would be the meaning. But if it were read as "*et*," then [the second phrase, starting "all that is written"] would refer only to what appears immediately prior to it (that is, all that Jeremiah himself has said)."

R. Yosef Kara raises the possibility of a textual emendation, even though he has not encountered any such textual support (he makes the acceptance of such a change dependent on its appearing in a reliable manuscript); but he still interprets the verse as it stands.

Thus, we are inclined to conclude, as does Prof. Menahem Cohen:

> The ideal of the sanctity of the textual version, down to the last letter, in our time, must be understood in its purely halakhic interpretation – i.e., it must draw its validity not from the assertion that human beings have managed to preserve the text in its exact form throughout its transmission, but rather from the faith that human beings are vested with the authority to make halakhic rulings as to the form of the authorized version, down to the last letter, and that the form thus determined is the halakhically binding one, even if historically speaking it is not "correct" or "accurate" in all its details.[117]

117. M. Cohen, 68.

However, one need not necessarily agree with the continuation of the passage:

> This being the case, the new religious approach to exegesis on the *peshat* level [of straightforward meaning] is accordingly committed to the method of textual criticism. Exegesis on the *peshat* level, which strives to grasp the meaning of the actual words, must – among other considerations – take into account every possible textual witness, weigh up the alternatives on their own merits, and decide on the basis of pure logic.

I would argue that our mandate is not to "decide," and our logic is not always the deciding factor in establishing the text.

Cohen seeks to illustrate his position using a specific example. In the list of Jacob's family members who go down to Egypt, the four sons of Issachar are named: וּבְנֵי יִשָּׂשכָר תּוֹלָע וּפֻוָּה וְיוֹב וְשִׁמְרוֹן, "And the sons of Issachar: Tola and Puva and Yov and Shimron" (Gen. 46:13). But the sons of Issachar are listed elsewhere in Tanakh, as well, and there, the name of the third son – Yov – appears in a slightly different form, with the addition of the letter *shin*. Consider *Parashat Pinhas*: בְּנֵי יִשָּׂשכָר לְמִשְׁפְּחֹתָם תּוֹלָע מִשְׁפַּחַת הַתּוֹלָעִי לְפֻוָה מִשְׁפַּחַת הַפּוּנִי. לְיָשׁוּב מִשְׁפַּחַת הַיָּשֻׁבִי לְשִׁמְרֹן מִשְׁפַּחַת הַשִּׁמְרֹנִי, "The sons of Issachar by their families: Tola – the Tola'i family; to Puva – the Puni family. To Yashuv – the Yashuvi family; to Shimron – the Shimroni family" (Num. 26:23–24). Similarly, in Chronicles: וְלִבְנֵי יִשָּׂשכָר תּוֹלָע וּפוּאָה ישיב [יָשׁוּב קרי] וְשִׁמְרוֹן אַרְבָּעָה, "And to the sons of Issachar – Tola and Pua, Yashiv [written 'Yashiv' but pronounced 'Yashuv'] and Shimron, four" (I Chr. 7:1).

The Septuagint and the Samaritan text present the name in Genesis as "*Yashuv*" as well. On the basis of these data, Cohen writes:

> All of these facts make it likely that "*Yashuv*" (spelled *yod, shin, vav, bet*) is indeed the name of Issachar's son, while "*Yov*" (spelled *yod, vav, bet*) is a corruption that found its way into the text over the course of transmission of the Masoretic version, prior to its canonization....

> Nevertheless, this historical conclusion is separate from the question of how a *Sefer Torah* should be written today. The word "*Yov*" has been sanctified as part of the canonized version down to its letters, by the power of halakhic ruling. Anyone who introduces any change into a *Sefer Torah* disqualifies it, for this version – and this alone – is halakhically binding in the copying of the text.

Cohen's clearly stated distinction between an exegetical emendation and the halakhic ruling as to the sanctity of the Masoretic text is, of course, important. But at the same time, the status of the Masoretic version goes beyond mere formal halakhic procedure. Preservation of the Masoretic version is also an expression of the position that Rabbi Hoffmann spelled out – namely, that no matter how logical a textual emendation may seem, it will always remain a question. It is, admittedly, logical to argue that the name of Issachar's son was "Yashuv," but it is also possible that the biblical text reflected in the Samaritan text and the Septuagint does not actually preserve an ancient version, but rather represents an emendation of the verse in Genesis, in light of the verses in Numbers and Chronicles.

Moreover, variation of names is a very common phenomenon in Tanakh, and it does not seem reasonable to propose a textual emendation for each and every such case. Similar names may have arisen for various unknown reasons. Therefore, the rejection of the textual emendation arises not only from our concern to defend the sanctity of the Masoretic text, but also because the emendation represents nothing more than exegesis – which is certainly reasonable, but cannot be proven.[118]

118. Various explanations have been offered on the midrashic level for the Yov/Yashuv alternatives: (1) "His name was Yov (and Shimron), so why is he called Yashiv? For he brought back (*heshiv*) the suggestion to the brothers to make chariots" (*Sifrei Zuta* 7, 18; Horowitz edition, 252–53). (2) "Yet it is written, 'Yashiv,' for they bring back (*meshivin*) Israel to their Father in heaven" (*Midrash HaGadol,* Genesis 46:13; Mosad HaRav Kook edition, 777). (3) "'And Yov' – [so called] for his voice sang with the words of Torah. And he is the same 'Yashuv' mentioned in Numbers.... So why was he called 'Yashuv'? Because he strengthened Torah study [the building

Thus, Cohen is correct in his assertion that "a contemporary religious commentator of the *peshat* will not have fulfilled his obligation if he fails to bring these facts and their like to the knowledge of the students," and familiarity with other versions is indeed important. However, students must be made aware of the entire range of considerations and factors involved in establishing the possible authentic text, with a cautious distinction being maintained between possible suggestions and proven conclusions.

SUMMARY

The text of the Tanakh was preserved rigorously over thousands of years. The close attention that was given to the precise transmission of the Tanakh is already evident in the Sages' teachings. The quest to preserve every word and letter in its proper place and form finds expression in the impressive cross-checking mechanism developed by the Masoretes, employing an extensive system of detailed notes. The Tanakh has been preserved in this manner with remarkable accuracy over many generations.

At the same time, the Tanakh was disseminated by means of many copies written by many scribes – and through this human activity, slight variations found their way into different manuscripts. The Sages acknowledged that they were not clear as to the exact textual version, and the Masoretic text of today does differ slightly, in several places, from the version that the Sages quote. In addition, the various textual witnesses – including the Qumran scrolls, the Samaritan version, the Septuagint, and the Aramaic translations – serve to support the thesis that in ancient times there existed versions that differed, in small details, from the Masoretic text (along with versions that differed more sub-

of *yeshivot*] in Egypt" (*Midrash Sekhel Tov*, Genesis 46:13, Buber edition, 290). And in the commentary attributed to Rashi on the verse in Chronicles: "His name was Yov, but since they settled down (*nityashvu*) to study Torah, as it is written, וּמִבְּנֵי יִשָּׂשכָר יוֹדְעֵי בִינָה לַעִתִּים, 'Of the sons of Issachar, men with understanding of the times' (I Chr. 12:33), he therefore merited being called 'Yashuv.'" A. Weisel, *HaPerush HaMeyuḥas LeRashi LeSefer Divrei HaYamim* (Jerusalem, 2010), 105, notes that the exegete himself may have arrived at this explanation, for there is no source for it either in the writings of *Ḥazal* or in the earlier commentaries.

stantially). During the period of the *Rishonim*, too, there were different manuscripts that were used by the various commentators. Rashi's version, for example, differs in dozens of small details from the Masoretic version. The editions of the Tanakh that are available today likewise show slight variations.

Determining with perfect accuracy the "original" version of each of the Tanakh's twenty-four books turns out to be unachievable. That simple fact converts textual emendations (a common phenomenon in biblical scholarship) from "corrections" to "interpretations," on the basis of Rabbi David Zvi Hoffmann's fundamental assumption that even emendations that are in fact corrections of a certain corrupted spelling, form, or structure cannot be proven as such. Moreover – and significantly – a version that appears at first glance to be problematic may actually reveal an important spiritual insight, when a hasty emendation would erase that level of meaning. In addition, being familiar with the style and language used in the Tanakh often renders what had appeared to be a need for textual emendation unnecessary.

Nevertheless, we are still left with instances where the text as we know it presents a very difficult textual problem, and here we cannot categorically refuse the possibility of a textual emendation – especially where it is based on other textual witnesses. That possible need for emendation does not negate the standing of the Masoretic text as the halakhically binding version, as the standard for writing Torah scrolls and for printing copies of the Tanakh. Moreover, a textual emendation can never be more than a hypothesis, which means students must labor to understand the Masoretic version as transmitted to us, on the level of religious scholarship.

Part II

Tanakh and Its World

Chapter 6

Tanakh and Archaeology

BACKGROUND

The study of the antiquities in the Land of Israel began in the nineteenth century, and since then, the relationship between Tanakh and archaeology has undergone many changes.[1] For example, when American and British scholars, such as Edward Robinson (1794–1863) and Charles Warren (1840–1927), were dispatched to Israel to conduct the earliest studies, their goal was find actual traces of the biblical narratives and thereby gain a deeper familiarity with the world of the Bible. At the beginning of the twentieth century, however, religious scholars such as William Albright (1891–1971) and G. Ernest Wright (1909–1974) introduced what became a central endeavor in the field: they sought, by means of archaeological findings, to demonstrate the authenticity of biblical narratives.

This type of archaeology received a boost from the rise of Zionism in Israel. Researchers like Yigael Yadin (1917–1984) and Benjamin Mazar (1906–1995) viewed archaeology as an important tool in the strengthening of the bond between the Jewish people and the Land of

1. Concerning the various trends in the relationship between Tanakh and archaeology, see, for example, W. G. Dever, *What Did the Biblical Writers Know and When Did They Know It? What Archaeology Can Tell Us about the Reality of Ancient Israel* (Grand Rapids, 2001), 1–96.

Israel. Their efforts included the search for evidence demonstrating the events and the activities of the various kings of Israel and Judah. Such findings attest to the reliability of Tanakh as a historical source.

Biblical archaeology as a field shifted again, toward the end of the twentieth century, in response to new trends. First, the school of research that became known as the "New Archaeology" sought to sever itself from the historical context of the Tanakh. This approach viewed archaeology as an independent discipline, dealing with the processes of cultural and social development that were borne out by the findings, independent of any particular reference to events recorded in the Tanakh. Then, some of the "New Archaeologists" adopted a more extreme approach that tended to negate the historical validity of the Tanakh, concerning everything up to the period of the divided kingdom, especially the period of Ahab (the first half of the ninth century BCE – see I Kings, ch. 16). Proponents of this view maintain that the Tanakh was written with a bias, long after the events actually took place.[2] They argue that the biblical record should not be regarded as historical fact unless there is positive archaeological evidence that supports the text. This school, related to some degree to trends among scholarly circles in Europe (especially in Scandinavia), is known as the "minimalist approach," and its more extreme exponents are pejoratively labelled the "nihilist school."[3] The narratives of the Torah, they maintain, along with the books of Joshua, Judges, Samuel, and even the beginning of the book of Kings, have almost no historical basis, and, more, they contradict the archaeological findings from the relevant periods. The books were therefore to be considered as mere myths and legends that had been created by the inhabitants of the Land of Israel to explain their national and social origins.

A certain school of contemporary Israeli scholars takes this same approach, one of the most prominent being Ze'ev Herzog. In a newspaper article that raised a storm of controversy, Herzog argued,

2. These claims are themselves addressed in chapter 3.
3. This so-called "nihilist" approach rejects completely the historical record of the Tanakh, claiming that it was written only in the Hellenistic or even the Roman period. This approach has sometimes been prompted by considerations that are not necessarily scientific and objective, and for this reason it has attracted vehement criticism; see Dever, 26–27.

> After seventy years of intensive excavation in the land of Israel, archaeologists are arriving at a frightening conclusion: the "deeds of the fathers" are a fable; we did not go down to Egypt nor did we come up from there; we did not conquer the land, and there is no trace of the empire of David and Solomon."[4]

Herzog's popular article led to extensive discussion of these questions, and conferences, articles, and books appeared in response to the minimalist approach.[5]

Yet many other scholars have distanced themselves from this position, regarding it as a passing trend. Herzog and others of his ilk argue not just from a historical perspective, but from a political one.

At the opposite end of the spectrum, there are scholars who maintain that everything in Tanakh should be accepted as historical truth, so long as there is no proof to the contrary – the "maximalist approach."[6] Most scholars, however, do not fall into either camp, and most treat each discovery on its own merits.

This chapter considers questions that have been raised by the minimalists, for the most part, and have received some media attention. It will also discuss a number of questions that have been raised by scholars who approach archaeological study not with a preconceived rejection of the authenticity of the Bible, but with an objective view appropriate to scientific enquiry.

---

4. Z. Herzog, "HaTanakh – Ein Mimtzaim BaShetaḥ," *Haaretz*, October 29, 1999. The article was translated into English and published in *Biblical Archaeology Review*. It can be found at http://www.freerepublic.com/focus/news/704190/posts.
5. Such as I. Finkelstein and A. Mazar, *The Quest for the Historical Israel: Debating Archaeology and the History of Early Israel* (Atlanta, 2007).
6. Such an approach characterizes the work of John Bright, *A History of Israel*, 3rd ed. (London, 1981). A more sophisticated approach can be found in Adam Zertal, who was one of the few archaeologists to investigate the highland cultures of northern Samaria in the Iron I period. Based on these studies, he concluded: "For most of the biblical descriptions of the nation's origins there exists a real basis, both archaeological and topographical" (*Am Nolad – HaMizbeaḥ BeHar Eival VeReshit Yisrael* [Tel Aviv, 2000], 12). This position does not necessarily accept the historicity of every event, but recognizes that the "*longue durée*" events lie behind many of the individual stories recorded in Joshua, Judges, and Samuel.

One might ask: Why would the questions arising from archaeological research interest someone who, independent of archaeology, already believes in the authenticity and reliability of the biblical account? Clearly, such an individual would approach this research with appropriate reservations and caution. For example, the archaeological approach that casts doubt on the reliability of the Tanakh is itself based on the conclusions prevalent in the world of Bible study – a realm that is far from offering unequivocal, decisive proofs, as already demonstrated in the previous chapters. Sometimes we find archaeologists who rely upon the findings of Bible critics, who themselves rely on the findings of different archaeologists.

Another reason for pause: There is doubt as to whether the discipline of archaeology may be defined as a "pure" science; indeed, many fundamental assumptions in the field, especially in the area of dating, are still open to debate. And the assumptions of "New Archaeology" are often based on the claim that there have been no findings in support of certain events recorded in Tanakh.

Finally, just as in the realm of the literary criticism of the Tanakh, it is difficult to ignore the bias – sometimes openly declared – on the part of many archaeologists of the minimalist school, who have joined together with the "new historians"[7] and follow a political agenda, both in Israel and elsewhere.[8] Herzog concludes his controversial article mentioned above with the words, "It turns out that Israeli society is partially ready to recognize the injustice done to the Arab inhabitants of the land…but is not yet sturdy enough to adopt the archaeological facts which shatter the biblical myth."[9]

---

7. This denotes a group of historians aligned with post-Zionism, including scholars such as Avi Shlaim, Benny Morris, Tom Segev and Ilan Pappe, who, since the 1980s, have sought to challenge the accepted version of Israeli and Zionist history.
8. For a discussion of this phenomenon see Y. Elitzur, "Al Ofnot BeḤeker Toldot Yisrael," *Al Atar* 7, 23–25.
9. Z. Talshir, "Matai Nikhtav HaTanakh," *Beit Mikra* 49, 1 (above, n. 5), 18, notes the statement by T. L. Thompson, a leading minimalist scholar in Denmark, that "current political developments indicate that an understanding of the heritage of Israel is extremely important not only for the academic community, but also for the community in general." She adds, "Against this background, we understand why the history of Israel has recently been taken out of the framework of Bible research and

In sum, bear in mind that many of the claims of the minimalist school are based on an absence of findings. The absence of artifacts from a certain time period, or place, or person, are construed as evidence that these never existed. The *argumentum ex silentio* is a major weakness of the approach: "'We have not found'... is not a proof" (see Ketubot 23b), and certainly not a solid foundation for major theories.[10]

As Bible scholar Sarah Japhet argues:

> Is history limited only to what archaeology is able to prove? If societies and cultures did not leave behind material artifacts, did they not exist? ... This bitter protest arises from the fact that the archaeology of the Land of Israel, and perhaps of the Ancient East in its entirety, started out by taking upon itself a task that it could not fulfill, nor should it have to: to "prove history" or to disprove it.... The role of archaeology is to expose the ancient material culture and to depict, as far as possible, the characteristics of the various cultures.... Nevertheless, it remains just one of the sources for reconstructing history, and it should by no means be entrusted with more than that task.... We must remind ourselves that archaeology, too, is a human science, with room for working assumptions and for discretion; whose data are incessantly changing, and whose conclusions change over time and are certainly not absolute."[11]

introduced as part of the all-encompassing, inter-disciplinary regional reviews of Palestine. The overt point of departure is 'on behalf of' and 'for the sake of,' rather than on study of the history for its own sake."

10. To illustrate this point, we might note that Jerusalem – one of the main foci of the controversy concerning the united monarchy (1050–930 BCE), as we shall see – is proof of the limitations of archaeological findings. We lack archaeological artifacts from Jerusalem in the fourteenth century BCE, but among the Amarna Letters, seven letters from this period were discovered which were sent by Abdi-Hepa, the Canaanite king of Jerusalem, to the king of Egypt, testifying to the importance of the city (B. Mazar, "Jerusalem" in the *Encyclopedia Mikra'it* 3 [Jerusalem, 1958], columns 795–96).
11. S. Japhet, "HaTanakh VeHaHistoria," in *HaPulmus Al HaEmet HaHistorit BaMikra*, 85–86, and see further in her discussion in "Can the Persian Period Bear the Burden?

Indeed, it can happen, and sometimes does, that an archaeological find, uncovered quite by accident, contradicts earlier theories. This will be discussed further in this chapter.

The minimalist approach has led some sectors of the religious world to dismiss biblical archaeology – and especially the "New Archaeology" – as unnecessary. The basic assumption is that the Tanakh describes an absolute reality, and there is therefore no need to become too excited over findings that sit well with the biblical narrative, and, conversely, no need to be overly agitated about findings that contradict the narrative. The question of the degree to which archaeological findings conform to the Tanakh is, to this view, simply a matter of time.

Nonetheless, a scornful attitude toward the study of archaeology is unwarranted. The questions that arise should be dealt with seriously and answered thoughtfully. Those findings that do not accord with the accounts in the Tanakh are not necessarily challenges to the faith; indeed, they may in fact lead to a new and deeper reading of the text, one that synthesizes the written account with the findings on the ground. Knowledge of archaeological findings serves not just to prove what is written in Tanakh, but to enhance the very enterprise of reading the text.

With regard to some of the various biblical periods that are subject to controversy, we will consider the seeming contradictions between the biblical account and the relevant archaeological discoveries. We will address the question of whether the findings represent a scientific consensus, and if so, how they may be reconciled with the biblical narrative and to what extent they require a new understanding of it. Thereafter, we will examine the issue from the opposite perspective – the correspondence between the archaeological findings of each period and the biblical narrative, and the arguments for the reliability of the text that arise from these discoveries.

Obviously, much has been written on these subjects and we will present only a few, brief, central points here, in the hope that they may serve as an introduction to understanding the broader discussion. I

Reflections on the Origins of Biblical History," in *From the Rivers of Babylon to the Highlands of Judah: Collected Studies on the Restoration Period* (Winona Lake, 2006), 342–52.

should also note here what may seem obvious: I am not an archaeologist, and, though I have read widely, I make no pretense to knowledge of archaeological methods or of all the extensive literature on the subject.

FROM AHAB ONWARDS

The most recent era we will discuss with regard to the relationship between the biblical text and the archaeological record is the reign of King Ahab, in the first half of the ninth century BCE.[12] This period is the time during which many scholars believe the books of the Torah and of the Prophets were written, and archaeological discoveries dating from then do generally match the biblical account, which has led scholars to acknowledge the basic reliability of the Tanakh's historical descriptions from this period onward.

For example, it is recorded in the book of Kings:

> וּמֵישַׁע מֶלֶךְ מוֹאָב הָיָה נֹקֵד וְהֵשִׁיב לְמֶלֶךְ יִשְׂרָאֵל מֵאָה אֶלֶף כָּרִים וּמֵאָה אֶלֶף אֵילִים צָמֶר. וַיְהִי כְּמוֹת אַחְאָב וַיִּפְשַׁע מֶלֶךְ מוֹאָב בְּמֶלֶךְ יִשְׂרָאֵל.
>
> And Mesha, king of Moab, was a sheepmaster, and he delivered to the king of Israel a hundred thousand lambs, and a hundred thousand rams, with the wool. But it was, when Ahab died, that the king of Moab rebelled against the king of Israel." (II Kings 3:4–5)

And in 1868, a stele (inscribed stone) dating to the ninth century BCE became an important addition to the archaeological record. It was discovered in what is now Jordan. Its inscription shows that it was established by this same Mesha, king of Moab.[13] It opens with the words, "I am Mesha,

12. See I Kings, ch. 16 onward.
13. Concerning the inscription and its interpretation, see S. Ahituv, *Echoes from the Past: Hebrew and Cognate Inscriptions from the Biblical Period* (Jerusalem, 2008), 389–418. At the end of his discussion he refers the reader to a bibliography pertaining to the inscription. See further on the organizational principles in this text, A. F. Rainey and S. Notley, *The Sacred Bridge: Carta's Atlas of the Biblical World* (Jerusalem, 2006), 203–4 and 211–12.

son of Kemosh, king of Moab."[14] Mesha records that the people of Moab were subservient to Omri, king of Israel, for a long time ["Omri, king of Israel, and they afflicted Moab for many days"], and Mesha describes at length how he prevailed against Omri's son, until Israel was annihilated. The Mesha Stele, then, is the earliest external evidence of Moab's battle against Israel, as recorded in the text, and of the existence of the House of Omri.[15]

Another archaeological find attesting to King Ahab is the Kurkh Monolith (Kurkh is located in southeastern Turkey), with its account describing the military campaigns of the Assyrian king Shalmanesser III.[16] That inscription is written in cuneiform, against an engraved image of a king. Extensive attention is given to the battle of Qarqar, which took place in the sixth year of Shalmanesser's reign (853 BCE). It records that an enormous army, led by twelve kings, was ranged against him, including "two thousand chariots, ten thousand foot-soldiers of Ahab the Israelite," and that among this alliance against him, Ahab was the king with the largest army.

There is no mention whatsoever of this battle in the Tanakh. The biblical silence can support the view that the Tanakh is not a history book, recording every event, but presents only those considered to have aspects worth recording for posterity. In any event, the inscription does

14. Kemosh is well known in the Tanakh as the god of Moab. For example, אוֹי לְךָ מוֹאָב אָבַדְתָּ עַם כְּמוֹשׁ, "Woe to you, Moab! You are done for, O people of Kemosh!" (Num. 21:29); and אָז יִבְנֶה שְׁלֹמֹה בָּמָה לִכְמוֹשׁ שִׁקֻּץ מוֹאָב, "Then Solomon built a high place for Kemosh, the abomination of Moab" (I Kings 11:7).
15. The inscription includes many other aspects and details of Moab's war against Israel that do not appear in the biblical text. *Inter alia*, the stele records that Moab conquered some cities in Israel, and destroyed others; it describes the "vessels of God's House" (apparently a reference to a local temple) being taken as spoils from the city of Nevo and being brought before Kemosh; and Mesha is documented as having taken captives from Israel and making them his slaves who took part in some of his fortification and construction projects. On this subject see E. Samet, *Pirkei Elisha* (Jerusalem, 2007), 99–100. Concerning the connection between the content of the Mesha Stele and the "burden of Moab" in Isaiah 15–16 and in Jeremiah 48, see Y. Elitzur, *Yisrael VeHaMikra* (Jerusalem, 2000), 175–82. For studies on the Mesha stele, see J. A. Dearman, *Studies in the Mesha Inscription and Moab* (Atlanta, 1989).
16. For more on the inscription see, *inter alia*, M. Cogan, *The Raging Torrent* (Jerusalem, 2008), 14–22, and Rainey and Notley, *The Sacred Bridge*, 199–209.

support the textual description of Ahab, king of Israel, as a warrior with a large and significant army.

A further example is an inscription found in Hezekiah's Tunnel in 1880, dating to the eighth century BCE, describing the final stages of the digging of the tunnel designed to lead water from the Gihon spring, outside of the city of Jerusalem, to a pool inside of the city.[17] And indeed, the book of Kings describes the water system devised by King Hezekiah: וַאֲשֶׁר עָשָׂה אֶת הַבְּרֵכָה וְאֶת הַתְּעָלָה וַיָּבֵא אֶת הַמַּיִם הָעִירָה, "and how he made the pool and the aqueduct, and brought water into the city" (II Kings 20:20). The book of Chronicles describes it in even greater detail:

> וַיַּרְא יְחִזְקִיָּהוּ כִּי בָא סַנְחֵרִיב וּפָנָיו לַמִּלְחָמָה עַל יְרוּשָׁלִָם. וַיִּוָּעַץ עִם שָׂרָיו וְגִבֹּרָיו לִסְתּוֹם אֶת מֵימֵי הָעֲיָנוֹת אֲשֶׁר מִחוּץ לָעִיר וַיַּעְזְרוּהוּ. וַיִּקָּבְצוּ עַם רָב וַיִּסְתְּמוּ אֶת כָּל הַמַּעְיָנוֹת וְאֶת הַנַּחַל הַשּׁוֹטֵף בְּתוֹךְ הָאָרֶץ לֵאמֹר לָמָּה יָבוֹאוּ מַלְכֵי אַשּׁוּר וּמָצְאוּ מַיִם רַבִּים.
>
> And when Hezekiah saw that Sennacherib had come, and that he intended to fight against Jerusalem, he took counsel with his ministers and his mighty men, to stop the water of the springs which were outside of the city, and they helped him. So a great many people gathered together, and they stopped up all the springs, and also the stream that ran through the midst of the land, saying, "Why should the kings of Assyria come and find abundant water?" (II Chr. 32:3–5)

The account continues: וְהוּא יְחִזְקִיָּהוּ סָתַם אֶת מוֹצָא מֵימֵי גִיחוֹן הָעֶלְיוֹן וַיַּישְּׁרֵם לְמַטָּה מַּעְרָבָה לְעִיר דָּוִיד, "And this same Hezekiah stopped up the upper watercourse of the Gihon, and brought it straight down to the west side of the city of David" (II Chr. 32:30). More explicit still is the description in the book of Ben Sira (48:22–23): "Hezekiah fortified his city by

---

17. Concerning the inscription, and for a bibliography in its regard, see Ahituv, *Echoes from the Past*, 19–24. Some scholars of the minimalist school sought to suggest that the inscription was from the Hasmonean period, but this possibility was rejected outright by paleographic experts; see Gary Rendsburg, "The Siloam Tunnel Inscription: Historical and Linguistic Perspectives," *Israel Exploration Journal* 60, 2 (2011): 188–203.

bringing water into its midst. He dug into the hard rock with iron, and made wells for water."[18]

The major disputes surrounding archaeology and the biblical text concern the eras that predate this time – from the era of the biblical forefathers until the united monarchy of David and Solomon. Granted, there were scholars of both the nihilist and minimalist schools who questioned even the historical existence of the House of David, but in 1993–1994, a delegation of researchers headed by Avraham Biran, at Tel Dan, found fragments of an Aramaic inscription.[19] The author of the Tel Dan Stele (apparently Hazael, king of Aram), which dates to the ninth or eighth century BCE, describes his victory over the king of Israel and over the king of the "House of David" – making the existence of the famous monarchy harder to write off.[20] This finding also shed light on the inscription on the Mesha Stele,[21] with the result that the existence of

18. *Book of Ben Sira*, 48:17, Kahana edition, 92.

19. For more on this inscription see A. Biran, "The Tel Dan Inscription: A New Fragment," *Israel Exploration Journal* 35 (1995): 1–18, and also the discussion in Ahituv, *Echoes from the Past*, 467–73.

20. The inscription is not intact, but scholars have concluded that, with the missing letters, it should read: "[And I killed Yeho]ram son of [Ahab] the king of Israel, and [I] killed [Ahaz]yahu son of [Yehoram, the ki]ng of the House of David." This would seem to contradict the textual record (II Kings 9:14–27) which attributes the killing of these two kings to Jehu. Some scholars have granted greater reliability to the account on the stele than to the biblical account, arguing that the story about Jehu is not historically correct. However, several solutions have been proposed: Ahituv (471–72) argues that the text can indicate that others killed Ahaziah and Jehoram, since the word "I" is broken (and therefore missing) at this point in the inscription, and W. Schneidewind proposed understanding the boast "[I] killed" as meaning "I supported the coup that killed" ("Tel Dan Stele: New Light on Aramaic and Jehu's Revolt," *Bulletin of the American Schools of Oriental Research* 302 (1996): 75–90), and Rainey and Notley, *The Sacred Bridge*, 212–13. The explanation supported by Schneidewind and Rainey may be derived directly from the text, especially from Elijah's prophecy at Horeb: וְהָיָה הַנִּמְלָט מֵחֶרֶב חֲזָאֵל יָמִית יֵהוּא, "He who escapes the sword of Hazael shall be slain by Jehu" (I Kings 19:17).

21. On the Mesha Stele, the king mentions his capture of "אראל דודה" (line 12). Many scholars have interpreted this expression, too, as being related to King David, perhaps meaning "Ariel of David" as a reference to one of David's warriors; compare וּבְנָיָהוּ בֶן יְהוֹיָדָע בֶּן אִישׁ חַי חַיִל רַב פְּעָלִים מִקַּבְצְאֵל הוּא הִכָּה אֵת שְׁנֵי אֲרִאֵל מוֹאָב, "And Benayahu, son of Yehoyada, the son of a valiant man of Kavtze'el, who had performed many acts,

the House of David is accepted as historical fact by the vast majority of scholars, including those affiliated with the minimalist school, although not those of the nihilist school.[22]

We shall now proceed by examining five periods prior to that of Ahab in which apparent conflict arises between archaeological findings and the biblical account: the period of the forefathers; the sojourn of the Children of Israel in Egypt; the conquest of the land; the period of settlement of the land; and the period of the united monarchy in the days of David and Solomon.

THE ERA OF THE FOREFATHERS

The first period that arouses controversy is the era of our forefathers Abraham, Isaac and Jacob.[23] We start out by noting that the very

---

killed two lion-hearted men (*shenei ariel*) of Moab" (II Sam. 23:20). Further on (line 31), the inscription records that "וחורנן ישב בה בת [ ] וד". Following the discovery of the Tel Dan Stele, many scholars have suggested that the full sentence is meant to read, "וחורנן ישב בה ב[ית ד]וד" – "the House of David dwelled in Houranen," i.e., the city (known to us as Horonayim – see Is. 15:5; Jer. 48:3) was under the rule of the House of David, as noted by André Lemaire, "'House of David' restored in Moabite Inscription," *Biblical Archaeology Review* 20, 3 (1994): 30–37.

22. See, for example, Dever, *What the Biblical Writers Know*, 134. Z. Talshir, 19, summarizes:

> The appearance of the House of David as a consolidated political concept represented a real problem for deniers of Ancient Israel. They went to great lengths to try to rid themselves of this most inconvenient evidence. Davis proposed impossible alternative readings, which no self-respecting scholar would dare to mention; Lemke, despairing of any other solution, decided that the inscription was a forgery. No other scholar in the academic world has cast the slightest doubt on the reliability of the inscription, the circumstances of its discovery, or its epigraphic identity. There is nothing problematic about this inscription, other than the fact that it deals a mortal blow to a priori claims against the history of the House of David.

23. There are some biblical scholars who declare this ancient period to lie "outside of the discussion," since there is "zero chance of discovering artifacts that would testify to the forefathers' wanderings in the land and in neighboring regions, and about the journey of the tribes of Israel through the wilderness; or of finding pharaonic monuments mentioning the mass enslavement of the men, and the Exodus. This, then, is a manifestly 'prehistoric' period, which lies beyond the reach of archaeological research.... Concerning this period there is no real possibility of bringing external proofs either in support or as refutation" (U. Simon, "Arkheologia Post-Mikrait U'Post Tzionit," in *HaPulmus Al HaEmet HaHistorit BaMikra*, 138). Nevertheless,

concept of the "era of the forefathers" is itself contested. The concept was accepted by the early archaeologists who studied the Land of Israel, led by William Albright,[24] as essentially equivalent to the Middle Bronze Age.[25] However, the minimalist school of biblical archaeology maintains that the historical and geographical depictions in Genesis do not conform to the periods of ancient history they claim to represent, but reflect a far later reality. Thus, for example, Nadav Na'aman writes:

> With regard to the era of the forefathers, which introduces the description of the period of the people of Israel in the Bible, there is widespread agreement among scholars. It is generally accepted that this is not a historical period, and that the vast majority, if not all, of the traditions included in the series of narratives about the forefathers, reflect a reality that is later, to a greater or lesser degree, than the beginning of the period of settlement.... The narratives include many elements which in no way conform to the ancient dating [attributed to them].[26]

---

there has been extensive discussion surrounding the period of the forefathers, not relating to specific events or personalities, but to the characteristics of the period as a whole – materially, geo-politically, culturally, and so on. In other words, archaeology does not get at the heart of the story, but to its outer trappings, to see if the background details (trivial as they may be) correspond to reality and thus confer reliability on the narrative as a whole.

24. See, for example, his book *The Archaeology of Palestine* (London, 1949).
25. The names of the different periods of ancient history derive from European archaeology and follow some of the raw material used in certain regions during that period: the Stone Age, the Chalcolithic Age (named for the word "bronze" in Greek), the Bronze Age, and the Iron Age. Since each of these periods lasted many hundreds of years, they are divided by convention into sub-periods (early, middle, and late), and even these are further subdivided. Obviously, the boundaries of these periods are not absolute, since the transition from the use of one type of utensils to another was gradual. In general, the Middle Bronze Age refers to the years 2000–1550 BCE.
26. N. Na'aman, "Parashat 'Kibbush HaAretz' BeSefer Yehoshua U'VaMetziut HaHistorit," in N. Na'aman and Y. Finkelstein (eds.), *MiNavadut LiMelukha* (Jerusalem, 1990), 286–87. The article also appeared in English as "The Conquest of Canaan in the Book of Joshua and in History," in *From Nomadism to Monarchy: Archeological and Historical Aspects of Early Israel*, ed ד. I. Finkelstein and N. Na'aman (Jerusalem, 1994), 218–81, but the relevant passage does not seem to appear in the English version.

Obviously, the stories of the forefathers in and of themselves cannot be proven or disproven from an archaeological point of view. There is no way to prove the existence of Abraham and Isaac, or the confrontation between Jacob and Laban. The main discussion in that regard, therefore, centers on the surrounding reality depicted in these narratives. We shall first examine some of the arguments from those who deny the reliability of the Torah's account of the era of the forefathers.[27] The main theme of their arguments is that the Torah's description is anachronistic – that is, it mentions phenomena dating from a later period than the period of the forefathers. Their claim is that the author of the accounts in the Torah used some details and information that he possessed from his own, later era, which did not belong to the biblical era that he described.

One of the best-known examples of the claim of anachronism – also an interesting reflection of the scholarly attitude in general – is the question of the domestication of camels. This issue was first raised at the end of the nineteenth century, but it received a renewed boost from none other than William Albright, who was generally motivated, as mentioned previously, by a desire to use archaeology to corroborate the biblical account. In this particular matter, however, Albright noted that the domestication of camels took place in the twelfth century BCE, with the stirrings of a fundamental change in the nature of nomadism, several hundred years after the era of the forefathers. Until that time, he argued, nomads had depended on donkeys for transport, since they lived in peripheral areas of civilization, and for this reason "our oldest certain evidence for the domestication of the camel cannot antedate the end of the twelfth century BC."[28] Only at a later stage did nomadism evolve into the form of tribes wandering deep into the wilderness, with occasional raids on camelback on settled agricultural territory, as described, for example, in the introduction to the story of Gideon:

27. A summary of most of these arguments is to be found in Na'aman, "The Conquest of Canaan," 225–26.

28. W. F. Albright, *The Archaeology of Palestine*, 207.

> וְהָיָה אִם זָרַע יִשְׂרָאֵל וְעָלָה מִדְיָן וַעֲמָלֵק וּבְנֵי קֶדֶם וְעָלוּ עָלָיו. וַיַּחֲנוּ
> עֲלֵיהֶם וַיַּשְׁחִיתוּ אֶת יְבוּל הָאָרֶץ עַד בּוֹאֲךָ עַזָּה וְלֹא יַשְׁאִירוּ מִחְיָה
> בְּיִשְׂרָאֵל וְשֶׂה וָשׁוֹר וַחֲמוֹר. כִּי הֵם וּמִקְנֵיהֶם יַעֲלוּ וְאָהֳלֵיהֶם יבאו וּבָאוּ
> כְדֵי אַרְבֶּה לָרֹב וְלָהֶם וְלִגְמַלֵּיהֶם אֵין מִסְפָּר וַיָּבֹאוּ בָאָרֶץ לְשַׁחֲתָהּ.

> And it was, when Israel had sown, that Midian and Amalek and the children of the east came up against them. And they encamped against them, and destroyed the produce of the earth as far as Gaza, and left no sustenance for Israel – neither sheep, nor oxen, nor donkeys. For they came up with their cattle and their tents, and they came like locusts for multitude, for both they and their camels were without number – and they entered the land to destroy it. (Judges 6:3–5)

Albright, admittedly, was cautious, noting that "these facts do not necessarily prove that earlier references to the camel in Genesis and Exodus are anachronistic, but they certainly suggest such an explanation." Albright's caution is justified, as his suggestion relies on the *argumentum ex silentio* (argument from silence). Namely, the absence of evidence that camels were domesticated in the Middle Bronze Age becomes evidence that they were not yet domesticated at that time. Certainly, many other (less cautious) archaeologists viewed the presence of camels in Genesis as an absolute proof of anachronism in Genesis.

In the years since Albright's time, however, more has been learned about the domestication of camels than he could have known. For example, a document discovered in Alalakh, in northern Syria, dated to the seventeenth century BCE, mentions "one portion of food for [each] camel."[29] In excavations carried out in Har HaNegev (Be'er Resisim), dating to the end of the third millennium BCE, camel bones were found along with bones of goats.[30] And there is also evidence specifically of

---

29. See W. Y. Wiseman, "Ration Lists from Alalakh VII," *JCS* 8 (1959): 29, line 59; R. W. Bulliet, *The Camel and the Wheel* (London 1975), 64.
30. R. Cohen, *HaYishuvim BeHar HaNegev*, doctoral dissertation submitted to the Hebrew University of Jerusalem, 1986, 303.

the early domestication of camels – from the fourth millennium BCE – from the deserts of Iran,[31] and elsewhere.[32]

The accumulation of this archaeological evidence demonstrates that the domestication of camels had, indeed, already begun in the days of the forefathers – if in a limited way. Later, of course, the phenomena expanded to include large numbers of camels. This finding sits well with the biblical account, in which camels did not play a central role, and their numbers stayed relatively small, until the time of the Judges. In the story of Abraham's servant and Rebecca, the Torah mentions עֲשָׂרָה גְמַלִּים מִגְּמַלֵּי אֲדֹנָיו, "ten of his master's camels" (Gen. 24:10). These impressed the greedy Laban (Gen. 24:30–31). Similarly, with regard to the gifts of camels that Jacob offers Esau: גְּמַלִּים מֵינִיקוֹת וּבְנֵיהֶם שְׁלֹשִׁים, "Thirty milk camels with their young" (Gen. 32:16).

Camels are absent from other narratives in the Torah. In the tale of the descent of Joseph's brothers to Egypt, the pack animals are donkeys and only donkeys (Gen. 42:26–27, and elsewhere); the spoils seized from Midian mention וַחֲמֹרִים אֶחָד וְשִׁשִּׁים אָלֶף, "sixty-one thousand asses" (Num. 31:34), but no camels. In contrast, from the period of the Judges onwards, a great many camels are found in the biblical text. In the war of the children of Gad and the children of Reuben against the Hagri'im: וַיִּשְׁבּוּ מִקְנֵיהֶם גְּמַלֵּיהֶם חֲמִשִּׁים אֶלֶף, "And they captured their cattle, [and] of their camels, fifty thousand" (I Chr. 5:21). And Job, at the end of his life, had "six thousand camels" (Job 42:12).

The issue of the domestication of camels illustrates the degree to which contemporary knowledge in the realm of biblical archaeology is weak and open to change. Albright himself changed his opinion and wrote, "In summary, the real domestication of the camel was no earlier than the end of the Bronze Age, although partial and sporadic domestication may already have existed a few hundred years earlier."[33] But the

31. Y. Bar-Yosef, "Reshitan Shel Ḥevrot Pastoraliot BaLevant," in S. Ahituv (ed.), *Meḥkarim BeArkheologia Shel Navvadim BaNegev U'VeSinai* (Beer Sheva, 1998), 7–25.
32. Other sources are cited by Y. M. Grintz, *Yiḥudo VeKadmuto shel Sefer Bereshit* (Jerusalem, 1983), 17, n. 32. L. Resnick, *HaTanakh Min HaShetaḥ* 1 (Jerusalem, 2011), 116–23, notes seventeen archaeological proofs for the domestication of camels in the ancient period.
33. Cited by Grintz.

later findings did not deter the minimalists[34] – whose earlier theory had been built on negative evidence – from propagating Albright's outdated theory that the mention of camels in the Torah represents an anachronism, though he himself had already retracted it.[35]

Some scholars have argued that the names of the various places that appear in the narratives of the forefathers are also anachronistic. For example, this opinion is raised especially in relation to the city of Beer Sheva (Beersheba), which, according to archaeological evidence, was not inhabited during the era of the forefathers, nor even during the period that followed.[36]

This position sounds quite convincing at first. It is based on two assumptions: (1) Beer Sheva is mentioned in the stories of the forefathers as a city, and (2) this ancient city is the place identified today at Tel Sheva.

The first assumption, however, does not conform to the biblical narrative. The Torah refers to Beer Sheva in two places, and in both cases it is clear that the reference is not to a city, but to an encounter at wells. Following the covenant and the oath between Abraham and Abimelekh, we are told, עַל כֵּן קָרָא לַמָּקוֹם הַהוּא בְּאֵר שָׁבַע כִּי שָׁם נִשְׁבְּעוּ שְׁנֵיהֶם, "Therefore they called that place Beer Sheva, for there they both swore (*nishbe'u*)" (Gen. 21:31). Thereafter, in the encounter between Isaac and Abimelekh, the city is named:

34. Such as Na'aman, who in 1990 could still write ("Parashat 'Kibbush HaAretz,'" 287), "The narratives contain many elements which are absolutely inconsistent with the ancient date. For example... the presentation of the camel as the forefathers' beast of wandering, although the domestication of the camel for labor and for wandering took place only in the last third of the second millennium BCE."

35. Here is it worth citing Kenneth Kitchen, a well-respected scholar of biblical archaeology and Professor Emeritus at Liverpool University, referred to by *The [London] Times* newspaper (October 13, 2002) as "the very architect of Egyptian chronology." In commenting on the approach of Finkelstein and Silberman, whom he mentions *inter alia* in note 30 and in various contexts throughout the chapter, Kitchen writes: "On the patriarchal and exodus periods our two friends are utterly out of their depth, hopelessly misinformed, and totally misleading.... Camels are *not* anachronistic in the early second millennium (Middle Bronze Age)." K. A. Kitchen, *On the Reliability of the Old Testament* (Grand Rapids and Cambridge, 2003), 465.

36. Na'aman, "Parashat 'Kibbush HaAretz,'" 287.

וַיַּשְׁכִּימוּ בַבֹּקֶר וַיִּשָּׁבְעוּ אִישׁ לְאָחִיו וַיְשַׁלְּחֵם יִצְחָק וַיֵּלְכוּ מֵאִתּוֹ בְּשָׁלוֹם. וַיְהִי בַּיּוֹם הַהוּא וַיָּבֹאוּ עַבְדֵי יִצְחָק וַיַּגִּדוּ לוֹ עַל אֹדוֹת הַבְּאֵר אֲשֶׁר חָפָרוּ וַיֹּאמְרוּ לוֹ מָצָאנוּ מָיִם. וַיִּקְרָא אֹתָהּ שִׁבְעָה עַל כֵּן שֵׁם הָעִיר בְּאֵר שֶׁבַע עַד הַיּוֹם הַזֶּה.

And they rose up early in the morning and they swore (*vayishavu*) to each other, and Isaac sent them, and they parted from him in peace. And it was on that day that the servants of Isaac came and told him about the well which they had dug, and they said to him, "We have found water." And he called it "Shiv'a"; therefore the name of the city is "Beer Sheva," until this day. (Gen. 26:31–33)

The Torah notes that the name given to the place was actually the name of the well – just as Isaac had named the other wells mentioned in the same chapter (Esek, Sitna, and Rehovot; Gen. 26:20–22). Only later was the city called "Beer Sheva" – owing to its proximity to the well (*be'er*) that was called Shiv'a. The notion that the Torah referred to a fortified city from the time of the forefathers, of which some sort of evidence might reasonably remain, is altogether unfounded.[37] Furthermore, the identification of the ancient city of Beer Sheva with Tel Sheva is extremely problematic. Ironically, it was Na'aman himself who proposed identifying the biblical city with the remains from ancient periods found in the modern-day city of Beer Sheva, which has been nearly continuously inhabited at least since the Byzantine period.[38] This argument was supported by the fact that this location "was suited to large-scale civilian settlement that was constantly growing, in terms of

37. See Rabbi Yoel Bin-Nun, "Historia U'Mikra – HaYelkhu Shenayim Yaḥdav? – Sefer Bereshit," *Al Atar* 7, 56; Y. Rosenson, "Sippur Avar – Sifrut VeHistoria BeTanakh – Stira O Hashlama?" *Al Atar* 7, 132. There is still room to question the Torah's mention of the city at this site, even if the reference is not to a city from the time of the forefathers, since according to archaeological evidence, Beer Sheva was settled only at the beginning of the period of the Judges, not at the time of Moses. This question relates to our discussion in chapter 2 of later verses in the Torah. All of this, however, assumes that the biblical Beer Sheva is in fact Tel Sheva, for which, see below.

38. See N. Na'aman, "The Inheritance of the Sons of Simeon," *ZDPV* 96 (1980): 132–52; Y. Meitlis, *Laḥpor et HaTanakh* (Jerusalem, 2006), 116.

proximity to far more accessible sources of water than Tel Sheva, whose water sources are poorer."[39]

Artifacts have been discovered in the city of Beer Sheva (near the site of the present-day city market) that date back to the Early Chalcolithic period, and to the Iron Age I, but the site has not been fully excavated.[40] While there are walls whose top level reveals remains from the Iron Age II, their foundations – as yet, unexposed – extend at least two meters further down. Artifacts from the Middle Bronze Period may yet be found one day at Beer Sheva.

Another claim of anachronism concerns the appearance of ethnic groups in Genesis – including the Philistines, Hivvites, and Hittites. According to Egyptian and other sources, the Philistines appeared in Israel only at the beginning of the Iron Age – that is, during the period of the Judges.[41] How, then, can they put in several appearances in Genesis?[42] At best, the author must be mistaken, say those who take this approach, for the Philistines migrated to the land only hundreds of years later.[43]

Yet closer examination of the biblical text shows clearly that there are significant differences in the ways that the biblical text refers to the Philistines during the period of the forefathers and the way it portrays the Philistines of the period of the Judges.[44] For example, during the

39. Y. Gilad and P. Fabian, "7,000 Shenot Hityashvut: HaSeridim HaArkheologiim BiVeer Sheva Min HaElef HaShishi Lifnei HaSefira Ad Shalhei HaElef HaRishon LaSefira," in Y. Gardos and A. Meir-Glitzenstein (eds.), *Beer Sheva: Metropolin BeHithavut* (Jerusalem, 2008), 314.

40. The Iron Age followed the Bronze Age (see above); it refers generally to the period from 1200 to 586 BCE. It is conventionally divided into the Iron Age I and Iron Age II, with the division between them paralleling the transition between the period of the Judges and the period of the Monarchy – i.e., around the year 1000 BCE.

41. See the discussion in Rainey and Notley, *The Sacred Bridge,* 104–10.

42. For instances, in the encounters between Abimelekh, king of the Philistines, with Abraham (Gen. 21:32) and with Isaac (Gen., ch. 26).

43. This well-known claim has been raised by many scholars. See, for example, T. Dotan, *HaPelishtim VeTarbutam HaḤomrit* (Jerusalem, 1967), 15; B. Mazar, *Kenaan VeYisrael – Meḥkarim Historiim* (Jerusalem, 1974), 136; Na'aman, "Parashat 'Kibbush HaAretz,'" 287; I. Finkelstein and N. A. Silberman, *The Bible Unearthed: Archaeology's New Vision of Ancient Israel and the Origin of Its Sacred Texts* (New York, 2001), 57–58.

44. My explanation here is based on Y. M. Grintz, *Motza'ei Dorot* (Jerusalem, 1969), 99–129.

earlier period, the Philistines are located in Gerar, in the Negev: וַיִּסַּע מִשָּׁם אַבְרָהָם אַרְצָה הַנֶּגֶב וַיֵּשֶׁב בֵּין קָדֵשׁ וּבֵין שׁוּר וַיָּגָר בִּגְרָר, "And Abraham journeyed from there to the land of the Negev, and he dwelled between Kadesh and Shur and he sojourned in Gerar" (Gen. 20:1). They were ruled by a king with a Semitic name (Abimelekh).[45] And at that time, recounts the Torah, the land that would later be the home of the Philistines in Judges was under the control of the Canaanite nations (Gen. 10:19; Num. 13:29). In contrast, those Philistines who appear during the period of the Judges lived in cities along the sea shore – Gaza, Ashkelon, and Ashdod – and not in the Negev region. They were led by "*seranim*" (local lords) who bore non-Semitic names, such as Achish (presumably from the Greek *akios*).

Were mention of the Philistines indeed anachronistic, we would have expected some overlap between the list of cities of the Philistines as they appear in the books of the Prophets, and the list of their cities from the narratives of the forefathers; likewise, we would have expected to find some consistency in their form of rule. The completely divergent lists seem to suggest a great distance between the two sets of Philistines, rather than anachronism.

In addition, the Philistines during the period of the Judges are described as a bitter enemy who wages war against Israel over parts of the Promised Land, whereas the Philistines during the earlier period forged covenants and swore oaths with Abraham and Isaac (it is for this reason, apparently, that the land of these ancient Philistines is not included within the boundaries of the Land of Israel). This strongly suggests that the later Philistines who would compete with the Israelites over the inheritance of the land were unknown when the Torah was written.

It is more likely that an ancient name, which first belonged to the ancient Philistines, was later adopted by the Philistine people who

45. The name of the commander of Abimelekh's army, Fikhol (Gen. 21:22), also appears to be of Western Semitic origin (see Tzadok, *Olam HaTanakh: Bereshit* [Tel Aviv, 2000], 139). Some scholars have argued that the name is Egyptian, although their arguments have been rejected (see Y. Yellin-Kalai, "Fikhol," *Encyclopedia Mikra'it* 6 [Jerusalem, 1972], column 456).

came to inhabit the coastal region.[46] The modern reader is then left with nothing more dramatic than the "phenomenon of the common name."

Indeed, there is much evidence that supports, rather than conflicts, with the depictions in Genesis. As we will see, there are many findings that do conform to the biblical narratives from the time of the forefathers, and indicate that these narratives were indeed written with a profound familiarity with the period.[47]

In chapter 5 we undertook a linguistic analysis showing that the language of the Torah is a more ancient form of Hebrew, different in several respects from the language during the period of the monarchy. This concept has ramifications pertaining directly to the language of Genesis, and particularly the names appearing in it. The names – such as Abram, Levi, Zebulun – follow the structure known to us from other cultures dating to the first half of the second millennium BCE, the same period identified as the period of the forefathers.[48] Theophoric names – those in which some form of God's name are embedded – are conspicuously absent in the Torah. Only two such names, Yehuda and Yehoshua (Judah and Joshua) appear – and it must be noted that Joshua's name was originally Hoshea. In contrast, the phenomenon of personal names containing some element of God's name was quite common during the

46. Meitlis, 123–24.

47. Our discussion here is based mainly on the following sources: S. Yevin, "Iyyunim BiTekufat HaAvot," *Beit Mikra* 7, 4 (16) (5727/1967): 13–47; Y. M. Grintz, 30–38; Bin-Nun, "Historia U'Mikra," 45–64. These articles cite dozens of other examples of the phenomena which they discuss; we will address only a few examples. In addition, in a future chapter we shall discuss at length the relationship between the story of the Flood and parallel narratives in the Mesopotamian culture, and especially in the Epic of Gilgamesh. The great similarity between the descriptions – not only in general content, but even in the more specific details – offers further proof of the ancient authorship of the biblical account.

48. See Yevin, 15–17. A. Mazar, "HaZika Bein HaArkheologia LeḤeker HaHistoria," in *HaPulmus Al HaEmet HaHistorit BaMikra*, 105, notes that "it is unthinkable that there appeared *ex nihilo* from the seventh century [BCE] onwards ... the 'Amorite' names characteristic of the second millennium BCE, in the narratives of Genesis." For further discussion, see E. A. Speiser, *Genesis*, Anchor Bible vol. 1 (Garden City, 1964).

period of the monarchy (e.g., in Hebrew, Yehoram, Yehoshafat, Yehoyakim, Yishayahu, Yirmiyahu, Yoel, and so on).

The great majority of the names mentioned in the stories of the forefathers do not appear again in Tanakh – at least not until the Second Temple Period, long after even the most revisionist estimations of the authorship of Genesis. Had the Torah indeed been written during the period of the monarchy, one might reasonably expect to find many names that were more common during that later era, including some that integrated an element of God's name. How could the later authors, as proposed by this approach, have known of the structure and nature of names from the period more than a thousand years earlier?

Additionally, many social and legal phenomena described in Genesis conform to what we know today about the laws and practices of various peoples in the ancient Near East – even though the Torah, given at a later time, explicitly forbade some of these practices. Presenting the forefathers as people who were active within a socio-legal framework that partly contravened the Torah demonstrates the familiarity of Genesis with the world within which its characters functioned. It is also testimony to the authenticity and honesty of the biblical account, which makes no pretense of presenting the forefathers as operating in accordance with the laws of the Torah, which came later. Consider the following examples of this phenomenon.

The relationship between Sarai and Hagar, as described in Genesis, chapter 16, is quite easily understood in light of the laws of the Laws of Hammurabi.[49] These laws state explicitly:

---

49. The Laws of Hammurabi are the most extensive literary legal document discovered and preserved from the ancient Near East. A stele discovered at the beginning of the twentieth century displays 282 laws, enacted at the command of the Babylonian king Hammurabi, who lived during the eighteenth century BCE. We will discuss the relationship between the laws of the Torah and these laws in a later chapter. For the time being, we refer to the Code as evidence that Genesis demonstrates familiarity with the world reflected in such findings. An accessible but authoritative translation, used below, appears in M. T. Roth, ed., *Law Collections from Mesopotamia and Asia Minor* (Atlanta, 1997), 71–142. The paragraph numbers of the laws remain identical in different translations.

> If a man takes a wife and she gives a slave woman to her husband, and she [that slave] bears children, after which that slave woman aspires to equal status with her mistress – because she bore children, her mistress will not sell her. She shall place upon her the slave-hairlock, and she shall reckon her with the slave women.[50]

This shows that taking a maidservant in the event that one's first wife did not bear children was indeed an accepted practice, although no such practice appears later in the Torah. This law from the Hammurabi Code also sheds light on Sarai's attitude toward Hagar:

> וַיָּבֹא אֶל הָגָר וַתַּהַר וַתֵּרֶא כִּי הָרָתָה וַתֵּקַל גְּבִרְתָּהּ בְּעֵינֶיהָ. וַתֹּאמֶר שָׂרַי אֶל אַבְרָם חֲמָסִי עָלֶיךָ אָנֹכִי נָתַתִּי שִׁפְחָתִי בְּחֵיקֶךָ וַתֵּרֶא כִּי הָרָתָה וָאֵקַל בְּעֵינֶיהָ יִשְׁפֹּט ה׳ בֵּינִי וּבֵינֶיךָ. וַיֹּאמֶר אַבְרָם אֶל שָׂרַי הִנֵּה שִׁפְחָתֵךְ בְּיָדֵךְ עֲשִׂי לָהּ הַטּוֹב בְּעֵינָיִךְ וַתְּעַנֶּהָ שָׂרַי וַתִּבְרַח מִפָּנֶיהָ.

> And he went in to Hagar, and she conceived; and when she saw that she had conceived, her mistress was despised in her eyes. And Sarai said to Abram: "My wrath is upon you: I gave my handmaid into your bosom, and when she saw that she had conceived, I was despised in her eyes; may God judge between me and you." And Abram said to Sarai: "Behold, your handmaid is in your hand; deal with her as you see fit." And Sarai dealt harshly with her, and she fled from before her. (Gen. 16:4–6)

It would seem that Sarai was familiar with the prevailing custom at the time, and that this was the basis for her conduct toward Hagar.

The Torah's fundamental law that לֹא יוּמְתוּ אָבוֹת עַל בָּנִים וּבָנִים לֹא יוּמְתוּ עַל אָבוֹת אִישׁ בְּחֶטְאוֹ יוּמָתוּ, "fathers shall not be slain for their sons, nor shall sons be slain for their fathers; a man shall be slain for his own sin" (Deut. 24:16) is absent from Reuben's efforts to persuade Jacob to send Benjamin together with his older brothers to Egypt. Indeed, his "convincing argument" is a most surprising assurance: אֶת שְׁנֵי בָנַי תָּמִית

50. "The Code of Hammurabi, King of Babylon," section 146. The translation is simplified from that in Roth, and uses the term "wife" instead of the Akkadian *nadītu*.

אִם לֹא אֲבִיאֶנּוּ אֵלֶיךָ, "You shall slay my two sons if I do not bring him [Benjamin] to you" (Gen. 42:37). What is the source for Reuben's very strange idea, which contravenes the position of the Torah? It turns out that the Hammurabi Code contains many expressions of the idea that someone who indirectly causes the death of another person's son is punished by having his own son put to death. For instance:

> If a builder builds a house for a man and does not make its construction firm, and the house which he has built collapses and causes ... the death of a son of the owner of the house, they shall put to death a son of that builder. (Sections 229–30)[51]

The Torah objects to this idea, but the very fact that Reuben expresses it arises from the prevalent practice at the time.

Another example: Abraham expresses his anguish before God at his lack of a son who can inherit from him: מַה תִּתֶּן לִי וְאָנֹכִי הוֹלֵךְ עֲרִירִי וּבֶן מֶשֶׁק בֵּיתִי הוּא דַּמֶּשֶׂק אֱלִיעֶזֶר... הֵן לִי לֹא נָתַתָּה זָרַע וְהִנֵּה בֶן בֵּיתִי יוֹרֵשׁ אֹתִי, "What will You give me, seeing that I go childless, and the steward of my house is Eliezer of Damascus.... Behold, to me You have given no seed, and now one who is born in my house is to be my heir" (Gen. 15:2–3). The Torah offers no basis for the idea that the steward of the house inherits. The laws of Nuzi and of Babylon do include several such instances, however.[52]

Geographically, the descriptions in the stories of the forefathers align well with archeological findings.[53] These findings indicate that the Middle Bronze Age had its own special characteristics, including, first and foremost, the existence of fortified settlements, as well as rural villages, around which nomads wandered. These nomads maintained

---

51. For additional examples, see sections 116, 209–10; Grintz, 58–59; and the detailed discussion in M. Greenberg, "Some Postulates of Biblical Criminal Law," *Yeḥezkel Kaufmann Jubilee Volume* (Jerusalem, 1960), 5–28, and subsequently, "More Reflections on Biblical Criminal Law," *Scripta Hierosolymitana* 31 (1986): 1–17.
52. See Grintz, 58. For an accessible discussion of the research on the patriarchs in their ancient Near Eastern setting, see I. Provan, V. Philips Long, and T. Longman III, *A Biblical History of Israel* (Louisville, 2003), 112–18.
53. For a discussion on this topic see Y. Meitlis, 117–18.

relations with the inhabitants of the villages, and their graves are located at a slight distance from them. Moreover, diverse groups, including the Amorites and the Hurrians, made their way from the north to the Judean mountains. By the time the Israelites returned for the sake of settling the Land of Israel, nomadic groups no longer lived in the land. Of course, the biblical narratives present the forefathers as nomads, maintaining contacts with the inhabitants of the towns (e.g., the story of Shekhem, in Genesis 34), as well as people of different ethnic origins who dwelled in the land, including Canaanites and Perizzites (Gen. 13:7), Amorites (Gen. 14:13), Hittites (Gen. 23:3), and Hivvites (Gen. 34:2; 36:2).

The reliability of the biblical descriptions of the period of the forefathers is found in these general demographic points. Rabbi Yoel Bin-Nun makes an important comment:

> The argument often offered by scholars, and hinted at by N. Na'aman,[54] according to which all of these data could also have been known to a later author, from the First Temple Period (or even writers of a later period), is unfounded and unscientific. No one, during the period of the monarchy, engaged in historical research of the sort that is undertaken by modern scholars, and no author at that time could have written a book so brimming with details, customs and names that had been common and well-known a thousand years previously.[55]

The scope of the present discussion does not allow for additional elaboration on proofs, one way or the other, concerning the authenticity of the narratives in Genesis. Rather, several examples, representative of this discussion, offer a basis for an understanding of the nature and limitations of this controversy.

54. N. Na'aman, *Hakibbush,* 287: "These undated elements may belong to ancient periods, but by the same token might also belong to much later periods."
55. Bin-Nun, "Historia U'Mikra," 54.

SLAVERY IN EGYPT AND THE EXODUS

Until recently, doubts as to the veracity of the story of the Exodus were rejected out of hand by most biblical scholars in Israel. This, for example, in the *Encyclopedia Mikra'it*, under "Exodus": "All in all, there is no doubting the slavery in Egypt and the exodus from Egypt, for no people would invent a tradition of subjugation at the very outset of their existence."[56]

The *Olam HaTanakh* series notes, in the introduction to the book of Exodus:[57]

> Reviews of the events of the past [as recorded] in the Bible recall the Exodus from Egypt as a central event in the life of the nation (Josh. 24; I Sam. 12; Ps. 105–6, and elsewhere). This refutes the claim that this important event in the history of Israel is nothing but a literary creation, devoid of any kernel of historical fact.

These two weighty arguments would seem to suffice to remove any doubt in this regard.[58] Nevertheless, a brief review of the arguments

56. S. A. Levinstam, "Yetziat Mitzrayim," *Encyclopedia Mikra'it* 3 (Jerusalem, 1958), column 754.
57. B. Oded, "Yisrael BeMitzrayim – HaReka HaHistori," in S. Talmon and Y. Avishur (eds.), *Olam HaTanakh: Shemot* (Tel Aviv, 1993), 12.
58. It should be noted that both arguments have been raised by many different scholars. See, for example, S. Yeivin, "Yetziat Mitzrayim," *Tarbiz* 31 (5731/1971): 1–7:

    > If a nation were to invent a fable about a "golden age" at the dawn of its consolidation, this would be perfectly understandable. However, the recounting of a legend about subjugation and oppression at the dawn of any nation is quite improbable, and the very illogic of it serves as faithful proof of the historical veracity of such an account. Moreover, the tradition concerning the forced sojourn in Egypt, and the exodus from there, from subjugation to redemption, is bound up with Jewish culture in all its shapes and forms, to such an extent that the nature and development of this culture over all the generations cannot be understood without it.

that are raised questioning the Exodus, and the responses to them, is worthwhile.[59]

59. The subsequent discussion is essentially unrelated to the question of the date of the Exodus, yet it is tangentially connected. Briefly, the issue of the date may be summarized as follows: On the one hand, in recording the construction of the Temple in the time of Solomon, the text notes that it was completed בִּשְׁמוֹנִים שָׁנָה וְאַרְבַּע מֵאוֹת שָׁנָה לְצֵאת בְּנֵי יִשְׂרָאֵל מֵאֶרֶץ מִצְרַיִם, "four hundred and eighty years after the Children of Israel left the land of Egypt" (I Kings 6:1), and since scholars generally agree that Solomon built the Temple approximately in the year 960 BCE, the Exodus would had to have taken place in the mid-fifteenth century BCE. This calculation sits well with Jephthah's words to the king of Amon, recalling how בְּשֶׁבֶת יִשְׂרָאֵל בְּחֶשְׁבּוֹן וּבִבְנוֹתֶיהָ וּבְעַרְעוֹר וּבִבְנוֹתֶיהָ וּבְכָל הֶעָרִים אֲשֶׁר עַל יְדֵי אַרְנוֹן שְׁלֹשׁ מֵאוֹת שָׁנָה, "Israel dwelled in Heshbon and its surrounding areas, and in Ar'or and its surrounding areas, and in all the cities around Arnon, for three hundred years" (Judges 11:26). Since Jephthah was active at the end of the period of the Judges (he seems to have been a contemporary of Samson; see Judges 10:7), i.e., the end of the twelfth or beginning of the eleventh century BCE, the settlement of Jews in the Gilead area would have been some three hundred years previously – around the year 1400 BCE, and the Exodus was forty years prior to that, in the mid-fifteenth century BCE. (See Y. Elitzur, *Yisrael VeHaMikra*, 51–53, and the discussion in Provan, Long, and Longman, *A Biblical History of Israel*, 131–33).

However, the more widely accepted view maintains that the Exodus took place during the thirteenth century BCE. The rationale behind this conclusion includes the fact that it makes sense to assume that construction of the city of Ramesses, as mentioned in Exodus (1:10), would have been undertaken at the order of Ramesses II, who ruled during the thirteenth century BCE. Egyptian documents indicate that the city of Pi-Ramesses was built at that time. In the mid-fifteenth century, the pharaoh who ruled over Egypt was Thutmose III, who conquered the land of Canaan and brought Egypt to immense political and military strength.

According to this approach, the verse from Judges concerning the construction of the Temple is viewed as a typological number which may refer to twelve generations (480 = 40 x 12), based on a calculation of forty years as a generation (as per Psalms 99:10 and elsewhere); this would then refer to the twelve generations of *kohanim* from Aaron until Ahimaatz, son of Zadok, as recorded in I Chr. 6:35–38.

Without preferring one approach the other, it must be noted that there need not be a direct contradiction between the dates as noted in the books of the Prophets and calculations accepted among most of the scholars. The phenomenon of symbolic numbers, which are not meant to reflect their actual value, appears in various places in the Tanakh. First and foremost, we might note the instance most relevant to our discussion – the length of the subjugation in Egypt. In Exodus (12:40) we read, וּמוֹשַׁב בְּנֵי יִשְׂרָאֵל אֲשֶׁר יָשְׁבוּ בְּמִצְרָיִם שְׁלֹשִׁים שָׁנָה וְאַרְבַּע מֵאוֹת שָׁנָה, "And the Children of Israel's dwelling which they dwelled in Egypt was four hundred and

The arguments of those who deny the servitude in Egypt and the Exodus are based, *inter alia,* on the following considerations.

1. The name "Israel" has not been found on any Egyptian artifact – neither walls of temples, inscriptions on graves, nor papyrus scrolls.[60]
2. Likewise, there is no archaeological evidence of the wandering in the wilderness of Sinai. Nowhere in this region – including in such locations as Kadesh Barne'a, where the nation encamped for lengthy periods – have there been any discoveries that might attest to the ancient encampment of such a large group of people.
3. Instances of anachronism are cited here as well: According to some scholars, the city of Pithom (mentioned in Ex. 1:11) was built only at the end of the seventh century BCE.[61] The description from the time of the Exodus – וְלֹא נָחָם אֱלֹהִים דֶּרֶךְ אֶרֶץ פְּלִשְׁתִּים כִּי קָרוֹב הוּא, "and God did not lead them on the route of the land of the Philistines, although it was close by" (Ex. 13:17) – cannot be reconciled with the knowledge that the Philistines arrived in the Land of Israel only at the end of the thirteenth century BCE (as discussed above).[62] The Torah records that Moses sends messengers to the king of Edom

---

thirty years," but the Sages already point out that this verse cannot be meant literally, and they therefore propose that the Jews dwelled in Egypt for only 210 years (see Rashi, ad loc.). In addition, in the verse introducing the rebellion of Absalom we find, וַיְהִי מִקֵּץ אַרְבָּעִים שָׁנָה וַיֹּאמֶר אַבְשָׁלוֹם אֶל הַמֶּלֶךְ אֵלֲכָה נָּא וַאֲשַׁלֵּם אֶת נִדְרִי אֲשֶׁר נָדַרְתִּי לַה' בְּחֶבְרוֹן, "And it was, at the end of forty years, that Absalom said to the king: 'Let me go, I pray you, and fulfill my vow which I vowed to God in Hebron'" (II Sam. 15:7); here too, since the entire period of David's reign was no longer than forty years (II Sam. 5:4–5), the verse cannot be meant literally. Similarly, the verse that repeats itself over and over in the book of Judges – "and the land was peaceful for forty years" – indicates that the number forty is used to refer to a generation, rather than a precise figure.

For more on this subject, see Y. Meitlis's extensive discussion, "LiShe'elat Tiarukh Yetziat Mitzrayim," in A. Bazak (ed.), *BeḤag HaMatzot* (Alon Shvut, 2015), 11–24.

60. With the exception of the Merneptah Stele, discussed below, and which speaks of Israel as a nation already dwelling in its own land.
61. Finkelstein and Silberman, *The Bible Unearthed,* 66.
62. Within the framework of the same discussion we pointed out the distinction that must be made between two different groups called Pelishtim/Philistines.

> (Num. 20:14), but the kingdom of Edom did not exist, according to these scholars, until the seventh century.[63]

First of all, it must be emphasized again that theories based on an *argumentum ad ignorantiam* – "we have not found evidence supporting" – must be treated with some reservation. Many of the central theories in the historio-archaeological world arose or were refuted on the basis of chance discoveries. Had these discoveries not been stumbled upon, the prevailing research assumptions would have been quite different. And if no traces of the Exodus were ever found, would that constitute a good argument that the Exodus had never happened? In the words of Kitchen: "It is silly to expect to find traces of everybody who ever passed through the various routes in that peninsula. The state of preservation of remains is very uneven... therefore the absence of possible Hebrew campsites is likewise meaningless."[64]

As for the absence of any mention of the Exodus in Egyptian records, note that that kings of the ancient world, including the pharaohs, used to construct monuments glorifying their victories and

63. This claim is actually baseless, as argued quite passionately by Kitchen, 467:

> Edom ***did*** exist [emphasis in the original] as a pastoral, tented kingdom... and was ***not*** a deserted land either then or in the thirteenth century, as the Edomites entering Egypt prove clearly. It was so much a land with active people that both Ramesses II and Ramesses III chose to attack it militarily. So Edom was no ghost in Moses's time. Tented kingdoms may be unknown to dumb-cluck socio-anthropologists, but they are solidly attested in the Near East from of old.

In recent years, studies have been undertaken that indicate the presence of copper mines and a fortress at Khirbat a-Nahas, dating to the eleventh century BCE and perhaps even earlier, and an organized entity dwelling permanently south of the Dead Sea. See T. E. Levy, "Iron Age Complex Societies, Radiocarbon Dates and Edom: Working with the Data and Debates," *Antiguo Oriente* 5 (2007): 13–34.

64. Kitchen, 467. Nadav Na'aman agrees with this specific argument: "Since nomads do not leave remains that scholars might trace, there is no significance to the fact that no remains of nomad-shepherds have been found thus far... archaeology is of no assistance in the argument of the historical veracity of the exodus" (N. Na'aman, "Sippur Yetziat Mitzrayim Bein Zikaron Histori LiYetzira Historiografit," *Tarbiz* 79, 3–4 [5770–5771/2010–11]: 360). In any event, Na'aman himself believes that the story of the Exodus was first committed to writing in the seventh century BCE and then later redacted, and that it does not reflect the reality of ancient Egypt.

achievements, not their defeats and failures.[65] The lack of mention does not signify.

From the opposite perspective, the narrative of the Exodus has been proven to include extensive knowledge about the details of the period in question, and especially the sort of details that changed in later times – just as in the case of the narratives about the forefathers. Had the biblical account indeed been written as late as the seventh century BCE, it surely would not have integrated such precise details of Egyptian reality some six hundred years prior to that narrator's own time. The following are some examples.[66]

The phenomenon of subjugating slaves for massive building projects, such as those described in the Torah immediately prior to the Exodus, is corroborated in several findings. One of the most important of these testaments is Papyrus Leiden 348, which describes the construction of the city of Ramesses by tribes "carrying stones to build the temple of Ramesses." Beyond the construction work, "the biblical account of the Jews in Egypt suggests that their socio-economic situation was remarkably similar to that of the Ḥabiru,"[67] according to Prof. Nili Shupak. A similar point may be expounded upon, with regard to other tribal groups known in Egypt during this period.

The Torah describes the backbreaking labor forced upon the Jews: וַיְמָרְרוּ אֶת חַיֵּיהֶם בַּעֲבֹדָה קָשָׁה בְּחֹמֶר וּבִלְבֵנִים וּבְכָל עֲבֹדָה בַּשָּׂדֶה, "And they embittered their lives with hard labor, with mortar and with bricks, and

65. As noted, for example, by N. Shupak, "Using Egyptian Elements in the Bible to Solve the Problem of Israel's Origins," *Bulletin of the Israeli Academic Center in Cairo* 26 (2003): 5–11; available at https://www.academy.ac.il/SystemFiles/21237.pdf.

66. In the last generation, several studies appeared that noted a very close correlation between the Torah's description of slavery in Egypt and the Exodus, and what we know of Egyptian culture at the time. For a brief review of these, see B. Mazar, *Kenaan VeYisrael – Meḥkarim Historiim*, 98–99, and Shupak, in her Hebrew discussion, "HaḤomer HaMitzri KiKheli LiLibbun Sugyat Reshit Yisrael" in *Beit Mikra* 49 (2003): 67–88. Penina Galpaz-Feller discusses these points in her book *Yetziat Mitzrayim: Metziut O Dimyon* (Jerusalem and Tel Aviv, 2003), 24; her concluding chapter is entitled "Did the Biblical Author Study Egyptian?" This sums up the essence of her argument that the precision in the description of Egyptian reality and culture must lead to the conclusion that "the exodus from Egypt did in fact take place" (135).

67. Shupak, "HaḤomer HaMitzri," 72.

all manner of labor in the fields" (Ex. 1:14). Later, the situation was further exacerbated at Pharaoh's command: לֹא תֹאסִפוּן לָתֵת תֶּבֶן לָעָם לִלְבֹּן הַלְּבֵנִים כִּתְמוֹל שִׁלְשֹׁם הֵם יֵלְכוּ וְקֹשְׁשׁוּ לָהֶם תֶּבֶן. וְאֶת מַתְכֹּנֶת הַלְּבֵנִים אֲשֶׁר הֵם עֹשִׂים תְּמוֹל שִׁלְשֹׁם תָּשִׂימוּ עֲלֵיהֶם לֹא תִגְרְעוּ מִמֶּנּוּ, "You shall no longer give straw to the people to bake bricks, as until now; let them go and gather straw for themselves. But the quantity of bricks that they made until now shall you lay upon them; you shall not diminish it" (Ex. 5:7–8).

The responsibility for making the bricks was placed upon the "officers of the Children of Israel": וַיֻּכּוּ שֹׁטְרֵי בְּנֵי יִשְׂרָאֵל אֲשֶׁר שָׂמוּ עֲלֵהֶם נֹגְשֵׂי פַרְעֹה לֵאמֹר מַדּוּעַ לֹא כִלִּיתֶם חָקְכֶם לִלְבֹּן כִּתְמוֹל שִׁלְשֹׁם גַּם תְּמוֹל גַּם הַיּוֹם, "And the officers of the Children of Israel, whom Pharaoh's taskmasters had set over them, were beaten, saying, 'Why have you not completed your quota for making bricks, both yesterday and today, as until now?'" (Ex. 5:14).

Many Egyptian papyri discuss the brick industry at length, and they also speak of supervisors who were required to maintain production of a daily quota. For instance, in one papyrus, a supervisor laments, "There are no men to make bricks or straw in the vicinity." Another notes, "They are making the daily quota of bricks."[68]

Furthermore, the biblical account of the subjugation in Egypt extensively uses words and expressions that archaeological discoveries have made familiar. For instance, in the description of the creation of the box for the baby Moses, we read: וַתִּקַּח לוֹ תֵּבַת גֹּמֶא וַתַּחְמְרָה בַחֵמָר וּבַזָּפֶת וַתָּשֶׂם בָּהּ אֶת הַיֶּלֶד וַתָּשֶׂם בַּסּוּף עַל שְׂפַת הַיְאֹר, "She took for him a box of sedge, and she coated it with tar and with pitch, and she put the child in it and placed it in the reeds by the bank of the Nile" (Ex. 2:3). Discoveries from Ancient Egypt indeed indicate that sedge was used to make mats and boats by binding it with ropes and coating it with pitch.

> The biblical author makes extensive use of words drawn from the Egyptian conceptual world – the Nile, sedge, reeds… and creates an authentic Egyptian atmosphere. Moreover, he even employs details borrowed from Egyptian social life – a wet-nurse,

68. See Galpaz-Feller, 27.

> procedures for adoption and raising a child in Pharaoh's palace – that are all suited to the period of the new kingdom."[69]

Similarly, Egyptian names, such as "Moses," are familiar to us from other sources.[70] And with regard to the plagues, there is clear evidence of a close familiarity with the culture and characteristics of ancient Egypt, such as the fear of snakes and crocodiles, the centrality of the Nile, and the responses of the magicians.[71] Likewise with the description of the route of the Exodus:

> וַיְהִי בְּשַׁלַּח פַּרְעֹה אֶת הָעָם וְלֹא נָחָם אֱלֹהִים דֶּרֶךְ אֶרֶץ פְּלִשְׁתִּים כִּי קָרוֹב הוּא כִּי אָמַר אֱלֹהִים פֶּן יִנָּחֵם הָעָם בִּרְאֹתָם מִלְחָמָה וְשָׁבוּ מִצְרָיְמָה.
>
> And it was, when Pharaoh had let the people go, that God did not lead them on the route of the land of the Philistines,[72] although it was close by, for God said, "Perhaps the people will change their minds when they see war, and return to Egypt." (Ex. 13:17)

Archaeological findings indicate a route along the northern coast of Sinai that was fortified with a network of fortresses, dating to the thirteenth

69. Galpaz-Feller, 45. With these words the author summarizes the findings that she cites from page 33 onwards. For more words and expressions that are unique to the story of the Exodus, and which relate to the reality of the period in question, see Shupak, "Using Egyptian Elements."
70. Moses's name seems to be derived from the Egyptian noun M-S, meaning "child," or from the Egyptian verb M-S-Y, meaning "to give birth" or "to be born." There are at least three known individuals with this name from the period of Ramesses II. (Of course, the biblical explanation of the name – כִּי מִן הַמַּיִם מְשִׁיתִהוּ, "for I drew him [*meshitihu*] from the water" [Exodus 2:10] – does not negate the Egyptian meaning of the name. For a discussion of the phenomenon of biblical explanation of names, see Galpaz-Feller, 39, and Shupak, "Using Egyptian Elements," 5–7.)
71. See Galpaz-Feller, 33–45.
72. Cassuto suggests that this verse refers not to the north-eastern road, the "sea route," but rather the more eastern route, which passes through the ancient land of the Philistines. In any event, even according to his interpretation, it is clear that the Jews could have entered Israel via a shorter route – the "sea route" – had this not been the most dangerous option.

century BCE.[73] In addition, a number of papyri have been found testifying to the very strict control over entry into and departure from Egypt.[74] Indeed, when the information from all of these sources is combined, it paints a clear picture as to why the Jews did not enter Israel via a shorter route. It also spotlights the impossibility of leaving Egypt without Pharaoh's approval.[75]

Shupak's summary is helpful in this regard:

> Analysis of the relevant Egyptian material indicates that the story includes material from the period of Ramesses.... Had the story been a fictitious creation...we would have expected to find elements from a later period mixed up in it. For example, the description of the Land of Egypt and its inhabitants would

---

73. See A. Malamat, "The Exodus: Egyptian Analogies," in *Exodus, the Egyptian Evidence*, eds. E. S. Frerichs and L. H. Lesko (Winona Lake, 1997), 15–26. Malamat cites additional sources which we have not mentioned here, concerning the corroboration between archaeological findings and the biblical account of the Exodus.
74. These papyri are named after Giovanni Anastasi, the Swedish consul who purchased them in 1839. Most of them date to the thirteenth century BCE.
75. In this regard it is puzzling that Finkelstein and Silberman, *The Bible Unearthed*, 59–63, try to use these findings to negate the veracity of the story of the Exodus. They argue that the remnants of the fortresses indicate the difficulty of escaping from Egypt via the border fortifications, and note without any apparent recognition of the contradictory nature of their claim, that "the biblical narrative hints at the danger of attempting to flee by the coastal route" (61). If this is so, where is the conflict between their version of the events and the biblical account? And how do they explain how an anonymous author in the seventh century BCE (as they claim) knew of the existence of this network of fortresses, which by his own account was the reason why the Jews did not take that route, preferring the route via the wilderness of Sinai?

    In fact, Finkelstein and Silberman's argument turns on a fundamental point of conflict between their view and the view of the believing reader of the biblical story. They argue, "Putting aside the possibility of divinely inspired miracles, one can hardly accept the idea of a flight of a large group of slaves from Egypt through the heavily guarded border fortifications into the desert and then into Canaan in the time of such a formidable Egyptian presence" (61). This is a sentence with which any religious believer can agree wholeheartedly. The whole question is whether we are to ignore the possibility of miraculous intervention, or to believe in Divine Providence and God's guidance of His nation. This argument, of course, has nothing to do with any question of archaeology.

> resemble that which appears in the writings of the Greek historian Herodotus, who lived and wrote during the Persian era; the Children of Israel would be engaged not in making bricks and labor in the field, but rather would be engaged in commerce; and the capital of Egypt would be Sais.... Even after the minimalist fashion dies out and passes from the world, to be replaced by a different theory, the tradition of the exodus will still continue to escort us.[76]

THE CONQUEST OF THE LAND

The conquest of the Land of Israel is described at length in the book of Joshua, and the conventional view, based on a superficial reading of the text, is that both the process of conquest and the subsequent settlement of the tribes of Israel in the land were completed in a short time. Various archaeological findings cast grave doubts on this view, however, and in fact a more in-depth reading of the relevant chapters likewise leads to a different conclusion.[77]

The view of the conquest and settlement as a quick transition was accepted among archaeologists of the previous generation, especially Albright and Yadin, who noted a wave of destruction that swept over Canaanite cities in the thirteenth century BCE and effectively ended the Middle Bronze Period. These celebrated archaeologists saw this destruction as the work of the tribes of Israel, in their conquest of the land.

One of the most important findings from this period pertains to the city of Hazor. In Joshua we read about Yavin, king of Hazor, who was the leader of the kings of the north, and about the conquest of the city by Joshua:

---

76. Shupak, "HaḤomer HaMitzri," 86–88. It is important to note that Shupak does not accept the biblical account as a description from the actual time of the events; she maintains that the story underwent later redactions which included "mythical and legendary elements" (86). Nonetheless, this again boils down to the question of a theological worldview, rather than to archaeological data.

77. For a review of the different approaches concerning the processes of conquest and settlement, see M. Weinfeld, *MiYehoshua Ve'ad Yoshiyahu*, 54–65; Dever, *What Did the Biblical Writers Know*, 108–24; and Provan, Long, and Longman, *A Biblical History of Israel*, 138–92.

> וַיָּשָׁב יְהוֹשֻׁעַ בָּעֵת הַהִיא וַיִּלְכֹּד אֶת חָצוֹר וְאֶת מַלְכָּהּ הִכָּה בֶחָרֶב כִּי חָצוֹר לְפָנִים הִיא רֹאשׁ כָּל הַמַּמְלָכוֹת הָאֵלֶּה. וַיַּכּוּ אֶת כָּל הַנֶּפֶשׁ אֲשֶׁר בָּהּ לְפִי חֶרֶב הַחֲרֵם לֹא נוֹתַר כָּל נְשָׁמָה וְאֶת חָצוֹר שָׂרַף בָּאֵשׁ... רַק כָּל הֶעָרִים הָעֹמְדוֹת עַל תִּלָּם לֹא שְׂרָפָם יִשְׂרָאֵל זוּלָתִי אֶת חָצוֹר לְבַדָּהּ שָׂרַף יְהוֹשֻׁעַ.

> And at that time Joshua turned back and he took Hazor, and he smote its king by the sword, for Hazor had until then been the chief of all of these kingdoms. And he smote all the souls who were in it by the sword; there remained no one breathing in it, and he burned Hazor with fire.... But all the cities that stood upon their mounds – Israel did not burn them, except for Hazor alone, which Joshua burned. (Josh. 11:10–13)

The wording suggests that Hazor had been a large and important center, but by the time of the redaction of the book of Joshua, long after the conquest, the city had lost its glory. The archaeological findings by Yigael Yadin, who excavated both the lower part and the upper part (acropolis) of Hazor in the years 1955–1958 and again in 1968–1969, indicated a large city, with impressive public structures, which existed hundreds of years before the conquest by Joshua. The importance of the city is attested to in archives discovered in the city of Mari, located on the western bank of the Euphrates. Mari maintained a written correspondence with various other cities, and about twenty of those letters relate to Hazor – the only city in Israel with which it maintained such correspondence.[78] Concerning the lower city, Yadin writes:

> We have evidence that this tremendous city, with thousands of inhabitants, came to an end with a sudden fire in the second half of the thirteenth century, and was not rebuilt.... The surprising similarity between the size of Hazor as revealed in the excavations, on one hand, and its description in the Bible as "the chief of all these kingdoms," on the other, and the emphasis of the biblical

78. See Y. Yadin, *Hazor* (Tel Aviv, 1975), 15, and A. Malamat, "Trade Relations between Mari and Hazor," in *Confronting the Past, Archaeological and Historical Essays on Ancient Israel in Honor of William Dever* (Winona Lake, 2006), 351–55.

> author that Hazor alone was destroyed by Joshua and set on fire, leave little doubt, to my mind, that we have indeed found the Canaanite city of Yavin, which was destroyed by Joshua.[79]

Likewise, concerning the definition of Hazor as "the chief of all these kingdoms," Amihai Mazar states, that "it is difficult to imagine that this definition would have been dreamed up from nowhere by an author in the seventh century, or even later."[80]

Then, starting in 1990, the city was excavated again, by a delegation led by Amnon Ben-Tor. Both Yadin and Ben-Tor discovered, among the ruins of the palace, fragments of statues whose heads and arms appeared to have been destroyed deliberately. Ben-Tor concluded, on the basis of this finding, that "it is only the settling tribes of Israel that could have been responsible for the conquest and destruction of Hazor."[81]

More recent developments have made clear that seeing the conquest and settlement of the land as a uniform, quick phenomenon contradicts the archaeological findings in several respects.[82] In most of the cities mentioned in the process of the conquest, along the coast and in the valleys, such as Megiddo, Aphek, and Gezer, no remains of Israelite settlement were found among the ruins of the Canaanite cities. By contrast, in most of the regions of settlement along the mountain range, where the major settlement revolution at that time took place, there are few Canaanite sites. From the evidence we may conclude that the Canaanite centers were not attacked all at the same time, but rather over a long period; also, while the period of settlement in the mountains was

79. Yadin, 145.
80. A. Mazar, "Devarim Al HaZika Bein HaArkheologia Shel Eretz Israel LeVein Ḥeker HaHistoria Shel Tekufat HaMikra," in Y. L. Levine and A. Mazar, *HaPulmus Al HaEmet HaHistorit BaMikra*, 105.
81. A. Ben-Tor, "HaḤafirot HaMeḥudashot BeTel Hazor," *Kadmoniot* 111 (5756/1996): 18. Later on, however, Ben-Tor changed his approach: "We may establish that Hazor still existed in the thirteenth century, and that it was destroyed not before the middle of this century. At present there is no archaeological evidence as to the identity of its destroyers" (Ben-Tor, "Ḥofrim BeHazor," *BeShevil HaAretz*, Dec. 2005, 24).
82. For a summary see I. Finkelstein, *The Archaeology of the Israelite Settlement* (Jerusalem, 1988), 295–314, especially 299.

already well underway, some Canaanite cities, such as Lachish,[83] were still standing.

Actually, these findings offer support for the picture created by a more comprehensive and careful reading of the biblical account of the settlement of the land. That is, had the book of Joshua been composed of only its first twelve chapters, it would have left the impression of a "uniform military conquest," with a string of victories and the complete annihilation of the Canaanites:

> וַיַּכֶּה יְהוֹשֻׁעַ אֶת כָּל הָאָרֶץ הָהָר וְהַנֶּגֶב וְהַשְּׁפֵלָה וְהָאֲשֵׁדוֹת וְאֵת כָּל מַלְכֵיהֶם לֹא הִשְׁאִיר שָׂרִיד וְאֵת כָּל הַנְּשָׁמָה הֶחֱרִים כַּאֲשֶׁר צִוָּה ה׳ אֱלֹהֵי יִשְׂרָאֵל. וַיַּכֵּם יְהוֹשֻׁעַ מִקָּדֵשׁ בַּרְנֵעַ וְעַד עַזָּה וְאֵת כָּל אֶרֶץ גֹּשֶׁן וְעַד גִּבְעוֹן. וְאֵת כָּל הַמְּלָכִים הָאֵלֶּה וְאֶת אַרְצָם לָכַד יְהוֹשֻׁעַ פַּעַם אֶחָת כִּי ה׳ אֱלֹהֵי יִשְׂרָאֵל נִלְחָם לְיִשְׂרָאֵל.
>
> And Joshua smote all of the hill country, and the Negev, and the plain, and the slopes, and all of their kings; he left none remaining, but destroyed completely all that breathed, as the Lord God of Israel had commanded. And Joshua smote them from Kadesh Barne'a to Gaza, and all the country of Goshen, as far as Giv'on. And Joshua took all these kings and their land at one time, because the Lord God of Israel fought for Israel. (Josh. 10:40–42)[84]

The text then goes on to paint a picture that is quite different: וִיהוֹשֻׁעַ זָקֵן בָּא בַּיָּמִים וַיֹּאמֶר ה׳ אֵלָיו אַתָּה זָקַנְתָּה בָּאתָ בַיָּמִים וְהָאָרֶץ נִשְׁאֲרָה הַרְבֵּה מְאֹד לְרִשְׁתָּהּ, "And Joshua was old and advanced in age, and God said to him, 'You are old and advanced in age, yet there remains much of the land still to be possessed'" (Josh. 13:1). That message is followed by a long list of the "land that remains" – namely, places in the land that the Jews

---

83. Lachish, too, was destroyed, but only during the second half of the twelfth century BCE, about a hundred years after the destruction of Hazor. D. Ussishkin, "Levels VII and VI at Tel Lachish and the End of the Bronze Age in Canaan," in J. N. Tubb (ed.), *Palestine in the Bronze and Iron Ages: Papers in Honor of Olga Tufnell* (London, 1985), 213–28.

84. The same idea is conveyed by the verses summarizing the inheritance of the land, in Josh. 21:41–42.

had yet to conquer and settle (Josh. 13:2–13). Likewise, throughout the verses detailing the inheritances, the text mentions again and again the places not yet conquered (Josh. 15:63; 16:10; 17:12–13). The partial nature of the conquest of the land is depicted even more sharply in the first chapter of Judges, which serves as an introduction to the period as a whole, including the problems that arose from the Israelites' failure to conquer the Canaanites in so many areas of the country.[85]

Some of the descriptions in the early chapters of Joshua therefore should be understood as referring to events that occurred later on. The value in describing these events out of order presumably lies in

---

85. The introductory chapters of Judges offer no fewer than four different answers to the question of why the conquest was so incomplete:
    1. Because the Jews forged a covenant with the inhabitants of the land and did not shatter their altars, they were punished by God: לֹא אֲגָרֵשׁ אוֹתָם מִפְּנֵיכֶם וְהָיוּ לָכֶם לְצִדִּים וֵאלֹהֵיהֶם יִהְיוּ לָכֶם לְמוֹקֵשׁ, "I shall not drive them out from before you, and they shall be as snares for you, and their gods shall be a trap for you" (Judges 2:3).
    2. As a punishment for the sins of the nation during the period of the Judges: יַעַן אֲשֶׁר עָבְרוּ הַגּוֹי הַזֶּה אֶת בְּרִיתִי אֲשֶׁר צִוִּיתִי אֶת אֲבוֹתָם וְלֹא שָׁמְעוּ לְקוֹלִי. גַּם אֲנִי לֹא אוֹסִיף לְהוֹרִישׁ אִישׁ מִפְּנֵיהֶם מִן הַגּוֹיִם אֲשֶׁר עָזַב יְהוֹשֻׁעַ וַיָּמֹת, "Because this nation has violated My covenant which I commanded to their forefathers, and they have not obeyed Me, I shall likewise not continue to drive out from before them any of the nations which Joshua left when he died" (Judges 2:20–21).
    3. As a test of Israel's loyalty: לְמַעַן נַסּוֹת בָּם אֶת יִשְׂרָאֵל הֲשֹׁמְרִים הֵם אֶת דֶּרֶךְ ה׳ לָלֶכֶת בָּם כַּאֲשֶׁר שָׁמְרוּ אֲבוֹתָם אִם לֹא, "To put Israel to the test, whether they will observe the way of God, to follow it, as their forefathers did, or not" (Judges 22).
    4. In order that the Jews will learn to fight in the future: רַק לְמַעַן דַּעַת דֹּרוֹת בְּנֵי יִשְׂרָאֵל לְלַמְּדָם מִלְחָמָה רַק אֲשֶׁר לְפָנִים לֹא יְדָעוּם, "Only that the generations of Israel might know, to teach them war, at least those who did not know of such things previously" (Judges 3:2).

    The first two reasons express punishments that come retroactively, while the last two represent a pre-planned reality. To these four reasons, we might add a fifth, which is actually the first, as set forth explicitly in the Torah: לֹא אֲגָרְשֶׁנּוּ מִפָּנֶיךָ בְּשָׁנָה אֶחָת פֶּן תִּהְיֶה הָאָרֶץ שְׁמָמָה וְרַבָּה עָלֶיךָ חַיַּת הַשָּׂדֶה. מְעַט מְעַט אֲגָרְשֶׁנּוּ מִפָּנֶיךָ עַד אֲשֶׁר תִּפְרֶה וְנָחַלְתָּ אֶת הָאָרֶץ, "I shall not drive them out from before you in a single year, lest the land become desolate and the wild beasts multiply against you. Little by little shall I drive them out from before you, until you grow numerous and inherit the land" (Ex. 23:29–30).

attributing these processes to Joshua himself, though he may have overseen only their earliest stages.

A good example of this approach may be found in the account of the conquest of Hebron and the inheritance of the "*anakim*" (giants) there. In Joshua 10:36–37, in the context of the war against the five kings of the south, the text records that Joshua conquered Hebron: וַיִּלְכְּדוּהָ וַיַּכּוּהָ לְפִי חֶרֶב וְאֶת מַלְכָּהּ וְאֶת כָּל עָרֶיהָ וְאֶת כָּל הַנֶּפֶשׁ אֲשֶׁר בָּהּ לֹא הִשְׁאִיר שָׂרִיד...וַיַּחֲרֵם אוֹתָהּ וְאֶת כָּל הַנֶּפֶשׁ אֲשֶׁר בָּהּ, "And they took it and they smote it with the sword, and its king, and all its cities, and all the souls that were in it; he left none remaining...but destroyed it utterly, and all the souls that were in it." Later, however, Caleb asks Joshua for Hebron, in accordance with God's promise following the sin of the spies (Josh. 14:6–15). Lo and behold, the city had not yet been conquered, and the *anakim* were still there: כִּי אַתָּה שָׁמַעְתָּ בַיּוֹם הַהוּא כִּי עֲנָקִים שָׁם וְעָרִים גְּדֹלוֹת בְּצֻרוֹת אוּלַי ה׳ אוֹתִי וְהוֹרַשְׁתִּים כַּאֲשֶׁר דִּבֶּר ה׳, "For you heard on that day that the *anakim* were there, and that the cities were great and fortified; if the Lord will be with me, perhaps I shall be able to drive them out, as God has spoken" (Josh. 14:12). Still later we read:

> וּלְכָלֵב בֶּן יְפֻנֶּה נָתַן חֵלֶק בְּתוֹךְ בְּנֵי יְהוּדָה אֶל פִּי ה׳ לִיהוֹשֻׁעַ אֶת קִרְיַת אַרְבַּע אֲבִי הָעֲנָק הִיא חֶבְרוֹן. וַיֹּרֶשׁ מִשָּׁם כָּלֵב אֶת שְׁלוֹשָׁה בְּנֵי הָעֲנָק אֶת שֵׁשַׁי וְאֶת אֲחִימַן וְאֶת תַּלְמַי יְלִידֵי הָעֲנָק.
>
> And to Caleb, son of Jefuneh, he gave a portion among the children of Judah, at God's command to Joshua – the city of Arba, the father of the *anak* – which is Hebron. And Caleb drove out from there the three sons of the *anak* – Sheshai and Ahiman and Talmai, the children of the *anak*. (Josh. 15:13–14)

Similarly, we find at the beginning of Judges: וַיִּתְּנוּ לְכָלֵב אֶת חֶבְרוֹן כַּאֲשֶׁר דִּבֶּר מֹשֶׁה וַיּוֹרֶשׁ מִשָּׁם אֶת שְׁלֹשָׁה בְּנֵי הָעֲנָק, "And they gave Hebron to Caleb, as Moses had spoken, and he expelled from there the three sons of the *anak*" (Josh. 1:20).

The question remains: When was Hebron conquered and the giants expelled? Was it during Joshua's time, or was it after his death?

It would seem that the original conquest was carried out by Caleb,[86] apparently after the death of Joshua. This account appears in Joshua 15, and Rashi notes there that these verses were written "after the death of Joshua, for during Joshua's time, the city of Hebron had not yet been captured, as we are told in Judges, and the matter is noted here only for the purposes of the division [of the land]." Nonetheless, these verses appear in Joshua as well, as part of the general literary aim of attributing the entire process of the conquest to Joshua, who led the nation at the start of its presence in the land.

It turns out, then, that the two descriptions of the conquest in Joshua express two aspects of the conquest of the land. One depicts the ideal picture – a uniform, continuous military conquest, representing God's willingness to give the land to the Children of Israel, and crediting Joshua, God's servant, with the entire process. The other shows the objective reality in which the process of conquering lasted several years; apparently, the Children of Israel were in no rush to take on the challenges awaiting them.[87]

86. It is highly symbolic that it is specifically Caleb who drives out the *anakim*, since it was this aspect of the spies' report that so concerned the Jews (Num. 13:28, 33; Deut. 1:28). It is Caleb son of Jefunah, who never feared the children of the *anak* from the outset, who drives three of them out.

87. Rabbi Yoel Bin-Nun, "HaMikra BeMabat Histori VeHaHitnaḥalut HaYisraelit BeEretz Kenaan," in *HaPulmus Al HaEmet HaHistorit BaMikra*, 13–16, argues that the description of the conquest in Joshua reflects not necessarily different literary aspects, but rather a distinction between military victory and conquest with settlement. Following the invasion and the great victories, especially against the kings of the south (Josh., ch. 10) and the kings of the north (Josh., ch. 11), there were effectively no large armies left to oppose the Israelites. These victories also prevented other kings in the region from waging war against Israel, and allowed the nation to embark on a decades-long program of settlement undisturbed – at least in the mountain region. Rabbi Bin-Nun arrives at this understanding on the basis of the difference between Hazor, which as noted above was the only city to be burned (other than Jericho and Ai), and the other cities, which remained intact: "But all the cities that stood upon their mounds – Israel did not burn them, except for Hazor alone, which Joshua burned" (Josh. 11:13). Although the text describes Joshua as taking and utterly destroying the other cities, too, the reference there is to military victory. For this reason, Joshua did not burn Lachish, as indeed is recorded in the text; its destruction, a hundred years later, appears to have taken place during the period of the Judges.

In addition to the complex picture that arises from the biblical description of the process of conquest alongside the archaeological evidence, two additional significant issues pertain to two of the better-known narratives in Joshua: the conquests of Jericho and of Ai.

Jericho

The book of Joshua (chapter 6) describes the conquest of Jericho in great detail, especially the miraculous collapse of the city walls. Yet archaeologist Kathleen Kenyon, who was involved in the excavations of the ancient site at Jericho in the 1950s, concluded that Jericho had not been fortified with a wall during the Late Bronze Period.[88] Her assertion is accepted by many scholars today.

The proofs of this view, however, are not absolute. In excavations carried out in Jericho during the 1930s by the British archaeologist John Garstang, fortifications were discovered dating back to the Early Bronze Period, and Kenyon herself agreed that "it is possible that this rampart served as fortification for the city from the Late Bronze Period, and it is possible that a new wall was built atop it, of which nothing remains."[89] Other scholars argued that a fortified city from this period can indeed be identified, disagreeing with Kenyon's conclusions.[90]

It should be noted that this view does not necessarily mean that the book of Joshua is not trying to convey two different perspectives. The practical resolution may well accord with Rabbi Bin-Nun's explanation.

88. K. M. Kenyon, *Digging Up Jericho* (London, 1957). A different discussion concerns the very existence of any habitation in Jericho during the Late Bronze Period, but a later study showed that the city had indeed been inhabited at this time, although it ceased to exist at the end of the fourteenth century or beginning of the thirteenth century BCE. See P. Bienkowski, *Jericho in the Late Bronze Age* (Warminster, 1986).
89. Kenyon, ibid.
90. See B. G. Wood, "Did the Israelites Conquer Jericho? A New Look at the Archeological Evidence," *Biblical Archeology Review* 16 (1990): 44–58. Wood rejects Kenyon's conclusions and brings various arguments in support of the authenticity of the biblical account. *Inter alia,* he relies on pottery shards from the Late Bronze Age that were found in clay from Jericho. He points to the remains of another brick wall, from around the year 1400 BCE, which in his view was destroyed in an earthquake, following which the city was burned. He also brings many more arguments for the authenticity of the biblical narrative. See also H. J. Bruins and J. Van der Plicht, "Tell el-Sultan (Jericho): Radiocarbon Results of Short-Lived Cereal and Multiyear

It is also possible that the remains of the city slowly eroded through natural phenomena, which have greatly influenced the discoveries in Jericho,[91] or even through human intervention. But whether one accepts such an explanation depends on the scholar's point of departure. Amihai Mazar argues that "in this case, the archaeological evidence does not run directly counter to the biblical tale, as is asserted by some scholars,"[92] even as Ze'ev Herzog takes the view that such arguments represent "invalid excuses that we would never dream of proposing in relation to any other period in which there are no walls."[93] Clearly, this debate is a controversy based on questions that are not purely academic in nature, but rather rest on one's fundamental view of the reliability of the biblical account.

In considering the degree of correlation between the archaeological evidence in Jericho and the biblical description in Joshua, another factor must be taken into account as well. According to the Tanakh, Jericho was completely abandoned under the threat of Joshua's curse (Josh. 6:26–27), and was not reinhabited until the time of King Ahab, when it was reestablished by Hiel of Beit El (I Kings 16:34). In light of the fact that Jericho was a central and important city, which had been inhabited for thousands of years, and which had access to convenient sources of water – the spring of Elisha and the spring of Naaran – this desertion of the city is noteworthy. More, the peculiar abandonment of Jericho is backed up by archaeological evidence,[94] and were it not for the biblical record of Joshua's curse, it would be quite inexplicable. In any event, the abandonment of Jericho may well have caused the erosion and erasing

---

Charcoal Samples from the End of the Middle Bronze Age," *Radiocarbon* 37, 2 (1995): 213–20; these scholars subjected the burned grain from Jericho IV to carbon dating, and concluded that the fire took place at the end of the fourteenth century BCE.

91. See Kenyon, 197–98.
92. The complete quote is: "Undoubtedly, the biblical story of the battle of Jericho is legendary, but in this case, the archaeological evidence does not run directly counter to the biblical tale, as is asserted by some scholars," A. Mazar, "The Iron Age I," *The Archaeology of Ancient Israel*, ed. A. Ben-Tor, transl. R. Greenberg (New Haven, 1992), 283.
93. Z. Herzog, "HaMahapekha HaMada'it BeArkheologia shel Eretz Yisrael," in *HaPulmus Al HaEmet HaHistorit BaMikra*, 57.
94. Kenyon, 200.

of many traces of the city, and for this reason the hypothesis that attributes the absence of remnants of the walls to the city's abandonment seems eminently reasonable.

Ai

A different controversy concerns the city of Ai, whose conquest is likewise described at length in Joshua (chaps. 7–8). The Tanakh offers a few topographical details that help us to identify the location of Ai: עִם בֵּית אָוֶן מִקֶּדֶם לְבֵית אֵל, "beside Beit Aven, to the east of Beit El" (Josh. 7:2), with a valley to its north: וַיַּחֲנוּ מִצְּפוֹן לָעַי וְהַגַּי בינו [בֵּינָיו קרי] וּבֵין הָעָי, "And they encamped to the north of Ai, with a valley between them and Ai" (Josh. 28:11).

Archaeological research has identified Ai with Khirbat A-Tel, northeast of Jerusalem, to the east of the biblical Beit El (which itself is identified with the village Bittin).[95] This identification rests on both the topographical conditions and the name of the place – "Tel" – in the sense of mounds of ruins. Note that the conquest of Ai concludes with the words, וַיִּשְׂרֹף יְהוֹשֻׁעַ אֶת הָעָי וַיְשִׂימֶהָ תֵּל עוֹלָם שְׁמָמָה עַד הַיּוֹם הַזֶּה, "Joshua burned Ai and made it an eternal mound [*tel*], a desolation to this very day" (Josh. 8:28).

The site yields extensive remains of a large city from the Early Bronze Age, which was destroyed about a thousand years before the story in Joshua, but there are no remains from the Late Bronze Age. This led even moderate scholars, such as Amihai Mazar, to the following conclusion:

> The narrative in Joshua, chapter 8, is not anchored in the historical reality matching the period of the conquest, even though the story is filled with topographical and tactical details.... In this instance there is no choice but to explain the biblical narrative as an etiological story,[96] created during a period in which the Jews

95. See S. Yeivin, "Ai, HaAi," in the *Encyclopedia Mikra'it* 6 (Jerusalem, 1972), columns 169–92.

96. A story that explains topographical or other phenomena by attributing them to some event that took place in the distant past, without necessarily having any historical basis.

> had already settled in Ai. Such settlement did in fact exist there during the period of the Judges; the inhabitants must have realized that their village was built on the ruins of a huge, destroyed city, and over time there developed a legend of the conquest of the city, which was attributed to Joshua son of Nun.[97]

This claim is based entirely on one single assumption, and that is the identification of Ai with Khirbat A-Tel. This identification has not been proven, however, and it presents several difficulties. For example, the biblical Giv'on (larger than Ai according to Joshua 10:2) is identified with Tel Giv'on in Al-Jib,[98] but the area of this mound is about half of that of Khirbat A-Tel, which is the largest archaeological site in the Binyamin region.[99]

Moreover, Grintz proves that there is no connection between the name "Ai" and the word "tel" in the sense of ruins; on the other hand, Grintz argues, there does exist a connection between the chronology of A-Tel and that of another city that was located close to Ai: Beit Aven.[100] That city was already in ruins during the period of Joshua's conquest, and there was therefore no need to conquer it. It is mentioned in the story of the conquest of Ai only for the purposes of marking the site – "Ai which was beside Beit Aven." While Grintz offers no alternative location for Ai, several other hypotheses have been raised in recent years

1. Rabbi Yoel Bin-Nun proposes that Ai be identified with Khirbat al-Marjama.[101] Excavations undertaken there revealed a fortified Israelite city from the period of the monarchy, but further exploration of a section of the southern wall exposed a layer of habitation from the Late Bronze Age.[102]

---

97. Mazar, 43.
98. See, for example, the entry for "Giv'on" (written by the editorial board), *Encyclopedia Mikra'it* 2 (Jerusalem, 1954), columns 417–18.
99. I heard this argument raised by Prof. Yoel Elitzur.
100. Grintz, 278–89.
101. Y. Bin-Nun, "Ba Al Ayat: Pitaron Ḥadash LeZihui HaAi," in Z. H. Ehrlich and Y. Eshel (eds.), *Meḥkerei Yehuda VeShomron* (Ariel, 1993), 63–64.
102. Some scholars have questioned this possibility; see Y. Elitzur's comments, ad loc., 63–64.

2. Y. Meitlis argues that many regions of settlement during the Middle Bronze Age were spread on a slope, rather than at the top of a hill.[103] It is therefore possible that Ai, which was indeed located at Khirbat A-Tel during the Early Bronze Age, and was destroyed, was later rebuilt on the slope, by the village of Deir Debwan. An archaeological survey at this site produced a pottery fragment from the Middle Bronze Age.

While neither of these suggestions has been proven, they nevertheless highlight that the hypothesis that the account of Ai is an etiological story rather than a historical record is not a simple matter. Consider that the small habitation at Khirbat A-Tel from the time of the Judges lasted only a short time – if the book of Joshua was indeed written as late as the seventh century BCE, how would its authors know of a city named Ai, to the east of Beit El, and provide such an accurate topographical description? Is it not preferable to locate Ai at a site other than Khirbet A-Tel, rather than to see the whole narrative as an etiology?

SETTLEMENT OF THE LAND

A significant process of settlement, recognized by all scholars working in the field of biblical archaeology, is evident in the central mountainous region of Israel, starting from the thirteenth century BCE. It is evident in the establishment of hundreds of small, similar points of settlement. These villages are notable for their modesty and simplicity, with no decorations on the clay vessels and almost no jewelry. The houses have a unique form of construction.[104]

But who were these new settlers? The answer to that question is the main controversy among archaeologists. The minimalist school maintains that what became known as the nation of Israel was actually formed out of a collection of local nomadic groups who abandoned

103. Meitlis, 62–64.

104. The building follows a "four spaces" or "house of pillars" plan, with three parallel oblong living areas and a fourth area stretching across the back of all three. These villages were also characterized by special pottery, including jugs and cooking pots with an outward-pointing folded rim; as well as various inscriptions, indicating that their inhabitants were literate (see Meitlis's summary, 147–50).

their villages on the coastal plain or in the Negev and settled in these new areas.[105] This approach contends that not only was there no sojourn in and no exodus from Egypt, but there was no invasion of the Land of Israel by an external population. Rather, the process of settlement described above is a phenomenon that began from within the country, by the ancient inhabitants of the land. These settlers slowly invented an Israelite identity for themselves, complete with stories about the origins of their existence, including those about the forefathers and the Exodus. Hundreds of years later, these stories were committed to writing, and the majority of the Tanakh came into being.

Scholars who disagree with the minimalist school raise several arguments against this approach. One of the main questions is whether the characteristics of these settlements are unique – indicating a specific national identity – or if the settlements are part of a more general phenomenon, with similar examples in other places.

One acknowledged unique characteristic of the communities formed in this region is the absence of pig bones – in clear contrast to the other inhabited areas in the land during the same period. A simple explanation of this phenomenon would be that the Israelite inhabitants observed the biblical prohibition against consuming pork (Lev. 11:7). Indeed, the minimalists, who maintain that the Torah was written only hundreds of years after the settlement of these communities, are forced to propose their own explanations, and ultimately they conclude that the phenomenon arises "for reasons that are not entirely clear."[106]

Moreover, the question of whether the form of settlement is unique likewise depends to some extent on the basic assumptions of the researcher, rather than on the findings themselves. In contrast to the conclusions drawn by Finkelstein and Silberman, Amihai Mazar writes:

> I claim that both the socio-economic status of the settlers and the historical-geographical data fit their identity as early Israelites. The socio-economic structure of the Iron I hill-country society

105. For a summary of this approach, see Finkelstein and Silberman, *The Bible Unearthed,* 97–122.
106. Finkelstein and Silberman, *The Bible Unearthed,* 120.

> coincides with the biblical description of Israel during the period of the Judges. This was a non-urban, sedentary society, living in small communities of farmers and herders, without a central political authority.... The archaeological evidence appears to indicate that this was an egalitarian society that was striving for subsistence in the harsh environmental conditions of the forested mountains and semi-arid regions of the land of Israel. Sites that, according to the biblical tradition, were major Israelite villages or towns during the period of the Judges, such as Shiloh, Mizpah (Tell en-Nasbeh), and Dan, do appear in the archaeological record as important Iron I sites. It is possible to identify them, as well as other sites with a similar material culture in the same region, as Israelite.[107]

As we have seen many times before, the interpretation given to identical material varies dramatically from one researcher to the next.

One piece of archaeological evidence represents a substantial challenge to the minimalist approach. One of the most important findings pertaining to this period is the Merneptah Stele (Israel Stele), discovered in 1896 during excavations in the ancient Egyptian capital of Thebes (the biblical No-Amon).[108] This large stone stele celebrates the victories of King Merneptah, son of Ramesses II, and it includes a list of conquests during the campaign undertaken by the king in the year 1208 BCE, including the following: "Ashkelon has been overcome; Gezer has been captured; Yanoam is made non-existent." The inscription then goes on to state, "Israel is laid waste and his seed is not."

Clearly, this claim represents a wild exaggeration – not only concerning Israel, but also in other aspects (a common feature of victory inscriptions in the Ancient East). The important point is the mention of an entity named "Israel," already living in the country by the end of the thirteenth century BCE, and the (exaggerated) pride of Merneptah

---

107. A. Mazar, *The Quest for the Historical Israel*, 92.
108. For more on this stele, the inscription, and its translation, see Provan, Long, and Longman, *A Biblical History of Israel*, 169–70, and Rainey and Notley, *The Sacred Bridge*, 99–100.

upon annihilating it.[109] This indicates that "Israel" was an independent body of some importance, on the northern border of Egypt, and this testimony is well suited to the period of settlement, before Israel became a real kingdom. The existence of the inscription is a considerable challenge to the minimalist approach, which is forced into various attempts at explaining or evading it.[110]

The claim that there are no traces of invasion by an external population and a specific process of expansion is likewise highly contentious. An extensive archaeological survey,[111] known as the "Manasseh hill-country survey,"[112] discovered thousands of previously unknown sites, including some 450 that were dated to the period of the settlement of the tribes of Israel. According to the survey, the direction of expansion of the Israelite villages was from the east westward, and from the center, both southward and northward. These findings accord with the biblical account, as does the shifting of the spiritual center of the Jews from Mount Ebal to Shiloh, and then from Shiloh to Jerusalem.

---

109. There is considerable historical irony in the fact that the two most ancient archaeological proofs concerning the existence of the Jewish people – the Merneptah Stele and the Mesha Stele – both describe the annihilation of Israel: "Israel is laid waste and his seed is not," says the former, while the latter asserts, "Israel has perished; it has perished forever!"
110. See, for example, Na'aman, 311–12, who concludes his discussion of this important finding with the words, "Despite the great importance attached to the very appearance of the name 'Israel' on an external document at the beginning of the proto-historic era of the People of Israel, and despite the temptation to try to integrate this ancient finding into Israelite history, it would seem that at this stage of the research it is advisable to avoid attaching to it any sort of hypothesis as to the nature of the Israelite settlement at the end of the thirteenth century BCE."
111. An archaeological survey examines a broad area; the historical sites discovered within it are mapped, measured, and dated by means of a careful gathering of the pottery shards found on the ground.
112. The survey, headed by Adam Zertal, was carried out over a period of thirty years, covering some three thousand square kilometers. The findings of the survey have been published in four volumes to date: A. Zertal, *The Manasseh Hill Country Survey*, from 2008 to 2017, with the fourth volume prepared by Zertal and Shay Bar, and published after Zertal's untimely death. Many of the results (up to 1994) are summarized in Adam Zertal's essay, "To the Land of the Perizzites and the Giants: On the Israelite Settlement in the Hill Country of Manasseh," in *From Nomadism to Monarchy*, 47–69.

The survey area included, among other sites, the strip stretching from Beit Shean to Wadi Petzael, the region through which the Israelites entered the land, according to the book of Joshua. More than a hundred sites have been discovered in this region with artifacts dating to the period of settlement (twelfth to thirteenth centuries BCE), most of them belonging to just a single period. Another important finding concerns the vessels discovered at these sites. The pottery vessels are rather primitive in the eastern sites, and show increasing sophistication as one follows the development of settlement westward.

All of the above suggests "gradual settlement from east to west, or an entry from the eastern side of the Jordan to the western side, toward the mountain range."[113] Indeed, some signs of settlement have also been discovered on the eastern side of the Jordan, to the north of the Dead Sea, that are very similar to the discoveries on the western side.[114]

In the 1980s, Zertal discovered a large rectangular structure (7 meters by 9 meters) at the Mount Ebal site.[115] The only access to the top of the structure is via a ramp that ascends to the center of it. To the left of the ramp there is another ramp, leading to the "*sovev*" – a foundation wall surrounding the central structure on three sides. Approximately one thousand burned bones of young male animals, all belonging to species defined as "pure" in the Torah, were found within this area. No figurines, bones of pigs, or any other familiar indications of Canaanite worship sites were discovered.[116] The findings at the site match the period of the beginnings of the settlement period – that is, the end of the thirteenth century BCE.[117] The altar belongs to just one

---

113. A. Zertal, "Tanakh, Arkheologia VeReshit Yisrael," in *HaPulmus Al HaEmet HaHistorit BaMikra*, 79.
114. See also Meitlis, 159.
115. See Zertal's essay, "To the Land of the Perizzites and the Giants: On the Israelite Settlement in the Hill Country of Manasseh," in *From Nomadism to Monarchy*, 47–69, here 61–65; a summary of the controversy appears in Finkelstein, *The Archaeology of the Israelite Settlement*, 82–85.
116. It should be noted that the architectural structure of the site is remarkably reminiscent of the description of the sacrificial altar described in the Mishna (Middot, chapter 3).
117. This conclusion is partly based on the discovery of Egyptian scarabs and pottery. The discovery of the Egyptian scarabs also indicates some sort of connection with Egypt.

period, and it was left in an orderly state, not destroyed. These data and others correspond almost perfectly[118] to the description in the Torah and the books of the Prophets regarding the structure of the altar in general,[119] and may even allow an identification of this structure with the altar that the Jews are commanded to build in Deuteronomy 27:4–5, the enactment of which is described in Joshua 8:30–35.[120]

These points and others show that there is a wide gap between the claim that there is no evidence of the entry of any external population into the land – itself a weak argument – and the evidence. We once again return to the issue of whether this debate is a genuine archaeological dispute, or a dispute over fundamental worldviews, the roots of which have nothing to do with archaeology.

In concluding our discussion of the conquest and settlement of the land, we note a further difficulty presented by the assumptions of

---

118. It should be noted that bones of deer were discovered at the site, and these are not mentioned in the Torah as animals suitable for sacrifice. Nevertheless it should be noted that the deer is in fact a "pure" animal (Deut. 14:5), and there is no explicit prohibition in the Torah against offering a pure animal (see Zertal, *Am Nolad – HaMizbeaḥ BeHar Eival VeReshit Yisrael*, 100). Rabbi Yoel Bin-Nun ("HaMivneh BeHar Eval VeZihuyo KeMizbeaḥ," *Lifnei Efraim U'Vinyamin U'Menashe* [Jerusalem, 1985], 137–62) argues that the source of these deer bones is "the remains of vessels and meals eaten in a state of purity or as sanctified meals, brought as a general mass free-will offering to fill the stone altar or the remains of the sanctified meal inaugurating the site."

119. The discovery of the altar gave rise to a great debate, since it presents a problem both for Bible critics (as we have seen in previous chapters) and for the minimalists, who date the texts to the seventh century and deny their historical authenticity. The minimalists, in response to the discovery of the structure on Mount Ebal, proposed that the site was a "watch tower" (Zertal, *Am Nolad*, 190–206). Zertal also discusses the political motivations behind the resistance to identifying the structure as an altar (ad loc., 133, 296, and more).

120. Zertal notes this. However, there are some scholars who oppose this identification because the altar at Mount Ebal shows initial worship upon natural rock, upon which the altar was later built (in a similar manner to the development of Saul's altar in I Sam. 14:33–35) and used for decades. The text, in contrast, speaks of an altar made of "whole stones" that was built for temporary use in the ceremony of the blessings and curses between Gerizim and Ebal. In any event, the assumption that this was an Israelite altar from the period of the settlement seems most probable.

the scholarly view that the book of Joshua, along with other books, was written in the seventh century at the earliest, and that the reliability of its account is therefore in question. Had the book indeed been written from within the perspective of the later Davidic monarchy, why would the author not include some hint to the future establishment of the Israelite kingdom? If anything, the author suggests that by the time of Joshua, the settlement was already in its ideal form: לֹא נָפַל דָּבָר מִכֹּל הַדָּבָר הַטּוֹב אֲשֶׁר דִּבֶּר ה׳ אֶל בֵּית יִשְׂרָאֵל הַכֹּל בָּא, "Nothing failed of all the good things [of] which the Lord had spoken to the house of Israel; it all came to pass" (Josh. 21:43). Could such a sentence have been written centuries after the events described, if the author knew all that was still to happen?[121]

THE UNITED MONARCHY

The final period under review in this context is the kingdom of David and Solomon, known as the period of the "united monarchy" (eleventh to tenth centuries BCE). Here, too, there are many facts that are universally agreed upon, and scholarly discussion turns mainly upon the interpretation of those facts.

All agree that in Israel during the period of the monarchy (referred to by archaeologists as Iron Age II-A), there was a real upheaval, with a new culture growing upon the ruins of the Canaanite cities. This culture was characterized by a higher quality of construction (use of hewn stone, pillars, etc.) and sophisticated ceramics. Fortified cities appeared, along with public structures and water supply systems, all showing evidence of a centralized government. This construction contrasts strongly with the meager, scattered construction of the Iron Age I. Another undisputed fact, with significant implications for the entire discussion, is the absence of any discovery of Egyptian, Assyrian, or Babylonian inscriptions mentioning Israel during this period.

The main question is when these changes took place – namely, when did the transition from Iron Age I (identified, as noted previously, with the period of the Judges) to Iron Age II occur? The classic view of biblical archaeology (known in this context as the "High Chronology") connected this phenomenon with David and Solomon, whose political

---

121. This point is noted by Y. Elitzur, "Al Ofnot BeḤeker Toldot Yisrael," 29–30.

and economic power is attested to in Tanakh. That prowess was evident most particularly in the extensive construction projects undertaken by Solomon throughout the country (I Kings 9:15–19), including Hazor, Megiddo, and Gezer. Support for this view came in part from artifacts that were discovered at the excavation sites of these three locations. In addition to the buildings being impressive, some of the structures found at the various locations were identical, consisting of large, six-chambered gates, with three chambers on each side of the opening. In each instance, the finding indicates Iron Age II. These structures came to be known as "Solomon's Gates."[122]

In recent years, however, this evidence has been rejected by some scholars.[123] The gate at Megiddo is connected to the wall built above the palaces, and since the wall necessarily dates from a period later than the palace, these scholars have assumed that the gate, too, is from a later period. They argue that additional six-chamber gates have been discovered in various cities, including Ashdod, Lachish, and Tel Ira, which were unquestionably later than Solomon's period. In addition, they claim that the gates attributed to Solomon cannot be dated, since the archaeological findings provide only a relative chronology – an indication of which came earlier and which came later – but absolute dating is possible only where there is some objective external datum. Since these scholars cast doubt on the reliability of the biblical narrative, they argue that the text cannot be relied upon for determining the dating of "Solomon's Gates," and hence there is no archaeological proof that they were built in Solomon's time.

Finkelstein and Silberman ask additional questions about the attribution of the construction in these cities to Solomon:

1. There is a disparity between the construction works evident in other cities, and the paucity of findings in Jerusalem and its environs. Admittedly, the entire area of study is plagued by the objective problem that no archaeological excavation is permitted on the Temple

122. The subject is expanded upon by Yigael Yadin; see, for example, *Hazor*, 187–205.
123. See D. Ussishkin, "Was the 'Solomonic' City Gate at Megiddo Built by King Solomon?" *Bulletin of the American Schools of Oriental Research* (1980): 1–18.

Mount itself, and therefore no evidence can be found supporting any dating of the First Temple. However, excavations in and around Jerusalem have not yielded significant findings from the tenth century BCE; the general impression is one of a "typical hill country village," with a sparse population living around it.[124] "Is it possible that a king who constructed fabulous ashlar palaces in a provincial city ruled from a small, remote, and underdeveloped village?"[125]

2. There are many similarities between the palaces discovered at Megiddo and the palace in the city of Shomron, which was built during the period of Omri and Ahab, at the beginning of the ninth century BCE. This would seem to indicate that they were built around the same time. These scholars thus conclude that the construction of Megiddo must also have been undertaken later, during the time of Omri.[126]

3. Carbon-14 samples from major sites attributed to Solomon, such as Megiddo and Hazor, indicate more uniform dates for the destruction of these cities – and hence also for their construction by the kings of Israel.[127] Finkelstein and Silberman contend that these tests represent

124. Finkelstein and Silberman, *The Bible Unearthed,* 133.

125. Ibid., 140.

126. Ibid., 141. The authors are aware of the internal contradiction in their attitude toward Tanakh (they reject its historical reliability concerning David and Solomon out of hand, while at the same time accepting its reliability concerning the construction of Shomron by Omri) but do not see this as a problem. In their view, "One may doubt the historicity of one verse and accept the validity of another" (Finkelstein and Silberman, *The Bible Unearthed,* 344). This is rather a weak argument, for even if one is able to understand the logic underlying the considerations for accepting some or other specific point, it is still difficult to accept a view that proposes accepting the reliability of one chapter of Tanakh, down to the tiniest details, while rejecting as later legend all information from preceding chapters.

127. The system of carbon dating was developed in 1950 by Nobel laureate Willard Frank Libby. The dating method is based on the fact that carbon is found in various forms, including the main stable isotope (C_{12}) and an unstable isotope (C_{14}). Through photosynthesis, plants absorb both forms from the atmosphere (in the form of carbon dioxide), and animals then feed on these plants. When any plant or animal organism dies, it contains a ratio of C_{14} to C_{12}, but this ratio decreases at a regular rate because the level of C_{12} remains constant, while the C_{14} decays. Carbon-14 has

> the "final nail in the coffin of the theory of the Solomonic period."[128] In fact, on the basis of these arguments and others, they conclude that the beginning of the Iron Age II must be postponed by a hundred years ("Low Chronology"). Thus, all the trappings of an opulent and well-developed kingdom should be moved from Solomon's days and attributed instead to the period of Omri. The period of David and Solomon should no longer be regarded as a "golden age." Instead of the tremendous unified kingdom described in Tanakh, Finkelstein proposes a view of Judah as a small, sparse, and isolated rural society. In his view, it was admiration for the figures cast by David and Solomon that led the authors of the Books of Samuel and Kings – some three hundred years later – to transform their small sovereign territory into a legend of a huge united kingdom, attributing the entire construction enterprise of the House of Omri to King Solomon.

The first argument, regarding the disparity between Jerusalem and other settlements, is based on an absence of findings for the reliability of the biblical account. Yair Hoffman has noted in this context, that "the attempt to draw conclusions from the absence of artifacts is highly

---

a relatively short half-life of 5,730 years, meaning that the fraction of carbon-14 in a sample is halved over the course of 5,730 years due to radioactive decay. Thus, a comparison between the carbon-14 and carbon-12 in any organic matter yields a fairly accurate estimate of its age.

128. Finkelstein and Silberman, *David and Solomon: In Search of the Bible's Sacred Kings and the Roots of the Western Tradition* (New York, 2006), 275–81. Despite these decisive pronouncements, the conclusions that they present are open to question. Amnon Ben-Tor, director of the excavation site at Hazor, has noted that six significant layers of construction have been discovered, the last of them dating unquestionably to the destruction of Hazor at the hands of Tiglat Pileser in the year 732 BCE. Given this, even if each layer represented only forty years, we would arrive at the conclusion that the layer of construction which Yadin attributed to Solomon does indeed date to the middle of the tenth century BCE. Finkelstein's proposal that the period of Hazor begins only in the ninth century would mean that only an extremely short period can be attributed to each layer. Such an example "does not appeal to common sense" (A. Ben-Tor, "Arkhaeologia-Mikra-Historia," in *HaPulmus Al HaEmet HaHistorit BaMikra*, 23). Finkelstein and Silberman's position is also questioned by other scholars; see A. Mazar, *Archaeology of the Land of the Bible* (Anchor Bible Reference Library, New York, 1990), 387.

questionable, for archaeological and epigraphic findings are sometimes extremely serendipitous."[129]

Beyond this objection, there is evidence in support of the biblical description that challenges the Low Chronology. An important basis for the discussion is an inscription found at the Temple of Amon at Karnak, in Egypt, describing Shishak's invasion of Israel, which brought destruction to several cities.[130] The campaign, somewhere around the year 925 BCE, was waged primarily against the Northern Kingdom of Israel, though it also affected the southern region of the Negev.[131] This inscription in and of itself represents real proof of the reliability of the narrative in the book of Kings, since the campaign is mentioned there explicitly:

> וַיְהִי בַּשָּׁנָה הַחֲמִישִׁית לַמֶּלֶךְ רְחַבְעָם עָלָה שושק [שִׁישַׁק קרי] מֶלֶךְ מִצְרַיִם עַל יְרוּשָׁלָם. וַיִּקַּח אֶת אֹצְרוֹת בֵּית ה׳ וְאֶת אוֹצְרוֹת בֵּית הַמֶּלֶךְ וְאֶת הַכֹּל לָקָח וַיִּקַּח אֶת כָּל מָגִנֵּי הַזָּהָב אֲשֶׁר עָשָׂה שְׁלֹמֹה.

> And it came to pass in the fifth year of King Rehoboam that Shishak, king of Egypt, came up against Jerusalem. And he took away the treasures of the House of God, and the treasures of the king's house, and he took all; and he took away all the shields of gold which Solomon had made (I Kings 14:25–26).[132]

---

129. Y. Hoffman, "Historia, Mitos, U'Politika," *HaPulmus Al HaEmet HaHistorit BaMikra*, 31.
130. In these inscriptions he is called "Shoshenk." The identity of Shoshenk with Shishak is universally accepted (see references in the next footnote).
131. On the inscription and its significance see A. Mazar, "The Search for David and Solomon: An Archaeological Perspective" in *The Quest for the Historical Israel* (Atlanta, 2007), 117–39; Rainey and Notley, *The Sacred Bridge*, 185–89; Yigal Levin, "Did Pharaoh Shoshenq Attack Jerusalem?" *Biblical Archaeology Review* 38, 4 (2012): 42–52; N. Na'aman, "Masa Shishak LeEretz Yisrael BeRe'i HaKetovot HaMitzriyot, HaMikra, VeHaMimtza HaArkheologi," *Tzion* 53 (5758/1998): 247–76. For the relationship between Shishak's campaign and the biblical narrative, see Y. Elitzur, *Yisrael VeHaMikra*, 152–56.
132. Even Finkelstein and Silberman, *The Bible Unearthed* (161), agree that this "provides the earliest correlation between external historical records and the biblical text." Nevertheless, they find it difficult to accept the reliability of the biblical narrative, even in this context. They attempt to claim that since there is no independent documentation of the chronology of the kings of Egypt during that period (the

In Chronicles, the account is expanded further. Shishak came up to Jerusalem בְּאֶלֶף וּמָאתַיִם רֶכֶב וּבְשִׁשִּׁים אֶלֶף פָּרָשִׁים וְאֵין מִסְפָּר לָעָם אֲשֶׁר בָּאוּ עִמּוֹ מִמִּצְרַיִם לוּבִים סֻכִּיִּים וְכוּשִׁים, "with twelve hundred chariots, and sixty thousand horsemen, and the people were without number who came with him from Egypt – Luvim and Sukkiyim and Kushim" (II Chr. 12:3). Thereafter: וַיִּלְכֹּד אֶת עָרֵי הַמְּצֻרוֹת אֲשֶׁר לִיהוּדָה וַיָּבֹא עַד יְרוּשָׁלָם, "he took the fortified cities which belonged to Judah, and he came to Jerusalem" (II Chr. 12:4).

But after the Jews repent, following the call by Shemaya the prophet, they are promised that Jerusalem will not be destroyed: וְנָתַתִּי לָהֶם כִּמְעַט לִפְלֵיטָה וְלֹא תִתַּךְ חֲמָתִי בִּירוּשָׁלַם בְּיַד שִׁישָׁק. כִּי יִהְיוּ לוֹ לַעֲבָדִים וְיֵדְעוּ עֲבוֹדָתִי וַעֲבוֹדַת מַמְלְכוֹת הָאֲרָצוֹת, "I shall grant them some deliverance, and My wrath shall not be poured out upon Jerusalem by the hand of Shishak. Nevertheless, they shall be his servants, that they may know My service and the service of the kingdoms of countries" (II Chr. 12:7–8). Thus, Shishak suffices with the plunder but does not destroy Jerusalem. His campaign is described in Tanakh only in this context.[133] Although Jerusalem is not mentioned in the Karnak inscription,[134] the existence of the Kingdom of Judah may be deduced from the route of the campaign:

---

chronology is determined as per the biblical narrative about Rehoboam), "Shoshenk's campaign could have been undertaken at almost any time in the late tenth century, not necessarily during Rehoboam's reign" (*David and Solomon*, 74).

133. It seems that the main purpose of the inclusion of this story of Shishak is to show the damage to the Temple, within a book that comes to describe the process leading from the building of the Temple to its destruction (see also A. Grossman, "HaShimush BeReka HaHistori BeHoraat Nevi'im Rishonim," *Maayanot 11 – Horaat HaMikra* [Jerusalem, 1986], 292–94).

134. Finkelstein and Silberman (n. 16) refuse to accept the biblical record of Shishak's having sufficed with the plunder, without going up against Jerusalem. They write, "And yet the urge to harmonize the Bible with the Karnak inscription has been persistent and has led some scholars to suggest that because Jerusalem was saved from destruction by a heavy ransom and left standing (according to the Bible), it was not included in the official list of conquered towns" (*David and Solomon*, 79). It is difficult to understand why this eminently reasonable hypothesis falls under the category of a "stubborn striving." In any event, Finkelstein and Silberman argue that the reason why Jerusalem and the Judean region in general are not included

> Unlike any of the earlier Egyptian New Kingdom military campaigns in Canaan, Sheshonq's list mentions sites north of Jerusalem, like Beth Horona and Gibeon. The only plausible explanation for this must be the existence of a political power in the central hill country that was significant enough in the eyes of the Egyptians to justify such an exceptional route for the campaign. The only sensible candidate for such a power is the Solomonic kingdom.... The fact that Jerusalem is not mentioned in the inscription does not mean much – if the city surrendered, perhaps there would have been no reason to mention it; or alternatively, its mention could have appeared on one of the broken parts of the inscription.[135]

The inscription about Shishak's campaign also contributes to the discussion surrounding the question of construction during the period of the unified kingdom.[136] It features about seventy unknown locations in the Negev region. This aligns well with the discovery of dozens of settlements in the Negev, each surrounded by a double wall, and the great majority of them belonging to just one period, no later than the tenth century BCE. These sites, which apparently existed until Shishak's campaign, are similar – in terms of both their architecture and the ceramics used in them – to other sites from the same period in the north of the country. The many sites of uniform pattern would seem to prove the existence of a strong kingdom that existed in the tenth century that invested concerted effort in building a network of fortifications in the kingdom's border regions.

These sites therefore can serve as an archaeological anchor, dating the type of ceramic found in them to the tenth century BCE. The ceramics in some of these locations parallel the layers of excavation at Hazor

---

in the inscription is because Jerusalem was at that time a small, sparse mountain village that would not have interested Shishak. We shall further address this point later on.

135. A. Mazar, *The Quest for the Historical Israel,* 124. Mazar argues that Shishak was trying to strike a blow against the emerging Israelite state, to protect Egyptian interests.

136. This paragraph is based on Meitlis, 203–5; and see the sources cited in the notes there.

and at Megiddo, which were, in fact, attributed to the time of Solomon, and thereby confirm the connection between the six-chambered gates in these cities and the kingdom of Solomon.

The archaeological findings leave the impression that Megiddo was indeed built up extensively by Solomon, and later destroyed by Shishak, as Ben-Tor suggests. At Megiddo, a fragment of Shishak's victory stele was discovered, which itself indicates the importance of the city during the tenth century, as it is difficult to imagine that Shishak would have constructed a victory stele in a village devoid of any importance.[137]

As to the absence of findings attesting to royal construction in Jerusalem and Judah – this issue has been radically reconsidered in recent years. From 2007 to 2012, excavations were undertaken at Khirbet Qeiyafa in the Ela Valley, by a team under the direction of Yosef Garfinkel, Saar Ganor, and Michael Hasel.[138] They discovered, upon a strategic hill 325 m high, the ruins of a fortified city occupying an area of twenty-three dunams (6 acres), surrounded by an impressive casemate wall.[139] Burned pits of olives discovered on-site and sent for carbon-14 testing led to the dating of the city to the early tenth century BCE – the period

137. See A. Bornstein, "HaIm Nifredu Darkei HaArkheologia U'Mekorot Tanakh? Al HaVikuaḥ He'Ḥadash' al Mamlekhet David U'Shlomo," *Talelei Orot* 8 (5758–5759/1998–99): 262.

138. On the findings, see Y. Garfinkel and S. Ganor, *Khirbet Qeiyafa* (Jerusalem, 2009); and more recently, the papers published in *Khirbet Qeiyafa in the Shephelah: Papers Presented at a Colloquium of the Swiss Society for Ancient Near Eastern Studies Held at the University of Bern, September 6, 2014*, S. Schroer and S. Münger (eds.) (Fribourg and Göttingen, 2017). A short summary article by Y. Garfinkel appeared in 2012: "The Iron Age City of Khirbet Qeiyafa after Four Seasons of Excavations," in *The Ancient Near East in the 12th–10th Centuries BCE* (2012), 149–74, and some of the inscriptions have been discussed by Christopher Rollston, "The Khirbet Qeiyafa Ostracon: Methodological Musings and Caveats," *Tel Aviv* 38, 1 (2011): 67–82, and Gershon Galil, "The Hebrew Inscription from Khirbet Qeiyafa/Netaim," *Ugarit-Forschungen* 41 (2009): 193–242.

139. The wall displays an interesting phenomenon – the presence of two gates. This led Garfinkel and his associates to conclude that the city that they uncovered was the biblical Shaarayim (literally, "two gates"). As proof of this, they cite the appearance of this city in the description of the battle between David and Goliath, which took place precisely in this region (I Sam. 17:52). Some have questioned this identification: see Galil, noted above.

of David. In addition, further discoveries have shown that the city was unquestionably an Israelite – not Philistine – habitation:

1. No pig bones were found among the thousands of animal bones found in the city. This follows the pattern of the Israelite settlement villages, and stands in contrast to Canaanite or Philistine towns.
2. Three rooms for religious ritual were discovered in the city, containing gravestones, a basalt altar, and libation vessels; no figurines depicting humans or animals were found. This contrasts with Canaanite and Philistine ritual sites, where both human and animal figurines are usually found in abundance.
3. The city is surrounded by a casemate wall – a double wall with the space in between partitioned into long, narrow rooms. The houses adjacent to the wall include these rooms within themselves. This sort of planning is familiar to us from other sites – all within the boundaries of the kingdom of Judah, while in the Canaanite and Philistine cultures, a double wall was uncommon.
4. The ceramic style is unique and characteristic of the Iron Age in Judea; it is different from the ceramics usually found at Philistine sites.
5. Finally, one of the fascinating discoveries at the site was an ostracon (an inscribed pottery shard) with five lines of proto-Canaanite script. These lines include words that were almost certainly written in Hebrew (using verbs that are unique to Hebrew),[140] representing the earliest evidence to date of an inscription with content and meaning in this language.[141]

---

140. The inscription is not clearly legible and is difficult to understand. One suggestion as to the original text is proposed by G. Galil; a more cautious proposal is offered by Chris A. Rollston. Both articles are cited above, note 138.

141. The Izbet Sartah ostracon, discovered in the region of Rosh HaAyin, is dated even earlier, to the period of the Judges, but its proto-Canaanite inscription consists only of the letters of the alphabet, apparently as a reading exercise. For more on the ostracon see Aaron Demsky, "A Proto-Canaanite Abecedary Dating from the Period of the Judges and Its Implications for the History of the Alphabet," *Tel Aviv* 4 (1977): 14–27. This inscription, too, is of great importance, since it proves the existence of an ancient scribal tradition, countering the claims of Na'aman and others – whose argument that biblical historiographic

The existence of a Judean city of this size attests to the fact that the wave of urbanization characterizing the transition to the Iron Age II did in fact occur at the beginning of the united monarchy. Moreover, it indicates that at the time of David's monarchy, fortified cities already existed in Judea. There is room to assume that the location of this city – at a walking distance from each of the two central cities of David's kingdom, Jerusalem and Hebron – arose from its position on the main road from the coastal plain to those cities, and from its position on the western border of the Israelite kingdom, facing the Philistines.

These new findings have had a significant impact, and the supporters of the Low Chronology have been hard-pressed to explain them.[142] Efraim Stern, one of the most senior archaeologists in Israel, summarizes as follows:

---

literature was written hundreds of years after the events described is based, *inter alia,* on the assumption that literacy in the earlier period was extremely rare. On this argument, see A. Demsky, *Yedi'at Sefer BeYisrael BaEt HaAtika* (Jerusalem, 2012), 28–33.

142. N. Na'aman, "Khirbet Qeiyafa in Context," *Ugarit-Forschungen* 42 (2010): 497–526, argues that the inhabitants of Khirbet Qeiyafa were Canaanites and not Israelites. He proposes that they refrained from eating pork as a way of distinguishing themselves from the Philistines, and that the ostracon discovered on-site was inscribed in an as-yet unidentified dialect of proto-Canaanite. For a discussion of the attempts by adherents of the school of Low Chronology to deal with the findings at Khirbet Qeiyafa, see A. Shtull-Trauring, "The Keys to the Kingdom," *Haaretz,* April 21, 2012, found online at http://www.haaretz.com/weekend/magazine/the-keys-to-the-kingdom-1.360222.

The article also provides an interesting description of the internal power struggles within archaeological circles, and principally between the Hebrew University of Jerusalem (with which Garfinkel is associated) and Tel Aviv University (the academic home of Na'aman and Finkelstein). This description illustrates the extent to which issues with no bearing whatsoever on science and objective truth become involved in the discussion. Garfinkel, Ganor, and Hasel (*Ikevot David HaMelekh BeEmek HaEla,* 49–50), describe the criticism with the following words:

> All of the writers are from Tel Aviv University, which is today a hothouse for flourishing minimalism. Why have no critical articles been penned to date by scholars based in London, Paris, or New York?… The original minimalist approach was a consolidated worldview, which argued that the ancient history of the Jewish People must be written only on the basis of extra-biblical data. All the approaches that came later… are simply patchwork additions that try desperately to solve difficulties which the earlier paradigm is incapable of addressing.

> Over the course of my lengthy involvement in the archaeology of the Land of Israel, I have seen a great many "fashions" that arrived from different places; most survived for short periods of time and then disappeared without a trace. It seems to me that the approach of the "minimalist chronology," with its harsh historical conclusions, represents one such "fashion." I believe that the sooner it disappears, the better, and the results of the excavations at Khirbet Qeiyafa are indeed aiding in this.[143]

The findings at Khirbet Qeiyafa join other discoveries of recent years that indicate the power and significance of the unified kingdom specifically through its manifestations on its outer borders. For example, excavations undertaken at Tel Beit Shemesh revealed that the city underwent significant changes during the Iron Age II, including construction, fortification, a water reservoir, and a workshop for iron processing:

> Thus, a "view from the border" serves to establish that over the course of the ninth and tenth centuries BCE, a central political entity was consolidated in Jerusalem. Even if the archaeological evidence of its existence at its seat of power is not yet sufficiently clear, the traces of its activity in the periphery of the area of its reign can tell us much about it.[144]

> These patchwork solutions are not the fruit of real research, in which data are gathered and examined with a view to reaching well-founded conclusions, but rather weak alternatives that run counter to logic, and whose strength lies in the absence of data and the negation of the value of the biblical tradition as a source of information about the period in question.

It should be noted that it is specifically the minimalists, who do not necessarily declare the Tanakh to be unreliable, but rather build their archaeological picture on the basis of actual findings (or lack thereof), who should have the easiest time changing their position once new findings appear. Surprisingly, however, they treat them with a suspicion that goes beyond the accepted archaeological norm – all of which calls their motives into question.

143. Editorial in *Kadmoniot* 141, 1.

144. S. Bunimowitz and Z. Lederman, "Yerushalayim U'Beit Shemesh: Bein Birah U'Gevulah," in A. Barukh and A. Faust (eds.), *Ḥiddushim BeḤekker Yerushalayim – HaKovetz HaAsiri* (Ramat Gan, 2005), 45.

The situation is changing even in Jerusalem. In 2005, Eilat Mazar, who heads the excavations in the City of David on behalf of the Hebrew University's Institute for Archaeology, discovered a large and impressive stone structure at the top of the mound of the City of David, apparently the result of a unique construction project of giant proportions.[145] While vessels discovered beneath this structure are from the Iron Age I period, the later additions to the structure have been dated, on the basis of the ceramics, to the Iron Age II period. The ceramic finding in conjunction with carbon dating led to the conclusion that the construction of a large stone building would have taken place around the year 1000 BCE. Mazar argues, on the basis of similar data, that the famous stepped stone structure located in Area G served as part of the supporting wall for this great stone structure. She argues that this is none other than the palace of King David, whose construction by Phoenician merchants is recorded in the Tanakh: וַיִּשְׁלַח חִירָם מֶלֶךְ צֹר מַלְאָכִים אֶל דָּוִד וַעֲצֵי אֲרָזִים וְחָרָשֵׁי עֵץ וְחָרָשֵׁי אֶבֶן קִיר וַיִּבְנוּ בַיִת לְדָוִד, "Hiram, king of Tyre, sent messengers to David, and cedar trees, and carpenters, and masons, and they built David a house" (II Sam. 5:11).[146]

Mazar's findings are contested, and others have argued that at least one of the relevant walls was built only in the eighth century BCE.[147] Finkelstein and Silberman maintain that the pottery within the stepped stone structure "includes types from the Early Iron Age to the ninth or even early eighth centuries BCE. It seems therefore that this monument was constructed at least a century later than the days of David and Solomon."[148]

145. See E. Mazar, *The Palace of King David: Excavations at the Summit of the City of David: Preliminary Report of Seasons 2005–2007* (Jerusalem, 2009).

146. Prior to the discovery of the large stone structure, it had been argued that the structure with the steps was a supporting wall of the citadel which David captured (rather than of his palace). To this view, too, the finding from the City of David accords with the biblical account of the conquest of Jerusalem.

147. Ronny Reich and Eli Shukron, "BeKhol Zot Ḥoma Mitekufat HaBarzel Bet," *Ḥiddushim BeḤekker Yerushalayim* 13, eds. E. Barukh, Ayelet Levi-Reifer, and A. Faust (Ramat Gan, 2008): 26–34. In the same volume are Eilat Mazar's article on this structure (7–26) and a further critique by David Ussishkin, Ze'ev Herzog, Lilly Zinger-Avitz, and Israel Finkelstein (35–45).

148. Finkelstein and Silberman, *David and Solomon*, 270.

It is certainly possible that Mazar's discoveries are only the tip of the iceberg, and that the future will provide further evidence of the united monarchy.[149] At the same time, we must address the question of why more artifacts from the period of the united monarchy have not been discovered to date in Jerusalem. It is reasonable to assume that this phenomenon is the result of Jerusalem's having undergone continuous construction from the Middle Bronze Age through the present day and that this accounts for the absence of more artifacts from the Davidic era.[150] It is relatively easy to find artifacts from destroyed layers of cities, and this explains why findings testifying to the destruction of the Second Temple have been discovered. By contrast, no buildings whatsoever have been found from the Persian or early Hellenistic periods, even though no one questions the existence of the city during these times. Likewise, there are no findings from within the city itself attesting to its existence during the much earlier period – the fourteenth century BCE. Note too that most of the artifacts that have been discovered in the City of David, from the Middle Bronze Age and Late Iron Age, were found on the eastern slope of the city – an area that had already been abandoned by the Second Temple Period.

The same phenomenon may apply to other Judean cities that had continuous Jewish settlement, in many cases lasting even through the Second Temple Period – in contrast to Dan and Hazor, which were almost completely abandoned, and Megiddo, where construction during the Assyrian period was scarce.

There are two final points that must be made concerning this issue.

The first is a question of knowledge. Throughout the book of Samuel, we find many descriptions of wars, including their geographical and strategic aspects, which suggest an author intimately familiar with the area. The notion that an author, during a later period, could

149. For more findings supporting Jerusalem's status as a significant city during the period of the united monarchy, see G. Kahil, "Tekufat HaMamlakha HaMeuḥedet: HaEdut HaArkheologit," in A. Faust and A. Barukh (eds.), *Ḥiddushim BeḤekker Yerushalayim – HaKovetz HaShevi'i* (Ramat Gan, 2002), 21–27, and A. de Groote, "HaIr HaNe'elma shel HaMea HaAsirit Lifnei HaSefira," in ibid., 29–34.

150. See Meitlis, 206–14; M. Garsiel, "Shelavei Ḥibburo shel Sefer Shmuel," *Beit Mikra* 54, 2, esp. 46–48.

have so accurately depicted events, field conditions, and roads that were sometimes far removed from the areas where these books are assumed to have been written, seems to stretch credulity.

The second point is about bias. The fundamental argument of adherents of the Low Chronology is that the narratives about David were created at a later time, with a view to glorifying the founder of the dynasty. The problem is that David is not glorified in these texts. There is no character in all of Tanakh who is criticized as closely and as sharply as David is. Consider the stories of Uriah and Bathsheba, Amnon and Tamar, Absalom and Adoniyahu – and the description of Solomon taking foreign wives and building altars for idolatry. Why would anyone seeking to glorify the royal house of David and Solomon want to describe the difficult and complex episodes involving its first two kings? What would a later author stand to gain by this? To date, no satisfactory explanation has been offered for this phenomenon.

SUMMARY

We have briefly reviewed some of the central points pertaining to different time periods where there is controversy about the integration of archaeological findings with the biblical account. We have seen that interpretation of the facts is highly dependent upon one's prior orientation. The biblical texts themselves often appear to point to a profound familiarity on the part of their authors with the historical and social background of the periods that they describe. Many archaeological artifacts accord with the biblical account as well, making it difficult to argue that the books of Tanakh were written much later than the events they record.

That said, there is an undeniable dearth of artifacts able to support the biblical account, and this phenomenon may be interpreted in different ways. Some scholars see the lack of artifacts as proof that the biblical account is unreliable, taking as their point of departure the assumption that the books are later creations, written to promote a particular point of view. Those who proceed from a different point of departure may view the lack of artifacts as a situation that will be remedied with time – or at least as a phenomenon that has a logical explanation.

Our review has also revealed the transience of some central theories in the world of archaeology. The Merneptah Stele is a proof of utmost significance as to the existence at that time of an entity known as "Israel," and had it not been discovered, quite coincidentally, "the research on this subject would be in a completely different situation from what it is today."[151]

Similarly, had the Dan Stele inscription not been discovered, some twenty years ago, many scholars today would probably still deny the existence of David and Solomon, arguing that "no findings that confirm their existence have yet been discovered." The amount of material that has been excavated and studied is extremely small, relative to what remains. We must also take into consideration the fact that in the most important regions, such as the City of David and the Temple Mount, excavations are highly problematic if not altogether impossible due to political considerations.

Archaeology has nonetheless contributed, and will continue to contribute greatly, to an understanding of and appreciation for Tanakh. Walking through the sites where the stories of the Tanakh took place, or standing before archeological findings from that period, is a powerful and moving experience. Archaeological research influences and deepens our understanding of different parts of Tanakh. Without the discoveries on the ground, it is doubtful whether we would be able to make the proper differentiation, for instance, between the descriptions of settlement in Joshua and those in Judges. In addition, archaeological findings have shed light on the events described in the text, such as the campaign of Shishak and the war against Mesha, king of Moab. It seems reasonable to assume that further discoveries with ramifications for this sphere of research still await us, and will continue to interest all those who hold the Tanakh dear.

---

151. Y. Hoffman, "Historia, Mitos U'Politika," in Y. L. Levine and A. Mazar, *HaPulmus Al HaEmet HaHistorit BaMikra*, 31–32.

Chapter 7

Tanakh and Literature of the Ancient Near East

BACKGROUND

In the nineteenth century, scholars turned to a scientific study of the ancient Near East – an investigation of the cultural, social, and religious world within which the personalities of the Tanakh were active. It gradually became apparent that the nations of this region, who lived hundreds of years prior to the giving of the Torah at Sinai, followed well-organized and clearly defined systems of law, and also created literary works expressing their religious worldviews. Certain similarities were discovered between the laws of the Torah and other legal systems from among the nations of the ancient Near East.[1] In addition, works were discovered with numerous parallels to the stories of Creation in the first part of Genesis (chapters 1–11), especially

1. Among the legal systems featuring parallels with Torah laws we can list (1) the Hammurabi Code; (2) the Laws of Eshnunna (a small kingdom in the northeastern part of what is today Iraq), written in Akkadian and dating to the eighteenth century BCE (i.e., predating the Code of Hammurabi; Hammurabi later conquered Eshnunna); (3) the Middle Assyrian Laws, dating to the eleventh century BCE; and (4) the Hittite laws, from the second half of the second millennium BCE. The parallels with the Torah, along with prefaces and comments, are treated in M. Maloul, *Kovtzei HaDinim VeOsafim Mishpati'im Aḥerim Min HaMizraḥ HaKadum* (Haifa, 2010).

the Enûma Eliš – the Babylonian story of creation – and the Epic of Gilgamesh, which shows striking similarities to the story of the Flood and Noah's Ark.[2]

These discoveries produced two opposite reactions. Initially, many people viewed these data as confirmation of the validity of the biblical account, and as a blow to Wellhausen's theory,[3] insofar as they demonstrated that the narratives of the Tanakh were written against this real background and were not a later development.[4] Simon Bernfeld, for example, a well-known German Jewish publicist, asserted in 1907 that the discoveries from Assyria and Babylon had brought about

> the collapse of the biblical criticism that had been adhered to by Jewish and gentile critics alike, all of whom had expressed the same idea – that the narratives of the Torah were written at a much later date, and had been composed for a specific purpose. We now know that the stories of the Torah are altogether genuine historical documents from a very ancient period.[5]

Similar conclusions were expressed by many at the end of the nineteenth century.

At the same time, however, an opposing trend developed – arguing that the strong similarities proved that the biblical narratives were in large part borrowed from Babylonian sources. The most prominent spokesman for this approach was Friedrich Delitzsch, a German Assyriologist, who also maintained that the Babylonian

---

2. For an anthology of Mesopotamian works on different topics, some similar to biblical literature, see S. Shifra and Y. Klein, *BaYamim HaReḥokim HaHem – Antologia MiShirat HaMizraḥ HaKadum* (Tel Aviv, 5757 [1997]), and B. Foster, *Before the Muses: An Anthology of Akkadian Literature* (Bethesda, 2006), as well as the many texts translated in W. W. Hallo, ed. *Context of Scripture*, vol. 1 (Canonical Literature) (Leiden, 1997).
3. We addressed the theory of biblical source criticism in chapter 3.
4. A description of these reactions among Jewish and Christian scholars is to be found in Y. Shavit and M. Eran, *Milḥemet HaLuḥot – HaHagana Al HaMikra BeMea Ha-19 U'Pulmus Bavel VeHaTanakh* (Tel Aviv, 2004), 81–86.
5. Cited by Shavit and Eran, *Milḥemet HaLuḥot*, 85.

culture was more spiritually and morally developed than that of the Torah.[6] In a series of lectures that Delitzsch delivered between 1902 and 1904, he ignited the "Babel and Bible" debate, in the wake of his book *Babel und Bibel*. He argued that even elements that had seemed unique to the Torah, such as the Sabbath, had their source in Babylonian culture. This aroused extensive public debate, which included no small measure of blatant anti-Semitism expressed by the scholar himself.

Although the original "Babel and Bible" debate receded long ago, the essence of the question of origins continues to occupy contemporary scholars. In this chapter we will address three central perspectives that pertain to the relationship between the Tanakh and the literature of the ancient Near East: first, the relationship between the commandments of the Torah and the laws of the ancient Near Eastern peoples; second, a comparison of the stories in Genesis and the parallel narratives; and third, the question of whether the Sabbath indeed appeared in Mesopotamian culture before it was presented in the Torah.

THE TORAH AND LEGAL SYSTEMS OF THE ANCIENT NEAR EAST

Among the ancient codes of law, the best known is the Code of Hammurabi, rediscovered in 1901. This legal system, dating to the eighteenth century BCE (the period of the forefathers, according to the prevailing view), includes 282 laws pertaining to all areas of life and setting forth social, legal, and punitive procedures. The laws relate to matters such as theft, slaves, pledges, adultery, divorce, damages caused by an ox, and inheritance. The following table shows some of the many parallels between the Code of Hammurabi and the commandments of the Torah.

6. Shavit and Eran's book is largely devoted to a detailed study of the polemic, its main arguments, and the various responses of Jewish scholars to Delitzsch's claims. The description below is based on their work.

Torah	Code of Hammurabi[7]
And if men strive together, and one smite another with a stone or with his fist, and he does not die, but is confined to his bed; if he rises and walks about upon his staff, then he that struck him shall be acquitted; he shall pay only for [the loss of] time, and shall cause him to be thoroughly healed. (Ex. 21:18–19) וְכִי יְרִיבֻן אֲנָשִׁים וְהִכָּה אִישׁ אֶת רֵעֵהוּ בְּאֶבֶן אוֹ בְאֶגְרֹף וְלֹא יָמוּת וְנָפַל לְמִשְׁכָּב. אִם יָקוּם וְהִתְהַלֵּךְ בַּחוּץ עַל מִשְׁעַנְתּוֹ וְנִקָּה הַמַּכֶּה רַק שִׁבְתּוֹ יִתֵּן וְרַפֹּא יְרַפֵּא.	If a gentleman should strike another gentleman during a brawl and inflict upon him a wound, that gentleman shall swear, "I did not strike intentionally," and he shall satisfy the physician [i.e., pay his fees]. (law 206)
If men strive, and hurt a pregnant woman, such that she miscarries, but there is no further loss of life, then he shall surely be punished in accordance with what the woman's husband imposes upon him, and he shall pay as the judges determine. (Ex. 21:22) וְכִי יִנָּצוּ אֲנָשִׁים וְנָגְפוּ אִשָּׁה הָרָה וְיָצְאוּ יְלָדֶיהָ וְלֹא יִהְיֶה אָסוֹן עָנוֹשׁ יֵעָנֵשׁ כַּאֲשֶׁר יָשִׁית עָלָיו בַּעַל הָאִשָּׁה וְנָתַן בִּפְלִלִים.	If a gentleman strikes a woman of the gentry-class and thereby causes her to miscarry her fetus, he shall weigh and deliver ten shekels of silver for her fetus. (209)
But if the ox had previously gored with its horn, and its owner had been warned but he had not kept it in, and it [now] killed a man or a woman, then the ox shall be stoned, and its owner shall also be put to death. If a sum of money is imposed on him, then he shall give it as a ransom for his life, whatever is imposed upon him. Whether it gored a son	If a man's ox is a known gorer and the authorities of his city quarter notify him that it is a known gorer, but he does not blunt [meaning uncertain] its horns or control his ox, and that ox gores to death

7. Translations based on Martha T. Roth, ed., *Law Collections from Mesopotamia and Asia Minor*, but use the word "gentleman" instead of the Akkadian *awīlum*.

Torah	Code of Hammurabi
or a daughter, according to this judgment shall it be done to him.... If the ox gores a manservant or a maidservant, he shall give to their master thirty shekels of silver, and the ox shall be stoned. (Ex. 21:29–32) וְאִם שׁוֹר נַגָּח הוּא מִתְּמֹל שִׁלְשֹׁם וְהוּעַד בִּבְעָלָיו וְלֹא יִשְׁמְרֶנּוּ וְהֵמִית אִישׁ אוֹ אִשָּׁה הַשּׁוֹר יִסָּקֵל וְגַם בְּעָלָיו יוּמָת. אִם כֹּפֶר יוּשַׁת עָלָיו וְנָתַן פִּדְיֹן נַפְשׁוֹ כְּכֹל אֲשֶׁר יוּשַׁת עָלָיו. אוֹ בֵן יִגָּח אוֹ בַת יִגָּח כַּמִּשְׁפָּט הַזֶּה יֵעָשֶׂה לּוֹ. אִם עֶבֶד יִגַּח הַשּׁוֹר אוֹ אָמָה כֶּסֶף שְׁלֹשִׁים שְׁקָלִים יִתֵּן לַאדֹנָיו וְהַשּׁוֹר יִסָּקֵל.	a member of the gentry, he [the owner] shall pay one half of a mina [i.e., thirty shekels] of silver. (251) If it is a man's slave [who is fatally gored], he shall pay one-third of a mina [i.e., twenty shekels] of silver. (252)
If a man maims his neighbor, as he has done, so shall it be done to him: a breach for a breach, an eye for an eye, a tooth for a tooth; as he has maimed a man, so shall be done to him. (Lev. 24:19–20) וְאִישׁ כִּי יִתֵּן מוּם בַּעֲמִיתוֹ כַּאֲשֶׁר עָשָׂה כֵּן יֵעָשֶׂה לּוֹ. שֶׁבֶר תַּחַת שֶׁבֶר עַיִן תַּחַת עַיִן שֵׁן תַּחַת שֵׁן כַּאֲשֶׁר יִתֵּן מוּם בָּאָדָם כֵּן יִנָּתֶן בּוֹ.	If a gentleman should blind the eye of another gentleman, they shall blind his eye. If he should break the bone of another gentleman, they shall break his bone. (196–97) If a gentleman should knock out the tooth of another gentleman, they shall knock out his tooth. (200)
If a false witness rises against any man to testify wrongly against him... then the judges shall diligently inquire, and behold, if the witness is a false witness, having lied about his fellow, then you shall do to him as he had thought to have done to his fellow, and so shall you put away the evil from among you. (Deut. 19:16–19)	If a gentleman comes forward to give false testimony in a case, but cannot bring evidence for his accusation, if that case involves a capital offense, that man shall be killed.

Torah	Code of Hammurabi
כִּי יָקוּם עֵד חָמָס בְּאִישׁ לַעֲנוֹת בּוֹ סָרָה... וְדָרְשׁוּ הַשֹּׁפְטִים הֵיטֵב וְהִנֵּה עֵד שֶׁקֶר הָעֵד שֶׁקֶר עָנָה בְאָחִיו. וַעֲשִׂיתֶם לוֹ כַּאֲשֶׁר זָמַם לַעֲשׂוֹת לְאָחִיו וּבִעַרְתָּ הָרָע מִקִּרְבֶּךָ.	If he comes forward to give [false] testimony for [a case whose penalty is] grain or silver, he shall be assessed the penalty for that case. (3–4)

The Laws of Eshnunna likewise feature parallels to the laws of the Torah. For example, concerning an ox that kills another ox belonging to someone else: "If an ox gores another ox and thus causes its death, the two ox-owners shall divide the value of the living ox and the carcass of the dead ox" (section 53). This is strongly reminiscent of the Torah law in this regard: וְכִי יִגֹּף שׁוֹר אִישׁ אֶת שׁוֹר רֵעֵהוּ וָמֵת וּמָכְרוּ אֶת הַשּׁוֹר הַחַי וְחָצוּ אֶת כַּסְפּוֹ וְגַם אֶת הַמֵּת יֶחֱצוּן, "If one man's ox hurt his neighbor's ox, and it dies, then they shall sell the live ox and divide the price of it, and they shall also divide [the value of] the dead [ox]" (Ex. 21:35).

It should be noted that copies of the Laws of Hammurabi have been found throughout the ancient Near East, including in the Land of Israel. The discoveries of these and other sets of laws gave rise to the claim that the laws of the Torah were in fact based on these external legal systems – seemingly supporting the position that the Torah laws are of human origin, by authors who had been influenced by external Babylonian sources.

Indeed, what are we to make of the connection between these codes of law and the commandments of the Torah?

First, it is important to note that the existence of systems of law that preceded the Torah is a fact that the Torah itself mentions explicitly. As Moses tells the Jewish people, in his speech at the beginning of Deuteronomy: וּמִי גּוֹי גָּדוֹל אֲשֶׁר לוֹ חֻקִּים וּמִשְׁפָּטִים צַדִּיקִם כְּכֹל הַתּוֹרָה הַזֹּאת אֲשֶׁר אָנֹכִי נֹתֵן לִפְנֵיכֶם הַיּוֹם, "And what nation is there so great, that has statutes and judgments so righteous as all this Torah, which I set before you today?" (Deut. 4:8). The Israelite leader explicitly compares the laws of the Torah with those of the other nations, and finds the Torah laws more "righteous" than the others. In fact, this verse would be meaningless were the Torah the only law code of its day.[8]

Truly, laws have accompanied mankind since its earliest stages. A reading of Genesis reveals an entire infrastructure of laws pertaining to all areas of life. The story of Judah and Tamar tells us that the accepted procedure was that a woman whose husband had died, leaving no children, could not marry someone else without conducting some form of *yibum* (levirate marriage) – a duty falling first and foremost to the brothers of the deceased, and even to their father. What is the source of this custom? Nahmanides (on Genesis 38:8) asserts:

> The ancient Sages, prior to the Torah, knew that there is great benefit in levirate marriage by the brother, and it is proper that he be the first to uphold it, and [only] after him [i.e., if he is unable to marry the widow] then the next closest family member, for any close blood relative from his family who inherits his portion will bring benefit. So it was customary to marry the widow of the deceased brother to the brother, or the father, or the next closest relative.[9]

Nahmanides's comment accords with what the laws of the ancient Near East have thus far revealed – an explicitly established possibility of *yibum*, including involving the father of the deceased.[10] Similarly, Abraham's purchase of the field containing the Cave of the Patriarchs

---

8. This understanding arises from the plain meaning of the text as well as from the commentaries of Sforno and Alshikh, among others. Nahmanides, however, in his treatise *Torat HaShem Temima* (*Kitvei HaRamban* I [Jerusalem, 1963], 143–44), understands from the verse that the other nations had no statutes and judgments at all. Yet as we will see, Nahmanides in his commentary to the Torah indicates a number of times that there were systems of law extant prior to the giving of the Torah.
9. The same idea appears in a more concise form in the *Pesikta Zutreta* (*Lekaḥ Tov*) on Genesis 38:8: "This teaches that they practiced '*yibum*' prior to the giving of the Torah, as a commandment that is logically self-evident."
10. For ancient laws in this regard see Y. M. Grintz, *Yiḥudo VeKadmuto Shel Sefer Bereshit* (Jerusalem, 1983), 57.

is instructive as to the accepted procedures for acquiring land;[11] the struggle between Jacob and Esau indicates the existence of the concept of a "birthright" as a legal status entailing more than just the chronological order of birth;[12] and so on. More generally, Nahmanides writes that the legal system in its entirety is one of the seven Noahide Laws:

> In my view, the *dinim* (laws) requirement that is incumbent upon the gentiles, as one of their seven commandments, entails more than just the appointment of judges in each and every place. [God] commands them concerning the laws of theft, deception, oppression, and paying wages, and the laws pertaining to guardians, coercion, and temptation, and the categories of damages, and injury to others, and the laws of lending and borrowing, and the laws of buying and selling, and the like, in a similar manner to the laws which Israel is commanded to observe. (Nahmanides on Gen. 34:13)

Moreover, the formulation of some of the commandments of the Torah indicates that these laws are based on previous knowledge assumed to be familiar to those receiving the Torah. The Torah is not formulated as a book that builds an entire system of laws and judgments from the very foundations up; rather, it adds layers onto an existing basis that does not require further elaboration – for those for whom the basis was familiar. Thus, for example, the Torah does not describe how the institution of marriage between man and woman comes into being. All that Moses says about marriage appears – paradoxically enough – in the context of discussing the procedure for divorce. From his lengthy "speech of the commandments" in Deuteronomy:

> כִּי יִקַּח אִישׁ אִשָּׁה וּבְעָלָהּ וְהָיָה אִם לֹא תִמְצָא חֵן בְּעֵינָיו כִּי מָצָא בָהּ עֶרְוַת דָּבָר וְכָתַב לָהּ סֵפֶר כְּרִיתֻת וְנָתַן בְּיָדָהּ וְשִׁלְּחָהּ מִבֵּיתוֹ. וְיָצְאָה מִבֵּיתוֹ וְהָלְכָה וְהָיְתָה לְאִישׁ אַחֵר. וּשְׂנֵאָהּ הָאִישׁ הָאַחֲרוֹן וְכָתַב לָהּ סֵפֶר כְּרִיתֻת וְנָתַן בְּיָדָהּ וְשִׁלְּחָהּ מִבֵּיתוֹ אוֹ כִי יָמוּת הָאִישׁ הָאַחֲרוֹן אֲשֶׁר לְקָחָהּ

11. Ibid., 60.
12. Ibid., 54.

לוֹ לְאִשָּׁה. לֹא יוּכַל בַּעְלָהּ הָרִאשׁוֹן אֲשֶׁר שִׁלְּחָהּ לָשׁוּב לְקַחְתָּהּ לִהְיוֹת
לוֹ לְאִשָּׁה אַחֲרֵי אֲשֶׁר הֻטַּמָּאָה כִּי תוֹעֵבָה הִוא לִפְנֵי ה׳ וְלֹא תַחֲטִיא אֶת
הָאָרֶץ אֲשֶׁר ה׳ אֱלֹהֶיךָ נֹתֵן לְךָ נַחֲלָה.

> If a man takes a wife and has relations with her, and it comes to pass that she does not find favor in his eyes, for he has found some unseemliness in her, then he shall write her a bill of divorce, and place it in her hand, and send her out of his house. And when she has left his house, she may go and become [the wife] of another. And if the latter man hates her and writes her a bill of divorce, and places it in her hand, and sends her out of his house – or if the latter husband, who took her to be his wife, dies – then her former husband, who sent her away, cannot take her again to be his wife, after she has been defiled, for that is an abomination before God, and you shall not cause the land which the Lord your God gives you for an inheritance, to be sinful. (Deut. 24:1–4)

The Torah clearly assumes its audience is familiar with the procedure for effecting marriage – the institution had in fact existed for hundreds of years prior to the giving of the Torah. Moreover, a close look at these verses indicates that the Torah is not introducing the idea of divorce either.[13] Rather, the Torah's innovation in these verses is the prohibition against remarrying a wife whom one had previously divorced after she was then married to someone else.[14]

Similarly, the Torah does not state directly that a firstborn son receives a double portion of his father's inheritance. This fact is deduced incidentally, from a passage concerning the firstborn, which comes to teach a different law:

---

13. For instance, we understand that Moses divorced his wife, Tzippora, from the verse: וַיִּקַּח יִתְרוֹ חֹתֵן מֹשֶׁה אֶת צִפֹּרָה אֵשֶׁת מֹשֶׁה אַחַר שִׁלּוּחֶיהָ, "And Jethro, Moses's father-in-law, took Tzippora, Moses's wife, after he had sent her away" (Ex. 18:2); this interpretation is proposed by Ibn Ezra (in his short commentary) there.
14. The Laws of Hammurabi likewise devote no attention to marriage and divorce per se; they address only certain details of the law (laws 128–43).

> כִּי תִהְיֶיןָ לְאִישׁ שְׁתֵּי נָשִׁים הָאַחַת אֲהוּבָה וְהָאַחַת שְׂנוּאָה וְיָלְדוּ לוֹ בָנִים הָאֲהוּבָה וְהַשְּׂנוּאָה וְהָיָה הַבֵּן הַבְּכוֹר לַשְּׂנִיאָה. וְהָיָה בְּיוֹם הַנְחִילוֹ אֶת בָּנָיו אֵת אֲשֶׁר יִהְיֶה לוֹ לֹא יוּכַל לְבַכֵּר אֶת בֶּן הָאֲהוּבָה עַל פְּנֵי בֶן הַשְּׂנוּאָה הַבְּכֹר. כִּי אֶת הַבְּכֹר בֶּן הַשְּׂנוּאָה יַכִּיר לָתֶת לוֹ פִּי שְׁנַיִם בְּכֹל אֲשֶׁר יִמָּצֵא לוֹ כִּי הוּא רֵאשִׁית אֹנוֹ לוֹ מִשְׁפַּט הַבְּכֹרָה.
>
> If a man has two wives, one beloved and the other hated, and they have borne him children – [both] the beloved and the hated – and the firstborn son is [born] of the hated [wife], then it shall be, when he bequeaths to his sons that which he has, he cannot give preference to the son of the beloved [wife] over the son of the hated [wife], who is the firstborn. Rather, he shall acknowledge the son of the hated [wife], giving him a double portion of all that he has, for he is the beginning of his strength; the birthright is his. (Deut. 21:15–17)

The entire discussion about the inheritance of the firstborn occurs within the framework of the discussion about a specific reality, in which the firstborn son is born to an unfavored wife. The Torah's demand is that even in such a situation, the status of the "birthright" must be reserved for the son of the unfavored wife, since "the birthright is his." This expression shows that the practice of the firstborn's inheritance was fixed and well known; there was no need to spell it out. The only innovation in the Torah law here is that the standard practice applies even in the unusual situation described in this text.[15]

That systems of justice existed among other nations prior to the giving of the Torah is a fact incorporated into the Torah's own narrative, and therefore presents no theological difficulty. The question of whether parts of the Torah that parallel ancient legal systems are the product of revelation, or are to be considered human documents, influenced by their

---

15. A similar situation pertains with regard to the verse: וְאִם לִבְנוֹ יִיעָדֶנָּה כְּמִשְׁפַּט הַבָּנוֹת יַעֲשֶׂה לָּהּ, "And if he designated her for his son, then he shall deal with her after the manner of daughters" (Ex. 21:9). Here, too, the Torah assumes knowledge of a familiar practice, which is not stated. Another example concerns the seducer of an unmarried woman, who is required to "pay money according to the marriage price of virgins" – כֶּסֶף יִשְׁקֹל כְּמֹהַר הַבְּתוּלֹת (Ex. 22:16).

surroundings, has nothing to do with the existence of the earlier laws and their efforts to organize society. Indeed, if the other ancient laws represent a valid articulation of justice that those societies had arrived at of their own accord, the Torah has no reason to seek to change them (or ignore them). This conclusion is set forth by Rabbi Abraham Isaac Kook, in his 1906 work *Eder HaYakar*:

> And, similarly, when Assyriology entered the world, it raised doubts in people's hearts through the similarities that it found, according to its baseless conjectures, between our holy Torah and what is found in the cuneiform inscriptions, with respect to doctrines, morals, and practices. Do these doubts have even the slightest rational basis? Is it not well known that among the ancients there were those who recognized God, prophets, and spiritual giants, such as Methuselah, Hanokh, Shem and Eber, and the like? Is it possible that they had no effect on the members of their generations? Even though their achievements do not compare with those of our forefather Abraham, how could their influence have left no impression whatsoever upon their generations? Surely [their teachings] must have resembled those that are found in the Torah! As for the similarity regarding practices, surely already in the days of Maimonides, and before him in the words of the Sages it was well known that prophecy operates upon man's nature. For man's natural inclinations must be raised through divine guidance, for the commandments were only given for the purpose of refining man. Therefore, anything that through the teaching that preceded the giving of the Torah found a place in the nation and the world, as long as it had a moral foundation and it was possible to elevate it to an eternal moral height, was retained in God's Torah .... It is fitting that these and similar ideas should enter the hearts of all those who immediately understand things. Then there would be no room whatsoever for fraudulent heresy to spread in the world and grow strong through such events.[16]

16. Rabbi Abraham Isaac Kook, *Eder HaYakar*, 2nd ed. (Jerusalem, 1967), 42–43, transl. David Strauss.

Rabbi Kook regards it as self-evident that, among the ancients who lived prior to the giving of the Torah, individuals of exceptional moral character influenced the society in which they lived, and created a moral system of laws. If those laws correspond with the Torah's view of morality and justice, then there is no reason, argues Rabbi Kook, for the Torah to reject such laws, and it should therefore come as no surprise that the study of the ancient Near East and its legal systems has discovered some similarities with certain laws in the Torah.[17]

Inasmuch as the commandments of the Torah and the laws of the Hammurabi Code are similar to one another, Rabbi Kook's words seem to offer a sufficient explanation for the phenomenon. That said, the fundamental contrasts between the two systems far outweigh their parallels, implying a tremendous philosophical and spiritual distance between the Torah and the Hammurabi Code. These differences recall Moses's words from Deuteronomy, asserting the superiority of the Torah over other existing systems of law. It is worth examining some of the substantial differences between the commandments of the Torah and the Laws of Hammurabi, in particular, and the laws of the ancient Near East, in general.[18]

First and foremost, it should be noted that the laws of the ancient Near East are presented explicitly as a human creation. For instance, although Hammurabi introduces his Code with a description of how the gods entrusted him with the role of legislating laws and bringing justice to the world, the laws themselves are his own doing. The laws of the Torah, in contrast, are presented as God's word; their source is God's command exclusively. Transgressing these laws is therefore perceived not merely as an affront to human conventions of truth and justice, but

17. Obviously, this sits well with Rabbi Kook's overall approach concerning the importance of natural morality, as expressed in many places in his writings. We discussed his view of the integration of scholarly research and Torah in an earlier chapter.
18. These differences have been treated in different forums. We might note, among others, Menahem Mordechai Soloveitchik (later Sulieli) and Zalman Rubashov (later Shazar), *Toldot Bikoret HaMikra* (History of Biblical Criticism) (Berlin, 1925), 108; M. Greenberg, "Some Postulates of Biblical Criminal Law," *Yeḥezkel Kaufmann Jubilee Volume* (Jerusalem, 1960), 5–28, and subsequently, "More Reflections on Biblical Criminal Law," *Scripta Hierosolymitana* 31 (1986): 1–17.

also as a violation of God's will. While in the ancient Near East, it was the king who issued laws in order to ensure justice in the land, in the Torah, the only connection between the king and the law is the king's obligation to write a copy of God's commandments for himself, and to obey them (Deut. 17:18–19). The sole Legislator is God, Israel's true King. This fundamental difference has many ramifications.

The Torah is unique in that it includes, within the same chapters and within the same collections of laws, both social legislation (pertaining to relations between man and his fellow) and religious legislation (pertaining to rituals specifically, and to the relationship between man and God more broadly). In fact, the division between these types of laws is irrelevant, since they belong to the same harmonious framework of performing God's will in the world. Only in the Torah is there such a phenomenon as *Parashat Mishpatim*, where social laws – similar to those in the Laws of Hammurabi, concerning thieves and robbers, monetary damages, pledges, and hiring – appear alongside laws such as the Sabbath, the three pilgrimage festivals, and the laws of sacrifices.

Moreover, even the social laws of the Torah contain a religious dimension, with many of them being set forth under the general heading, קְדֹשִׁים תִּהְיוּ כִּי קָדוֹשׁ אֲנִי ה׳ אֱלֹהֵיכֶם, "You shall be holy, for I, the Lord your God, am holy" (Lev. 19:2). In Mesopotamian literature, collections of laws and narrative texts are found in separate works. The Torah is the only ancient work in which the two spheres coexist.

Another difference concerns the way in which the laws are formulated. The laws of the ancient Near East are not formulated in absolute terms, instructing a person what he must do and what he must not do. Instead, they are almost always set forth in casuistic fashion – that is, in the form of a case in relation to which a law is set down: if someone does X, then the legal consequence is Y. This approach is rooted in a fundamental view of the law as addressing problems and setting down solutions for instances of conflict between people. In the Torah, in contrast, alongside casuistic formulations there are apodictic laws – absolute "dos" and "don'ts," such as the Ten Commandments: "Remember the Sabbath day to sanctify it"; "Honor your father and your mother"; "You shall not kill"; "You shall not commit adultery"; "You shall not steal"

(Ex. 20:7–12). There is no parallel phenomenon in the laws of the ancient Near East.[19] Yet the two models coexist in the Torah in close proximity.

Parashat Mishpatim contains both casuistic formulations and apodictic commands. The first are apparent in such statements as, "If you acquire a Hebrew slave…"; "If a man sells his daughter as a maidservant…"; "If a man plots against his neighbor, to kill him with cunning…" (Ex. 21:2–14). The latter appear in: "You shall not suffer a witch to live"; "You shall not vex a stranger"; "You shall not afflict any widow"; "You shall not revile the judges, nor curse the ruler of your people. You shall not delay to offer the first of your ripe fruits and of your liquors; the firstborn of your sons shall you give to Me"; "And you shall be holy men unto Me, and you shall not eat any meat that is torn by beasts in the field; you shall cast it to the dogs" (Ex. 22:17–30). This difference between the law codes of the ancient Near East and the Torah is a function of the fact that the Torah intends not merely to set forth rules and regulations concerning various situations that may arise, but aims to guide human behavior. Even when one's actions do not give rise to any offense or complaint on the part of another, one may nevertheless be transgressing that which is prohibited in the eyes of God.

This contrast is also evident in the regulations concerning adultery. According to the laws of the ancient Near East, if a woman commits adultery, her husband may choose to waive punishment, which would also exempt the man with whom she had shared intimate relations from punishment: "If a man's wife should be seized lying with another male,

19. See U. Cassuto, *A Commentary on the Book of Exodus* (Jerusalem, 1967), especially on *Parashat Mishpatim*; M. Weinfeld, "The Origins of Apodictic Law," *Vetus Testamentum* 23 (1973): 63–75, who notes that what is unique in Israelite law is "the formulation of the command in second person" (63); Samuel E. Loewenstamm, "Mishpat, Mishpat HaMikra" in *Encyclopedia Mikra'it* 5 (Jerusalem, 1978), columns 625–28. Weinfeld and Loewenstamm point out that the laws of the ancient Near East include some apodictic commands or prohibitions formulated in the third person, pertaining to the status of and procedures concerning inferior categories – such as, for example, in the Laws of Eshnunna 51: "A slave or slave-woman (belonging to a resident) of Eshnunna… will not exit the main city-gate of Eshnunna without his owner" (Roth, *Law Collections from Mesopotamia and Asia Minor*). However, these are not universal positive and negative commandments directed toward the entire nation, as we find in the Torah.

they shall bind them and cast them into the water. If the wife's master allows his wife to live, the king shall pardon his subject [i.e., the other male]" (Laws of Hammurabi, para. 129).[20] In the Torah, no such possibility of clemency exists (see Lev. 20:10; Deut. 22:22–23).

Once again, this difference arises from a fundamental distinction between the two systems of laws: The specific law in question is formulated, in its ancient Near Eastern versions, with a view to protecting the husband, such that if he is willing to forego his rights and prefers to ignore the offense, there is no need for compensation. The Torah, however, regards adultery not only as an injustice toward the husband, but also as a sin against God. The Torah's narratives relating to this issue reflect this sense as well. For example, God prevents Abimelekh from touching Sarah because it is a sin against God: וָאֶחְשֹׂךְ גַּם אָנֹכִי אוֹתְךָ מֵחֲטוֹ לִי עַל כֵּן לֹא נְתַתִּיךָ לִנְגֹּעַ אֵלֶיהָ, "I also withheld you from sinning against Me; therefore I did not permit you to touch her" (Gen. 20:6). Similarly, Joseph's refusal to accede to Potiphar's wife when she tries to seduce him acknowledges the extent of the offense: וְאֵיךְ אֶעֱשֶׂה הָרָעָה הַגְּדֹלָה הַזֹּאת וְחָטָאתִי לֵאלֹהִים, "How can I perform this great evil, for I would be sinning to God" (Gen. 39:9).

Another example of the differences between the legal systems is with regard to the case of taking another's life. According to some ancient Near Eastern law systems, a family that has had one of its members killed may choose monetary payment instead of the death penalty for the killer. For example, the Middle Assyrian laws state, "If either a man or a woman enters another man's house and kills either a man or a woman, they shall hand over the manslayers to the head of the household; if he so chooses, he shall kill them, or if he chooses to come to an accommodation, he shall take their property."[21] It is the head of the household, representing the next of kin, who is considered the injured

20. Translation based on Roth, *Law Collections from Mesopotamia and Asia Minor*; the last clause can be translated literally (as Roth does): "the king shall allow his subject to live," but the meaning is the same. Similar clauses are to be found in the Assyrian Laws (14) and the Laws of the Hittites (197). An extensive discussion appears in M. Greenberg, "Some Postulates of Biblical Criminal Law."
21. Roth, *Law Collections from Mesopotamia and Asia Minor*. The text is broken, and the translation represents the accepted restoration of the text.

party – partly owing to the monetary damage incurred against the family's work force – making it his choice to have the murderer put to death, or to take his property. In the Laws of the Hittites (1–4), different circumstances of a murder result in different rates for ransoms. By contrast, the Torah does not consider gradations of punishment for one who is guilty of murder: וְלֹא תִקְחוּ כֹפֶר לְנֶפֶשׁ רֹצֵחַ אֲשֶׁר הוּא רָשָׁע לָמוּת כִּי מוֹת יוּמָת, "You shall not take a ransom for the life of a murderer who is guilty of death; for he shall surely be put to death" (Num. 35:31).[22] The murder is not only an offense against the victim and his family, but also against the Creator, as the Torah recounts immediately after the description of the Flood: שֹׁפֵךְ דַּם הָאָדָם בָּאָדָם דָּמוֹ יִשָּׁפֵךְ כִּי בְּצֶלֶם אֱלֹהִים עָשָׂה אֶת הָאָדָם, "One who sheds the blood of man shall have his own blood shed by man, for God created man in His image" (Gen. 9:6).

The difference between the two systems also finds expression in the treatment of animals that have caused loss of human life. Owing to the great value that the Torah attaches to human life, it is emphasized that an animal that kills a person must be put to death. This appears along with the law of a murderer: וְאַךְ אֶת דִּמְכֶם לְנַפְשֹׁתֵיכֶם אֶדְרֹשׁ מִיַּד כָּל חַיָּה אֶדְרְשֶׁנּוּ, "But the blood of your lives shall I require; at the hand of every beast shall I require it" (Gen. 9:5). An ox that has killed a person, therefore, is put to death: וְכִי יִגַּח שׁוֹר אֶת אִישׁ אוֹ אֶת אִשָּׁה וָמֵת סָקוֹל יִסָּקֵל הַשּׁוֹר וְלֹא יֵאָכֵל אֶת בְּשָׂרוֹ, "If an ox gores a man or a woman, that they die, then the ox shall surely be stoned, and its flesh shall not be eaten" (Ex. 21:28). According to the Torah, whoever or whatever has cut short human life shall not itself be left alive. In the laws of the ancient Near East, by contrast, the focus is on the monetary compensation that the owner of the ox must pay, but the ox is left alive.

---

22. A ransom is possible, in Torah law, only in a situation where it was not a person who directly performed the act of killing. For example, in the case of an ox that is known to gore and that killed someone, the law is: הַשּׁוֹר יִסָּקֵל וְגַם-בְּעָלָיו יוּמָת, "the ox shall be stoned and its owner, too, shall be put to death" (Ex. 21:29); but there is another possibility: אִם כֹּפֶר יוּשַׁת עָלָיו וְנָתַן פִּדְיֹן נַפְשׁוֹ כְּכֹל אֲשֶׁר יוּשַׁת עָלָיו, "If a sum of money is laid upon him, he shall give for the ransom of his life whatever is laid upon him" (Ex. 21:30). The topic of ransom is discussed by Moshe Greenberg in "The Biblical Grounding of Human Value," in *The Samuel Friedland Lectures 1960–66* (New York, 1966), 39–51, here 43–44.

> If an ox gores to death a man while it is passing through the streets, that case has no basis for a claim.
>
> If a man's ox is a known gorer and the authorities of his city quarter notify him that it is a known gorer, but he does not blunt [meaning uncertain] its horns or control his ox, and that ox gores to death a gentleman, he [the owner] shall pay a half-mina [thirty shekels] of silver. (Laws of Hammurabi, 250–51)[23]

The Torah maintains a stricter standard when it comes to loss of human life, going beyond the monetary loss entailed by damage to property. The laws of the ancient Near East blur this distinction, from both directions. On the one hand, the laws are more lenient in certain instances of murder, imposing only a monetary fine. On the other hand, they are sometimes stricter in the realm of property, imposing the death sentence. Thus, for example, the Laws of Hammurabi state:

> If a man should purchase silver, gold, a slave, a slave woman, an ox, a sheep, a donkey, or anything else whatsoever, from a gentleman or from a gentleman's slave without witnesses or a contract – or if he accepts the goods for safekeeping – that man is a thief, he shall be killed. (7)

> If a fire breaks out in a house of a man, and a man who came to help put it out covets the household furnishings belonging to the householder and takes household furnishings belonging to the householder, that man shall be cast into that very fire. (25)

This contrasts sharply with Torah law, which does not impose the death penalty for theft or monetary damage of any sort. Rather, the Torah clearly distinguishes between loss of life, which justifies the death penalty, and loss of or damage to property, which is not serious enough to warrant the taking of human life.

---

23. Roth, *Law Collections from Mesopotamia and Asia Minor.*

The contrast between the Torah and the Laws of Hammurabi is most prominent in the law of a thief who lacks the means to repay what he has stolen. The Laws of Hammurabi state: "If a man steals an ox or sheep, or an ass … if the thief does not have anything to give, he shall be killed." It would seem that this is precisely the practice that the Torah seeks to avoid: **שַׁלֵּם יְשַׁלֵּם אִם אֵין לוֹ וְנִמְכַּר בִּגְנֵבָתוֹ**, "He shall make full restitution; if he has nothing, then *he shall be sold for his theft*" (Ex. 22:2). The Torah proposes indenture as a way of dealing with a thief who lacks the wherewithal to pay what he owes, in marked contrast to the thief paying with his life.

Likewise, concerning a robber or a thief who comes stealthily: "If a man breaks into a house, they shall kill him and hang him in front of that very breach. If a man commits a robbery and is then seized, that man shall be killed" (Laws of Hammurabi 21–22). In this case as well, the Torah rules out the death penalty for one who comes stealthily or who is caught in an attempted burglary, owing to the importance of human life – unless the life of the owner of the house is in danger: אִם בַּמַּחְתֶּרֶת יִמָּצֵא הַגַּנָּב וְהֻכָּה וָמֵת אֵין לוֹ דָּמִים. אִם זָרְחָה הַשֶּׁמֶשׁ עָלָיו דָּמִים לוֹ, "If a thief be found breaking in [stealthily], and be smitten that he die, there shall be no blood shed on his account. If the sun was shining upon him, then blood shall be shed on his account" (Ex. 22:1–2).[24]

The commandments of the Torah also emphasize not only the technical law, but also the plight of the weaker members of society, who must be treated with consideration that goes beyond the letter of the law. For example, the Torah is very strict concerning the laws of a pledge, out of concern for the situation of a poor person who is in need of the loan, and therefore prohibits the taking of an object as a guarantee if it is needed by the borrower:

---

24. The distinction between a situation of "stealth" and one of "the sun shining upon him" concerns the question of whether the burglar comes with the knowledge that the homeowner is likely to be present and to defend his property – the burglar thus presents a threat to the life of the homeowner, such that it is permissible to kill him – or whether he comes with the presumption that the homeowner will not be encountered, such that the burglar comes unarmed and presents no threat (see Sanhedrin 72a).

אִם חָבֹל תַּחְבֹּל שַׂלְמַת רֵעֶךָ עַד בֹּא הַשֶּׁמֶשׁ תְּשִׁיבֶנּוּ לוֹ. כִּי הִוא כסותה [כְסוּתוֹ קרי] לְבַדָּהּ הִוא שִׂמְלָתוֹ לְעֹרוֹ בַּמֶּה יִשְׁכָּב וְהָיָה כִּי יִצְעַק אֵלַי וְשָׁמַעְתִּי כִּי חַנּוּן אָנִי.

> If you take your neighbor's garment for a pledge, you shall deliver it to him by sundown. For that is his only covering; it is his garment for his skin; in what shall he sleep? And it shall be, when he cries out to Me, that I shall hear, for I am gracious. (Ex. 22:25–26)

The Torah emphasizes that harm to the elementary needs of the borrower represents a violation of God's will. The same message arises from the command, לֹא יַחֲבֹל רֵחַיִם וָרָכֶב כִּי נֶפֶשׁ הוּא חֹבֵל, "No one shall take either an upper or a lower millstone for a pledge; for he [who does so] takes a life for a pledge" (Deut. 24:6). In the Laws of Hammurabi, in contrast, even the debtor himself may be taken, in person, as a pledge.

> If a man has a claim of grain or silver against another man, and therefore takes a member of the debtor's household, and the one taken dies a natural death while in the house of the one who has taken him, that case has no basis for a claim. (115)[25]

Another example concerns a slave who escapes from his master's house. The Torah warns: לֹא תַסְגִּיר עֶבֶד אֶל אֲדֹנָיו אֲשֶׁר יִנָּצֵל אֵלֶיךָ מֵעִם אֲדֹנָיו, "You shall not deliver to his master a slave who has fled to you from his master" (Deut. 23:16). The plain reason for this prohibition seems to be moral: if the slave has fled from his master, he must have suffered acutely – and therefore the Torah prohibits returning him.[26] The Laws of Hammurabi, however, view the returning of the slave to his master as a positive obligation: "If a man should harbor a fugitive slave or slave woman of either the palace or of a commoner in his house and not bring out at the herald's public proclamation, that householder shall be killed" (16).

25. The technical term for the taking of the member of the debtor's household is "distraint." See Roth, *Law Collections from Mesopotamia and Asia Minor*, 103.
26. Admittedly, the Sages mitigate this law, applying it only to a non-Jewish slave who has fled from a different country to Israel: he is not returned, so that he will not have to return to idolatry (Gittin 45a).

In the Laws of Hammurabi, formal ownership trumps the value of compassion.

As a final example, in the laws of the ancient Near East, the prevailing view of the family is that it is a single legal unit, to the extent that sons may pay for the misdeeds of their fathers. For example, the Laws of Hammurabi include the possible scenario in which a person is seized (for labor) in lieu of money that he owes if he is unable to pay (a situation which is legally possible, according to these laws):

> If the one taken should die from the effects of a beating or other physical abuse while in the house of the one who took him, the owner of the one taken shall charge and convict the merchant, and if the one taken is the man's son, they shall kill the son of the one who took him. (116)

Elsewhere: "If a gentleman strikes a woman of the gentry-class, and thereby causes her to miscarry her fetus, he shall weigh and deliver ten shekels of silver for her fetus" (209–10).[27]

Against this background, the Torah's prohibition stands out in stark contrast: לֹא יוּמְתוּ אָבוֹת עַל בָּנִים וּבָנִים לֹא יוּמְתוּ עַל אָבוֹת אִישׁ בְּחֶטְאוֹ יוּמָתוּ, "Fathers shall not be put to death for sons, and sons shall not be put to death for fathers; every one shall be put to death for his own sin" (Deut. 24:16).[28] Individuals are judged for their own conduct, and a child is not considered a parent's property to allow a parent to be punished through the child. For this reason, the Torah emphasizes, after stating the law regarding an ox that kills a person: אוֹ בֵן יִגָּח אוֹ בַת יִגָּח כַּמִּשְׁפָּט

27. Another example of vicarious punishment appears in paragraphs 229–30 of the Laws of Hammurabi, which ordain that if a builder erred in building a house, and the house collapsed and killed the homeowner's son, the builder's son is to be killed.

28. One might be prompted to point out that the Torah also states that God "visits the transgressions of fathers on sons, and on sons of sons, upon the third and the fourth generation" (Ex. 34:7), but the distinction between the two statements is clear, as pointed out by Ibn Ezra in his commentary on the verse in Deuteronomy: there, the command is directed to the court, which may not punish a person for the sins of others. In the heavenly accounting, however, the possibility exists. The Sages teach (Berakhot 7a) that sons receive punishment for the sins of their fathers only when they "maintain their forefathers' deeds in their own actions."

הַזֶּה יֵעָשֶׂה לּוֹ, "Whether it has gored a son, or gored a daughter, according to its judgment shall it be done to it" (Ex. 21:31).[29]

The Torah appears to be making the point that, despite living in a world where children may, or even must, pay for the sins of their parents, Jews follow a different law. The owner of the ox himself, rather than one of his children, is punished.

We have seen that there are commonalities between the laws of the Torah and the laws of the ancient Near East, yet the distinctions between the two are telling. We may conclude that the Torah displays awareness of the existence of other ancient codes of law, and perhaps even specific laws, such as those discussed above. However, even in instances where there is a clear connection between the two systems, the Torah is not a replica of existing laws.

On the contrary, the Torah adopts those laws that conform to the dictates of morality and uprightness, while altering radically some of the basic principles upon which those laws are based, as well as their foundation in limited human perceptions of justice. From the Torah's divine point of view, the emphases on the value of life, on individual responsibility, and so on, contrast with the underlying principles of the other systems of laws.[30] The Torah represents, even in the social sphere, a wondrous legal structure based on social justice, supporting and illustrating Moses's declaration cited above: וּמִי גּוֹי גָּדוֹל אֲשֶׁר לוֹ חֻקִּים וּמִשְׁפָּטִים צַדִּיקִם כְּכֹל הַתּוֹרָה הַזֹּאת אֲשֶׁר אָנֹכִי נֹתֵן לִפְנֵיכֶם הַיּוֹם, "What nation is there so great, that has statutes and judgments so righteous as all this Torah, which I set before you today?" (Deut. 4:8).

29. The commentators explain that the Torah's intention here is to rule out the possibility of a complete exemption in the case of the goring of a child. Such a thought might arise either (as Rashi suggests) on the basis of the claim that a child is not defined as a legal entity, or (as Nahmanides posits) because an ox that has gored a child uses less force than one that gores an adult.

30. Hence, the similarity between the Torah and the Laws of Hammurabi need not be presented as a dilemma, necessitating a choice between asserting either the moral superiority of the Torah (as reflected in these similarities) or the essence of Torah as Revelation (thus ignoring the similarities), as proposed by Shavit and Eran, 177. The similarities exist, but their comparison need not come at the expense of regarding the Torah as Divine Revelation – reflected precisely from within these similarities.

All of this serves to demonstrate the value to the Tanakh scholar of comparing and contrasting the laws of the Torah with those found in legal codes of the ancient Near East. Namely, familiarity with the laws of the latter may help one to understand the context or possibility that the Torah is protesting, revealing the innovation of the Torah law. As Maimonides writes:

> I say that my knowledge of the belief, practice, and worship of the Sabians [i.e., an ancient idolatrous nation] has given me an insight into many of the divine precepts, and has led me to know their reason.... I will mention to you the works from which you may learn all that I know of the religion and the opinions of the Sabians; you will thereby obtain a true knowledge of my theory as regards the purpose of the divine precepts.... All these books which I have mentioned are works on idolatry translated into Arabic; there is no doubt that they form a very small portion in comparison to that which has not been translated, and that which is no longer extant, but has been lost in the course of time.... They describe how temples are built and... many other things which you can learn from the books mentioned by us. The knowledge of these theories and practices is of great importance in explaining the reasons of the precepts. For it is the principal object of the Law and the axis round which it turns, to blot out these opinions from man's heart and make the existence of idolatry impossible. (*Guide of the Perplexed* III:29)

THE NARRATIVES IN GENESIS AND THEIR PARALLELS IN ANCIENT NEAR EASTERN LITERATURE

Given the parallels between laws of the ancient Near East and some of the laws of the Torah – and the demonstration of how the similarities serve to highlight fundamental differences between them – it is worth noting the narratives in Genesis that similarly parallel narratives in ancient Near Eastern literature.[31]

31. A classic study of the book of Genesis in its ancient Near Eastern context is Nahum Sarna's *Understanding Genesis* (New York, 1966).

The story of the Flood, as recounted in Genesis 6–8, is an especially striking example. The most extensive parallel is found in the *Epic of Atrahasis,* composed in Babylonia in the eighteenth to seventeenth centuries BCE, but the narrative most similar to the biblical story appears in the *Epic of Gilgamesh.*[32] The narrative describes how Gilgamesh asks the immortal man Utnapishtim (paralleling the biblical Noah) to reveal how the gods came to grant him eternal life. In response, Utnapishtim recounts at length the story of how he was saved from a flood. According to his account, the gods decided to bring a flood upon the world, and vowed not to broadcast this imminent catastrophe. Ea, the god of wisdom and magic, wanted to save his beloved Utnapishtim, however, and therefore decided to reveal this secret decision. Ea instructs Utnapishtim to build a boat, and then:

> Put on board the boat the seed of all living creatures
> The boat that you are going to build,

32. The *Epic of Giglamesh* began to develop as a written text already in the third millennium BCE, around the time that the first known texts were written. From these early texts, written in Sumerian, it developed into something approaching its currently known form in Akkadian in the Old Babylonian period (close to the eighteenth century BCE), and continued to develop until it reached what is known as its "Standard Babylonian" form. Most of the tablets containing the standard form of this text derive from the seventh-century BCE library of Assurbanipal, in Assyria. For a detailed discussion of the literary history of this epic, see A. R. George, *The Babylonian Gilgamesh Epic: Introduction, Critical Edition and Cuneiform Texts,* 2 vols. (Oxford, 2003), 1:5–55, and more briefly in U. Cassuto, *A Commentary on the Book of Genesis,* part 2, transl. I. Abrahams (Jerusalem, 1964), 5–10. The different stories in the standard version of the epic are all connected in some way to Gilgamesh, a historical figure who is thought to have served as a king in southern Mesopotamia. (For a discussion of his historicity or lack thereof, see George 1:91–137.) Many of the different stories in the epic relate to the question of death and the conflict between the human world and the natural world.

   Tablet XI of the twelve tablets in the standard version of the epic discusses the flood story. It draws heavily on the Atrahasis epic, known to us from Old Babylonian versions. For a translation of the Atrahasis epic, see B. Foster, *Before the Muses: An Anthology of Akkadian Literature,* 2 vols. (Bethesda, 1993), 1:158–200. For a discussion of how Atrahasis relates to the Epic of Gilgamesh in its standard form, see J. Tigay, *The Evolution of the Gilgamesh Epic* (Philadelphia, 1982).

> Her dimensions should all correspond. (lines 27–29)[33]

Utnapishtim builds the boat:

> I gave her six decks, I divided her into seven parts....
> Three times 3,600 (buckets) of bitumen I poured into the furnace. (lines 61–65)

And ultimately:

> I loaded aboard it whatever seed I had of living things, each and every one.
> All my kith and kin I sent aboard the boat. (lines 84–85)

Once everyone is inside, a flood lasts six days and seven nights. When it ends, the ship comes to rest on Mount Nisir for seven days. Then,

> When the seventh day arrived –
> I brought out a dove, setting it free:
> Off went the dove;
> No perch was available for it and it came back to [me].
> I brought out a swallow,
> Off went the swallow;
> No perch was available for it and it came back to [me].
> I brought out a raven, setting it free;
> Off went the raven and it saw the waters receding.
> It was eating, bobbing up and down, it did not come back to me. (lines 147–56)

After leaving the ship, Utnapishtim offers sacrifices, and "the gods smelled the savor" (line 161). The story concludes with Enlil, the chief god of the pantheon, becoming very angry at Ea for revealing the secret to Utnapishtim, but Ea defends himself, arguing:

33. Translations from George, *The Babylonian Gilgamesh Epic*, 1:705–25.

How could you lack counsel and cause the deluge?
On him who commits sin, inflict his crime!
On him who does wrong, inflict [his] wrong-doing. (lines 184–86)

Sinners should be punished, but there is no need to destroy all of humanity. Ultimately, Enlil accepts Ea's advice not to destroy the human race, and he blesses Utnapishtim and his wife with eternal life.

There are many points of similarity between the *Epic of Gilgamesh* and the story of the Flood as recounted in Genesis.[34] On the one hand, the great similarity to a source that is unquestionably more ancient may serve to substantiate the authenticity of the story of the Flood.[35] If there were no other known traditions of this event, with its impact on the entire world, at the very dawn of human existence, the reliability of the biblical account might be undermined. On the other hand, the biblical story was seen as no more than a duplication of the earlier Mesopotamian tradition, by Delitzsch and others.[36]

As with the comparison of the legal systems, however, the similarities between the narratives serve to highlight the substantial differences between them. These differences find expression both in a comparison between the description of God and the description of the pagan gods, and in a comparison between the description of Noah and that of Utnapishtim. Consider some of the central differences between the accounts, and their significance:[37]

1. First and foremost, the biblical story centers on the monotheistic Noah, as opposed to the pagan Gilgamesh. God operates as a single divine power, as compared to several gods producing the flood collectively, with disagreement between them.

---

34. For additional similarities, including those in other Mesopotamian sources, and a discussion of those sources, see U. Cassuto, *A Commentary on the Book of Genesis*, part 2, transl. I. Abrahams (Jerusalem, 1964), 5–14.
35. Indeed, in the Christian world the parallel was perceived by Protestant orthodoxy as absolute proof of the biblical tradition (see Shavit and Eran, 83).
36. Shavit and Eran, 171.
37. These differences have been discussed in many different works; see especially Cassuto, 5–14; Sarna, 37–63; and T. Frymer-Kensky, "The Atrahasis Epic and Its Significance for Our Understanding of Genesis 1–9," *Biblical Archaeologist* 40 (1977): 147–55.

2. The *Epic of Gilgamesh* gives no reason for the decision of the gods to bring a flood upon the world. In the story of Atrahasis, the noise produced by human beings disturbs the rest of Enlil, who declares,

   The clamor of mankind has become burdensome to me,
   I am losing sleep to their uproar.
   Cut off provisions for the peoples.[38]

   In the story of Noah, God decides to wipe out mankind after seeing that they have become irredeemably corrupt.

3. The different versions of the Gilgamesh story offer no explanation why specifically Utnapishtim was saved,[39] while, in the Torah, Noah's personal ethical conduct is distinguished from that of his generation: כִּי אֹתְךָ רָאִיתִי צַדִּיק לְפָנַי בַּדּוֹר הַזֶּה, "For I have seen you righteous before Me in this generation" (Gen. 7:1).

4. In the *Epic of Gilgamesh* the gods themselves are fearful of the flood that they have brought upon the world:

   Even the gods took fright at the deluge....
   They withdrew, they went up to the heaven of Anu (the sky-god)
   The gods were curled up like dogs, lying out in the open.
   The goddess, screaming like a woman in childbirth....
   The gods, the Anunnaki (the chief gods) were weeping with her
   Wet-faced with sorry, they were weeping
   Their lips were parched, being stricken with fever. (lines 113–26)

---

38. Tablet II, lines 6–7, from Foster, *Before the Muses* 1:171, representing one of several attempts to control the human population before the bringing of the flood. For different approaches to the question of the reason for the flood in Mesopotamian literature, see J. Klein, "A New Look at the Theological Background of the Mesopotamian and Biblical Flood Stories," in *A Common Cultural Heritage: Studies on Mesopotamia and the Biblical World in Honor of Barry L. Eichler*, ed. G. Frame, et al. (Bethesda, 2011), 151–76, as well as Frymer-Kensky, "The Atrahasis Epic."
39. The story of Atrahasis even states that man is actually saved from the flood for the sake of the gods – "Behold, I have done this for your sakes" – apparently, because the gods need man to work for them.

The gods are unable to control the mighty forces of nature that they had unleashed. They themselves dwell within nature, and may themselves be harmed by the flood. It also appears that the gods do not anticipate the results of their decision. In the story of Noah, God controls nature and is completely independent of it.

5. In the Gilgamesh story there are disagreements and arguments between the gods. No such reality can exist in the story of Noah, where God's will is the only will that has any influence on the world.

6. In the story of Gilgamesh, following the offering of sacrifices by Utnapishtim, the gods smell the sweet aroma, and then they "collected like flies over the sacrifice" (line 161). According to the pagan view, the gods need to eat and drink the sacrifices that humans offer to them. During the week-long flood, during which no sacrifices were offered, the gods became hungry and thirsty. In sharp contrast, the Torah says of God only that וַיָּרַח ה׳ אֶת רֵיחַ הַנִּיחֹחַ, "God smelled the sweet aroma" (Gen. 8:21). God has no "need" for the sacrifice, and there is certainly no physical aspect involved. The biblical expression denotes divine acceptance of man's actions, the sole result of which is the decision, לֹא אֹסִף לְקַלֵּל עוֹד אֶת הָאֲדָמָה בַּעֲבוּר הָאָדָם כִּי יֵצֶר לֵב הָאָדָם רַע מִנְּעֻרָיו, "I shall not again curse the earth anymore because of man, for the inclination of man's heart is evil from his youth" (Gen. 8:21).

7. The Mesopotamian story ends with the survivor being "promoted" to the rank of a god. Noah remains a mortal man after the Flood.

We may therefore summarize as follows: the basic facts of the story – a man saved from annihilation by a flood, through advice given from on high that he build an ark into which he should take all types of living things, the conclusion of the flood, and the way in which the man leaves the ark – parallel one another, offering support for the authenticity and the ancient origins of the narratives themselves.

The contrasts between the stories point to the fundamental differences between the pagan and the monotheistic worldviews, and to our mind demonstrate the superior moral message of the story of Noah over that of the pagan story. The fact that the tradition of the great flood was familiar to the nations of the ancient Near East presents no contradiction to the Torah, and there is no reason that the Torah should refrain from recording it just because it was already well-known. To the contrary, it is specifically the comparison of the messages arising from the respective descriptions that strengthens the distinction between them. In any event, chronological precedence has nothing to do with the authenticity of the story, one way or the other.

We may adopt a similar attitude to the parallels in the Creation narrative appearing in Mesopotamian literature. Among the various works that have been discovered, of special note is the Babylonian *Enûma Eliš (Enuma Elish)*, which appears to have been written toward the end of the second millennium BCE, but which may be assumed to preserve more ancient Mesopotamian traditions. The similarities between this text and the description of the creation of the world (Gen., ch. 1) include the following:[40]

Enuma Elish is introduced with the following words:

> When on high no name was given to heaven,
> Nor below was the netherworld called by name
> Primeval Apsu, their progenitor
> And matrix-Tiamat, who bore them all,
> Were mingling their waters together
> No cane break was intertwined, nor thicket matted close (to create solid ground)
> When no gods at all had been brought forth. (First Tablet, lines 1–7)[41]

The two gods mentioned here represent the two entities that existed prior to the creation of the world: "Apsu," representing the waters of the deep, and "Tiamat," the primordial sea goddess. There is a clear similarity here to the description at the beginning of Genesis:

---

40. For more on parallels between the Mesopotamian creation stories and the account in Genesis, as well as the differences between them, see Frymer-Kensky, "The Atrahasis Epic," and Y. Kaufmann, *The Religion of Israel: From Its Beginnings to the Babylonian Exile,* transl. and abridged by M. Greenberg (London, 1960), 7–148.

41. From Foster, *Before the Muses,* 1:351–401.

בְּרֵאשִׁית בָּרָא אֱלֹהִים אֵת הַשָּׁמַיִם וְאֵת הָאָרֶץ. וְהָאָרֶץ הָיְתָה תֹהוּ וָבֹהוּ
וְחֹשֶׁךְ עַל פְּנֵי תְהוֹם וְרוּחַ אֱלֹהִים מְרַחֶפֶת עַל פְּנֵי הַמָּיִם.

> In the beginning God created the heavens and the earth. And the earth was formless and void, and darkness was over the face of the deep. And a wind from God moved over the surface of the waters. (Gen. 1:1–2)

Both descriptions mention water as the primordial material preceding the rest of creation, and this substance is given a similar name in both traditions (*teḥom – tiamat*).

Further on, the Babylonian myth describes the splitting of Tiamat into two, with a separation between the primordial sea and the sky, by means of a firmament:

> He split (Tiamat) in two, like a fish for drying
> Half of her he set up and made as a cover, like heaven
> He stretched out the hide and assigned watchmen.
> And ordered them not to let her waters escape. (Fourth Tablet, lines 137–40)

Here, too, the description is similar to the one in Genesis:

וַיֹּאמֶר אֱלֹהִים יְהִי רָקִיעַ בְּתוֹךְ הַמָּיִם וִיהִי מַבְדִּיל בֵּין מַיִם לָמָיִם. וַיַּעַשׂ
אֱלֹהִים אֶת הָרָקִיעַ וַיַּבְדֵּל בֵּין הַמַּיִם אֲשֶׁר מִתַּחַת לָרָקִיעַ וּבֵין הַמַּיִם אֲשֶׁר
מֵעַל לָרָקִיעַ וַיְהִי כֵן. וַיִּקְרָא אֱלֹהִים לָרָקִיעַ שָׁמָיִם.

> And God said: Let there be a firmament in the midst of the waters, and let it divide water from water. And God made the firmament, and divided the waters which were under the firmament from the waters which were above the firmament, and it was so. And God called the firmament "*shamayim.*" (Gen. 1:6–8)

In the Fifth Tablet of *Enuma Elish,* a description of the creation of the sun and the moon serves *inter alia* to establish the calendar (lines 1–46), and in the Sixth Tablet, at the end of the process of creation, the creation of man is described (lines 35–38). These descriptions and their parallels in Genesis (1:14–18; 26–27) also contain other similarities, both in terms of the order of creation and in certain additional details.

Once again, the similarities, on the one hand, support the credibility of the Creation account, which was known to different cultures in the ancient world. On the other hand, there are some fundamental differences. First and foremost, in the Babylonian version, all the gods (including the creator god), representing the forces of nature, are themselves created out of nature, out of a mixture of the sweet water of "Apsu, the oldest of beings, their progenitor" with the salty water of "Mummu" Tiâmat, who bore each and all of them. The Torah presents a single, transcendent God, having no progeny and not influenced by nature, devoid of any physical aspects or influences. Here again, the similarities between the descriptions by the respective cultures sharpens the difference between the Torah and the pagan perceptions that preceded it.

It should be noted that, while the universal narratives recorded in Genesis up to chapter 11 may have parallels to a greater or lesser degree in ancient Near Eastern literature, once the text shifts to stories of the forefathers, starting from chapter 12 in Genesis, there are almost no parallel texts. This is especially evident with regard to the two central narratives of the Torah – the exodus from Egypt and the giving of the Torah – which have no parallels in ancient Near Eastern literature, and for good reason. These narratives indicate the unique national story of the Jewish people and their special relationship with God. There is no reason that they would appear in the stories of other nations. Moreover, these narratives deviate from the pagan worldview to a considerable extent: a spiritual divine revelation to an entire nation, as part of the forging of a covenant between God and the people, stands in opposition to the scornful pagan attitude toward mankind.[42]

42. Concerning the uniqueness of the story of the Revelation at Mount Sinai in this context, specifically against the backdrop of Hittite Vassal Treaties of the same period, see J. Berman, "God's Alliance with Man," *Azure* 25 (5766/2006); "The Biblical Origins of Equality," *Azure* 37 (5769/2009).

THE SABBATH

Let us briefly address the question of the Sabbath in the Mesopotamian sources. The Torah testifies to the uniqueness of the Sabbath in relation to the Jews:

> וְשָׁמְרוּ בְנֵי יִשְׂרָאֵל אֶת הַשַּׁבָּת לַעֲשׂוֹת אֶת הַשַּׁבָּת לְדֹרֹתָם בְּרִית עוֹלָם. בֵּינִי וּבֵין בְּנֵי יִשְׂרָאֵל אוֹת הִוא לְעֹלָם כִּי שֵׁשֶׁת יָמִים עָשָׂה ה׳ אֶת הַשָּׁמַיִם וְאֶת הָאָרֶץ וּבַיּוֹם הַשְּׁבִיעִי שָׁבַת וַיִּנָּפַשׁ.

> The Children of Israel shall observe the Sabbath, to perform the Sabbath for their generations; an eternal covenant. Between Me and the Children of Israel, it is a sign forever, for [in] six days God made the heavens and the earth, and on the seventh day He ceased, and rested. (Ex. 31:16–17)

For this reason, if the Sabbath is not an original innovation of the Torah, we have a more difficult question than that posed by the laws or narratives discussed thus far.

Delitzsch's argument[43] was that the institution of the Sabbath in the Torah was borrowed from Mesopotamian culture, where we find concepts of "*šapattu*" in the context of rest on the seventh day. However, Delitzsch's claims were misleading, and his argument in this regard is not accepted by biblical scholars. The concepts that he names do indeed appear in the ancient sources, but in contexts quite different from those of the Torah.[44]

In fact, two separate sources are involved. The first is the day referred to as "*šapattu*" in the Mesopotamian calendar, defined as the "day of rest for the heart." This is generally understood as the day when the hearts of the gods are set at rest through the performance of ritual ceremonies. This day falls on the fifteenth of the month – the day of

43. See Shavit and Eran, 116, 172–75.

44. On this subject see Cassuto, 40–42; J. Tigay, s.v. "*Shabbat*," *Encyclopedia Mikra'it* 7 (Jerusalem, 1976), columns 511–13; the brief discussion by M. Greenberg, s.v. "Sabbath," *Encyclopedia Judaica* (Jerusalem, 1972) 14:562; B. Oppenheimer, "Shabbat-Shemitta-Yovel: Semikhut HaParshiot bein Shabbat, Shemitta VeYovel," *Beit Mikra* 100 1 (5745/1985): 33–35.

the full moon. The second source is related to the phenomenon of the division of the lunar month into quarters, each consisting of approximately seven days. In ancient Assyrian calendars the 7th, 14th, 21st, and 28th days are "evil days," when kings and officials were forbidden from certain activities: they were prohibited from eating cooked meat or baked bread, they were not permitted to travel in a chariot, and so on. However, these days are related mainly to the New Moon and pertain to kings or rulers, rather than to the nation as a whole.

Whatever similarities exist between the Sabbath, as it appears in the Torah, and the ancient elements appearing in Mesopotamian culture are therefore weak. For that matter, we might propose[45] that the Torah presents a "Sabbath" that is diametrically opposed to its apparent parallels: the Sabbath is not related to the lunar calendar and the appearances of the moon, but rather to the "seventh day" – it is independent of the heavenly spheres. It is not a day of bad luck, but one of blessing. It is not a day for appeasing the gods, but a day for desisting from creative labor, as an expression of faith in the Creator of the world, and more. Most essentially, it is not a day solely for the societal elite, but a radically egalitarian institution applying to servants, strangers, and even animals, as much as to rulers. Thus, while the concept of a Sabbath may not be unique to the Torah, the very significant differences between the Sabbath in the Torah and the institution in Mesopotamian culture emphasize the unique nature of the former. The partial parallels may indicate historical roots at the foundation of the Sabbath, but whatever the nature of these roots may have been, they were molded among the Jewish people into a new and unique institution.[46]

SUMMARY

The Torah was given to the Jewish people – a nation that lived in the ancient Near East, where the influence of Mesopotamian culture was widespread. They were therefore aware of ancient systems of law and worldviews, and the generations preceding the giving of the Torah followed these to a considerable extent. The Torah given to the Jews was

45. As do, for example, Cassuto and Oppenheimer.

46. Tigay, 513.

likewise written with an awareness of the legal systems in practice at the time, and for this reason, its own unique system of laws does not proceed from an assumption that the people were a *tabula rasa*. Various aspects of the ancient laws are left intact in the Torah, others are amended, while still others are erased entirely.

The Torah represents a religious view of the laws that is morally superior, discernable specifically through comparison to the ancient legal systems. A familiarity with the laws of the ancient Near East, along with its culture and concepts, can shed light on and help to clarify the intention of the Torah in various instances. That said, the fact that certain concepts existed long before the giving of the Torah in no way supports the claim of duplication. At most, it offers an interesting basis for an important comparison between systems, which are fundamentally different from one another religiously and morally.

Part III

Between *Peshat* and *Derash*

Chapter 8

"*Peshat*" and "*Derash*" – *Midrash Aggada*

INTRODUCTION

Much ink has been spilled in the attempt to define the terms "*peshat*" (the plain meaning of the text) and "*derash*" (a homiletical lesson representing a different level of interpretation),"[1] which have their origin in the teachings of the Sages.[2] These terms are debated to the extent that, in a given discussion of the explanation of a verse, everyone might

1. See, for example, E. Touitou, *Rabbi Haim Ben Attar U'Perusho Ohr HaḤayim Al HaTorah* (Jerusalem, 1982), 48, 13; S. Kamin, "Rashi's Exegetical Categorization with Respect to the Distinction Between 'Peshat' and 'Derash' According to His Commentary to the Book of Genesis and Selected Passages from His Commentaries to Other Books of the Bible," *Immanuel* 11 (1980): 16–32; M. Ahrend, *Parshanut HaMikra VeHoraato* (Jerusalem, 2006), 9–31; S. Japhet, "The Pendulum of Exegetical Methodology: From 'Peshat' to 'Derash' and Back," in *Midrash Unbound: Transformations and Innovations*, eds. M. Fishbane and J. Weinberg (Oxford, 2013), 249–66.
2. For discussion of the Sages' use of these terms and their meaning, see D. Weiss Halivni, *Peshat and Derash* (New York, Oxford, 1991), 54–76; J. L. Kugel, "Two Introductions to Midrash," *Prooftexts* 3, 2 (1983), 131–55; D. Stern, "Midrash and Jewish Exegesis" in *The Jewish Study Bible* (Oxford, 2014), 1879–91. It is unanimously agreed that it is difficult to find a distinct and clear system in the way the Sages related to the differences between the two concepts.

agree that one of the proposed interpretations is "*peshat*" and the other interpretation "*derash*," and yet disagree as to which is which! In fact, a well-known aphorism says, "My interpretation of the verse is the *peshat* – and yours is the *derash*." For the purposes of this discussion, therefore, the following definitions will be used:

> *Peshat* assumes that "the Torah speaks in the language of human beings,"[3] and that it should be understood in the same manner in

---

3. Originally, the statement that "the Torah speaks in the language of human beings" was meant in a rather limited context. Rabbi Akiva's exegetical approach was that it is necessary to seek the reason for every instance where the Torah uses an expression involving a repetitious phrase – such as "*hikaret tikaret*" (Num. 15:31); "*bashel mevushal*" (Ex. 12:9); "*shaleaḥ teshalaḥ*" (Deut. 22:7), etc. – while Rabbi Yishmael rejected this exegetical principle, maintaining that "the Torah speaks in the language of human beings" – i.e., in using these grammatical forms, the Torah does not mean to teach us anything extra; rather, the situation is "Just as when a person is telling his friend to do something, if he wishes to urge him, he repeats himself and commands him twice over; thus, the text doubles its language, in order to urge [us]" (*Torat Ḥayim*, Bava Metzia 31b). For instance, concerning the verse הִכָּרֵת תִּכָּרֵת הַנֶּפֶשׁ הַהִוא עֲוֺנָה בָה, "That soul shall surely be cut off (*hikaret tikaret*), its iniquity is upon it" (Num. 15:31), Rabbi Akiva teaches: "'*Hikaret*' [teaches that the soul will be cut off] from this world; '*tikaret*' – [it will be cut off] from the World to Come" (Sanhedrin 64b), but Rabbi Yishmael rejects this interpretation, maintaining that the Torah is simply "speaking in the language of human beings."

This debate is related to the Sages' broader exegetical approaches: while R. Akiva tended toward extensive, far-reaching exegesis, R. Yishmael adhered more closely to the plain meaning of the text. On the differences between their respective approaches concerning midrash, see A. J. Heschel, *Heavenly Torah as Refracted through the Generations*, 32–45.

It should be noted that many of the *Rishonim* extended the use of the principle that "the Torah speaks in the language of human beings" to apply also to the expressions in the Torah that seem to attribute some corporeality to God. Thus, for example, Maimonides writes (*Hilkhot Yesodei HaTorah* 1:12): "All such [descriptions] and the like which are related in the Torah and the words of the Prophets – all these are metaphors and imagery. [For example,] יוֹשֵׁב בַּשָּׁמַיִם יִשְׂחָק, 'He Who sits in the heavens shall laugh' (Ps. 2:4); כִּעֲסוּנִי בְּהַבְלֵיהֶם, 'They angered Me with their emptiness' (Deut. 32:21); and כַּאֲשֶׁר שָׂשׂ ה', 'As God rejoiced' (Deut. 28:63). With regard to all such statements, our Sages said: 'The Torah speaks in the language of man.'" Similarly, Radak writes (in his commentary on Jeremiah 14:8), "In many places the Torah speaks about the Creator using the language of man, attributing to Him sight and hearing and smell, a hand, a foot – in the manner of human speech – but all is

> which human speech is usually understood – i.e., in accordance with the rules of grammar and syntax, with consideration for textual context, and within the framework of that which human rational thought deems plausible,[4] of social convention, and of the laws of nature. *Derash* assumes that the Torah does not speak in the language of man,[5] and it must be understood in special ways, with attention paid to elaboration and superfluities, and using the hermeneutical laws.[6]

A huge body of midrashic literature was created, starting from the time of the Sages and continuing throughout the Middle Ages. Midrashim were widely disseminated and highly popular among Torah scholars – especially those midrashim made familiar by Rashi, who was fond of integrating them into his commentaries. For many scholars, a large number of midrashim became integral to the content of the text itself.

Midrashim may be divided into two main types: *midreshei halakha*, pertaining to laws that are derived from the verses or based upon them, and *midreshei aggada*, which focus less on legal aspects of the text. In this chapter we will discuss *midreshei aggada* and the prevailing attitude toward them; in the next chapter we will turn our attention to *midreshei halakha*.

---

meant metaphorically, so that people can understand." For an in-depth discussion on the use of this phrase from the period of the Talmud through to Maimonides and its connection to the philosophy of religious language, see A. Margalit and M. Halbertal, *Idolatry* (Cambridge, MA, 1992), 54–62.

4. Obviously, it is clear that the biblical commentator lives within a certain cultural world, and his understanding of the *peshat* is inseparable from this world. Nevertheless, this does not mean that we cannot apply the same definition to the aim of his study (within the world that he is coming from): the desire to understand the text from within its authentic context.
5. The intention here is that *derash* assumes that the Torah does not speak *only* in the language of human beings; it does not mean to negate the plain meaning of the text.
6. E. Touitou, *HaPeshatot HaMitḥadshim BeKhol Yom – Iyyunim BePerusho Shel Rashbam LaTorah* (Jerusalem, 2003), 55. His insightful comment concerning other definitions (ibid., 54, n. 8) is worthy of note: "Words about the 'objectivity' of the *peshat* as opposed to the 'subjectivity' of *derash* are in fact the evaluation of [the respective interpretations on the part of] the scholars, and not definitions reflecting the view of the commentators."

Recent years in Israel have witnessed two different trends within the Religious-Zionist community. On the one hand, there are rabbis and religious Tanakh scholars (many of them graduates of Yeshivat Har Etzion and associated institutions) who promote the study of Tanakh on the level of *peshat*, sometimes making cautious use of academic tools and the accumulated knowledge of the academic world. Among this group, special mention should be made of Rabbi Mordekhai Breuer, *zt"l*, and – may they merit long lives – Rabbi Yoel Bin-Nun and Rabbi Yaakov Medan, who have raised a generation of students and students' students who study Tanakh in its *peshat* dimension in depth as an integral part of the world of the *beit midrash*.

On the other hand, there are rabbis and scholars of a more *ḥaredi*-national orientation, who view the study of Tanakh on the level of *peshat* as a dangerous innovation, and therefore rule out the study of *peshat* of Tanakh in the present generation. Tanakh is not studied much in these circles, and the main approach to such study relies on *midreshei Ḥazal* or exegesis in hasidic or kabbalistic style.[7]

This chapter seeks to demonstrate that the approaches that ignore the level of *peshat* represent a substantial deviation from the path of most of the major medieval biblical commentators. These commentators interpret the text on the level of *peshat*, proceeding from the assumption that God's word, as recorded in the books of Tanakh, finds expression on the level of *peshat*, too – perhaps principally so[8] – and one who

7. The following statements, for instance, express this view: "We are fortunate enough to have *Ḥazal*, whose insight was close to the level of prophecy. In the Oral Law it is they who teach us greater depth than what we, with our meager abilities, are able to grasp ourselves. It is essential to know this, that through *Ḥazal* we see more depth.... One can stand in front of a mirror and talk to himself, but this has nothing to do with what the Tanakh is saying" (Rabbi Tzvi Tau, *Tzaddik BeEmunato Yiḥyeh* [Jerusalem, 2002], 13–14); "In our *beit midrash* we emphasize the indispensable adherence to *Ḥazal* in studying Tanakh. Without this, the Book of Books is not complete" (Y. Rosen, *Sefer Shoftim BeGova Ḥazal* [Jerusalem, 2005], 9). In the United States, sentiments along similar lines were expressed by Rabbi Aharon Kotler; see *Mishnat Rabbi Aharon* III:179.

8. As we shall see below, there are different views among the medieval commentators as to whether *peshat* represents the most important level of understanding, or whether it is an additional level subservient to *derash*.

wants to study God's word therefore must know how to understand the meaning of the text on its plain level. They emphasize that the complementary insights offered by *derash* do not obligate the scholar of *peshat*, and they do not rule out the legitimacy of an interpretation that ignores these insights. This chapter cites some comments in this spirit from the classical biblical commentators, and examines the ramifications of this approach for Tanakh study in the current generation.

THE ATTITUDE OF THE *GEONIM* TO *MIDRASH AGGADA*

The distinction between *peshat* and *derash* is already apparent in the writings of the *Geonim* of Babylonia (roughly 500–1038 CE), who in many instances were reluctant to be bound to midrashic interpretations of verses.[9]

It appears that it was Rabbi Saadia Gaon,[10] the first rabbinic author of a running biblical commentary, who established the principle that "we do not rely on aggada,"[11] setting the precedent for many of the *Geonim* to take a different view from that expressed in the midrash – obviously, with a clear distinction between halakha, where rabbinic interpretation is binding, and aggada, where it need not be so. Rabbi Sherira Gaon writes explicitly:[12]

---

9. See Y. Fraenkel, *Darkei HaAggada VeHaMidrash*, vol. 2 (Givatayim, 1991), 504–7; Y. Elbaum, *Lehavin Divrei Ḥakhamim* (Jerusalem, 2001), 47–64; R. Brody, "The Geonim of Babylonia as Biblical Exegetes," *Hebrew Bible / Old Testament: The History of Its Interpretation*, 2nd ed. (Magne Saebø, Göttingen, 2000), 74–88.

   Among the reasons for this attitude, as Fraenkel and Elbaum note, was the considerable attention invested in polemics against Karaites and even Muslims, who attacked aggada from a rationalist position.
10. Known by his initials, RaSaG (882–942), he was one of the greatest Jewish scholars in the post-talmudic era, and the leader of the yeshiva in Sura, one of the two Babylonian yeshivot that were preeminent in the Jewish world in the centuries following the redaction of the Talmud. The leaders of these yeshivot were given the title Gaon. Rabbi Saadia wrote books in the areas of halakha, Tanakh, philosophy, and grammar, and these were a basis for later Jewish scholarship.
11. See B. M. Levin, *Otzar HaGeonim: Berakhot* (Haifa, 1928), *Ḥelek HaPerushim*, 91, and n. 10.
12. Rabbi Sherira Gaon (906–1006) was the head of the other preeminent Babylonian yeshiva, in Pumbedita, and the author of a great number of responsa. The well-known

> Those matters which are inferred from biblical verses, known as midrash and aggada, are but conjecture; some of them are substantiated ... but many are not – such as R. Akiva's teaching that the "gatherer" [of wood on the Sabbath, referred to in Numbers 15] was Zelofehad,[13] or R. Shimon's assertion that "the fast of the tenth month" refers to the tenth of Tevet,[14] and they mention each opinion; but as for us – לְפִי שִׂכְלוֹ יְהֻלַּל אִישׁ, "a man is praised according to his reason" (Prov. 12:8). Likewise, the aggadot brought by their disciples' disciples – such as Rabbi Tanḥuma and Rabbi Ushia and the like – most of them are not substantiated, and therefore we do not rely on the words of aggada. The correct interpretations among them are those that may be backed up by logic and by the text, but there is no limit or end to aggadot."[15]

According to Rabbi Sherira Gaon, aggada should be regarded as an educated opinion, not as an authoritative received tradition, giving the exegete every right to accept or reject it. The guiding principle, in his view, is the extent to which the aggada is based on reason and grounded

---

Iggeret Rav Sherira Gaon (Letter of Rabbi Sherira Gaon) deals with the development of rabbinic literature, and the history of the Talmud and legal scholars of the immediate post-Talmud era, the *Savoraim* and the *Geonim*.

13. See Shabbat 96b. Rabbi Akiva bases his opinion on the hermeneutical principle of the *gezera shava*: "Here the text says, וַיִּהְיוּ בְנֵי יִשְׂרָאֵל בַּמִּדְבָּר וַיִּמְצְאוּ אִישׁ, 'And the Children of Israel were in the wilderness, and they found a man' (Num. 15:32), and later on, Zelofehad's daughters say, אָבִינוּ מֵת בַּמִּדְבָּר, 'Our father died in the wilderness' (Num. 27:3). Just as the later quote refers to Zelofehad, so does the earlier one." We may assume that R. Sherira's reservations concerning this identification related to the fact that if it had indeed been Zelofehad who had gathered wood on the Sabbath, the text would have mentioned him by name – as indeed the continuation of the discussion there would suggest: "R. Yehuda ben Beteira said to him: Akiva, either way you will have to answer for this in the future. If the matter is as you say, then the situation is that the Torah chose to conceal his identity, but you have revealed it. And if it is not as you say, then you are slandering a righteous man."
14. See Rosh HaShana 18b, where the opposing view is cited.
15. Cited in *Sefer HaEshkol, Hilkhot Sefer Torah,* Albeck edition 60b. *Sefer HaEshkol* is a halakhic code by R. Abraham b. Isaac of Narbonne, Provence (c. 1110–1158), which includes extensive geonic as well as talmudic sources.

in the text. Where the connection is strong, the aggada may be accepted; where it is not, "we do not rely on the words of aggada."

A similar view was adopted by R. Samuel ben Hofni Gaon,[16] who drew a clear distinction between matters of halakha and matters of aggada, in terms of the obligation to accept them:

> Aggada is any interpretation brought in the Talmud that does not explain a commandment. This is aggada, and one should rely on it only within reason. You should know that all laws that the rabbis [of the Talmud] enacted on the basis of a commandment come directly from Moses our Teacher, may he rest in peace, who received them from the Almighty. One may neither add nor detract from them. But when [the rabbis] interpreted [non-legal] verses, they were expressing their own opinions and what happened to occur to them. We rely on these interpretations only when they are reasonable.[17]

16. R. Samuel ben Hofni (the Gaon of Sura from the year 997, d. 1013) wrote works in different spheres, including a commentary on the Torah and philosophical works. For more about him, see A. Greenbaum's introduction to *Perush HaTorah LaRav Shmuel ben Ḥofni Gaon* (Jerusalem, 1979), 11–23.
17. Translation by Dr. Moshe Simon-Shoshan: https://www.etzion.org.il/en/lecture-2-what-aggada-part-iiaggada-medieval-thought. This excerpt is from *Mavo LaTalmud*, which is erroneously attributed to Rabbi Shmuel HaNaggid. The work is actually an abridged translation of a work by Rabbi Samuel ben Hofni Gaon, entitled *Mavo El Mada HaMishna VeHaTalmud*; see Elbaum, 52, no. 11, and the bibliography listed there. Further on there are more quotations from the writings of R. Samuel ben Hofni Gaon, the most strident among them being an excerpt from a letter (originally published by S. Asaf, *Tekufat HaGeonim VeSifruta* [Jerusalem, 1977], 283), in which he states, with rhyming literary finesse, that while some of the early *Geonim* would write aggadot to draw the hearts of readers, "we have adopted different paths in writing halakhot and traditions, and these are like fine flour, while the aggadot are like chaff."

 In his commentary on the story of the woman medium consulted by Saul (I Sam. 28), R. Samuel ben Hofni Gaon maintains that it is inconceivable that the woman actually conjured up the spirit of Samuel. In his view, the entire story is one of deceit on the part of the woman, and she herself invents all the messages conveyed to Saul. He is well aware that the Sages understand the episode according to its plain meaning (see, for instance, Ḥagiga 4b; Sanhedrin 65b) – i.e., that the woman did indeed raise the spirit of Samuel – but he writes: "Even though what *Ḥazal* say in the

A similar view is expressed by his son-in-law, R. Hai Gaon:[18]

> Rabbi Hai was asked concerning the distinction between aggadot written in the Talmud, regarding which we are charged to remove their corruptions, and other written aggadot outside of the Talmud. He replied: Everything included in the Talmud is clearer than that which was omitted. Nonetheless, with respect to the aggadot included therein, if it cannot be reconciled or it has been corrupted, one should not rely upon it, for we have a principle that one does not rely upon aggada. Yet, we are charged to correct the distortions in anything included in the Talmud, for if a teaching did not contain a midrash, it would not have been included in the Talmud. But if a text lies so corrupted, beyond anyone's ability to edit it, then we must treat it as words which are not legally binding. But regarding other aggadot we are not obligated to pay so much attention: if they are true and correct, they should be studied and preached; if not, they should be ignored.[19]

R. Hai Gaon maintains that a distinction should be drawn between the aggadot found in the Babylonian Talmud, and those that do not appear there. In the case of the latter, the guiding principle is that "if they are true and correct, they should be studied and preached; if not, they should be ignored." Concerning the midrashim that appear in the Gemara, however, greater effort should be exerted to understand them. Nonetheless, here too, "if it cannot be reconciled or it has been corrupted, one should not rely upon it."

Gemara suggests that the woman truly raised up Samuel, such statements cannot be accepted where they run counter to rational thought" (quoted in the commentaries of R. Yehuda ben Balaam and Radak on I Sam. 28).

18. R. Hai Gaon (939–1038), son and heir of R. Sherira Gaon of Pumbedita, and son-in-law of R. Samuel ben Hofni, Gaon of Sura, is considered the last of the *Geonim*. His best-known works include the halakhic writings *Mishpetei Shevuot* and *Sefer HaShetarot*.

19. Translation by Mark Goldenberg, found online at http://www.cardozo.yu.edu/sites/default/files/Berachyahu%20Lifshitz,%20Aggadah%20Versus%20Haggadah,%20Towards%20a%20More%20Precise%20Understanding%20of%20the%20Distinction.pdf.

Elsewhere the *Geonim* discuss the midrashic interpretation of the verse: וְהָיָה בַּיּוֹם הַהוּא לֹא יִהְיֶה אוֹר יְקָרוֹת יקפאון (וְקִפָּאוֹן), "And it shall be on that day that there shall be no bright light (*ohr yekarot*) but thick darkness (*vekipaon*)" (Zechariah 14:6):

> What is the meaning of the terms "*yekarot*" and "*kipaon*"? Rabbi Elazar taught: This means that the light that is precious (*yakar*) in this world, is considered of no value (*kapuy*) in the World to Come. R. Yoḥanan taught: These refer to the laws concerning leprosy and the ritual impurity of a tent in which there lies a corpse; these are dear [i.e., acquired at great cost, requiring great effort to understand] in this world, but are cheap [i.e., easily understood] in the World to Come. R. Yehoshua ben Levi taught: These refer to people who are honored in this world, but will be considered unimportant in the World to Come. (Pesaḥim 50a)

The *Geonim* devote brief discussion to these interpretations, and conclude: "These are all midrashim and aggadot… and there are other ways of understanding this verse."[20]

To conclude, consider Rabbenu Hananel's statement in his commentary on Ḥagiga (12a) concerning the many midrashim cited there:[21] "These are all midrashim, and we should not be too exacting with them, holding them up to rational evaluation."

The critical attitude of the *Geonim* toward midrash was not passed down to later generations. During the Middle Ages, for example, midrash came to occupy a central and significant place in Jewish scholarship. In his Introduction to the Commentary on the Mishna, Maimonides writes:

> Do not imagine that the midrashim brought in the Talmud are of little importance or of little value. They serve an important purpose, insofar as they include some profound allusions to

20. *Teshuvot HaGeonim Harkaby*, siman 353.
21. Rabbenu Hananel ben Hushiel (965–1055) was the first to write a commentary on the majority of the Babylonian Talmud. He was one of the greatest scholars in the early period of the *Rishonim*.

> wondrous matters, accessible to those who study these midrashim in depth. From them we understand something of the absolute, unsurpassed good, and they reveal some Godly matters, matters of truth, which these wise men concealed within them, and which have been sought by generations of philosophers.

Nevertheless, despite the value given to midrashim, the distinction between *derash* and *peshat* is still maintained, and the legitimacy of *peshat* as an independent level of interpretation in its own right is preserved. Indeed, the medieval biblical commentators maintained the distinction systematically, throughout their commentaries.

PESHAT COMMENTATORS IN FRANCE

As noted earlier, Rashi often incorporates midrashim in his biblical commentary. He was the first commentator to draw a clear distinction between commentary on the level of *peshat* and teachings on the level of *derash*. He sets forth his exegetical approach most concisely:

> There are many *midreshei aggada*, and our Sages have set them down and ordered them in Genesis Rabba and the other midrashic collections. My intention is only [to teach] the plain meaning of the text and such aggada that clarifies the words of the verses, so that each word is properly understood in context. (Rashi on Genesis 3:8)

Rashi sets himself a dual objective: to explain "the plain meaning of the text" and also to cite midrashic interpretations when they answer to the definition of "clarifying the words of the verses so that each word is properly understood." In so doing, Rashi implicitly expresses the view that there is aggada that belongs to a new category – teachings that do not match the plain meaning of the text. The distinction between them is not clear-cut; it is not always certain how Rashi selects the midrashim that he cites, in light of this criterion.[22] In any event, he often proposes alternate interpretations

22. On this issue, see Kamin's article; N. Leibowitz and M. Ahrend, *Perush Rashi LaTorah – Iyyunim BeShitato*, vol. 2 (Tel Aviv, 1990), 363–406; A. Grossman, *Emunot VeDeot*

for the text both in accordance with "the plain meaning" and in accordance with "its midrashic interpretation," and in many instances he notes explicitly that he is refraining from citing a *midrash aggada* that does not match the plain meaning of the text. Some examples include:

> There are *midreshei aggada* [on this matter], but they cannot be resolved with the plain meaning (Rashi on Gen. 3:22);
>
> There is a *midrash aggada*, but I seek only to address the plain meaning (Gen. 3:24);
>
> And there are *midreshei aggada* on this matter, but this is how the text is to be understood (Gen. 4:8);
>
> And there is a *midrash aggada*, yet this is how the text is to be understood (Gen. 19:15).

Rashi elaborates somewhat in explaining his approach at the beginning of *Parashat Va'era*. The verse reads,

> וָאֵרָא אֶל אַבְרָהָם אֶל יִצְחָק וְאֶל יַעֲקֹב בְּאֵל שַׁדָּי; וּשְׁמִי ה׳, לֹא נוֹדַעְתִּי לָהֶם וְגַם הֲקִמֹתִי אֶת בְּרִיתִי אִתָּם, לָתֵת לָהֶם אֶת אֶרֶץ כְּנָעַן.
>
> And I appeared to Abraham, to Isaac, and to Jacob, by [the Name] El Shadai, but My Name [the Tetragrammaton] I did not make known to them. And I also established My covenant with them, to give them the land of Canaan. (Ex. 6:3–4)

Rashi (commenting on verse 9) addresses the question of why mention is made here of the forefathers, and he cites the midrash (from Sanhedrin 111a):

BeOlamo Shel Rashi (Alon Shvut, 2008), 43–60; Y. Jacobs, "Peshutam shel Mikraot," *Shenaton LeḤeker HaMikra VeHaMizraḥ HaKadum* 22; E. Lawee, "Words Unfitly Spoken: Late Medieval Criticism of the Role of Midrash in Rashi's Commentary on the Torah," in *Between Rashi and Maimonides: Themes in Medieval Jewish Thought, Literature and Exegesis*, eds. E. Kanarfogel and M. Sokolow (New York, 2010), 401–30.

> Our Sages interpret this in connection with what is written previously, where Moses said, לָמָה הֲרֵעֹתָה לָעָם הַזֶּה, "Why have You dealt badly" (Ex. 5:22). The Holy One, blessed be He, said to him: "Alas for those who are gone and no more to be found! I should mourn the deaths of the forefathers, for many times I revealed Myself to them by the name of El Shadai, yet they did not say to Me: 'What is Your Name?' You say, [if the Jews question whether you are truly sent by God, and they ask,] וְאָמְרוּ לִי מַה שְּׁמוֹ, מָה אֹמַר אֲלֵהֶם, '"What is His Name?" – what shall I tell them?' (Ex. 3:13). When Abraham sought a burial plot for Sarah, he did not find one, until he was forced to purchase a plot for a great sum of money. Likewise, Isaac was challenged concerning the wells that he dug [but he did not question Me], and in the same way, Jacob purchased the piece of land, in order to have somewhere to pitch his tent (Gen. 33:19). Yet they did not question My character. You, on the other hand, ask, 'Why have You dealt badly…'" (Ex. 5:22).

However, Rashi addresses a difficulty with regard to this midrash:

> The midrash does not match the text, for several reasons: first, the verse does not say, "But they *did not ask* concerning My Name"; [rather, it says "I did not make it known to them"].… And furthermore, how does this understanding fit in with what comes next in the verse – וְגַם אֲנִי שָׁמַעְתִּי...לָכֵן אֱמֹר לִבְנֵי יִשְׂרָאֵל, "And also I have heard.… Therefore, say to the Children of Israel…" (Ex. 6:5–6)?

Rashi therefore establishes the following principle:

> Therefore I say that the verse should be explained in accordance with its plain meaning, each word being understood in its context, while the midrashic interpretation may be expounded upon, as it is written, הֲלוֹא כֹה דְבָרִי כָּאֵשׁ נְאֻם ה׳ וּכְפַטִּישׁ יְפֹצֵץ סָלַע, "Is My word not like fire, says the Lord, and like a hammer shattering the rock?" (Jer. 23:29) – i.e., God's word is like the splintering of a rock into many fragments.

With these words Rashi lays the foundations for the simultaneous parallel existence of different levels in biblical exegesis, and the legitimacy of independent exegesis on the level of *peshat*. His basic assumption is that the text is polysemous – that is, it contains multiple meanings, accessible through different levels and modes of interpretation, without one level cancelling out the significance of another. For this reason, the level of *peshat* has value and significance in its own right.

Rashi's commentary had a tremendous impact on his generation, and the *peshat* school of exegesis in France grew and flourished.[23] Prominent Jewish scholars of the late eleventh and twelfth centuries who wrote *peshat* commentaries include Rabbi Yosef Kara and Rashbam, whose approaches will be examined presently. However, it should first be noted that Rashi himself was aware of the processes that his generation had undergone in the return to a study of the plain level of the text – as evidenced by the testimony of his grandson, Rashbam, in his commentary at the beginning of *Parashat Vayeshev* (Gen. 37:2):

> Let those who love reason know and understand that which our Sages taught us: "A verse never departs from its plain meaning" (Shabbat 63a). It is still true that in essence, the Torah's purpose is to teach us and relate to us teachings, rules of conduct, and laws, which we derive from hints [hidden] in the plain meaning of Scripture, through superfluous wording, through the thirty-two principles of R. Eliezer the son of R. Yose the Galilean, or the thirteen principles of R. Yishmael.

---

23. For the reasons behind this expansion, see A. Grossman, "The School of Literal Jewish Exegesis in Northern France," in *Hebrew Bible / Old Testament: The History of Its Interpretation* I, 2, 321–71, especially 327–9; Touitou, 11–47, and idem, "Rashi's Commentary on Genesis 1–6 in the Context of Judeo-Christian Controversy," *HUCA* 61 (1990): 159–83, and "Rashi and His School: The Exegesis on the Halakhic Part of the Pentateuch in the Context of the Judeo-Christian Controversy," in *Bar-Ilan Studies in History*, vol. 4, ed. B. Albert et al. (Ramat Gan, 1995), 231–51. Both scholars note that the two principal factors were the twelfth-century renaissance and the increasing phenomenon of Jewish-Christian disputations. Grossman adds also the influence of the Judeo-Spanish heritage, with the gradual liberation of the Jews of northern France from subservience to German traditions.

> Due to their piety, the earliest scholars tended to devote their time to midrashic explanations, which are the essence of Torah; as a result, they never became attuned to the profundities of the plain meaning of Scripture.
>
> Furthermore, the Sages said, "Keep your children away from [too much] *higgayon*" (Berakhot 28b; Rashi there interprets the term as meaning biblical study). They also said, "Studying the Bible has only incomplete merit, but there is nothing more meritorious than studying Talmud" (Bava Metzia 33a). Accordingly, they never became entirely attuned to the plain meaning of Scriptural verses. As [Rabbi Kehana] says in Shabbat (63a), "I was eighteen years old and I had studied the entire Talmud, and I had never realized that 'a verse never departs from its plain meaning.'"
>
> Similarly, Rabbenu Shlomo, my mother's father, the great light of the exile, who wrote commentaries on Torah, *Nevi'im*, and *Ketuvim*, dedicated himself to explain the plain meaning of Scripture, and I, Shmuel, son of his son-in-law Meir, of blessed memory, argued with him, in his presence, and he conceded to me that if only he had the time, he would have written new [revised] commentaries based on the insights into the plain meaning of Scripture that are newly thought of day by day.[24]

Rashbam seeks to explain why it was that, until Rashi's time, Jews were not heavily involved in biblical commentary. In his view, since the *derashot* – the midrashic lessons derived from the text – represented the "essence of Torah," earlier commentators focused on those lessons, and neglected the study of the plain level, the *peshat,* of the text. Rashi represented a turning point: he awarded extensive attention to the plain meaning of the text in his commentaries on Tanakh. However, Rashi himself was aware that his exegesis was not the "last word" in the realm of *peshat*; he acknowledged that if he were to have time, he would indeed compose new commentaries, since "the plain meaning is renewed anew

24. Translation based on M. Lockshin, *Rabbi Samuel ben Meir's Commentary on Genesis: An Annotated Translation* (Lewiston, 1989), 240–42.

each day." In fact, there is evidence that, in certain places, Rashi indeed amended his commentary in light of Rashbam's comments.[25]

The *peshat* approach in biblical exegesis is set forth most clearly and unequivocally by Rashi's disciple and colleague, Rabbi Yosef Kara.[26] R. Kara (c. 1050–c. 1125) occupied himself with commentary on Tanakh and on liturgical poetry, and was among the *Rishonim* who upheld the importance of studying the plain level of the text. Rashi, who was slightly his senior, mentions him several times in his commentaries,[27] as does Rashbam.[28] R. Yosef Kara engaged most markedly in *peshat*, and expressed his opposition to approaches that supported interpretations deviating from the plain meaning of the text. The foundation of his view may be gleaned from the following (commentary on I Sam. 1:17):

> Know that when the prophetic text was written, it was written whole and complete, so that future generations would not stumble in it, and in its place it lacks nothing. There is no need to bring proofs from elsewhere, nor midrash, for the Torah was given whole – it was written whole and lacks nothing. The purpose of the midrashim proposed by the Sages is to glorify the Torah and to enhance it. But one who is not proficient in the plain meaning of the text, and inclines toward a midrashic interpretation of it, may be compared to one who is drowning in a river, being swept away by its waters, and he grabs whatever comes his way in order to save himself. Whereas had he paid attention to God's word, he would have sought the meaning of the text in its context, and would thereby have fulfilled that which is written: אִם תְּבַקְשֶׁנָּה

25. An example is cited by M. Sabbato, "Perush Rashbam LaTorah," *Maḥanayim* 3 (5753/1993): 123.
26. For a discussion of R. Yosef Kara and his exegetical approach, see A. Grossman, "The School of Literal Jewish Exegesis in Northern France," 346–55; concerning his *peshat* approach see G. Brin, *Meḥkarim BePerusho shel R. Yosef Kara* (Tel Aviv, 1990), 37–45.
27. For example, "So I heard from R. Yosef" (Rashi on Is. 64:3); "R. Yosef told me this, in the name of R. Menahem" (Rashi on Is. 10:24) – the reference here is to R. Menahem ben Helbo, the uncle of R. Yosef Kara. (For more about him, see Grossman, 331.)
28. For example, "This I heard from my friend R. Yosef Kara" (Rashbam on Gen. 37:13).

> כַּכָּסֶף וְכַמַּטְמוֹנִים תַּחְפְּשֶׂנָּה אָז תָּבִין יִרְאַת ה׳ וְדַעַת אֱלֹהִים תִּמְצָא, "If you seek it as you do silver, and search for it as for treasures, then you will understand the awe of the Lord, and attain knowledge of God" (Prov. 2:4–5).

Rabbi Kara argues that the interpretation of the biblical text must be based solely on the data that appear in the verses themselves; Tanakh is transmitted whole, with all the details required to be understood. Hence, his fierce opposition to the interpretation of verses based on information that is found only in midrash. R. Yosef Kara expresses himself in a similar vein elsewhere, too.[29] Consider the verse at the beginning of the Song of Deborah:

> ה׳ בְּצֵאתְךָ מִשֵּׂעִיר בְּצַעְדְּךָ מִשְּׂדֵה אֱדוֹם אֶרֶץ רָעָשָׁה גַּם שָׁמַיִם נָטָפוּ גַּם עָבִים נָטְפוּ מָיִם. הָרִים נָזְלוּ מִפְּנֵי ה׳ זֶה סִינַי מִפְּנֵי ה׳ אֱלֹהֵי יִשְׂרָאֵל.
>
> God, when You went out of Se'ir, marching out of the field of Edom, the earth trembled, and the heavens dripped; the clouds, too, dripped water. The mountains melted from before God; this Sinai, before the Lord God of Israel. (Judges 5:4–5)

R. Yosef Kara cites a midrash that interprets these verses as a reference to the day of the giving of the Torah: the nations of the world did not wish to receive the Torah, and "the entire world turned on its inhabitants... believing that [God] would return the entire world to its primordial chaos."[30] He goes on to comment:

29. We have already examined one example of his approach, in an earlier chapter, as part of our discussion of the identity of the author of the book of Samuel.
30. I have not found the source of this midrash. S. Epstein, in his *Perushei Rabbi Yosef Kara LeNevi'im Rishonim* (Jerusalem, 1973), 24, n. 2, writes: "See Avoda Zara 2b," but fails to note that the Gemara there is connected only in a most general way to the idea that God approached the other nations to give them the Torah, and they did not accept it; there is no reference at all there to the Song of Deborah. *Mikraot Gedolot HaKeter, Yehoshua-Shoftim* (Jerusalem, 1992), 107, is unfortunately even more misleading in this regard, since the reference there is simply to tractate Avoda Zara, without even the qualifying "see."

> This is the midrashic interpretation, but I am unable to reconcile this with the plain text in its context; this is not its plain meaning. Furthermore, the astonishing question is, what does this [verse, in its context,] have to do with the giving of the Torah? ...Moreover, it is not the practice of the prophets, in any of the twenty-four books [of Tanakh], to obscure their words in such a way that their meaning must be derived from an aggadic teaching.

Here, too, R. Yosef Kara's assumption is that all that is needed to understand a prophecy is to be found within the words of the prophecy itself. One cannot arrive at what the prophet means by relying on aggada that is not explicit in the text.

The verse, וַיְהִי לִתְקֻפוֹת הַיָּמִים וַתַּהַר חַנָּה וַתֵּלֶד בֵּן, "And in due course (*litekufot hayamim*) Hannah conceived, and she bore a son" (I Sam. 1:20), is interpreted by the Sages as a precise accounting of the period of Hannah's pregnancy, lasting six months and two days: "The minimum number of seasons [quarters] that can be referred to by the plural form '*tekufot*'[31] is two; and the minimum number of days that can be referred to by the plural form '*yamim*' is two" (Rosh HaShana 11a).

R. Yosef Kara, however, maintains that this expression simply means, "at that season, when Elkana was accustomed to going up to Shilo." He adds:

> I am aware that all those who uphold the aggada and the Talmud will scoff at this, for they will not abandon the teaching of the Sages in Rosh HaShana and in some other tractates, and they will follow their interpretation, but those who think will think on the proper path to establish the true meaning.

R. Yosef Kara is aware that his interpretation is likely to arouse opposition among scholars who are accustomed to reliance on aggada and the

31. According to *Ḥazal*, a "*tekufa*" (season, period of time) means a quarter of a year – i.e., three months.

Talmud, but he holds fast to his view that scholars of the *peshat* – "those who think" – will strive to understand the truth through study of the plain meaning of the text.

In his commentary on Isaiah 5:9, R. Yosef Kara takes his approach one step further:

> Incline your ear and make yourself subservient to the text. For each and every verse expounded by our Sages, may they rest in peace, although they teach a midrash about it, they ultimately say of it, "No verse loses its simple meaning." Thus, we have no better exegetical approach to the verse than its simple meaning.... And thus Solomon, king of Israel, said, הַט אָזְנְךָ וּשְׁמַע דִּבְרֵי חֲכָמִים וְלִבְּךָ תָּשִׁית לְדַעְתִּי, "Incline your ear and hear the words of the wise, and apply your heart to My knowledge" (Prov. 22:17) – meaning, even though one is commanded to ["incline one's ear" and] listen to the Sages, ultimately the intention is to "apply your heart to My knowledge." The verse does not say, "their [the Sages'] knowledge," but rather "My [God's] knowledge."

Here R. Yosef Kara asserts that interpretation of the text in accordance with *peshat* is not only a legitimate exegetical approach, but is in fact *preferable* to interpretations that turn to *derash*.[32]

32. A similar view is expressed by Rabbi Isaiah di Trani (the Younger), who lived in thirteenth-century Italy (for more about him see Y. Lipschitz [ed.], *Sanhedri Gedola V*, part II [Jerusalem, 1972], 5–10): "And they taught, 'The text never loses its plain meaning'; this is the essence. Of the midrashim that are expounded around it, some are essentially closer to the *peshat*, while others are [removed from the plain meaning] almost to the level of '*remez*'" (*Piskei R. Yeshayahu Aharon z"l*, Sanhedrin 11:7, Wertheimer edition [Jerusalem, 1994], 194; for more on his assertion here, see Elbaum, 96–104); "And the Torah Sages taught that 'the text never loses its plain meaning' – i.e., although any person is entitled to expound on the text in any matter that may be expounded.... Nevertheless, the plain meaning of the text is its essence, and this is the truth, for the text never loses its plain meaning" (*Kuntres HaRaayot leR. Yeshayahu Aharon z"l*, Sanhedrin 90a, Wertheimer edition, 91).

Let us now turn to the view of Rashbam,[33] one of the greatest of the biblical commentators.[34] Rashbam, too, asserted the independent status of exegesis on the basis of *peshat*, but, unlike R. Yosef Kara, he stated that the midrashic messages, rather than the *peshat* understanding, represented the essence of the Torah. For example, at the beginning of his commentary on the Torah, Rashbam writes:[35]

> Let those who think understand that all the words of our Sages, and their midrashic interpretations, are correct and true. And this is as we find in Tractate Shabbat (63a), "Yet I did not know that a verse cannot depart from its plain meaning." The essence of the laws and teachings are deduced from [seeming] superfluities in the text, or from linguistic peculiarities, which are apparent in the plain text, in such a way that the essence of the teaching may

---

33. R. Samuel b. Meir (c. 1080 – c. 1160), one of the early Tosafists, who authored commentaries on several tractates of the Talmud (including those printed in the Gemara, Bava Batra starting from 29a, and the tenth chapter of Pesaḥim). However, his principal contribution was in the area of biblical commentary, where he left his unique stamp on *peshat*. On Rashbam and his oeuvre, see Urbach, *Baalei HaTosafot*, vol. 1, 45–59; on his exegetical approach see E. Z. Melamed, *Mefarashei HaMikra – Darkeihem VeShitoteihem*, vol. 1 (Jerusalem, 1975), 449–514; Y. Z. Moskowitz, *Parshanut HaMikra LeDoroteiha* (Jerusalem, 1998), 52–65; S. Japhet, "The Tension between Rabbinic Legal Midrash and the 'Plain Meaning' ('*Peshat*') of the Biblical Text – an Unresolved Problem? In the Wake of Rashbam's Commentary on the Pentateuch," in *Sefer Moshe: The Moshe Weinfeld Jubilee Volume*, eds. Chaim Cohen et al. (Winona Lake, IN: Eisenbrauns, 2004); M. Lockshin, "Rashbam as a 'Literary' Exegete," in *With Reverence for the Word*, ed. J. D. McAuliffe et al. (Oxford, 2003), 83–91; J. Jacobs, "Rashbam's Major Principles of Interpretation as Deduced from a Manuscript Fragment Discovered in 1984," *Revue des Etudes Juives* 170, 3–4 (2011): 443–63.
34. See, for example, A. Hakham, "Perushei Rabbi Avraham ben Ezra LaMikra," *Maḥanayim* 3, who notes that "a select group of commentators has made its mark on the national consciousness"; study of their commentaries "is considered mandatory for any Jew seeking to study Tanakh in-depth." He includes within this group Rashi, Rashbam, Ibn Ezra, Radak, and Nahmanides.
35. He adopts a more strident tone in his commentary on Genesis 37:2, as cited above: "The essence of the Torah comes to teach and make known to us – through allusion in the literal text – aggada, and principles, and laws.... The earlier scholars, owing to their piety, were inclined to focus on the lessons to be derived, which are the essence."

> be deduced from it. For example, תוֹלְדוֹת הַשָּׁמַיִם וְהָאָרֶץ בְּהִבָּרְאָם, "These are the generations of the heavens and the earth when they were created (*behibaram*)" (Gen. 2:4) – our Sages understand the seemingly superfluous word *behibaram* as an allusion to Abraham [whose name is made up of the same letters].

Both Rashbam and R. Yosef Kara base their opinions on the teaching of the Sages that "the text never departs from its plain meaning," but they understand this statement in different ways. According to R. Yosef Kara, it is a testament to the superiority of *peshat* over *derash*, while according to Rashbam, it is simply a stamp of legitimacy granted to study the *peshat*. In addition, while R. Yosef Kara regards the *derash* as separate from the text, according to Rashbam, it represents a certain level – even a central dimension – of the text itself, arising from "[seeming] superfluities in the text, or from linguistic peculiarities," in keeping with the principle of polysemy established by Rashi, his grandfather. In any event, both commentators share a fundamental approach that draws a distinction between *peshat* and *derash*, and views the study of *peshat* as a legitimate realm of study in its own right.

Consider a few examples of the many instances in which Rashbam rejects a midrashic interpretation, offering instead an interpretation on the level of *peshat*.[36]

1. Concerning the verse וַיֹּסֶף אַבְרָהָם וַיִּקַּח אִשָּׁה וּשְׁמָהּ קְטוּרָה, "Avraham once again took a wife, and her name was Ketura" (Gen. 25:1), Rashi cites the midrashic teaching that Ketura was Hagar.[37] Rashbam comments laconically that "according to the plain text, this was not Hagar." Presumably, what he means is that, surely, were the Torah referring to the person who is already known by the name of Hagar using a different name, it would also explicitly mention the name that is already known.

36. Melamed (see above), 458–60, presents a detailed list of examples.
37. Genesis Rabba 68, 12, Theodor-Albeck edition, 788–89.

2. Concerning the verse וְהִנֵּה מַלְאֲכֵי אֱלֹהִים עֹלִים וְיֹרְדִים בּוֹ, "And behold, angels of God were ascending and descending upon it" (Gen. 28:12), Rashi cites the midrash:[38]

> First "ascending" and then "descending" [although seemingly the order should be reversed, since we would expect the angels to emerge first from the heavens]: the angels who had accompanied him in the Land of Israel do not depart from the land, so they ascend heavenward, and the angels appointed over areas outside the Land of Israel descended, in order to accompany him."

Rashbam comments, "On the level of *peshat*, there is nothing to be deduced from the fact that 'ascending' is mentioned before 'descending,' for it is a matter of normal manners [*derekh eretz*] to mention ascent prior to descent."

The term "*derekh eretz*" is often invoked by Rashbam as a means of clarifying the plain meaning of the text, in the sense of "what people usually do," social manners, social reality, or laws of nature.[39] Since a person would usually say "ascending and descending," no special attention should be paid to the fact that the Torah describes the movement of the angels in this order.

3. Following the deaths of Nadav and Avihu, Moses tells Aaron, הוּא אֲשֶׁר דִּבֶּר ה׳ לֵאמֹר בִּקְרֹבַי אֶקָּדֵשׁ וְעַל פְּנֵי כָל הָעָם אֶכָּבֵד וַיִּדֹּם אַהֲרֹן, "This is that of which God spoke, saying, 'I shall be sanctified among those who come near to Me, and before all the people shall I be glorified'" (Lev. 10:3). The commentators try to ascertain what statement of God Moses is referring to here. Rashi, citing the midrash,[40] maintains that this is a reference to the conclusion of the command concerning the building of the Mishkan, the Sanctuary: וְנֹעַדְתִּי שָׁמָּה לִבְנֵי יִשְׂרָאֵל וְנִקְדַּשׁ בִּכְבֹדִי, "And I shall meet there with the Children of Israel, and it shall be sanctified through My glory" (Ex. 29:43). He adds:

38. Genesis Rabba 61, 4, Theodor-Albeck edition, 61.
39. See Touitou, 31.
40. Leviticus Rabba 12, 2, Margaliot edition, 257.

> Do not read "*bikhevodi*" ("through My glory"), but rather "*bimekhubadai*" ("through My honored ones"). Moses said to Aaron: "Aaron, my brother, I knew that the Mishkan would be sanctified through those especially appointed by God, but I believed that it would be either through myself or through you. Now I see that they were greater than me or you."

Rashbam rejects this interpretation on logical grounds: "This is not in accordance with the plain meaning. Would God have announced to Moses, 'Make Me a Sanctuary' – and on that very day [that the Sanctuary is ready] the greatest among you will die?" He therefore proposes a different understanding of the verse.[41]

Although Rashbam accepts the importance of *derash* as a dimension of Torah in its own right – perhaps even as the central dimension – this does not prevent him from expressing sharp criticism of interpretations that are based on *derash*, when he believes they contradict the meaning of the text. In several places, Rashbam attacks such interpretations, as well as the commentators preceding him who proposed them – including even Rashi. For example, concerning the verse, דָּן יָדִין עַמּוֹ כְּאַחַד שִׁבְטֵי יִשְׂרָאֵל, "Dan shall judge his people, as one of the tribes of Israel" (Gen. 49:16), Rashi comments (basing himself on the midrash):[42] "It

41. He proposes that what Moses is saying is that Aaron should continue his service despite his mourning: "It is through the service of the high priest who is close to Me, serving Me, that I wish to be sanctified, and that My Name and My service not be profaned." He explains: "For the verse reads, וְהַכֹּהֵן הַגָּדוֹל מֵאֶחָיו, 'And he who is the high priest among his brethren … אֶת רֹאשׁוֹ לֹא יִפְרָע וּבְגָדָיו לֹא יִפְרֹם, he shall not allow his hair to grow long, nor rend his clothes … וּמִן הַמִּקְדָּשׁ לֹא יֵצֵא וְלֹא יְחַלֵּל אֵת מִקְדַּשׁ אֱלֹהָיו, nor shall he depart from the Sanctuary, nor shall he profane the Sanctuary of his God'" (Lev. 21:10–12). Thus, if the high priest does not depart from the Sanctuary [even under such circumstances as have befallen Aaron], he has thereby sanctified God. And [this interpretation is possible because although these specific commands to Aaron appear later on,] there is no chronological order in the units of the Torah. Therefore – 'Do not abandon the divine service, for you are the high priest; do not depart from the Sanctuary and do not profane it; rather, let God and His service be sanctified through you.'"

42. Genesis Rabba 98, 14, Theodor-Albeck edition, 1265.

was concerning Samson that [Jacob] uttered this prophecy." Rashbam comments:

> He who interprets this as a reference to Samson did not possess a thorough grasp of the plain meaning of the text. Would Jacob have meant to prophesy here about a single individual, who fell into the hands of the Philistines, and had his eyes gouged by them, and met his death together with the Philistines – i.e., in such a negative vein? Heaven forefend.

Elsewhere, he writes:

> One who wishes to arrive at the essence of the plain meaning of the text here should think about this interpretation that I have proposed, for my predecessors did not understand it at all.... Those who interpret [the text here] in reference to other matters are completely misguided. (Rashbam on Ex. 3:11)

Furthermore, in several places, Rashbam labels the midrashic interpretations offered by his predecessors as "*hevel*" (nonsense).[43]

The commentaries of Rabbi Yosef Kara and Rashbam influenced later sages of France, including Rabbi Joseph b. Isaac Bekhor Shor,[44] who proposed dozens of *peshat* interpretations that were alternatives to the midrashim taught by the Sages – even where Rashi and Rashbam had not done so, as well as Rabbi Hizkiya ben Manoah, in his commentary *Ḥizkuni*.[45]

---

43. See his commentaries on Genesis 1:1; 37:2 (immediately after the excerpt cited above, concerning the arguments between him and Rashi, which serves as an introduction to his criticism of Rashi's interpretation there); Gen. 45:28; Lev. 26:21; Deut. 15:18.
44. R. Joseph b. Isaac Bekhor Shor of Orleans was a disciple of Rabbenu Tam and one of the twelfth-century Tosafists of northern France. For more about him, see Grossman, 367–69, and Urbach, 132–42; on his exegetical approach in the context of *peshat*, see Y. Nevo, *Bekhor Shor – Perushei HaTorah*, Introduction, 4–5.
45. R. Hizkiya ben Manoah lived in France in the second half of the thirteenth century (c. 1250–1310). For more about his commentary, see Rabbi Chavel's introduction to *Perushei HaḤizkuni Al HaTorah* (Jerusalem, 2006), 5–13; Y. Ofer, "Perush HaḤizkuni LaTorah VeGilgulav," *Megadim* 8 (5749/1989): 69–83; S. Japhet, "Perush

PESHAT COMMENTATORS IN SPAIN AND IN PROVENCE

Biblical commentary on the level of *peshat* was also prevalent among the *Rishonim* of Spain and Provence, including Ibn Ezra, Radak, and Nahmanides. Indeed, the approaches of these prominent commentators in this regard merit a brief review.

Rabbi Abraham ibn Ezra[46] was a commentator who adopted a clear and explicit path with regard to the significance of *peshat* interpretations of the text.[47] He addresses the subject briefly in the introduction to his commentary on the Torah: "The way of *peshat* does not step aside for *derash*, for 'there are seventy faces to the Torah'" (that is, the Torah can be interpreted in a myriad of ways).[48] Throughout his commentary, he rejects interpretations that represent *derash*. The following are some examples:

HaḤizkuni LaTorah – LiDemuto Shel HaḤibbur U'LeMatarato," in *Sefer HaYovel LeRav Mordekhai Breuer*, ed. M. Bar Asher, vol. 1 (Jerusalem, 1992), 91–111. For more about his exegetical approach with regard to *peshat*, see Japhet, 107–10.

46. Ibn Ezra (c. 1089–1164) was a scholar whose knowledge was wide-ranging and diverse. In addition to being a biblical commentator he was also a poet, grammarian, philosopher, translator, astronomer, and astrologer. For more about his exegetical approach, see U. Simon, "Abraham Ibn Ezra," *Hebrew Bible / Old Testament* I, 2 (2000), 377–87, and the essays collected in *Rabbi Abraham Ibn Ezra: Studies in the Writings of a Twelfth-Century Jewish Polymath*, eds. I. Twersky and J. Harris (Cambridge, 1993).

47. It should be noted that unlike Rashbam – who, as we have seen, maintained that *derash* has its basis in the text, being deduced from "[seeming] superfluities in the text, or from linguistic peculiarities," Ibn Ezra held the view that the text had one single meaning. He maintained that not all the information necessary for the proper understanding was to be found in the text itself (unlike the view of R. Yosef Kara), and that the supplementary data is transmitted through the Oral Law. Nevertheless, in his view the information transmitted orally is not derived from the text – even if the *midrash aggada* appears to derive the information from the text – since the midrashic method is not actually the source for the information that the Sages convey. We will discuss the significance of this view in terms of *midreshei halakha* in the next chapter.

48. The expression "seventy faces to the Torah" was popular among biblical commentators from the Middle Ages onwards, although it does not appear in the talmudic literature. For the history of this expression see H. Mack, "Shiv'im Panim LaTorah: LeMahalakho shel Bitui," in *Sefer HaYovel LeRav Mordekhai Breuer*, vol. 2, 449–62.

1. Commenting on the verse, וַיִּשְׁמַע אַבְרָם כִּי נִשְׁבָּה אָחִיו וַיָּרֶק אֶת חֲנִיכָיו יְלִידֵי בֵיתוֹ שְׁמֹנָה עָשָׂר וּשְׁלֹשׁ מֵאוֹת, "Abram heard that his brother had been taken captive, and he led forth his trained servants, born in his own house – three hundred and eighteen [of them]" (Gen. 14:14), Rashi cites the midrash (Nedarim 32b) that this is a reference to Eliezer alone, since the *gematriya* (numerical value of the name) of "Eliezer" is 318. Ibn Ezra understands the verse literally, as a reference to "his disciples, whom he had trained regularly in warfare, although they have not previously been mentioned." He adds, "And the [interpretation based on] the numerical value of the name 'Eliezer' is arrived at through *derash*, for the text does not speak in *gematriya*, since anyone wishing to interpret any name in either a positive or negative light [on this basis] is able to do so; hence, a name should be treated as just that."[49]

2. Concerning the verse, וְאַבְרָהָם זָקֵן בָּא בַּיָּמִים וַה׳ בֵּרַךְ אֶת אַבְרָהָם בַּכֹּל, "And Abraham was old, advanced in age, and God had blessed Abraham with everything (*bakol*)" (Gen. 24:1), the Gemara cites an opinion that Abraham had a daughter whose name was "*Bakol*" (בַּכֹּל) (Bava Batra 16b). Ibn Ezra explains the verse in its literal sense, as meaning that God had blessed Abraham "with long life, and wealth, and honor, and children, and this is all that a person desires." He adds, "And as for the midrashic teaching that 'Bakol' was the name of his daughter – [were this indeed indicated by the text,] it would require the addition of a prepositional '*bet*.'" In other words, the teaching does not sit well with the language of the verse; if this were the intention, it would read, "God had blessed Abraham with *bakol* (*be-bakol*)."

3. Jacob swears an oath in Beit El: וְכֹל אֲשֶׁר תִּתֶּן לִי עַשֵּׂר אֲעַשְּׂרֶנּוּ לָךְ, "And all that You give me, I will surely tithe for You" (Gen. 28:22). The Sages teach that Jacob set aside his son Levi, too, as a tithe – as one of the first ten sons born to him.[50] Here, too, Ibn Ezra understands

49. Concerning Ibn Ezra's negative view of *gematriya* as an exegetical approach unconnected to the plain meaning of the text, see A. Mondshein, "LeYaḥaso Shel Ibn Ezra El HaShimush HaParshani BeMidat HaGematriya," *Te'uda* 8 (5752/1992): 137–62.

50. Genesis Rabba 70, 7, Theodor-Albeck edition, 804.

the verse in the plain sense: "[This means,] to deduct a tithe of all the wealth that You give me, to give it to whoever is worthy to receive it in honor of God." He adds, "As for the midrashic teaching that Levi was set aside as one-tenth [of his sons] – nowhere in the Torah do we find that a person offers a tithe from among his children; tithes are taken only from cattle and sheep and produce."

Sometimes, Ibn Ezra draws a distinction between details that appear in a midrash as part of a conceptual or symbolic idea, and details that have their source in historical tradition and are therefore binding even when they do not match the plain meaning of the text.[51] Other times, Ibn Ezra expresses his reservations with regard to an interpretation that represents *derash*, but declares that if the interpretation has become an accepted tradition, he withdraws his reservation. The following are some examples:

1. וַיָּמָת הָרָן עַל פְּנֵי תֶּרַח אָבִיו בְּאֶרֶץ מוֹלַדְתּוֹ בְּאוּר כַּשְׂדִּים, "Haran died before his father, Terah, in the land of his birth, in Ur Kasdim" (Gen. 11:28). Ibn Ezra understands "Ur Kasdim" literally, as the name of a place located in a valley. With regard to midrashim about Abraham in his youth, prior to God's revelation to him, he adds: "The Sages taught that [this alludes to the fact that] Abraham was cast into a fiery furnace. This is not indicated in the text, but if it is an accepted tradition, we accept it as we do the words of Torah."
2. Ibn Ezra addresses the question of Isaac's age at the time of his binding:

51. Concerning *derash* as an expression of ideas on different levels, the following is a loose translation of Ibn Ezra's rhyming words at the beginning of the introduction to his commentary on Lamentations: "There are many diverse types of *midrashim*: some are esoteric riddles, secrets, and parables; others come to offer support for weary hearts with profound teachings; others still come to train the feeble [in faith] and to fill those who are empty [of knowledge]. Therefore the [plain] meaning of the verses may be viewed as the body, while the *midrashim* are like the garments that clothe it – some sheer as silk, others coarse as sackcloth. The path of *peshat* is the body, with its specific wording and its laws, and hence the ancient teaching [of the Sages] that 'the text is [to be understood] in accordance with its plain meaning.'"

> Our sages taught that Isaac was thirty-seven years old when he was bound upon the altar. If this represents an accepted tradition, we accept it. According to reason, however, it seems improbable, for [if so] it is proper that Isaac's righteousness should be apparent, and his reward should be double that of his father, for he give himself willingly to be slaughtered, but the text says nothing about [this act of supreme religious devotion on the part of] Isaac (Gen. 22:4).

On the basis of this logic, Ibn Ezra rules out the possibility that Isaac could already have been an adult, for the text notes explicitly that this was a test for Abraham, not for Isaac. However, he notes that if this is indeed an accepted tradition, he accepts it. Ibn Ezra then offers his own opinion on the matter:

> It seems reasonable that he was close to the age of thirteen, and his father forced him and bound him against his will. This is evidenced in the fact that his father hid this secret [the object of their journey] from him, saying, "God will provide Himself a lamb" – for had he told him, "You yourself will be the sacrifice," he probably would have fled.

3. The Sages teach that the Jewish people were surrounded by seven clouds during their wanderings in the wilderness, since the word "*anan*" (cloud) appears seven times in the text.[52] Ibn Ezra maintains, on the basis of the plain text, that there were only the pillar of fire and the pillar of cloud that are mentioned in the verses (Ex. 14:24 and elsewhere), but adds, "Thus, there are these two alternating pillars over the Mishkan, but if it is an accepted tradition that there were clouds of glory, we relinquish our view and rely on the tradition" (Ibn Ezra in his long commentary, Ex. 15:22).

---

52. *Mekhilta DeRabbi Yishmael, Beshalaḥ, Petiḥta LeMasekhta DeVayeḥi,* Horowitz-Rabin edition, 80.

Even when Ibn Ezra acknowledges the possibility that the midrashic teaching rests on accepted tradition, however, he does not refrain from proposing different interpretations of the text, in accordance with its plain meaning. It is an approach that he regards as exegetically preferable – as long as it is not conclusively proven that the details introduced in the midrash are indeed accepted tradition.

Let us turn now to the well-known commentary of Nahmanides on the Torah.[53] This commentary is unique and also revolutionary in many respects, including its integration of kabbalistic teachings. For the purposes of discussion, it should be noted that Nahmanides was more consistent than any other commentator in distinguishing between *peshat* and *derash*, usually by stating, "*al derekh hapeshat*" (namely, that the interpretation in question reflects the plain meaning of the text) – an expression that he uses some 160 times. In the vast majority of cases, Nahmanides cites the *peshat* interpretation as an alternative to the midrash, and in dozens of instances he does so after noting some difficulty in the *derash* (although he usually also tries to resolve the verse in accordance with the midrashic teaching). The following are some examples.

1. The commentators debate what causes Isaac to suspect Jacob, who is dressed up as Esau, and to demand: גְּשָׁה נָּא וַאֲמֻשְׁךָ בְּנִי, הַאַתָּה זֶה בְּנִי עֵשָׂו אִם לֹא, "Draw near, I pray you, that I may feel you, my son, whether you are really my son Esau, or not" (Gen. 27:21). Rashi, based on a midrash, explains that it surprised Isaac that "Esau" made reference to God: "Isaac said to himself, Esau does not usually mention God, but here he said, 'Because the Lord your God sent me good speed'" (Gen. 27:20).[54] Nahmanides questions this interpretation, pointing out, "But Esau was not viewed as

53. Rabbi Moses ben Nahman (Nahmanides, Spain, c. 1194 – c. 1270) is regarded as one of the greatest Jewish thinkers of all time. He authored commentaries on the Torah, some parts of Tanakh, and many tractates of Talmud. He also authored works in the spheres of halakha, kabbala, and Jewish philosophy. For more about his exegetical approach, see Y. Elman, "Moses ben Nahman/Nahmanides," in *Hebrew Bible / Old Testament* I, 2 (2000), 416–32; Melamed, vol. II, 937–1021; Moskowitz, 98–116.
54. The source of the midrash is Genesis Rabba 65, 19, Theodor-Albeck edition, 732.

wicked [that is, someone who lacks a consciousness of God] by his father!" He immediately offers an explanation that could resolve this question:

> Perhaps he thought to himself that since Esau was a man of the field, whose mind was trained on hunting, he avoided mentioning God's name for fear that he might come to utter it inadvertently in a place that was not clean. In the eyes of his father, this [habit of not mentioning God's name] would be viewed [in a positive light,] as a sign of Esau's fear of Heaven.

Nevertheless, Ramban offers an alternative interpretation: "According to the plain meaning, this [suspicion] would arise because of the sound of his voice." Indeed, this is supported by Isaac's words: הַקֹּל קוֹל יַעֲקֹב, וְהַיָּדַיִם יְדֵי עֵשָׂו, "The voice is the voice of Jacob, while the hands are the hands of Esau" (Gen. 27:22).

2. Following the story of Joseph and Potiphar's wife: וַיְהִי כִשְׁמֹעַ אֲדֹנָיו אֶת דִּבְרֵי אִשְׁתּוֹ אֲשֶׁר דִּבְּרָה אֵלָיו לֵאמֹר, כַּדְּבָרִים הָאֵלֶּה עָשָׂה לִי עַבְדֶּךָ וַיִּחַר אַפּוֹ, "And it was, when his master heard the words of his wife, which she spoke to him, saying, 'After the manner of these things (*kadevarim ha'eleh*) your servant did to me'" (Gen. 39:19). Rashi cites the midrashic teaching:[55] "It was during intercourse that she said this to him, and this is the meaning of her words, 'After the manner of these things your servant did to me' – i.e., engaging in intercourse like this." Here, too, Nahmanides questions:

> But Joseph's master was a eunuch, and his wife had married him when he was young.... Moreover, how is it possible that she would have implicated herself, and made herself loathsome in the eyes of her husband, telling him that she had engaged in sexual relations – whether under duress or willingly? For he would surely kill her: Why did she then not cry out at the beginning, and flee, as she ultimately did?

55. Genesis Rabba 87, 9, Theodor-Albeck edition, 1074.

Again Nahmanides tries to answer his own question: "Perhaps what [the Sages] meant by 'after the manner of these things' is other acts of sexual immorality, not actual intercourse." Nevertheless, he also offers an explanation on the level of *peshat*: "According to the *peshat* no such explanation is necessary, for the letter *kaf* (in the expression '*kadevarim ha'eleh*') need not imply a comparison to something else; it simply means, 'these things.'"

3. When Moses rebukes the Hebrew man striving with his fellow, the man retorts, מִי שָׂמְךָ לְאִישׁ שַׂר וְשֹׁפֵט עָלֵינוּ הַלְהָרְגֵנִי אַתָּה אֹמֵר כַּאֲשֶׁר הָרַגְתָּ אֶת הַמִּצְרִי, "Who made you a prince and judge over us? Do you intend [literally, 'say'] to kill me, as you killed the Egyptian?" (Ex. 2:14). Rashi cites the midrash, "From here we learn that Moses had killed the Egyptian by uttering God's name."[56] Nahmanides asks, "If this is so, who told the Hebrew aggressor that Moses had killed him?" To this, he proposes the possible answer:

> Perhaps Moses had laid a hand upon him and then cursed him in God's name; this would explain why the text states, "He smote the Egyptian" Or perhaps when he fell dead before him, Moses was afraid that he would be reported, so he buried him in the sand, and [the Hebrew man] saw him doing so, and knew that he was the cause [of the man's death], or assumed that he had killed him with a sword, for he saw only the burial.

Once again, he proposes an alternative interpretation:

> But on the plain level of the text, when one says, "Do you *say* to do such and such," it means, "do you *intend* to," for "saying" sometimes refers to one's inner thoughts.... But here there is no need for such an explanation, for he says, "Who made you a prince and judge over us?" – i.e., is it because you seek to kill me, as you killed the Egyptian, that you rebuke me and say, "Why do you smite your fellow?"

---

56. Exodus Rabba 1, 30, Shinan edition, 91.

We see from these examples that Nahmanides endeavors to explain the midrashic interpretation in such a way as to reconcile it with the text. Like Rashi and Rashbam, he does not regard *derash* as a form of exegesis that is not intended to match the text. At the same time, Nahmanides tries to explain the verses on the level of *peshat*, even where he is able to reconcile the midrashic teaching. He expresses this guiding principle himself:

> However, since Rashi sometimes takes pains, after citing midrashim, to explain the plain meaning of the text, he thereby permitted us to do the same, for there are "seventy faces to the Torah," and there are many midrashim that are not unanimous among the Sages. (Nahmanides on Genesis 8:4)

Nahmanides continues the same principle that Ibn Ezra upheld – the "seventy aspects of the Torah," adding that, even among the midrashim of the Sages, there are many disagreements, which is why midrash should not be viewed as the single, necessary interpretation.

Moving on from Spain leads to the greatest of the Provencal commentators – Radak.[57] Radak cites many midrashim, as he acknowledges in the introduction to his commentary on the Early Prophets: "I will also bring some midrashim, for those who enjoy midrashim." However, he too notes the need to draw a distinction between *peshat* and *derash*, and rejects midrashic interpretations that do not match the plain meaning of the text. Consider some examples:

57. R. David Kimhi (1160–1235) was a major biblical commentator and one of the greatest of Hebrew grammarians. He is most famous for his commentaries on the Prophets and Writings, which appear in *Mikra'ot Gedolot* editions, but Radak also wrote a commentary on Genesis which has been widely disseminated over the past generation in the wake of its inclusion in the *Torat Ḥayim* edition (published by Mosad HaRav Kook). Concerning Radak and his exegetical approach, see Melamed, vol. 2, 719–932; Moskowitz, 84–97; M. Cohen, "The Qimhi family" in *Hebrew Bible / Old Testament* I, 2 (2000), 396–415; Y. Berger, "Radak's Commentary to Chronicles and the Development of his Exegetical Programme," *Journal of Jewish Studies* 57, 1 (2006): 80–98; N. Grunhaus, *The Challenge of Received Tradition: Dilemmas of Interpretation in Radak's Biblical Commentaries* (Oxford, 2013).

1. In the chapter on David's valiant men:

וַיִּתְאַוֶּה דָוִד וַיֹּאמַר מִי יַשְׁקֵנִי מַיִם מִבּאר בֵּית לֶחֶם אֲשֶׁר בַּשָּׁעַר. וַיִּבְקְעוּ שְׁלֹשֶׁת הַגִּבֹּרִים בְּמַחֲנֵה פְלִשְׁתִּים וַיִּשְׁאֲבוּ מַיִם מִבֹּאר בֵּית לֶחֶם אֲשֶׁר בַּשַּׁעַר וַיִּשְׂאוּ וַיָּבִאוּ אֶל דָּוִד וְלֹא אָבָה לִשְׁתּוֹתָם וַיַּסֵּךְ אֹתָם לַה'.

David longed, and he said, "Who will give me water to drink from the well of Bethlehem, which is by the gate?" And the three warriors broke through the camp of the Philistines, and drew water out of the well of Bethlehem, which was by the gate, and they took it and brought it to David. But he would not drink it, and he poured it out to God. (II Sam. 23:15–16)

In his commentary on these verses, Radak discusses the following midrash, found in Bava Kamma 60b:

> That which our Sages taught in this regard is most puzzling.... They interpreted the words, "Who will give me water to drink?" in a metaphorical sense, equating water with Torah.... Thus, the expression, "Who will give me water?" means that he had a halakhic question that he needed to ask of the Sanhedrin, who were in Bethlehem.... The halakha concerned a plot of a field full of lentils and barley... and David asked if it was permissible for him to set fire to the sacks of lentils, with the intention of burning the Philistines who were hiding among them. They answered him, "It is generally forbidden for one to save himself through the destruction of property belonging to someone else, but you are a king, and a king may break through [private fields] to make a road for himself, and nobody may prevent him from doing so." And the meaning of the words "But David would not drink" is that he did not quote this teaching in the name of the three [warriors], for he said: "It has been conveyed to me from the court of Samuel in Ramah that anyone who is ready to die for words of Torah – one does not quote him on matters of halakha."

Radak then goes on to comment:

> But this is very far from the plain meaning of the verses, which recount the story of David's valiant men.... And the text recounts the brave acts of each of these three men in the beginning, and what the three later did in bringing water. There was no halakhic question concerning a field, rather, there was fierce battle, until the Israelites fled from before the Philistines, as recorded in the text.... In all of this, what one should understand is the plain meaning of the text, as it stands.

Indeed, this is a rare case where the Sages' teaching includes wide-ranging elaboration that deviates very far from the plain meaning of the text, and Radak expresses himself quite sharply. Nevertheless, Radak adopts the same approach even in instances where the midrash is less removed from the simple meaning of the text.

2. In Joshua (5:14), Joshua encounters God's angel in Jericho, and the angel says: כִּי אֲנִי שַׂר צְבָא ה' עַתָּה בָאתִי, "But I am captain of the host of God; I am now come." The Sages understand this as meaning that he had come to rebuke the Jews:

> He [the angel] said to him, "You had already done away with the daily sacrifice offered at twilight; now you have done away with Torah study!" He [Joshua] replied, "For which of these [sins] have you come?" He answered, "I am *now* come [i.e., because of the latter sin]." Therefore we read immediately thereafter, "And Joshua tarried that night in the midst of the valley (*emek*)."[58] Rabbi Yoḥanan taught: "This teaches that he tarried that night in the depths (*omkah*) of halakha." (Megilla 3a–b)

Radak interprets the words of the angel in accordance with their plain meaning: "'I am now come' – at the moment that you saw me,

58. The verse in this form does not exist in the Masoretic version; it is a combination of two separate verses, as Radak notes in his words cited below.

which is not what happens in the case of humans. This was meant to convince Joshua that he was in fact an angel." Radak then goes on to quote the midrash, but expresses reservations:

> But this midrash is far removed [from the plain meaning of the text], for the time of war is not a time for Torah study; furthermore, the verse "And Joshua tarried" is located far from this verse, in the context of the battle against Ai.

Radak also adds a further sharp comment:

> Furthermore, whoever wrote this midrash was mistaken concerning the verse "And he tarried," for he confused two different verses: the verse that starts "Joshua tarried (*vayalen*)" – וַיָּלֶן יְהוֹשֻׁעַ בַּלַּיְלָה הַהוּא בְּתוֹךְ הָעָם – ends with the words, "amongst the people" (Josh. 8:9); while a different verse reads, וַיֵּלֶךְ יְהוֹשֻׁעַ בַּלַּיְלָה הַהוּא בְּתוֹךְ הָעֵמֶק, "Joshua went (*vayelekh*) that night into the midst of the valley" (Josh. 8:13).[59]

3. Before crossing the Jordan, Joshua tells the people:

> וַיֹּאמֶר יְהוֹשֻׁעַ אֶל בְּנֵי יִשְׂרָאֵל גֹּשׁוּ הֵנָּה וְשִׁמְעוּ אֶת דִּבְרֵי ה׳ אֱלֹהֵיכֶם. וַיֹּאמֶר יְהוֹשֻׁעַ בְּזֹאת תֵּדְעוּן כִּי אֵל חַי בְּקִרְבְּכֶם וְהוֹרֵשׁ יוֹרִישׁ מִפְּנֵיכֶם אֶת הַכְּנַעֲנִי וְאֶת הַחִתִּי וְאֶת הַחִוִּי וְאֶת הַפְּרִזִּי וְאֶת הַגִּרְגָּשִׁי וְהָאֱמֹרִי וְהַיְבוּסִי. הִנֵּה אֲרוֹן הַבְּרִית אֲדוֹן כָּל הָאָרֶץ עֹבֵר לִפְנֵיכֶם בַּיַּרְדֵּן. וְעַתָּה קְחוּ לָכֶם שְׁנֵי עָשָׂר אִישׁ מִשִּׁבְטֵי יִשְׂרָאֵל אִישׁ אֶחָד אִישׁ אֶחָד לַשָּׁבֶט. וְהָיָה כְּנוֹחַ כַּפּוֹת רַגְלֵי הַכֹּהֲנִים נֹשְׂאֵי אֲרוֹן ה׳ אֲדוֹן כָּל הָאָרֶץ בְּמֵי הַיַּרְדֵּן מֵי הַיַּרְדֵּן יִכָּרֵתוּן הַמַּיִם הַיֹּרְדִים מִלְמָעְלָה וְיַעַמְדוּ נֵד אֶחָד.

> Come here, and hear the words of the Lord your God.... Hereby shall you know that the living God is among you, and

59. The *Tosafot* (Megilla 3a, "*vayalen*"), propose a solution to this problem that does not assume a mistaken reading on the part of the author of the midrash: "It is the style of the Talmud to abbreviate verses and to combine them." For more on this instance see R. Margaliot, *HaMikra VeHaMesora* (Jerusalem, 1989), 11–12; D. Rosenthal, "Ḥazal VeḤilufei Nusaḥ BaMikra," in Y. Zakovitch and A. Rofe (eds.), *Sefer Yitzchak Aryeh Zeligman* (Jerusalem, 1983), 414–15.

> that He will surely drive out from before you the Kenaani.... Behold, the Ark of the Covenant of the Lord of all the earth passes before you into the Jordan.... And it shall be, when the soles of the feet of the priests who bear the Ark ... shall rest ... then the water of the Jordan shall be cut off: those waters that come down from above, and they shall stand in a heap. (Josh. 3:9–13)

Radak interprets, in accordance with the plain meaning, that the words "hereby shall you know" refer to what follows:

> The meaning of this phrase is explained – that the Ark will pass before them and the waters of the Jordan will be cut off. Through this great sign they will know that God is in their midst, and will drive out the nations from before them.

Afterwards, he cites the midrashic teaching that these words refer to what the text had mentioned previously, with the addition of a description that does not appear explicitly in the text:[60]

> A midrash teaches that this refers to that which is written, "Come here" – that is, he brought them all between the two poles of the Ark, and this is one of the places where something small contained something larger, and he said to them, "Hereby shall you know" – by means of this wonder, where you see that you all manage to squeeze between the poles of the Ark.

To this, Radak comments, "This *derash* seems far from the plain meaning, for had this been the wonder that he referred to, it would be mentioned [explicitly] in the text."

Thus far, we have seen that the best-known biblical commentators have all taken approaches that recognize the vital distinction between *peshat* and *derash*. With the exception of R. Yosef Kara and Ibn Ezra, they all

---

60. The source is Genesis Rabba 5, 7, Theodor-Albeck edition, 36–37.

viewed *derash* as a dimension of interpretation that is independent and no less important than *peshat,* and they nevertheless emphasize that *peshat* is an interpretative level in its own right, such that the *derash* cannot and must not obscure or negate the *peshat.*

MAIMONIDES AND HIS SON, RABBI ABRAHAM

Maimonides did not write a systematic commentary on the Torah, but among his various compositions are places where he addresses the relationship between *peshat* and *derash.* His approach was continued by his son, Rabbi Abraham, who did write a commentary on the Torah and thereby devoted more extensive attention to this question.

Maimonides had sought to compose a commentary on *midreshei Ḥazal,* and in presenting this quest, he drew a distinction between two types: "I hope to write a book collecting all the Sages' teachings in this regard from the Talmud and other works. I shall interpret them systematically, showing which must be understood literally and which metaphorically" (introduction to *Perek Ḥelek*).

We do not know if Maimonides ever wrote that book, but he did repeat, in many places, the same distinction between midrashim that should be understood literally and others that should be understood metaphorically. In the continuation of the passage above, he speaks of midrashim that "seem impossible" and should be understood "as riddles and parables." Elsewhere he speaks of midrashim that are "figurative descriptions," noting: "This style was prevalent in ancient days; everyone adopted it in the same way as poets adopt poetic, figurative expressions."

It appears that in all these statements, Maimonides referred specifically to midrashim where the gap between *peshat* and *derash* is clearly apparent. As an example of this type of midrash, he cites Bar Kappara's teaching:

> וְיָתֵד תִּהְיֶה לְךָ עַל אֲזֵנֶךָ, "A paddle (*yated*) shall you have upon your weapon (*azanekha*)" (Deut. 23:14): Do not read the word as *azanekha,* but rather as *oznekha* (your ear). This teaches that if a person hears something which is improper, he should place his finger in his ear. (Ketubot 5a–b)

Maimonides argues that it is clear, in this instance, that Bar Kappara does not mean to indicate that this is the actual meaning of the verse: "I cannot imagine that any person whose intellect is sound would admit this. The author employs the text as a beautiful poetical phrase, in teaching an excellent moral lesson…. This lesson is poetically connected with the above text."

Maimonides's son, R. Abraham, expanded on his father's view.[61] In his *Maamar al Derashot Ḥazal,*[62] he divides midrashim into five categories, maintaining that most belong to the fourth category: lyrical or metaphorical interpretation of verses. He emphasizes that those *midreshei Ḥazal* that do not pertain to principles of faith or to matters of halakha, are not to be regarded as binding tradition that must be accepted:

> Know, however, that there are interpretations of verses that do not involve principles of faith, nor any law of the Torah, that have not been passed down as tradition (i.e., as part of Torah). Some of these are logical suggestions, while others are pleasant teachings that are meant figuratively or metaphorically, teaching uplifting messages concerning the words…. And it would seem that most of the midrashim of *Ḥazal* belong to this category, for it is universally recognized and agreed by all except for the misguided

61. Rabbi Abraham, son of Rambam, or Abraham Maimonides (1186–1237), succeeded his father as Nagid (head) of the Jews of Cairo after Maimonides died in 1204. He authored several works on halakha and Jewish philosophy, including responsa, the work *HaMaspik LeOvdei Hashem* (moral and halakhic teachings relating to prayer, with some teachings that go against the approach of his father), and the monograph *Milḥamot Hashem,* which he wrote in defense of his father's writings and especially *Moreh Nevukhim.* For more about him and his oeuvre, see P. B. Fenton, "The Post-Maimonidean Schools of Exegesis in the East," in *Hebrew Bible / Old Testament* I, 2 (2000), 433–41; Rabbi Reuven Margaliot's introduction to *Milḥamot Hashem* (Jerusalem, 1953), 11–44; the introduction to N. Dana's edition of Rabbi Avraham's *HaMaspik LeOvdei Hashem* (Ramat Gan, 1989), 11–48, and the sources he cites on 14, n. 1. *HaMaspik LeOvdei Hashem,* originally written in Arabic, was translated into English in the early twentieth century by Samuel Rosenblatt under the title *The High Ways to Perfection.* See also below.
62. In *Milḥamot Hashem* (see previous note), 81–88.

> and the simple-minded that this category of their teachings comprises a mosaic of views.[63]

Thus, R. Abraham draws a distinction between those midrashim that flow from reasoned consideration of the verse, and those for which the intention is not to explain the meaning of the verse, but to use it as a springboard to teach a different lesson. It is this latter sort to which Maimonides refers.

R. Abraham brings a similar example: "That which our Sages taught in the Gemara, in Taanit (9a): 'R. Yoḥanan said: The text states, "You shall surely tithe (*aser te'aser*)." This teaches: Take a tithe (*aser*) in order that you will become wealthy (*tit'asher*).'" Clearly, in such instances, "the teaching does not indicate that the Sage believed this to be what the verse actually meant, Heaven forefend."

Concerning midrashim whose interpretation of verses are "logical suggestions," R. Abraham emphasizes that the teachings are not to be considered as binding, received tradition. For example, he addresses the Sages' debate (Zevaḥim 116a) as to what Jethro heard that caused him to come to Moses in the desert (Ex. 18:1):

> I do not doubt R. Yehoshua's teaching concerning "And Jethro heard," with regard to what it was he heard that caused him to arrive – that what he heard about was the war against Amalek. For this arises from reasoning, not from a received teaching. Proof of this lies in the fact that he cites textual evidence to support his claim,[64] whereas if this were a received teaching, he would need no support for it. Further proof lies in the fact that other Sages offer different possibilities for what he might have heard, and if this had been a received teaching they would not have expressed divergent opinions. R. Eliezer states that what Jethro heard about

63. Ibid., 91.
64. Rabbi Yehoshua teaches: "It was the war against Amalek that he heard about, for this verse follows after the conclusion of that episode, with the words, 'Joshua harried Amalek and his people with the edge of the sword.'"

was the giving of the Torah, and he, too, cites evidence in support of his position.

R. Abraham makes two arguments in support of his claim that some midrashim do not fall under the category of "received teachings." First, there is the very fact that the Sages find it necessary to cite verses in support of their interpretations; second, there is disagreement between them – and if these midrashim had been handed down as a Torah tradition, there would be no need for proof texts, nor would there be debate about them.[65]

As noted, R. Abraham wrote a commentary on the Torah, in which he implements his approach.[66] Because he believes that the midrash reflects the thinking of the Sages rather than a received tradition, he does not regard *midreshei aggada* as exegetically binding, and he therefore explains many verses in accordance with their plain meaning.

65. In this regard, R. Abraham applies to biblical commentary a well-known principle set down by his father in the context of halakha: that no law that had been given to Moses at Sinai as part of the Oral Law can be subject to disagreement. (See, for example, *Mishneh Torah, Hilkhot Mamrim* 1:3: "There can never be any difference of opinion with regard to matters received through the Oral Tradition. Whenever there arises a difference of opinion with regard to some matter, it shows that the matter was not received as a tradition from Moses.")

66. The commentary was originally written in Arabic, and was translated by Efraim Yehuda Weisenberg on the basis of a sole manuscript dating to 1375. The work was unknown until the discovery of the manuscript in the nineteenth century, and therefore while R. Abraham's other writings were known throughout the Diaspora, neither the *Rishonim* nor later scholars make any mention of his commentary on the Torah. The extant commentary includes Genesis (except for chapters 2–20) and Exodus. It is not clear whether the original work included more.

Concerning the exegetical approach of R. Avraham, see Y. Nevo, "Perusho Shel R. Avraham ben HaRambam LaTorah," *Sinai* 113 (5753/1993): 230–54; C. Cohen, *BeShalom U'VeMishor – Middot VeDeot BePerush HaTorah Shel Rabbi Avraham ben HaRambam* (Jerusalem, 1999); A. Bazak, "Perusho LaTorah Shel Rabbi Avraham ben HaRambam," in M. Bar Asher, et al. (eds.), *Teshura LeAmos* (Alon Shvut, 2007), 109–24; N. Ilan, "Hanaḥot Teologiot VeEkronot Parshani'im: LeTivo U'LeYiḥudo Shel Perush R. Avrhaam ben HaRambam LaTorah," *Davar Davur al Ofanav* (Jerusalem, 2007), 31–70; Y. Yinon-Fenton, "HaRambam U'Beno, Rabbi Avraham ben Moshe – Hemshekhiut VeShoni," in A. Ravitzky (ed.), *HaRambam – Shamranut, Mekoriut, Mahapkhanut*, vol. 1 (Jerusalem, 2009), 17–42.

We will first note some examples of places where R. Abraham argues that the midrash is offered as "figurative ornamentation," rejecting any possibility of using it to explain the text and even negating any connection between them.

1. In the introduction to the story of the sale of the birthright, it is written: וַיָּבֹא עֵשָׂו מִן הַשָּׂדֶה וְהוּא עָיֵף, "Esau came from the field, and he was faint" (Gen. 25:29). The midrash posits that Esau returned from an act of murder,[67] or that he was spent after "having engaged in relations with a girl who was betrothed." R. Avraham explains the verse in the plain sense: "'He was faint' – the road was long, and he exerted great effort in hunting, and perhaps it had been a long time since he had eaten." He then offers the two possibilities set forth in the midrash:

   > The midrashic teaching that he killed someone is similar to the teaching that he engaged in relations with a girl who was betrothed: these are teachings that bestow figurative, metaphoric beauty, and they are pleasant and make sense to those who involve themselves with such midrash, but they are not necessarily so, nor do they approximate the actual meaning of the verse, for those seeking its true meaning.

2. Commenting on the verse וַיֶּאֱהַב יִצְחָק אֶת עֵשָׂו כִּי צַיִד בְּפִיו, "Isaac loved Esau, for game was in his mouth (*ki tzayid befiv*)" (Gen. 25:28), Rashi cites the midrashic teaching that Esau "would entrap [Isaac] and deceive him with his words."[68] R. Avraham writes:

   > There are some beautiful teachings which treat the word "*befiv*" as referring back to Esau – in other words, that he pursued Isaac's love by means of his words, which indicated his observance of

67. The source of the midrash is Genesis Rabba, *parasha* 63, 12, Theodor-Albeck edition, 694–95.
68. The source of the midrash is Genesis Rabba, *parasha* 63, 9, Theodor-Albeck edition, 693.

the way of God. This is a wonderfully apt description of a certain nature, even though it is not the meaning of the verse.

3. Isaac's blessing to Jacob includes the words, וְיִתֶּן לְךָ הָאֱלֹהִים מִטַּל הַשָּׁמַיִם וּמִשְׁמַנֵּי הָאָרֶץ, "May God give you of the dew of the heavens and of the fat places of the earth" (Gen. 27:28). The midrash teaches: "'Of the dew of the heavens' – this is the manna, as it is written, וַיֹּאמֶר ה' אֶל מֹשֶׁה הִנְנִי מַמְטִיר לָכֶם לֶחֶם מִן הַשָּׁמָיִם, 'God said to Moses: Behold, I will rain bread from the heaven for you' (Ex. 16:4)."[69] Here R. Avraham comments, "How sweet is the midrashic teaching of the Sages that 'of the dew of the heavens' hints to the manna ... but it is a wonderful and beautiful metaphor, not a true interpretation."[70]

R. Abraham does not view these midrashim as interpretations of the text per se; rather, he regards them as teachings that are pleasing in their own right.

With regard to the other types of midrashim, too – those which he defines as being based on "reasoned consideration" – R. Abraham maintains that one may disagree with them on the basis of one's own reasoning. Consider the following two examples:

1. Recall Ibn Ezra's discussion of Isaac's age at the time of his binding. R. Abraham, too, citing his father, rejects the midrashic teaching that Isaac was thirty-seven years old at the time.[71] He writes:

> But my father and teacher, of blessed memory ... said that if this were so, then Isaac's obedience in this act would truly have been a greater act than Abraham's obedience, and Isaac should have received an even greater promise and reward than what was promised to Abraham, yet there is nothing in the text to suggest that this is what happened.

69. Genesis Rabba, 66, 3, Theodor-Albeck edition, 747.
70. For additional examples of similar comments on *midrashim*, see R. Avraham's commentary on Genesis 25:22, 28:22, 38:15, and Exodus 8:10.
71. See Genesis Rabba, 56, 8, Vilna edition.

2. Concerning the verse that lists the children of Leah who went down to Egypt: כָּל נֶפֶשׁ בָּנָיו וּבְנוֹתָיו שְׁלֹשִׁים וְשָׁלֹשׁ, "All the souls of his sons and daughters were thirty-three" (Gen. 46:15), there is extensive commentary, particularly since a count of the names adds up to only thirty-two. The Sages explain that Yocheved, who "was conceived in Canaan and born in the land of Egypt," is included in the total.[72] R. Abraham writes:

> That which the Sages taught about this ... has no support in the text; if it is halakha, we accept it, but the opinion of Ibn Ezra is that it was Jacob himself who completed the total of thirty-three, and this is the most proper of the commentaries. Support for this is to be found in the verse at the beginning of the count: "Jacob and his sons" – indicating that the number is completed with his inclusion.[73]

Thus Rabbi Abraham, son of Maimonides, joins the prevailing spirit of the medieval commentators, in explaining the text in accordance with its plain meaning, maintaining a clear separation between *peshat* and *derash*.

SUMMARY

The classical commentators insisted that the *peshat,* the plain meaning of the text, be viewed as an independent form of interpretation from *derash.* It followed, for all of them, that the attempt to understand the text on the plain level constitutes a highly significant part of the overall goal of understanding God's word as embodied in the Torah. The *derash* is perceived as a level distinct from the *peshat,* and there are different views regarding its significance – ranging from opinions that do not regard it as requiring in-depth study, to opinions that view it as an even more important level than the *peshat.* Yet, according to all the views examined, the distinction between *peshat* and *derash* is a vital one.

---

72. Genesis Rabba, 94, 9, Theodor-Albeck edition, 1180.

73. See also what he writes in this regard on Ex. 2:1.

The commentators used logical considerations in the distinctions that they drew between *peshat* and *derash*, and thereby bequeathed a legacy for future generations, as to how the text should be approached and in which ways the plain meaning of the text distinguishes itself from the midrashic lessons derived from it.

Moreover, they also paved the way for the innovative insights of all future generations into the *peshat*, in accordance with Rashi's assertion quoted by Rashbam that the "plain meaning of the text is refreshed each day." Or, as Rabbi Yom-Tov Lipman Heller, author of the *Tosefot Yom Tov* (in his commentary on Nazir 5:5), puts it: "One is entitled to interpret the text, as we see that commentators have been doing since the times of the Gemara." Rabbi Haim ben Attar, in the introduction to his *Ohr HaḤayim* on the Torah, writes:

> Sometimes I expound on the plain meaning of the text in a manner that is different from the teaching of the Sages, and I have already stated my position that I do not disagree even to the tiniest degree, Heaven forefend, with the *Rishonim*, but those who expound on the Torah are entitled to "cultivate it and sow it" – [it is] "a light sown for the righteous," and the Land of the Living produces fruit from each and every seed that is sown in it by one who studies the Torah.

In view of this, we must conclude that the path proposed in the present era, by those in the *ḥaredi*-nationalist camp, which negates the legitimacy of study of *peshat* and denies its distinction from *derash*, is therefore actually a deviation from the classic exegetical tradition. The protest against the study of *peshat* is a protest against the path followed by the greatest of Torah commentators throughout history.

The ability of every generation to study the plain text and to arrive at new insights is a most tangible expression of the relevance of Torah to our lives. The *peshat* commentaries never ceased to express new insights and illumination – not in the time of the Sages, nor during the Middle Ages. The text continues to be illuminated anew, day after day, using new tools that shed bright light on it in every generation, and the current generation is no exception.[74]

It should be clear that none of the classical commentators ever would have thought to argue – as some do today – that even if in the past it was permissible to interpret the text in accordance with the *peshat*, in the present doing so is no longer possible, owing to the inferior level of our generation. On the contrary, Rashi's comment to his grandson, Rashbam, admitting that if he lived longer he would need to write new commentaries in accordance with "the meaning of the plain text, which is refreshed every day anew," is a demand and a challenge directed to each and every generation.

If we see ourselves as the proud descendants and inheritors of those who lived Torah and learned Torah, we dare not forego our responsibility to give our own generation's interpretation to the text, as has every other generation before us.

74. See U. Simon, "Mashma'utam HaDatit Shel HaPeshatot HaMitḥadeshim," in U. Simon (ed.), *HaMikra VeAnaḥnu* (Tel Aviv, 1979), 149–52; English translation here: http://www.lookstein.org/articles/simon_peshat.htm ("The Religious Significance of the *Peshat*").

Chapter 9

Peshat and *Midrash Halakha*

INTRODUCTION

Having established, in the previous chapter, that the biblical commentators saw fit to draw a distinction between the *peshat* (plain meaning) of the text and midrashim, we will now examine the more complicated issue of the relationship between *peshat* and *midrash halakha*[1] – i.e., between the simple reading of the text and the readings of classical works which mine the biblical verses for their practical halakhic significance.[2] This complexity arises from the fact that the way "halakhic" verses are interpreted would appear to have practical, normative significance.

1. I use the term "*midrash halakha*" in reference to the rabbinic works that explain the biblical verses for their practical halakhic import. The central works are the *Mekhilta* on Exodus, the *Sifra* on Leviticus, and the *Sifrei* on Numbers and Deuteronomy. Excerpts from *midreshei halakha* are regularly quoted throughout the Talmud.
2. Much has been written on this topic and I will refer to some of the literature below. Important reviews are to be found in M. Ahrend, "Al Peshuto Shel Mikra U'Midrash HaHalakha," in S. Vargon et al. (eds.), *Iyyunei Mikra U'Parshanut* 8 (Ramat Gan, 2008), 19–32; M. Lockshin, "Iyyun BeGishot Shonot LeFitron Baayat HaYaḥas She-Bein HaPeshat LeVein Midrash HaHalakha," in ibid., 33–45. An accessible English discussion of this topic can be found in D. Weiss Halivni, *Midrash, Mishnah, and Gemara: The Jewish Predilection for Justified Law* (Cambridge, 1986), especially 18–37.

The discrepancies between the *peshat* and *midrash halakha* can be divided into two groups.

1. The more common scenario is where the midrash derives a certain law that is not necessarily suggested by the plain meaning of the text. In such instances, one might well ask whether we may also interpret the verse in accordance with *peshat* – in a way that does not match the *midrash halakha.*
2. There are instances where the halakhic instruction indicated by the text is not merely different from the one established in accordance with the *midrash halakha,* but actually contradicts it. Here the question of the legitimacy of exegesis in accordance with *peshat* becomes more acute, and also gives rise to a different question: If indeed one may understand the verse on the basis of *peshat,* even in these cases, as some of the greatest commentators certainly did, then why does the discrepancy between *peshat* and *midrash halakha* exist, and how are we to relate to this phenomenon?

We will first examine *midreshei halakha* that merely differ from the *peshat;* afterwards we will deal at greater length with the complex issue of *midreshei halakha* that contradict the *peshat.*

MIDRESHEI HALAKHA THAT DIFFER FROM *PESHAT*

Among the early biblical commentators there are two main approaches in explaining the gap between *midreshei halakha* and the plain meaning of the text.

The majority approach adopts the Sages' well-known teaching concerning the verse הֲלוֹא כֹה דְבָרִי כָּאֵשׁ נְאֻם ה׳ וּכְפַטִּישׁ יְפֹצֵץ סָלַע, "Is not My word like fire, says the Lord, and like a hammer that shatters the rock?" (Jer. 23:29) – "Just as a hammer produces many sparks, so a single verse has many interpretations" (Sanhedrin 34a). That is, the nature of the divine word is such that it contains many different meanings. The Torah, which is God's word, therefore has many valid interpretations and meanings, rather than a single one.

The previous chapter saw how Rashi uses this principle to justify explaining a verse in accordance with *peshat,* as well as citing a *midrash aggada*. Similarly, the principle of textual polysemy is also widely accepted among the commentators with regard to *midreshei halakha*.[3] Nahmanides sets forth this principle very clearly. He proposes a straightforward understanding of the verse כָּל חֵרֶם אֲשֶׁר יָחֳרַם מִן הָאָדָם לֹא יִפָּדֶה מוֹת יוּמָת, "Any *herem* that has been banned from man shall not be redeemed; he shall surely be put to death" (Lev. 27:29), indicating that the king, or the Sanhedrin, is entitled to declare certain items *herem*, and anyone who violates this dedication is to be put to death, as in the story of Saul and the honeycomb (I Sam. 14:24–45). Nahmanides notes that the Sages propose other possible ways of understanding the *peshat*, and writes:

> Do not silence this explanation just because our Sages interpreted this verse in a different way – some understanding it (Arakhin 6b) in the context of estimating the value of someone who is condemned to death, while others understand from it that those deserving of *karet* (spiritual excision) and those sentenced to death at the hands of the court cannot be redeemed with money, as taught in Ketubot (35a). Despite these interpretations, this verse cannot be stripped of its plain meaning – as it is written, אַחַת דִּבֶּר אֱלֹהִים שְׁתַּיִם זוּ שָׁמָעְתִּי, "God spoke one utterance, yet two things have I heard" (Ps. 62:12). The verse supports both

3. Rashi himself often explains verses in accordance with *peshat* and then in accordance with *derash*, even in matters of halakha. One example concerns the verse, וְכִי יִגַּח שׁוֹר אֶת אִישׁ אוֹ אֶת אִשָּׁה וָמֵת סָקוֹל יִסָּקֵל הַשּׁוֹר וְלֹא יֵאָכֵל אֶת בְּשָׂרוֹ וּבַעַל הַשּׁוֹר נָקִי, "If an ox gores a man or a woman, that they die, then the ox shall surely be stoned, and its flesh shall not be eaten, but the owner of the ox shall be acquitted" (Ex. 21:28). Rashi cites *Hazal* (Pesahim 22b), who conclude from the words "*baal hashor naki*" (literally, 'the owner of the ox is clear' – i.e., acquitted) that the carcass of the ox cannot be used for any benefit, "Like someone telling his friend: So-and-so has been cleared of (i.e., lost) his assets and cannot enjoy any benefit from them." However, Rashi goes on to add that this interpretation follows the *derash*, but according to *peshat* the verse comes to establish that the owner of the ox is not deserving of death – in contrast to the situation of a "goring ox" (i.e., one known already to be dangerous): "Its plain meaning is as it says. Since in the case of the goring ox, the Torah states, וְגַם בְּעָלָיו יוּמָת, 'its owner, too, shall be put to death' (Ex. 29), it is therefore necessary to stipulate here that 'the owner of the ox is acquitted.'"

> interpretations. Take note that our Sages teach (Sanhedrin 27b), concerning the verse לֹא יוּמְתוּ אָבוֹת עַל בָּנִים וּבָנִים לֹא יוּמְתוּ עַל אָבוֹת, "Fathers shall not be put to death for sons" (Deut. 24:16) – "at the testimony of their sons"; and similarly, "sons shall not be put to death for fathers" (Deut. 24:16) is understood to mean, "at the testimony of their fathers."... Nevertheless, a verse cannot be stripped of its plain meaning,[4] as it is written, וְאֶת בְּנֵי הַמַּכִּים לֹא הֵמִית כַּכָּתוּב בְּסֵפֶר תּוֹרַת מֹשֶׁה אֲשֶׁר צִוָּה ה׳ לֵאמֹר לֹא יוּמְתוּ אָבוֹת עַל בָּנִים וּבָנִים לֹא יוּמְתוּ עַל אָבוֹת, "But he did not put to death the children of the murderers, as it is written in the Torah of Moses, 'Fathers shall not be put to death for sons, and sons shall not be put to death for fathers'" (II Kings 14:6). Thus we learn that *the Torah has several facets of truth.* (Nahmanides, *Mishpat HaḤerem*)

The conventional approach among the commentators is thus that all of the Sages' interpretations are halakhically binding, but they do not void the validity of the *peshat* reading of the text.[5]

---

4. In the previous chapter, we addressed this principle and the two approaches to understanding it: one maintains that it shows a preference for the plain meaning of the text, while the other approach understands it as merely granting legitimacy to the plain meaning, alongside the midrashic interpretation. Clearly, Nahmanides here tends toward the second approach.
5. The Sages note an exception where the plain meaning of the text is not to be understood as its message. In the case of a man entering a levirate marriage, the Torah states, וְהָיָה הַבְּכוֹר אֲשֶׁר תֵּלֵד יָקוּם עַל שֵׁם אָחִיו הַמֵּת וְלֹא יִמָּחֶה שְׁמוֹ מִיִּשְׂרָאֵל, "And it shall be that the firstborn that she [the widow] bears shall stand in the name of his brother who is dead, so his name will not be erased from Israel" (Deut. 25:6). Rabba states: "Although throughout the entire Torah the text never loses its plain meaning, here the *gezera shava* comes and removes the text entirely from its plain meaning" (Yevamot 24a). Rashi explains: Although the plain meaning of the verse would seem to suggest that the son born from the levirate marriage should be named for the brother who has died, in this case we do not do so. Ritva explains at greater length: "In any place where there is not an outright contradiction (between the simple reading and that derived from an exegetical principle), we fulfill both interpretations, yet in this case although it would be possible to fulfill both, we are not obligated to fulfill the simple reading of the text at all." This would seem to indicate that in all other cases, the *peshat* is also binding.

For those who do not accept the principle of polysemy, and believe that the text has only one authoritative meaning, a different approach must be sought. Ibn Ezra explains the gap between *peshat* and *derash* as arising from the fact that the *derash* is not meant as an interpretation of the verse, and the halakha is in fact not derived from the verse. Rather, the source of the halakha is the oral tradition, while its attachment to the verse came at a later stage, as an "*asmakhta*."[6] This principle is stated explicitly in his short commentary on Exodus 21:8: "And I state here the general rule that in the Torah there are instances where the Sages are known to utilize an *asmakhta*, but they know the essence of the matter."

Ibn Ezra cites a few examples of this principle, the first concerning the verse: וְאִם אֵין אַחִים לְאָבִיו וּנְתַתֶּם אֶת נַחֲלָתוֹ לִשְׁאֵרוֹ הַקָּרֹב אֵלָיו מִמִּשְׁפַּחְתּוֹ וְיָרַשׁ אֹתָהּ, "And if his father has no brothers, then you shall give his inheritance to his kinsman who is next to him of his family, and he shall possess it" (Num. 27:11). According to the plain meaning of the verse, the Torah states that if the deceased has no first-degree relatives (sons, daughters, or brothers), nor even second-degree (father's brothers), then his inheritance passes to even more distant family members. The Sages arrive at a completely different understanding of the verse: from the words "of his family, and he shall possess it" they conclude that a husband inherits from his wife (Bava Batra 111b and elsewhere).[7] This teaching is not based on the plain meaning of what the verse says, but rather on the seemingly redundant phrase, "and he shall possess it" (*otah* – the feminine form, seemingly referring to the inheritance – *naḥala* – which is a feminine noun).

Ibn Ezra has no argument with the law that a husband inherits from his wife; he simply disagrees with the manner in which this law is derived, since it does not sit well with the plain meaning of the text:

6. An *asmakhta* traditionally refers to an independent teaching which is nevertheless associated with a verse. This association can serve as a memory aid, as an indication of the truth of the teaching, or some other purpose.
7. Rashi (commenting on this discussion in Ketubot 83a) explains this in accordance with his own approach, discussed above, in which the teaching of *Ḥazal* is an expression of the multiple facets of textual meaning: "Although the word 'family' here does not mean to indicate his wife."

> It was known through the oral tradition that a husband inherits from his wife, and the Sages interpreted this verse as a hint. For all of Israel knows that the verse should be understood in accordance with its plain meaning, for it is impossible that someone should say, "Give Reuben's inheritance to Simeon," while intending exactly the opposite – that Simeon's inheritance be given to Reuben.... So the proper understanding of the verse is in accordance with its plain meaning, while the Sages add another layer of meaning that is part of the oral tradition.

Since the midrash here indeed contradicts the plain meaning of the verse – which deals with the question of *to whom a person leaves his inheritance,* and not *from whom he inherits* – it should not be regarded as an interpretation of the verse, but rather as a known law relying upon the verse only[8] as *asmakhta.*[9]

From this perspective it is possible to understand verses in accordance with their plain meaning, contrary to the *midrash halakha.* In the realm of exegesis, the *peshat* is the only way of understanding the text,

---

8. See Ibn Ezra, ad loc., for more examples; also see his commentary on Leviticus 19:20, 23:40, and elsewhere. Ralbag adopts a similar approach. In the introduction to his commentary on the Torah he writes:

   > In our explanation of the commandments and the roots from which all their particular laws emerge, as set forth in the talmudic wisdom, we shall not consistently associate those roots with the textual verses which the Sages of the Talmud associated with them, through one of the thirteen hermeneutical principles, as was their custom. For they associated the truths that had been handed down to them concerning the commandments of the Torah, to those verses, with a view to the verses serving as allusions, or *asmakhta,* to those truths. They did not mean to suggest that these specific laws were actually derived from those verses – for a person could in fact turn all the laws of the Torah on their head on the basis of such logic.... Rather, we shall associate them with the plain meaning of the verses from which these laws might in fact arise, for this is more easily accepted by the mind. This does not represent any deviation from the teachings of our Sages, for, as stated, their intention was not that those laws are derived from the verses which they associate with them; rather, the laws were handed down to them, from one person to another, all the way back to Moses – and they simply sought allusions to them in the text.

9. Ibn Ezra is innovative in his use of the expression "*asmakhta,*" using the term far more broadly than *Ḥazal* do, as Lockshin points out in "Iyyun BeGishot Shonot," 38.

but when it comes to halakha, the Oral Law is binding – even where it does not match the plain meaning. The source and authority of the halakha do not arise from the verse, but rather from the oral tradition; the connection to the verse serves only as an *asmakhta*.[10]

In summary, we have discussed two broad approaches to the relationship between *peshat* and *midrash halakha*. The first, championed by Rashi, Nahmanides, and others, focuses on the multiple valid interpretations of the text, making room for both the *peshat* and the legal inference. The second, put forward by Ibn Ezra and others, maintains that the *peshat* is the only correct way to read the text, and that the conclusions of the *midrash halakha* are not to be viewed as readings of the text in and of themselves, but rather as independently received traditions, which are then hinted at or alluded to in the biblical verses.

MIDRESHEI HALAKHA THAT CONTRADICT THE *PESHAT*

As noted, the relationship between the straightforward reading of the text (*peshat*) and the halakhic ramifications derived in the midrash becomes more complicated when they appear to directly contradict each other. When halakha is not decided in accordance with the literal meaning, the question arises: Is it nevertheless legitimate to understand the verses literally; and if so, what is the significance of a *peshat* understanding that is not followed as halakha?

---

10. In recent generations this approach has been broadened even further. Rabbi Yitzchak Isaac HaLevi (Rabinowitz) (1847–1914) wrote:

> For all the disputes among the *Tanna'im* arose only from the fundamental understanding of each of them, and the traditions that had been received. But the midrashim themselves are merely allusions to these…. For in all their teachings they use midrash only for one of two purposes: either to associate the received tradition with a verse, with the understanding that "there is nothing that is not alluded to in the Torah," or to support the position they had arrived at on the basis of their understanding of the fundamental principles set forth in the Mishna, or received tradition, or logical deduction, or knowledge of the foundations of the Torah. (*Dorot Rishonim* I, part 5, 244)

Today, this approach is referred to as "*midrash mekayyem*" ("preservative/restorative midrash"); see M. Elon, *Jewish Law: History, Sources, Principles*, transl. B. Auerbach and M. Sykes, 4 vols. (Philadelphia, 1994), 2:283–99.

One possible way of dealing with the problem is suggested by Ibn Ezra. Since, in his view, a verse has only one meaning (as discussed previously), he opts to reject the *peshat* and to adopt the *derash* as the sole interpretation of the verse. Indeed, this is his general approach, as he declares explicitly:

> Only when it comes to teachings, laws, and statutes, if a verse has two different interpretations – one in accordance with the teachings of the *maatikim* ["relayers," a reference to the Sages, who relay the traditions received at Sinai to future generations], who were all righteous (and we may place our full reliance on their truth), then Heaven forefend that we should lend an ear to the Sadducees, who claim that the relayers contradict the details of the text; rather, our predecessors embody truth and all their words are truth, and the Lord God of Truth shall guide His servant on the way of truth. (Introduction to Commentary on the Torah, the "fifth way")

When there is a blatant contradiction between the *peshat* and *midrash halakha*, Ibn Ezra systematically interprets the verses in accordance with the midrash.[11]

11. At the same time, he sometimes offers an interpretation in accordance with the *peshat*. Although he is quick to clarify that he accepts the view of the Sages, the very fact that he brings the *peshat* shows that he views such an interpretation as having some value. The following are two examples.
    a. In the matter of leaning (*semikha*) on a sacrifice, Ibn Ezra writes in his commentary on Leviticus 1:4: "'And he shall lean his hands'(וְסָמַךְ יָדוֹ) – the plain meaning of the verse would seem to be that he leans only one hand [the verse says '*yado*,' not '*yadav*'], for the procedure concerning the goat that is condemned to die in the wilderness [where the verse specifies, וְסָמַךְ אַהֲרֹן אֶת שְׁתֵּי יָדָו עַל רֹאשׁ הַשָּׂעִיר הַחַי, 'Aaron shall lean his two hands (*shetei yadav*) upon the head of the goat that is alive' – Lev. 16:21] is not the same procedure that governs the other sacrifices; therefore the Torah changes the formulation. It is only in light of the teaching of the Sages, who taught that every instance of *semikha* involves both hands, that we rely on them."
    b. Concerning the punishment of lashes, the Torah states, וְהִכָּהוּ לְפָנָיו כְּדֵי רִשְׁעָתוֹ בְּמִסְפָּר אַרְבָּעִים יַכֶּנּוּ לֹא יֹסִיף, "He [the accused] shall be lashed in his [the judge's] presence, according to his wrongdoing, by a certain number. Forty stripes he may give him, but no more" (Deut. 25:2–3). Ibn Ezra comments

However, other commentators maintain the distinction between *peshat* and *derash* even in matters of halakha. Most prominent among them is Rashbam, who, in dozens of instances, interprets verses in accordance with their plain meaning, rather than in accordance with the *midrash halakha.*[12] Naturally, many of these instances are to be found in *Parashat Mishpatim,* which includes a great many laws. Therefore, at the beginning of his commentary on this *parasha,* Rashbam sees fit to set forth the following fundamental principle:

> Let those who love wisdom know and understand that my purpose, as explained in Genesis, is not to offer halakhic interpretations, wherein haggadot and halakhot are derived from superfluities in Scriptural language, even though such interpretations are the most essential ones. Some of those explanations can be found in the works of my mother's father, Rashi. But my purpose is to explain the plain meaning of Scripture. I will explain the laws and rules [of the Torah] in a manner that conforms to the [natural] way of the world. Nevertheless, it is the halakhic level of interpretation that is the most essential one, as the rabbis said (Sota 16a): Halakha uproots

---

that the plain meaning of the verse suggests that the number of stripes administered varies in accordance with the severity of the sin, and the Torah stipulates "forty" as the maximum number that is permissible: "We would think that there are some sins for which he might receive ten, or twenty, or less than that, or more, based on the words, 'according to his wrongdoing.' Only, he must receive no more than forty." However, the Sages stipulate that for any sin, the punishment of forty lashes is fixed (or, rather, thirty-nine – see, for example, Mishna Makkot 3:10). Ibn Ezra therefore negates what would have seemed to be the plain meaning of the text, "on account of the received wisdom, which alone is truth."

12. Rashbam's attitude toward *midreshei aggada* was discussed in the previous chapter. As to his approach to *midreshei halakha,* see E. Touitou, "*HaPeshatot HaMit'ḥaddeshim BeKhol Yom*" – *Iyyunim be-Perusho shel Rashbam LaTorah* (Jerusalem, 2003), 53–56; 177–88; M. Lockshin, *Rabbi Samuel ben Meir's Commentary on Genesis,* 9–23.

> [the plain meaning of] the biblical text.[13] (Rashbam, commentary on Ex. 21:1)[14]

Rashbam maintained that the principle of polysemy, of multiple valid interpretations of the text, is relevant even in these instances. He emphasizes that the laws derived from seeming superfluities in the text are the "essence" – and by this he would seem to be saying that the midrashic teaching is binding, in practical, halakhic terms, but, nevertheless, the plain sense of the verse still has its value and role. The gap between the *peshat* and the *derash* arises from their being the products of two different reading strategies: *derash* is what is derived from superfluities and other noteworthy aspects of the text, as well as through the

---

13. The translation is taken from Lockshin, *Rashbam's Commentary on Exodus: An Annotated Translation* (Atlanta, 1997). Many editions preserve the final phrase quoted here as "*halakha okeret mishna.*" This formula presents a problem, since no such expression appears in *Ḥazal,* nor does it appear suited to the context. Lockshin therefore suggests that Rashbam's comment should read, "*halakha okeret mikra*" (the halakha uproots the literal verse). As noted, Rashbam would then be referring to the Gemara in Sota 16a:

    > Rabbi Yoḥanan said in the name of R. Yishmael: In three places the halakha uproots the literal verse: The Torah says [that the blood must be covered] "with dust" (Lev. 17:13), while the halakha is that it may be covered with any substance; the Torah says [that a Nazirite may not shave] "with a blade" (Num. 6:5), while the halakha is that he may not shave with anything; and the Torah says "a writ" (literally "book," Deut. 24:1), while the halakha is that he may write on anything.

    Rabbi Yishmael's words do indeed apply to the instances where the halakha supersedes the plain meaning of the text. Rashbam's term, "*okeret*" (uproots), in contrast to the term used in the Gemara, "*okevet*" (circumvents), also appears in the *Tosafot* in various places (Kiddushin 16a; Ḥullin 88b); see Rabbi M. M. Kasher's addenda to *Torah Shelema* 17 (New York, 1956), 293.
14. In the same vein, see his commentary at the end of Exodus (40:35) and at the beginning of Leviticus (1:1). Rashbam (Lev. 13:2) presents the units discussing *tzaraat* as an exception: "With regard to all the units concerning *tzaraat* of a person, and of clothing, and of houses, and their various appearances, and the calculations of how long they are to be shut up, and white hairs and hair that is black or yellow – we have no basis for understanding the plain meaning of the text at all, nor [interpreting it] on the basis of proficiency in these matters as they affect people; rather, the essence here is the teaching of the Sages, with their laws and received wisdom from the early Sages."

hermeneutical laws, while *peshat* is studied "in a manner that conforms to the way of the world."[15]

The following are some of the better-known instances where Rashbam interprets the text in accordance with *peshat*, even where this runs counter to halakha:

1. The Sages understand the verse, וְהָיָה לְךָ לְאוֹת עַל יָדְךָ וּלְזִכָּרוֹן בֵּין עֵינֶיךָ, "And it shall be a sign for you upon your hand, and as a remembrance between your eyes" (Ex. 13:9), as the source for the commandment of *tefillin*. Rashbam, in his commentary, writes that the plain meaning of the text is metaphorical: "According to the profound plain meaning of Scripture, it will always be a reminder for you, as if it were written on your hand. Like the verse שִׂימֵנִי כַחוֹתָם עַל לִבֶּךָ, 'Let me be a seal upon your heart' (Song of Songs 8:6)."[16]

   Other commentators vehemently reject Rashbam's audacious proposal. Without mentioning him by name, Ibn Ezra writes:

   > There are those who dispute our holy ancestors (*Ḥazal*), teaching that "a sign ... a remembrance" is to be understood in the sense of, כִּי לִוְיַת חֵן הֵם לְרֹאשֶׁךָ וַעֲנָקִים לְגַרְגְּרֹתֶךָ, "For they are a wreath upon your head, a necklace upon your throat" (Prov. 1:9);

15. It should be noted that this complex approach does entail some danger. During the Middle Ages, the Karaites aroused great controversy by deciding halakha in accordance with the plain reading of the text. (For further reading, see *inter alia:* M. Corinaldi, "Karaites," in *HaEncyclopedia HaIvrit* 30 [Jerusalem-Tel Aviv, 1978], columns 36–50; N. Schorr, *Toledot HaKara'im* [Jerusalem, 2003].) Biblical interpretation of the *peshat* even where this goes against halakha, as per Rashbam's approach, may create the impression of legitimizing Karaite positions. Therefore Rashbam's approach was opposed by some – first and foremost among them Ibn Ezra, as we shall see below.
16. Translation based on Lockshin, *Rashbam's Commentary on Exodus.* It is possible that Rashbam's interpretation follows that of the tenth-century Spanish philologist and linguist Menahem ben Saruk, who offers this meaning in his *Maḥberet Menaḥem,* a work which was likely the first dictionary of biblical Hebrew. It should be noted that Rashbam mentions Menahem's explanations in several places in his commentary, although not in this particular instance.

> that וְקָשַׁרְתָּם לְאוֹת עַל יָדֶךָ, "You shall bind them as a sign upon your hand" (Deut. 6:8) is similar to קָשְׁרֵם עַל לִבְּךָ תָמִיד, "bind them upon the tablet of your heart always" (Prov. 6:21); and that וּכְתַבְתָּם עַל מְזֻזוֹת בֵּיתֶךָ, "And you shall write them upon the doorposts of your house" (Deut. 6:9), follows the idea, כָּתְבֵם עַל לוּחַ לִבֶּךָ, "Inscribe them upon the tablet of your heart" (Prov. 3:3).... But this is not the proper way [of interpretation], for at the beginning of the Book [of Proverbs] it states, מִשְׁלֵי שְׁלֹמֹה, "the parables of Solomon" (Prov. 1:1) – meaning that all that is included in it is meant metaphorically. But nowhere in the Torah is it written that it is meant metaphorically, Heaven forefend; rather, it is to be understood literally. Therefore, the verse should not be severed from its literal meaning. (Long commentary on Exodus 13:9)

Ibn Ezra rejects the possibility of interpreting these verses in a metaphoric sense, and brands commentators who do so as "disputing our holy ancestors." It is not clear whether Ibn Ezra refers here specifically to Rashbam[17] or whether he is combatting the Karaite

17. Perhaps Ibn Ezra's polemic is actually directed against Menahem ben Saruk. Some of the verses that Ibn Ezra cites as being erroneously interpreted by others in a metaphoric sense (such as "bind them upon the tablet of your heart") are not cited by Rashbam, while the specific verse that Rashbam does cite ("Set me as a seal upon your heart") appears nowhere in Ibn Ezra's comment. In addition, Ibn Ezra asserts that the commentators to whom he is referring also propose a metaphoric understanding of the verse, "And you shall inscribe them upon the doorposts of your house" – which, as we know, is the textual basis upon which *Ḥazal* teach the commandment of mezuza, but this is not Rashbam's understanding of the verse at all.

R. Yosef Bekhor Shor, in his commentary on Numbers 12:8 and on Deuteronomy 6:9, likewise attacks sharply the metaphoric interpretation of these verses. He, too, makes no explicit mention of Rashbam (nor of ben Saruk), but he does note (in his commentary on Numbers, ad loc.) the negative impact of such interpretations: "I have heard even from some Jews that they question [the commandments of] *tefillin* and mezuza."

On the question of whom the criticism of Ibn Ezra and other commentators is directed against, see Lockshin, *Rashbam's Commentary on Exodus*, 129.

commentators.[18] In any event, it is clear that Rashbam's intention was not to challenge the commandment of wearing *tefillin*; rather, he points out that the halakhic derivation from the text, while authoritative, is not necessarily identical with the true *peshat* reading of the verses, keeping with his consistent theoretical approach.[19]

2. According to halakha, the day begins at nighttime (Mishna Ḥullin 5:6), and in the Sages' teachings, this principle is based on the formula repeated over and over in the account of the Creation, "And it was evening and it was morning, a…day" (see, for example, Berakhot 26a). However, commenting on this verse, Rashbam writes:

> The text does not write, "There was night and there was day." Rather, it writes, "There was evening," i.e., the light of the first day subsided and the darkness fell, "and there was morning," that morning (that came at the end) of the night when dawn broke. At that point, one day of those six described in the Decalogue (Ex. 20:11) was completed. Then, the second day began when God said: "Let there be an expanse" (Gen. 1:6). The text has no interest in stating that an evening and a morning regularly constitute one day. The text is interested only in describing how those six days were constituted, that when the night finished and the dawn broke, one day was completed and the second day began (Gen. 1:5).[20]

According to his approach, the plain meaning of the verse is that the day begins in the morning, and ends on the following morning. This

18. The Karaites did indeed interpret the verses in Exodus and in Deuteronomy in a metaphoric sense, and they did not wear *tefillin*. See J. Tigay, s.v. "*tefillin*," *Encyclopedia Mikra'it* 8 (Jerusalem, 1982), columns 890–91.
19. Some have argued that Rashbam maintains this position only in relation to the verse in Exodus, which was uttered prior to the giving of the Torah, but even he would agree that the verses in Deuteronomy represent the basis for the commandment of *tefillin* even according to *peshat* (see N. Leibowitz, *Iyyunim Ḥadashim BeSefer Shemot* [Jerusalem, 1973], 157, n. 1; Touitou, 187). For further discussion of this debate, see S. Japhet, *Dor Dor U'Parshanav* (Jerusalem, 2008), 44–46.
20. Translation from Lockshin, *Rabbi Samuel ben Meir's Commentary on Genesis.*

has extremely important halakhic ramifications, since it seemingly suggests that, according to the plain meaning of the text, the Sabbath and the festivals begin in the morning, rather than on the previous evening.

This interpretation, too, drew sharp criticism from Ibn Ezra. In his commentary on the verse, אִכְלֻהוּ הַיּוֹם כִּי שַׁבָּת הַיּוֹם לַה׳ הַיּוֹם לֹא תִמְצָאֻהוּ בַּשָּׂדֶה, "Eat it today, for today is the Sabbath unto God; today you shall not find it in the field" (Ex. 16:25), he writes:

> Many faithless ones have a corrupted understanding of this verse, claiming that one must observe the day of the Sabbath and the night that follows it, for Moses says, "for today is the Sabbath unto God," rather than "last night,"… and they have interpreted the verse, "And it was evening and it was morning," as they wish – that the first day was not complete until the morning of the second day.

Ibn Ezra connects the approach arguing that the Sabbath should be observed starting from the morning, with the interpretation cited above concerning the verse, "And it was evening and it was morning," and rejects both outright:

> And now, consider the folly of those who explain, "And it was evening and it was morning," as I set forth above; for the text says, וַיִּקְרָא אֱלֹהִים לָאוֹר יוֹם, "And God called the light day" (Gen. 1:5), extending from when the sun rises until it sets; וְלַחֹשֶׁךְ קָרָא לָיְלָה, "And the darkness He called night" (Gen. 1:5) – from when the sun sets until it rises; and night is thus the opposite of day, just as darkness is the opposite of light. This being so, how can one call [the period] from evening, which is when the sun goes down, until the morning, "day," when it is in fact night?

In addition, Ibn Ezra wrote a letter, while in London, in 1158, known as *Iggeret HaShabbat*, in which he imagines receiving a letter sent to him by the Sabbath herself.[21] He portrays her as berating him, claiming that,

21. Published in the book *Kerem Ḥemed* 4 (Prague 5599 [1839]), with comments by Shadal. The fascinating text of the *Iggeret HaShabbat* can be read at www.daat.co.il/daat/shabat/luach/igeret-2.htm.

although in his youth he honored and observed the Sabbath, in his later years he offended her: "Yesterday your disciples brought books of Torah commentaries to your house, and in them, it was written that the eve of the Sabbath should be desecrated." Ibn Ezra recounts that he was deeply shocked, and found that, indeed, in the books that he had received, "there appeared a commentary concerning the verse, 'And it was evening and it was morning,' arguing that, when the morning of the second day arrived, one whole day was complete, since the night follows the day." Ibn Ezra testifies, "I almost rent my garments, and I also rent this commentary, for I said, 'Better to desecrate one Sabbath, and not have the Jewish people desecrate many Sabbaths,' [which might happen] should they see this evil commentary." Ibn Ezra concludes this figurative introduction by explaining at length why the proposed commentary on the verse is not to be accepted.[22]

Here, too, Rashbam's intention was of course merely to explain the *peshat* of the verses; he certainly would never have dreamed of suggesting that this interpretation should be the basis of any halakhic ruling. However, his knowledge of the halakha and his clear position that the *midrash halakha* is the "main point" did not prevent him from interpreting the verses as he understood them, even where this ran counter to the practical halakha associated with the verse.[23]

3. Regarding the scapegoat on Yom Kippur, the Torah commands us לְשַׁלַּח אֹתוֹ לַעֲזָאזֵל הַמִּדְבָּרָה, "to send it to Azazel in the wilderness" (Lev. 16:10). The Mishna explains that the goat is put to death: "They would push it from behind, and it would roll and fall, and before it had fallen halfway down the mountain it would already be torn limb from limb" (Yoma 6:6).

   Sifra, or *Torat Kohanim* (the *midrash halakha* to the book of Leviticus) rejects the possibility of the goat's being sent into the wilderness without killing it:

22. Here again, it is not entirely clear whether Ibn Ezra meant his words as a direct attack on Rashbam, but it is reasonable to assume that he is alluding to Rashbam's commentary (as Lockshin in *Rabbi Samuel ben Meir's Commentary on Genesis,* 38).
23. For more on this subject see Japhet, 48–49, and the sources listed ad loc., n. 34.

> "It shall remain alive before God" – what does this teach us? Since the text previously says, "to send it" – it is sent to its death. Could the expression not perhaps mean that it was "sent to life"? [No,] as we learn from the expression יָעֳמַד חַי לִפְנֵי ה׳ לְכַפֵּר עָלָיו, "it shall remain alive before God, to make atonement upon it" (Lev. 16:10). How so? It [first] stands alive before God, and [then] is put to death [by being thrown] off a cliff.[24]

However, Rashbam states explicitly,

> According to the simple meaning, it is sent away alive, to the goats that live in the wilderness – as we find in relation to the birds brought by one who had *tzaraat*: וְשִׁלַּח אֶת הַצִּפֹּר הַחַיָּה עַל פְּנֵי הַשָּׂדֶה, "And he shall let the living bird loose into the open field" (Lev. 14:7), to cleanse him of his impurity. Here, too, to cleanse the Jewish people of their sins, the goat is sent into the wilderness, which is a place where animals graze.[25]

As noted, Rashbam was not the only commentator to adopt this path. *Peshat* interpretations that go against *midreshei halakha* appear many times in the commentaries of Nahmanides, Rabbi Yosef Bekhor Shor, and other Tosafists and *Rishonim,* discussed below.[26] All, of course, emphasized that in terms of practical halakha, the *midrash halakha* is binding.[27] Below, in an effort to understand the significance of this

24. *Torat Kohanim, Dibbura DeAḥarei Mot, parasha* 2, 2, Weiss edition 81a.
25. Concerning this interpretation, see Touitou, 187–88.
26. R. Kasher, 298–302, notes many examples of such interpretations in *Parashat Mishpatim.*
27. There is an exceptional case in which one of the *Rishonim* seemingly suggests a halakhic ruling in accordance with the plain meaning of the text, contrary to the *midrash halakha.* In the unit describing a thief who comes in secret, the Torah stipulates: אִם בַּמַּחְתֶּרֶת יִמָּצֵא הַגַּנָּב וְהֻכָּה וָמֵת אֵין לוֹ דָּמִים. אִם זָרְחָה הַשֶּׁמֶשׁ עָלָיו דָּמִים לוֹ שַׁלֵּם יְשַׁלֵּם אִם אֵין לוֹ וְנִמְכַּר בִּגְנֵבָתוֹ, "If a thief is found breaking in with stealth, and he is struck and he dies, no blood is shed on his account. If the sun had risen upon him, blood shall be shed on his account; he shall make full restitution; if he has nothing, he shall be sold for his theft" (Ex. 22:1–2). The plain meaning of the text suggests that the license to kill a thief who "breaks in with stealth" (*bamaḥteret*) applies specifically

phenomenon, we will examine other examples of Rashbam's interpretations in accordance with *peshat* that run contrary to *midreshei halakha*.

One of the most prominent *Aḥaronim* (rabbinic scholars from the post-medieval era) who took the same approach as Rashbam was Rabbi Elijah of Vilna, the Vilna Gaon. In his commentary on the Torah, *Aderet Eliyahu*, he often interprets verses according to their plain sense,

---

where he breaks in at night, but not by day. However, the Sages concluded that the expression "if the sun has risen upon him" is not meant literally, as a reference to daylight hours, but rather as a metaphor: "Did the sun rise upon him alone? [Obviously not; rather,] this is the meaning: 'If it is as clear to you as the sun that his intentions are not peaceable, slay him; if not, do not slay him'" (Sanhedrin 72a). The question of whether or not the homeowner is permitted to kill the thief depends on the extent to which his life is threatened by him: if it is as "clear as day" that the thief has no intention of killing the homeowner and that he means only to steal his belongings, then it is forbidden to kill him – even at night. However, Nahmanides interprets the verse in accordance with its plain meaning:

> The plain meaning is well known – stating that if the thief was breaking into houses by night, and was found breaking in stealthily by night, he is to be killed. But if the sun has risen upon the thief, and a person sees him and identifies him, he is not to be killed; rather, he repays that which he stole and removed by day. And the meaning of the word "sun" here is light for the eyes of those who see. The word is used in the same sense in the verse לְעֵינֵי הַשֶּׁמֶשׁ הַזֹּאת, "in the sight of this sun" (II Sam. 12:11) – i.e., openly.

Moreover, in his gloss on Maimonides (*Hilkhot Geneva* 3:9), Raavad writes:

> I shall not hold back from writing my view, which is that even though our Sages interpreted the verse, "if the sun has risen upon him" in a metaphorical sense, meaning – "if it is clear as day to you that the thief has not come with the intention of killing you," etc. – nevertheless, the text is not to be severed from its plain meaning: by day, the homeowner is not permitted to kill him, for a thief comes by day only to grab what he can; he grabs and then flees immediately. He does not stay there to steal a great quantity of money, [which might entail] confronting the homeowner and killing him. A thief who comes at night, on the other hand, since he steals at night, he knows that the homeowner is at home; thus, he comes with the intention of killing or being killed. But a thief by day [assumes that] the homeowner is not usually at home, so it is simply a matter of removing something.

In his view, even where, according to the homeowner's estimation, it is possible that the thief did indeed mean to kill him, the plain meaning of the text is that he must not be killed by day under any circumstances, since the assumption is that the thief does not come by day with murderous intentions. For a discussion of this exceptional approach, see R. Kasher, 301.

even when doing so means going against *midrash halakha*.[28] Throughout *Parashat Mishpatim*, there are many instances in which he follows the same interpretation as Rashbam. Near the beginning of the *parasha*, he sets forth his fundamental approach, albeit in somewhat opaque terms:

> אוֹ אֶל הַמְּזוּזָה, "Or to the mezuza" (Ex. 21:6) – according to the plain text, the doorpost is valid [for boring through the slave's ear]. But the halakha supersedes the [plain] text,[29] and this is the case for most of this *parasha* and in many *parshiot* of the Torah. This is the greatness of the Oral Torah, which is passed down as a tradition from Moses at Sinai, and is inverted like sealing-wax.... As it is written (Makkot 22b), "How foolish are those who rise [out of respect] for a Torah scroll, but not for a Torah scholar."[30] And likewise concerning *piggul*,[31] and most of the Torah.

28. A partial list appears in *Torah Shelema*, 302.
29. Note that the Vilna Gaon uses this expression, as does Rashbam. What the Vilna Gaon means is that according to the *peshat* of the verse, the ear of the slave may be driven though at the door or the doorpost, but the Sages teach that it may done only at the door, and not at the doorpost; the doorpost, in their understanding, is mentioned only to teach that "just as a doorpost stands upright, so the door must be standing upright" (Kiddushin 22b).
30. Here the Vilna Gaon refers to another instance of a gap between the *peshat* and *midrash halakha*: Concerning the punishment of lashes, the Torah states, אַרְבָּעִים יַכֶּנּוּ לֹא יֹסִיף, "Forty stripes shall he give him, but he shall not exceed this" (Deut. 25:3). The Sages conclude (Mishna Makkot 3:10) that the maximum punishment is actually thirty-nine stripes ("forty less one"), based on a reading that includes the final word of the previous verse – "*... bemispar. Arba'im...*" ("by a [certain] number. Forty") – implying, "by a number that is proximate to forty." The Gemara offers the following explanation: "Were the text to read, 'forty by number,' it would mean a count of forty; since it reads, 'by a number – forty,' it means a number coming up to forty." (Admittedly, in the Mishna, Rabbi Yehuda opposes this view, maintaining that the law here is in accordance with the plain text: "He receives a full forty stripes.") Concerning this view, the Gemara comments: "Rabba said: How foolish are those people who stand up in deference to a *Sefer Torah*, but do not arise in deference to a great personage [Torah scholar], for a *Sefer Torah* states 'forty,' while the Sages came and [through interpretation] reduced them by one."
31. *Piggul* is a clear example of the gap between *peshat* and *midrash halakha*. According to the plain meaning of the text, the law of *piggul* is that if the meat of a sacrifice is

> Therefore one must understand the plain meaning of the text, in order to be able to make sense of the "seal."[32]

The Vilna Gaon maintains that the Written Law is, in many instances, a sort of "seal" – which, in order to be read and properly understood, is turned over and impressed. He therefore considers study of the plain meaning of the text important – a "seal," of sorts – independently of the Oral Law, which sometimes overturns, or reverses, the meaning of the "seal."

Surprisingly enough, nowhere in the writings of Rashbam, the Vilna Gaon, or any of the other commentators who follow their approach, is there any explanation of the reason for this phenomenon. If the literal text indeed suggests one understanding, why do the Sages not rule in

---

eaten past the set time during which it may be consumed, the sacrifice itself retroactively becomes *piggul* – an "abomination":

> וְאִם נֶדֶר אוֹ נְדָבָה זֶבַח קָרְבָּנוֹ בְּיוֹם הַקְרִיבוֹ אֶת זִבְחוֹ יֵאָכֵל וּמִמָּחֳרָת וְהַנּוֹתָר מִמֶּנּוּ יֵאָכֵל. וְהַנּוֹתָר מִבְּשַׂר הַזָּבַח בַּיּוֹם הַשְּׁלִישִׁי בָּאֵשׁ יִשָּׂרֵף. וְאִם הֵאָכֹל יֵאָכֵל מִבְּשַׂר זֶבַח שְׁלָמָיו בַּיּוֹם הַשְּׁלִישִׁי לֹא יֵרָצֶה הַמַּקְרִיב אֹתוֹ לֹא יֵחָשֵׁב לוֹ פִּגּוּל יִהְיֶה וְהַנֶּפֶשׁ הָאֹכֶלֶת מִמֶּנּוּ עֲוֹנָהּ תִּשָּׂא.

> If the sacrifice of his offering is a vow, or a voluntary offering, then it may be eaten on the same day that he offers his sacrifice, and on the next day, too, the remainder of it may be eaten. But that which remains of the flesh of the sacrifice on the third day shall be burnt with fire. And if any of the flesh of the sacrifice of his peace offering is eaten at all (*he'akhol ye'akhel*) on the third day, it shall not be accepted; it shall not be attributed to him who brought it, it shall be an abomination, and the person who eats of it shall bear his iniquity. (Lev. 7:16–18; see also Lev. 19:5–8)

According to the Sages (Zevaḥim 29a and elsewhere), however, the definition of a sacrifice as *piggul* is not dependent on whether the meat of the sacrifice was actually eaten within its specified time or beyond its specified time; rather, it is dependent on the intentions of the person who brings the offering, at the time of its sacrifice: if his *intention* had been to eat it beyond the set time, then it is considered *piggul* – even if it was, in fact, eaten in time. But if he intended to eat it within the set time, then it is not considered *piggul* – even if it was, in fact, eaten after its set time. In this latter instance, the *midrash halakha* deviates from the plain meaning of the text, in the direction of a more lenient interpretation. Rashbam also discusses this disparity: "The Sages uprooted [this law] from its plain meaning, explaining it in reference to entertaining the thought of eating of the sacrifice on the third day, while performing one of the four sacrificial labors." For further discussion, see my article, "Din Piggul BiFeshuto Shel Mikra U'VeMidrash HaHalakha," in *Maamar HaZevaḥ* (Alon Shvut, 2010), 209–15.

32. For an explanation of what the Vilna Gaon means here, see *Torah Shelema*, 302; D. Hanschke, "Ein Mikra Yotzi Midei Peshuto," *HaMaayan* 17, 3 (5737/1977): 15–17.

accordance with it? If, on the other hand, the Sages' interpretation is binding in any case, what is the status and value of the *peshat* understanding?

I will suggest an answer to this question by addressing three types of cases where the *midrash halakha* stands in contrast to the *peshat*, with each category representing a different reason for the discrepancy.

Contradictions That Arise from Rabbinic Authority

The first category concerns instances where the contradiction between *peshat* and *derash* arises from the authority of the Sages to interpret the verses in a way that differs from their plain meaning.

Sometimes the differences between *peshat* and *derash* involve moral considerations. For example, consider one of the best-known cases of a discrepancy between the *peshat* and the *midrash halakha*: "an eye for an eye," *lex talionis*. This law is stated explicitly in the Torah in several places, including Leviticus 24:19–20:

> וְאִישׁ כִּי יִתֵּן מוּם בַּעֲמִיתוֹ - כַּאֲשֶׁר עָשָׂה, כֵּן יֵעָשֶׂה לּוֹ. שֶׁבֶר תַּחַת שֶׁבֶר, עַיִן תַּחַת עַיִן, שֵׁן תַּחַת שֵׁן - כַּאֲשֶׁר יִתֵּן מוּם בָּאָדָם כֵּן יִנָּתֶן בּוֹ.
>
> If a man maims his neighbor, then as he has done, so shall be done to him: A breach for a breach; an eye for an eye; a tooth for a tooth; as he has caused a man to be maimed, so shall it be caused to him.

The Talmud interprets the verse to mean that the person who inflicted the injury must provide monetary compensation, rather than actually receiving a physical punishment that parallels that injury he himself inflicted.[33]

---

33. The Talmud indeed questions, "Why [pay compensation]? God said, 'an eye for an eye,' so why not take this literally to refer to his actual eye?" (Bava Kamma 83b), and then goes on to list no less than ten ways of explaining the Sages' interpretation, including teachings derived from the verses and proofs based on logic. Out of the ten answers offered, five are rejected on the basis of questions which are not answered. S. Friedman, "Hosafot VeKitei 'Sevara' BePerek HaḤovel (Bava Kamma Perek 8)," *Tarbiz* 40 (5731/1971): 423, argues that all of the rejected answers are based on logic, while those that are accepted are derived from the verses themselves.

However, the plain meaning of the verse does suggest a physical punishment, as Maimonides notes:

> "As he has caused a man to be maimed, so it shall be caused to him" (Num. 35:33). You should not engage in cogitation concerning the fact that in such a case we punish by imposing a fine. For at present, my purpose is to give reasons for the [biblical] texts and not for the pronouncements of the halakha (Arabic, *fiqh*). Nevertheless, I have an opinion concerning this provision of the halakha which should only be expressed by word of mouth.[34]

Maimonides's son, Rabbi Avraham, likewise wrote in his Bible commentary on Exodus 21:24: "The plain meaning of the text is clear, and the traditional interpretation is that the text calls for the monetary value of a tooth as payment for a tooth, and so on concerning each instance."[35]

More intriguingly, just as Maimonides asserts that he has an explanation for the discrepancy between the plain meaning of the text and the Oral Law, but preferred not to set it down in writing, his son, too, writes, "Also my father and teacher, of blessed memory, in his *Guide*,

---

N. Zohar, *BeSod HaYetzira Shel Sifrut Ḥazal* (Jerusalem, 2007), 123–39, questions this assertion and argues instead that common to the rejected answers is that they are formulated by way of negation.

34. *Moreh Nevukhim* III:41 – *The Guide of the Perplexed*, transl. S. Pines (Chicago, 1963), 558. Onkelos, who often interprets verses in accordance with *midrash halakha*, also adheres to the plain meaning in this instance. For discussion of a systematic relationship between *peshat* and *midrash halakha* in Onkelos's translation, see R. B. Posen, *HaAkivut HaTirgumit BeTargum Onkelos* (Jerusalem, 2008), 114–19.

35. A similar phenomenon is to be found in relation to the law, כִּי יִנָּצוּ אֲנָשִׁים יַחְדָּו אִישׁ וְאָחִיו וְקָרְבָה אֵשֶׁת הָאֶחָד לְהַצִּיל אֶת אִישָׁהּ מִיַּד מַכֵּהוּ וְשָׁלְחָה יָדָהּ וְהֶחֱזִיקָה בִּמְבֻשָׁיו, וְקַצֹּתָה אֶת כַּפָּהּ לֹא תָחוֹס עֵינֶךָ, "If men strive together, one against the other, and the wife of one of them draws near to deliver her husband from the hand of he who smites him, and, in sending forth her hand, takes hold of his private parts, then you shall cut off her hand; your eye shall have no pity" (Deut. 25:11–12). Here, too, the plain meaning of the text suggests a bodily punishment, but the Sages teach that she is to pay monetary damages: "Rabbi Yehuda said: Here the text says, 'your eye shall have no pity,' and there (Deut. 19:21), it said, 'your eye shall have no pity.' Since the latter instance refers to monetary payment, so the same phrase here also refers to monetary payment" (*Sifrei* Deuteronomy 293, Finkelstein edition, 312).

hinted at an oral interpretation with a wondrous resolution between the received tradition and the plain meaning of the text, but it may not be written down, because he concealed it."

What is this secret that was concealed by Maimonides? Why, in fact, is there a discrepancy – even a contradiction – between the *peshat* and the *midrash halakha* in this regard?[36] In order to answer this question, we will need to review the relevant passages concerning the law of "an eye for an eye," both in the talmudic context, as well as in the writings of Maimonides and other commentators.

It must be noted at the outset that Maimonides's writings elsewhere give the reader a different impression. Maimonides writes in his *Mishneh Torah*:

> How do we know that, when the Torah states, concerning the limbs, "an eye for [*taḥat*] an eye," etc., it refers to financial restitution? For it is written, "a blow for [*taḥat*] a blow" (Ex. 21:25), and [concerning the administering of a blow] it states explicitly,

36. Admittedly, according to the second derivation in the above-cited passage in Bava Kamma, it is possible that the *peshat* and the *midrash halakha* are not necessarily contradictory. According to this teaching, the source of the law that monetary compensation is to be made, rather than bodily punishment, is the verse, וְלֹא תִקְחוּ כֹפֶר לְנֶפֶשׁ רֹצֵחַ אֲשֶׁר הוּא רָשָׁע לָמוּת כִּי מוֹת יוּמָת, "You shall take no ransom for the life of a murderer, who is guilty of death; rather, he shall surely be put to death" (Num. 35:31). Here the Sages explain, "'For the life of a murderer' you do not take a ransom – but you do take a ransom for the various types of limbs that cannot be restored." According to this understanding, the punishment in principle is indeed a physical one, but it may be exchanged for monetary payment, which is viewed not as compensation to the victim, but rather as a "ransom" for the limb of the offender.

However, further on the Gemara explains that it is precisely for this reason that this explanation alone cannot suffice, for it would seem to suggest that the choice of the alternative rests with the offender: "If he wishes he may pay with the loss of his eye, or if he desires otherwise he may pay the value of the eye" – and this is a reality that the Gemara cannot accept. It is interesting to note that Ibn Ezra – who, as noted, views halakha as binding even on the exegetical level, interprets the verse in this spirit: "Thus, 'an eye for an eye' means that the offender should indeed pay an eye for an eye, if he does not pay its ransom," and he offers a similar interpretation of the law that "you shall cut off her hand": "If her hand is not ransomed, it is cut off" – even though the Gemara categorically rules out the possibility of severing limbs, even if there is no payment of a ransom.

> "If a man strikes his fellow[37] with a stone or a fist…he shall pay for his idleness, and he shall surely be healed" [i.e., he pays also for his medical expenses] (Ex. 21:18–19). Since we learn that the word "*taḥat*," mentioned with regard to a blow, indicates financial restitution, we conclude that the same word used in relation to the eye and other limbs has the same meaning. (*Hilkhot Ḥovel U'Mazik* 1:5)[38]

Maimonides goes on to add:

> Although these interpretations are implicit in the Written Law, they are all also set forth in the tradition handed down by Moses from Mount Sinai, and they are all accepted as the practical ruling. This is what our ancestors saw [carried out] in the court of Joshua, and in Samuel's court in Ramah, and in each Jewish court that has functioned from the days of Moses until the present time.[39]

37. The wording of the verse as we have it is, "If men strive together and one smites another with a stone or with a fist."
38. It is not clear why Maimonides goes to the trouble of making this argument (to prove that the intent of the verse is financial restitution), which does not appear in the talmudic discussion, rather than simply bringing one of the non-rejected arguments that does appear there. Just prior to this (*Hilkhot Ḥovel U'Mazik* 1:3), he does in fact cite the second argument that appears in the talmudic discussion: "The meaning of the Torah's statement, 'as he has caused a man to be maimed, so shall it be caused to him,' is not that the offender should actually be injured in the same way that he injured his fellow. Rather, it means that he deserves to lose a limb, or to suffer the same injury that he inflicted – and therefore he should make financial restitution. Support for this is to be found in the fact that the verse states, וְלֹא תִקְחוּ כֹפֶר לְנֶפֶשׁ רֹצֵחַ, 'You shall not take a ransom for the life of a murderer' (Num. 35:31) – meaning that only a murderer has no ransom, but when it comes to the loss of a limb, or an injury, a ransom is paid." However, as noted, the Talmud goes on to reject this derivation as a sufficient source for the law. See *Leḥem Mishneh*, ad loc., who concludes that "the matter requires further study."
39. Maimonides sets forth the same idea in the introduction to his Commentary on the Mishna:

    This is a fundamental principle that you should know: The interpretations that have been handed down from Moses are not subject to any dispute, because until now we find no dispute among the Sages at any time in all the period from Moses until Rav Ashi, with one side claiming that someone who blinds

Maimonides seems to be contradicting himself. In *Moreh Nevukhim,* he writes that the plain meaning of the text is that the offender's eye is actually to be put out, while in *Mishneh Torah,* he writes that the Sages' conclusion that the reference is to monetary restitution is "implicit in the Written Law."[40] Moreover, asks the author of *Dor Revi'i,*[41] what is

---

> someone else must be [punished by being] blinded himself, in accordance with God's word, 'an eye for an eye,' and the other side arguing that this entails only monetary restitution.

But perhaps the matter is not so simple. At the end of the discussion in the Gemara, following the ten proofs that the punishment specified in the Torah actually refers to monetary restitution, a *baraita* is cited: "It was taught – Rabbi Eliezer said, 'An eye for an eye' refers to an actual eye." The Gemara rejects a literal understanding of this statement – "Do you mean this literally? Does Rabbi Eliezer then go against the view of all the *Tanna'im* [whose various explanations have already been discussed]?" It concludes with Rav Ashi's explanation: "This teaches that the value that is paid is calculated not in accordance with the victim, but rather in accordance with the offender." According to this view, the payment that Rabbi Eliezer has in mind is indeed not a matter of monetary compensation, calculated in accordance with the reduced value of the victim, but rather a payment made in accordance with the value of the offender. Hence, the payment does indeed function as a ransom.

In *Midrash Lekaḥ Tov (Pesikta Zutreta)* on Exodus 21:24, however, Rabbi Eliezer's approach is presented differently: "Since he [the perpetrator] sought to maim his fellow, he does not pay money, but rather has an actual injury inflicted upon him." Addressing the relationship between the midrash and the discussion in the Gemara, Rabbi Yerucham Fischel Perlow explains that Rabbi Eliezer's approach is indeed that a ransom is paid, and therefore if the money is not actually handed over, the law reverts to the original bodily punishment: "The law requires an actual 'eye for an eye,' but the Torah offers [the offender] the possibility of paying a ransom. If there is no way of getting the offender to pay the ransom, then the basic law remains that he pays an actual eye for an eye" (*Commentary on R. Saadia Gaon's Sefer HaMitzvot,* part III, *parasha* 29). This suggests that there was indeed some dispute over the question of whether the Torah is commanding a physical punishment with the option of a ransom, or whether the punishment is a monetary one in the first place. Hence, Maimonides's claim that there was never any dispute in this regard is problematic.

40. There is no room to draw a distinction between "what the verses mean" and that which is "implicit in the Written Law," as Y. Levinger shows in *HaRambam KeFilosof U'KePosek* (Jerusalem, 2010), 63–64, n. 8.

41. Rabbi Moses Shemuel Glasner (1856–1924) chose the title "*Dor Revi'i*" for his well-known work on Masekhet Ḥullin and for his book of responsa because he was the eldest great-grandchild of the Ḥatam Sofer. Rabbi Glasner was the rabbi of Klausenberg, and was one of the few religious leaders in Hungary who supported

the source for claiming that the law stating "an eye for an eye [means] monetary restitution" is a law handed down from Moses at Sinai (*halakha leMoshe miSinai*)?

> I find the claim that at no time in history did the court's sentence ever involve the [perpetrator's] actual eye very difficult to understand. Maimonides himself writes that with regard to all rabbinical interpretations, it is possible to rule contrary to the ruling of a previous court, but [argues that] this [particular law] is a law handed down by Moses from Sinai – which, according to the opinion of Maimonides, cannot be disputed. But the Sages taught their interpretation [that the reference is to monetary restitution] based on a logical deduction from "a blow for a blow," as Maimonides himself writes there. And in such an instance some court at some point in time must surely have had the power [to rule differently].[42]

The author of *Dor Revi'i* raises the possibility that at some point, "an eye for an eye" was observed literally, and only later did the Sages interpret it to mean money. If that is the case, however, then we must ask why the Sages moved away from the literal interpretation and instead define the punishment monetarily.

Similarly, Rabbi Kook establishes a principle that sheds light on the issue:

Zionism, going so far as to join the Mizrahi movement. Toward the end of his life he moved to Palestine and developed strong ties with Rabbi Kook, who supported him against the tide of opposition that he faced from the rabbis of Hungary (see "Perek BeHilkhot Tzibbur" in *Maamarei HaRe'aya* 1 [Jerusalem, 1984], 55–61). He was not afraid to publish original opinions, and in the introduction to his book he wrote, "I have been greatly scorned during my life, but thanks to the blessed God I have found no wrongdoing in myself or in the members of my household; they rose up against me to oppose me – but only because my way of study was not to their liking, and it was difficult for them to accept my reasoning, which went against those who came before me, with no prejudice. Therefore many joined together to oppose me, with no justification."

42. Introduction to *Dor Revi'i* (Jerusalem, 2004), 7.

> What I say is that the divine knowledge which sees everything, from the beginning to the end of time, encompasses the entire Torah. This belief is the true acceptance of God's absolute sovereignty: that all the causes which form and influence understanding, and the feelings leading to decisions in every generation, were prepared from the beginning, in the proper and correct way. Therefore, the truth of the Torah can be revealed only when the entire nation of God is in its land, perfected in all its spiritual and physical manners. Then the Oral Law will regain its essential condition, according to the understanding of the Great Court [Sanhedrin], which will sit "in the place that God will choose," and deal with matters too difficult for lower courts to judge. At that time, we may be certain that any new interpretation will be crowned with might and holiness, because Israel is holy to the Lord. And if a question arises about some law of the Torah, which ethical notions indicate should be understood in a different way, then truly, if the Sanhedrin decides that this law pertains only to conditions that no longer exist, a source in the Torah will certainly be found for it. The conjunction of events with the power of the courts and interpretation of the Torah is not a coincidence. They are rather signs of the light of the Torah and the truth of the Oral Law, for we are obligated to accept [the rulings of] the judge that will be in those days, and this is not a negative "development."
>
> But whoever wishes to judge in these times[43] – when we are in a poor state and our economic life is not ordered as it would be were the state of the nation in its proper form – according to the same exalted requirements, "it is ready for those whose foot slips." May God save us from such a view."[44]

Rabbi Kook raises a number of important principles here. The multiplicity of potential readings of the text means that the Torah anticipates different possibilities for interpretation in accordance with changing

43. That is, prior to the re-establishment of the Sanhedrin.

44. *Iggerot HaRe'aya*, vol. 1, letter 90 (Jerusalem, 1977), 103.

circumstances. The Torah proceeds from the assumption that, over time, the practical halakha may change in accordance with the circumstances of each generation, and no single criterion of practice can be applied to all generations or to all circumstances. In fact, this fundamental principle is set forth explicitly in the Jerusalem Talmud:

> Had the Torah been given in the form of clear-cut instructions, the world would have been unable to exist. What does this mean? "And the Lord said to Moses" – [Moses] said to Him: "Master of the Universe, tell me the halakha!" [God] said to him: "Incline in accordance with the majority" – if there are more who favor acquittal, he is acquitted; if there are more who favor conviction, he is convicted. Thus the Torah may be explained in forty-nine ways to arrive at a conclusion of ritual impurity and in forty-nine to arrive at a conclusion of ritual purity." (Y. Sanhedrin 4:2, 22a)

According to the Jerusalem Talmud, God refused to give Moses a Torah that was unequivocal in its interpretation, for if He had, it would have not been fit for "eternal existence" (*Penei Moshe*, ad loc.).[45] Instead, God gave him an eternal Torah of life, in which there are many different interpretative possibilities, all of them correct, and the decisions as to how to interpret it are the responsibility of the Sanhedrin in each generation.

The possibility of interpreting the Torah in accordance with the manner appropriate to it in each and every generation rests exclusively with the *Beit Din HaGadol* (Sanhedrin), in the ideal situation and conditions of the Jews dwelling in the land. Under those conditions, the Sanhedrin may rule, in accordance with their "ethical notions," that a certain law of the Torah "pertains only to situations that no longer exist," and, in light of changed circumstances, they are able to reinterpret the verses and God's will in a manner that is appropriate to the new conditions that have arisen. It is the conjunction of the interpretation of the text and the decision of the Sanhedrin, in view of contemporary events,

45. Commentary on the Talmud Yerushalmi by R. Moshe Margaliot (1710–1781), of Keidan in Lithuania.

that allows for changes in halakha that are made on the basis of moral considerations, in step with changes in human society.[46] Thus, Rabbi Kook maintained faith in the divine source of the Torah, along with its ability to be changed by the Sanhedrin in every generation, in accordance with changing circumstances. Rabbi Kook was well aware of the potential risks in stating such a view, and saw fit to emphasize that no such possibility exists at this time, in the absence of a Sanhedrin. "May God save us from such a view," he said.[47]

---

46. Rabbi Kook mentions this principle elsewhere, too. His approach to the biblically prescribed animal sacrifices was that in a future period, all of humanity might revert to vegetarianism, and then animal sacrifices would be annulled and only plant-based sacrifices would remain, such as the *minḥa* (see, for example, *Otzarot HaRe'aya* 2 [Tel Aviv, 1988], 755–56; *Olat Re'iya* 1 [Jerusalem, 1989], 292). Rabbi Kook raises the possibility that the Sanhedrin will then see fit, in keeping with their power to uproot from the Torah in the form of *shev ve'al taaseh* (omission of a certain action), to find an exemption from the mandatory animal sacrifices, since the killing of animals will already have ceased as a voluntary practice. And the text supports this, for the Torah calls a sacrifice "*leḥem*" (literally, "bread") – אֶת קָרְבָּנִי לַחְמִי לְאִשַּׁי, "My offering, the provision (*leḥem*) of My sacrifices made by fire" (Num. 28:2), but then it goes on to say, אֶת הַכֶּבֶשׂ אֶחָד, "the one lamb" (Num. 28:4). How can this be? So long as animals are killed for personal consumption, they should be offered as sacrifices to God. But when animals are not consumed voluntarily – then bring sacrifices of bread (Rabbi Kook, *Kevatzim MiKetav Yad Kodsho* 2 [Jerusalem, 2008], 15).

    In this context Rabbi Kook employs a different mechanism – that of *shev ve'al taaseh* (which may indeed be invoked here with no need for or possibility of interpreting the verses in any other way) – but here too he cites the principle that the Written Law already hints at the possibility of changing the halakha such that only plant-based sacrifices are to be brought.

47. Rabbi Kook's reservation here is, of course, an allusion to Reform Judaism's assertion that certain laws of the Torah are no longer relevant and must be reinterpreted. Rabbi Kook's argument with this position is that it is not tenable without the mechanism of the Sanhedrin, whose authority permits them to base changes upon reinterpretation of the biblical verses.

    It should be noted that Rabbi Kook's words here, concerning the possibility of interpreting verses in a different way in light of moral considerations, express a most audacious view that was not generally accepted and was not stated explicitly by Maimonides or any other great authorities over the course of the generations. It seems that fear of the possible effects of this view, leading to practical ramifications in keeping with the Reform approach, is what led to a new exegetical school in the nineteenth century which rejected outright the distinction between *peshat* and *derash*, thereby nullifying Rabbi Kook's point of departure.

In the biblical period, of course, there was little compunction about severing limbs as a form of corporal punishment,[48] allowing for the possibility that "an eye for an eye" was indeed followed literally at that time, as suggested by the author of *Dor Revi'i.* As the generations passed, and moral norms shifted, one who had maimed his fellow no longer had to have his own limb removed. The Sanhedrin therefore used

---

An outspoken representative of this school was the Malbim (Rabbi Meir Leibush Weiser, 1809–1879), who sets forth his theoretical approach to this question in the introduction to his commentary on Leviticus:

> In this commentary I have trodden a new path, clothed in sanctity, to explain the teachings of the Sages and their wisdom, the words of our teachers as handed down to them, in accordance with the rules of language and in accordance with the laws of rhetoric and logic, in wondrous new ways... I have shown and clarified with reliable proofs that the midrashic teaching is the simple *peshat* which is the inescapable meaning anchored in the depth of the language and the foundation of the Hebrew tongue. And all of the Oral Law is written explicitly in the Book of God's Torah. Application of the intellect leads to an understanding, through the text, of all the traditions handed down at Sinai, in accordance with the rules of language.... With this I have built a strong edifice to God's Name in which righteous and lofty ones may run; where the commanders of the forces might wage war against the Karaites and those who deny the traditions of *Ḥazal.* There they may refute the enemies of the tradition, confronting them face-to-face, bringing their claim and arguing their case, disputing and discerning and hearing and speaking the truth: Moses is truth and his Torah is truth, and his tradition is truth – all given from a Single Shepherd."

Malbim makes no attempt to conceal the fact that his commentary is directed against "the Karaites and those who deny the traditions of *Ḥazal*" – i.e., Reformers who argue for development of halakha. His approach to dealing with them is to prove that there had never been any development, and that the *midreshei halakha* are themselves the *peshat* of the text. This approach, which goes against the path of the *Rishonim* that we have previously examined, arose from the reality in which Malbim lived and the religious struggles of his era. For more about Malbim's approach see E. Touitou, "Bein Peshat LeDerash – Iyyun BeMishnato HaParshanit Shel HaMalbim," *Deot* 48 (5740/1980): 193–98; D. Berger, "Malbim's Secular Knowledge and His Relationship to the Spirit of the Haskalah," *Yavneh Review* 5 (1966): 24–46; and more recently, A. Frisch, "From Distinguishing between Synonyms to Revealing the Coherence of the Literary Unit: On the Interpretive Method of Malbim," *Judaica* 69 (2013): 393–429.

48. We see such behavior in a number of instances in Tanakh. Thus do the Jews act toward Adoni-Bezek (Judges 1:6), the Philistines put out the eyes of Samson (Judges 16:21), and the Babylonians blind Tzidkiyahu (II Kings 25:7).

its authority to interpret the verses in a different way, with the faith that this was God's will and that the Torah had permitted this change from the outset.[49]

Rabbi Kook's argument that halakha can and must change in accordance with the circumstances of each generation is unquestionably shared by Maimonides, in his *Guide of the Perplexed*. He writes:

> Since God, may He be exalted, knew that in every time and place the laws of the Torah – as far as some of them are concerned – will need to be added to or subtracted from, according to the places, happenings, and conjunctures of circumstances, He forbade adding to them or subtracting from them.... He permitted the men of knowledge of every period, i.e., the Sanhedrin, to take precautions with a view to consolidating the ordinances of the Torah, by means of regulations which they innovate with a view to repairing breaches.... Similarly, they were permitted in certain circumstances, or with a view to certain events, to abolish certain actions prescribed by the Torah or to permit some of the things forbidden by it; but these measures may not be perpetuated, as we have explained in the Introduction to the Commentary on the Mishnah, in speaking of temporary decisions. In this way, the Torah remains one, and one is governed in every time and with a view to every happening in accordance with that happening.... He, may He be exalted, has forbidden all men of knowledge with the single exception of the Sanhedrin to undertake this.[50]

Here, Maimonides addresses the need for the Sanhedrin to apply the Torah in changing circumstances, but he explicitly mentions only the mechanism of rabbinic enactments ("regulations" or "temporary measures"), which does not include the possibility of the reinterpretation

49. Thus it would seem that the Sadducees, who interpreted the verse "an eye for an eye" in the literal sense (see *Megillat Taanit*, 4 Tammuz, Noam edition [Jerusalem, 2004], 78–79), did not accept the principles of polysemy of the text and authority of the Sages to interpret the text, and therefore they believed that the law arising from the plain sense of the verses should be upheld for all generations.

50. *Guide* III:41; translation based on Pines, 563.

of verses, as mentioned by Rabbi Kook.[51] It may be this mechanism that Maimonides hinted to, when he stated, regarding "an eye for an eye" that he had an opinion which "I shall make known orally," for fear of possible misunderstanding.[52]

If, indeed, this was the "secret" view of Maimonides in his *Guide*, then it differed most radically from his words in the *Mishneh Torah*,[53] and

51. Maimonides's fundamental approach concerning the adaptation of mitzvot to changing circumstances also finds expression in his well-known views concerning the Temple and its sacrifices. Maimonides insists that many laws in the Torah were given to Israel at the time, since "it is impossible to move from one extreme to the other in a single jump. Accordingly, man's nature will not allow him to abandon all that he is used to, all at once." Since at the time of the Exodus "the accepted practice throughout the world at that time, and the conventional manner of worship that we were accustomed to, involved sacrificing different types of animals in those temples," God consequently did not require "the rejection of these manners of worship, to abandon them and nullify them, for in those days this would have been unthinkable, in terms of human nature – which is always comfortable with that which it is accustomed to" (*Guide* III:32). This suggests that the commandments concerning the Temple and the sacrifices were given to the Jews against the background of their particular time and place. Maimonides himself was aware of the radical nature of this theory, and he writes there: "I know that you will at first thought reject this idea and find it strange." Indeed, his explanation is attacked most vehemently by Nahmanides, in his commentary on Leviticus 1:9, as well as many other commentators. On this issue and its connection to our discussion, see A. Ravitzky, "HaRambam VeAlfarabi Al Hitpat'ḥut HaHalakha," in A. Ravitzky and A. Rosenak, *Iyyunim Ḥadashim BeFilosofia shel HaHalakha* (Jerusalem, 2008), 228–29.
52. The importance of presenting the halakhic approach in all its complexity, on the one hand, balanced against the danger of presenting apologetic explanations that may collapse when challenged by other worldviews, on the other, is the "justification" for our efforts to suggest what it was that Maimonides sought to keep hidden.
53. See especially the end of his *Hilkhot Me'ila* (8:8): "The decrees (*ḥukim*) are those laws whose rationale is not known. Our Sages taught, 'I ordained decrees for you, and you have no license to question them.'... All of the sacrifices are in the category of decrees. Our Sages said: 'The world exists for the sake of the sacrificial service.' For it is through the performance of the decrees and the judgments that the righteous merit the life of the World to Come." There are many sources that address this contradiction; see, e.g., Rabbi Y. Epstein, "LeShitat HaRambam BeTaamei HaKorbanot," in Rabbis Y. Y. Weinberg and P. Bieberfeld (eds.), *Yad Shaul* (Tel Aviv, 1953), 145–52; Rabbi Y. Cherlow, "Taamei HaKorbanot Shel HaRambam BeMishnat HaRav Kook," *Daat* 39 (5757/1997): 123–48.

this phenomenon occurs in other places, too.[54] Thus, according to the *Mishneh Torah*, the original intention of the Torah was that monetary restitution be given for bodily injury, while in the *Guide* he explains that the plain meaning of the verses is indeed corporal punishment – and it may be that he alludes to the idea proposed by Rabbi Kook, according to which the halakhic exegesis is part of the Torah's way of responding to changes in moral sensibility.[55]

One of the most important works of Hasidism, *Degel Maḥaneh Efraim*, which likewise reflects the view that *midreshei Ḥazal* are intended to adapt the Torah to every generation in accordance with its conditions and needs, says as follows:[56]

> The Written Law, without the Oral Law, is not a complete Torah; is it like half of a book – until the Sages came and interpreted the Torah, revealing its hidden matters. Sometimes they uproot something from the Torah, as in the matter of [the punishment of] lashes, concerning which the Torah says "forty," but the Sages

54. It should be noted that there are many places in which we find attitudes toward the mitzvot in *Mishneh Torah* different from those in the *Guide of the Perplexed*. A review of twelve such instances is undertaken by Y. Levinger, *HaRambam KeFilosof UKhePosek* (Jerusalem, 1992), 177–81. Levinger lists instances where it would seem that "the Rambam justifies – or seems to justify – the commandments of the Torah in a manner that is different from their interpretation in talmudic halakha."
55. Rabbi Mordekhai Breuer, "Ayin Taḥat Ayin," *Megadim* 24 (5755/1995): 21–25, rejects this sort of explanation. He argues, "We find no other instance where the Oral Law deviates from the Written Law solely out of compassion and human consideration." Instead, he raises a different possible resolution of the contradiction: "The Written Law expresses the punishment that is 'appropriate' to administer for the physical maiming, while the Oral Law expresses the compensation for the monetary loss. Since it is impossible to carry out both judgments simultaneously, the Sages ruled that the monetary restitution takes preference over the corporal punishment" (23). However, this explanation raises the obvious question: If the Written Law stipulates that corporal punishment takes preference, then why do the talmudic Sages reverse this? According to the explanation we have proposed, the reason for their innovation is understandable, since it is a response and reflection of changing circumstances, as described by Rabbi Kook.
56. *Degel Maḥaneh Efraim* was written by Rabbi Moshe Haim Efraim of Sadilkov (c. 1742–1800), grandson of the Baal Shem Tov. His work is one of the primary texts of *Ḥasidut*, in general, and of the teachings of the Baal Shem Tov in particular.

came and removed one,[57] all through the divine inspiration they received, which enabled them to do this.... The homiletic teachings of the Sages complement the Torah, such that it may be called a whole book. And likewise in every generation with its sages, they complete the Torah. For the Torah is interpreted in each and every generation in accordance with that which is needed for that generation, and in accordance with the root of the soul of that generation. Thus God illuminates the eyes of the sages of that generation with His holy Torah."[58]

In summary, we have discussed instances in which the Sanhedrin used its authority to reinterpret verses, so as to arrive at a broader understanding of what the Torah demands of us as circumstances change. This assumes that laws were bound to the social and historical realities in which they were given and are subject to reinterpretation as those conditions change.

There exists a second reason that the Sanhedrin might wield its authority to use a *midrash halakha* against the plain meaning of the text, and that is a practical consideration.

For example, consider the discussion about the time for sacrificing the *omer*. The time that the *omer* is brought has ramifications for the timing of the Shavuot festival. The Torah teaches that the *omer* offering must be waved מִמָּחֳרַת הַשַּׁבָּת, "on the day after the Sabbath" (Lev. 23:11), and then a count is immediately commenced, leading up to the festival when a new meal offering is brought:

וּסְפַרְתֶּם לָכֶם מִמָּחֳרַת הַשַּׁבָּת מִיּוֹם הֲבִיאֲכֶם אֶת עֹמֶר הַתְּנוּפָה שֶׁבַע שַׁבָּתוֹת תְּמִימֹת תִּהְיֶינָה. עַד מִמָּחֳרַת הַשַּׁבָּת הַשְּׁבִיעִת תִּסְפְּרוּ חֲמִשִּׁים יוֹם וְהִקְרַבְתֶּם מִנְחָה חֲדָשָׁה לַה׳.

And you shall count for yourselves from the day after the Sabbath, from the day that you brought the *omer* of the wave-offering,

57. See above. Intriguingly, this position of the grandson of the Baal Shem Tov echoes the words of the Vilna Gaon, the arch-opponent of the hasidic movement.

58. *Degel Maḥaneh Efraim* (Jerusalem, 1985), 5.

> seven complete Sabbaths shall there be. Until the day after the seventh Sabbath, you shall count fifty days, and you shall offer a new meal offering to God. (Lev. 23:15–16)

When the text speaks of "the Sabbath," it usually refers to the seventh day; thus, "the day after the Sabbath" would be Sunday. This interpretation is supported by the verses that follow, which speak of counting seven weeks leading to "the day after the seventh Sabbath," where the expression once again indicates Sunday, the day that follows the seventh Sabbath. Since the counting of the *omer* is not attached to any specific calendar date, there is no way of knowing the date of the end of the counting.[59] For this reason, the timing of the Shavuot festival – the fiftieth day of the counting – would not be defined by the date on which it falls (as the other festivals are), but rather by the day of the week.

However, the Sages taught that "from the day after the Sabbath" means "from the day after the festival" (Menaḥot 65b and elsewhere). On this basis, the *omer* is offered not on the Sunday of the week after Passover (nor on the Sunday of any week after that), but rather on the first day of Ḥol HaMoed (the intermediate days) of Passover – namely, on the sixteenth day of Nissan, the day after the first day of the festival. Thus, Shavuot will always fall fifty days after Passover. Here too, as in the discussion regarding the verse of "an eye for an eye," the Gemara cites many different proofs for this law, most of which are rejected. And this matter, likewise, was at the center of a great controversy with the Sadducees,[60] who maintained that the verse should be understood in its

59. It should be noted that in the period when the New Moon was sanctified and declared on the basis of testimony by witnesses, the exact date of Shavuot could not be calculated even if the date for the start of the count was given, since the date of the festival depended on the number of days in the months of Nissan and Iyar. (See Tosefta Arakhin 1:9 [Zukermandel edition, 543], noting that the festival can fall on the 5th, 6th, or 7th of Sivan: if Nissan and Iyar each have 30 days, Shavuot will fall on the 5th of Sivan; if one has 30 days and the other 29, then Shavuot will fall on the 6th; and if both months have 29 days then Shavuot will fall on the 7th of Sivan.)

60. It was owing to this controversy that the reaping of the *omer* was carried out on the sixteenth of Nissan with special pomp and ceremony, as described in the Mishna (Menaḥot 10:3): "And [the inhabitants of] all the neighboring towns would gather there in order that the reaping of the *omer* would be with great ceremony. When it

plain sense – that the reaping of the *omer* and the festival of Shavuot should both fall on Sundays.[61]

The Sages' interpretation was accepted by all of the commentators (including those like Rashbam, who adhere to the *peshat*), but it is difficult to ignore the fact that this understanding seems somewhat forced. First, nowhere else in Tanakh is the word "Shabbat," on its own, used to mean "festival."[62] Second, the word "Shabbat," if understood as a reference to the festival, makes no sense in relation to verse 16 – "until the day of the seventh Sabbath shall you count fifty days," since there is no additional festival ("Sabbath") on the forty-ninth day of the count. One must therefore conclude that the word "Sabbath" is used in two (!) unusual ways in these two verses: In verse 15, it means "festival," and in verse 16, it means "the end of the seventh week from the start of the

---

became dark he would say to them, 'Has the sun set?' They said, 'Yes.' [Again,] 'Has the sun set?' And they say – 'Yes.' '[With] this sickle?' They say, 'Yes.' [Again,] '[With] this sickle?' And they say – 'Yes.' 'In this basket?' They say, 'Yes.' 'In this basket?' They say – 'Yes.' On the Sabbath he says to them, 'On the Sabbath?' They say, 'Yes.' 'On the Sabbath?' They say, 'Yes.' 'Shall I reap?' And they say to him, 'Reap.' 'Shall I reap?' And they say to him, 'Reap.' [Thus] three repetitions for each and every detail, and they say to him, 'Yes,' 'yes,' 'yes.' Why all this ceremony? Because of the Boethusians, who said, 'There is no reaping of the *omer* at the conclusion of the festival.'"

61. The conflict is described in *Megillat Taanit* (Noam edition, 59–63, 174–79), and it is cited in the discussion in Menaḥot 65a–b: "The Boethusians said: 'Shavuot is [celebrated] on the day after the Sabbath [i.e., Sunday].' Rabban Yoḥanan ben Zakkai contended with them, saying: 'Fools, from where do you deduce this?' And none of them was able to answer him, except for one old man who began prattling before him, saying: 'Moses our teacher loved Israel, and he knew that Shavuot was only one day, so he fixed it on the day after the Sabbath so that the Jewish people could enjoy two days [of festivity].' He [Rabban Yoḥanan ben Zakkai] then quoted them this verse: אַחַד עָשָׂר יוֹם מֵחֹרֵב דֶּרֶךְ הַר שֵׂעִיר עַד קָדֵשׁ בַּרְנֵעַ, 'It is a journey of eleven days from Horeb by way of Mount Se'ir to Kadesh Barnea' (Deuteronomy 1:2); if Moses loved the Jewish people, why did he keep them in the wilderness for forty years?" This anecdote presents the Sadducees in an ironic light, for the simple answer to Rabbi Yoḥanan ben Zakkai's question should have been that that is the plain meaning of the text.

62. A festival is sometimes referred to as "*Shabbaton*," but even this appellation is used only with reference to the festivals in the month of Tishrei (the "day of sounding of the shofar" [Rosh HaShana], Yom Kippur [the only day that is referred to as "*Shabbat Shabbaton*"], Sukkot, and *Shemini Atzeret*; see Lev. 23:24, 32:39); it is never used with reference to Passover.

counting" (see Rashi). How are we to understand this rather significant discrepancy between the plain meaning of the text and the Sages' interpretation of it?[63]

The key to understanding this puzzle is to be found in the words of Rabbi Yehuda HaLevi (1075–1141), in his great work, *The Kuzari*:

> Even if we accept the Karaite[64] interpretation of the verses, "From the day after the Sabbath" and "until the day after the Sabbath" (Lev. 23:11, 15, 16), to refer to Sunday, we submit that one of the judges, or *kohanim*, or kings who were righteous in the eyes of God, interpreted the verse thus, and the Sanhedrin and all of the Sages were in agreement with him, that the counting is intended to create an interval of fifty days between "the first fruits of the barley harvest" and "the first fruits of the wheat harvest," and to maintain "seven weeks," which are "seven complete Sabbaths." The first day of the week is only mentioned as an example, as if to say: If the beginning – the day of "putting the sickle to the standing corn" – is a Sunday, then you will reach the end of your count on a Sunday. From this we deduce that if the beginning [of the count] is on a Monday, then we count until a Monday. But the time of "putting the sickle to the standing corn" is in our hands: we may start [putting the sickle to the corn] whenever we see fit, and count from that day. And indeed, that day was fixed as the second day of Passover. This in no way contradicts the Torah, and we are obligated to accept this ruling as a commandment, since it emerged from "the place which the Lord shall choose."[65]

63. The question is discussed at length and in detail by Rabbi David Zvi Hoffmann in his *Perush LeSefer Vayikra*, vol. II (Jerusalem, 1959), 113–51. For a different direction see Rabbi Y. Bin-Nun, "Ḥametz U'Matza BePesaḥ, BeShavuot U'VeKorbanot HaLeḥem," *Megadim* 13 (5751/1991), 32–37.
64. On this point there is a connection between the Karaites and the Sadducees (a fairly rare occurrence), since the Karaites also interpreted "the day of the Sabbath" as a reference to Sunday (Corinaldi, "Karaites," *HaEncyclopedia HaIvrit* 30 [Jerusalem-Tel Aviv, 1978], column 45).
65. *Sefer HaKuzari*, part III, section 41.

Rabbi Yehuda HaLevi raises the possibility that in an earlier period, Shavuot did indeed fall on a Sunday every year, as suggested by the plain meaning of the expression "from the day after the Sabbath." However, at a later stage, "one of the judges, or *kohanim*, or kings who were righteous in God's eyes" changed this practice, and this change was accepted by the Sages of the Sanhedrin.

Rabbi Yehuda HaLevi's suggestion here makes two assumptions: first, in using the expression "from the day after the Sabbath," the Torah means only to illustrate the manner in which the date of Shavuot is to be calculated, rather than give instruction that the *omer* be sacrificed and the counting commenced specifically on a Sunday.[66] In other words, the verse is descriptive rather than prescriptive. Second, he assumes that it was agreed, and confirmed by the Sanhedrin, that the beginning of the

---

66. Seemingly, an argument could be brought against Rabbi Yehuda HaLevi from the verse, וַיֹּאכְלוּ מֵעֲבוּר הָאָרֶץ מִמָּחֳרַת הַפֶּסַח מַצּוֹת וְקָלוּי בְּעֶצֶם הַיּוֹם הַזֶּה, "They ate of the corn of the land on the day after the Passover, unleavened bread and parched corn, on that very day" (Josh. 5:11), which would appear to parallel the verses relating to the counting of the *omer*: וְהֵנִיף אֶת הָעֹמֶר לִפְנֵי ה׳ לִרְצֹנְכֶם מִמָּחֳרַת הַשַּׁבָּת יְנִיפֶנּוּ הַכֹּהֵן... וְלֶחֶם וְקָלִי וְכַרְמֶל לֹא תֹאכְלוּ עַד עֶצֶם הַיּוֹם, "And he shall wave the *omer* before God to be accepted for you; on the day after the Sabbath shall the *kohen* wave it.... And you shall eat neither bread nor parched corn nor green ears until that very day" (Lev. 23:11–14). From here we see that already by the time of Joshua it was established that "on the morrow of *the Sabbath*" means "on the morrow of Passover" (see Maimonides, *Hilkhot Temidin U'Musafin* 4:11). However, the verse in Joshua is difficult to understand in light of the Sages' interpretation, since the expression "Passover," as a date, always refers to the fourteenth of Nissan (see, for example, Num. 28:16; Josh. 5:10). Thus, in this context "the morrow after the Passover" means the fifteenth day of Nissan, and this appears explicitly: וַיִּסְעוּ מֵרַעְמְסֵס בַּחֹדֶשׁ הָרִאשׁוֹן בַּחֲמִשָּׁה עָשָׂר יוֹם לַחֹדֶשׁ הָרִאשׁוֹן מִמָּחֳרַת הַפֶּסַח יָצְאוּ בְנֵי יִשְׂרָאֵל בְּיָד רָמָה לְעֵינֵי כָּל מִצְרָיִם, "They journeyed from Ramesses in the first month, on the fifteenth day of the first month; on the morrow of the Passover the Jews went out with a high hand in the sight of all of Egypt" (Num. 33:3). Indeed, the Sages are divided as to whether the expression, "on the morrow of the Passover" in Joshua refers to the fifteenth or the sixteenth of Nissan (Y. Ḥalla 2:1; 58b), and whether the prohibition on the "new" produce was observed already at this stage, or whether it came into effect only after the inheritance of the land. Even the "*peshat*" commentators agree that the plain meaning of the verse in Joshua refers to the fifteenth of Nissan, and therefore the text is not talking about eating of the new produce, but rather about eating of the old produce (see Radak on Josh. 5:11; Ibn Ezra on Lev. 23:11).

counting – "when the sickle is put to the standing corn" (Deut. 16:9) – would always be from the second day of Passover.

Rabbi Yehuda HaLevi's words make a substantial contribution to reconciling the discrepancy between the *peshat* and the *midrash halakha.* When the Sages declared that "from the day after the Sabbath" means "from the day after the festival," they did not mean this as an *interpretation* of the verse in Leviticus; rather, they meant it as a *halakhic ruling,* by virtue of the authority of the Sanhedrin to decide the beginning of the count on a particular date – though the Torah itself makes no such stipulation.

That said, Rabbi Yehuda HaLevi's solution does not explain why in fact it was decided that the count would begin specifically on the sixteenth of Nissan, rather than on another date. The answer to this question is found in a *baraita:*

> "On the day of the Sabbath" – that is, on the day of the festival. Or perhaps it is not so, but rather on the day after the Sabbath of Creation [i.e., the seventh day]? Rabbi Yossi ben Yehuda said: "The text says, 'You shall count fifty days': the whole count that you make will be only fifty days." For if you were to say that the verse refers to the day after the Sabbath of Creation, then it would sometimes come to 51, sometimes to 52, 53, 54, 55, or 56. (Menaḥot 65b)[67]

This seems rather opaque. How does one get to these larger counts from the command to count fifty days?[68] The explanation, however, is quite simple: these numbers (51 to 56) testify to the varying interval between

67. The discussion in the Gemara brings several proofs for the assertion that "the morrow of the Sabbath" means the morrow of the festival. The very attempt to cite proofs would seem to weaken Rabbi Yehuda HaLevi's argument that this is a halakhic ruling that does not have a basis in the verses. However, according to Rabbi Yehuda HaLevi one could suggest that the Gemara is seeking "*asmakhtaot,*" i.e., attempts to find allusions to a law which is not actually derived from the verses.
68. In light of this question, the Gemara argues at the end of the discussion at Menaḥot 56a that indeed this claim can be disproved, since "perhaps the verse intends fifty days, not including these other six days" (see Rashi ad loc.).

the first day of Passover and Shavuot. If the counting begins on the first Sunday after the first day of Passover, then the interval between the first day of Passover and Shavuot changes from year to year: when the fifteenth of Nissan falls on a Sabbath, the count will begin on the sixteenth, and Shavuot will be celebrated fifty days later. But if the fifteenth of Nissan falls on a Friday, then the count will begin only on the seventeenth of Nissan (the following Sunday), and Shavuot will fall fifty-one days from the first day of Passover. If the fifteenth of Nissan falls on Thursday, the count will begin on the eighteenth of Nissan, and Shavuot will fall fifty-two days after the first day of Passover, and so on.

Why was maintaining a fixed period of time between Passover and Shavuot important? Perhaps the motive was simply practical. Fixing the beginning of the count on the sixteenth of Nissan yielded a (relatively) fixed date for Shavuot, given its exceptional status of no set calendar date, as compared to the other Torah festivals.[69] In ancient times, according to Rabbi Yehuda HaLevi, Shavuot would fall on a different date each year, and there would be a varying number of days between Passover and Shavuot. In that era, two variables affected the date of Shavuot: the day of the week on which the first day of Passover occurred, and the respective lengths of the months of Nissan and Iyar. In a later period, however, only the length of the months of Nissan and Iyar affected the date of Shavuot.[70] Fixing the number of days between Passover and Shavuot meant Jews were able to know when Shavuot would fall without having to conduct complex calculations every year. Thus, the Sages' aim arose from practical considerations.

This discussion offers us the possibility of understanding other instances in which we find a discrepancy between the *peshat* of the verses

69. The date of the festival was still not altogether fixed, because in those times, before the calendar itself was fixed, a count of fifty days after the first day of Passover could lead to any one of three dates, depending on whether the months of Nissan and Iyar had 30 days or 29 days: "Shavuot can fall on the 5th, the 6th, or the 7th [of Sivan] – no earlier and no later" (Tosefta Arakhin 1:9, Zukermandel edition, 543).
70. The process of fixing the date of Shavuot in the calendar as the sixth of Sivan was only completed with the transition from sanctification of the new month on the basis of testimony from eyewitnesses, to the adoption of the fixed calendar year.

and *midreshei halakha*[71] as stemming from practical considerations as well.[72] These considerations were viewed as important by *Ḥazal*, and therefore some of their *midreshei halakha* were intended to serve these purposes.

Contradictions between Different Texts

The second category of tensions between *peshat* and *derash* are contradictions that arise between different *parshiot* in the Torah itself. In an earlier chapter, the phenomenon of contradictions within the text, and the aspects approach of Rabbi Mordechai Breuer that attempts to explain them, were discussed at length. The following discussion will be limited to those contradictions that influence and affect *midreshei halakha*.

---

71. It may be that the same idea applies also to other instances where the Written Law leaves room for maneuver, which is then limited by the Oral Law. For instance, the Torah gives no definition of the quantity of bread that must be consumed for the Blessing after Meals to be obligatory; it states merely, וְאָכַלְתָּ וְשָׂבָעְתָּ וּבֵרַכְתָּ אֶת ה' אֱלֹהֶיךָ עַל הָאָרֶץ הַטֹּבָה אֲשֶׁר נָתַן לָךְ, "You shall eat and you shall be satisfied and you shall bless the Lord your God for the good land which He has given you" (Deut. 8:10), but the Oral Law gives objective measurements – a "*kezayit*" or a "*kebeitza*" (the volume of an olive or the volume of an egg). As the Sages teach: "God said to [the ministering angels]: And shall I not lift up My countenance to Israel, seeing that I wrote for them in the Torah, 'You shall eat and be satisfied and bless the Lord your God,' but they take care [to recite Grace after Meals] even over the quantity of a mere olive or a mere egg" (Berakhot 20b).

    Likewise concerning the quantity of produce from which *teruma* (a tithe) must be taken: the Torah offers no definition of the quantity that must be given to the *kohen*, but gives a general instruction, כֹּל חֵלֶב יִצְהָר וְכָל חֵלֶב תִּירוֹשׁ וְדָגָן רֵאשִׁיתָם אֲשֶׁר יִתְּנוּ לַה' לְךָ נְתַתִּים, "All the best of the oil and all the best of the wine, and of the wheat, the first of them which they shall offer to God – to you have I given them" (Num. 18:12). However, the Sages provide defined guidelines: "One part in forty is considered generous... a medium measure is one in fifty, while one part in sixty is considered meager" (Terumot 4:3). Therefore we might propose that underlying these *midreshei halakha* is the desire to establish defined halakhic norms.

72. The idea of explaining some of the contradictions between *midreshei halakha* and the *peshat* as arising from practical considerations is developed at length by Shadal. For a discussion of his approach in this realm, see S. Vargon, "Shadal's Critical Attitude Towards *Chazal*'s Halakhic Interpretations that Run Counter to the Simple Meaning of the Text," *JSIS* 2 (2003): 97–122; Lockshin, 39–45.

Recall the earlier discussion on the contradiction in the text concerning the freeing of the *eved Ivri*, the Hebrew indentured servant. Leviticus states explicitly that a Hebrew servant is always freed in the Jubilee year (Lev. 25:40–42), but according to Deuteronomy, after the servant's ear is bored through, he remains in his master's house "forever" (*le'olam*) (Deut. 15:17). The plain meaning of the latter verse is that he remains a servant to his master until his death.[73]

It was explained that the contradictions between the two textual units arise from the fact that each expresses a different perspective on the master-servant relationship. Leviticus adopts a theocentric perspective, emphasizing God's sovereignty and direct "ownership" of the Jewish people. From this point of view, a Jew cannot be a true servant to another Jew, since fundamentally the Jew is God's servant, and so the Hebrew servant will always go free in the Jubilee year. In Deuteronomy, by contrast, the focus is anthropocentric. Within this framework, once the master has fulfilled his moral obligation to free the servant in the seventh year, and the servant has refused this freedom and asked to remain in his master's house, then, according to this perspective, the servant must indeed remain forever.

Given this backdrop, the Sages' interpretation of serving "forever" in Exodus and in Deuteronomy as meaning "until the Jubilee" makes sense. "For all time" is thereby defined as "for all the time, until the Jubilee." It is not meant as a narrow interpretation of the word "forever" (*le'olam*),[74] but as an understanding of the *parshiot* in the Torah as a whole that deal with the topic, each of which expresses an independent value or ideal, and which together form a single coherent instruction on the practical halakhic level.

---

73. As explained, for example, by Rashbam (Ex. 21:6): "According to the plain meaning, this means 'for his whole life,' as it is written concerning Samuel, 'and he will abide there forever (*ad olam*)' (I Sam. 1:22)."

74. Admittedly, Ibn Ezra, who – as we have noted – regards the *midrash halakha* as the decisive interpretation of the text, argues that "*olam*" actually means "*yovel*" (Jubilee): "We know that the word '*le'olam*' in the holy tongue means a [defined] time… and likewise 'he shall serve him forever' means – 'for all the time until the Jubilee,' for there is no Jewishly defined period of time longer than that."

Rabbi Breuer regarded this as a model for many instances of contradiction between *peshat* and *midrash halakha*:

> Many contradictions between different *parshiot* in the Torah may be resolved in a similar way. In each case, we must first seek the starkly contrasting objectives [of the different *parshiot*]. Then we must seek that which they share, which bridges the aforementioned contrasts. It will usually turn out that the *midreshei Ḥazal* that resolve the contradictions actually sit well with a deeper understanding of the plain meaning of the text. They do not accord with the separate plain meanings that contradict one another, but they do accord with the plain meaning that bridges the contradictory units.[75]

Consider another example. With regard to a firstborn animal, Deuteronomy (15:19–20) stipulates:

> כָּל הַבְּכוֹר אֲשֶׁר יִוָּלֵד בִּבְקָרְךָ וּבְצֹאנְךָ הַזָּכָר תַּקְדִּישׁ לַה׳ אֱלֹהֶיךָ, לֹא תַעֲבֹד בִּבְכֹר שׁוֹרֶךָ וְלֹא תָגֹז בְּכוֹר צֹאנֶךָ. לִפְנֵי ה׳ אֱלֹהֶיךָ תֹאכְלֶנּוּ שָׁנָה בְשָׁנָה בַּמָּקוֹם אֲשֶׁר יִבְחַר ה׳ אַתָּה וּבֵיתֶךָ.
>
> Every firstborn male of your herd and of your flock shall you sanctify to the Lord your God; you shall do no work with the firstborn of your bullock, nor shear the firstborn of your sheep. You shall eat it before the Lord your God year by year in the place which the Lord shall choose, you and your household.

According to the plain meaning of the verse, every person who has a firstborn male born in his herd or his flock must consume it before God.[76] Why, then, do Rashi, Ibn Ezra, and others explain that the verse

75. *Shitat HaBeḥinot shel HaRav Mordekhai Breuer* (Alon Shvut, 2005), 69–70.
76. This is also the plain meaning arising from the verse in Deut. 12:17: לֹא תוּכַל לֶאֱכֹל בִּשְׁעָרֶיךָ מַעְשַׂר דְּגָנְךָ וְתִירֹשְׁךָ וְיִצְהָרֶךָ וּבְכֹרֹת בְּקָרְךָ וְצֹאנֶךָ, "You may not eat within your gates the tithe of your corn or of your wine or of your oil, or the firstborn of your herds or of your flocks."

is actually addressing itself to the priest, based on the Sages' teaching that "the firstborn is eaten by the priests" (Mishna Zevaḥim 5:8)?[77] It seems that the reason for this is that Numbers (18:17–18) states explicitly that it is the priests who eat the firstborn animals:

> אַךְ בְּכוֹר שׁוֹר אוֹ בְכוֹר כֶּשֶׂב אוֹ בְכוֹר עֵז לֹא תִפְדֶּה קֹדֶשׁ הֵם אֶת דָּמָם תִּזְרֹק עַל הַמִּזְבֵּחַ וְאֶת חֶלְבָּם תַּקְטִיר אִשֶּׁה לְרֵיחַ נִיחֹחַ לַה׳ וּבְשָׂרָם יִהְיֶה לָּךְ כַּחֲזֵה הַתְּנוּפָה וּכְשׁוֹק הַיָּמִין לְךָ יִהְיֶה.
>
> But the firstborn of an ox, or the firstborn of a sheep, or the firstborn of a goat, you shall not redeem, for they are holy. You shall sprinkle their blood upon the altar, and you shall burn their fat as a fire offering, a pleasing aroma unto God. And their flesh shall be yours, as the breast of the waving and as the right thigh, it shall be yours.

The contradiction lies not between the Sages' teaching and the verses, but between the two biblical passages themselves. The contradiction arises from the different perspectives of Numbers and Deuteronomy, with regard to the relative statuses of the priests and the Jews.[78] The halakhic ruling therefore combines the two perspectives, in practice, permitting

---

77. In this instance there is no explicit *midrash halakha* that explains the verse in this way, but the interpretation offered by Rashi and Ibn Ezra (that the verse is talking about the priest) is the unavoidable conclusion of the mishna.
78. This is a subject worthy of extensive discussion in its own right, but suffice it to mention briefly that the general view of Deuteronomy is that the Jewish people as a whole was worthy of being a עַם קָדוֹשׁ...לִהְיוֹת לוֹ לְעַם סְגֻלָּה מִכֹּל הָעַמִּים, "holy nation…a nation chosen from among all nations" (Deut. 14:2), as indeed was promised before the Revelation at Sinai: וְאַתֶּם תִּהְיוּ לִי מַמְלֶכֶת כֹּהֲנִים וְגוֹי קָדוֹשׁ, "And you shall be for Me a kingdom of *kohanim* and a holy nation" (Ex. 19:6). Therefore, according to the text of Deuteronomy, there are prohibitions that apply to the nation as a whole by virtue of its status as a holy nation – even though in the other books of the Torah these prohibitions are specified as applying only to the *kohanim* or the *leviim* (such as the prohibition of making a bald patch and eating a carcass; cf. Lev. 21:5 and 22:8 with Deut. 14:1, 21). Deuteronomy presents a reality in which all Jews eat the firstborn animals, as well as the tithes (14:22–23). Furthermore, the tithe of Deuteronomy is referred to by the Sages as

only the priests to eat the firstborn animals, though the plain meaning of the verse in Deuteronomy indicates that ordinary Jews, too, may eat of the firstborn animals.

In conclusion, this category of contradictions includes instances where the Sages implement a broad view that takes into account even contradictory *parshiot* in the Torah, to establish a system of unified halakhic behavior.

Different Approaches to the *Peshat*

The third category where the *midrash halakha* stands in contrast to the *peshat* can be illustrated by the textual unit dealing with guardians. In Exodus we read:

> כִּי יִתֵּן אִישׁ אֶל רֵעֵהוּ כֶּסֶף אוֹ כֵלִים לִשְׁמֹר וְגֻנַּב מִבֵּית הָאִישׁ אִם יִמָּצֵא הַגַּנָּב יְשַׁלֵּם שְׁנָיִם. אִם לֹא יִמָּצֵא הַגַּנָּב וְנִקְרַב בַּעַל הַבַּיִת אֶל הָאֱלֹהִים אִם לֹא שָׁלַח יָדוֹ בִּמְלֶאכֶת רֵעֵהוּ.
>
> If a man gives his neighbor money or vessels to keep for him, and it is stolen from that man's house, then if the thief is found, he pays double. If the thief is not found, then the master of the house is brought to the judges [to swear] that he did not put his hand to his neighbor's goods. (Ex. 22:6–7)

And shortly after this passage follows:

> כִּי יִתֵּן אִישׁ אֶל רֵעֵהוּ חֲמוֹר אוֹ שׁוֹר אוֹ שֶׂה וְכָל בְּהֵמָה לִשְׁמֹר וּמֵת אוֹ נִשְׁבַּר אוֹ נִשְׁבָּה אֵין רֹאֶה. שְׁבֻעַת ה׳ תִּהְיֶה בֵּין שְׁנֵיהֶם אִם לֹא שָׁלַח יָדוֹ בִּמְלֶאכֶת רֵעֵהוּ וְלָקַח בְּעָלָיו וְלֹא יְשַׁלֵּם. וְאִם גָּנֹב יִגָּנֵב מֵעִמּוֹ יְשַׁלֵּם לִבְעָלָיו.
>
> If a man gives his neighbor a donkey or an ox or a sheep, or any animal, to keep for him, and it dies, or is hurt, or is taken away,

---

"*maaser sheni,*" which is different from the "*maaser rishon*" referred to in Numbers 18:21. The tithe of Numbers is given to the *leviim*, while Deuteronomy mentions only the *maaser* that is eaten by all Jews.

> with no one seeing, then an oath of God shall be between both of them that [the guardian] did not put his hand to his neighbor's goods, and the owner shall accept this, and [the guardian] shall not pay. But if it was stolen from him, he shall make restitution to its owner. (Ex. 22:9–11)

In the first passage, the guardian swears that the object was stolen from him, and he is exempt from payment. In the second, the guardian is obligated to pay – even in the event that the object was stolen; he is exempt, following his oath, only where what happened was unavoidable. What is the difference between the two types of guardians? A *baraita* explains: "The first unit is talking about an unpaid guardian, while the second refers to a paid guardian.... Thus, it must be that the second instance refers to a paid guardian, for he is liable in the case of both theft and loss" (Bava Metzia 94b).

The plain meaning of the text suggests that the difference between the two passages is not whether the guardian is being paid for his services (as that is not explicitly mentioned at all), but what he is watching over. The first passage starts with the words, "If a man gives his neighbor money or vessels to keep for him," while the second speaks of "a donkey or an ox or a sheep or any animal." That is, are objects or animals being watched over? Rashbam explains the discrepancy between the verses as follows:

> In this [first] section (vv. 6–8), the keeper is described as not being liable in a case of theft or loss. In the second section (vv. 9–12), the keeper is described as being responsible in a case of theft or loss. The rabbis explained that the first unit refers to a keeper who is not being paid, while the second refers to a paid keeper. However, following the plain meaning of Scripture, the first section – "If a man gives his neighbor money or vessels to keep" – refers to the guarding of movables that are commonly kept inside one's house, and that were given to him so that he would guard them in the same way that he guards his own possessions. That is why, if they were stolen from his house, the keeper is not responsible, for he guarded them as he guards

> his own possessions. But in the second section (vv. 9–12), "If a man gives his neighbor a donkey, or an ox, or a sheep, or any animal, to guard," since animals commonly graze in the field, it is to be assumed that when he entrusted them [to the keeper], he expected that the keeper would protect them from thieves. Accordingly, if they were stolen, the keeper is responsible.[79]

According to Rashbam, a person who is watching over some objects and keeps them together with his own possessions is exempt in the case of a burglary, because he gives them the same care he gives his own possessions.[80] But when one is asked to watch over animals, one accepts the responsibility with the intention of keeping them outside, and therefore a higher level of protection is required from the outset.[81]

Rashbam's explanation appears to be a straightforward and compelling reading of the verses. The question remains, however, why the

79. Based on the translation in Lockshin, *Rashbam's Commentary on Exodus*, 253–54.

80. Rashbam's criterion, according to which it suffices that a person take the same care of the object that he does of his own possessions, is not a simple one; there are many authorities who demand a higher level of protection for objects that he is keeping for someone else. See Lockshin, *Rashbam's Commentary on Exodus*, 253–54, notes 17 and 18.

81. Rashbam's comment here differs from its citation in the *Tosafot* on Bava Metzia 41b: "And Rabbenu Shmuel (Rashbam) explained that we can logically deduce that the first section (verses 6–7), which speaks of guarding 'money or vessels,' is speaking about an unpaid guardian since people do not usually take money for looking after these sorts of objects, since guarding them does not require much exertion. In the second section (verses 9–11), which speaks of an 'animal,' we can deduce that this is speaking of a paid guardian, since greater exertion is involved in guarding animals."

This explanation suggests that there is in fact no discrepancy between the plain meaning of the text, as set forth above, and the *midrash halakha*, because guarding money or vessels means (or may be defined as) guarding for free, while guarding animals is called (or may be defined as) guarding for payment. This approach is adopted by many of the commentators, including Nahmanides, *Ḥizkuni*, and Sforno. However, Rashbam, in his Commentary on the Torah, maintains that according to the plain level of the text, if a person is guarding objects – even if he is receiving payment for his services – he is exempt in the event of a burglary, in contrast to his opinion as cited by *Tosafot*. Likewise the corollary – if he is guarding animals, he will always be obligated to pay restitution in the event of burglary, even if he was guarding them for free.

Sages did not take his approach and differentiate between the two passages on the basis of what is being guarded, and instead distinguished between the two cases on the basis of whether payment is made to the guardian.[82]

It would seem that the explanation hinges upon the question of what, in fact, represents the "*peshat.*" To complicate matters, yet another verse seems to blur the distinction between watching over objects and watching over animals:

> עַל כָּל דְּבַר פֶּשַׁע עַל שׁוֹר עַל חֲמוֹר עַל שֶׂה עַל שַׂלְמָה עַל כָּל אֲבֵדָה אֲשֶׁר יֹאמַר כִּי הוּא זֶה עַד הָאֱלֹהִים יָבֹא דְּבַר שְׁנֵיהֶם אֲשֶׁר יַרְשִׁיעֻן אֱלֹהִים יְשַׁלֵּם שְׁנַיִם לְרֵעֵהוּ.
>
> For all manner of wrongdoing – whether it be for an ox, for a donkey, for a sheep, for a garment, or for any lost thing concerning which one might say, "This is it" – the cause of both parties shall come before the judges, and whomever the judges condemn – he shall pay double to his neighbor. (Ex. 22:8)

It seems, then, that the Sages indeed viewed this verse, which treats objects and animals in the same light, as definitively negating any categorical distinction between different types of possessions given for keeping:

> The text is speaking about two kinds of guardians. [Do we conclude that it is speaking about two kinds of guardians,] or that the text means to draw a distinction between money and vessels, on

82. Shadal, in his commentary on this verse, adopts the same view as Rashbam, and adds – in keeping with his general approach, which we have discussed previously: "Our Sages rule leniently, stating that he is not guilty of any wrongdoing if he was not paid [for guarding]." This suggests that the Sages did indeed deliberately introduce a change in the law, rendering it more lenient – but he offers no explanation as to why they would do this. It must be remembered that a leniency in the obligations of the guardian entails, at the same time, a stricter liability on the part of the person who deposits the object with the guardian; for this reason, I find this explanation problematic.

> the one hand, and animals, on the other? The key here lies in the word "garment" – a "garment" would seemingly be included in the first category (money and objects), but it is singled out – to teach that just as the text is talking about two kinds of guardians with regard to a garment, which is a singular object, so likewise the text is talking about two kinds of guardians with regard to any object; the text does not mean to draw a distinction between money and vessels, on the one hand, and animals, on the other.[83]

Rashbam, of course, addresses this verse, and explains it in a different way:

> "For all manner of wrongdoing," when the pledged item was stolen, whether that pledge was an ox, a sheep, a garment, or any other lost thing, and the depositor [owner] says "this is it – [that is,] the money that was stolen from me," then either the thief or the [thieving] keeper "shall pay double to his neighbor."[84]

Rashbam understands that the point of the verse is not to determine who pays, but to stipulate that whenever an owner claims that a given object belongs to him, and the court accepts his claim, then the guilty party must pay double, whether it is the guardian or a thief.

The difference between the *peshat* (as Rashbam understands it) and the *midrash halakha,* therefore, may well arise from different ways of understanding the literal meaning of the text. Indeed, Exodus 22:8 can be understood in different ways. The Sages regard it as blurring the distinction between a guardian of objects and a guardian of animals, to the extent that a different distinction must be sought between the two types of guardianship, in order to justify the two different verdicts. In contrast, Rashbam views this verse as a sort of parenthetical addition that does not affect the main distinction between the two cases in any way.

83. *Mekhilta DeRabbi Yishmael, Mishpatim, masekhta denezikin parasha* 15; Horowitz-Rabin edition, 301.
84. Translation based on Lockshin, *Rashbam's Commentary on Exodus,* 255–56.

Therefore, in any instance of contradiction between the plain meaning of the text and *midrash halakha,* we must ask whether it is indeed these two elements that constitute the discrepancy, or whether some earlier tension between different parts of the biblical text underpins the *midrash halakha.*

SUMMARY

Some commentators who distinguish between the plain meaning of the text and *midreshei halakha* will sometimes interpret a verse according to what they consider to be *peshat,* even when doing so contradicts the halakha. It goes without saying that these commentators all regarded themselves as committed to halakhic practice, yet they did not view the Sages' interpretation underlying the practical halakha as binding on the exegetical level. At the same time, these commentators do not directly address how they understand the nature of, or the reason for, the gap between the *peshat* and the *midrash halakha.*

We have addressed three types of instances of such gaps, with an attempt to explain them using three different models. In the first model, the Torah is recognized to be a living law, not given in a fixed and one-dimensional form, but rather embodying – from the outset – "forty-nine aspects indicating ritual purity and forty-nine aspects indicating ritual impurity" (Jerusalem Talmud), with the Sanhedrin possessing the authority to interpret the verses "in accordance with what is needed for that generation" (*Degel Maḥaneh Efraim*). Their decision may be based on moral considerations – "for in accordance with moral principles it would seem … that this law was given within conditions that no longer exist" (Rabbi Kook), or practical considerations. The second model sees the midrash as offering a practical resolution of contradictions between different textual units in the Torah that present conflicting ideals. The third model views the discrepancy as arising from different exegetical approaches to the plain meaning of the text.

It is therefore very important to understand the plain level of the text in its own right: "One must understand the plain meaning of the text, in order to be able to make sense of the 'seal'" (Vilna Gaon). Once we are able to distinguish between the *peshat* and the *derash,* we can go on to try and understand why, in each separate instance, the discrepancy exists.

Chapter 10

The Sins of Biblical Figures

INTRODUCTION

The return to the study of the *peshat* – the plain meaning – of the biblical text leads to a discussion about the proper attitude toward central characters in Tanakh.

A plain reading of the text makes it clear that the biblical figures are simply flawed: the forefathers, Moses, the kings, and the prophets all display human complexity. In many instances, they make mistakes or even sin – including some who commit major transgressions. How, then, is one to reconcile the depiction of our biblical ancestors in the plain text with the Sages' teachings concerning their greatness? Fundamentally, how is one to understand the complex picture of the biblical heroes that emerges from a *peshat*-oriented reading of the text?[1]

1. The contemporary polemic surrounding this question is known in Israel by the misnomer, "*Tanakh begova ha'enayim*" (Bible at eye-level). This was in fact the title of an article published by Rabbi Shlomo Aviner in the weekly publication *BeAhava UVe'emuna*, no. 338 (5762/2002): 5–6. Rabbi Yoel Bin-Nun responded in an article entitled, "Yes, Tanakh at Eye-Level," published in *HaTzofeh*, 12 Shevat 5762 (2002), 12. Thus the debate gained a title that does not represent the positive position of either side. Many opinions have been voiced in this debate, some profound and others superficial. My aim in this chapter will be to examine some of the fundamental questions raised by the plain text, without engaging in polemics.

The key question in this regard revolves around the conflict between the plain meaning of the text and the degree to which it does not match the reader's basic assumptions. On the one hand, a reading of the plain text leads to conclusions that do not necessarily accord with traditional views emerging from acknowledged Jewish thought over the course of history. These conclusions demand certain rethinking of traditional positions – as has been the case with the issues addressed in previous chapters. On the other hand, when preconceived basic assumptions are regarded as unassailable, one attempts to adapt the text to fit those assumptions. Thus, the text presents an inherent source of tension for the reader.[2]

The Sages were aware of this tension, as a midrash on the following verse makes clear: וַתֵּרֶא שָׂרָה אֶת בֶּן הָגָר הַמִּצְרִית אֲשֶׁר יָלְדָה לְאַבְרָהָם

---

2. To illustrate, let us consider two areas in which this sort of phenomenon occurs.

In the case of the medium consulted by Saul (I Sam. 28), there is no question that the plain text indicates that the medium did indeed succeed in raising up Samuel, and Samuel prophesies what will happen in battle. However, some of the *Geonim* refused to accept this, and their views are cited in Radak's summary of this chapter: "There is some debate among the *Geonim* on this matter: they all agree that the act of raising up spirits is vanity, emptiness, and misleading falsehood, but some say that Samuel did not speak to Saul; that Samuel did not, Heaven forefend, ascend from his grave, nor did he speak; rather, the woman performed the entire procedure deceitfully, for she recognized Saul immediately, and in order to give him the impression that she recognized this through her supernatural wisdom, she said, 'Why have you deceived me? For you are Saul.'" (The continuation of the commentary on that chapter continues the same line of interpretation.) The basic assumption that Samuel could not have risen from the grave led the *Geonim* to interpret the chapter in a way that does not accord with the plain reading, maintaining that their rather forced interpretation is ideologically inescapable.

There are numerous instances where the text records that a prophet is required to perform a symbolic act – sometimes quite extreme and morally questionable – in order to illustrate and reinforce his message. Maimonides maintains that these symbolic acts were perceived as being carried out as part of the prophetic vision, but were not performed in reality. Thus, for example, he explains the command to Ezekiel that he shave all the hair of his head and his beard (Ezekiel 5:1): "And likewise the command, 'and cause it to pass over your head and upon your beard': it was in a prophetic vision that he saw himself performing all these actions which he was commanded to do. The great God would not cause His prophets to become the object of ridicule and sport in the eyes of the ignorant, by commanding them to perform foolish acts. In addition, this command would entail transgression, for

מְצַחֵק, "Sarah saw the son of Hagar, the Egyptian, whom she had borne to Abraham, making sport (*metzaḥek*)" (Gen. 21:9). The obvious question is what exactly was Ishmael doing? Indeed, the midrash cites three different interpretations of the root TZ-Ḥ-K, as morally objectionable behavior, or sinning, based on how the term was used in other contexts:

> R. Akiva taught: "Sarah saw the son of Hagar, the Egyptian, whom she had borne to Abraham, *metzaḥek*"; the "*tzeḥok*" referred to here is idolatry, as it is written, וַיֵּשֶׁב הָעָם לֶאֱכֹל וְשָׁתוֹ וַיָּקֻמוּ לְצַחֵק, "And the people sat down to eat, and they drank and they got up to make sport (*letzaḥek*)" (Ex. 32:6).
>
> R. Eliezer, son of R. Yossi HaGelili taught: The "*tzeḥok*" referred to here is sexual immorality, as it is written, [when Potiphar's wife complains about Joseph:] בָּא אֵלַי הָעֶבֶד הָעִבְרִי אֲשֶׁר הֵבֵאתָ לָּנוּ לְצַחֶק בִּי, "The Hebrew slave whom you brought to us came to me to make sport (*letzaḥek*) with me" (Gen. 39:17).
>
> R. Yishmael taught: "*Tzeḥok*" refers to bloodshed, as it is written, וַיֹּאמֶר אַבְנֵר אֶל יוֹאָב יָקוּמוּ נָא הַנְּעָרִים וישַׂחֲקוּ לְפָנֵינוּ... וַיַּחֲזִקוּ אִישׁ בְּרֹאשׁ רֵעֵהוּ וְחַרְבּוֹ בְּצַד רֵעֵהוּ וַיִּפְּלוּ יַחְדָּו, "Abner said to Yoav: 'Let the young men arise and make sport (*veyitzaḥaku*)[3] before us....' Each man caught each his fellow by the head, and thrust his sword in his fellow's side, so they fell down together" (II Sam. 2:14–16). (Tosefta Sota 6:6, Lieberman edition, 185–86)

But then the midrash takes a different tack, and these opinions are followed by the opinion of R. Shimon bar Yoḥai:

> But I say, Heaven forefend that such actions would be carried out in the household of that righteous man. Is it possible that the man

Ezekiel was a *kohen*, and would thus have transgressed two prohibitions concerning the corners of his beard or the corners of his head. Rather, all of this took place only in his prophetic vision" (*Guide of the Perplexed* II:46).

3. The text as we have it reads "*viyisaḥaku*."

> concerning whom we read, כִּי יְדַעְתִּיו לְמַעַן אֲשֶׁר יְצַוֶּה אֶת בָּנָיו וְאֶת בֵּיתוֹ, "For I know him, that he will instruct [his children and his household after him...to do righteousness and justice]" (Gen. 18:19) would have idolatry, sexual immorality, or bloodshed committed within his household? [Surely not.] Rather, the "*tzeḥok*" referred to here concerns the matter of inheritance: When Isaac was born to Abraham, everyone was joyful and said, "A son has been born to Abraham" – a son has been born to Abraham who will inherit the world and take both portions. Ishmael scorned this (*metzaḥek*) in his thoughts, saying, "Do not be fools. Do not be fools! I am the firstborn, and I shall take both portions!" For it is from this response that we understand [the continuation of the description concerning Sarah] – כִּי לֹא יִירַשׁ בֶּן הָאָמָה הַזֹּאת, "For the son of this handmaid shall not inherit [with my son, with Isaac]" (Gen. 21:10).

R. Shimon bar Yoḥai does not interpret the biblical text by means of linguistic comparisons or an etymological analysis of the word *metzaḥek*. Rather, he begins with the assumption that no one of Abraham's stature could have raised a child who would commit those most serious transgressions. After all, God Himself says about Abraham that "he will instruct his children and his household after him, that they will keep the way of God, to do righteousness and justice." R. Shimon bar Yoḥai therefore interprets the verse at some remove from its plain meaning, suggesting that Ishmael merely contested the status of the firstborn and the inheritance. Were it not for his underlying assumption, this verse would not necessarily lead to his conclusion – even considering his citation of the preceding verse as support.

The other interpretations cited in the midrash seek instead to understand the meaning of the word *metzaḥek* by means of linguistic comparison – considering the meaning of the term in various other contexts, and applying that meaning to this verse as well. They conclude that Ishmael was indeed guilty of a major transgression. While their interpretations of the nature of Ishmael's wrongdoing are not strictly in accordance with the plain sense of the verse, they proceed from the impression gleaned from the plain meaning of the text – that Ishmael's actions were morally wrong.

These Sages do not address R. Shimon b. Yoḥai's argument directly, but it appears that they do not perceive any contradiction between God's statement that Abraham will instruct his progeny in the way of God, and the fact that one of his sons in fact deviated from that path.[4]

The debate continues in the midrash concerning Moses's plea to God:

> וַיֹּאמֶר מֹשֶׁה שֵׁשׁ מֵאוֹת אֶלֶף רַגְלִי הָעָם אֲשֶׁר אָנֹכִי בְּקִרְבּוֹ וְאַתָּה אָמַרְתָּ בָּשָׂר אֶתֵּן לָהֶם וְאָכְלוּ חֹדֶשׁ יָמִים. הֲצֹאן וּבָקָר יִשָּׁחֵט לָהֶם וּמָצָא לָהֶם אִם אֶת כָּל דְּגֵי הַיָּם יֵאָסֵף לָהֶם וּמָצָא לָהֶם.
>
> The people in whose midst I am are 600,000 footmen, and You have said, "I will give them meat, that they may eat a whole month." Shall flocks and herds be slain for them, would it suffice for them? Or shall all the fish of the sea be gathered together for them, would it suffice for them? (Num. 11:21–22)

According to the plain meaning of the text, Moses appears to doubt God's ability to provide meat for such a large population for an entire month. Hence, God responds: הֲיַד ה׳ תִּקְצָר עַתָּה תִרְאֶה הֲיִקְרְךָ דְבָרִי אִם לֹא, "Is God's hand too short? Now you shall see whether My word will come to pass, or not" (Num. 11:23). R. Akiva understood the text in this way, too, but this immediately raises the question of why Moses was not punished for his brazen words – if anything, his reaction in this context seems far more problematic than his actions at Mei Meriva, when he struck the rock, rebuked the people, and was barred from entering the Land of Israel. The midrash explains:

4. Rashi, in his usual fashion (as we shall see), cites all the different opinions of the *Tanna'im* mentioned in the midrash. However, the commentators who adhere to the *peshat* suggest exegetical directions different from those of the *Tanna'im*. Ibn Ezra maintains that the text implies no improper action on Ishmael's part: "'*Metzaḥek*' – for such is the way of all youth. And she [Sarah] was zealous [to protect Isaac] because he [Ishmael] was older than her son." Others suggest that Ishmael mocked Isaac in different ways. Nahmanides suggests that he "scorned Isaac, or the great banquet" (i.e., the banquet mentioned in Gen. 21:8), while Radak proposes that "he scorned Isaac for being born of this elderly couple."

> R. Akiva taught: "Shall flocks and herds be slain for them, would it suffice for them"; which is more serious – this argument, or שִׁמְעוּ נָא הַמֹּרִים, "Hear now, you rebels" (Num. 20:10)? We must conclude that although this questioning is more severe than [the outburst of anger in] "Hear now, you rebels," nevertheless, one who causes a desecration of God's name in private may be treated leniently, but one who does so in public is punished. The instance that occurred in private was overlooked by God.[5]

On this verse, R. Shimon bar Yoḥai again takes a different interpretive approach – and, again, because of his basic assumption about Moses's character:

> But I say, Heaven forefend that this righteous man would even think of saying that God "cannot provide for all of us and for our livestock." Could someone concerning whom the text testifies with the words, לֹא כֵן עַבְדִּי מֹשֶׁה, "Not so My servant Moses" (Num. 12:7), even think of saying that God could not provide for all the people and their livestock? After all, when the Jews were in Egypt, the Nile River provided sufficient fish for them and for the Egyptians, and the livestock in Egypt were likewise sufficient for them and for the Egyptians. Rather, [Moses's words] concerned that which is written, לֹא יוֹם אֶחָד תֹּאכְלוּן...עַד חֹדֶשׁ יָמִים, "Not one day shall you eat it ... but a whole month" (Num. 11:19–20). Moses said to the Holy One, blessed be He: "Master of the Universe, is it fair that You give this to them only to then kill them? Does one say to a person, 'Take already, and go down to Sheol'? Does one say to a donkey, 'Take this measure of barley' – and then cut off its head?"... To which God responded, "Is it then proper that they say, 'God cannot provide enough for us and for our livestock'? Rather, they and thousands like them should die rather than My hand be considered too short even for a short time." As it is written, "And God said to Moses, 'Is God's hand too short?'" (Num. 21:23).

5. Tosefta Sota 6:7.

R. Shimon bar Yoḥai assumes that Moses would not have voiced any doubt as to God's ability to provide food for the Israelites – the Sage uses the expression, as he did with regard to Abraham, "Heaven forefend." He therefore has no choice but to interpret Moses's words as a moral argument: "Is it proper to feed them such prodigious quantities and then kill them?" To this God responds that it is better than to risk the Israelites doubting God's ability to provide. As an interpretation of the verses, this approach is rather forced, but inescapable, given R. Shimon's need to avoid what he considers unthinkable.[6]

Based on this midrash, it would seem that R. Akiva and R. Shimon bar Yoḥai disagree, with the former willing to accept that even Moses was not immune to questioning and doubt – and that the Torah does not hide it. Thus, the debate among the *Tanna'im* again concerns not only exegetical possibilities, but also basic assumptions regarding the text, including the fundamental question of the extent to which the human qualities that indicate imperfection may be attributed to the great characters of the Tanakh.

The two disagreements we have cited here are representative of our dilemma and the different approaches to dealing with it. In general, these two fundamental approaches may be found throughout Tanakh, along with some intermediate approaches, in keeping with the particular circumstances of each case. In many cases, there are *midrashim* that seek to view favorably actions that seem, on the level of *peshat*, to be greater or lesser sins.[7] At the same time, the opposite phenomenon also appears – when the Sages take a harsh view of the actions of biblical

6. Here, too, Rashi cites both sides of the Tannaitic debate without stating his own preference. The other *peshat* commentators (Rashbam, Ibn Ezra, Nahmanides, Radak) tend to accept R. Akiva's view in terms of understanding the verse, but they do not accept with equanimity the conclusion that Moses is questioning God's abilities; rather, they explain why in this particular instance there was indeed room for Moses to wonder. Thus, they mitigate the seriousness of his questioning.
7. For a detailed list of such instances, see A. Margaliot, *HaḤayavim BaMikra VeZaka'im BaTalmud U'VaMidrashim* (London, 1949). R. Kalmin, "Portrayals of Kings in Rabbinic Literature of Late Antiquity," *Jewish Studies Quarterly* 3, 4 (1996): 320–41, provides a close study of several of these instances.

characters – even the patriarchs – even though the plain meaning of the text seems not to imply any wrongdoing.[8]

ABRAHAM AND SARAH

Let us examine three episodes in the lives of Abraham and Sarah where their actions seem to be presented in a questionable light. Two fundamental approaches will be presented: one maintains that the plain reading of the text suggests the acts in question were wrong – perhaps even serious sins – and were recorded with a view to instructing readers how not to behave; the other approach seeks to recast the biblical figures' actions in a positive light and regards them as models to emulate.

During a famine in Canaan, Abraham goes down to Egypt and asks Sarah to pretend that she is his sister (Gen. 12:10–20). Both decisions arouse lively debate among the Sages and commentators alike. Consider first Abraham's leaving the land. Some say this departure was a test that he passed successfully, as Radak explains (Gen. 12:10):[9]

> This is one of the tests with which God tested Abraham, and he withstood all of them, never questioning the Holy One, blessed be He, saying, "Yesterday, [God] told me, 'Through you shall all the families of the earth be blessed,' but today there is famine in the land in which I am dwelling, such that I am forced to leave it for a different place." Rather, he accepted everything with love.

According to Radak, Abraham's test consisted of dealing with the conflict between the divine promise of the land and the severe famine that was forcing him to leave the land. A lesser man than Abraham might have blamed or questioned God, but Abraham bore the contradiction in a silence that expressed his faith.[10]

8. For a detailed list, see A. Y. Chwat, "HaZaka'im BaMikra VeḤayavim BeḤazal," *Talelei Orot* 12 (5766/2006): 13–99. Various explanations are offered for this phenomenon, with a discussion of the educational messages of the *midrashim* that may sometimes come at the price of textual accuracy or even the esteem shown to the forefathers.
9. See also *Pirkei DeRabbi Eliezer*, chapter 26, and Rashi, ad loc.
10. According to Radak's explanation, the structure of the test here resembles that of the binding of Isaac: In both instances God makes a significant promise to Abraham

In contrast, the Zohar presents a negative view of the descent to Egypt:

> R. Yehuda said: Come and see – because Abraham moved to Egypt without permission, the Jews were enslaved in Egypt for four hundred years. For it is written, "Abraham went down to Egypt," but not [a command,] "Go down to Egypt," and it was for that reason that he was troubled all that night on account of Sarah. (Zohar, *Lekh Lekha* 71b)

The negative judgment of Abraham's action, as interpreted by the Zohar, arises from the fact that the patriarch was not commanded by God to go to Egypt. The fact that Sarah is seized immediately thereafter should be viewed as a direct punishment. Furthermore, inasmuch as Abraham's act has ramifications for future generations, in its wake, God decreed that the Jews would be enslaved in Egypt. In a similar vein, Nahmanides writes in his commentary (ad loc.):

> Also, his leaving the land, concerning which he had originally been commanded [to go to], owing to the famine, was a misdeed that he committed, for God would have delivered him from death in the midst of the famine. And for this act his descendants suffered exile in Egypt at the hand of Pharaoh, where instead of justice there was wickedness and sin.

Because God had commanded Abraham to go to the land, says Nahmanides, he was implicitly forbidden to leave it; he should have trusted in God even under conditions of famine. In other words, Abraham failed this test – a failure that brought about the subjugation of the Jews in Egypt. Thus, where Radak sees the patriarch's descent to Egypt as a test that Abraham withstood, Nahmanides believes it was a test he failed.

(the land / progeny), which starts to be fulfilled (he reaches the land / Isaac is born). In both cases there is then a divine decree that negates the fulfillment of the promise (famine / binding of Isaac). Ultimately, Abraham passes both tests, and the promises remain valid.

Opinions are similarly divided concerning Abraham's presenting Sarah as his sister. Radak again views Abraham's decision as correct:

> Abram feared this and did not rely on God's promise to him, for he said, "Perhaps my sins will cause [the promise to be annulled]." Likewise Jacob feared even after God had made a promise to him, and so it is proper that every righteous man not rely on miracles in a situation of danger, but rather protect himself with every possible tactic. Concerning this Solomon said, אַשְׁרֵי אָדָם מְפַחֵד תָּמִיד, "Happy is the man who is always fearful" (Prov. 28:14), and so the Sages taught that one should not rely on a miracle.

Radak is aware that Abraham's act might be perceived as evidence of a lack of faith, and so he is quick to assert at the outset that when "Abraham feared and did not rely on God's promise," he committed no wrongdoing. The commentator even goes on to present Abraham's actions as a model for future generations: "And so it is proper that every righteous man not rely on miracles."

Nahmanides, in contrast, and consistent with his position above, criticizes Abraham:

> Know that Abraham unwittingly committed a great transgression in exposing his righteous wife to the possibility of sin owing to his own fear of being killed. He should have trusted that God would save him, and his wife, and all that he had, for God has the power to help and to deliver.

According to Nahmanides, Abraham's act was a transgression that brought suffering upon his descendants when they were subjugated in Egypt.[11] Thus, while Radak thinks that there is nothing wrong with

---

11. Compare, for example, Abraham's words (Gen. 12:12), וְהָרְגוּ אֹתִי וְאֹתָךְ יְחַיּוּ, "They shall kill me but leave you alive," and Pharaoh's words (Ex. 1:22), כָּל הַבֵּן הַיִּלּוֹד הַיְאֹרָה תַּשְׁלִיכֻהוּ וְכָל הַבַּת תְּחַיּוּן, "Every son that is born you shall cast into the Nile, but every daughter you shall leave alive."

Abraham "not relying on God's promise," Nahmanides insists that the patriarch "should have trusted in God."

In a different episode involving Abraham and Sarah, Radak joins Nahmanides in criticizing their behavior. After Sarah, who is barren, gives her handmaid Hagar to Abraham, and the handmaid becomes pregnant, the text relates:

> וַתֵּרֶא כִּי הָרָתָה וַתֵּקַל גְּבִרְתָּהּ בְּעֵינֶיהָ. וַתֹּאמֶר שָׂרַי אֶל אַבְרָם חֲמָסִי עָלֶיךָ אָנֹכִי נָתַתִּי שִׁפְחָתִי בְּחֵיקֶךָ וַתֵּרֶא כִּי הָרָתָה וָאֵקַל בְּעֵינֶיהָ יִשְׁפֹּט ה׳ בֵּינִי וּבֵינֶיךָ וַיֹּאמֶר אַבְרָם אֶל שָׂרַי הִנֵּה שִׁפְחָתֵךְ בְּיָדֵךְ עֲשִׂי לָהּ הַטּוֹב בְּעֵינָיִךְ וַתְּעַנֶּהָ שָׂרַי וַתִּבְרַח מִפָּנֶיהָ.

> And when [Hagar] saw that she had conceived, her mistress was despised in her eyes. And Sarai said to Abram, "My anger be upon you; I gave my handmaid into your bosom, but when she saw that she had conceived, I was despised in her eyes; may God judge between me and you." And Abram said to Sarai, "Behold, your maid is in your hand; do to her as it pleases you." So Sarai dealt harshly with her, and she fled from before her. (Gen. 16:4–6)

Nahmanides regards the treatment of Hagar as a sin, not only on the part of Sarah, but also on the part of Abraham:

> Our matriarch sinned in this harsh dealing, and so did Abraham, in permitting her to do so. And God heard [Hagar's] affliction, and gave her a son who would be a wild man who would afflict the progeny of Abraham and Sarah with all kinds of harsh dealings.

Nahmanides asserts that this misdeed, too, had long-term historic ramifications, for it resulted in the birth of Ishmael, who was destined to afflict the descendants of Abraham and Sarah over many generations.

Radak preempts Nahmanides in criticizing Sarah's actions, though he refrains from attributing any wrongdoing to Abraham:

> What Sarai did here was neither proper nor pious behavior. Not proper – because even though Abraham was willing to forego his

> own honor, and told her, "Do to her as it pleases you," she should have restrained herself out of honor for him, and not dealt with [Hagar] harshly. Nor was it pious behavior reflecting a good soul, for it is not proper for a person to do all that he can against those who are subject to his authority.... And that which Sarai did was not good in God's eyes, as the angel tells Hagar: "For God has heard your affliction," and he gave her a blessing to compensate for her affliction. Yet Abram did not prevent Sarai from afflicting [Hagar] even though it was evil in his eyes, in order to preserve peace in their home. And this entire story is written in the Torah in order for a person to learn good traits from it, and to distance himself from evil ones.

Radak concludes his commentary with a most important comment: the stories of the patriarchs and matriarchs are recorded not only so that we can learn from and imitate their positive actions, but also so that we can learn from and avoid repeating their misdeeds.

It should be noted that the critical view of Sarah is not universally accepted. The Tosefta notes that the second time that Sarah asks to banish Hagar, together with Ishmael (Gen. 21:9–21), after she sees him "making sport" (as above), God intervenes in the disagreement between her and Abraham, telling him, כֹּל אֲשֶׁר תֹּאמַר אֵלֶיךָ שָׂרָה שְׁמַע בְּקֹלָהּ כִּי בְיִצְחָק יִקָּרֵא לְךָ זָרַע, "All that Sarah tells you, listen to her, for in Isaac shall your seed be called" (Gen. 21:12). According to the Tosefta, this divine ruling retroactively justifies Sarah's original banishment of Hagar:

> God decided between her words and his, as it is written, "All that (*kol asher*) Sarah tells you, listen to her" – for what extra meaning is added by the word "*kol*" ("all")? This teaches that God ruled in the first instance [i.e., the expulsion of Hagar in Gen. 16, where no explicit Divine acceptance of Sarah's actions is recorded in the text] as He did in the second instance [i.e., the expulsion of Hagar and Ishmael in Gen. 21, where the statement "All that Sarah tells you, listen to her" appears].[12]

12. Tosefta Sota 5:12, Lieberman edition, 181.

This approach is adopted by R. Yehuda ben Elazar, one of the Tosafists, in his work *Minḥat Yehuda*:[13]

> And R. Elyakim gave a reason for this: "How could so righteous a woman as our matriarch Sarah behave this way? Because Hagar first afflicted Sarah, in accordance with R. Shimon's explanation concerning, "Her mistress was scorned in her eyes" (Gen. 16:4), and therefore Sarah afflicted her lawfully, for in the *Sefer Mitzvot HaGadol* it is written, in the commandment of לֹא תוֹנוּ "You shall not afflict" (Lev. 19:33), that if someone behaved in that way toward you, you may act in the same way toward him, for he is not "your fellow," since he has afflicted you.[14]

We consequently see that the different commentators are at odds with one another in their interpretation of the stories of Abraham and Sarah. These include commentators who do not shy away from criticizing Abraham and Sarah's actions when they deem them improper, despite the certainty that overall the Torah clearly stresses the greatness of Abraham's and Sarah's characters.

"ANYONE WHO SAYS THAT SO-AND-SO SINNED IS SIMPLY MISTAKEN"

Those who seek a favorable interpretation of all questionable actions by biblical characters rely, as one of their central sources, on a well-known discussion in Tractate Shabbat (55b–56b). The Talmud lists six figures who seem, according to the plain text, to have committed various transgressions – some of them extremely serious ones. In each case, R. Shmuel bar Naḥmani teaches, in the name of R. Yonatan, that "anyone who says that so-and-so sinned is simply mistaken."

The discussion in the Gemara of the first three figures makes it clear that R. Yonatan's view is not the only view – sometimes not even

13. His commentary on the Torah was written in 1313. For more about him and his commentary, see H. Touitou's introduction to his critical edition of the commentary: *Minḥat Yehuda: Perush LeRabbi Yehuda ben Elazar MiBaalei HaTosafot* (Jerusalem, 2012), 11–40.
14. *Minḥat Yehuda* on Genesis 16; Touitou edition, 54–55.

the majority view – in rabbinic literature, and even among the later commentators, the issue is subject to debate. Let us examine these three figures, and try to arrive at the messages arising from the plain reading of the text, according to those views that maintain that a transgression was indeed committed.

Reuben

The first source discussed in the Gemara is about Jacob's son Reuben: וַיְהִי בִּשְׁכֹּן יִשְׂרָאֵל בָּאָרֶץ הַהִוא וַיֵּלֶךְ רְאוּבֵן וַיִּשְׁכַּב אֶת בִּלְהָה פִּילֶגֶשׁ אָבִיו וַיִּשְׁמַע יִשְׂרָאֵל וַיִּהְיוּ בְנֵי יַעֲקֹב שְׁנֵים עָשָׂר, "And it was, when Israel dwelled in that land, that Reuben went and lay with Bilha, his father's concubine; and Israel heard [of it]; and the sons of Jacob were twelve" (Gen. 35:22). The plain text suggests a very serious transgression. Although Bilha was only Jacob's concubine and not his wife, she was forbidden to any other man, and especially to Jacob's son. According to R. Yonatan, however, Reuben did not actually engage in relations with Bilha:

> R. Shmuel bar Naḥmani said in the name of R. Yonatan: "Anyone who says that Reuben sinned is simply mistaken. As it is written, 'And the sons of Jacob were twelve' – this teaches that they were all considered equal. So what are we meant to learn from the words, 'and lay with Bilha, his father's concubine'? This teaches that he moved or overturned his father's bed, and the text compares this to lying with her."[15]

R. Shimon ben Elazar expands on R. Yonatan's approach:

> It was taught: R. Shimon b. Elazar said: "That righteous man [Reuben] was saved from that sin, and he did not come to perform that deed. Is it possible someone whose descendants were destined to stand on Mount Ebal and proclaim, אָרוּר שֹׁכֵב עִם אֵשֶׁת אָבִיו, 'Cursed is one who lies with his father's wife' (Deut. 27:20) could himself have committed this sin? But how do I then

15. See the lengthy discussion in the article by Rabbi Yaakov Medan, "Anyone Who Says That Reuven Sinned...," *Alei Etzion* 14 (2006): 95–126.

> understand the words 'and lay with Bilha, his father's concubine'? He demanded [redress for] his mother's humiliation. He said, '[Even] if my mother's sister was a rival to my mother, shall the handmaid of my mother's sister be a rival to my mother?' [Thereupon] he arose and moved her bed.... Thus it is written, כִּי עָלִיתָ מִשְׁכְּבֵי אָבִיךָ אָז חִלַּלְתָּ יְצוּעִי עָלָה, 'Because you went up to your father's bed, you defiled it; you went up to my couch' (Gen. 49:4)."

Those who wish to argue that Reuben did not lie with Bilha cite two arguments. First, from the verse "and the sons of Jacob were twelve," they deduce that all were equal in righteousness, and so it cannot be that one of them committed such a terrible transgression. Second, the tribe of Reuben was among those who stood at Mount Ebal, as witnesses to the curse against a man who lies with his father's wife; hence, Reuben himself could not have committed this sin (not even with his father's concubine).

On the plain level of the text, neither of these arguments is particularly compelling, and their weaknesses are evident.[16] It seems, therefore, that the effort to clear Reuben of apparent sin arises not from the plain reading of the text, but from fundamental assumptions concerning the righteousness of biblical characters. As Genesis Rabba puts it: "Did Reuben then engage in forbidden sexual relations? God spare the righteous man!"[17] In other words, it is unthinkable that so righteous an individual as Reuben would commit such a terrible sin. If the text appears to imply otherwise, then the text must be reread accordingly.

Many people present the above view as "the view of the Sages," but in doing so, they underestimate the diversity of opinions among the Sages. R. Eliezer and R. Yehoshua maintain that the text is meant to be understood literally: Reuben indeed engaged in sexual relations

16. Concerning the first proof, we might argue that the twelve tribes included also Simeon and Levi, who were sharply criticized by Jacob prior to his death. Concerning the second proof, we might counter that the division of the tribes for the blessings and curses was part of an event that included the entire nation; the entire tribe of Reuben could not have been barred from it.
17. Genesis Rabba, *parasha* 97 (new system), Theodor-Albeck edition, 1205.

with Bilha. Each explains Jacob's words to Reuben, פַּחַז כַּמַּיִם אַל תּוֹתַר, "Unstable (*paḥaz*) as water, you shall not excel" (Gen. 49:4), as an acronym suggesting three aspects of his sin. "R. Eliezer said, 'You were impetuous, you were liable, you were contemptuous.' R. Yehoshua said, 'You transgressed, you sinned, you were promiscuous.'"[18] Although they do not question Reuben's righteousness, they maintain that his level of piety did not prevent him from sinning.

The debate surrounding the story of Reuben and Bilha rages on among the medieval biblical commentators. While Rashi adopts the approach of R. Yonatan, who clears Reuben of wrongdoing, Radak understands the account in the literal sense:

> "Reuben went" – He went to the tent of Bilha and lay with her. "His father's concubine" – she was his father's wife, but she is referred to here as his "concubine" because Reuben thought that she was not forbidden to him, since she had first been a handmaid and afterwards his father took her as his concubine; but the text testifies that she became his wife, as it is written, וַתִּתֶּן לוֹ אֶת בִּלְהָה שִׁפְחָתָהּ לְאִשָּׁה, "And she gave him Bilha, her handmaid, as a wife" (Gen. 30:4), so she was forbidden to him, for the children of Noah were commanded concerning forbidden sexual relations ... and how much more so the children of Jacob. Therefore his birthright was taken from him, as it is written, וּבְחַלְּלוֹ יְצוּעֵי אָבִיו נִתְּנָה בְּכֹרָתוֹ לִבְנֵי יוֹסֵף, "But when he defiled his father's bed, his birthright was given to Joseph"[19] (I Chr. 5:1).

18. Rashi there explains: You rushed to sin, you were disrespectful. The Gemara continues, providing supporting arguments for R. Yonatan, and explaining Jacob's words differently. R. Eliezer HaModa'i reverses the letters of the word *paḥaz* and explains homiletically: You trembled, you recoiled, and the sin flew away. Rava quotes R. Yirmiya bar Abba as saying: You remembered the punishment, you made yourself ill, you separated yourself from sin.

19. Our Masoretic version reads, "But when he defiled his father's bed, his birthright was given to *the sons of* Joseph, son of Israel."

Radak explains Reuben's act as a "halakhic" mistake, in an attempt to mitigate somewhat the severity of his transgression. Ibn Ezra, Ralbag, and Rabbi Yosef Bekhor Shor explain the verse in the literal sense without seeking any sort of favorable interpretation.

What is the meaning of Reuben's sin? Perhaps his act is meant to express his desire to be designated his father's heir already at this stage. Indeed, several sons in Tanakh take their father's concubines as a means of proclaiming themselves successors to their fathers. The most prominent example is Absalom – who, taking Ahitophel's advice, lies with his father's concubines upon the roof in the sight of all of Israel (see II Sam. 16:20–22). The same thinking prompts Solomon's anger toward Adonijah, when the latter seeks to take Avishag the Shunamite as his wife (I Kings 2:13–25). Ish Boshet likewise accuses Abner of taking his father's concubine (II Sam. 3:7).

The continuation of the description of Reuben is therefore most instructive. Given that Reuben is the only one among the brothers who tries to save Joseph, to return him, alive, to his father (Gen. 37:21–22), this effort may be understood as a profoundly restorative act, a *tikkun,* or repair, for his sin concerning Bilha.

While Reuben's motive in sinning with Bilha may well have been a desire to press forward in the struggle for the status of his father's successor, he moves to save his brother even though he had heard Joseph's dreams expressing the younger brother's own desire to become the central figure of the family. In contrast to his actions with Bilha, with Joseph Reuben acts contrary to his personal interests and is motivated by a spirit of repentance and responsibility. In fact, the connection between these two situations is noted by the midrash. When the brothers conspired to sell Joseph, Reuben was not present, as evidenced by the verse, וַיָּשָׁב רְאוּבֵן אֶל הַבּוֹר וְהִנֵּה אֵין יוֹסֵף בַּבּוֹר וַיִּקְרַע אֶת בְּגָדָיו, "Reuben returned to the pit and behold, Joseph was not in the pit; and he tore his garments" (Gen. 37:29). The midrash asks where he was, and answers: "R. Eliezer said: He was busy with sackcloth and fasting. When he was finished, he went and looked into the pit." The midrash thereby draws a direct connection between Reuben's regret over his behavior with Bilha and his behavior in the episode of Joseph, and concludes by conveying the main message of the story:

> The Holy One, blessed be He, said to him: "No one has ever sinned before Me and then repented; you are the first to introduce repentance! By your life, a descendant of yours will likewise spearhead a call to repentance." And who was that? It was Hosea, who said: שׁוּבָה יִשְׂרָאֵל עַד ה' אֱלֹהֶיךָ, "Return, O Israel, to the Lord your God" (Hosea 14:2).[20]

This approach does not attempt to minimize or exonerate Reuben's sin, but rather appreciates his repentance.

The Sons of Eli

The conduct of the sons of Eli is described in detail in the second chapter of I Samuel, along with their father's half-hearted rebuke, and the heavy punishment that the house of Eli incurs as a result of their sins. Nevertheless, they appear on the Talmud's list of those who did not sin:

> R. Shmuel bar Naḥmani said in the name of R. Yonatan: "Anyone who says that the sons of Eli sinned, is simply mistaken. As it is written, וְשָׁם שְׁנֵי בְנֵי עֵלִי חָפְנִי וּפִנְחָס כֹּהֲנִים לַה', 'And there the two sons of Eli, Hofni and Pinhas, ministered unto God'" (I Sam. 1:3).

Later in the Gemara, it becomes clear that this conclusion is reached in two stages. First, Pinhas is cleared of sin, as Rav argues:

> Pinhas did not sin, as it is written, וַאֲחִיָּה בֶן אֲחִטוּב אֲחִי אִיכָבוֹד בֶּן פִּינְחָס בֶּן עֵלִי כֹּהֵן ה', "And Ahiya son of Ahituv, brother of I-Khavod, son of Pinhas son of Eli, a *kohen* unto God" (I Sam. 14:3). Is it possible that he could have come to sin, if the text traces his [respected] lineage?

The second stage deduces that Hofni did not sin either, from the verse cited by R. Yonatan, since "the text juxtaposes Hofni and Pinhas; hence, if Pinhas did not sin, neither did Hofni."

---

20. Genesis Rabba, *parasha* 84, 19, Theodor-Albeck edition, 1023.

This midrash raises questions. Although we have seen that there is a tendency to defend biblical figures against accusations that they had sinned, even when such defense goes against the plain meaning of the text, what sort of interest is there in defending Hofni and Pinhas on this account? They are characterized quite plainly in the text as "worthless men" (בְּנֵי בְלִיָּעַל, *benei beliyaal*) (I Sam. 2:12), whose actions are recorded in great detail.

Rashi and the Tosafists explain that the discussion in the Gemara concerns not the cheapening of the sacrificial offerings as documented in the story, but rather the specific sin concerning the women, which is mentioned subsequently in the talmudic discussion:

> What, then, are we to understand from the words יִשְׁכְּבוּן אֶת הַנָּשִׁים, "they lay with the women" (I Sam. 2:22)? Since [Hofni and Pinhas] delayed [the women's] bird offerings, such that they could not return to their husbands, the text regards them as though they had lain with them.

According to this explanation, the attempt to mitigate the transgressions of the sons of Eli pertains only to the part of the account that appears most serious – engaging in sexual relations with the women visiting the Mishkan. But again, here, too, we must ask why R. Yonatan tries to mitigate the impression arising from the textual description of the sins of these "worthless men."[21] The simple answer is given in another midrash:

21. Ralbag (on I Sam. 2:22) raises an additional argument as to why the description of sexual immorality should not be taken literally: "For if it were so, the prophet who came to Eli would have denounced this tremendous sin, but we find him denouncing only the sin mentioned at the outset." The rebuke conveyed by the man of God to Eli (I Sam. 2:27–32) mentions only the sins concerning the sacrificial offerings, but not the women (the source for this is in Y. Sota 1:4, 16d). It must be acknowledged that the prophet's avoidance of any mention of the matter of the women in his rebuke is indeed surprising, but it seems that the same surprise remains even according to R. Yonatan's interpretation, for if the text takes so negative a view of the sin of delaying the women that it depicts Hofni and Pinhas as though they had engaged in relations with them, why would the prophet not rebuke them for such serious wrongdoing?

> Is it possible that the sons of the righteous Eli would behave in this way? How can that be? Rather, when the women brought their bird offerings they would cause them to spend a night away from their homes, and by virtue of that, the Holy One, blessed be He, considers them as though they had committed forbidden acts with them.[22]

The mitigation of their sin therefore arises from a desire to alleviate the righteous Eli of responsibility. This is turn reflects not only a general tendency to defend the upbringing of the children of central characters in Tanakh, as we have seen in relation to Abraham and Ishmael, but also the special circumstances of the story of Eli's sons, where Eli himself is punished for not rebuking them effectively: בַּעֲוֹן אֲשֶׁר יָדַע כִּי מְקַלְלִים לָהֶם בָּנָיו וְלֹא כִהָה בָּם, "for the iniquity that he knew that his sons were blaspheming, but he did not restrain them" (I Sam. 3:13). The more limited the description of the sin, the stronger the defense of Eli for failing to rebuke his sons as he should have.

This episode also evokes different opinions among the Sages. Rav maintains that Pinhas alone did not sin, but he too is punished: "Because Pinhas should have protested Hofni's behavior but did not do so, the text considers him as though he himself had sinned." His wording suggests that no attempt was made to mitigate Hofni's sin.[23] Moreover, R. Yoḥanan ben Torta asks: "Why was Shiloh [the site of the Mishkan] destroyed? Because of two things that happened there: sexual immorality and dishonor toward the sacrificial offerings" (Yoma 9a). According

22. Genesis Rabba, *parasha* 85, 12, Theodor-Albeck edition, 1046–47.

23. The Gemara discusses Rav's opinion and reduces all expressions that are written in the plural, to the singular – even at the expense of clear speech: "Pinhas did not sin. But what about the verse that states, אֲשֶׁר יִשְׁכְּבוּן אֶת הַנָּשִׁים, 'that they lay [*yishkevun*, in the plural] with the women' (I Sam. 2:22)? It is written as ישכבן, [without the *vav*, alluding to something less than a plural]. But it is written, 'No, my sons [*banai*, in the plural]; for it is not a good report that I hear.' [To this] R. Naḥman b. Yitzḥak responded: The word can also be read as 'my son' [*beni*, in the singular]. But it is written, 'You cause the people to transgress' [*maavirim*, in the plural]. To which R. Huna, son of R. Yehoshua, answered, 'It is written without the *yod*' [alluding to something less than a plural]." Rav's opinion is that Hofni alone sinned, "but R. Yonatan disagreed and said that neither of them sinned" (*Tosafot*, ad loc.).

to R. Yoḥanan ben Torta, the description of sexual immorality should be understood literally.[24]

The commentators cite both opinions. Rashi writes, "'That they lay' – literally; but our Sages taught that because they delayed the women's bird offerings…the text considers them as though they lay with them." Radak's commentary appears to take a middle path between the two approaches: "This is meant literally, but some of our Sages interpreted it not in accordance with the plain meaning." Rabbi Yosef Kara suggests only the *peshat* interpretation, while Ralbag and Metzudat David adopt R. Yonatan's interpretation that the text does not refer to actual sexual relations.

Thus, among both the Sages and the medieval commentators, there are some who understand the account about Eli's sons literally. Of course, the literal understanding raises concerns about unworthy individuals holding senior positions, and it teaches of the need to avoid corruption among those in positions of power. The dynasty of the house of Eli is destined to be replaced by כֹּהֵן נֶאֱמָן כַּאֲשֶׁר בִּלְבָבִי וּבְנַפְשִׁי יַעֲשֶׂה, "a faithful *kohen* who shall do according to that which is in My heart and in My mind" (I Sam. 2:35),[25] who will lead in the way of truth and uprightness and will not be blinded and corrupted by the power that he wields.

The Sons of Samuel

The text refers only briefly to the sins of the sons of Samuel: וַיְהִי כַּאֲשֶׁר זָקֵן שְׁמוּאֵל וַיָּשֶׂם אֶת בָּנָיו שֹׁפְטִים לְיִשְׂרָאֵל...וְלֹא הָלְכוּ בָנָיו בִּדְרָכָו וַיִּטּוּ אַחֲרֵי הַבָּצַע וַיִּקְחוּ שֹׁחַד וַיַּטּוּ מִשְׁפָּט, "And it was, when Samuel was old, that he made his sons judges over Israel… but his sons did not walk in his ways; they turned

24. Concerning the dishonor of sacrifices there is no argument, but with regard to sexual immorality this source is formulated as follows: "But nevertheless R. Shmuel bar Naḥmani said in the name of R. Yoḥanan [R. Yonatan in Shabbat] that 'Anyone who says that the sons of Eli sinned, is simply mistaken,' because they merely delayed the women's bird-offerings, and the text therefore regards them as though they had engaged in forbidden relations with them." According to this version, even R. Yoḥanan ben Torta accepts Rabbi Yonatan's interpretation, but he still sees some justification for referring to this sin as sexual immorality. However, the Ritva cites a different version: "But he disagrees with R. Shmuel bar Naḥmani."

25. For the identity of this *kohen* see my book, *Shmuel Alef: Melekh BeYisrael* (Maggid, 2013), 41–44.

aside after unjust gain, and took bribes, and perverted justice" (I Sam. 8:1–3). Here again, R. Yonatan seeks to mitigate the description of their behavior:

> R. Shmuel bar Naḥmani said in the name of R. Yonatan: "Anyone who says that the sons of Samuel sinned, is simply mistaken, for it is written, 'And it was, when Samuel was old... but his sons did not walk in his ways' – it says merely that they did not walk in his ways, but it does not say that they sinned. What, then, are we to understand from the words, 'They turned aside after unjust gain'? That they did not act as their father did. The righteous Samuel would travel to all the places in Israel and would judge the people in their own cities, as it is written, וְהָלַךְ מִדֵּי שָׁנָה בְּשָׁנָה וְסָבַב בֵּית אֵל וְהַגִּלְגָּל וְהַמִּצְפָּה וְשָׁפַט אֶת יִשְׂרָאֵל, 'And he went each year on circuit to Beit El and Gilgal and Mitzpa, and he judged Israel' (I Sam. 7:16). But they did not do so; rather, they remained in their own cities, so as to increase the income of their clerks and scribes."

The sin explicitly identified in the text is diminished: the seeking of unjust gain and taking of bribes is interpreted as abandoning the unusual habit followed by Samuel, their father. The attempt to mitigate the sin seems again to arise from a desire to protect the honor of Samuel himself. Indeed, the midrash asks, "Is it then possible that the sons of the righteous Samuel could act in this way?"

Here again, "the Sages' view" includes not only those who clear Samuel's sons of sin, but also others who understand that their actions were indeed as described explicitly in the text:

> There is disagreement among the Sages concerning the words, "turned aside after unjust gain." R. Meir said, "[That means] they openly demanded their portions."[26] R. Yehuda said: "They forced

26. Rashi explains: "The *maaser rishon,* to which, as Levites, they were entitled, they demanded openly, as the leaders of the generation and as the judges, and no one objected, and the other Levites, who were left without (*maaser*), suffered on account of this. According to R. Meir, the sons of Samuel did not actually commit the sin of perverting justice."

> goods on private people."[27] R. Akiva said: "They took an extra basket of tithes by force." R. Yossi said: "They took the gifts by force."

Commentators address both views, and Radak concludes his discussion with an interesting comment:

> Our Sages taught that the sons of Samuel did not sin; rather, because they did not visit all the places in Israel, but remained in their places so as to increase the wages of their clerks and scribes, the text considers them as though they had taken bribes. Some of the Sages maintain that they demanded their portion outright; others say that they took it by force; but the plain meaning of the verse seems to indicate that they sinned.

Similarly, Ralbag and Rabbi Yosef Kara understand the verse in accordance with its plain meaning.

DAVID

The fourth figure defended by R. Yonatan is King David (Shabbat 55b–56b). David's greatness and holiness, on the one hand, along with the severity of his actions concerning Bathsheba and Uriah, on the other, make this episode the classic test case for how to approach the apparent failings of biblical heroes.

A reading of the eleventh chapter of II Samuel creates a very negative impression of David's deeds. First, he sleeps with Bathsheba, wife of Uriah the Hittite, thereby transgressing the prohibition against adultery; then, he sends Uriah to his death at the hands of Ammon. The chapter concludes with the words, וַיֵּרַע הַדָּבָר אֲשֶׁר עָשָׂה דָוִד בְּעֵינֵי ה׳, "And the thing that David had done was evil in the eyes of God" (II Sam. 11:27), and immediately afterwards David is chastised by Nathan the prophet:

27. Rashi explains: "They gave them merchandise in which to trade and to bring them profit, and this caused their hearts to incline their rulings toward them when they came before them in judgment, and this was their sin." Meiri adds, "This is no justification for the sin, since there is no greater bribery than this."

כֹּה אָמַר ה׳ אֱלֹהֵי יִשְׂרָאֵל, אָנֹכִי מְשַׁחְתִּיךָ לְמֶלֶךְ עַל יִשְׂרָאֵל, וְאָנֹכִי הִצַּלְתִּיךָ מִיַּד שָׁאוּל. וָאֶתְּנָה לְךָ אֶת בֵּית אֲדֹנֶיךָ וְאֶת נְשֵׁי אֲדֹנֶיךָ בְּחֵיקֶךָ וָאֶתְּנָה לְךָ אֶת בֵּית יִשְׂרָאֵל וִיהוּדָה, וְאִם מְעָט וְאֹסִפָה לְּךָ כָּהֵנָּה וְכָהֵנָּה. מַדּוּעַ בָּזִיתָ אֶת דְּבַר ה׳ לַעֲשׂוֹת הָרַע בעינו (בְּעֵינַי) אֵת אוּרִיָּה הַחִתִּי הִכִּיתָ בַחֶרֶב וְאֶת אִשְׁתּוֹ לָקַחְתָּ לְּךָ לְאִשָּׁה וְאֹתוֹ הָרַגְתָּ בְּחֶרֶב בְּנֵי עַמּוֹן. וְעַתָּה לֹא תָסוּר חֶרֶב מִבֵּיתְךָ עַד עוֹלָם, עֵקֶב כִּי בְזִתָנִי וַתִּקַּח אֶת אֵשֶׁת אוּרִיָּה הַחִתִּי לִהְיוֹת לְךָ לְאִשָּׁה. כֹּה אָמַר ה׳ הִנְנִי מֵקִים עָלֶיךָ רָעָה מִבֵּיתֶךָ וְלָקַחְתִּי אֶת נָשֶׁיךָ לְעֵינֶיךָ וְנָתַתִּי לְרֵעֶיךָ, וְשָׁכַב עִם נָשֶׁיךָ לְעֵינֵי הַשֶּׁמֶשׁ הַזֹּאת. כִּי אַתָּה עָשִׂיתָ בַסָּתֶר וַאֲנִי אֶעֱשֶׂה אֶת הַדָּבָר הַזֶּה נֶגֶד כָּל יִשְׂרָאֵל וְנֶגֶד הַשָּׁמֶשׁ.

So says the Lord God of Israel: "I appointed you king over Israel, and I delivered you out of the hand of Saul. And I gave you your master's house, and your master's wives into your bosom, and gave you the house of Israel and of Judah; if that had been too little, I would have given you as much again. Why have you despised God's command, to do evil in His sight? You have killed Uriah the Hittite with the sword, and have taken his wife to be your wife, and have slain him with the sword of the children of Ammon. Now therefore the sword will never depart from your house, for you have despised Me, and have taken the wife of Uriah the Hittite to be your wife." So says the Lord: "Behold, I will raise up evil against you out of your own house, and I will take your wives before your eyes, and give them to your neighbor, and he shall lie with your wives in the sight of this sun. For you acted in secrecy, but I will do this thing before all of Israel, and before the sun." (II Sam. 12:7–12)

This episode illustrates the dilemma in all its intensity and complexity. A straightforward reading of the chapter evokes confusion: Who is this David, the king chosen by God to establish the eternal royal house of Israel? How is one to reconcile God's positive attitude toward His chosen king throughout the grand sweep of the David narratives, with the plain meaning of the verses in chapters 11 and 12? This question underlies R. Yonatan's words in the continuation of the discussion in the Gemara (Shabbat 56a):

> R. Shmuel bar Naḥmani said in the name of R. Yonatan: "Anyone who says that David sinned is simply mistaken, for it is written: וַיְהִי דָוִד לְכָל דְּרָכָו מַשְׂכִּיל וַה' עִמּוֹ, 'And David succeeded in all his ways, and the Lord was with him' (I Sam. 18:14). Is it possible that he sinned and yet the Divine Presence was with him? [Surely not.] What, then, are we to understand from the words מַדּוּעַ בָּזִיתָ אֶת דְּבַר ה' לַעֲשׂוֹת הָרַע, 'Why have you despised God's command, to do evil in His sight' (II Sam. 12:9)? That he wanted to commit this act, but did not do so."

R. Yonatan argues that it is unthinkable that David would have sinned, for "the Lord was with him." What, then, is the meaning of the verse? The Gemara noted above proceeds with an interesting comment by Rav: "Rav said: 'R. Yehuda HaNasi, who himself was a descendant of the house of David, parses the matter and offers an interpretation that is favorable toward David.'"

It is difficult to know whether Rav's comment is meant as praise or as criticism of R. Yehuda HaNasi for trying to judge his ancestor David favorably.[28] Either way, R. Yehuda HaNasi takes the most strongly incriminating verse in the speech by Nathan the prophet – "Why have you despised God's command, to do evil in His sight? You have killed Uriah the Hittite with the sword, and have taken his wife to be your wife, and have slain him with the sword of the children of Ammon" (II Sam. 12:9) – and interprets it, phrase by phrase, in such a way as to clear David of the most severe aspects of his sin:

> "Why have you despised God's command, to do evil" (מַדּוּעַ בָּזִיתָ אֶת דְּבַר ה' לַעֲשׂוֹת הָרַע בעינו [בְּעֵינַי קרי]): Rabbi (i.e., R. Yehuda HaNasi) said: "This 'evil' is different from all other 'evils' in the Torah, for in every other place mentioning evil, the text says,

28. Abrabanel writes, in his commentary on this chapter, "Rabbi [Yehuda HaNasi] interprets as he does owing to the fact that he is descended from David's house, *and not in accordance with the truth.*"

'he did (*vayaas*) [evil],' whereas here it says, 'to do (*laasot*)' – suggesting that he intended to do it, but did not."[29]

"You have killed Uriah the Hittite with the sword" (אֵת אוּרִיָּה הַחִתִּי הִכִּיתָ בַחֶרֶב): You should have submitted him to judgment by the Sanhedrin, but you did not.

"And you have taken (*lakaḥta*) his wife to be your wife" (וְאֶת אִשְׁתּוֹ לָקַחְתָּ לְּךָ לְאִשָּׁה): You had marriage rights (*likuḥin*) concerning her, for as R. Shmuel bar Naḥmani taught in the name of R. Yonatan: "Everyone who went out to war for the house of David would write a bill of divorce for his wife."

"And have slain him with the sword of the children of Ammon" (וְאֹתוֹ הָרַגְתָּ בְּחֶרֶב בְּנֵי עַמּוֹן): Just as you are not liable for punishment for the sword of the children of Ammon, so you are not liable for punishment for [the death of] Uriah the Hittite. Why is this so? Because he rebelled against the king, saying to him, "And my lord Yoav, and the servants of my lord, are encamped in the open field" (II Sam. 11:11).

According to R. Yehuda HaNasi, David's two sins are not as severe as one might think. He did not actually commit adultery, since Uriah the Hittite had given his wife a bill of divorce before he went out to war, like every other soldier in David's army. Nor was there any unlawful bloodshed, since one who rebels against the king is subject to the death sentence, and Uriah the Hittite rebelled against David's monarchy.[30]

29. This argument is difficult to accept, for many times in Tanakh we find the expression "to do (*laasot*) evil," where the intention is clearly to indicate that the evil is in fact performed. Thus, for example, we find in Deuteronomy 9:18: וָאֶתְנַפַּל לִפְנֵי ה׳ כָּרִאשֹׁנָה אַרְבָּעִים יוֹם וְאַרְבָּעִים לַיְלָה לֶחֶם לֹא אָכַלְתִּי וּמַיִם לֹא שָׁתִיתִי עַל כָּל חַטַּאתְכֶם אֲשֶׁר חֲטָאתֶם לַעֲשׂוֹת הָרַע בְּעֵינֵי ה׳ לְהַכְעִיסוֹ "And I fell down before the Lord, as on the earlier occasion, forty days and forty nights; I did not eat bread, nor did I drink water, owing to all your sins which you sinned, *to do evil* in the eyes of God, to provoke Him to anger." See also Judges 3:12, 4:1, 10:6, 13:1; I Kings 16:19, 21:20, 25 (Maharsha notes this verse in his discussion of the topic, but does not mention the others); II Kings 17:17, 21:6, 16; II Chr. 33:6.

30. Further on, the Gemara discusses the circumstances of his rebellion: "He rebelled against the king, for he said (II Sam. 11:11), וַאדֹנִי יוֹאָב וְעַבְדֵי אֲדֹנִי עַל פְּנֵי הַשָּׂדֶה חֹנִים,

Nevertheless, R. Yehuda HaNasi does attribute two lesser sins to David. One concerns his psychological state – "He intended to do so" – that is, he wanted to commit the sin, but was prevented from doing so. The other is a procedural matter: "He should have submitted him [Uriah] to judgment by the Sanhedrin" – that is, the rightful execution of Uriah was not carried out according to the proper legal procedure. Moreover, even R. Yehuda HaNasi does not argue that so righteous an individual as David could not have sinned; rather, he maintains that God was with David, which prevented him from actually committing the sin.

The argument that "anyone who went out to war for the house of David gave a bill of divorce to his wife" is a key claim in the discussion, and the *Rishonim* debate how it should be understood. Rashi explains that it was a conditional bill of divorce: if the husband was killed in war, or did not return from the battlefield, his wife would be considered retroactively divorced from the time he gave her the bill. This arrangement offered a twofold benefit. First, because the wife would be considered divorced, no *yibum* (levirate marriage) would be required if her husband died childless; and second, if her husband did not return (for example, if he were taken captive or missing) she would be divorced and free to remarry, rather than remaining an *aguna* ("chained" wife).[31]

The Tosafists (Ketubot 9b; Gittin 74a) argue that when David engaged in relations with Bathsheba, he could not yet have known whether Uriah would return from the battlefield, so Rashi's explanation cannot justify David's behavior. Yet their position clarifies what

'And my lord Yoav and the servants of my lord are encamped upon the open field.'" The *Rishonim* are divided as to how these words reflect his rebellion. Rashi maintains that the very fact that he refers to Yoav as 'my lord,' while standing before the king, represents a rebellion. According to Rabbenu Meir (Rashi's son-in-law), it is Uriah's refusal to go down to his house, as David had commanded him, that constitutes the rebellion (see *Tosafot* on Shabbat 56a).

31. *Tosafot* contest Rashi's interpretation, citing the Mishna in Gittin (73a) where R. Yehuda rules that a woman who receives a conditional divorce is considered "a married woman for all intents and purposes." This being so, the conditional divorce given by Uriah would not mitigate David's sin in any way.

Rashi is saying: he maintains that R. Yonatan was not attempting to justify David's actions, but that ultimately God was with David, as attested to in the text, which prevented the king from lying with a married woman. That is not meant to minimize the severity of what he did, however.

The Tosafists disagree with Rashi, maintaining, in accordance with the plain meaning of R. Shmuel bar Naḥmani's words, that the bill of divorce was altogether valid, and Bathsheba was divorced when David lay with her. The Tosafists do not explain the prophet's severe rebuke of David's actions, but Rashba (Ketubot 9b) clarifies: "The fact that the prophet rebukes him is because he acted improperly, for the husbands issued the bill of divorce only in order that their wives would not end up as *agunot*; they trusted that their wives would be faithful to them."

The Tosafists' position is problematic for several reasons. David sent Uriah home to be with his wife – how could he have done so if Bathsheba was divorced from him at the time? And while David may not have transgressed the prohibition of adultery in the formal sense, he still sinned in the moral sense. He lay with a woman whose husband trusted that she would remain faithful to him, even if at that particular moment, they were formally divorced.

We find, then, that even those Sages who defend David do not seek to clear him of all sin; rather, they merely diminish the severity of his actions, whether by cancelling the sin retroactively (as in Rashi's explanation) or by transferring it from the formal plane to the moral one (as proposed by the *Tosafot*).[32]

As we have seen, the cornerstone of the approach adopted by R. Yehuda HaNasi and R. Yonatan is the claim that "anyone who went out to war for the house of David wrote a bill of divorce for his wife"; but is this an uncontested historical fact?

---

32. Rabbi Yaakov Medan expands on this in *David U'Batsheva: HaḤet, HaOnesh VeHaTikkun* (Alon Shvut, 2002). An alternate reading of the rabbinic discussions of David's sin may be found in J. A. Diamond, "King David of the Sages: Rabbinic Rehabilitation or Ironic Parody?" *Prooftexts*, vol. 27(3) (2008): 373–426.

> R. Shmuel bar Naḥmani said in the name of R. Yonatan: "Anyone who went out to war for the House of David wrote a writ of divorce for his wife, as it is written (I Sam. 17:18), וְאֵת עֲשֶׂרֶת חֲרִצֵי הֶחָלָב הָאֵלֶּה תָּבִיא לְשַׂר הָאָלֶף וְאֶת אַחֶיךָ תִּפְקֹד לְשָׁלוֹם וְאֶת עֲרֻבָּתָם תִּקָּח, 'Bring these ten cheeses to the captain of their thousand, and inquire as to your brothers' welfare, and take their token.' What is meant by 'their token'? R. Yosef taught, 'Such things as are tokens between husband and wife.'"

Thus, R. Yonatan himself presents his teaching as a *midrash aggada,* rather than as a historic fact passed down by tradition.[33] It is therefore no surprise that there is no consensus among the talmudic Sages concerning this bill of divorce.

A direct contradiction of the idea that Bathsheba was divorced is found in a passage in Ketubot (9a). The Gemara asks: How could David have married Bathsheba? After all, a married woman who commits adultery is thereafter forbidden both to her husband and to the adulterer. Two explanations are offered: The first is that David forced himself on Bathsheba. Since she was coerced, she was not forbidden to her husband – and therefore, by the same token, was not forbidden afterwards to David. The second is that Bathsheba was indeed divorced, by virtue of the bill of divorce that David's soldiers would give to their wives. While the second explanation relies on the existence of a bill of divorce, the first explanation ignores it altogether. Not only does it assume that Bathsheba retained her status as a married woman, but it increases the severity of David's act, with the claim that he forced himself on her.[34]

The explanation that "he forced himself on her" is rather startling, especially in light of "the Sages' view" that David did not sin. Of course,

---

33. This midrash is rejected out of hand by Abrabanel: "How can I accept their claim that the men gave bills of divorce to their wives? For the verse that they bring as proof is far from suggesting this. [Furthermore,] David told Uriah to go to his home that night, and then return [to the battlefield] in the morning, which indicates that there was no divorce [in effect], and their relations would be proper and appropriate."

34. It is possible that what the Sages mean is not rape in the physical sense of overpowering a woman and forcing oneself on her, but rather a reference to the power differential between a king and a woman who feels that she is not free to refuse him.

many midrashim stress his sin, so alleging that David did sin does not actually oppose the Sages' position – indeed, they do not have one unified opinion.

Consider the following (Sanhedrin 107a):

> R. Yehuda said in the name of Rav: "A person should not put himself in a situation where he will be tempted, for David, king of Israel, placed himself in temptation – and failed. He said: 'Master of the Universe, why do they say, "God of Abraham, God of Isaac, and God of Jacob," but they do not say, "God of David"?' [God] said, 'Them I placed in temptation, but I did not place you in temptation.' He said, 'Master of the Universe, You tested me and tried me, as it is written: "Examine me, O Lord, and try me" (Ps. 26:2).' He said, 'I shall test you, and I shall grant you a special privilege, for I did not make known to them [what sort of test they would face], but I make known to you that I will test you concerning sexual relations.'"
>
> Rabba taught: "What is the meaning of the verse, וּבְצַלְעִי שָׂמְחוּ וְנֶאֱסָפוּ עָלַי נֵכִים וְלֹא יָדַעְתִּי קָרְעוּ וְלֹא דָמּוּ, 'When I stumble they rejoice, and wretches gather themselves that I have not known, they tear me in pieces without ceasing' (Ps. 35:15)? David said to the Holy One, blessed be He: Master of the Universe, it is clear and known to You that if they were to tear my flesh, my blood would not flow. And furthermore, while they discuss the four deaths inflicted by the court they pause in their study and say to me (tauntingly): 'David, one who engages in relations with a married woman – what death sentence does he receive?' I said to them, 'One who engages in relations with a married woman dies by strangulation, yet he still has a place in the World to Come, but one who publicly shames his neighbor – he has no place in the World to Come.'"
>
> He said: "Master of the Universe, forgive me this sin in its entirety!" [God] said, "Your son, Solomon, is destined to say, in his wisdom, הֲיַחְתֶּה אִישׁ אֵשׁ בְּחֵיקוֹ וּבְגָדָיו לֹא תִשָּׂרַפְנָה? אִם יְהַלֵּךְ אִישׁ עַל הַגֶּחָלִים וְרַגְלָיו לֹא תִכָּוֶינָה? כֵּן הַבָּא אֶל אֵשֶׁת רֵעֵהוּ לֹא יִנָּקֶה כָּל הַנֹּגֵעַ בָּהּ, 'Can a man take fire in his bosom, and his clothes not be

burned? Can one go upon hot coals, and his feet not be burned? So he that goes in to his neighbor's wife – whoever touches her shall not be innocent' (Prov. 6:27–30)."

Furthermore:

> It is written, וְאֶת הַכִּבְשָׂה יְשַׁלֵּם אַרְבַּעְתָּיִם, "He shall repay the worth of the lamb fourfold" (II Sam. 12:6). R. Yehuda bar Ḥanina said, "The Holy One, blessed be He, said to David: 'You committed adultery once; sixteen adulteresses shall come to you. You murdered once; sixteen murdered ones shall come to you' – 'fourfold' (*arbatayim*), [meaning] four times four."[35]

The talmudic discussion may therefore be summarized as follows: The Sages did not try to clear David of all sin; rather, the prevailing view largely aligns with the plain reading of the text – namely, that Bathsheba was a married woman. That said, some partially exonerate David (R. Yehuda HaNasi and R. Yonatan), while others take a harsher view of his behavior (the first opinion cited in the Gemara in Ketubot).

Just as there is no uniform view among the Sages concerning David's sin, so too there is no uniform view among the medieval commentators.

Rashi (II Sam. 11:15) adopts R. Yonatan's view and adds a surprising element – that the dispatching of Uriah to his death on the battlefield was meant to overcome the halakhic problem of Bathsheba's being married: "In order that she would be divorced retroactively, such that he would not have engaged in relations with a married woman. For anyone who went out to war for the house of David would write his wife a conditional bill of divorce, in case he died in battle."

Radak, in contrast, suggests two different approaches:

35. *Midrash Tehillim* (*Shoḥar Tov*) *mizmor* 3, 4, Buber edition 19a–b; see Buber's comment that the basis for this calculation is unclear.

1. "She had purified herself of her impurity" – This teaches that he did not lie with her while she was menstrually impure, for she had already purified herself of her impurity, just as the text had previously said "washed" – to tell us that this washing was for the purposes of purification from menstrual impurity. Thus, the transgression did not involve sexual relations with a woman who was menstrually impure, but with a woman who was married.
2. But our Sages taught: "Anyone who went out to war for the house of David would write a bill of divorce for his wife, in case he died in battle. Therefore David brought about the death of Uriah, so that she would be retroactively divorced."

According to the first explanation, Bathsheba was indeed married, and therefore immersed herself to be purified of her menstrual impurity. Only according to the second approach was Bathsheba divorced retroactively after the death of Uriah.

Other commentators, such as Ralbag and Rabbi Yosef Kara, understand the verses in accordance with their plain meaning. But they, and all who understand the story in its plain sense, must address the question of the unique status occupied by David, if he indeed committed such terrible sins as the plain text suggests. How are we to understand and respond to this story?

Many scholars have suggested an understanding that arises directly from the text itself and that views the crux of the story as a message about the power of repentance. When David hears Nathan's rebuke, he utters only two words: חָטָאתִי לַה', "*Ḥatati laShem*" – I have sinned to God (II Sam. 12:13). Unquestionably, this is a very powerful statement. Other kings, confronted by the rebuke of prophets, responded very differently. Some grew angry and ordered that the prophet be put to death, as happened in the case of Jeroboam (see I Kings 13:4) and Ahaziah (see II Kings 1). Others tried to evade blame – a phenomenon clearly demonstrated in the case of Saul, who tries again and again to justify himself rather than accept blame for his actions.[36] David, in contrast, acknowledges his sin; he does not

36. See I Sam. 13:11–12, 15:14–30, 28:15.

show anger toward the prophet, nor does he make any attempt to justify himself. His response is appreciated by God Himself, and Nathan tells David that his repentance has been effective in the immediate term, saving him from death: "The Lord has commuted your sin; you shall not die."[37] Thus we learn that even when a person has committed very serious transgressions, the gates of repentance are not closed; even when the person involved is a king, he still has the potential to acknowledge his sin and accept responsibility.

Rabbi Yehuda ben Natan (Riban) adopts this line in explaining why David did not lose his kingdom for his sin, while Saul, whose misdeeds appear less severe, did lose the kingdom.[38] Riban offers his views in rhyme.[39]

> Know that Saul's judgment was sealed
> His rule was ended and he died for his sin
> While David's judgment was torn up, not even put on the scales
> Even though his sin with Bathsheba was far greater
> And though our sainted rabbis declared him innocent
> They are praiseworthy, but the text must be read according to its meaning
> Why did he merit forgiveness
> While Saul died with his wrongdoing?
> When his only sin was in the matter of Amalek
> Leaving them alive and not disagreeing with the prophet
> For Samuel shouted and passed a restless night
> And God did not listen to his prayers
> But Saul did not accept blame graciously

37. David's response here is expanded upon in Psalms 51, which opens with the words, בְּבוֹא אֵלָיו נָתָן הַנָּבִיא כַּאֲשֶׁר בָּא אֶל בַּת-שָׁבַע, "When Nathan the prophet came to him, after he had come in to Bathsheba." This psalm deals with asking forgiveness and regretting sin.

38. Riban, son-in-law of Rashi, composed commentaries on various tractates. See Y. N. Epstein, "Perushei HaRiban U'Perushei Vermeiza," *Tarbiz* 4, 5693 (1933): 11–24, 153–78, and the appendices, 179–92; for a more concise review see E. E. Urbach, *Baalei HaTosafot*, vol. 1, 38–41.

39. To be found in *Shu"t Hakhmei Provence*, siman 71.

> But protested
> And after evading the issue
> Explained that he had mercy on the best of the flocks
> He blamed the people and excused himself
> As though he were innocent
> For this God punished him, to demonstrate how serious
> It is to sin and evade responsibility
> And act as one who has not sinned
> For he was distracting
> But David took responsibility when Nathan rebuked him with the parable of the sheep
> He admitted without shame, the young anointed one
> Did not look for excuses or to blame the elders
> He said, I sinned to God
> And so Nathan responded to the admission and the perfection
> God will pass over your sin and you shall not die

Riban agrees that that the text must be read in accordance with its plain meaning. David therefore retains his kingship not because he does not sin, but because he confesses to the wrongdoing.[40]

Abrabanel, too, is sharply critical of exegetical approaches that try to mitigate the severity of David's deeds in this episode:

> The teachings of our Sages in this matter are midrashic explanations, and I will not address them.... How can we propose that "he sought to commit [the transgression] but did not commit it"? The text testifies explicitly to this evil act in its entirety. If David had not sinned, why would he say, "I have sinned unto God"? And

40. Riban's explanation that David does not lose his kingdom gives rise to a certain difficulty owing to the fact that a review of the verses shows that even prior to his admission and his repentance, there is no mention of David losing his kingdom. The text states explicitly that David's repentance cancels only the death penalty that would otherwise have awaited him, but nothing is said concerning the continuation of his royal dynasty. Therefore we must find a different explanation for why he and his descendants retain the monarchy, while Saul loses his. I examine this question in my book *Shmuel Bet: Malkhut David* (Maggid, 2013).

why would he have engaged in such sincere repentance, saying, כִּי פְשָׁעַי אֲנִי אֵדָע וְחַטָּאתִי נֶגְדִּי תָמִיד, "For I know my wrongdoing, and my sin is before me always" (Ps. 51:5)? Furthermore, the verse that they cite in support of [the approach seeking to exonerate him] – וַיְהִי דָוִד לְכָל דְּרָכָו מַשְׂכִּיל וַה׳ עִמּוֹ, "And David succeeded in all his ways, and the Lord was with him" (I Sam 18:14) – comes prior to this episode, such that it does not rule out the possibility of him sinning afterwards. For even if at that time he was prudent, wise, and successful in all his undertakings, and God was with him in whatever he did, then certainly if he did in fact sin, God would be with him, since he accepted his punishment and engaged in repentance.

Therefore my thinking cannot accept a minimizing of David's sin, and I shall not deny the simple truth. Likewise, how can I accept their claim that the men gave bills of divorce to their wives? For the verse that they bring as proof is far from suggesting this. [Furthermore,] David told Uriah to go to his home that night, and then return [to the battlefield] in the morning, which indicates that there was no divorce [in effect], and their relations would be proper and appropriate. This is a further reflection of the Sages' teaching, in the Gemara there, that Uriah rebelled against the king, and was deserving of death, for he had said, "and my lord Yoav" – calling Yoav "my lord" while standing before the king.

In summary, if the text calls him a sinner and he acknowledges his own sin, then how could anyone make any mistake in believing him? It seems to me better to say that he did indeed sin very gravely, and he acknowledged his sin very profoundly, and returned in complete repentance, and accepted his punishment – and it was for this reason that his sins were atoned for.

Abrabanel rejects outright the midrashic interpretation as a substitute for the *peshat*, drawing a very clear distinction between *midrash aggada* and "the simple truth." In his view, the greatness of David finds expression in his complete, wholehearted repentance, which brings atonement for his sins.

Other *Rishonim* conclude that David's misdeed is of great importance because it leads to consideration of the precautions one must take to prevent falling prey to temptation. Those who adopt this approach offer two possibilities as to the message of the story. Ralbag writes:

> This teaches that a person should not turn to pleasure while his fellow is in distress. We see that Uriah himself did not agree to go home, to lie with his wife, while Yoav and all of Israel were in distress – i.e., encamped on the open field to lay siege to Rabba. And see what happened to David, as a result of the evil of permitting himself pleasures at that time – to the point where he desired Bathsheba, even knowing that she was married, and he came in to her and she conceived; and this in turn caused him to sin even further and to make efforts to have Uriah killed by the sword by the children of Ammon, when he saw that what he had hoped would happen – that Uriah would lie with his wife, such that David's disgrace would be concealed – would not come to pass.[41]

In Ralbag's view, the story's message concerns the sense of solidarity and identification with the troubles of the nation: when the nation is in distress, frivolous pleasures – at the root of David's sin – are not proper.

R. Yehuda HeHasid suggests a different message:

> Likewise, the stories of Samson's, David's, and Solomon's sins are recorded, in order to teach us the overwhelming power of love for women, such that the evil inclination was able to overcome these righteous men.... And the story of David comes to teach that this greatest of the pious ones, whose entire occupation was for the sake of Heaven, nevertheless stumbled when he saw a woman, although he was nearing old age. How much more so, then, must a young man take care not to look at a woman, and to distance himself from women. (*Sefer Ḥasidim, siman* 619)

41. From Ralbag's list of "*toalot*" at the end of II Sam. 21, item 42.

If even King David could succumb to sexual temptation, then clearly everyone needs to be careful. Obviously, this warning assumes that David did indeed sin.

Several of the *Rishonim* – Radak, Ralbag, Rabbi Yosef Kara, Rabbi Yehuda HeHasid, and Abrabanel – understand the account on the plain level, and then draw different conclusions as to the themes and moral lessons that it conveys. This reading was not an innovation on the part of the medieval scholars, but the continuation of a view prevalent among the Sages who did not seek to clear David of the sin attributed to him in the text. Hence, those seeking to address this complex story on the plain level of the text do not deviate from the path of the Sages and of the great Jewish scholars of previous generations; to the contrary, they are continuing the prevailing view among the Sages and the path adopted by many of the medieval commentators.

OUR APPROACH TO UNDERSTANDING SINS OF BIBLICAL CHARACTERS

Since the earliest times, there have been two main approaches to understanding the sins and errors of biblical heroes. One takes the straightforward meaning of the text as its starting point, while the other proceeds from the fundamental assumption that such negative actions cannot be attributed to such great figures. Both approaches can be found in the commentaries, such that neither may be presented as the decisively and unequivocally accepted mode of interpretation. Nevertheless, we shall conclude with a final observation concerning the *peshat* approach and its significance for the present generation.

Reasonably enough, those who study Tanakh in accordance with the plain meaning of the text will not suddenly adopt other approaches, upon encountering narratives that record transgressions committed by central, generally positive, figures. One who believes that God's word must be understood first and foremost in accordance with its plain meaning, as elaborated in the previous chapters, will try to apply this approach in every chapter that he or she encounters, with no preconceived notions. One who seeks to understand the messages arising from the text must approach it with great humility, without presumption, and without forcing the text to mean things that sit more comfortably with his or her personal worldview. Rather, the reader must mold his or her worldview in light of Tanakh and not seek to mold Tanakh in light of his or her worldview. Only in this way is one able to internalize the messages that the text conveys – through its presentation of the story as it appears.

At the same time, it is important to emphasize that this approach in no way diminishes the tremendous stature of these biblical figures, given that the *peshat* approach views the plain understanding of the text as God's word. The greatness of Abraham, Moses, and David arises not only from Jewish tradition and teachings over the generations, but – first and foremost – from the many chapters of Tanakh that explicitly describe God as choosing them or relating to them, thanks to their unique qualities. For this reason, even where the text indicates that they erred or transgressed, those incidents cannot be severed from the broader context of their character and stature.

The Tanakh teaches that even great people make mistakes, succumb to temptation, and commit transgressions. Moreover, it teaches that the way to deal with sin is through genuine repentance, which should always be accepted. This important educational message emerges from the study of the text – and not as a premise for which support is found in the text. Indeed, biblical characters are complex, and it is difficult to find a single one of them who is described and depicted in a purely positive manner throughout. The Sages' teaching "if someone is greater than his fellow, then his evil inclination is likewise greater" (Sukka 52a) is no empty statement. This message is central both in the midrashim and in the approach of the commentators over the generations. It is no coincidence that the Sages name only four individuals who died without sin[42] – and all four of them play only a very minor role in the narratives of the Tanakh.

42. The *baraita* states, "Four died on account of the snake" – in other words, they died on account of the sin of Adam and Eve which introduced death into the world, but they had not sinned and they personally were worthy of eternal life: "And these are they: Benjamin, son of Jacob; Amram, the father of Moses; Jesse, the father of David; and Kilav, son of David" (Shabbat 55b). Further on, the Gemara notes that this list is based on a tradition handed down, rather than on biblical evidence (except for the case of Jesse; see the discussion there).

Rabbi Samson Raphael Hirsch, one of the greatest commentators in recent generations, expressed this view most eloquently:

> The Torah never presents our great men as being perfect.... The Torah never hides from us the faults, errors, and weaknesses of our great men. Just by that it gives the stamp of veracity to what it relates. But in truth, by the knowledge which is given us of their faults and weaknesses, our great men are in no wise made lesser but actually greater and more instructive. If they stood before us as the purest models of perfection we should attribute them as having a different nature, which has been denied to us.... It may never be our task to whitewash the spiritual and moral heroes of our past, to appear as apologists for them. Truth is the seal of our Torah, and truthfulness is the principle of all its true and great commentators and teachers. (Commentary on Genesis 12:10–13)[43]

---

43. Translation from *The Pentateuch: Translation and Commentary*, transl. I. Levy (Gateshead, 1976), 236. R. Samson Raphael Hirsch (1808–1888, Germany) expresses the same idea in other places in his commentary, such as: "Our Sages, who never objected to drawing attention to the small and great mistakes and weaknesses in the history of our great forefathers, and thereby reflected the greatness of the Torah and upheld its lessons for all generations" (Gen. 25:27); "We follow the opinion of our sages, and do not consider it our task to be apologists for our great men and women, just as the Word of God, the Torah itself, never refrains from informing us of their errors and weaknesses" (Gen. 27:1). For more about R. Hirsch's philosophy in this regard, see A. Frisch, "Shitato Shel RSh"R Hirsch BeSugyat Ḥatei HaAvot," in M. Ahrend and S. Feuerstein (eds.), *Derakhim BaMikra U'VeHoraato* (Jerusalem, 1997), 181–97.

Similar points have been made by academic scholars of biblical literature. Eric Auerbach, in his classic essay "Odysseus' Scar," contrasts the presentation of biblical heroes with those of Greek myth in the following terms:

> And how much wider is the pendulum swing of their lives than that of the Homeric heroes! For they are bearers of the divine will, and yet they are fallible, subject to misfortune and humiliation – and in the midst of misfortune and in their humiliation their acts and words reveal the transcendent majesty of God. There is hardly one of them who does not, like Adam, undergo the deepest humiliation – and hardly one who is not deemed worthy of God's personal intervention and personal inspiration. Humiliation and elevation go far deeper and far higher than in Homer, and they belong basically together. The poor beggar Odysseus is only masquerading, but Adam is really cast down, Jacob really

Paradoxically, it is precisely the tendency to diminish the significance of the *peshat* in these episodes that plays into the hands of those who do not accept the divine origin of the Tanakh. For it is specifically the complexity of the great biblical characters and the awareness that they, too, were not perfect, that conveys a very solid sense of the reliability of the text. In and of itself, this is a strong argument against those who question the authenticity of the Tanakh. As the midrash teaches:

> Moses said to the Holy One, blessed be He: "Master of the Universe, any transgression that I have committed – attribute it to me, so that people will not say, 'Moses appears to have falsified matters in the Torah,' or 'He wrote something that he was not commanded to.'" (*Sifre* Deuteronomy, *piska* 26, Finkelstein edition, 36)[44]

The Tanakh is a text that is altogether exceptional within the world of ancient literature, insofar as it presents its characters in all their complexity, describing their greatness as well as their shortcomings.

When confronted with stories such as Judah and Tamar, the sale of Joseph, the waters of Meriva (where Moses struck the rock), David and Bathsheba, Solomon and his foreign wives, and others, many biblical critics maintain that these episodes cannot be from the same original source as the narratives that describe the positive attributes of the

---

a refugee, Joseph really in the pit and then a slave to be bought and sold. The reader clearly feels how the extent of the pendulum's swing is connected with the intensity of the personal history – precisely the most extreme circumstances, in which we are immeasurably forsaken and in despair, or immeasurably joyous and exalted, give us, if we survive them, a personal stamp which is recognized as the product of a rich existence, a rich development. (Erich Auerbach, *Mimesis: The Representation of Reality in Western Literature* [Princeton, 1973])

44. A similar idea appears in a different midrash: "A Roman matron asked R. Yossi: 'Is it possible that Joseph, at the age of seventeen, at the height of physical maturity, would have acted in this way?' R. Yossi brought out the book of Genesis and began to read the stories of Reuben and Judah. He said to her, 'If with regard to these two, who were older than he and were in their father's house, the text makes no effort to cover up their deeds, then concerning Joseph, who was younger than they and was all alone – how much more credence is thereby bestowed on this account'" (Genesis Rabba, *parasha* 87, 10, Theodor-Albeck edition, 1070–71).

aforementioned characters. What the religious opponents of the *peshat* approach and the secular Bible critics share is an inability to accept that the Tanakh can depict its heroes as complex individuals whose greatness exists alongside their fallibility. In contrast with both of these schools, the acceptance of the mistakes of biblical characters is a more intellectually honest and less reductive approach to the text. But it is also far more than that. It is a more religiously enriching message, for it accepts human complexity in the lives of biblical heroes, and maintains the integrity and unity of the biblical text.

Other Books in the
Maggid Tanakh Companions Series

Textual Tapestries: Explorations of the Five Megillot
Gabriel Cohn

Creation: The Story of Beginnings
Jonathan Grossman

Abraham: The Story of a Journey (forthcoming)
Jonathan Grossman

Subversive Sequels in the Bible:
How Biblical Stories Mine and Undermine Each Other
Judy Klitsner

Tribal Blueprints
Nechama Price

Elijah (forthcoming)
Elchanan Samet

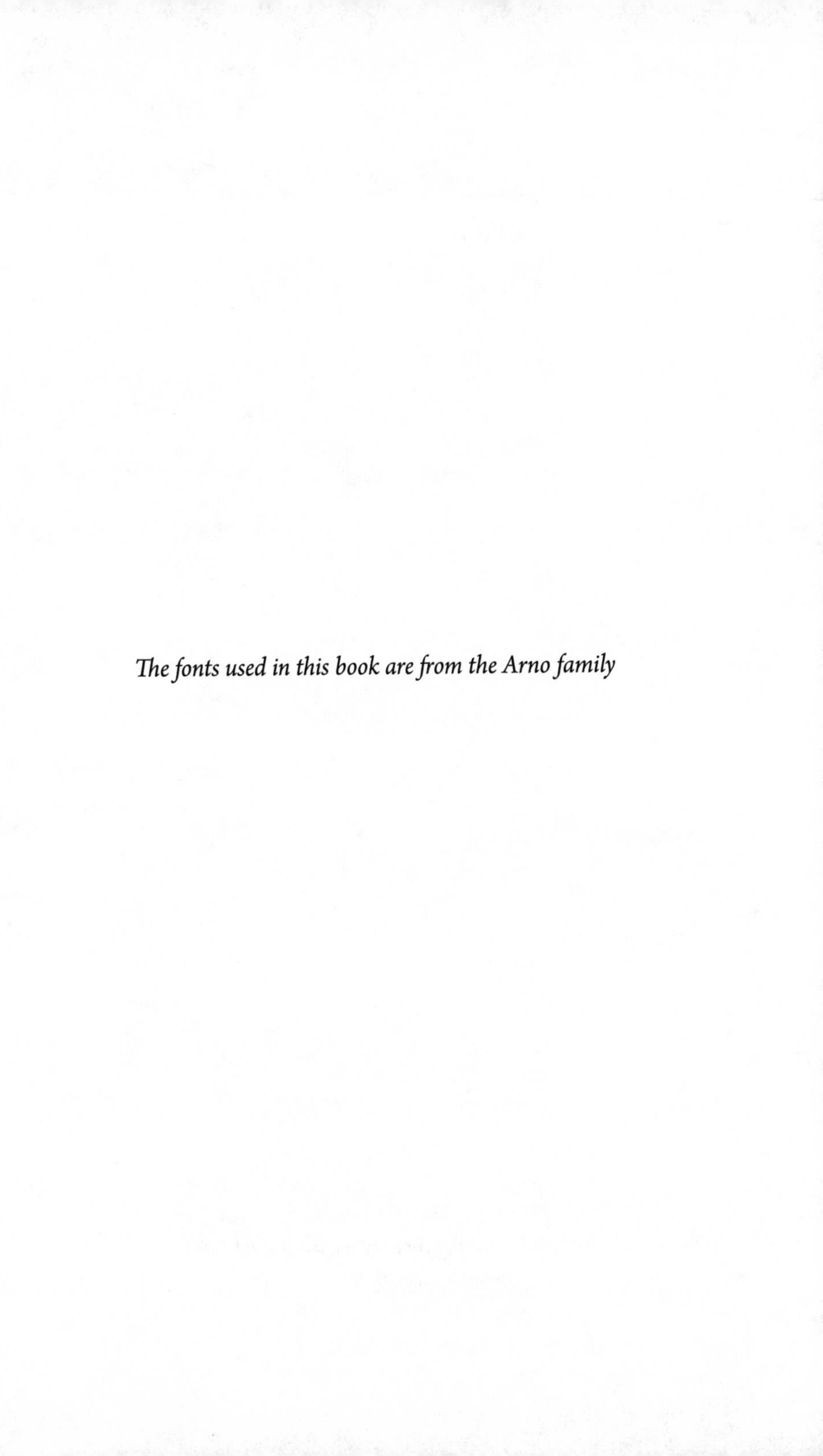

The fonts used in this book are from the Arno family

Maggid Books
The best of contemporary Jewish thought from
Koren Publishers Jerusalem Ltd.